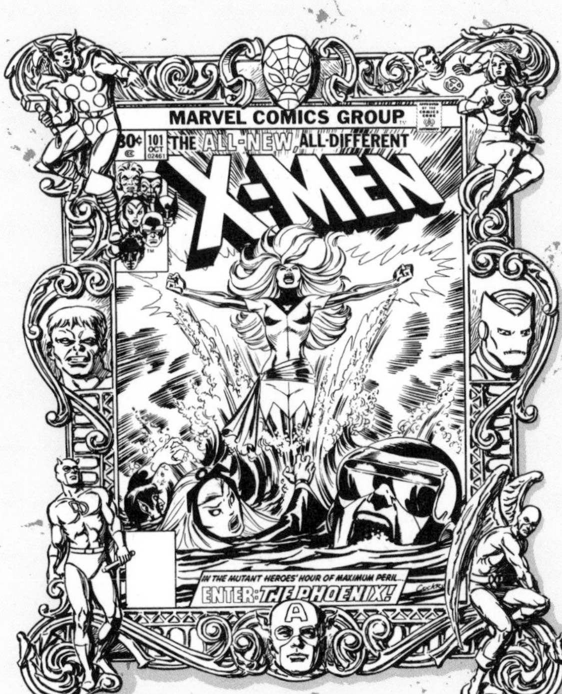
MARVEL COMICS GROUP
30¢ 101 OCT
THE ALL-NEW ALL-DIFFERENT
X-MEN
IN THE MUTANT HEROES' HOUR OF MAXIMUM PERIL...
ENTER: THE PHOENIX!

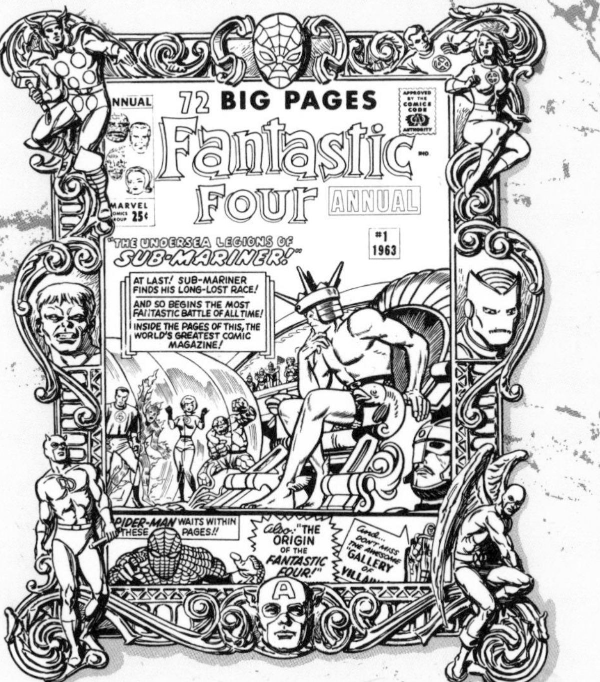
ANNUAL
72 BIG PAGES
Fantastic Four ANNUAL
#1 1963
"THE UNDERSEA LEGIONS OF SUB-MARINER!"
AT LAST! SUB-MARINER FINDS HIS LONG-LOST RACE!
AND SO BEGINS THE MOST FANTASTIC BATTLE OF ALL TIME!
INSIDE THE PAGES OF THIS, THE WORLD'S GREATEST COMIC MAGAZINE!
SPIDER-MAN WAITS WITHIN THESE PAGES!!
Also: "THE ORIGIN OF THE FANTASTIC FOUR!"

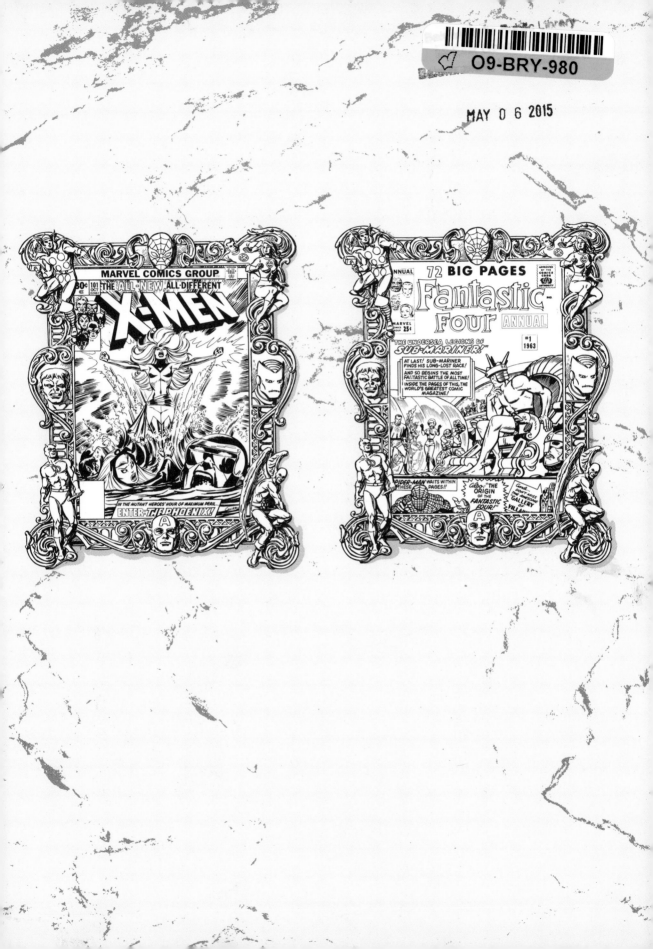

MARVEL MASTERWORKS

PRESENTS

THE X-MEN

VOLUME 12

REPRINTING X-MEN NOS. 101–110

MARVEL MASTERWORKS

CREDITS

THE X-MEN

Written by: Chris Claremont, Bill Mantlo (Co-plotter, Issue No. 106)
Penciled by: Dave Cockrum (Issue Nos. 101–105, Co-penciler on
Issue Nos. 106, 110) Bob Brown (Co-penciler, Issue No. 106),
John Byrne (Issue Nos. 108, 109) Tony DeZuniga (Issue No. 110)
Inked by: Frank Chiaramonte (Issue No. 101)
Sam Grainger (Issue Nos. 102–104) Bob Layton (Issue No. 105)
Tom Sutton (Issue No. 106) Dan Green (Issue No. 107)
Terry Austin (Issue Nos. 108, 109) Tony DeZuniga (Issue No. 110)
Lettered by: John Costanza (Issue Nos. 101–103)
Gaspar Saladino (Co-letterer, Issue Nos. 102–105)
Bruce Patterson (Issue No. 104) Tom Orzechowski (Issue No. 105,
Co-letterer, Issue No. 108) Joe Rosen (Issue Nos. 106, 107, 109)
Denise Wohl (Co-letterer, Issue No. 108) Annette Kawecki (Issue No. 110)
Colored by: Andy Yanchus
Art Restoration by: Phil Lord

Editor in Chief: Tom DeFalco
Special Projects Editor: Bob Budiansky
Editor: Gregory Wright
Assistant Editor: Evan Skolnick
Editorial Assistant: Tom Brevoort
Book Design: Lillian Lovitt
Logo Design: Ken Lopez
Dust Jacket Frame: Sandy Plunkett with Tom Palmer

VOLUMES AVAILABLE

MARVEL® MASTERWORKS VOLUME 12: THE X-MEN® Nos. 101–110 Copyright © 1976, 1977, 1978 and 1990 by Marvel Entertainment Group, Inc. All rights reserved. Published by Marvel Comics, 387 Park Avenue South, New York, N.Y. 10016.

PRINTED IN THE UNITED STATES OF AMERICA

ISBN 0-87135-628-7

MARVEL MASTERWORKS

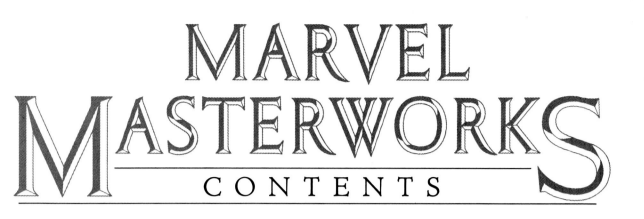

CONTENTS

MARVEL MASTERWORKS

INTRODUCTION

BY STAN LEE

Hi, Heroes!

Wait'll you see what we have in store for you this time around! You remember that our last X-Men Masterwork (as we so modestly refer to these valiant little volumes) featured the introduction of our new team of merry mutants in answer to an overwhelming amount of your requests. "Requests" did I say? "Threats" might be a better word, and you know how easy we are to intimidate!

That's why last ish, in our unstinting benevolence, we afforded you the chance to meet our great new team of extraordinary evil-smashers. But now that the intros are over, fasten your seat belt, frantic one! You're about to see them in blazing, burgeoning, bombastic action against some of the most fantastic foes any battling bevy of do-gooders has ever faced!

Naturally, each and every story is a certifiable winner, and it's tough to pick the best one from among the dramatically dazzling array of contemporary classics contained within these two deliciously-designed covers. However, I must confess that I have one special favorite, because as you've probably already guessed, we here in the Marvel Bullpen are the biggest fans of all! There's no way we could create and produce these epic adventures day after day, year after year, if we didn't love the myths and legends and fantasy and foul-ups every bit as much as you do!

But getting back to my own particular favorite, it's actually the very first story in the book, the one that so powerfully presents the birth of Phoenix.

Look, we all know there are countless ways to tell any story. Give the same plot to any dozen writers, and you'll end up with twelve totally different versions of the same theme. Bearing that in mind, I've a hunch when you read "Greater Love Hath No X-Man . . ." and see the way one of my all-time favorite comic book scribes, the oh-so-talented Chris Claremont, dreamed up the death of Jean Grey and the birth of Phoenix, you'll agree with me that no one, but *no one* writing comics today could have done it in such a dramatic, unique and truly original manner. If you've read it before, you'll enjoy it twice as much this time around; and if you haven't yet thrilled to one of the truly great superhero sagas of our time, I envy you. You're in for a treat you won't soon forget!

MARVEL MASTERWORKS

INTRODUCTION

But I can't close this passionate paean of praise without including a few well-deserved words for the artistry of Dave Cockrum and John Byrne, whose illustrations abound throughout these glamour-packed pages. No matter how thrilling a story may be, it needs artwork to match in order to create a successful comic book epic. Well, as you're about to see, we've got the artwork for you—and thanks to the brilliance of Dave and John, we've got it in abundance!

Incidentally, I think you'll get a kick out of the little note which John put at the end of one of the stories, praising Dave for his illos. John was so flattering that his little accolade read somewhat like an epitaph. The part that cracked me up was the line below, where Dave added the terse response: "I'm not dead.—Dave Cockrum"!

Well, I've made no secret of the way I feel about the stories that follow. But why spend time reading my comments when you could be gleefully plunging into the dynamite yarns themselves? In fact, I'll cut this short because I've managed to whet my own appetite for the ever exotic X-Men brand of extravagant excitement! So let's dispense with the chatter and get to the heavy stuff.

Or, as we are ever wont to say here in the hallowed halls of Marvel—the best lies just ahead!

Excelsior!

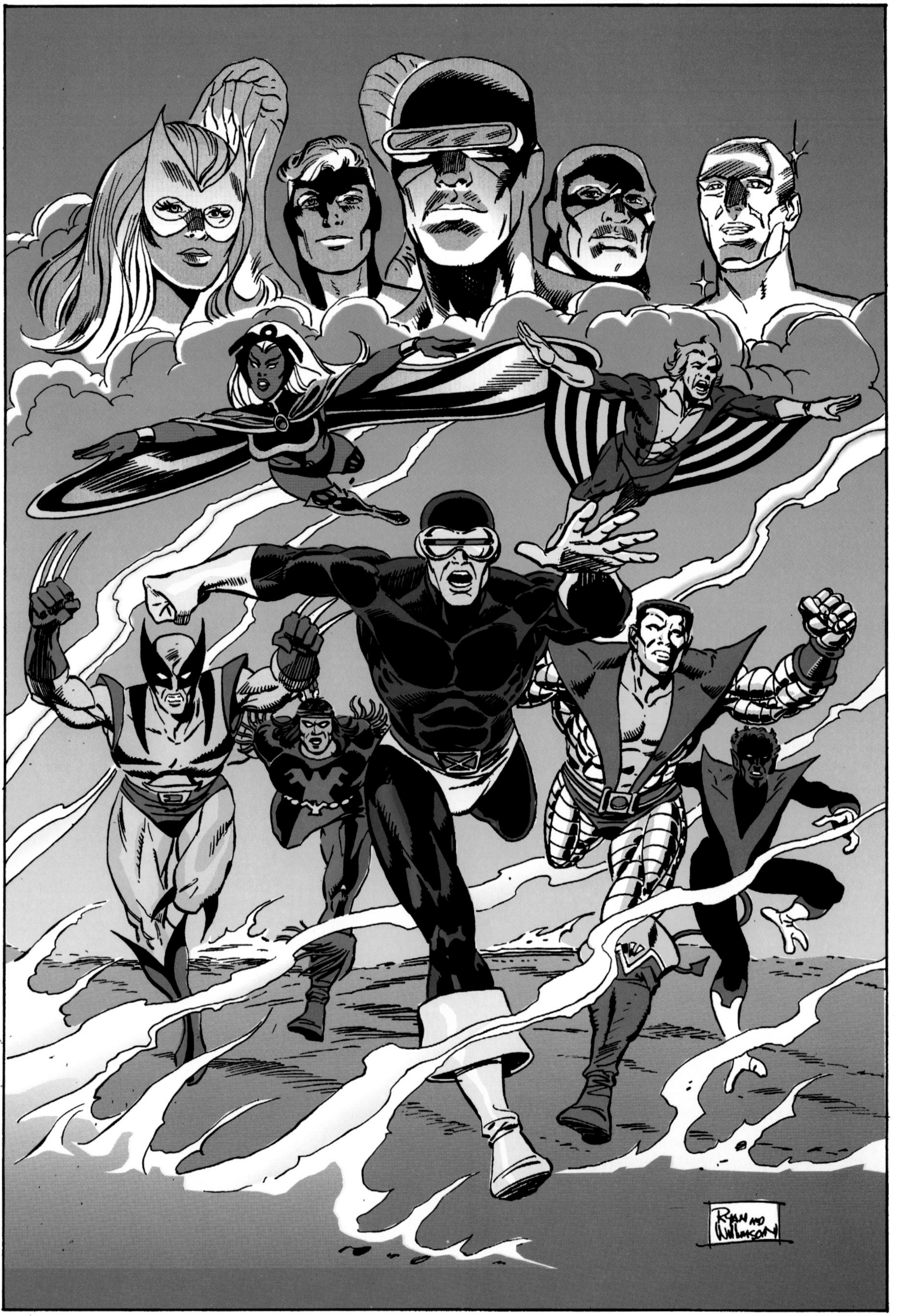
RYAN AND WILLIAMSON

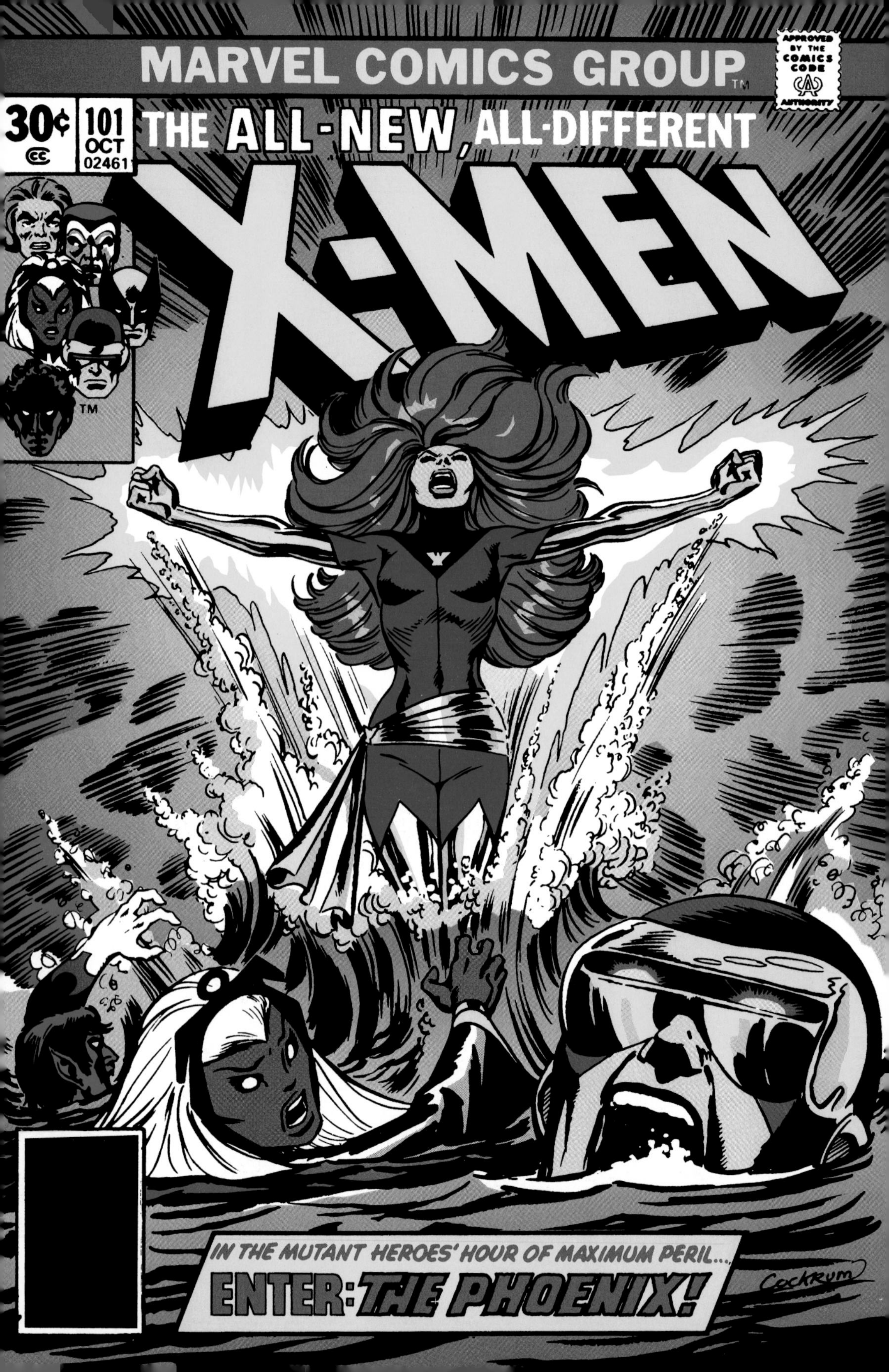
MARVEL COMICS GROUP
APPROVED BY THE COMICS CODE AUTHORITY
30¢
101 OCT 02461
THE ALL-NEW, ALL-DIFFERENT
X-MEN
IN THE MUTANT HEROES' HOUR OF MAXIMUM PERIL...
ENTER: THE PHOENIX!
Cockrum

Cyclops. Storm. Banshee. Nightcrawler. Wolverine. Colossus. Children of the atom, students of Charles Xavier, MUTANTS––feared and hated by the world they have sworn to protect. These are the STRANGEST heroes of all!

Stan Lee PRESENTS: THE UNCANNY X-MEN!™

CHRIS CLAREMONT, AUTHOR. DAVE COCKRUM, ARTIST. FRANK CHIARAMONTE, INKER. J. COSTANZA, letterer. A. YANCHUS, colorist. ARCHIE GOODWIN, EDITOR

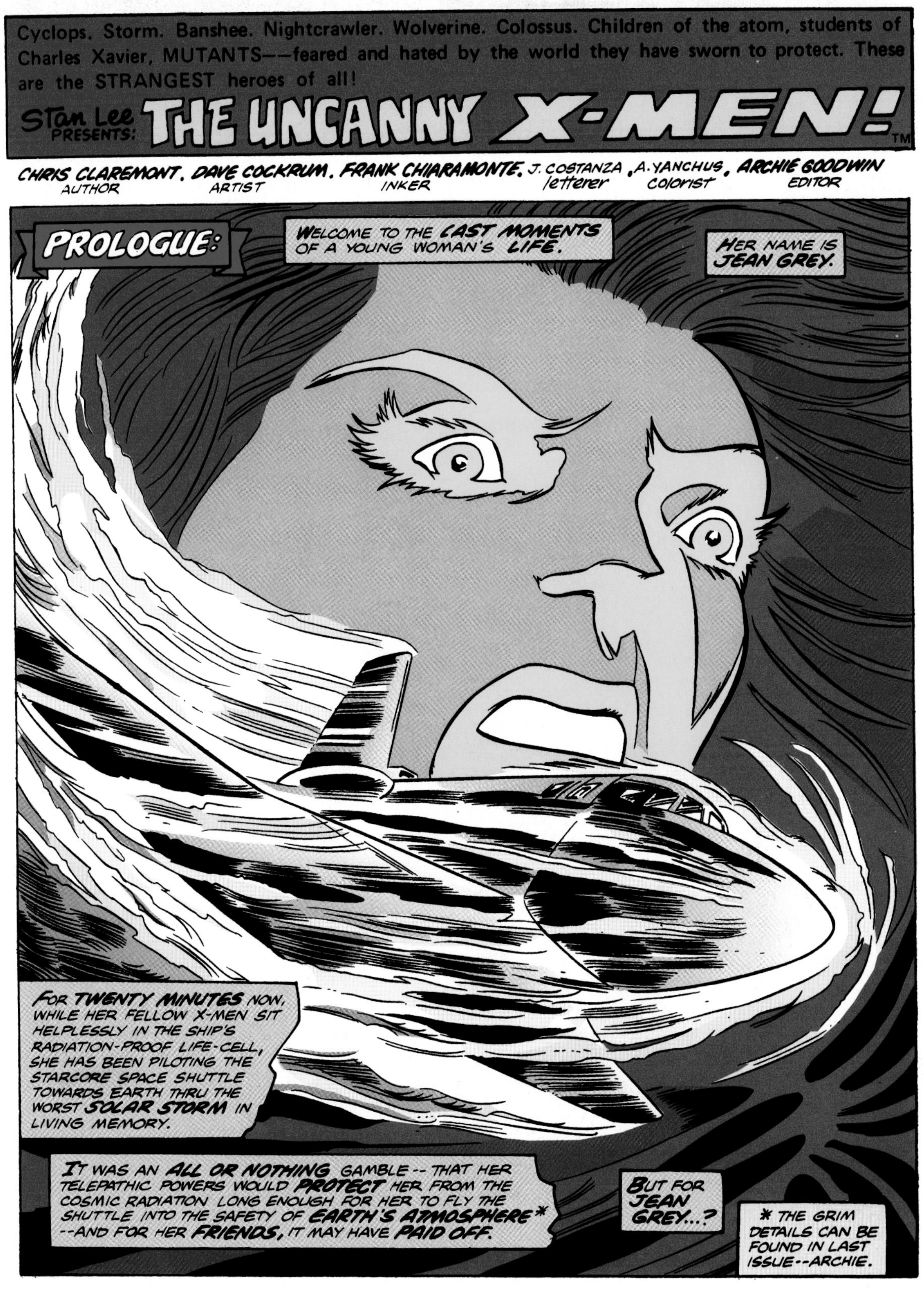

PROLOGUE:
WELCOME TO THE LAST MOMENTS OF A YOUNG WOMAN'S LIFE.
HER NAME IS JEAN GREY.
FOR TWENTY MINUTES NOW, WHILE HER FELLOW X-MEN SIT HELPLESSLY IN THE SHIP'S RADIATION-PROOF LIFE-CELL, SHE HAS BEEN PILOTING THE STARCORE SPACE SHUTTLE TOWARDS EARTH THRU THE WORST SOLAR STORM IN LIVING MEMORY.
IT WAS AN ALL OR NOTHING GAMBLE -- THAT HER TELEPATHIC POWERS WOULD PROTECT HER FROM THE COSMIC RADIATION LONG ENOUGH FOR HER TO FLY THE SHUTTLE INTO THE SAFETY OF EARTH'S ATMOSPHERE* --AND FOR HER FRIENDS, IT MAY HAVE PAID OFF.
BUT FOR JEAN GREY...?
* THE GRIM DETAILS CAN BE FOUND IN LAST ISSUE--ARCHIE.

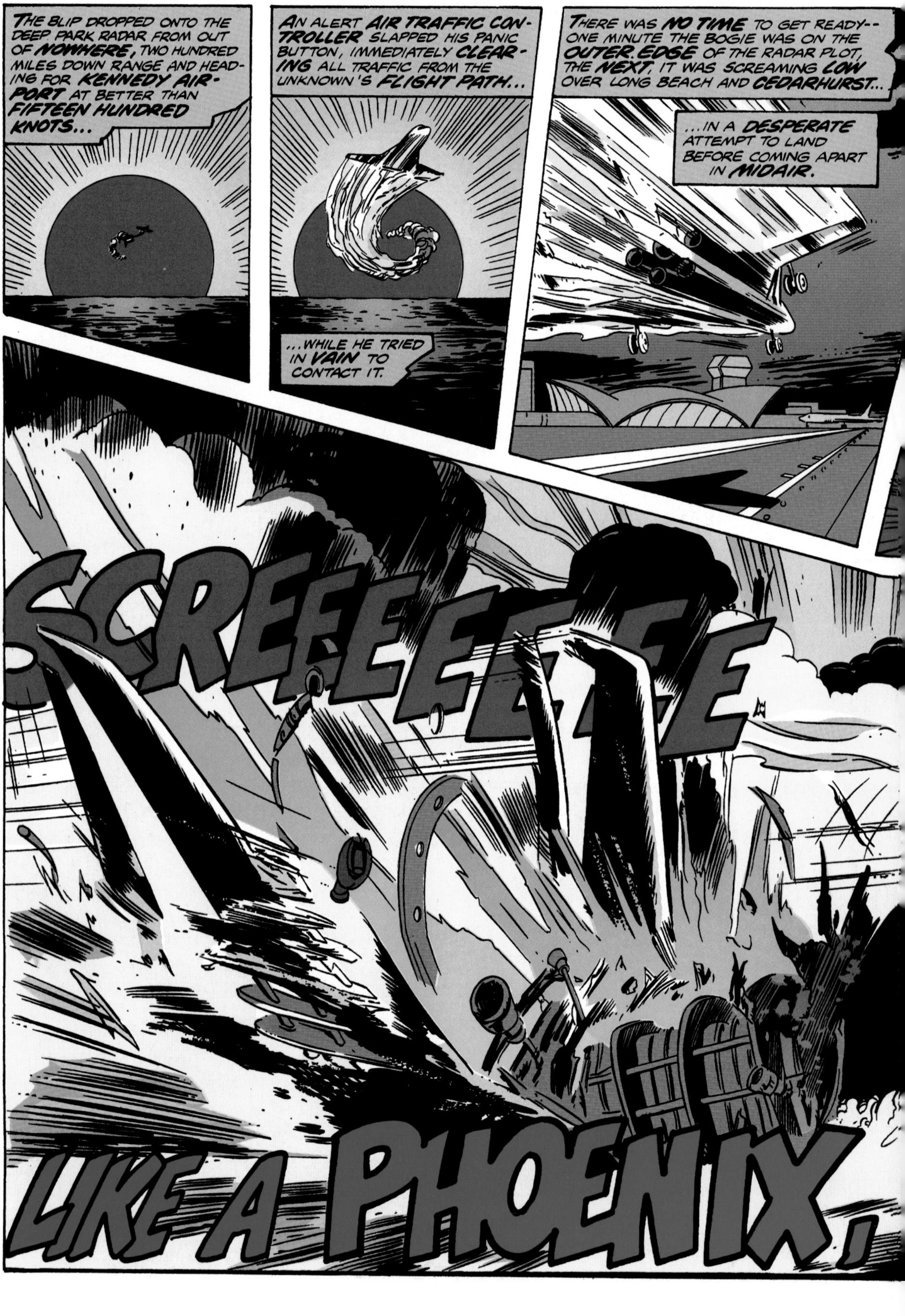

THE BLIP DROPPED ONTO THE DEEP PARK RADAR FROM OUT OF NOWHERE, TWO HUNDRED MILES DOWN RANGE AND HEADING FOR KENNEDY AIRPORT AT BETTER THAN FIFTEEN HUNDRED KNOTS...
AN ALERT AIR TRAFFIC CONTROLLER SLAPPED HIS PANIC BUTTON, IMMEDIATELY CLEARING ALL TRAFFIC FROM THE UNKNOWN'S FLIGHT PATH...
...WHILE HE TRIED IN VAIN TO CONTACT IT.
THERE WAS NO TIME TO GET READY-- ONE MINUTE THE BOGIE WAS ON THE OUTER EDGE OF THE RADAR PLOT, THE NEXT, IT WAS SCREAMING LOW OVER LONG BEACH AND CEDARHURST...
...IN A DESPERATE ATTEMPT TO LAND BEFORE COMING APART IN MIDAIR.
SCREEEEEEE
LIKE A PHOENIX,

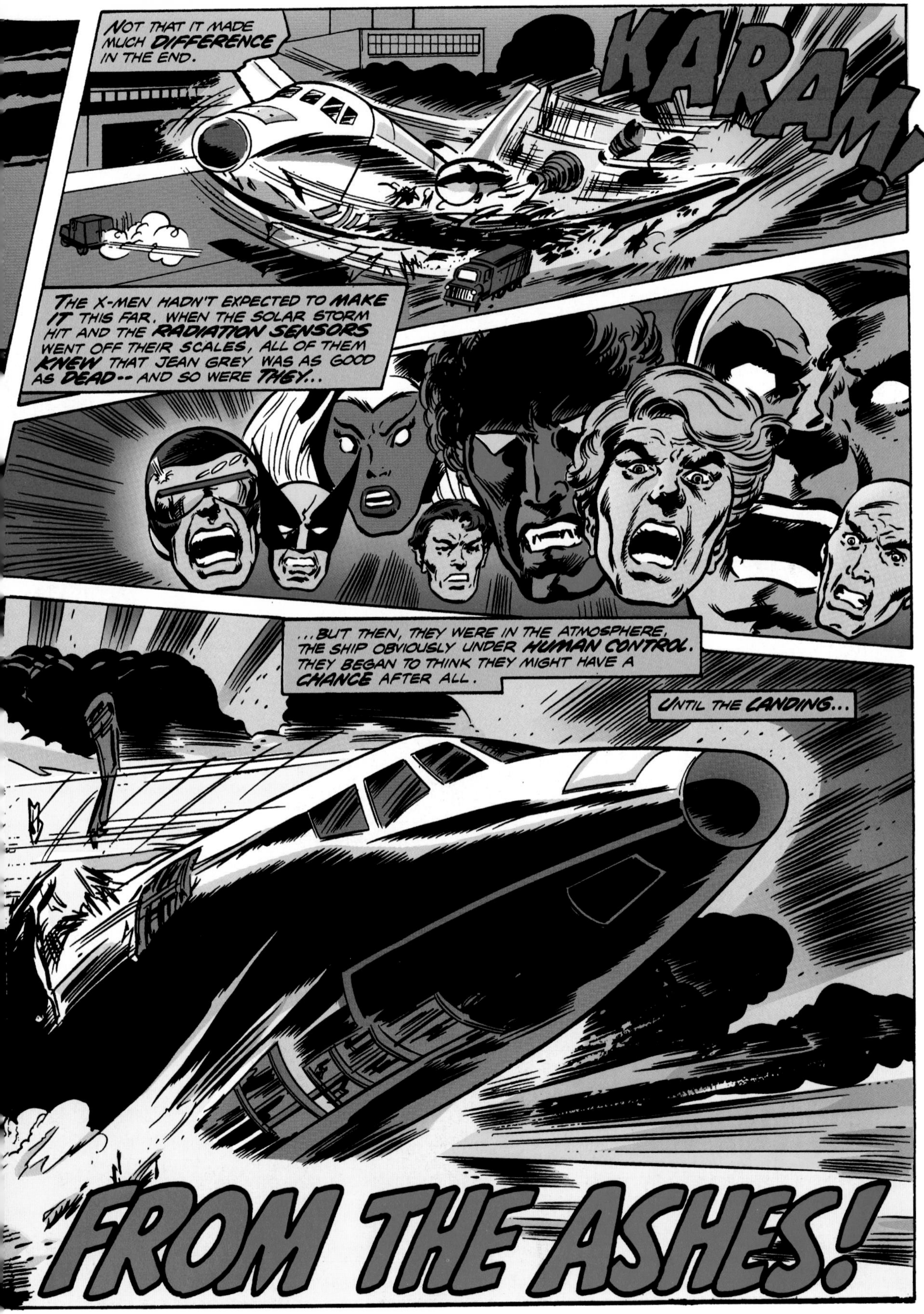
NOT THAT IT MADE MUCH DIFFERENCE IN THE END.
KARAM!
THE X-MEN HADN'T EXPECTED TO MAKE IT THIS FAR. WHEN THE SOLAR STORM HIT AND THE RADIATION SENSORS WENT OFF THEIR SCALES, ALL OF THEM KNEW THAT JEAN GREY WAS AS GOOD AS DEAD-- AND SO WERE THEY...
...BUT THEN, THEY WERE IN THE ATMOSPHERE, THE SHIP OBVIOUSLY UNDER HUMAN CONTROL. THEY BEGAN TO THINK THEY MIGHT HAVE A CHANCE AFTER ALL.
UNTIL THE LANDING...
FROM THE ASHES!

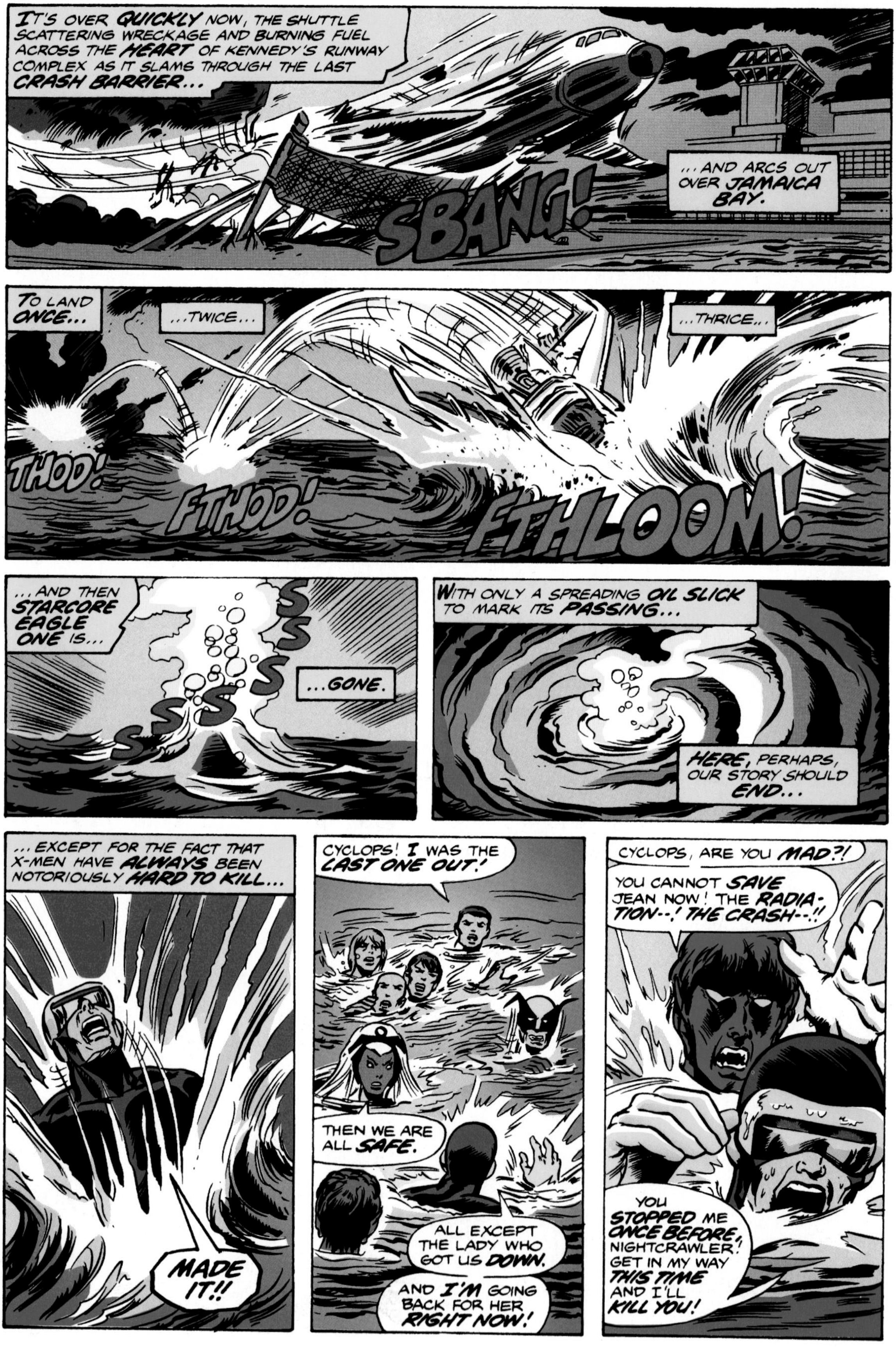

IT'S OVER QUICKLY NOW, THE SHUTTLE SCATTERING WRECKAGE AND BURNING FUEL ACROSS THE HEART OF KENNEDY'S RUNWAY COMPLEX AS IT SLAMS THROUGH THE LAST CRASH BARRIER...
SBANG!
...AND ARCS OUT OVER JAMAICA BAY.
TO LAND ONCE...
...TWICE...
...THRICE...
THOD!
FTHOD!
FTHLOOM!
...AND THEN STARCORE EAGLE ONE IS...
SSSSSSS
...GONE.
WITH ONLY A SPREADING OIL SLICK TO MARK ITS PASSING...
HERE, PERHAPS, OUR STORY SHOULD END...
...EXCEPT FOR THE FACT THAT X-MEN HAVE ALWAYS BEEN NOTORIOUSLY HARD TO KILL...
MADE IT!!
CYCLOPS! I WAS THE LAST ONE OUT!
THEN WE ARE ALL SAFE.
ALL EXCEPT THE LADY WHO GOT US DOWN.
AND I'M GOING BACK FOR HER RIGHT NOW!
CYCLOPS, ARE YOU MAD?!
YOU CANNOT SAVE JEAN NOW! THE RADIATION--! THE CRASH--!!
YOU STOPPED ME ONCE BEFORE, NIGHTCRAWLER! GET IN MY WAY THIS TIME AND I'LL KILL YOU!

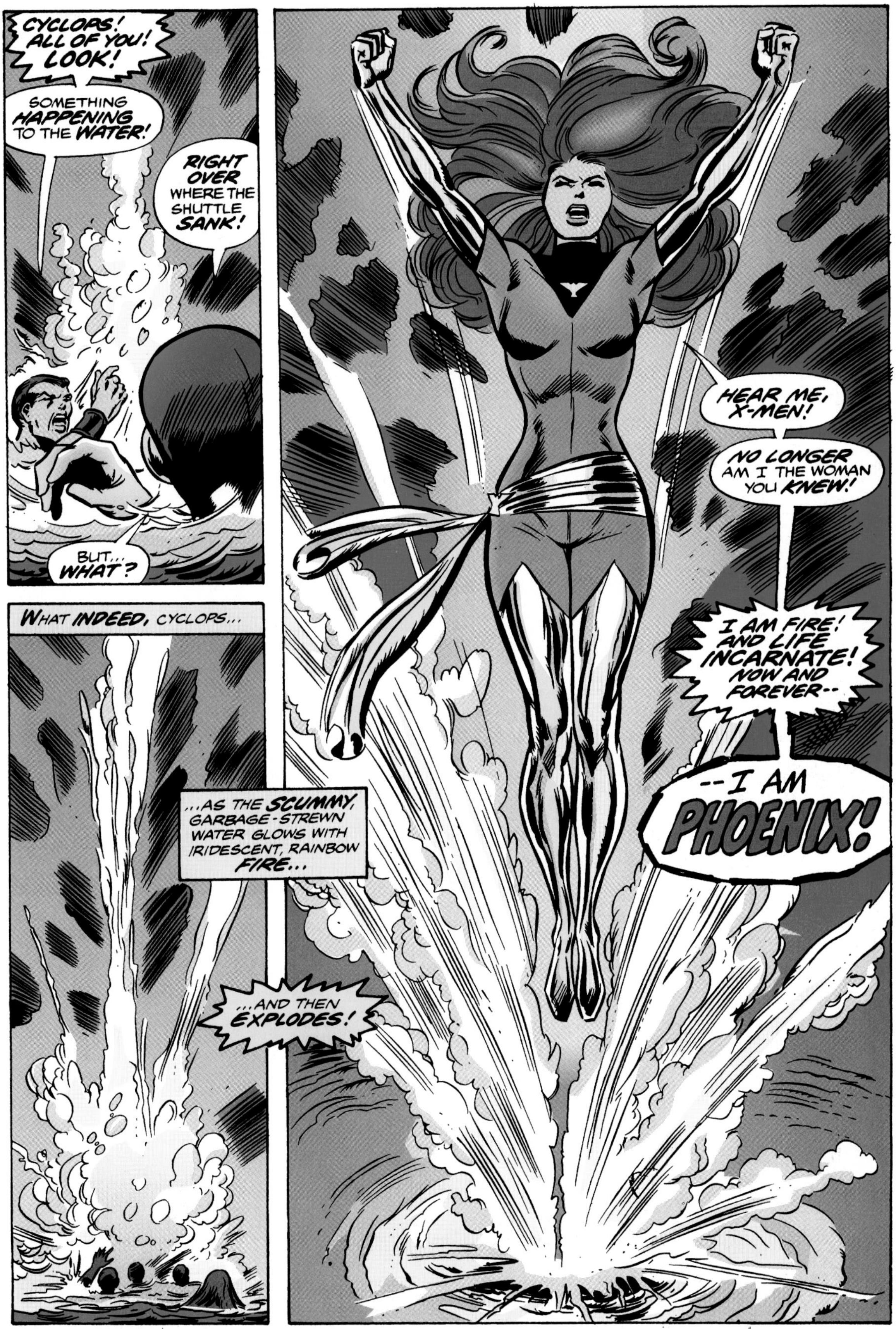
CYCLOPS! ALL OF YOU! LOOK!
SOMETHING HAPPENING TO THE WATER!
RIGHT OVER WHERE THE SHUTTLE SANK!
BUT... WHAT?
WHAT INDEED, CYCLOPS...
...AS THE SCUMMY, GARBAGE-STREWN WATER GLOWS WITH IRIDESCENT, RAINBOW FIRE...
...AND THEN EXPLODES!
HEAR ME, X-MEN!
NO LONGER AM I THE WOMAN YOU KNEW!
I AM FIRE! AND LIFE INCARNATE! NOW AND FOREVER--
--I AM PHOENIX!

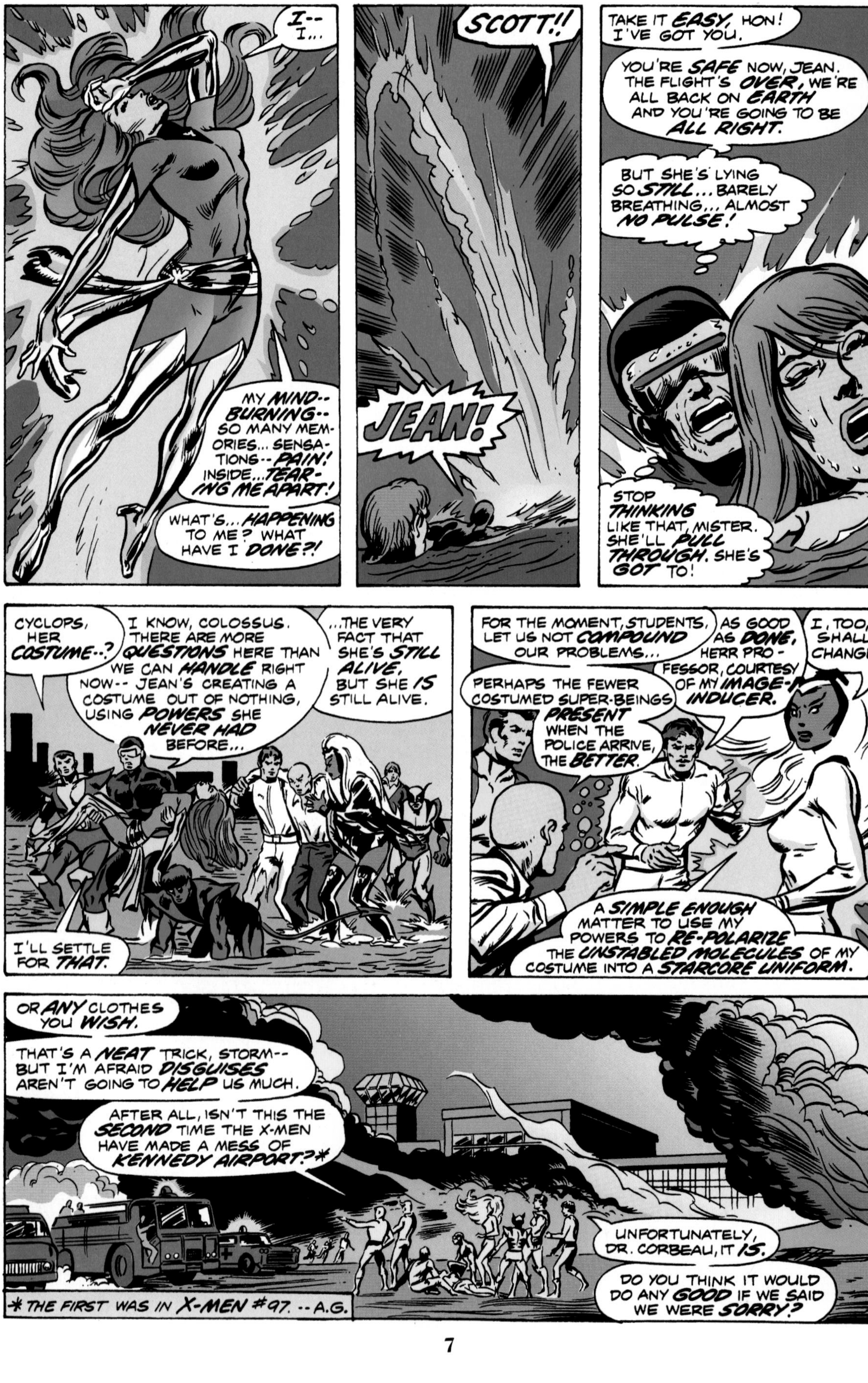

I-- I...
MY MIND-- BURNING-- SO MANY MEMORIES... SENSATIONS-- PAIN! INSIDE... TEARING ME APART!
WHAT'S... HAPPENING TO ME? WHAT HAVE I DONE?!
SCOTT!!
JEAN!
TAKE IT EASY, HON! I'VE GOT YOU.
YOU'RE SAFE NOW, JEAN. THE FLIGHT'S OVER, WE'RE ALL BACK ON EARTH AND YOU'RE GOING TO BE ALL RIGHT.
BUT SHE'S LYING SO STILL... BARELY BREATHING... ALMOST NO PULSE!
STOP THINKING LIKE THAT, MISTER. SHE'LL PULL THROUGH. SHE'S GOT TO!
CYCLOPS, HER COSTUME--?
I KNOW, COLOSSUS. THERE ARE MORE QUESTIONS HERE THAN WE CAN HANDLE RIGHT NOW-- JEAN'S CREATING A COSTUME OUT OF NOTHING, USING POWERS SHE NEVER HAD BEFORE...
...THE VERY FACT THAT SHE'S STILL ALIVE, BUT SHE IS STILL ALIVE.
I'LL SETTLE FOR THAT.
FOR THE MOMENT, STUDENTS, LET US NOT COMPOUND OUR PROBLEMS...
PERHAPS THE FEWER COSTUMED SUPER-BEINGS PRESENT WHEN THE POLICE ARRIVE, THE BETTER.
AS GOOD AS DONE, HERR PROFESSOR, COURTESY OF MY IMAGE-INDUCER.
I, TOO, SHALL CHANGE!
A SIMPLE ENOUGH MATTER TO USE MY POWERS TO RE-POLARIZE THE UNSTABLED MOLECULES OF MY COSTUME INTO A STARCORE UNIFORM.
OR ANY CLOTHES YOU WISH.
THAT'S A NEAT TRICK, STORM-- BUT I'M AFRAID DISGUISES AREN'T GOING TO HELP US MUCH.
AFTER ALL, ISN'T THIS THE SECOND TIME THE X-MEN HAVE MADE A MESS OF KENNEDY AIRPORT?*
UNFORTUNATELY, DR. CORBEAU, IT IS.
DO YOU THINK IT WOULD DO ANY GOOD IF WE SAID WE WERE SORRY?
* THE FIRST WAS IN X-MEN #97. --A.G.

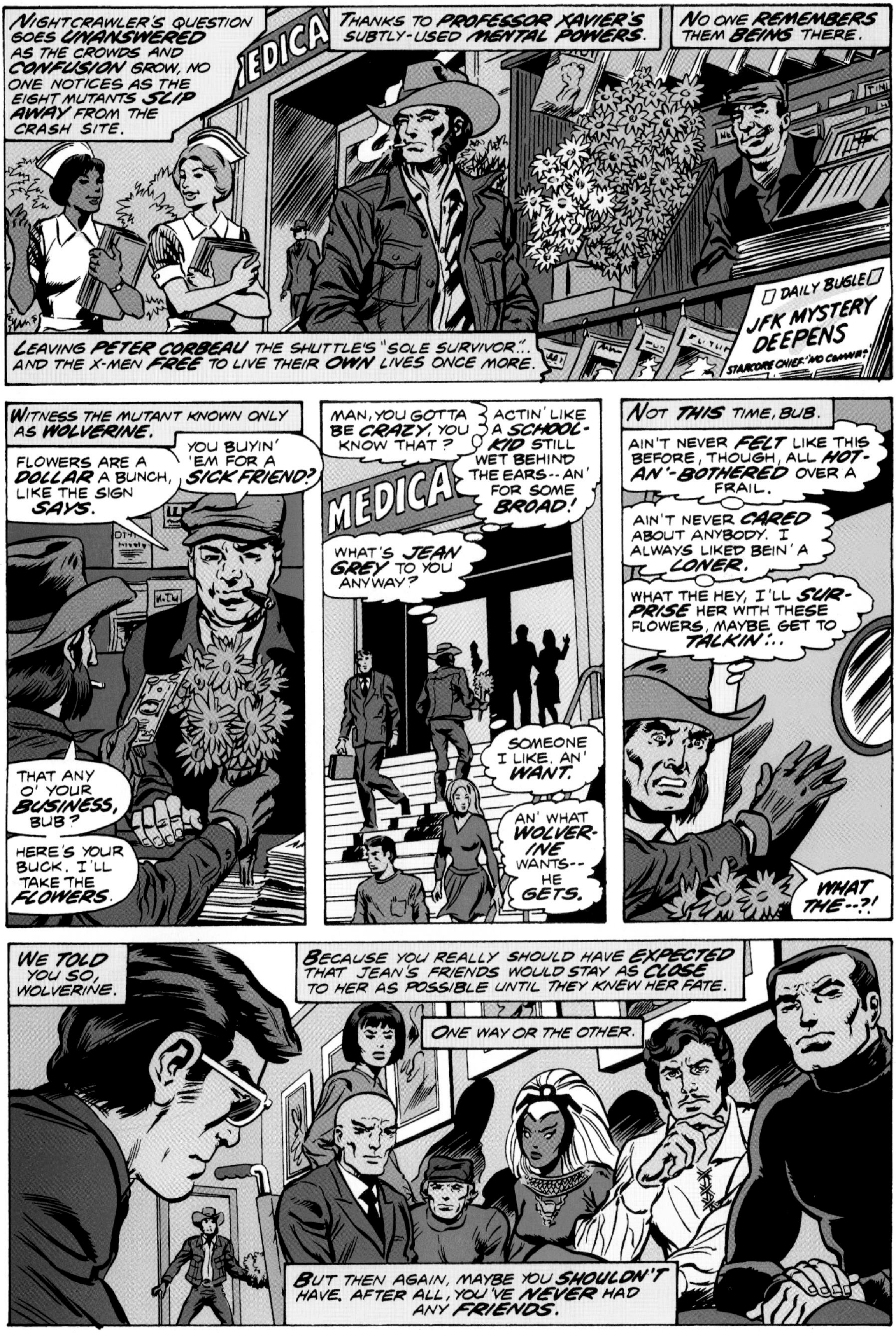

NIGHTCRAWLER'S QUESTION GOES UNANSWERED AS THE CROWDS AND CONFUSION GROW, NO ONE NOTICES AS THE EIGHT MUTANTS SLIP AWAY FROM THE CRASH SITE.
THANKS TO PROFESSOR XAVIER'S SUBTLY-USED MENTAL POWERS.
NO ONE REMEMBERS THEM BEING THERE.
MEDICA
DAILY BUGLE
JFK MYSTERY DEEPENS
LEAVING PETER CORBEAU THE SHUTTLE'S "SOLE SURVIVOR"... AND THE X-MEN FREE TO LIVE THEIR OWN LIVES ONCE MORE.
WITNESS THE MUTANT KNOWN ONLY AS WOLVERINE.
FLOWERS ARE A DOLLAR A BUNCH, LIKE THE SIGN SAYS.
YOU BUYIN' 'EM FOR A SICK FRIEND?
THAT ANY O' YOUR BUSINESS, BUB?
HERE'S YOUR BUCK. I'LL TAKE THE FLOWERS.
MAN, YOU GOTTA BE CRAZY, YOU KNOW THAT?
ACTIN' LIKE A SCHOOL-KID STILL WET BEHIND THE EARS--AN' FOR SOME BROAD!
MEDICA
WHAT'S JEAN GREY TO YOU ANYWAY?
SOMEONE I LIKE. AN' WANT.
AN' WHAT WOLVER-INE WANTS-- HE GETS.
NOT THIS TIME, BUB.
AIN'T NEVER FELT LIKE THIS BEFORE, THOUGH, ALL HOT-AN'-BOTHERED OVER A FRAIL.
AIN'T NEVER CARED ABOUT ANYBODY. I ALWAYS LIKED BEIN' A LONER.
WHAT THE HEY, I'LL SUR-PRISE HER WITH THESE FLOWERS, MAYBE GET TO TALKIN'...
WHAT THE--?!
WE TOLD YOU SO, WOLVERINE.
BECAUSE YOU REALLY SHOULD HAVE EXPECTED THAT JEAN'S FRIENDS WOULD STAY AS CLOSE TO HER AS POSSIBLE UNTIL THEY KNEW HER FATE.
ONE WAY OR THE OTHER.
BUT THEN AGAIN, MAYBE YOU SHOULDN'T HAVE. AFTER ALL, YOU'VE NEVER HAD ANY FRIENDS.

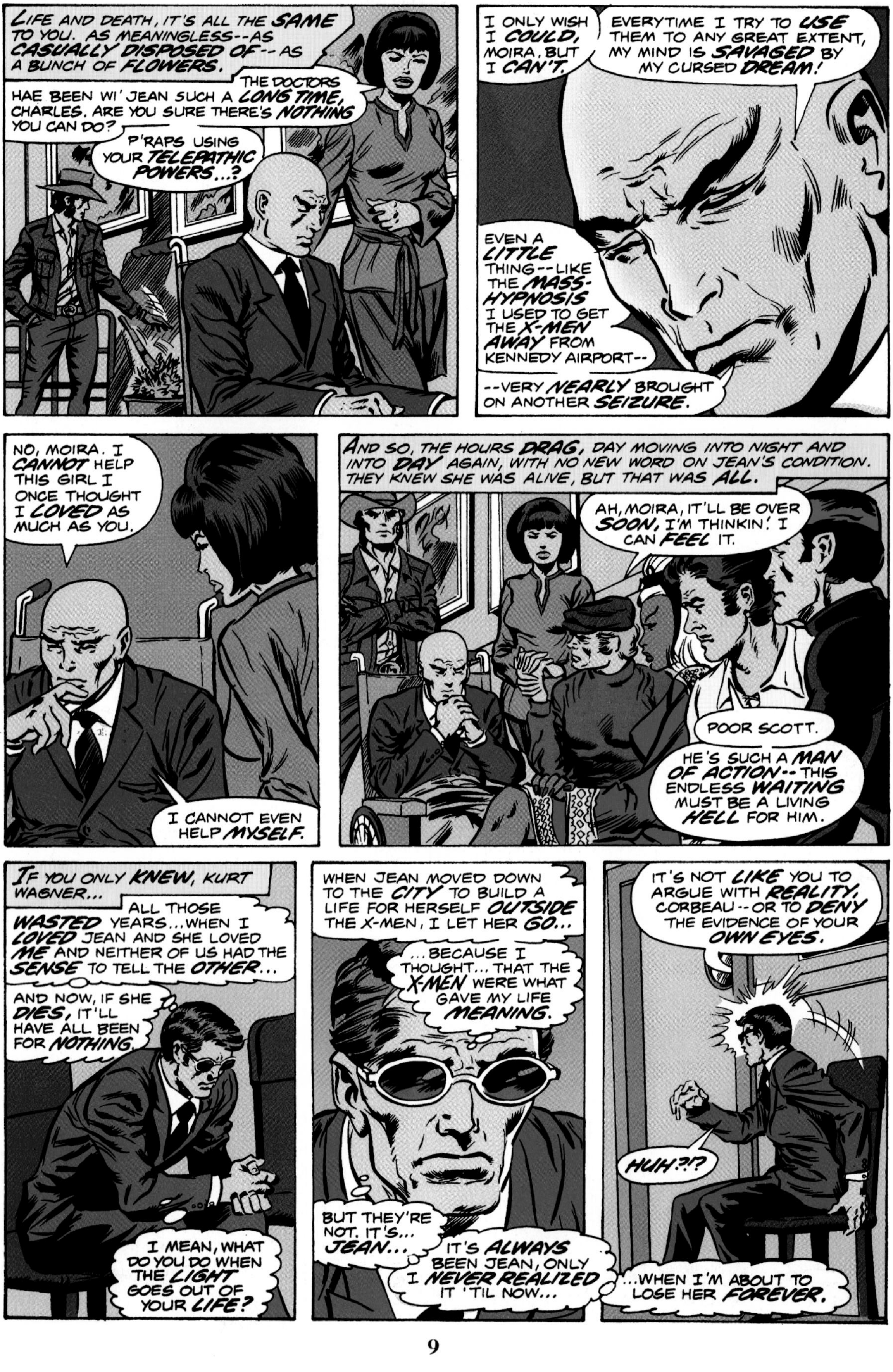
LIFE AND DEATH, IT'S ALL THE SAME TO YOU. AS MEANINGLESS--AS CASUALLY DISPOSED OF--AS A BUNCH OF FLOWERS.
THE DOCTORS HAE BEEN WI' JEAN SUCH A LONG TIME, CHARLES. ARE YOU SURE THERE'S NOTHING YOU CAN DO?
P'RAPS USING YOUR TELEPATHIC POWERS...?
I ONLY WISH I COULD, MOIRA, BUT I CAN'T.
EVERYTIME I TRY TO USE THEM TO ANY GREAT EXTENT, MY MIND IS SAVAGED BY MY CURSED DREAM!
EVEN A LITTLE THING--LIKE THE MASS-HYPNOSIS I USED TO GET THE X-MEN AWAY FROM KENNEDY AIRPORT--
--VERY NEARLY BROUGHT ON ANOTHER SEIZURE.
NO, MOIRA. I CANNOT HELP THIS GIRL I ONCE THOUGHT I LOVED AS MUCH AS YOU.
I CANNOT EVEN HELP MYSELF.
AND SO, THE HOURS DRAG, DAY MOVING INTO NIGHT AND INTO DAY AGAIN, WITH NO NEW WORD ON JEAN'S CONDITION. THEY KNEW SHE WAS ALIVE, BUT THAT WAS ALL.
AH, MOIRA, IT'LL BE OVER SOON, I'M THINKIN'. I CAN FEEL IT.
POOR SCOTT.
HE'S SUCH A MAN OF ACTION--THIS ENDLESS WAITING MUST BE A LIVING HELL FOR HIM.
IF YOU ONLY KNEW, KURT WAGNER...
ALL THOSE WASTED YEARS...WHEN I LOVED JEAN AND SHE LOVED ME AND NEITHER OF US HAD THE SENSE TO TELL THE OTHER...
AND NOW, IF SHE DIES, IT'LL HAVE ALL BEEN FOR NOTHING.
I MEAN, WHAT DO YOU DO WHEN THE LIGHT GOES OUT OF YOUR LIFE?
WHEN JEAN MOVED DOWN TO THE CITY TO BUILD A LIFE FOR HERSELF OUTSIDE THE X-MEN, I LET HER GO...
...BECAUSE I THOUGHT... THAT THE X-MEN WERE WHAT GAVE MY LIFE MEANING.
BUT THEY'RE NOT. IT'S... JEAN...
IT'S ALWAYS BEEN JEAN, ONLY I NEVER REALIZED IT 'TIL NOW...
IT'S NOT LIKE YOU TO ARGUE WITH REALITY, CORBEAU--OR TO DENY THE EVIDENCE OF YOUR OWN EYES.
HUH?!?
...WHEN I'M ABOUT TO LOSE HER FOREVER.

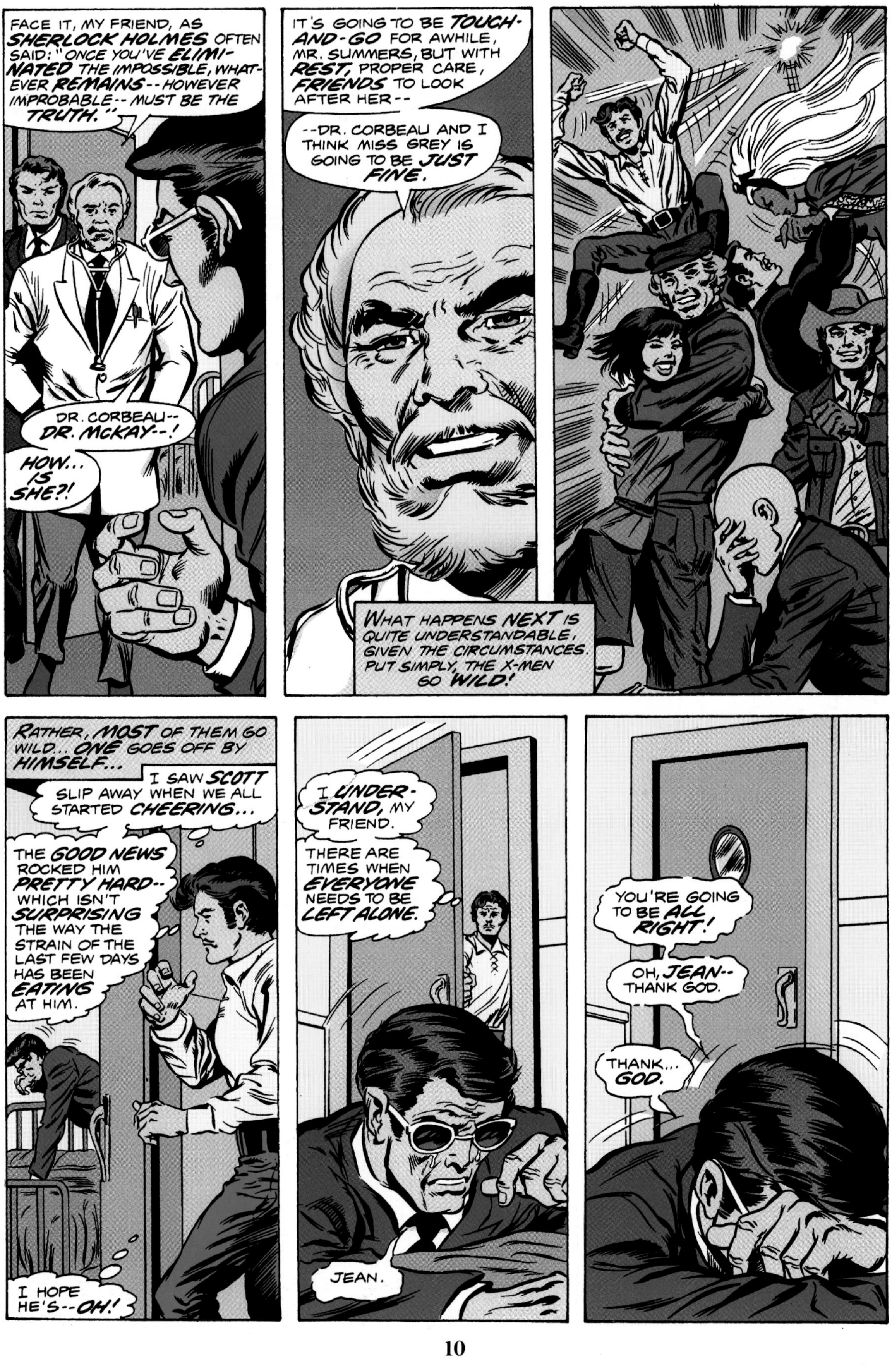

FACE IT, MY FRIEND, AS SHERLOCK HOLMES OFTEN SAID: "ONCE YOU'VE ELIMINATED THE IMPOSSIBLE, WHATEVER REMAINS--HOWEVER IMPROBABLE--MUST BE THE TRUTH."
DR. CORBEAU--DR. MCKAY--!
HOW... IS SHE?!
IT'S GOING TO BE TOUCH-AND-GO FOR AWHILE, MR. SUMMERS, BUT WITH REST, PROPER CARE, FRIENDS TO LOOK AFTER HER--
--DR. CORBEAU AND I THINK MISS GREY IS GOING TO BE JUST FINE.
WHAT HAPPENS NEXT IS QUITE UNDERSTANDABLE, GIVEN THE CIRCUMSTANCES. PUT SIMPLY, THE X-MEN GO WILD!
RATHER, MOST OF THEM GO WILD... ONE GOES OFF BY HIMSELF...
I SAW SCOTT SLIP AWAY WHEN WE ALL STARTED CHEERING...
THE GOOD NEWS ROCKED HIM PRETTY HARD--WHICH ISN'T SURPRISING THE WAY THE STRAIN OF THE LAST FEW DAYS HAS BEEN EATING AT HIM.
I HOPE HE'S--OH!
I UNDERSTAND, MY FRIEND.
THERE ARE TIMES WHEN EVERYONE NEEDS TO BE LEFT ALONE.
JEAN.
YOU'RE GOING TO BE ALL RIGHT!
OH, JEAN--THANK GOD.
THANK... GOD.

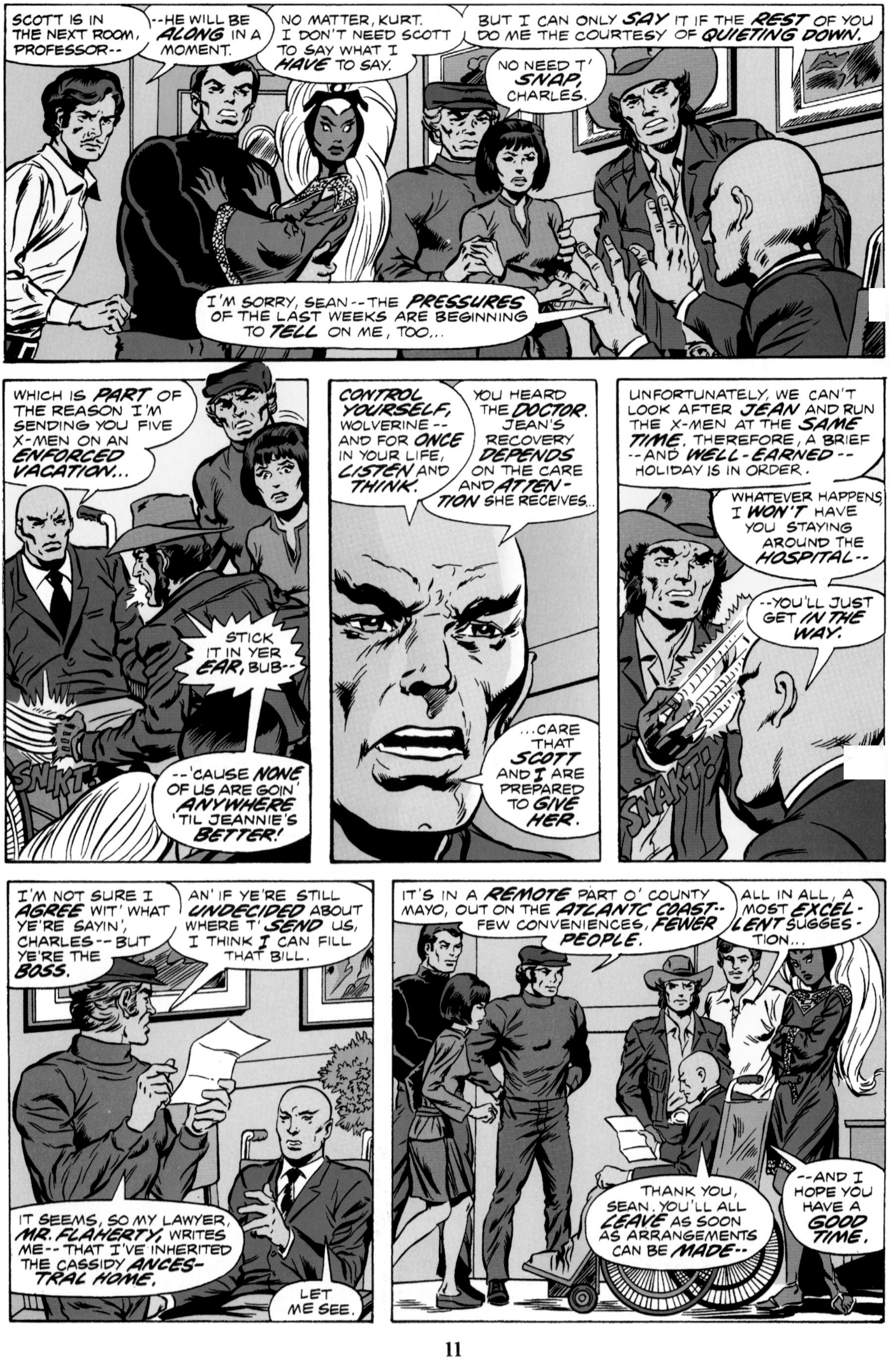
SCOTT IS IN THE NEXT ROOM, PROFESSOR--
--HE WILL BE ALONG IN A MOMENT.
NO MATTER, KURT. I DON'T NEED SCOTT TO SAY WHAT I HAVE TO SAY.
BUT I CAN ONLY SAY IT IF THE REST OF YOU DO ME THE COURTESY OF QUIETING DOWN.
NO NEED T' SNAP, CHARLES.
I'M SORRY, SEAN--THE PRESSURES OF THE LAST WEEKS ARE BEGINNING TO TELL ON ME, TOO...
WHICH IS PART OF THE REASON I'M SENDING YOU FIVE X-MEN ON AN ENFORCED VACATION...
STICK IT IN YER EAR, BUB--
SNIKT!
--'CAUSE NONE OF US ARE GOIN' ANYWHERE 'TIL JEANNIE'S BETTER!
CONTROL YOURSELF, WOLVERINE--AND FOR ONCE IN YOUR LIFE, LISTEN AND THINK.
YOU HEARD THE DOCTOR. JEAN'S RECOVERY DEPENDS ON THE CARE AND ATTENTION SHE RECEIVES...
...CARE THAT SCOTT AND I ARE PREPARED TO GIVE HER.
UNFORTUNATELY, WE CAN'T LOOK AFTER JEAN AND RUN THE X-MEN AT THE SAME TIME. THEREFORE, A BRIEF --AND WELL-EARNED-- HOLIDAY IS IN ORDER.
WHATEVER HAPPENS, I WON'T HAVE YOU STAYING AROUND THE HOSPITAL--
--YOU'LL JUST GET IN THE WAY.
SNAKT!
I'M NOT SURE I AGREE WIT' WHAT YE'RE SAYIN', CHARLES--BUT YE'RE THE BOSS.
AN' IF YE'RE STILL UNDECIDED ABOUT WHERE T' SEND US, I THINK I CAN FILL THAT BILL.
IT SEEMS, SO MY LAWYER, MR. FLAHERTY, WRITES ME--THAT I'VE INHERITED THE CASSIDY ANCESTRAL HOME.
LET ME SEE.
IT'S IN A REMOTE PART O' COUNTY MAYO, OUT ON THE ATLANTC COAST--FEW CONVENIENCES, FEWER PEOPLE.
ALL IN ALL, A MOST EXCELLENT SUGGESTION...
THANK YOU, SEAN. YOU'LL ALL LEAVE AS SOON AS ARRANGEMENTS CAN BE MADE--
--AND I HOPE YOU HAVE A GOOD TIME.

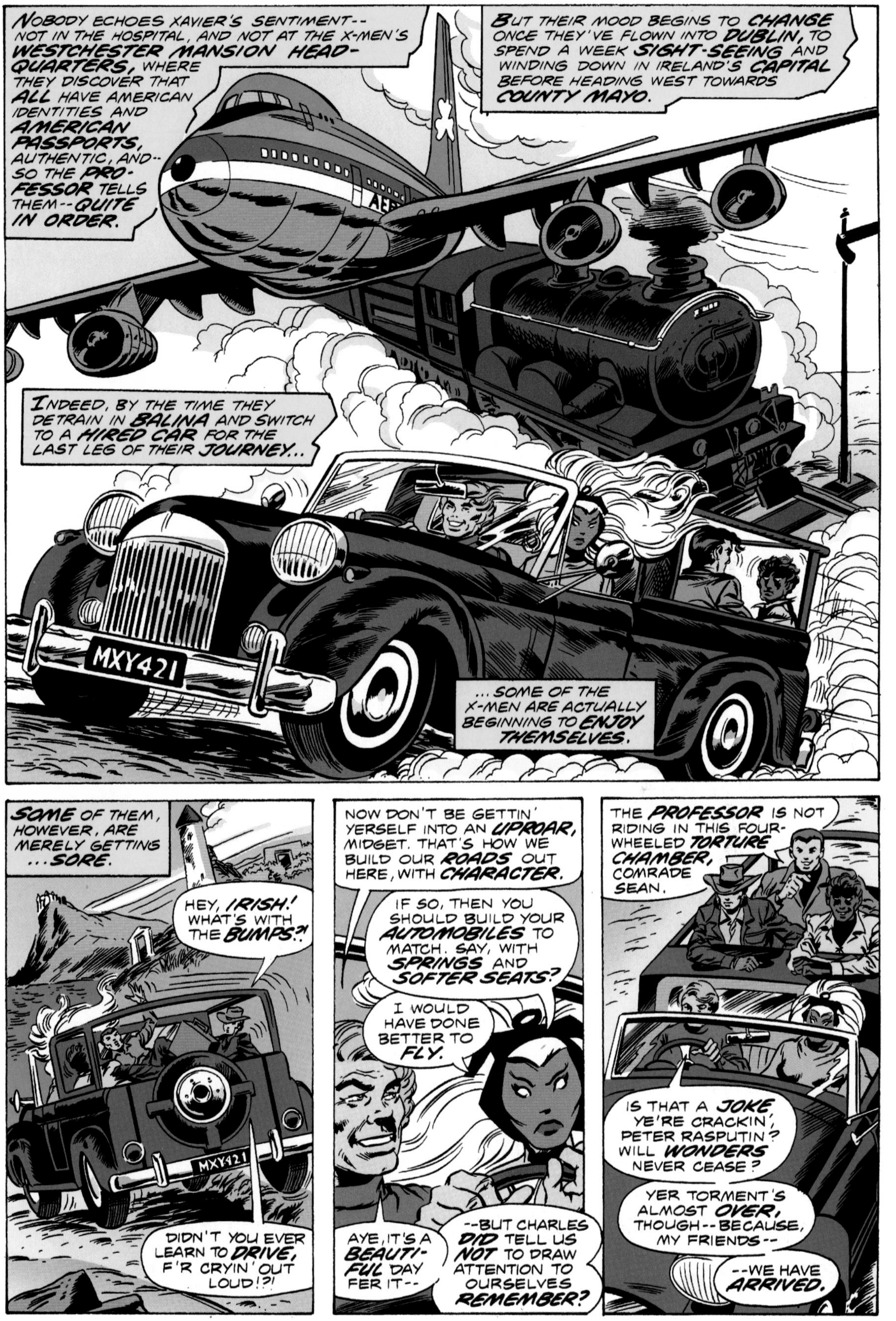
NOBODY ECHOES XAVIER'S SENTIMENT-- NOT IN THE HOSPITAL, AND NOT AT THE X-MEN'S WESTCHESTER MANSION HEAD-QUARTERS, WHERE THEY DISCOVER THAT ALL HAVE AMERICAN IDENTITIES AND AMERICAN PASSPORTS, AUTHENTIC, AND-- SO THE PRO-FESSOR TELLS THEM--QUITE IN ORDER.
BUT THEIR MOOD BEGINS TO CHANGE ONCE THEY'VE FLOWN INTO DUBLIN, TO SPEND A WEEK SIGHT-SEEING AND WINDING DOWN IN IRELAND'S CAPITAL BEFORE HEADING WEST TOWARDS COUNTY MAYO.
INDEED, BY THE TIME THEY DETRAIN IN BALINA AND SWITCH TO A HIRED CAR FOR THE LAST LEG OF THEIR JOURNEY...
MXY421
...SOME OF THE X-MEN ARE ACTUALLY BEGINNING TO ENJOY THEMSELVES.
SOME OF THEM, HOWEVER, ARE MERELY GETTING ...SORE.
HEY, IRISH! WHAT'S WITH THE BUMPS?!
MXY421
DIDN'T YOU EVER LEARN TO DRIVE, F'R CRYIN' OUT LOUD!?!
NOW DON'T BE GETTIN' YERSELF INTO AN UPROAR, MIDGET. THAT'S HOW WE BUILD OUR ROADS OUT HERE, WITH CHARACTER.
IF SO, THEN YOU SHOULD BUILD YOUR AUTOMOBILES TO MATCH. SAY, WITH SPRINGS AND SOFTER SEATS?
I WOULD HAVE DONE BETTER TO FLY.
AYE, IT'S A BEAUTI-FUL DAY FER IT--
--BUT CHARLES DID TELL US NOT TO DRAW ATTENTION TO OURSELVES REMEMBER?
THE PROFESSOR IS NOT RIDING IN THIS FOUR-WHEELED TORTURE CHAMBER, COMRADE SEAN.
IS THAT A JOKE YE'RE CRACKIN', PETER RASPUTIN? WILL WONDERS NEVER CEASE?
YER TORMENT'S ALMOST OVER, THOUGH--BECAUSE, MY FRIENDS--
--WE HAVE ARRIVED.

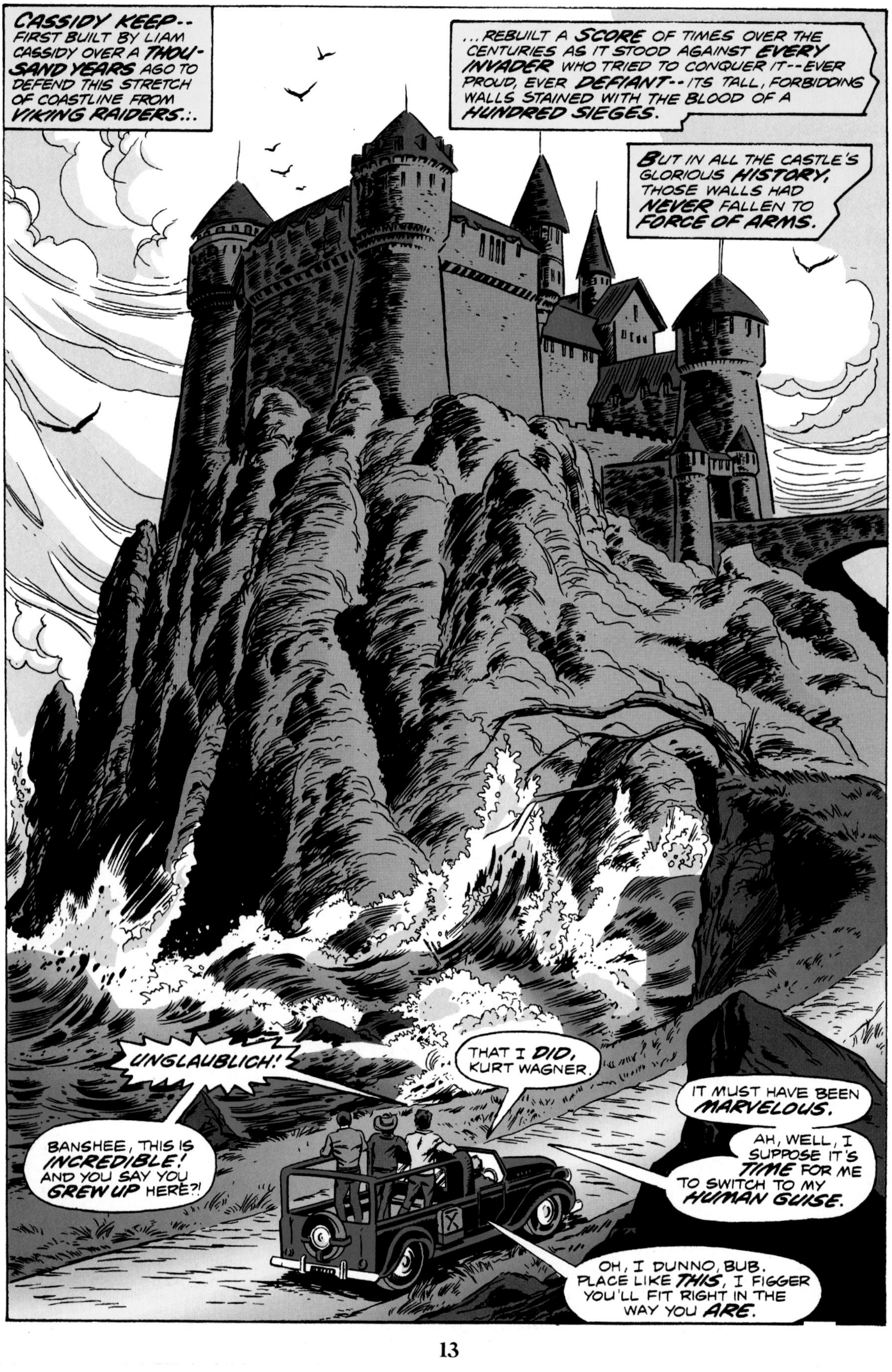
CASSIDY KEEP.. FIRST BUILT BY LIAM CASSIDY OVER A THOUSAND YEARS AGO TO DEFEND THIS STRETCH OF COASTLINE FROM VIKING RAIDERS...
...REBUILT A SCORE OF TIMES OVER THE CENTURIES AS IT STOOD AGAINST EVERY INVADER WHO TRIED TO CONQUER IT--EVER PROUD, EVER DEFIANT--ITS TALL, FORBIDDING WALLS STAINED WITH THE BLOOD OF A HUNDRED SIEGES.
BUT IN ALL THE CASTLE'S GLORIOUS HISTORY, THOSE WALLS HAD NEVER FALLEN TO FORCE OF ARMS.
UNGLAUBLICH!
BANSHEE, THIS IS INCREDIBLE! AND YOU SAY YOU GREW UP HERE?!
THAT I DID, KURT WAGNER.
IT MUST HAVE BEEN MARVELOUS.
AH, WELL, I SUPPOSE IT'S TIME FOR ME TO SWITCH TO MY HUMAN GUISE.
OH, I DUNNO, BUB. PLACE LIKE THIS, I FIGGER YOU'LL FIT RIGHT IN THE WAY YOU ARE.

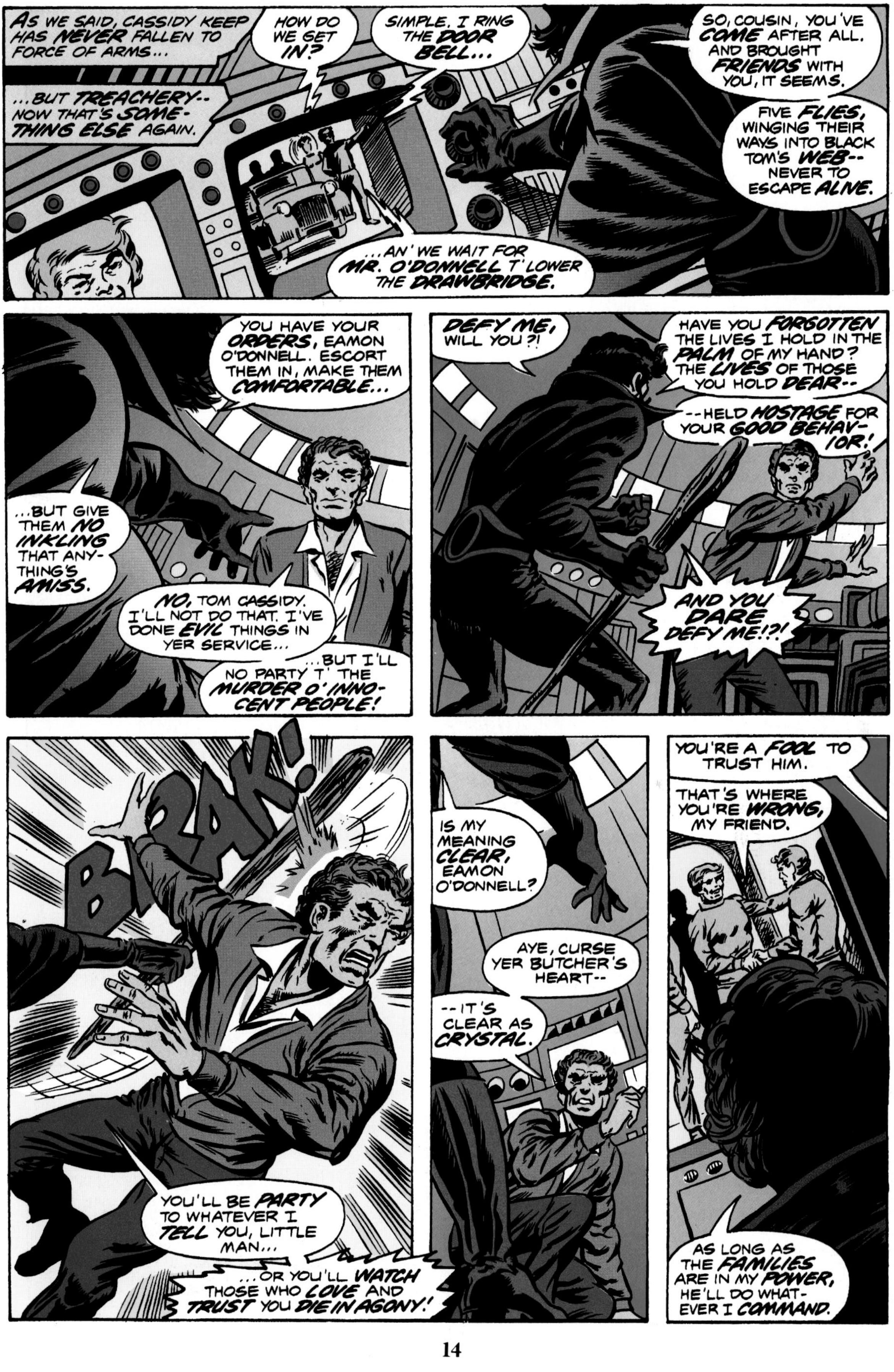
AS WE SAID, CASSIDY KEEP HAS NEVER FALLEN TO FORCE OF ARMS...
...BUT TREACHERY-- NOW THAT'S SOMETHING ELSE AGAIN.
HOW DO WE GET IN?
SIMPLE. I RING THE DOOR BELL...
...AN' WE WAIT FOR MR. O'DONNELL T' LOWER THE DRAWBRIDGE.
SO, COUSIN, YOU'VE COME AFTER ALL. AND BROUGHT FRIENDS WITH YOU, IT SEEMS.
FIVE FLIES, WINGING THEIR WAYS INTO BLACK TOM'S WEB-- NEVER TO ESCAPE ALIVE.
YOU HAVE YOUR ORDERS, EAMON O'DONNELL. ESCORT THEM IN, MAKE THEM COMFORTABLE...
...BUT GIVE THEM NO INKLING THAT ANYTHING'S AMISS.
NO, TOM CASSIDY. I'LL NOT DO THAT. I'VE DONE EVIL THINGS IN YER SERVICE...
...BUT I'LL NO PARTY T' THE MURDER O' INNOCENT PEOPLE!
DEFY ME, WILL YOU?!
HAVE YOU FORGOTTEN THE LIVES I HOLD IN THE PALM OF MY HAND? THE LIVES OF THOSE YOU HOLD DEAR--
--HELD HOSTAGE FOR YOUR GOOD BEHAVIOR!
AND YOU DARE DEFY ME!?!
BRAK!
YOU'LL BE PARTY TO WHATEVER I TELL YOU, LITTLE MAN...
...OR YOU'LL WATCH THOSE WHO LOVE AND TRUST YOU DIE IN AGONY!
IS MY MEANING CLEAR, EAMON O'DONNELL?
AYE, CURSE YER BUTCHER'S HEART--
--IT'S CLEAR AS CRYSTAL.
YOU'RE A FOOL TO TRUST HIM.
THAT'S WHERE YOU'RE WRONG, MY FRIEND.
AS LONG AS THE FAMILIES ARE IN MY POWER, HE'LL DO WHATEVER I COMMAND.

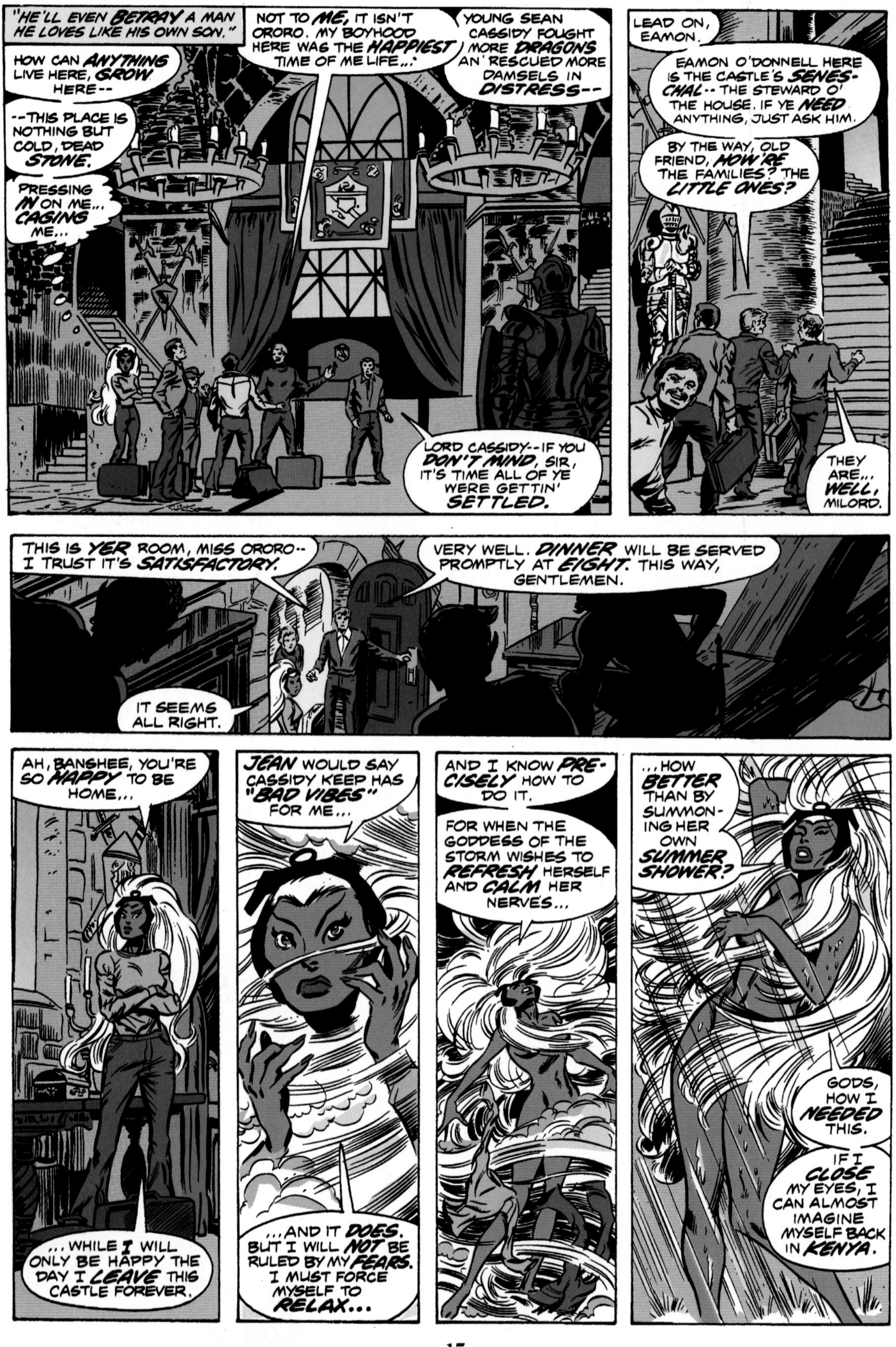
"HE'LL EVEN BETRAY A MAN HE LOVES LIKE HIS OWN SON."
HOW CAN ANYTHING LIVE HERE, GROW HERE--
--THIS PLACE IS NOTHING BUT COLD, DEAD STONE.
PRESSING IN ON ME... CAGING ME...
NOT TO ME, IT ISN'T ORORO. MY BOYHOOD HERE WAS THE HAPPIEST TIME OF ME LIFE...
YOUNG SEAN CASSIDY FOUGHT MORE DRAGONS AN' RESCUED MORE DAMSELS IN DISTRESS--
LORD CASSIDY-- IF YOU DON'T MIND, SIR, IT'S TIME ALL OF YE WERE GETTIN' SETTLED.
LEAD ON, EAMON.
EAMON O'DONNELL HERE IS THE CASTLE'S SENESCHAL -- THE STEWARD O' THE HOUSE. IF YE NEED ANYTHING, JUST ASK HIM.
BY THE WAY, OLD FRIEND, HOW'RE THE FAMILIES? THE LITTLE ONES?
THEY ARE... WELL, MILORD.
THIS IS YER ROOM, MISS ORORO-- I TRUST IT'S SATISFACTORY.
IT SEEMS ALL RIGHT.
VERY WELL. DINNER WILL BE SERVED PROMPTLY AT EIGHT. THIS WAY, GENTLEMEN.
AH, BANSHEE, YOU'RE SO HAPPY TO BE HOME...
...WHILE I WILL ONLY BE HAPPY THE DAY I LEAVE THIS CASTLE FOREVER.
JEAN WOULD SAY CASSIDY KEEP HAS "BAD VIBES" FOR ME...
...AND IT DOES. BUT I WILL NOT BE RULED BY MY FEARS. I MUST FORCE MYSELF TO RELAX...
AND I KNOW PRECISELY HOW TO DO IT.
FOR WHEN THE GODDESS OF THE STORM WISHES TO REFRESH HERSELF AND CALM HER NERVES...
...HOW BETTER THAN BY SUMMONING HER OWN SUMMER SHOWER?
GODS, HOW I NEEDED THIS.
IF I CLOSE MY EYES, I CAN ALMOST IMAGINE MYSELF BACK IN KENYA.

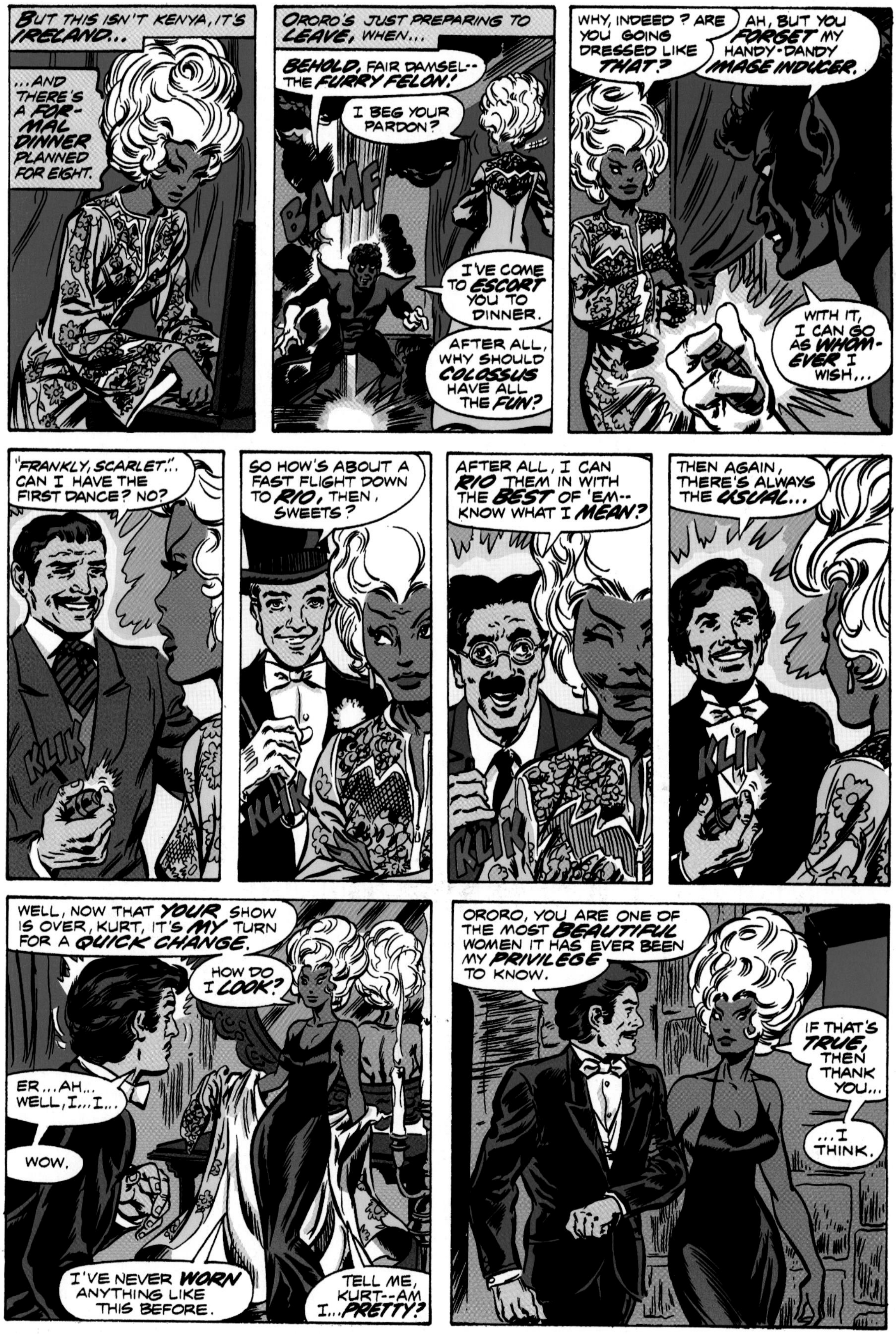
BUT THIS ISN'T KENYA, IT'S IRELAND...
...AND THERE'S A FORMAL DINNER PLANNED FOR EIGHT.
ORORO'S JUST PREPARING TO LEAVE, WHEN...
BEHOLD, FAIR DAMSEL-- THE FURRY FELON!
I BEG YOUR PARDON?
BAMF
I'VE COME TO ESCORT YOU TO DINNER.
AFTER ALL, WHY SHOULD COLOSSUS HAVE ALL THE FUN?
WHY, INDEED? ARE YOU GOING DRESSED LIKE THAT?
AH, BUT YOU FORGET MY HANDY-DANDY IMAGE INDUCER.
WITH IT, I CAN GO AS WHOMEVER I WISH...
"FRANKLY, SCARLET"... CAN I HAVE THE FIRST DANCE? NO?
KLIK
SO HOW'S ABOUT A FAST FLIGHT DOWN TO RIO, THEN, SWEETS?
KLIK
AFTER ALL, I CAN RIO THEM IN WITH THE BEST OF 'EM-- KNOW WHAT I MEAN?
KLIK
THEN AGAIN, THERE'S ALWAYS THE USUAL...
KLIK
WELL, NOW THAT YOUR SHOW IS OVER, KURT, IT'S MY TURN FOR A QUICK CHANGE.
HOW DO I LOOK?
ER...AH... WELL, I...I...
WOW.
I'VE NEVER WORN ANYTHING LIKE THIS BEFORE.
TELL ME, KURT--AM I...PRETTY?
ORORO, YOU ARE ONE OF THE MOST BEAUTIFUL WOMEN IT HAS EVER BEEN MY PRIVILEGE TO KNOW.
IF THAT'S TRUE, THEN THANK YOU...
...I THINK.

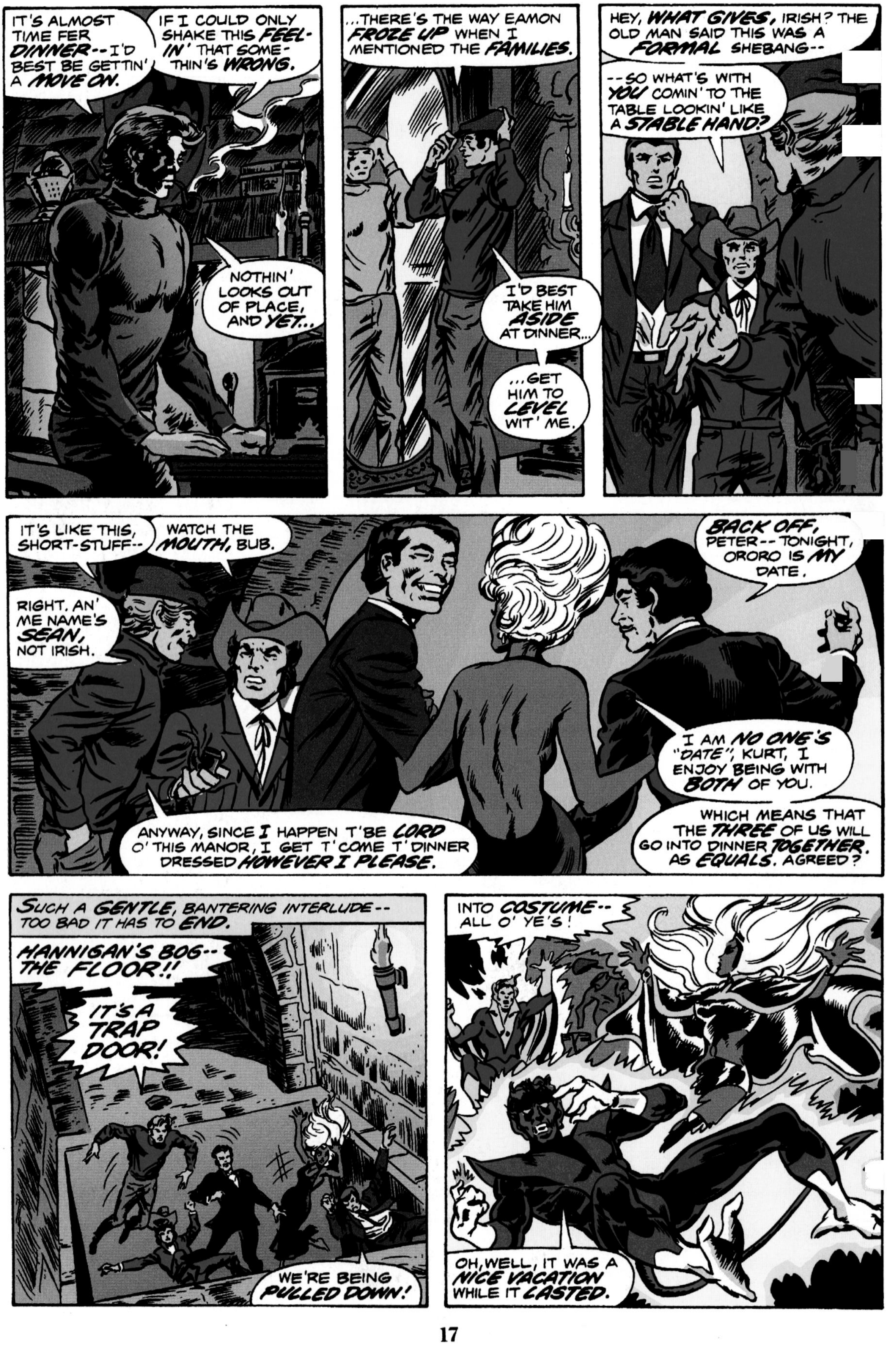

IT'S ALMOST TIME FER DINNER--I'D BEST BE GETTIN' A MOVE ON.
IF I COULD ONLY SHAKE THIS FEEL-IN' THAT SOME-THIN'S WRONG.
NOTHIN' LOOKS OUT OF PLACE, AND YET...
...THERE'S THE WAY EAMON FROZE UP WHEN I MENTIONED THE FAMILIES.
I'D BEST TAKE HIM ASIDE AT DINNER...
...GET HIM TO LEVEL WIT' ME.
HEY, WHAT GIVES, IRISH? THE OLD MAN SAID THIS WAS A FORMAL SHEBANG--
--SO WHAT'S WITH YOU COMIN' TO THE TABLE LOOKIN' LIKE A STABLE HAND?
IT'S LIKE THIS, SHORT-STUFF--
WATCH THE MOUTH, BUB.
RIGHT. AN' ME NAME'S SEAN, NOT IRISH.
ANYWAY, SINCE I HAPPEN T'BE LORD O' THIS MANOR, I GET T'COME T'DINNER DRESSED HOWEVER I PLEASE.
BACK OFF, PETER--TONIGHT, ORORO IS MY DATE.
I AM NO ONE'S "DATE", KURT, I ENJOY BEING WITH BOTH OF YOU.
WHICH MEANS THAT THE THREE OF US WILL GO INTO DINNER TOGETHER. AS EQUALS. AGREED?
SUCH A GENTLE, BANTERING INTERLUDE--TOO BAD IT HAS TO END.
HANNIGAN'S BOG--THE FLOOR!!
IT'S A TRAP DOOR!
WE'RE BEING PULLED DOWN!
INTO COSTUME--ALL O' YE'S!
OH, WELL, IT WAS A NICE VACATION WHILE IT CASTED.

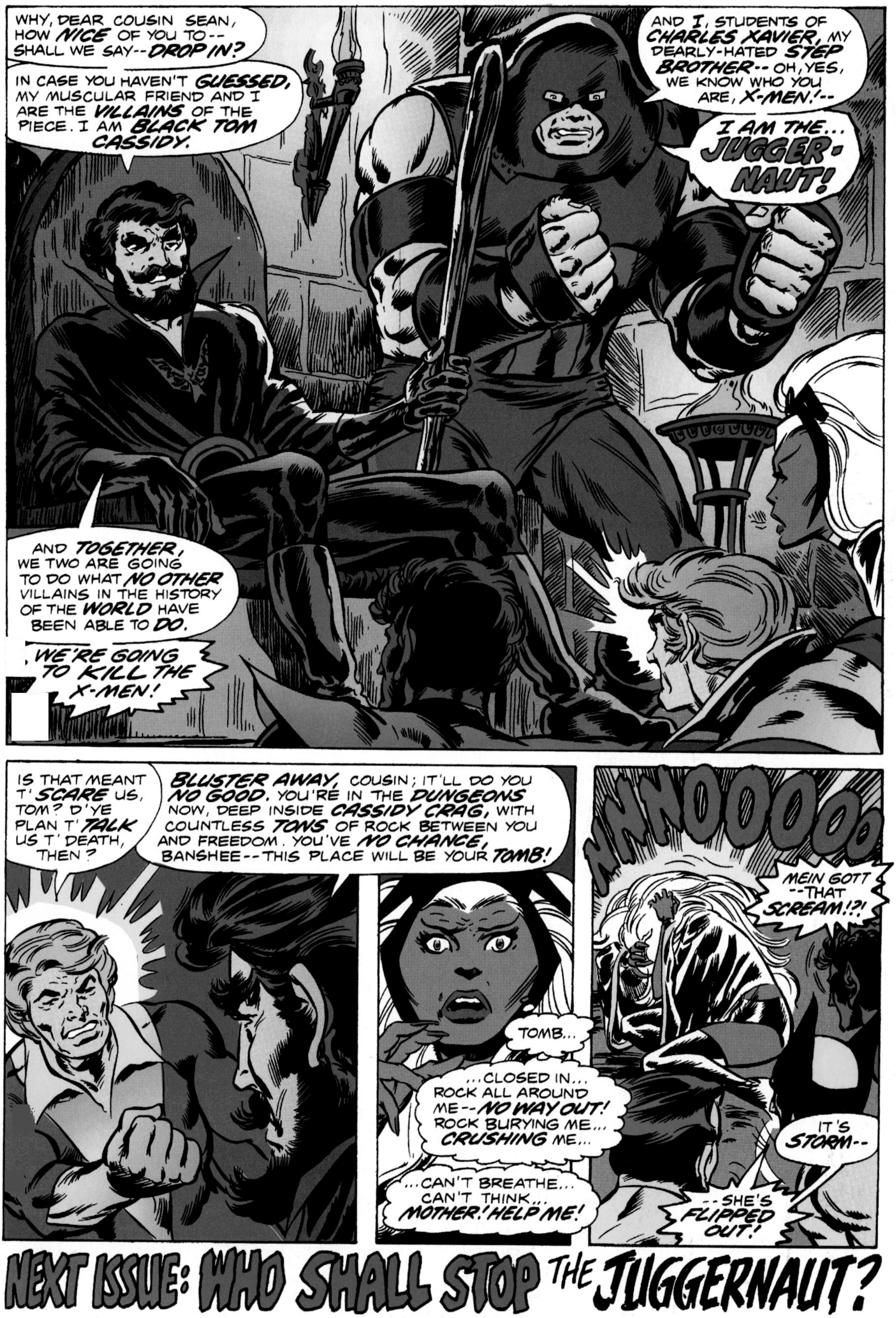

WHY, DEAR COUSIN SEAN, HOW NICE OF YOU TO-- SHALL WE SAY--DROP IN?
IN CASE YOU HAVEN'T GUESSED, MY MUSCULAR FRIEND AND I ARE THE VILLAINS OF THE PIECE. I AM BLACK TOM CASSIDY.
AND I, STUDENTS OF CHARLES XAVIER, MY DEARLY-HATED STEP BROTHER-- OH, YES, WE KNOW WHO YOU ARE, X-MEN!--
I AM THE... JUGGER-NAUT!
AND TOGETHER, WE TWO ARE GOING TO DO WHAT NO OTHER VILLAINS IN THE HISTORY OF THE WORLD HAVE BEEN ABLE TO DO.
WE'RE GOING TO KILL THE X-MEN!
IS THAT MEANT T' SCARE US, TOM? D'YE PLAN T' TALK US T' DEATH, THEN?
BLUSTER AWAY, COUSIN; IT'LL DO YOU NO GOOD. YOU'RE IN THE DUNGEONS NOW, DEEP INSIDE CASSIDY CRAG, WITH COUNTLESS TONS OF ROCK BETWEEN YOU AND FREEDOM. YOU'VE NO CHANCE, BANSHEE--THIS PLACE WILL BE YOUR TOMB!
TOMB...
...CLOSED IN... ROCK ALL AROUND ME--NO WAY OUT! ROCK BURYING ME... CRUSHING ME...
...CAN'T BREATHE... CAN'T THINK... MOTHER! HELP ME!
NNNOOOOOOO
MEIN GOTT --THAT SCREAM!?!
IT'S STORM--
--SHE'S FLIPPED OUT!

NEXT ISSUE: WHO SHALL STOP THE JUGGERNAUT?

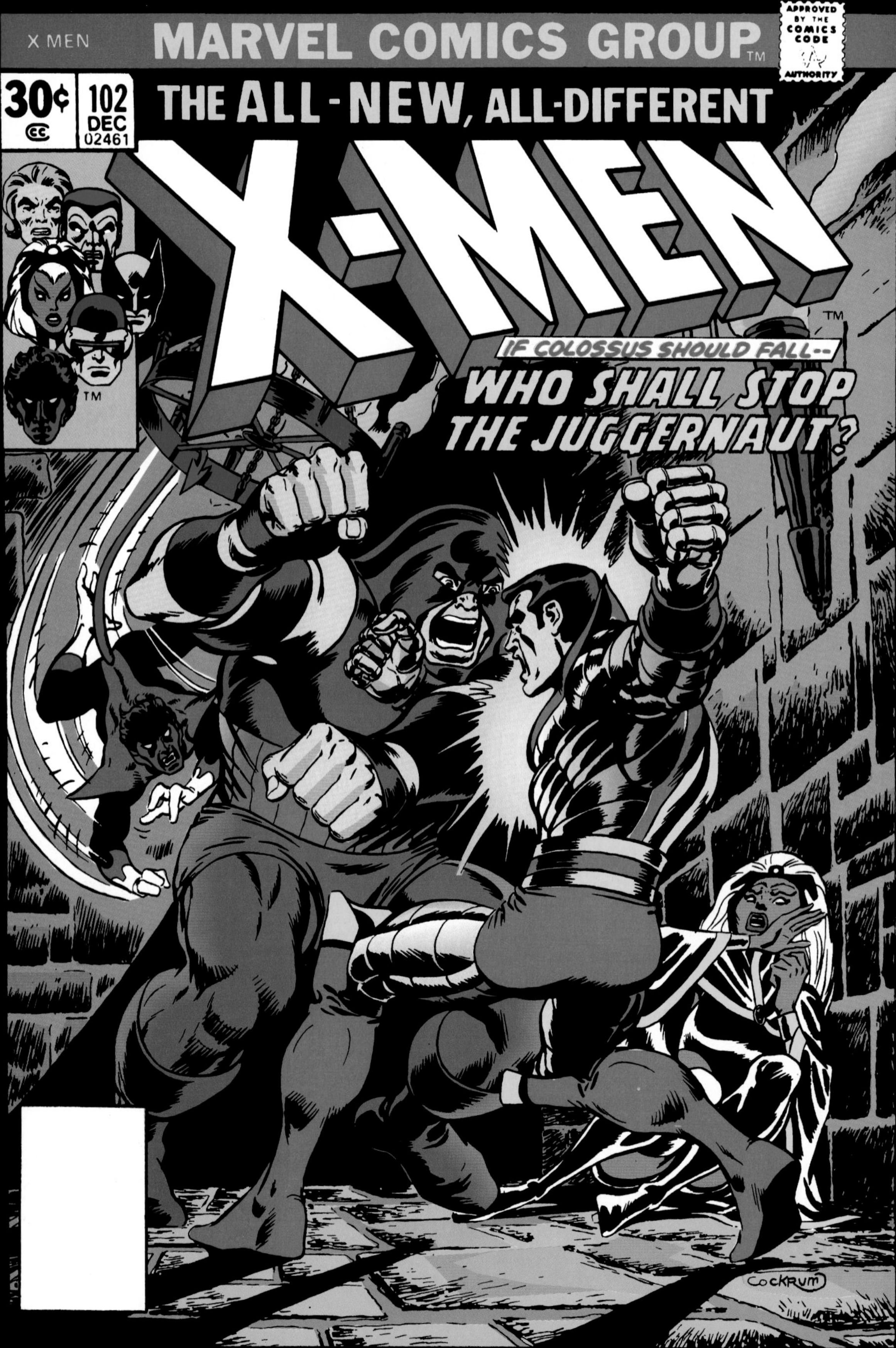
X MEN
MARVEL COMICS GROUP
APPROVED BY THE COMICS CODE AUTHORITY
30¢
102
DEC
02461
THE ALL-NEW, ALL-DIFFERENT
X-MEN
IF COLOSSUS SHOULD FALL--
WHO SHALL STOP THE JUGGERNAUT?
COCKRUM

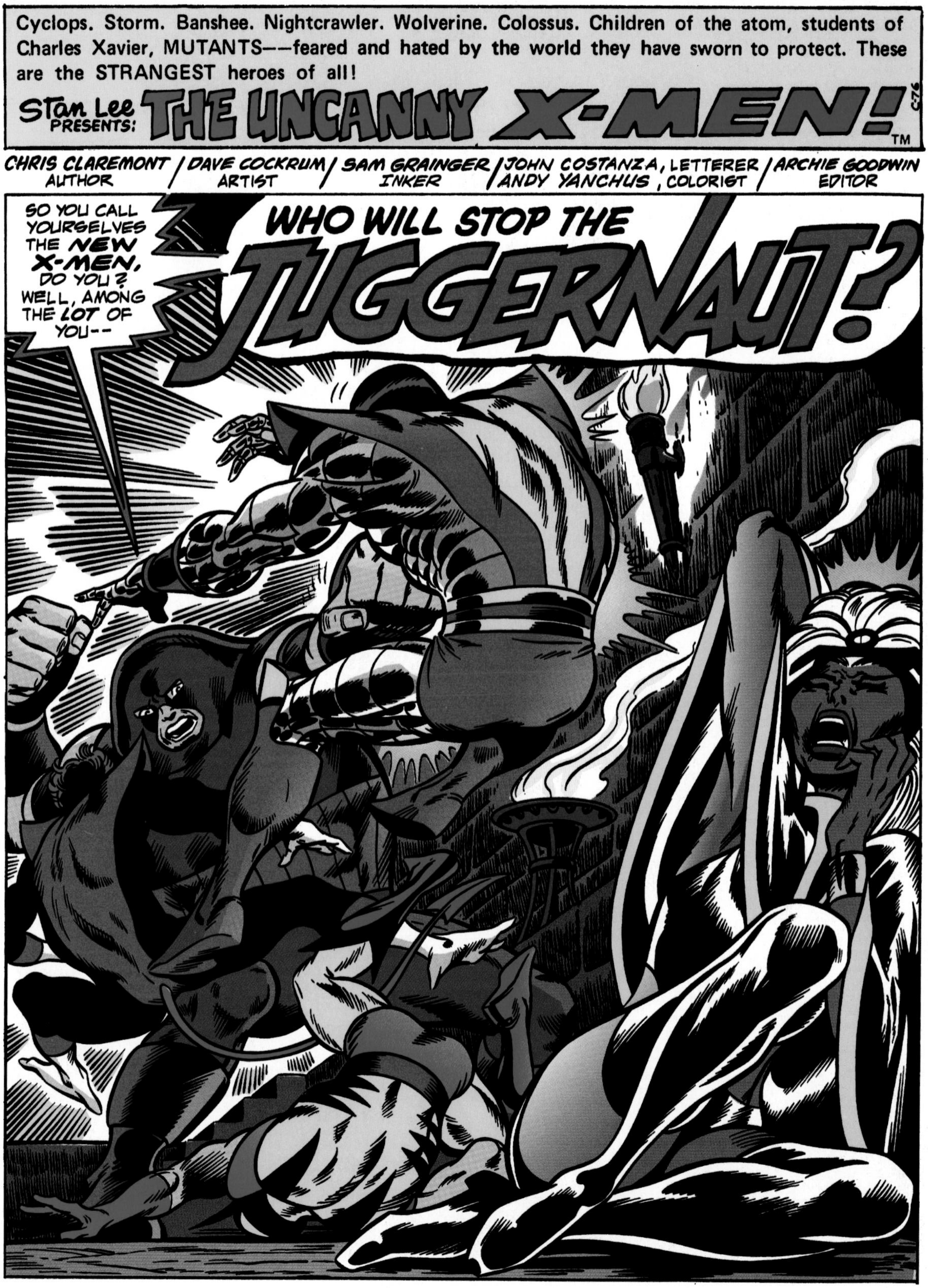

Cyclops. Storm. Banshee. Nightcrawler. Wolverine. Colossus. Children of the atom, students of Charles Xavier, MUTANTS––feared and hated by the world they have sworn to protect. These are the STRANGEST heroes of all!
Stan Lee PRESENTS: THE UNCANNY X-MEN!
CHRIS CLAREMONT AUTHOR / DAVE COCKRUM ARTIST / SAM GRAINGER INKER / JOHN COSTANZA, LETTERER / ANDY YANCHUS, COLORIST / ARCHIE GOODWIN EDITOR
SO YOU CALL YOURSELVES THE NEW X-MEN, DO YOU? WELL, AMONG THE LOT OF YOU--
WHO WILL STOP THE JUGGERNAUT?

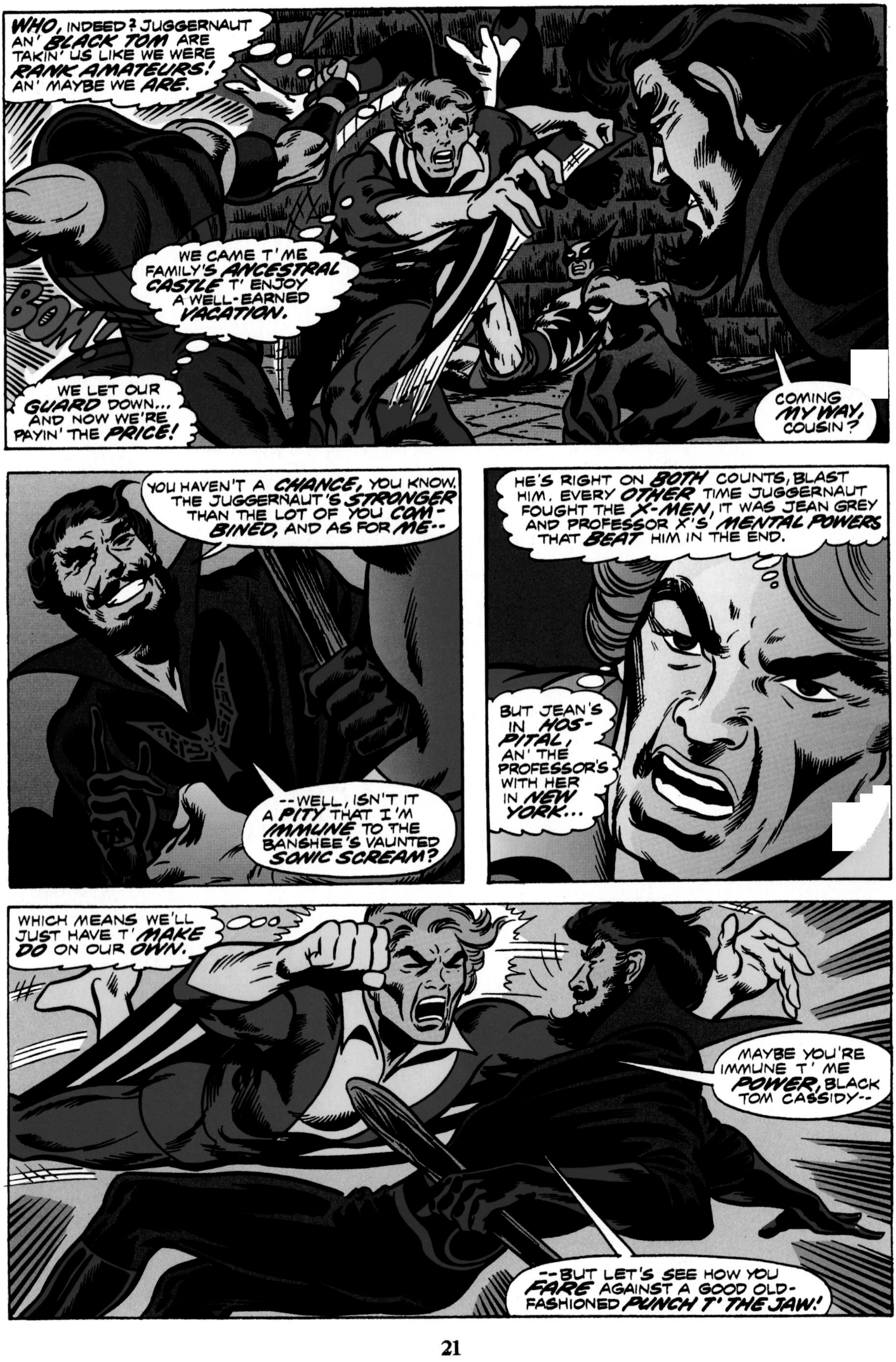
WHO, INDEED? JUGGERNAUT AN' BLACK TOM ARE TAKIN' US LIKE WE WERE RANK AMATEURS! AN' MAYBE WE ARE.
WE CAME T'ME FAMILY'S ANCESTRAL CASTLE T' ENJOY A WELL-EARNED VACATION.
BOM!
WE LET OUR GUARD DOWN... AND NOW WE'RE PAYIN' THE PRICE!
COMING MY WAY, COUSIN?
YOU HAVEN'T A CHANCE, YOU KNOW. THE JUGGERNAUT'S STRONGER THAN THE LOT OF YOU COMBINED, AND AS FOR ME--
--WELL, ISN'T IT A PITY THAT I'M IMMUNE TO THE BANSHEE'S VAUNTED SONIC SCREAM?
HE'S RIGHT ON BOTH COUNTS, BLAST HIM. EVERY OTHER TIME JUGGERNAUT FOUGHT THE X-MEN, IT WAS JEAN GREY AND PROFESSOR X'S MENTAL POWERS THAT BEAT HIM IN THE END.
BUT JEAN'S IN HOSPITAL, AN' THE PROFESSOR'S WITH HER IN NEW YORK...
WHICH MEANS WE'LL JUST HAVE T' MAKE DO ON OUR OWN.
MAYBE YOU'RE IMMUNE T' ME POWER, BLACK TOM CASSIDY--
--BUT LET'S SEE HOW YOU FARE AGAINST A GOOD OLD-FASHIONED PUNCH T' THE JAW!

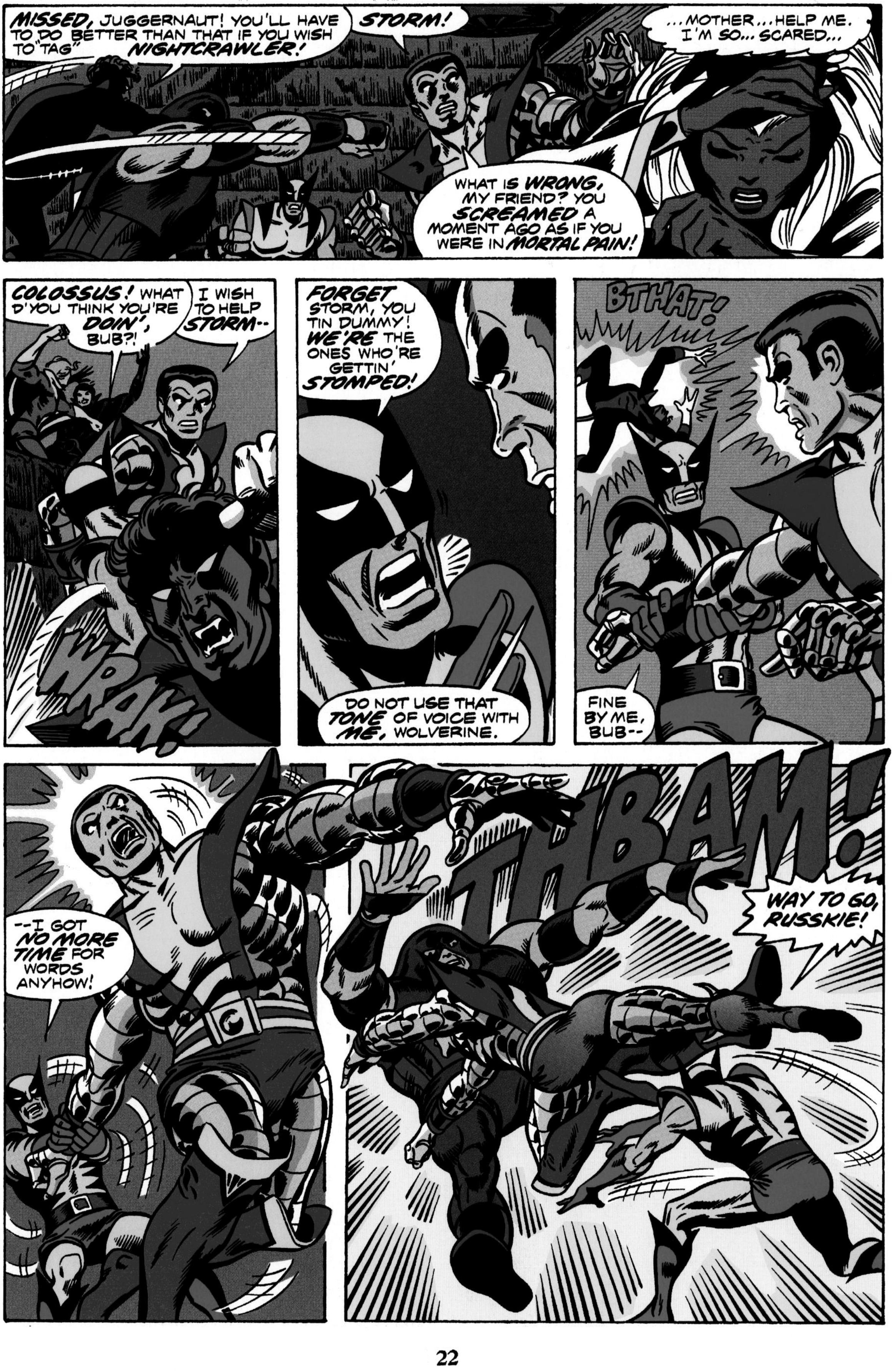
MISSED, JUGGERNAUT! YOU'LL HAVE TO DO BETTER THAN THAT IF YOU WISH TO "TAG" NIGHTCRAWLER!
STORM!
...MOTHER...HELP ME. I'M SO... SCARED...
WHAT IS WRONG, MY FRIEND? YOU SCREAMED A MOMENT AGO AS IF YOU WERE IN MORTAL PAIN!
COLOSSUS! WHAT D'YOU THINK YOU'RE DOIN', BUB?!
I WISH TO HELP STORM--
WRAK!
FORGET STORM, YOU TIN DUMMY! WE'RE THE ONES WHO'RE GETTIN' STOMPED!
DO NOT USE THAT TONE OF VOICE WITH ME, WOLVERINE.
BTHAT!
FINE BY ME, BUB--
--I GOT NO MORE TIME FOR WORDS ANYHOW!
THBAM!
WAY TO GO, RUSSKIE!

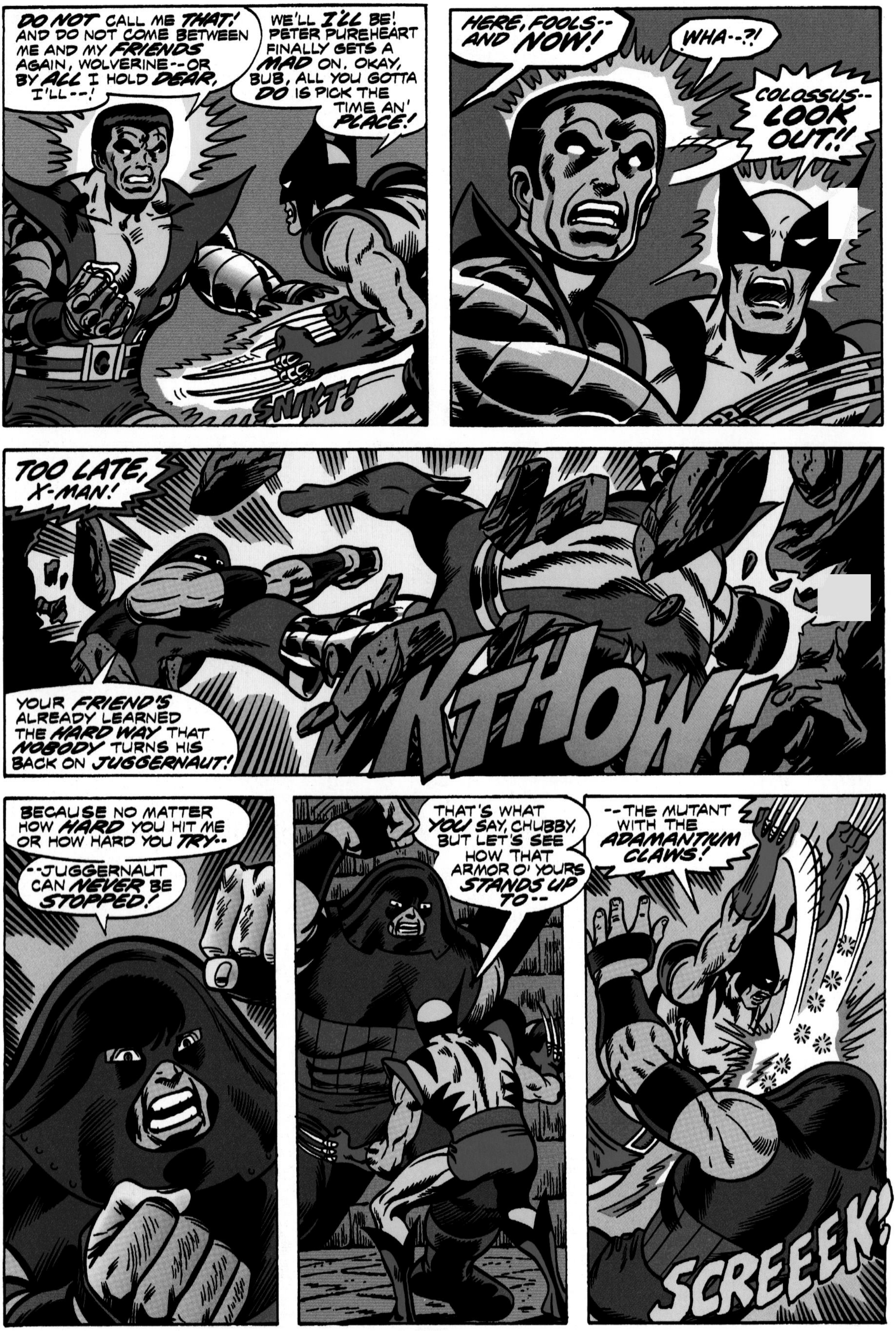
DO NOT CALL ME THAT! AND DO NOT COME BETWEEN ME AND MY FRIENDS AGAIN, WOLVERINE--OR BY ALL I HOLD DEAR, I'LL--!
WE'LL I'LL BE! PETER PUREHEART FINALLY GETS A MAD ON. OKAY, BUB, ALL YOU GOTTA DO IS PICK THE TIME AN' PLACE!
SNIKT!
HERE, FOOLS--AND NOW!
WHA--?!
COLOSSUS--LOOK OUT!!
TOO LATE, X-MAN!
YOUR FRIEND'S ALREADY LEARNED THE HARD WAY THAT NOBODY TURNS HIS BACK ON JUGGERNAUT!
KTHOW!
BECAUSE NO MATTER HOW HARD YOU HIT ME OR HOW HARD YOU TRY--
--JUGGERNAUT CAN NEVER BE STOPPED!
THAT'S WHAT YOU SAY, CHUBBY, BUT LET'S SEE HOW THAT ARMOR O' YOURS STANDS UP TO--
--THE MUTANT WITH THE ADAMANTIUM CLAWS!
SCREEEK!

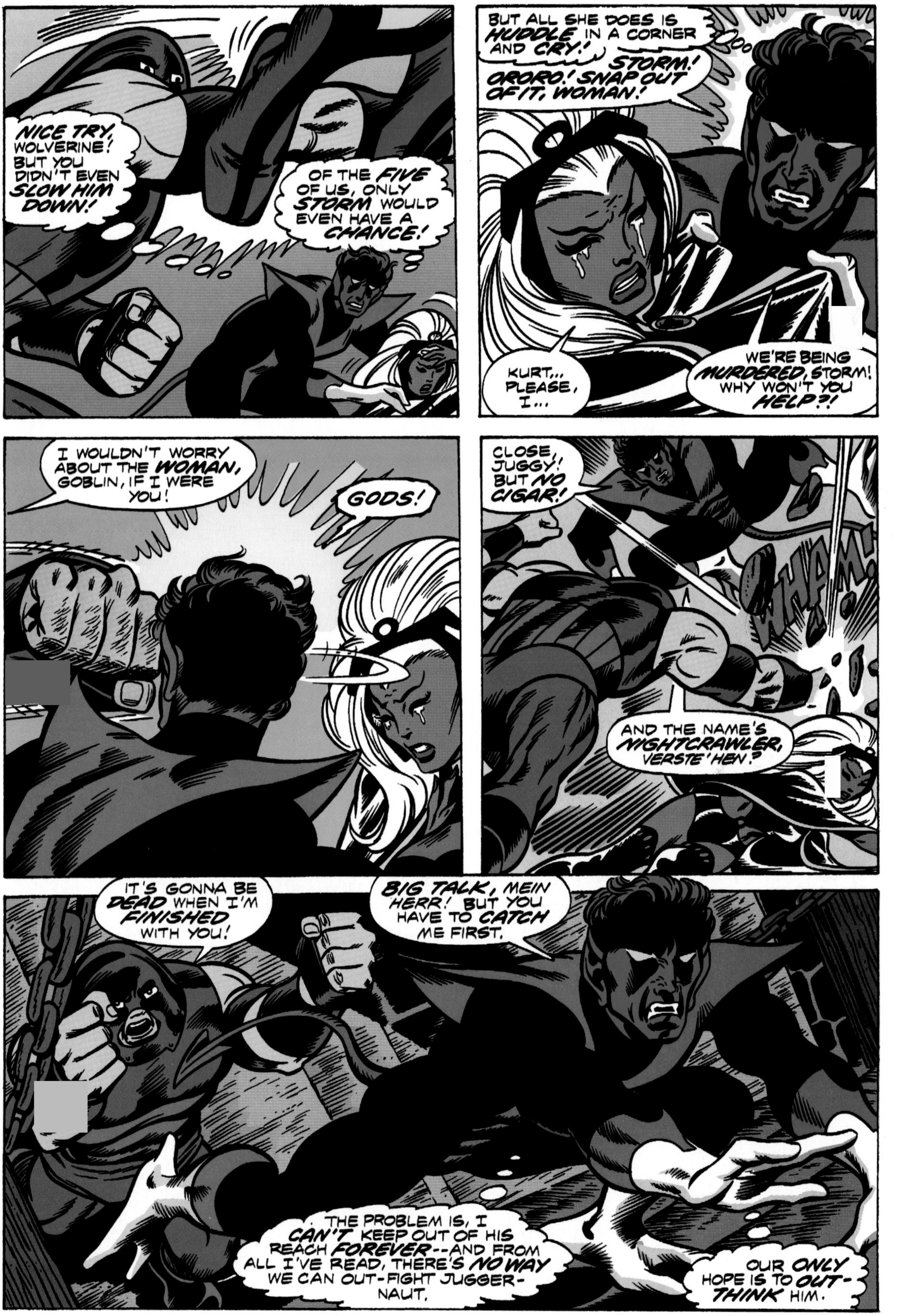
NICE TRY, WOLVERINE! BUT YOU DIDN'T EVEN SLOW HIM DOWN!
OF THE FIVE OF US, ONLY STORM WOULD EVEN HAVE A CHANCE!
BUT ALL SHE DOES IS HUDDLE IN A CORNER AND CRY!
STORM! ORORO! SNAP OUT OF IT, WOMAN!
KURT... PLEASE, I...
WE'RE BEING MURDERED, STORM! WHY WON'T YOU HELP?!
I WOULDN'T WORRY ABOUT THE WOMAN, GOBLIN, IF I WERE YOU!
GODS!
CLOSE, JUGGY! BUT NO CIGAR!
WHAM!
AND THE NAME'S NIGHTCRAWLER, VERSTE'HEN?
IT'S GONNA BE DEAD WHEN I'M FINISHED WITH YOU!
BIG TALK, MEIN HERR! BUT YOU HAVE TO CATCH ME FIRST.
THE PROBLEM IS, I CAN'T KEEP OUT OF HIS REACH FOREVER--AND FROM ALL I'VE READ, THERE'S NO WAY WE CAN OUT-FIGHT JUGGER-NAUT.
OUR ONLY HOPE IS TO OUT-THINK HIM.

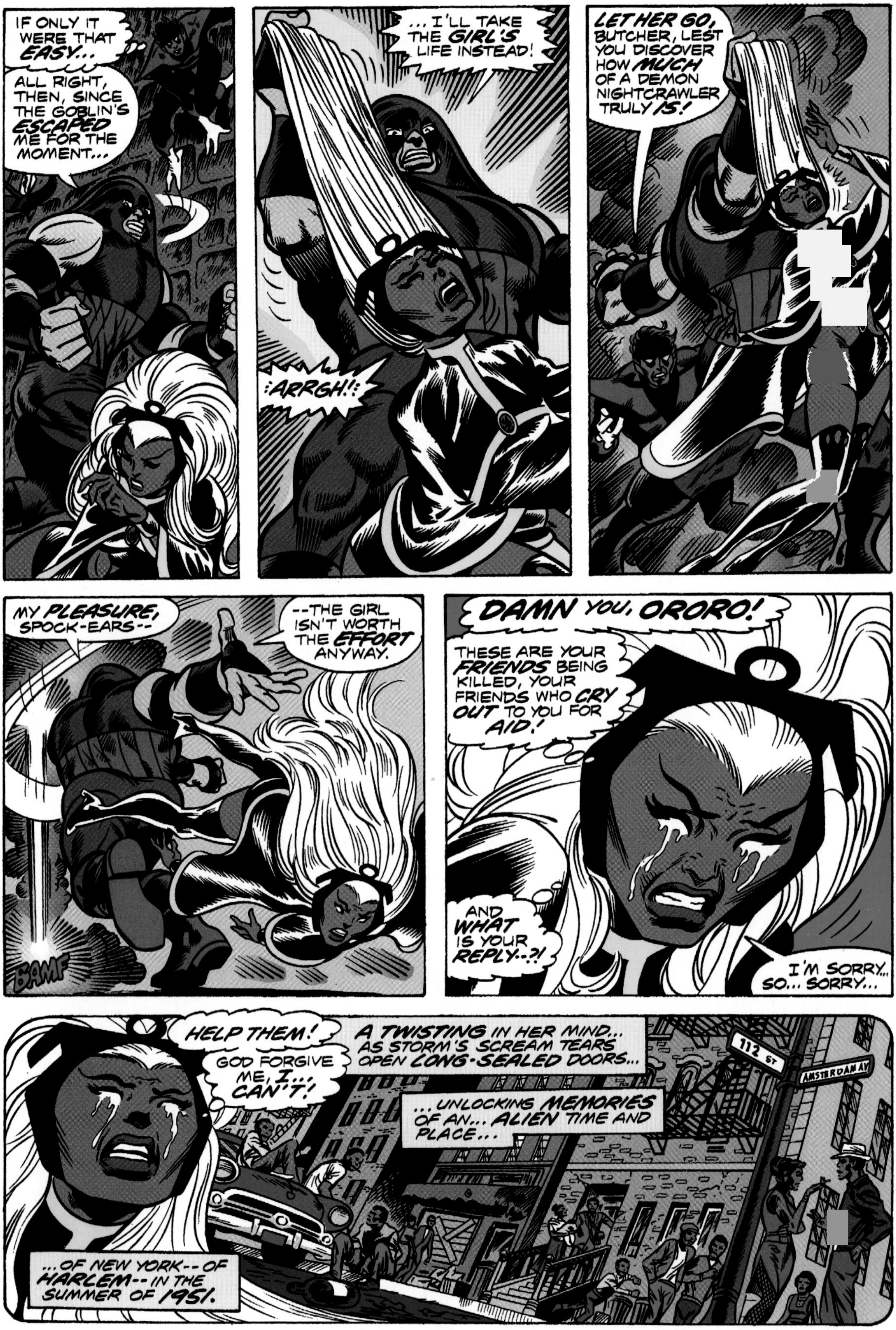

IF ONLY IT WERE THAT EASY...
ALL RIGHT, THEN, SINCE THE GOBLIN'S ESCAPED ME FOR THE MOMENT...
... I'LL TAKE THE GIRL'S LIFE INSTEAD!
ARRGH!!
LET HER GO, BUTCHER, LEST YOU DISCOVER HOW MUCH OF A DEMON NIGHTCRAWLER TRULY IS!
MY PLEASURE, SPOCK-EARS--
--THE GIRL ISN'T WORTH THE EFFORT ANYWAY.
BAMF
DAMN YOU, ORORO!
THESE ARE YOUR FRIENDS BEING KILLED, YOUR FRIENDS WHO CRY OUT TO YOU FOR AID!
AND WHAT IS YOUR REPLY..?!
I'M SORRY... SO... SORRY...
HELP THEM!
GOD FORGIVE ME, I... CAN'T!
A TWISTING IN HER MIND... AS STORM'S SCREAM TEARS OPEN LONG-SEALED DOORS...
112 ST
AMSTERDAM AV
...UNLOCKING MEMORIES OF AN... ALIEN TIME AND PLACE...
...OF NEW YORK-- OF HARLEM-- IN THE SUMMER OF 1951.

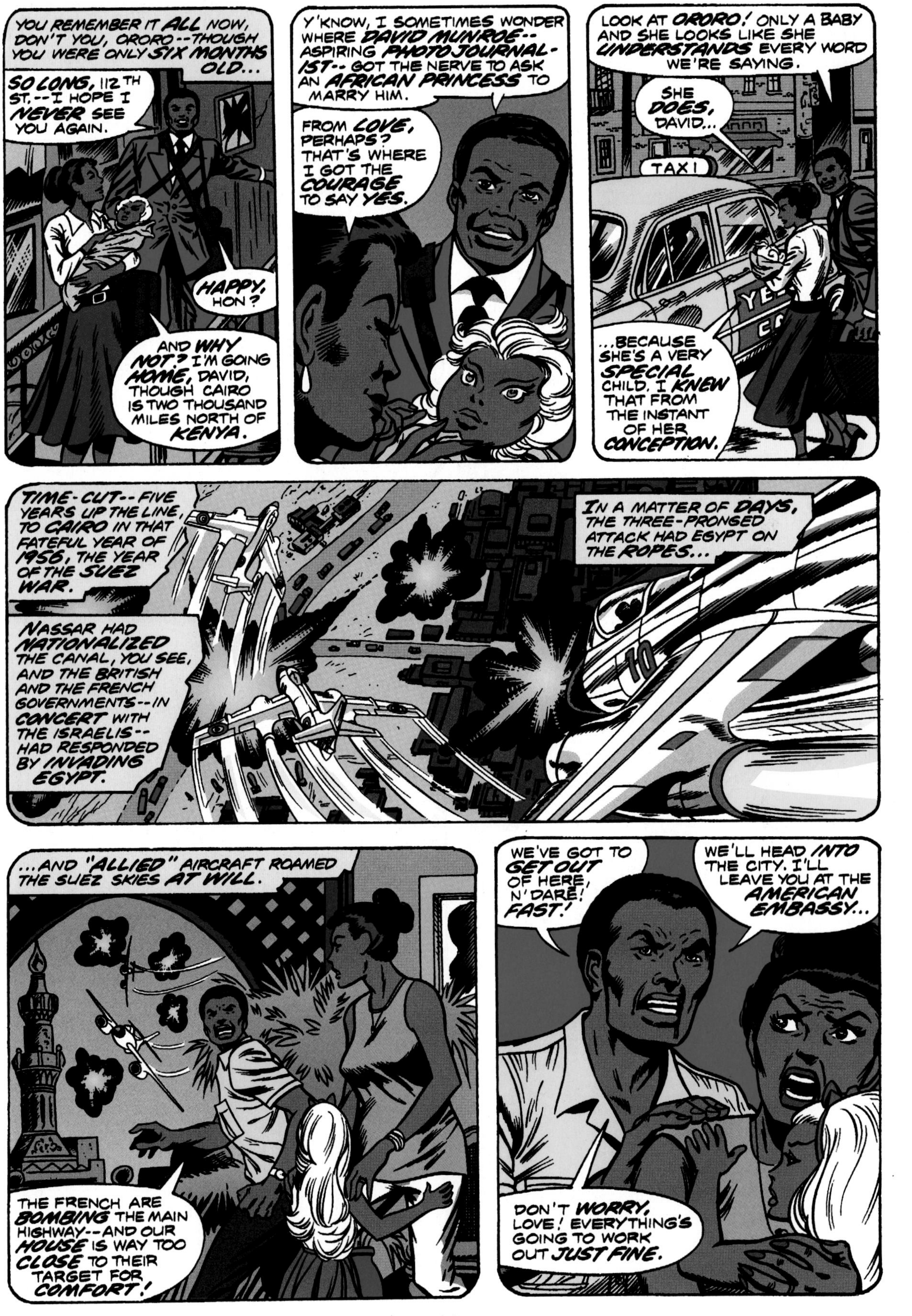
YOU REMEMBER IT ALL NOW, DON'T YOU, ORORO--THOUGH YOU WERE ONLY SIX MONTHS OLD...
SO LONG, 112TH ST.--I HOPE I NEVER SEE YOU AGAIN.
HAPPY, HON?
AND WHY NOT? I'M GOING HOME, DAVID, THOUGH CAIRO IS TWO THOUSAND MILES NORTH OF KENYA.
Y'KNOW, I SOMETIMES WONDER WHERE DAVID MUNROE--ASPIRING PHOTOJOURNALIST--GOT THE NERVE TO ASK AN AFRICAN PRINCESS TO MARRY HIM.
FROM LOVE, PERHAPS? THAT'S WHERE I GOT THE COURAGE TO SAY YES.
LOOK AT ORORO! ONLY A BABY AND SHE LOOKS LIKE SHE UNDERSTANDS EVERY WORD WE'RE SAYING.
SHE DOES, DAVID...
TAXI
...BECAUSE SHE'S A VERY SPECIAL CHILD. I KNEW THAT FROM THE INSTANT OF HER CONCEPTION.
TIME-CUT--FIVE YEARS UP THE LINE, TO CAIRO IN THAT FATEFUL YEAR OF 1956, THE YEAR OF THE SUEZ WAR.
NASSAR HAD NATIONALIZED THE CANAL, YOU SEE, AND THE BRITISH AND THE FRENCH GOVERNMENTS--IN CONCERT WITH THE ISRAELIS--HAD RESPONDED BY INVADING EGYPT.
IN A MATTER OF DAYS, THE THREE-PRONGED ATTACK HAD EGYPT ON THE ROPES...
...AND "ALLIED" AIRCRAFT ROAMED THE SUEZ SKIES AT WILL.
THE FRENCH ARE BOMBING THE MAIN HIGHWAY--AND OUR HOUSE IS WAY TOO CLOSE TO THEIR TARGET FOR COMFORT!
WE'VE GOT TO GET OUT OF HERE, N'DARÉ! FAST!
WE'LL HEAD INTO THE CITY. I'LL LEAVE YOU AT THE AMERICAN EMBASSY...
DON'T WORRY, LOVE! EVERYTHING'S GOING TO WORK OUT JUST FINE.

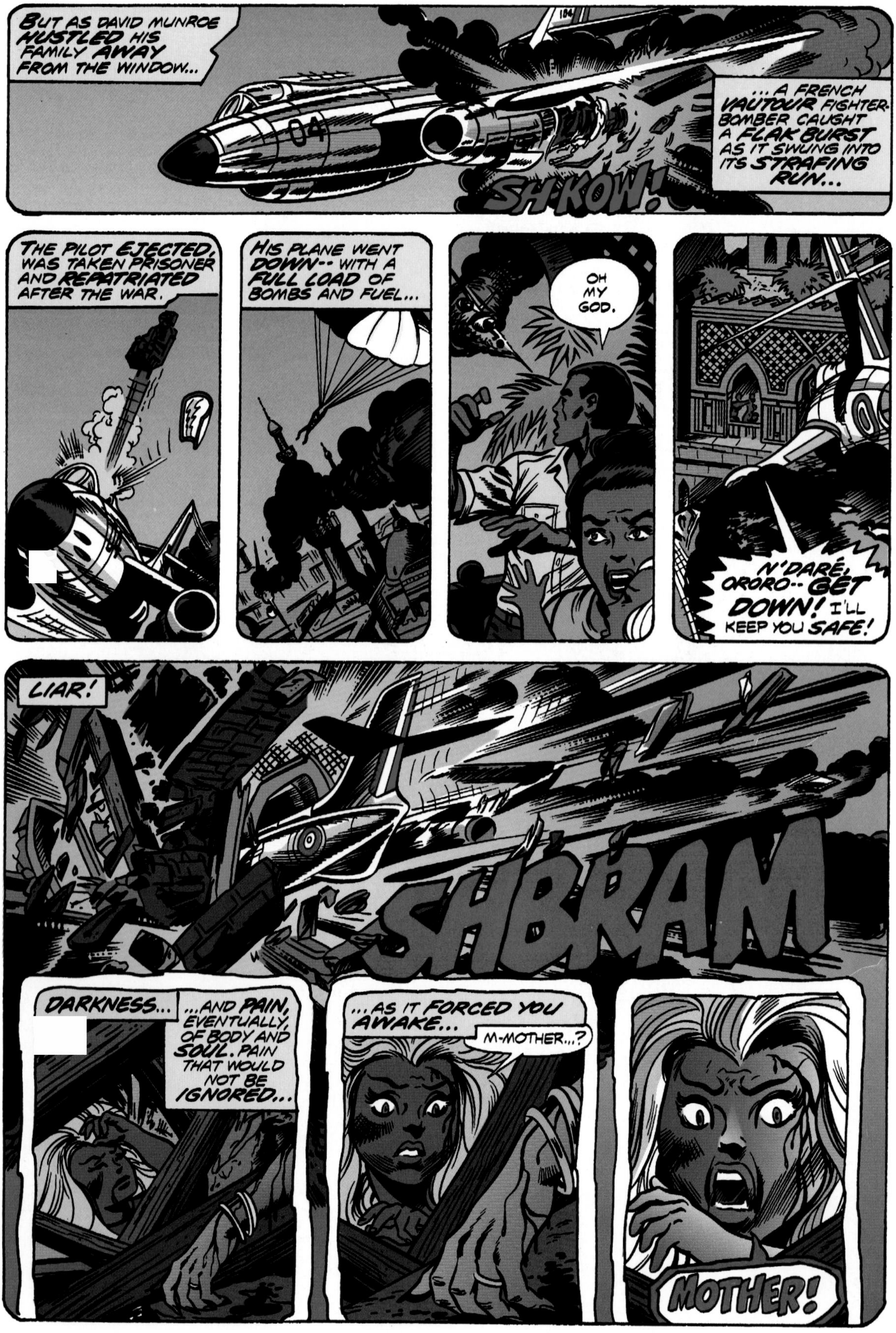

BUT AS DAVID MUNROE HUSTLED HIS FAMILY AWAY FROM THE WINDOW...
...A FRENCH VAUTOUR FIGHTER-BOMBER CAUGHT A FLAK BURST AS IT SWUNG INTO ITS STRAFING RUN...
SH-KOW!
THE PILOT EJECTED, WAS TAKEN PRISONER AND REPATRIATED AFTER THE WAR.
HIS PLANE WENT DOWN-- WITH A FULL LOAD OF BOMBS AND FUEL...
OH MY GOD.
N'DARÉ, ORORO-- GET DOWN! I'LL KEEP YOU SAFE!
LIAR!
SHBRAM
DARKNESS...
...AND PAIN, EVENTUALLY, OF BODY AND SOUL. PAIN THAT WOULD NOT BE IGNORED...
...AS IT FORCED YOU AWAKE...
M-MOTHER...?
MOTHER!

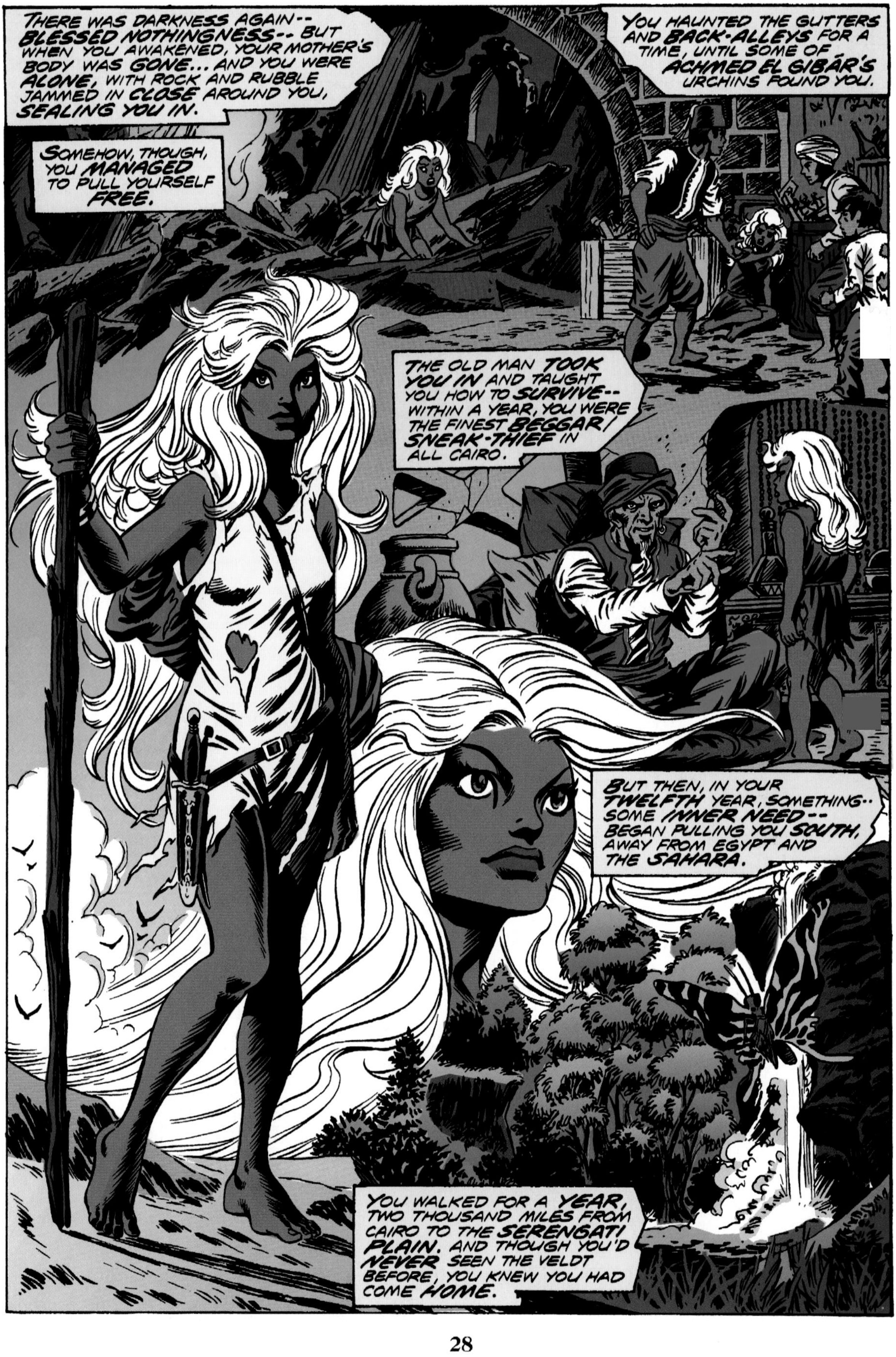
THERE WAS DARKNESS AGAIN-- BLESSED NOTHINGNESS-- BUT WHEN YOU AWAKENED, YOUR MOTHER'S BODY WAS GONE... AND YOU WERE ALONE, WITH ROCK AND RUBBLE JAMMED IN CLOSE AROUND YOU, SEALING YOU IN.
SOMEHOW, THOUGH, YOU MANAGED TO PULL YOURSELF FREE.
YOU HAUNTED THE GUTTERS AND BACK-ALLEYS FOR A TIME, UNTIL SOME OF ACHMED EL GIBÁR'S URCHINS FOUND YOU.
THE OLD MAN TOOK YOU IN AND TAUGHT YOU HOW TO SURVIVE-- WITHIN A YEAR, YOU WERE THE FINEST BEGGAR/ SNEAK-THIEF IN ALL CAIRO.
BUT THEN, IN YOUR TWELFTH YEAR, SOMETHING-- SOME INNER NEED-- BEGAN PULLING YOU SOUTH, AWAY FROM EGYPT AND THE SAHARA.
YOU WALKED FOR A YEAR, TWO THOUSAND MILES FROM CAIRO TO THE SERENGATI PLAIN. AND THOUGH YOU'D NEVER SEEN THE VELDT BEFORE, YOU KNEW YOU HAD COME HOME.

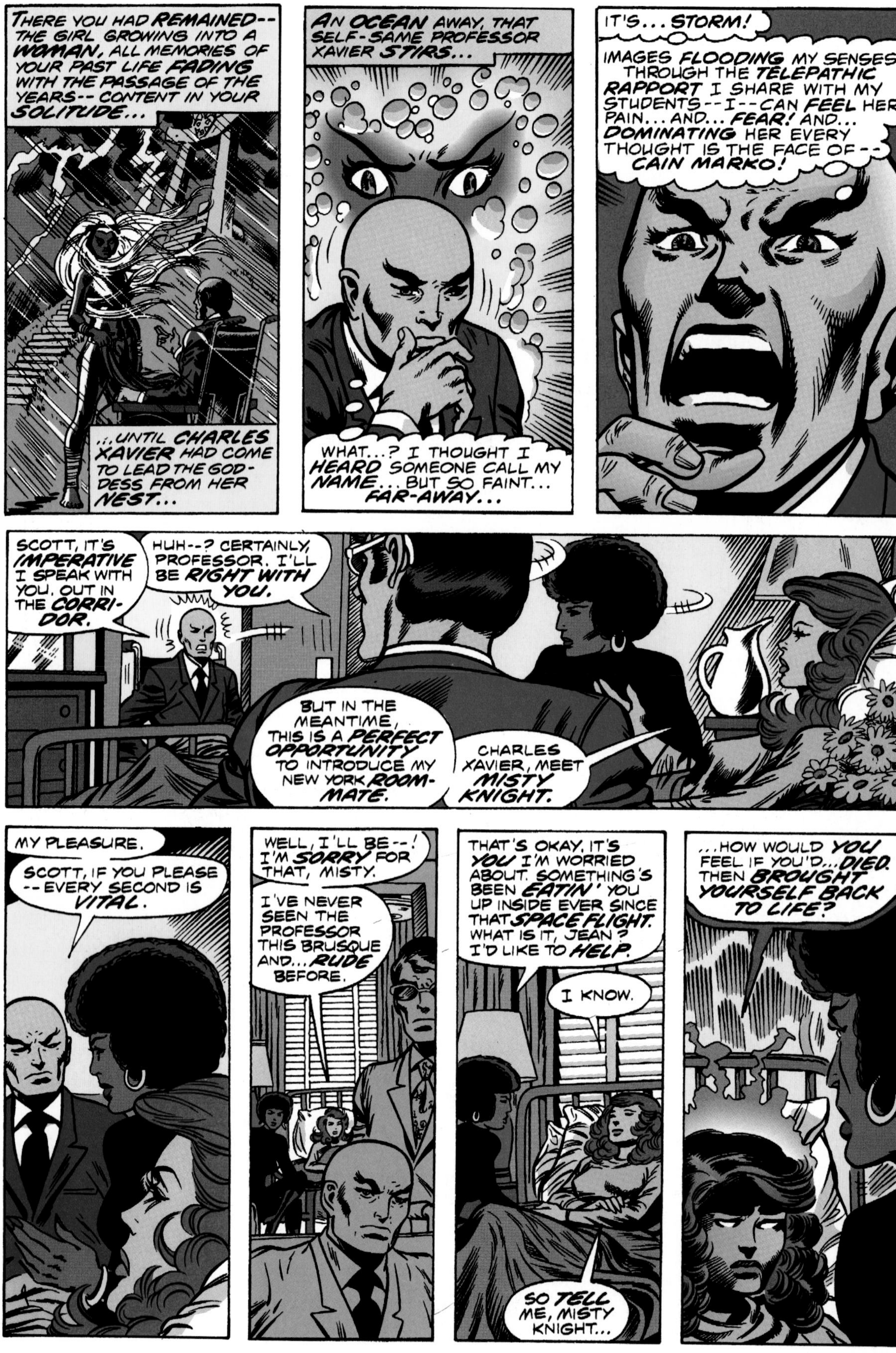
THERE YOU HAD REMAINED-- THE GIRL GROWING INTO A WOMAN, ALL MEMORIES OF YOUR PAST LIFE FADING WITH THE PASSAGE OF THE YEARS-- CONTENT IN YOUR SOLITUDE...
...UNTIL CHARLES XAVIER HAD COME TO LEAD THE GOD-DESS FROM HER NEST...
AN OCEAN AWAY, THAT SELF-SAME PROFESSOR XAVIER STIRS...
WHAT...? I THOUGHT I HEARD SOMEONE CALL MY NAME... BUT SO FAINT... FAR-AWAY...
IT'S... STORM!
IMAGES FLOODING MY SENSES THROUGH THE TELEPATHIC RAPPORT I SHARE WITH MY STUDENTS--I--CAN FEEL HER PAIN... AND... FEAR! AND... DOMINATING HER EVERY THOUGHT IS THE FACE OF-- CAIN MARKO!
SCOTT, IT'S IMPERATIVE I SPEAK WITH YOU. OUT IN THE CORRI-DOR.
HUH--? CERTAINLY, PROFESSOR. I'LL BE RIGHT WITH YOU.
BUT IN THE MEANTIME, THIS IS A PERFECT OPPORTUNITY TO INTRODUCE MY NEW YORK ROOM-MATE.
CHARLES XAVIER, MEET MISTY KNIGHT.
MY PLEASURE.
SCOTT, IF YOU PLEASE --EVERY SECOND IS VITAL.
WELL, I'LL BE--! I'M SORRY FOR THAT, MISTY.
I'VE NEVER SEEN THE PROFESSOR THIS BRUSQUE AND... RUDE BEFORE.
THAT'S OKAY, IT'S YOU I'M WORRIED ABOUT. SOMETHING'S BEEN EATIN' YOU UP INSIDE EVER SINCE THAT SPACE FLIGHT. WHAT IS IT, JEAN? I'D LIKE TO HELP.
I KNOW.
SO TELL ME, MISTY KNIGHT...
...HOW WOULD YOU FEEL IF YOU'D... DIED. THEN BROUGHT YOURSELF BACK TO LIFE?

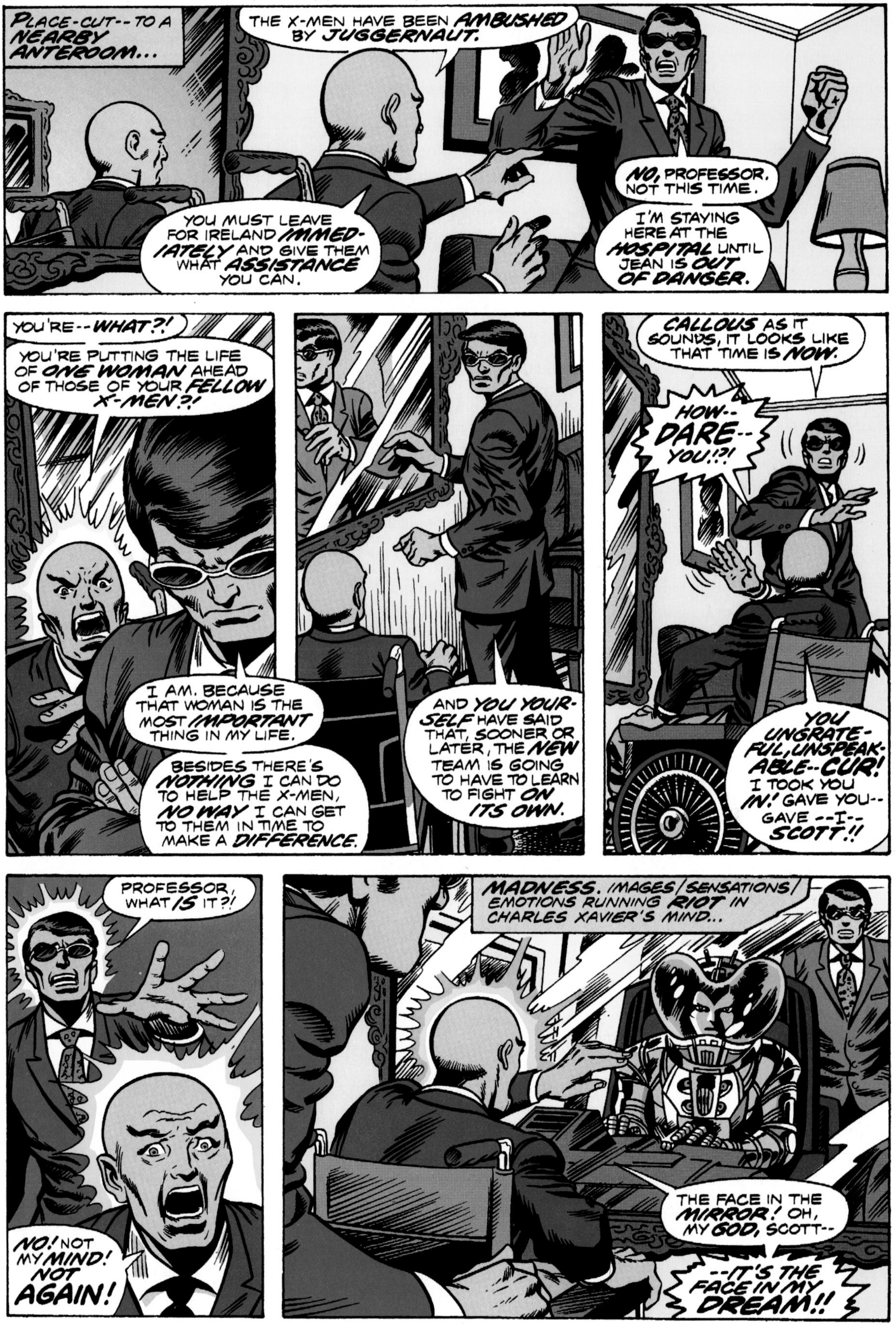

PLACE-CUT--TO A NEARBY ANTEROOM...
THE X-MEN HAVE BEEN AMBUSHED BY JUGGERNAUT.
YOU MUST LEAVE FOR IRELAND IMMED-IATELY AND GIVE THEM WHAT ASSISTANCE YOU CAN.
NO, PROFESSOR. NOT THIS TIME.
I'M STAYING HERE AT THE HOSPITAL UNTIL JEAN IS OUT OF DANGER.
YOU'RE--WHAT?!
YOU'RE PUTTING THE LIFE OF ONE WOMAN AHEAD OF THOSE OF YOUR FELLOW X-MEN?!
I AM. BECAUSE THAT WOMAN IS THE MOST IMPORTANT THING IN MY LIFE.
BESIDES THERE'S NOTHING I CAN DO TO HELP THE X-MEN, NO WAY I CAN GET TO THEM IN TIME TO MAKE A DIFFERENCE.
AND YOU YOURSELF HAVE SAID THAT, SOONER OR LATER, THE NEW TEAM IS GOING TO HAVE TO LEARN TO FIGHT ON ITS OWN.
CALLOUS AS IT SOUNDS, IT LOOKS LIKE THAT TIME IS NOW.
HOW--DARE--YOU!?!
YOU UNGRATE-FUL, UNSPEAK-ABLE--CUR! I TOOK YOU IN! GAVE YOU--GAVE --I-- SCOTT!!
PROFESSOR, WHAT IS IT?!
NO! NOT MY MIND! NOT AGAIN!
MADNESS. IMAGES/SENSATIONS/EMOTIONS RUNNING RIOT IN CHARLES XAVIER'S MIND...
THE FACE IN THE MIRROR! OH, MY GOD, SCOTT--
--IT'S THE FACE IN MY DREAM!!

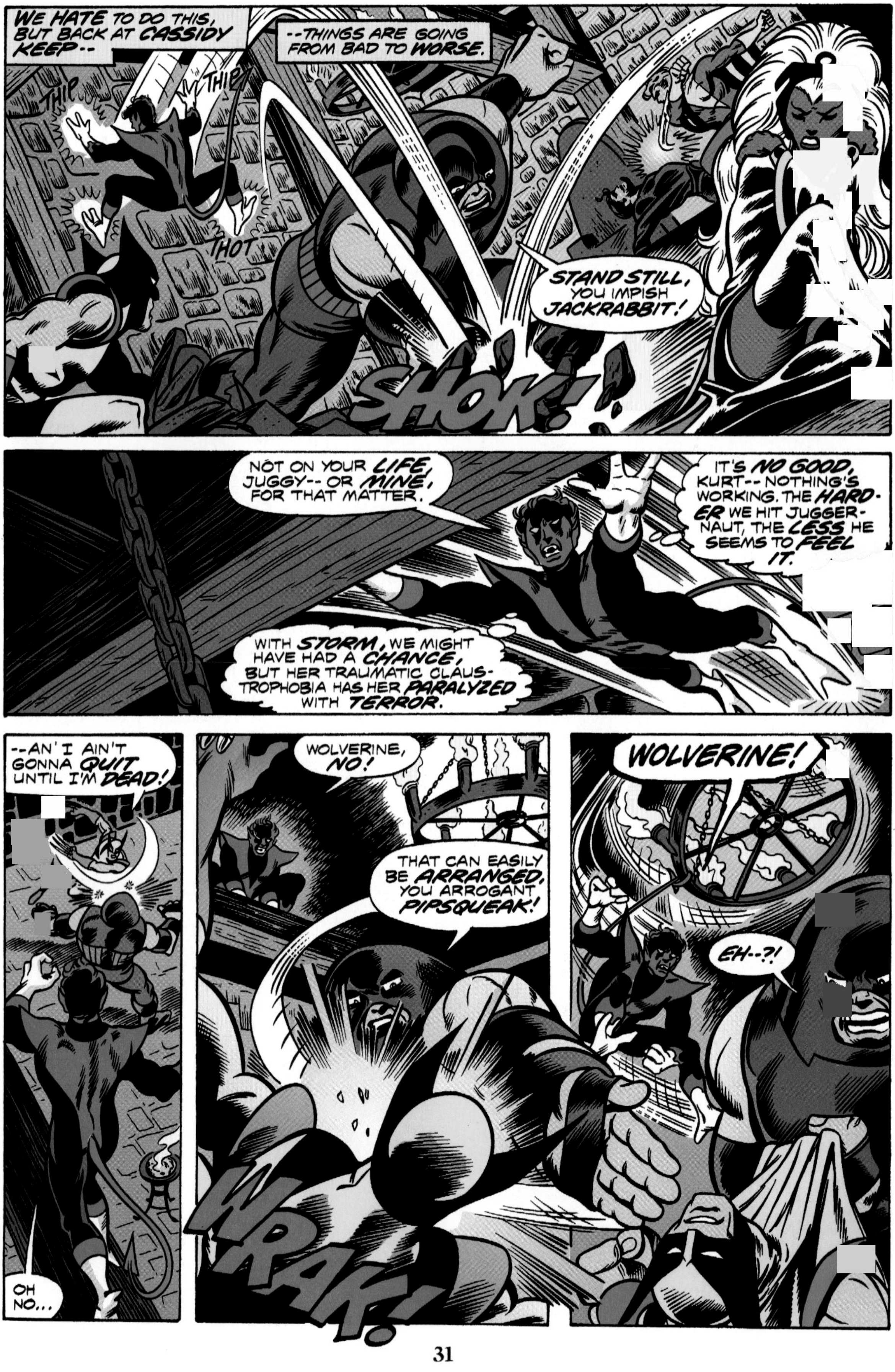

WE HATE TO DO THIS, BUT BACK AT CASSIDY KEEP--
--THINGS ARE GOING FROM BAD TO WORSE.
THIP
THIP
THOT
STAND STILL, YOU IMPISH JACKRABBIT!
SHOK!
NOT ON YOUR LIFE, JUGGY-- OR MINE, FOR THAT MATTER.
IT'S NO GOOD, KURT-- NOTHING'S WORKING. THE HARDER WE HIT JUGGERNAUT, THE LESS HE SEEMS TO FEEL IT.
WITH STORM, WE MIGHT HAVE HAD A CHANCE, BUT HER TRAUMATIC CLAUSTROPHOBIA HAS HER PARALYZED WITH TERROR.
--AN' I AIN'T GONNA QUIT UNTIL I'M DEAD!
OH NO...
WOLVERINE, NO!
THAT CAN EASILY BE ARRANGED, YOU ARROGANT PIPSQUEAK!
WRAK!
WOLVERINE!
EH--?!

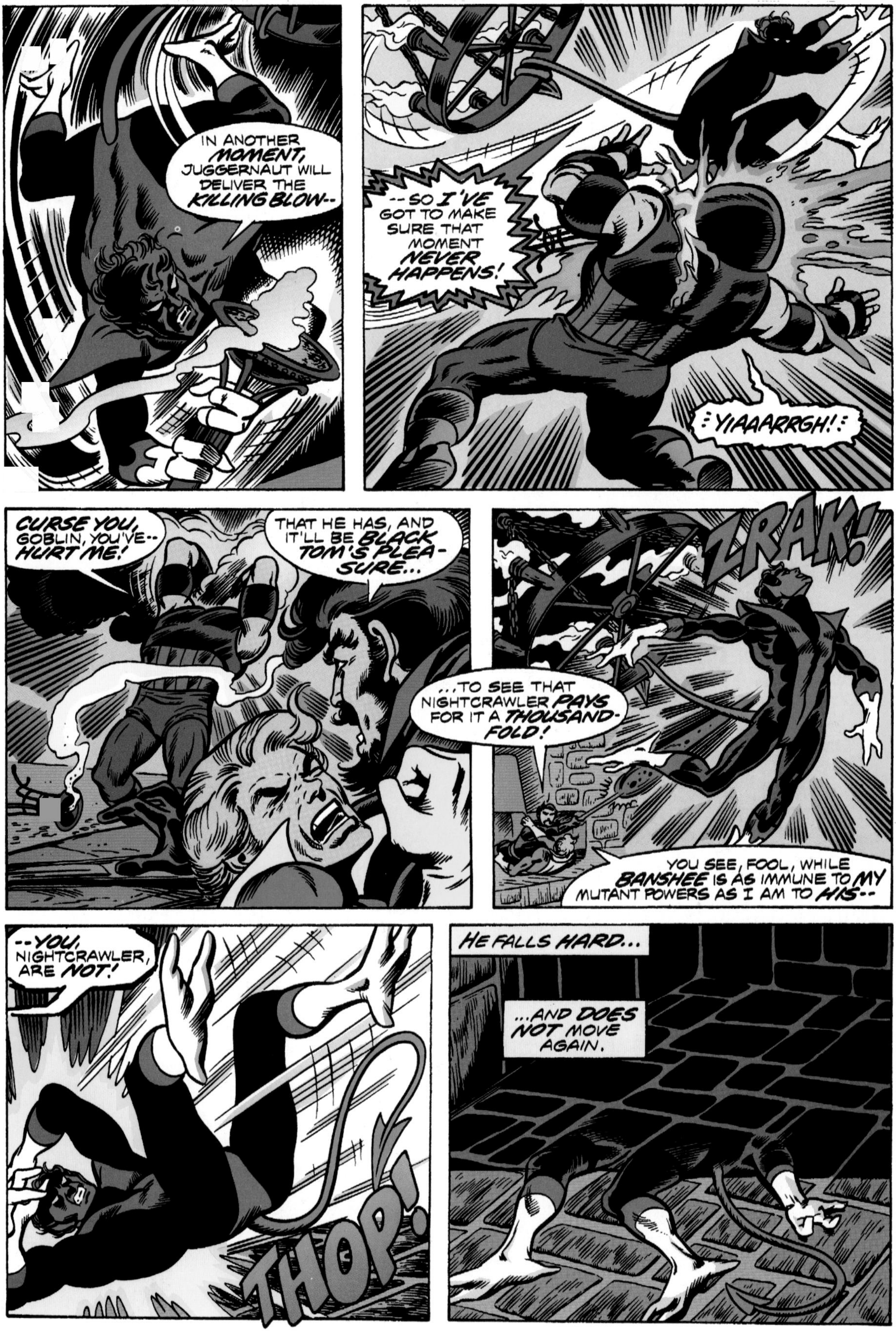

IN ANOTHER MOMENT, JUGGERNAUT WILL DELIVER THE KILLING BLOW--
--SO I'VE GOT TO MAKE SURE THAT MOMENT NEVER HAPPENS!
YIAAARRGH!
CURSE YOU, GOBLIN, YOU'VE-- HURT ME!
THAT HE HAS, AND IT'LL BE BLACK TOM'S PLEA-SURE...
...TO SEE THAT NIGHTCRAWLER PAYS FOR IT A THOUSAND-FOLD!
ZRAK!
YOU SEE, FOOL, WHILE BANSHEE IS AS IMMUNE TO MY MUTANT POWERS AS I AM TO HIS--
--YOU, NIGHTCRAWLER, ARE NOT!
THOP!
HE FALLS HARD...
...AND DOES NOT MOVE AGAIN.

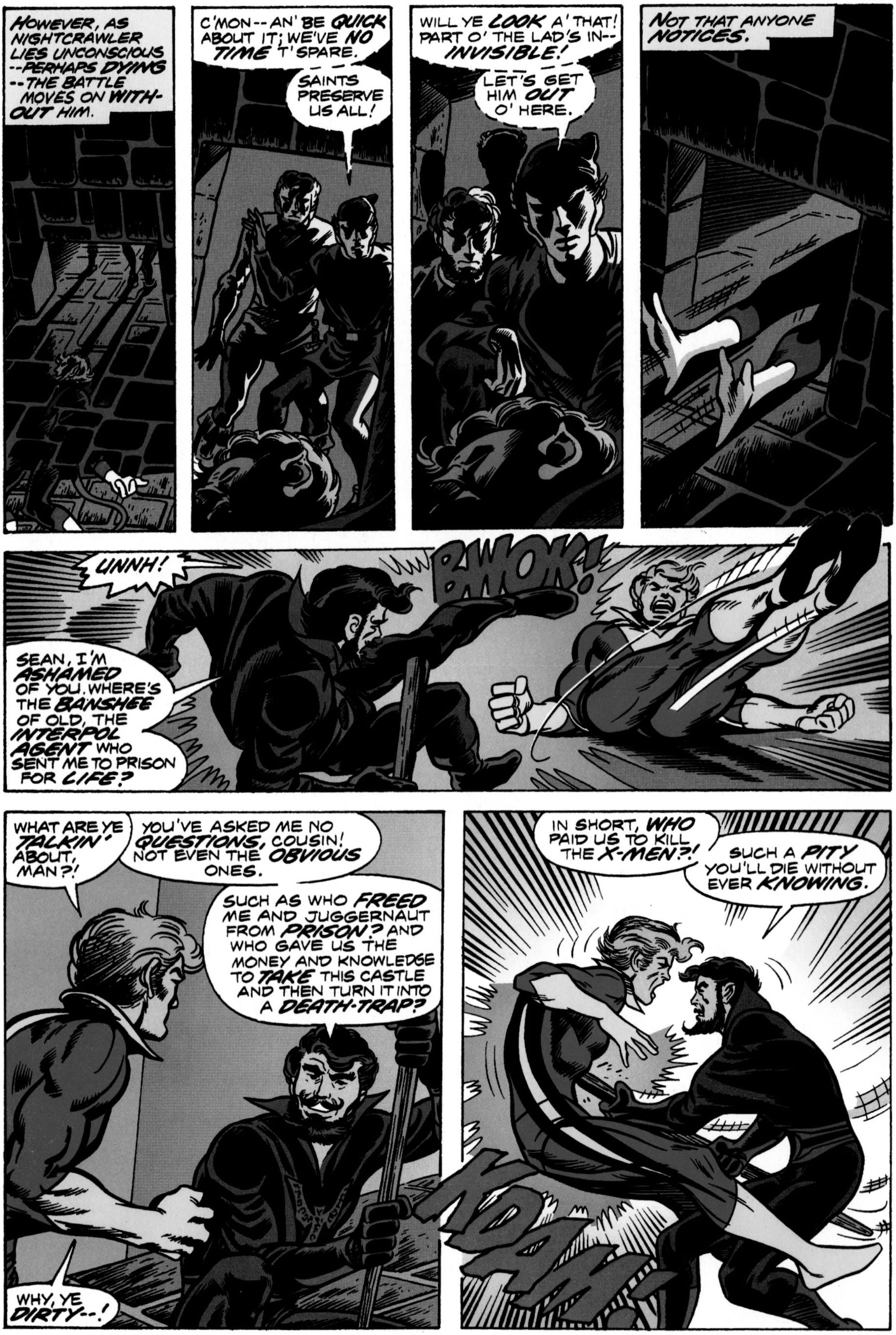
However, as Nightcrawler lies unconscious --perhaps dying --the battle moves on without him.
C'mon--an' be quick about it; we've no time t' spare.
Saints preserve us all!
Will ye look a' that! Part o' the lad's in-- invisible!
Let's get him out o' here.
Not that anyone notices.
Unnh!
BWOK!
Sean, I'm ashamed of you. Where's the Banshee of old, the Interpol agent who sent me to prison for life?
What are ye talkin' about, man?!
You've asked me no questions, cousin! Not even the obvious ones.
Such as who freed me and Juggernaut from prison? And who gave us the money and knowledge to take this castle and then turn it into a death-trap?
Why, ye dirty--!
In short, who paid us to kill the X-Men?!
Such a pity you'll die without ever knowing.
KWAM!

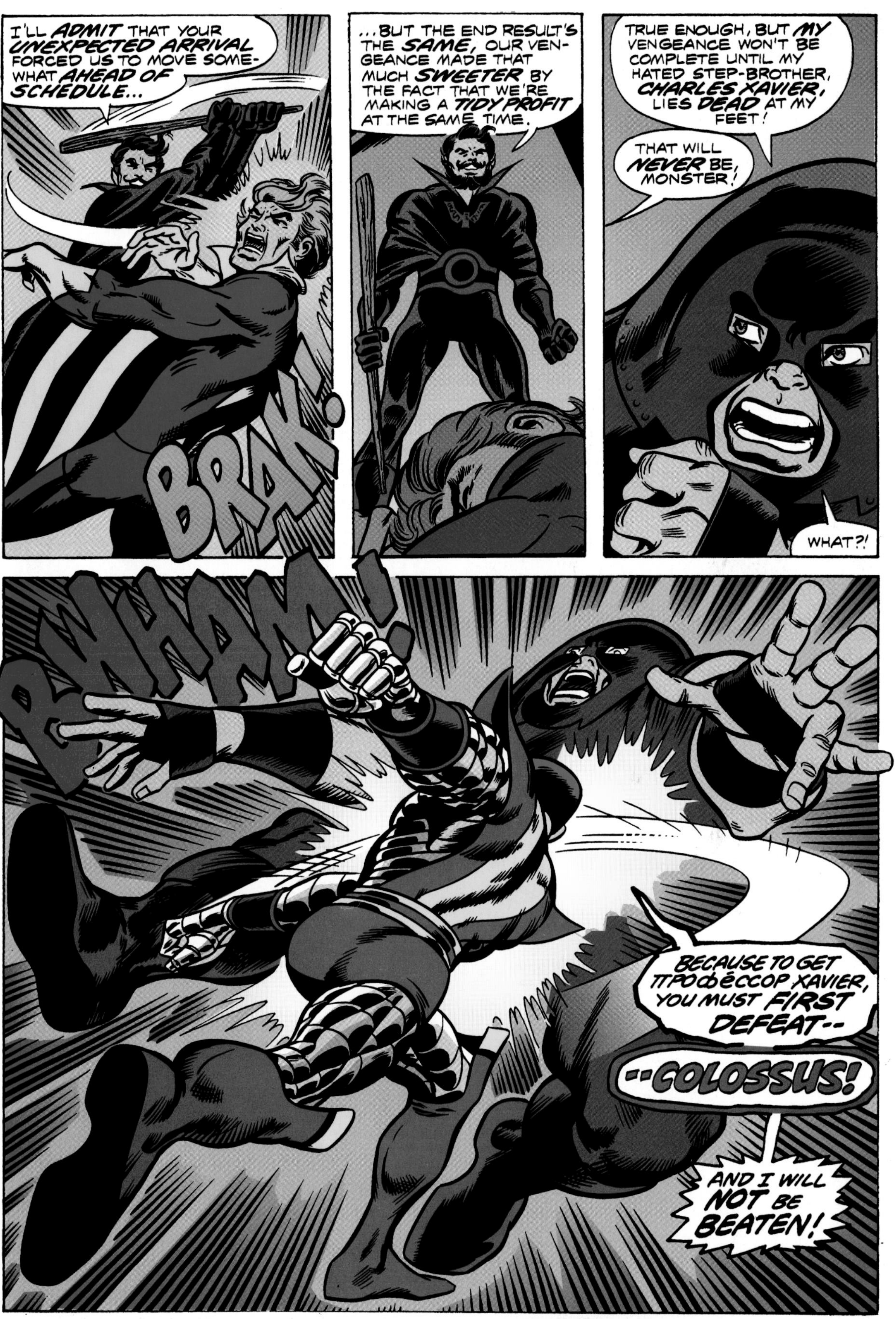
I'LL ADMIT THAT YOUR UNEXPECTED ARRIVAL FORCED US TO MOVE SOMEWHAT AHEAD OF SCHEDULE...
BRAK!
...BUT THE END RESULT'S THE SAME, OUR VENGEANCE MADE THAT MUCH SWEETER BY THE FACT THAT WE'RE MAKING A TIDY PROFIT AT THE SAME TIME.
TRUE ENOUGH, BUT MY VENGEANCE WON'T BE COMPLETE UNTIL MY HATED STEP-BROTHER, CHARLES XAVIER, LIES DEAD AT MY FEET!
THAT WILL NEVER BE, MONSTER!
WHAT?!
BWHAM!
BECAUSE TO GET ПРОФЕССОР XAVIER, YOU MUST FIRST DEFEAT--
--COLOSSUS!
AND I WILL NOT BE BEATEN!

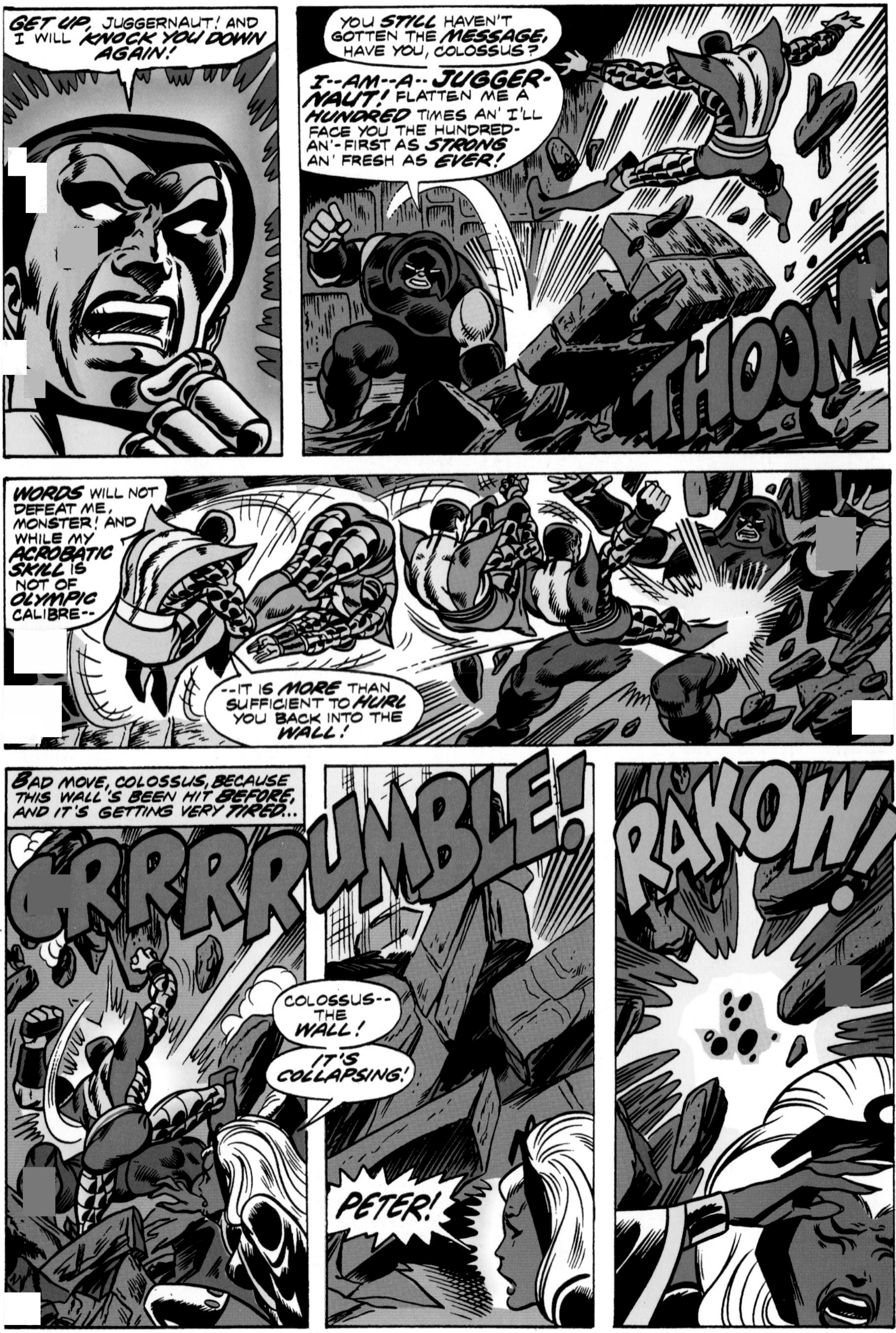

GET UP, JUGGERNAUT! AND I WILL KNOCK YOU DOWN AGAIN!
YOU STILL HAVEN'T GOTTEN THE MESSAGE, HAVE YOU, COLOSSUS?
I--AM--A--JUGGERNAUT! FLATTEN ME A HUNDRED TIMES AN' I'LL FACE YOU THE HUNDRED-AN'-FIRST AS STRONG AN' FRESH AS EVER!
THOOM!
WORDS WILL NOT DEFEAT ME, MONSTER! AND WHILE MY ACROBATIC SKILL IS NOT OF OLYMPIC CALIBRE--
--IT IS MORE THAN SUFFICIENT TO HURL YOU BACK INTO THE WALL!
BAD MOVE, COLOSSUS, BECAUSE THIS WALL'S BEEN HIT BEFORE, AND IT'S GETTING VERY TIRED...
CRRRRRUMBLE!
COLOSSUS--THE WALL!
IT'S COLLAPSING!
PETER!
RAKOW!

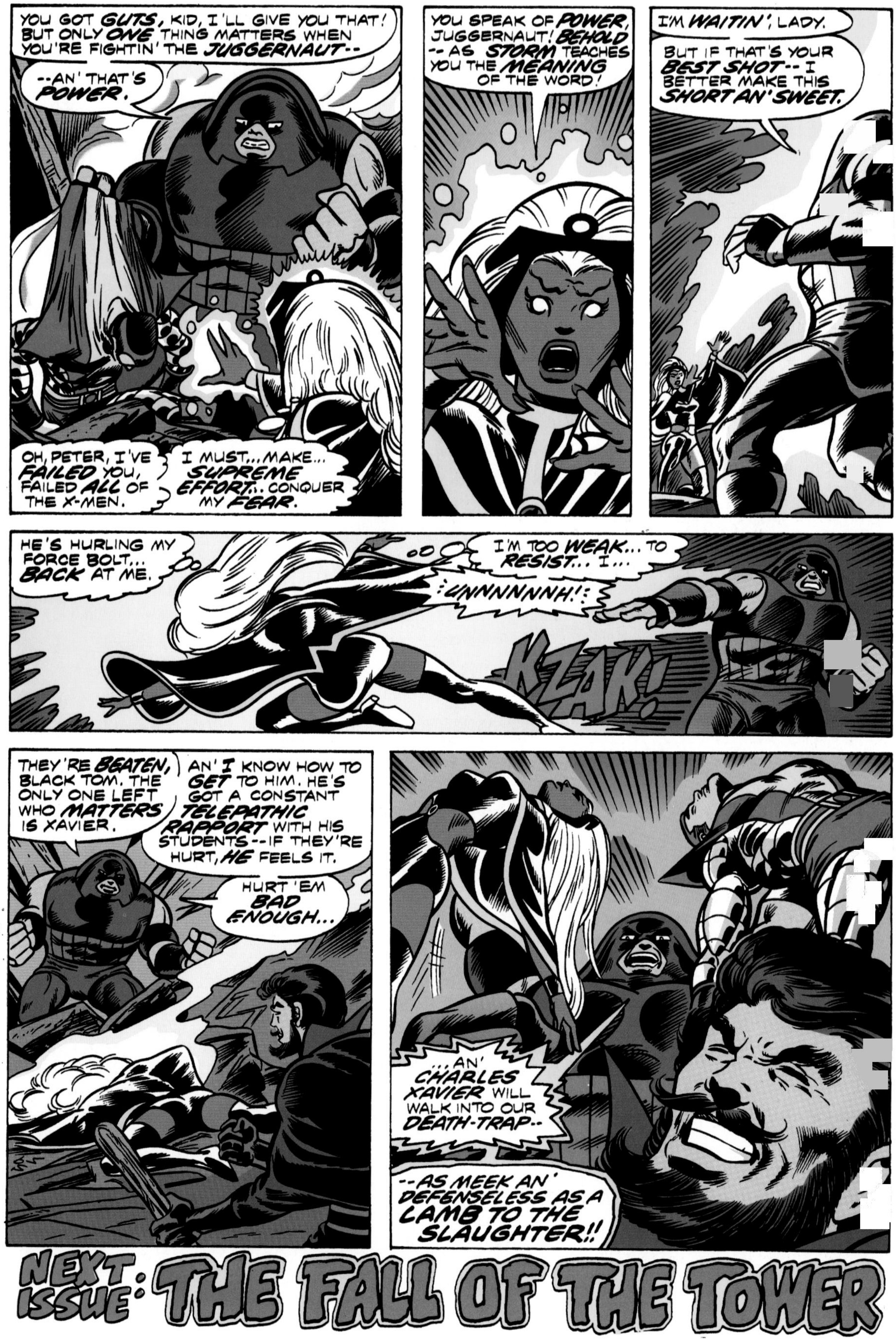
YOU GOT GUTS, KID, I'LL GIVE YOU THAT! BUT ONLY ONE THING MATTERS WHEN YOU'RE FIGHTIN' THE JUGGERNAUT--
--AN' THAT'S POWER.
OH, PETER, I'VE FAILED YOU, FAILED ALL OF THE X-MEN.
I MUST... MAKE... SUPREME EFFORT.. CONQUER MY FEAR.
YOU SPEAK OF POWER, JUGGERNAUT! BEHOLD -- AS STORM TEACHES YOU THE MEANING OF THE WORD!
I'M WAITIN', LADY.
BUT IF THAT'S YOUR BEST SHOT-- I BETTER MAKE THIS SHORT AN' SWEET.
HE'S HURLING MY FORCE BOLT... BACK AT ME.
I'M TOO WEAK... TO RESIST... I...
UNNNNNNH!
KZAK!
THEY'RE BEATEN, BLACK TOM. THE ONLY ONE LEFT WHO MATTERS IS XAVIER.
AN' I KNOW HOW TO GET TO HIM. HE'S GOT A CONSTANT TELEPATHIC RAPPORT WITH HIS STUDENTS--IF THEY'RE HURT, HE FEELS IT.
HURT 'EM BAD ENOUGH...
...AN' CHARLES XAVIER WILL WALK INTO OUR DEATH-TRAP--
--AS MEEK AN' DEFENSELESS AS A LAMB TO THE SLAUGHTER!!
NEXT ISSUE: THE FALL OF THE TOWER

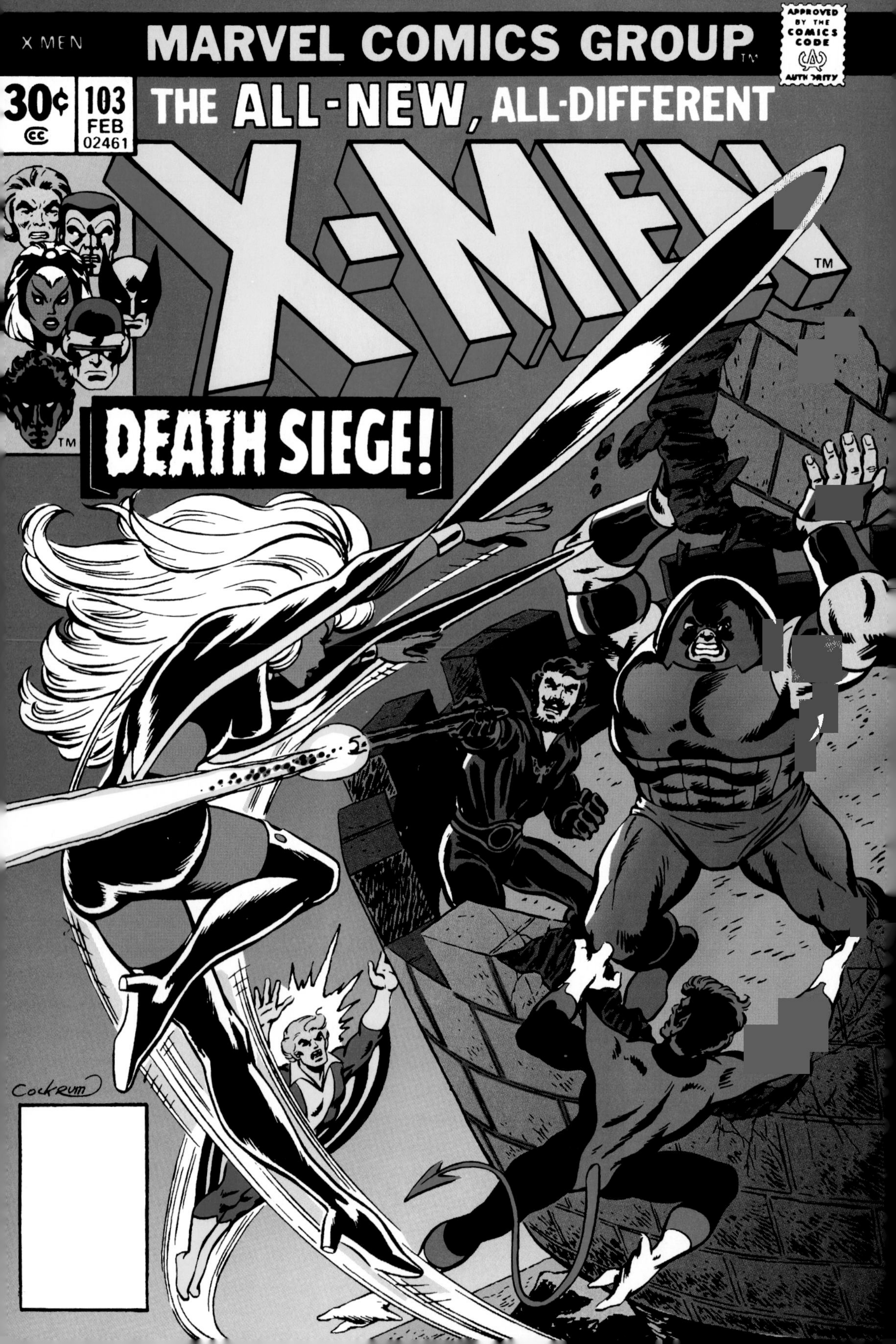
X MEN
MARVEL COMICS GROUP
APPROVED BY THE COMICS CODE AUTHORITY
30¢
CC
103
FEB
02461
THE ALL-NEW, ALL-DIFFERENT
X-MEN
DEATH SIEGE!
COCKRUM

Cyclops. Storm. Banshee. Nightcrawler. Wolverine. Colossus. Children of the atom, students of Charles Xavier, MUTANTS——feared and hated by the world they have sworn to protect. These are the STRANGEST heroes of all!

Stan Lee PRESENTS: **THE UNCANNY X-MEN!** TM

CHRIS CLAREMONT, AUTHOR / DAVE COCKRUM, ARTIST / SAM GRAINGER, INKER / JOHN COSTANZA, letterer / ANDY YANCHUS, colorist / ARCHIE GOODWIN, EDITOR

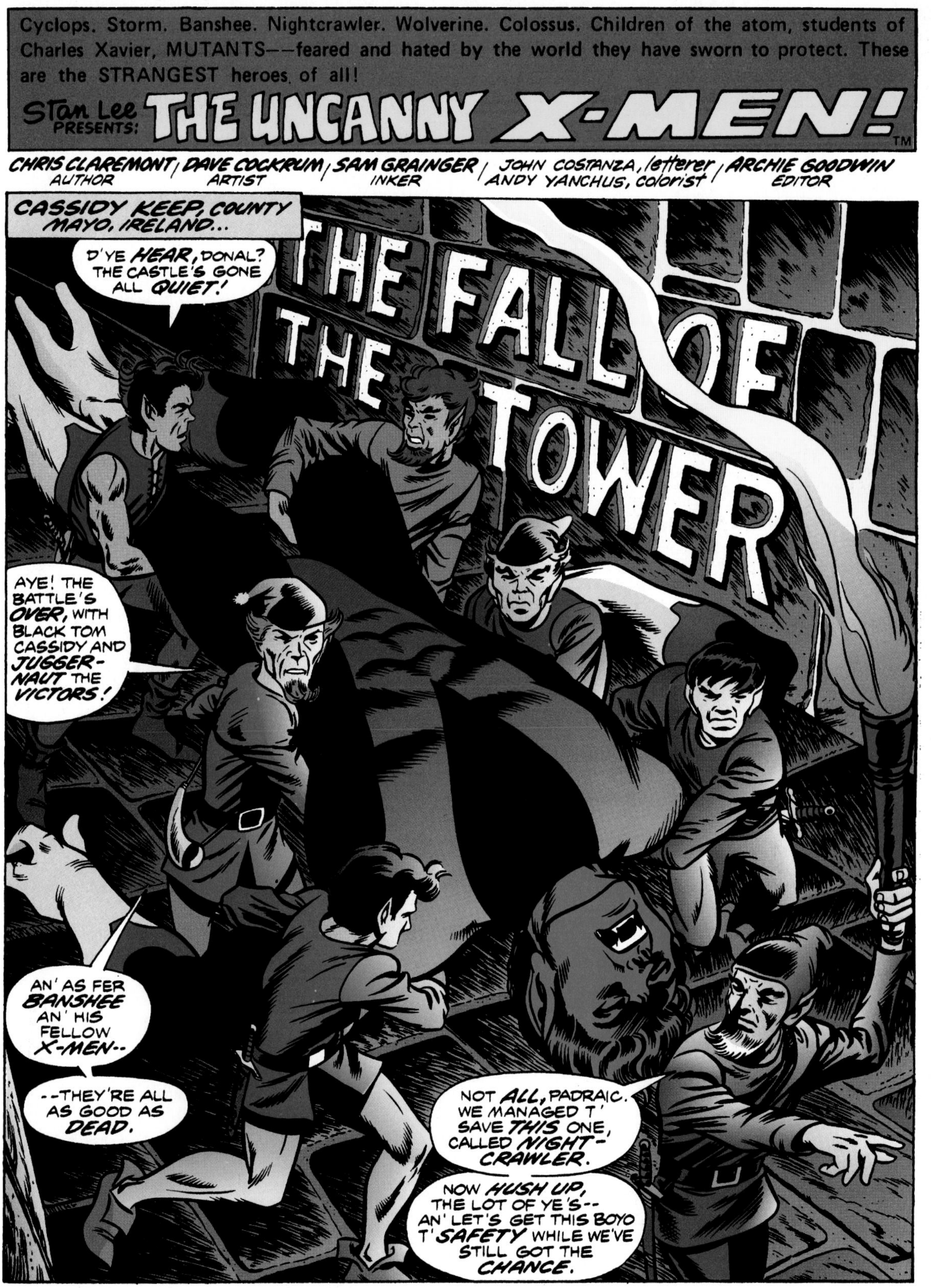
CASSIDY KEEP, COUNTY MAYO, IRELAND...
THE FALL OF THE TOWER
D'YE HEAR, DONAL? THE CASTLE'S GONE ALL QUIET!
AYE! THE BATTLE'S OVER, WITH BLACK TOM CASSIDY AND JUGGER-NAUT THE VICTORS!
AN' AS FER BANSHEE AN' HIS FELLOW X-MEN--
--THEY'RE ALL AS GOOD AS DEAD.
NOT ALL, PADRAIC. WE MANAGED T' SAVE THIS ONE, CALLED NIGHT-CRAWLER.
NOW HUSH UP, THE LOT OF YE'S-- AN' LET'S GET THIS BOYO T' SAFETY WHILE WE'VE STILL GOT THE CHANCE.

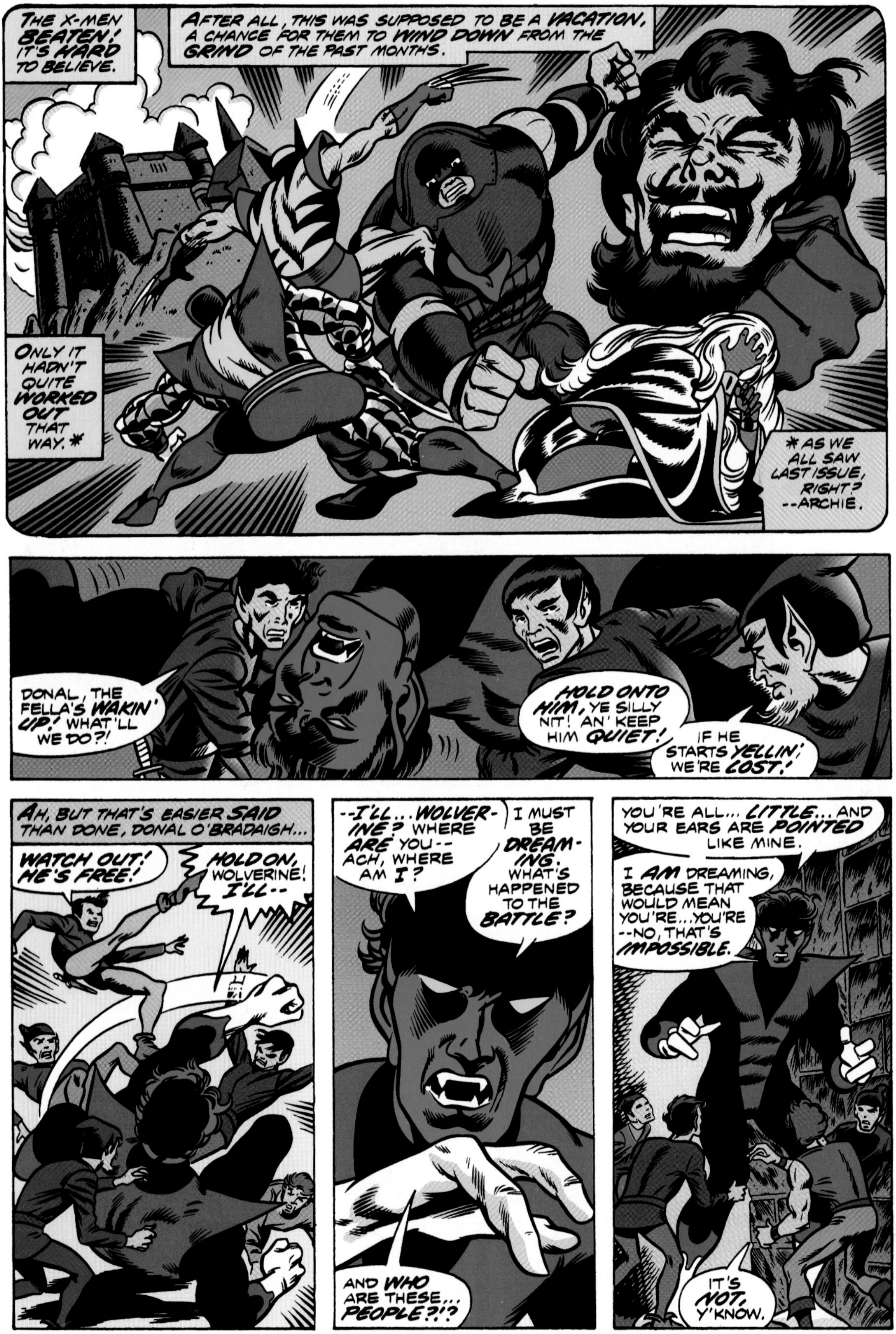
THE X-MEN BEATEN! IT'S HARD TO BELIEVE.
AFTER ALL, THIS WAS SUPPOSED TO BE A VACATION, A CHANCE FOR THEM TO WIND DOWN FROM THE GRIND OF THE PAST MONTHS.
ONLY IT HADN'T QUITE WORKED OUT THAT WAY.*
*AS WE ALL SAW LAST ISSUE, RIGHT? --ARCHIE.
DONAL, THE FELLA'S WAKIN' UP! WHAT'LL WE DO?!
HOLD ONTO HIM, YE SILLY NIT! AN' KEEP HIM QUIET!
IF HE STARTS YELLIN', WE'RE LOST!
AH, BUT THAT'S EASIER SAID THAN DONE, DONAL O'BRADAIGH...
WATCH OUT! HE'S FREE!
HOLD ON, WOLVERINE! I'LL--
--I'LL... WOLVERINE? WHERE ARE YOU-- ACH, WHERE AM I?
I MUST BE DREAMING. WHAT'S HAPPENED TO THE BATTLE?
AND WHO ARE THESE... PEOPLE?!?
YOU'RE ALL... LITTLE... AND YOUR EARS ARE POINTED LIKE MINE.
I AM DREAMING, BECAUSE THAT WOULD MEAN YOU'RE... YOU'RE --NO, THAT'S IMPOSSIBLE.
IT'S NOT, Y'KNOW.

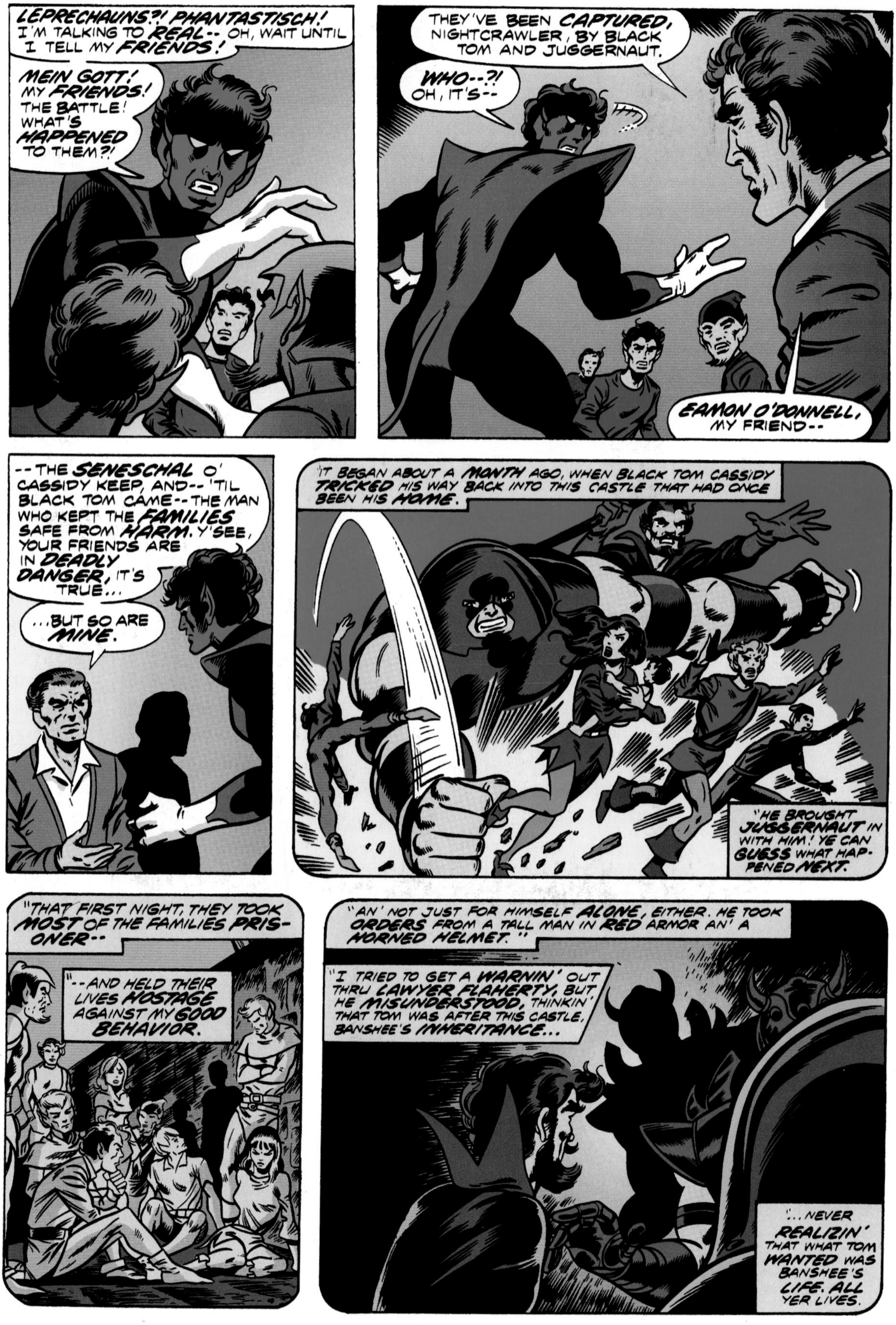
LEPRECHAUNS?! PHANTASTISCH! I'M TALKING TO REAL-- OH, WAIT UNTIL I TELL MY FRIENDS!
MEIN GOTT! MY FRIENDS! THE BATTLE! WHAT'S HAPPENED TO THEM?!
THEY'VE BEEN CAPTURED, NIGHTCRAWLER, BY BLACK TOM AND JUGGERNAUT.
WHO--?! OH, IT'S--
EAMON O'DONNELL, MY FRIEND--
--THE SENESCHAL O' CASSIDY KEEP, AND--'TIL BLACK TOM CAME--THE MAN WHO KEPT THE FAMILIES SAFE FROM HARM. Y'SEE, YOUR FRIENDS ARE IN DEADLY DANGER, IT'S TRUE...
...BUT SO ARE MINE.
"IT BEGAN ABOUT A MONTH AGO, WHEN BLACK TOM CASSIDY TRICKED HIS WAY BACK INTO THIS CASTLE THAT HAD ONCE BEEN HIS HOME.
"HE BROUGHT JUGGERNAUT IN WITH HIM! YE CAN GUESS WHAT HAPPENED NEXT.
"THAT FIRST NIGHT, THEY TOOK MOST OF THE FAMILIES PRISONER--
"--AND HELD THEIR LIVES HOSTAGE AGAINST MY GOOD BEHAVIOR.
"AN' NOT JUST FOR HIMSELF ALONE, EITHER. HE TOOK ORDERS FROM A TALL MAN IN RED ARMOR AN' A HORNED HELMET."
"I TRIED TO GET A WARNIN' OUT THRU LAWYER FLAHERTY, BUT HE MISUNDERSTOOD, THINKIN' THAT TOM WAS AFTER THIS CASTLE, BANSHEE'S INHERITANCE...
"...NEVER REALIZIN' THAT WHAT TOM WANTED WAS BANSHEE'S LIFE. ALL YER LIVES.

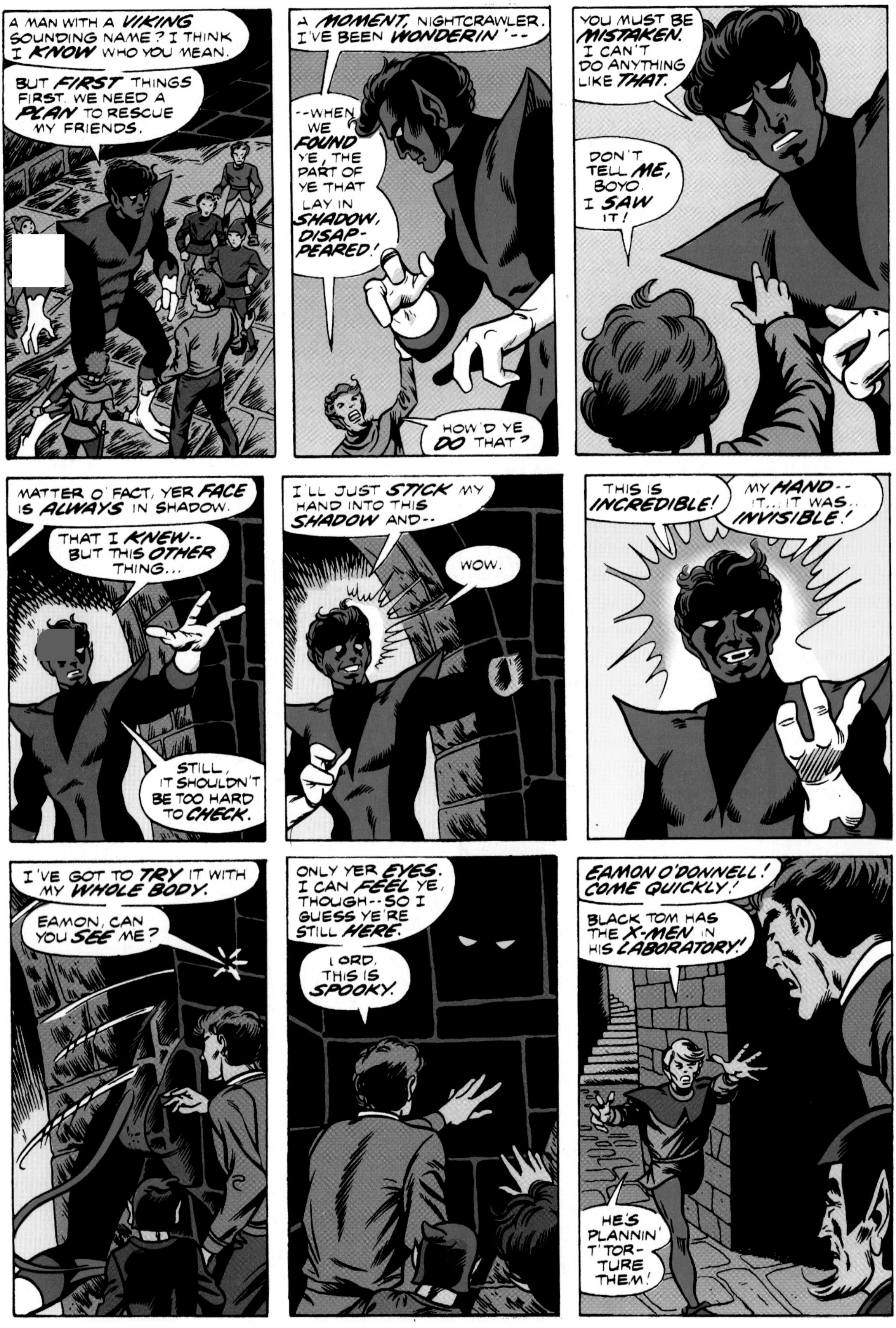
A MAN WITH A VIKING SOUNDING NAME? I THINK I KNOW WHO YOU MEAN.
BUT FIRST THINGS FIRST. WE NEED A PLAN TO RESCUE MY FRIENDS.
A MOMENT, NIGHTCRAWLER. I'VE BEEN WONDERIN'--
--WHEN WE FOUND YE, THE PART OF YE THAT LAY IN SHADOW, DISAPPEARED!
HOW'D YE DO THAT?
YOU MUST BE MISTAKEN. I CAN'T DO ANYTHING LIKE THAT.
DON'T TELL ME, BOYO. I SAW IT!
MATTER O' FACT, YER FACE IS ALWAYS IN SHADOW.
THAT I KNEW-- BUT THIS OTHER THING...
STILL, IT SHOULDN'T BE TOO HARD TO CHECK.
I'LL JUST STICK MY HAND INTO THIS SHADOW AND--
WOW.
THIS IS INCREDIBLE!
MY HAND-- IT... IT WAS... INVISIBLE!
I'VE GOT TO TRY IT WITH MY WHOLE BODY.
EAMON, CAN YOU SEE ME?
ONLY YER EYES. I CAN FEEL YE, THOUGH-- SO I GUESS YE'RE STILL HERE.
LORD, THIS IS SPOOKY.
EAMON O'DONNELL! COME QUICKLY!
BLACK TOM HAS THE X-MEN IN HIS LABORATORY!
HE'S PLANNIN' T'TORTURE THEM!

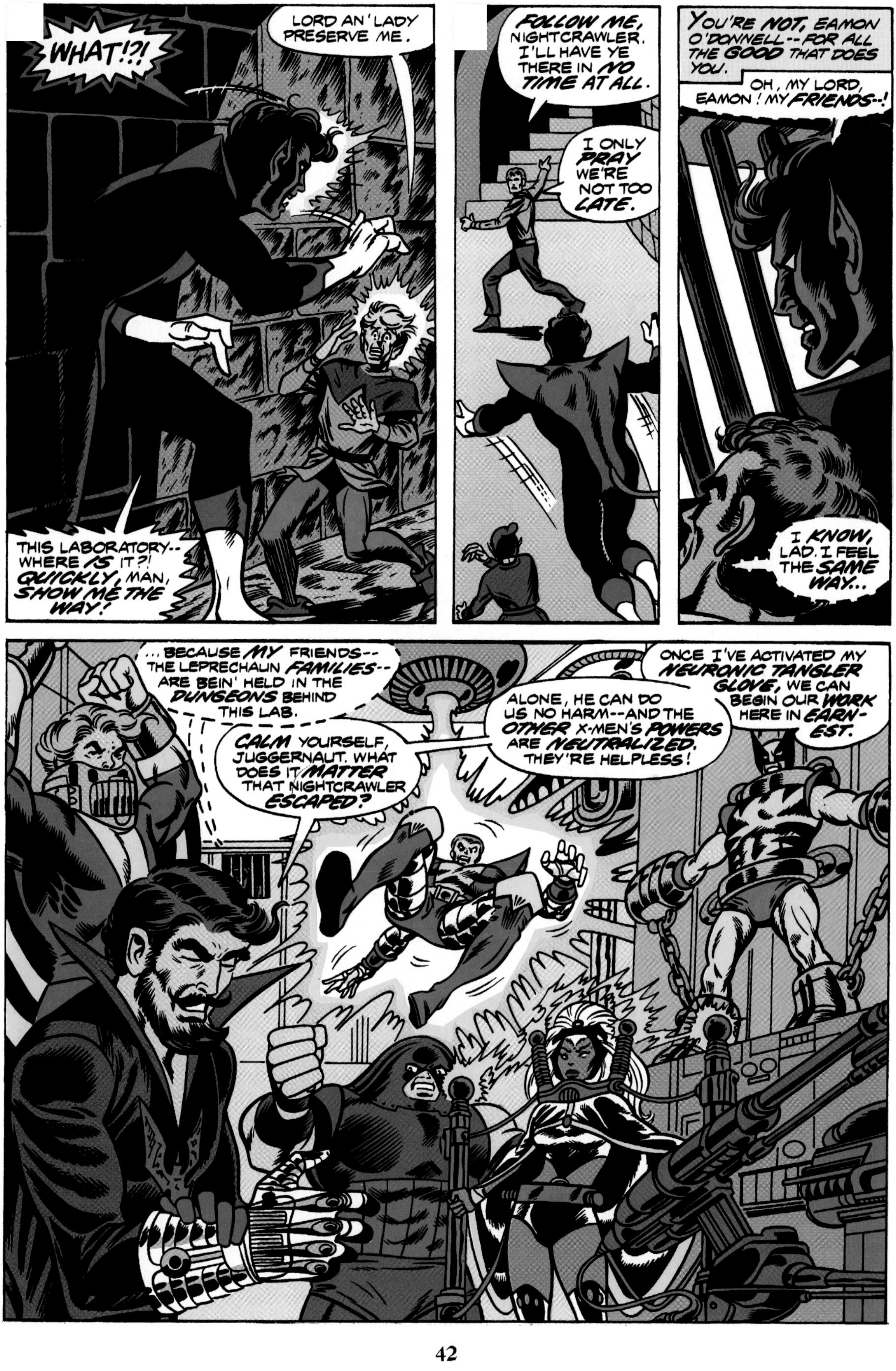
WHAT!?!
LORD AN' LADY PRESERVE ME.
THIS LABORATORY-- WHERE IS IT?! QUICKLY, MAN, SHOW ME THE WAY!
FOLLOW ME, NIGHTCRAWLER. I'LL HAVE YE THERE IN NO TIME AT ALL.
I ONLY PRAY WE'RE NOT TOO LATE.
YOU'RE NOT, EAMON O'DONNELL--FOR ALL THE GOOD THAT DOES YOU.
OH, MY LORD, EAMON! MY FRIENDS--!
I KNOW, LAD. I FEEL THE SAME WAY...
...BECAUSE MY FRIENDS-- THE LEPRECHAUN FAMILIES-- ARE BEIN' HELD IN THE DUNGEONS BEHIND THIS LAB.
CALM YOURSELF, JUGGERNAUT. WHAT DOES IT MATTER THAT NIGHTCRAWLER ESCAPED?
ALONE, HE CAN DO US NO HARM--AND THE OTHER X-MEN'S POWERS ARE NEUTRALIZED. THEY'RE HELPLESS!
ONCE I'VE ACTIVATED MY NEURONIC TANGLER GLOVE, WE CAN BEGIN OUR WORK HERE IN EARN-EST.

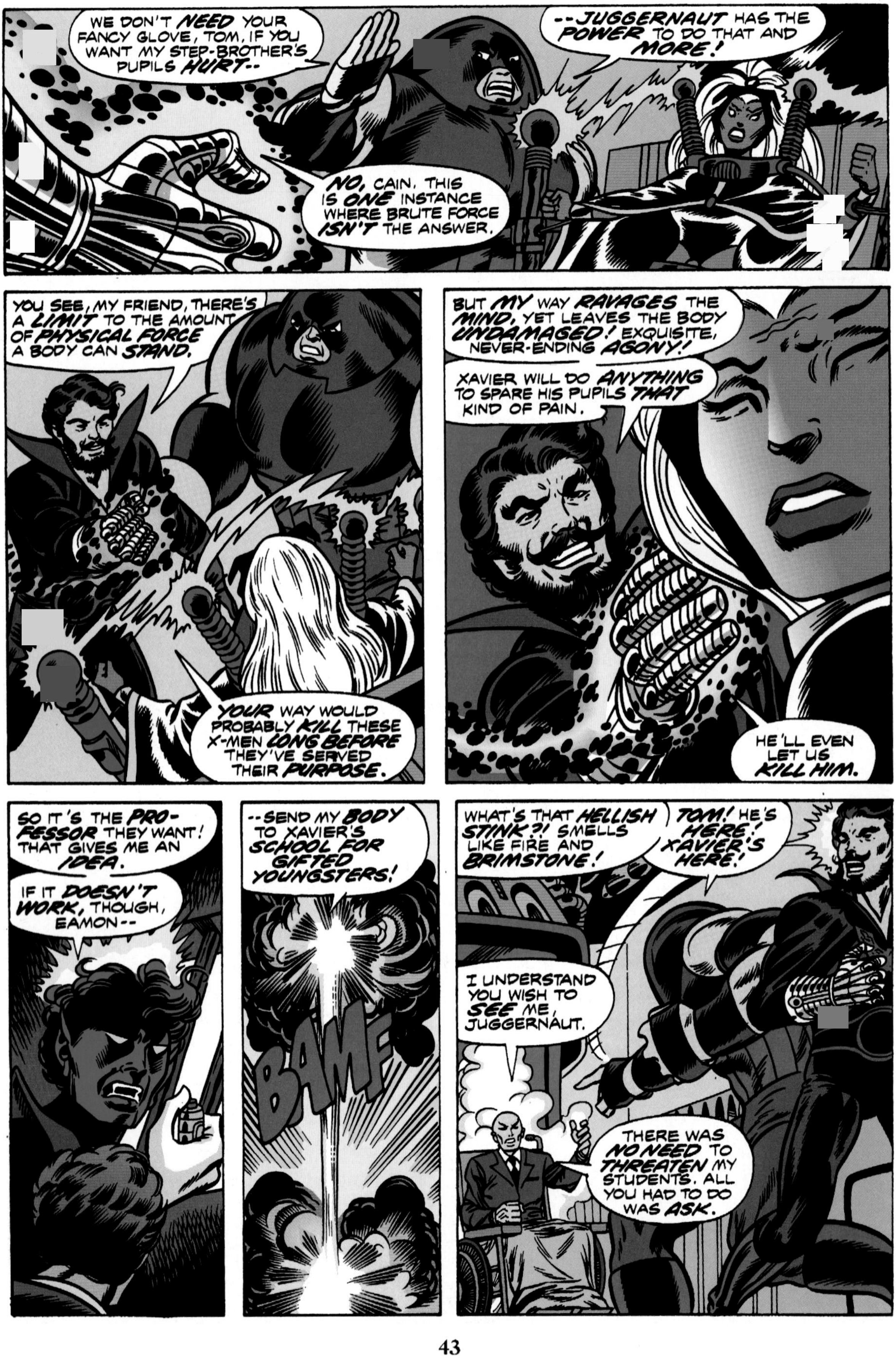
WE DON'T NEED YOUR FANCY GLOVE, TOM, IF YOU WANT MY STEP-BROTHER'S PUPILS HURT--
--JUGGERNAUT HAS THE POWER TO DO THAT AND MORE!
NO, CAIN. THIS IS ONE INSTANCE WHERE BRUTE FORCE ISN'T THE ANSWER.
YOU SEE, MY FRIEND, THERE'S A LIMIT TO THE AMOUNT OF PHYSICAL FORCE A BODY CAN STAND.
YOUR WAY WOULD PROBABLY KILL THESE X-MEN LONG BEFORE THEY'VE SERVED THEIR PURPOSE.
BUT MY WAY RAVAGES THE MIND, YET LEAVES THE BODY UNDAMAGED! EXQUISITE, NEVER-ENDING AGONY!
XAVIER WILL DO ANYTHING TO SPARE HIS PUPILS THAT KIND OF PAIN.
HE'LL EVEN LET US KILL HIM.
SO IT'S THE PRO-FESSOR THEY WANT! THAT GIVES ME AN IDEA.
IF IT DOESN'T WORK, THOUGH, EAMON--
--SEND MY BODY TO XAVIER'S SCHOOL FOR GIFTED YOUNGSTERS!
BAMF
WHAT'S THAT HELLISH STINK?! SMELLS LIKE FIRE AND BRIMSTONE!
TOM! HE'S HERE! XAVIER'S HERE!
I UNDERSTAND YOU WISH TO SEE ME, JUGGERNAUT.
THERE WAS NO NEED TO THREATEN MY STUDENTS. ALL YOU HAD TO DO WAS ASK.

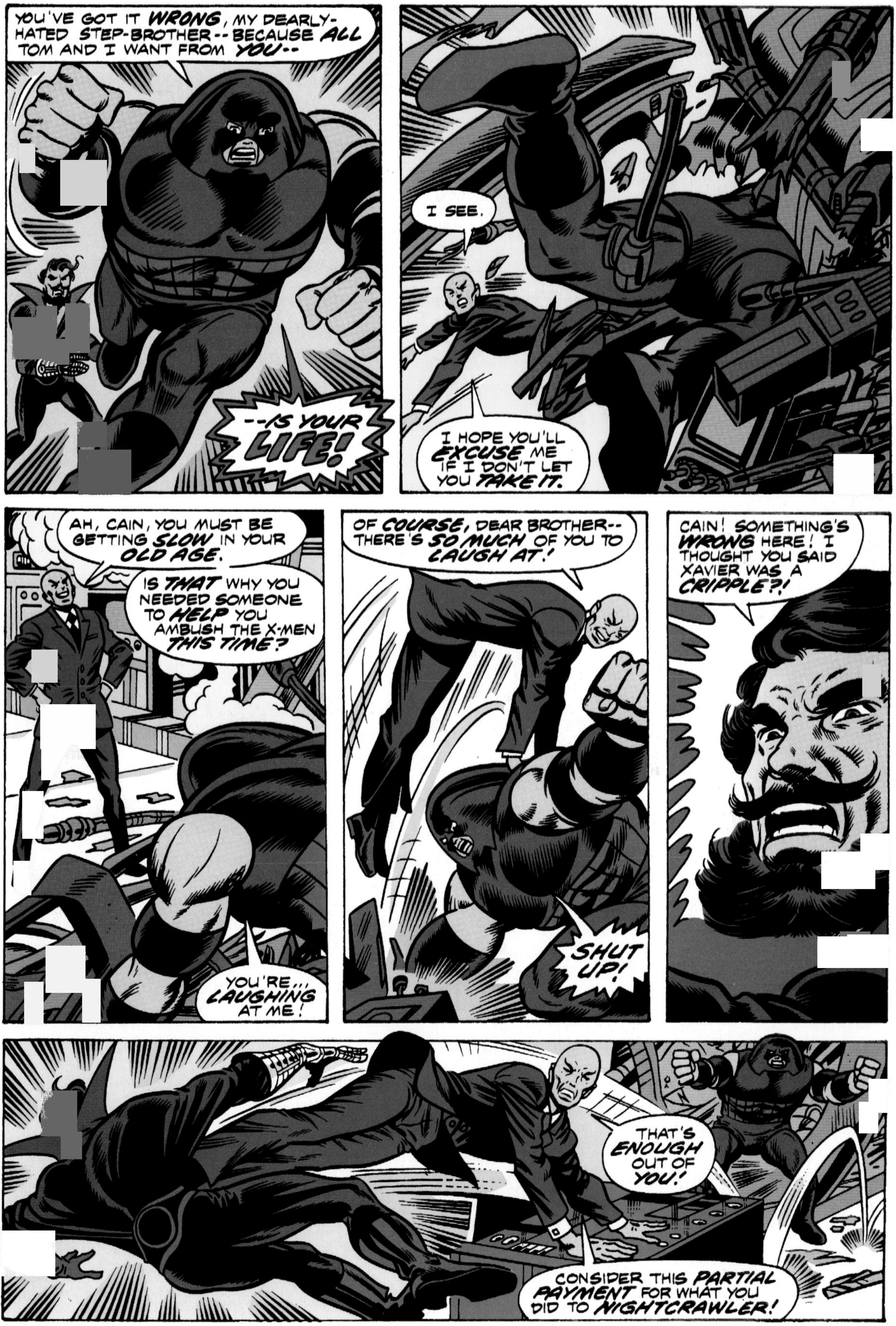
YOU'VE GOT IT WRONG, MY DEARLY-HATED STEP-BROTHER -- BECAUSE ALL TOM AND I WANT FROM YOU --
-- IS YOUR LIFE!
I SEE.
I HOPE YOU'LL EXCUSE ME IF I DON'T LET YOU TAKE IT.
AH, CAIN, YOU MUST BE GETTING SLOW IN YOUR OLD AGE.
IS THAT WHY YOU NEEDED SOMEONE TO HELP YOU AMBUSH THE X-MEN THIS TIME?
YOU'RE... LAUGHING AT ME!
OF COURSE, DEAR BROTHER -- THERE'S SO MUCH OF YOU TO LAUGH AT!
SHUT UP!
CAIN! SOMETHING'S WRONG HERE! I THOUGHT YOU SAID XAVIER WAS A CRIPPLE?!
THAT'S ENOUGH OUT OF YOU!
CONSIDER THIS PARTIAL PAYMENT FOR WHAT YOU DID TO NIGHTCRAWLER!

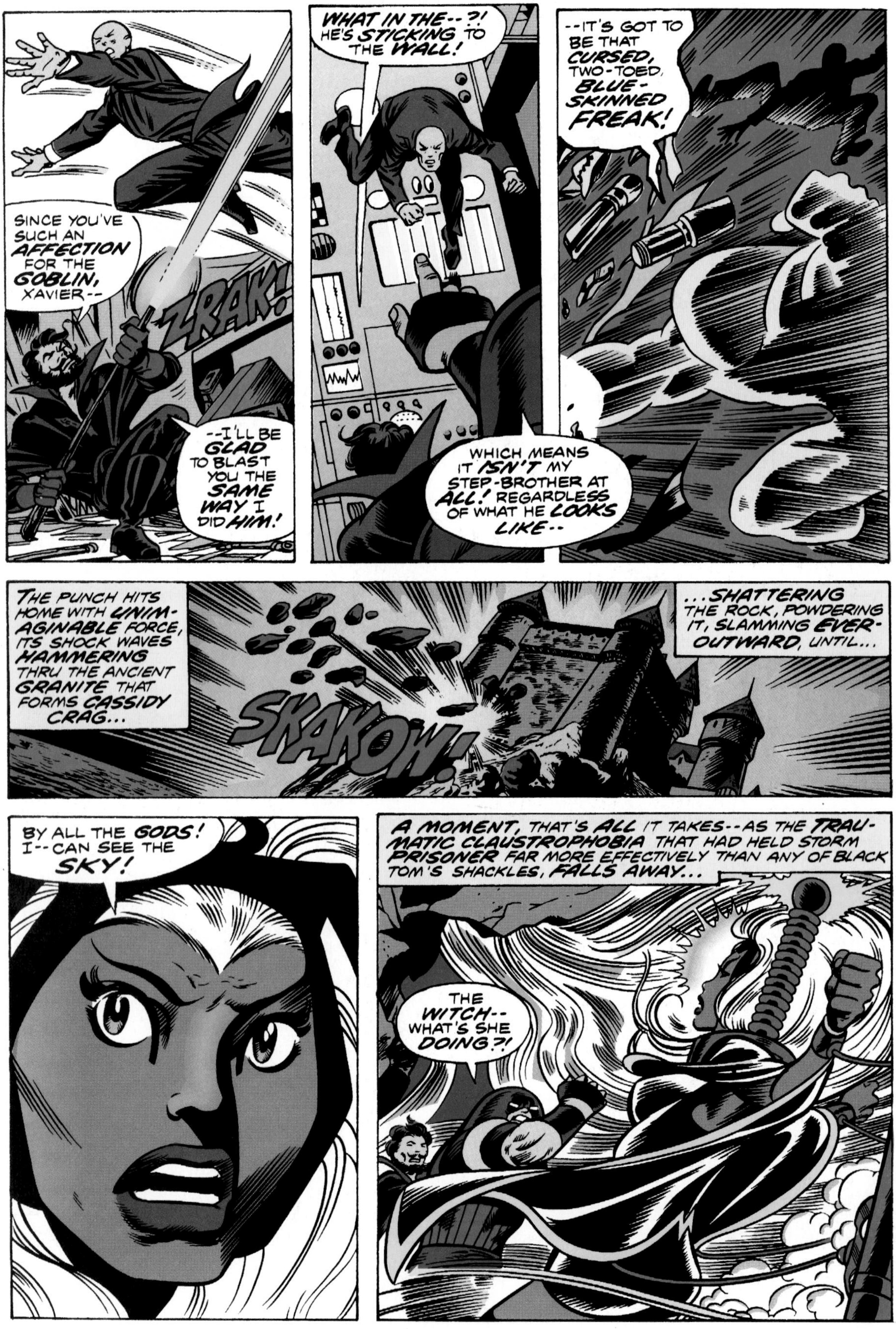
SINCE YOU'VE SUCH AN AFFECTION FOR THE GOBLIN, XAVIER--
ZRAK!!
--I'LL BE GLAD TO BLAST YOU THE SAME WAY I DID HIM!
WHAT IN THE--?! HE'S STICKING TO THE WALL!
--IT'S GOT TO BE THAT CURSED, TWO-TOED, BLUE-SKINNED FREAK!
WHICH MEANS IT ISN'T MY STEP-BROTHER AT ALL! REGARDLESS OF WHAT HE LOOKS LIKE--
THE PUNCH HITS HOME WITH UNIMAGINABLE FORCE, ITS SHOCK WAVES HAMMERING THRU THE ANCIENT GRANITE THAT FORMS CASSIDY CRAG...
SKAKOW!
...SHATTERING THE ROCK, POWDERING IT, SLAMMING EVER-OUTWARD, UNTIL...
BY ALL THE GODS! I--CAN SEE THE SKY!
A MOMENT, THAT'S ALL IT TAKES--AS THE TRAUMATIC CLAUSTROPHOBIA THAT HAD HELD STORM PRISONER FAR MORE EFFECTIVELY THAN ANY OF BLACK TOM'S SHACKLES, FALLS AWAY...
THE WITCH--WHAT'S SHE DOING?!

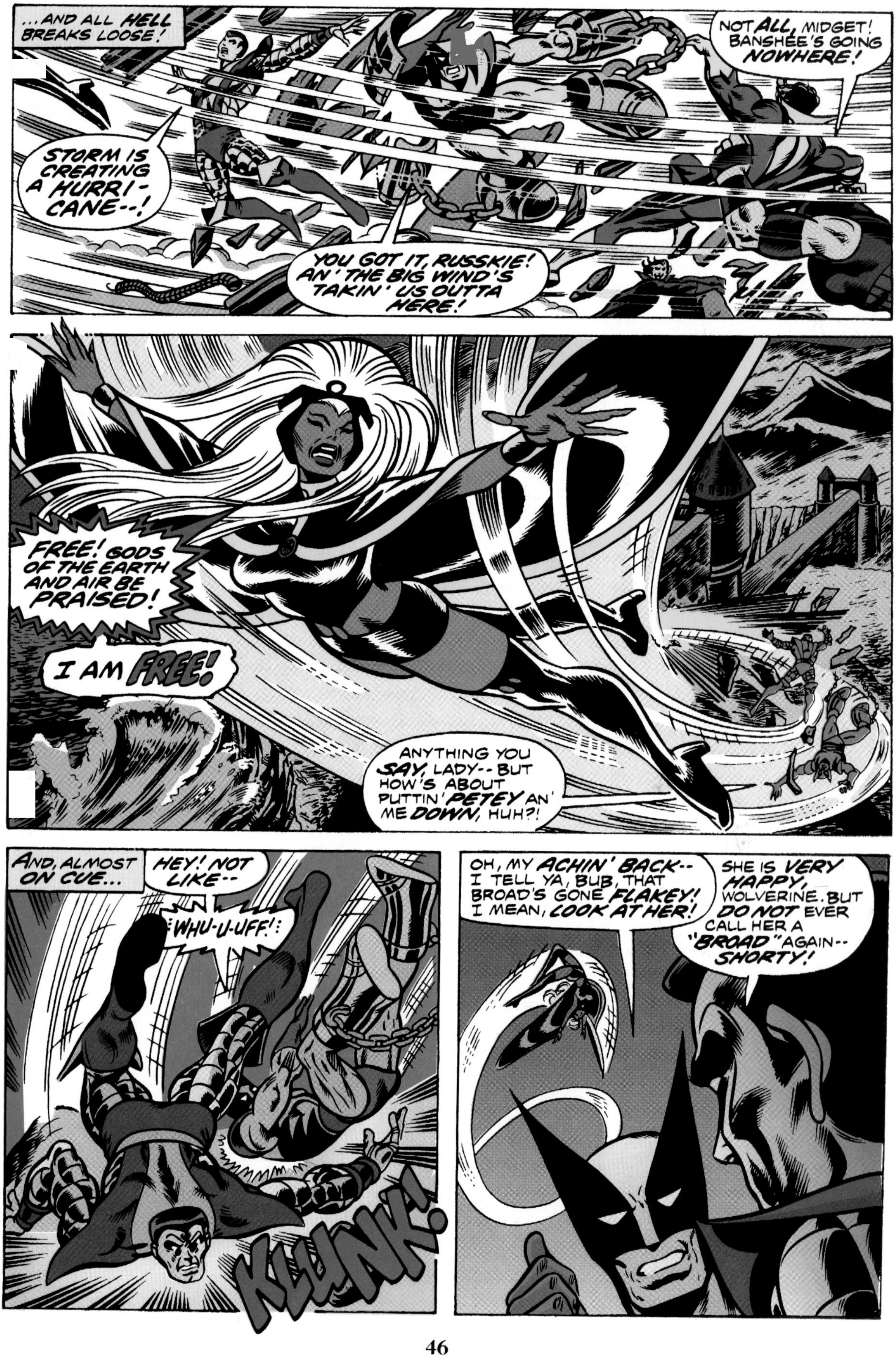

...AND ALL HELL BREAKS LOOSE!
NOT ALL, MIDGET! BANSHEE'S GOING NOWHERE!
STORM IS CREATING A HURRI-CANE--!
YOU GOT IT, RUSSKIE! AN' THE BIG WIND'S TAKIN' US OUTTA HERE!
FREE! GODS OF THE EARTH AND AIR BE PRAISED!
I AM FREE!
ANYTHING YOU SAY, LADY-- BUT HOW'S ABOUT PUTTIN' PETEY AN' ME DOWN, HUH?!
AND, ALMOST ON CUE...
HEY! NOT LIKE--
WHU-U-UFF!
KLUNK!
OH, MY ACHIN' BACK-- I TELL YA, BUB, THAT BROAD'S GONE FLAKEY! I MEAN, LOOK AT HER!
SHE IS VERY HAPPY, WOLVERINE. BUT DO NOT EVER CALL HER A "BROAD" AGAIN-- SHORTY!

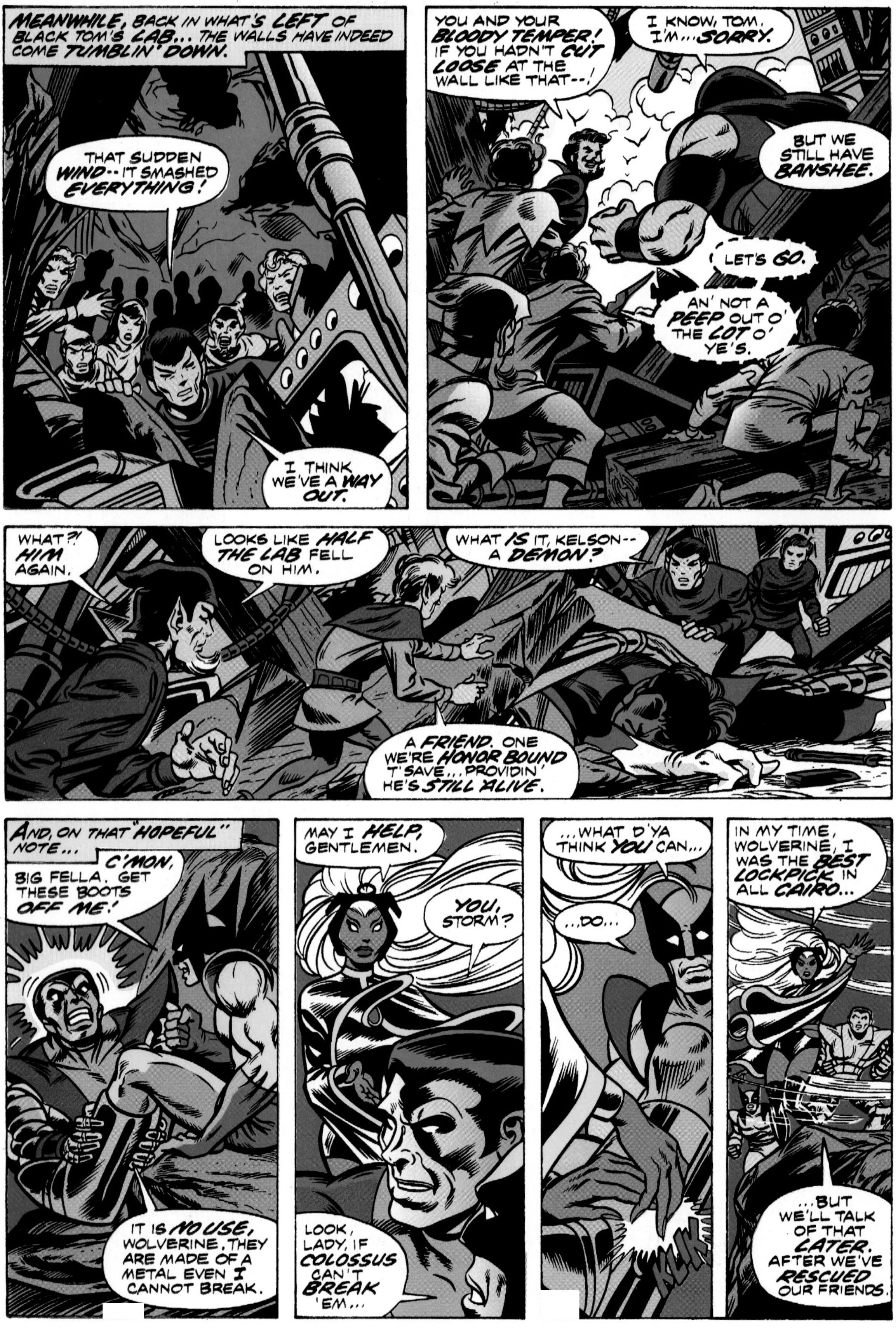
MEANWHILE, BACK IN WHAT'S LEFT OF BLACK TOM'S LAB... THE WALLS HAVE INDEED COME TUMBLIN' DOWN.
THAT SUDDEN WIND--IT SMASHED EVERYTHING!
I THINK WE'VE A WAY OUT.
YOU AND YOUR BLOODY TEMPER! IF YOU HADN'T CUT LOOSE AT THE WALL LIKE THAT--!
I KNOW, TOM. I'M... SORRY.
BUT WE STILL HAVE BANSHEE.
LET'S GO.
AN' NOT A PEEP OUT O' THE LOT O' YE'S.
WHAT?! HIM AGAIN.
LOOKS LIKE HALF THE LAB FELL ON HIM.
WHAT IS IT, KELSON-- A DEMON?
A FRIEND. ONE WE'RE HONOR BOUND T'SAVE... PROVIDIN' HE'S STILL ALIVE.
AND, ON THAT "HOPEFUL" NOTE...
C'MON, BIG FELLA. GET THESE BOOTS OFF ME!
IT IS NO USE, WOLVERINE. THEY ARE MADE OF A METAL EVEN I CANNOT BREAK.
MAY I HELP, GENTLEMEN.
YOU, STORM?
LOOK, LADY, IF COLOSSUS CAN'T BREAK 'EM...
...WHAT D'YA THINK YOU CAN...
...DO...
KLIK
IN MY TIME, WOLVERINE, I WAS THE BEST LOCKPICK IN ALL CAIRO...
...BUT WE'LL TALK OF THAT LATER. AFTER WE'VE RESCUED OUR FRIENDS.

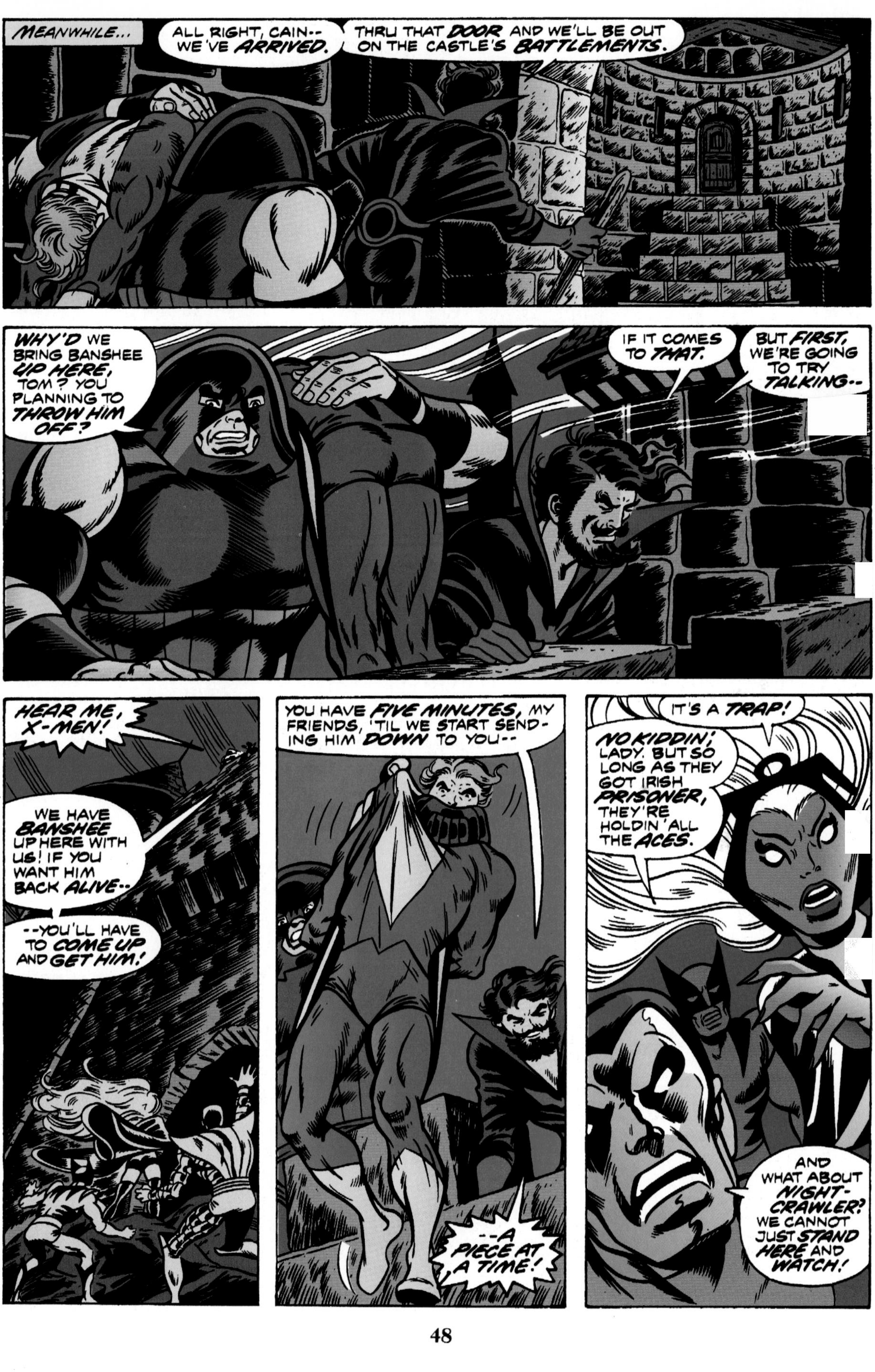
MEANWHILE...
ALL RIGHT, CAIN-- WE'VE ARRIVED.
THRU THAT DOOR AND WE'LL BE OUT ON THE CASTLE'S BATTLEMENTS.
WHY'D WE BRING BANSHEE UP HERE, TOM? YOU PLANNING TO THROW HIM OFF?
IF IT COMES TO THAT.
BUT FIRST, WE'RE GOING TO TRY TALKING--
HEAR ME, X-MEN!
WE HAVE BANSHEE UP HERE WITH US! IF YOU WANT HIM BACK ALIVE--
--YOU'LL HAVE TO COME UP AND GET HIM!
YOU HAVE FIVE MINUTES, MY FRIENDS, 'TIL WE START SENDING HIM DOWN TO YOU--
--A PIECE AT A TIME!
IT'S A TRAP!
NO KIDDIN', LADY. BUT SO LONG AS THEY GOT IRISH PRISONER, THEY'RE HOLDIN' ALL THE ACES.
AND WHAT ABOUT NIGHTCRAWLER? WE CANNOT JUST STAND HERE AND WATCH!

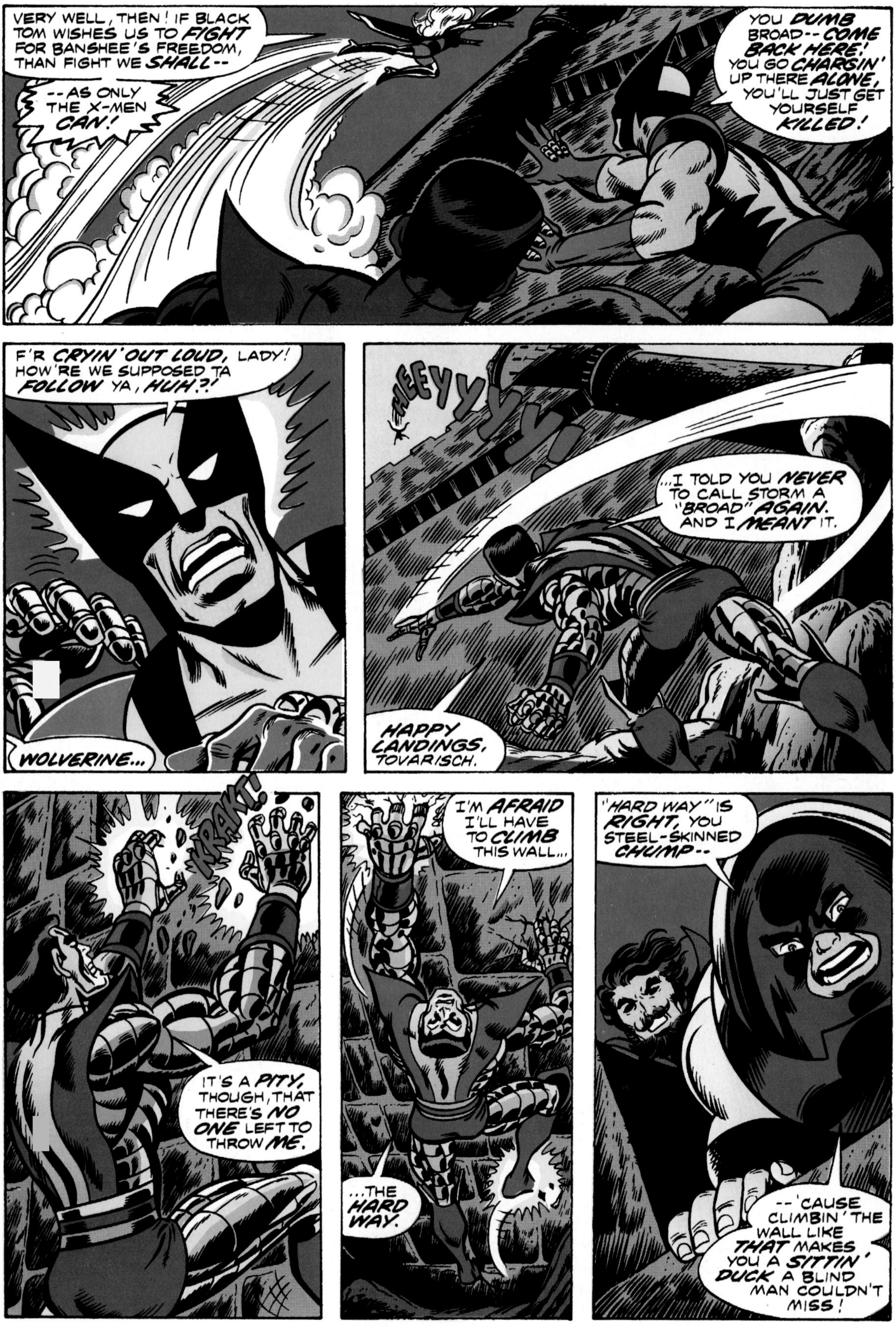

VERY WELL, THEN! IF BLACK TOM WISHES US TO FIGHT FOR BANSHEE'S FREEDOM, THAN FIGHT WE SHALL--
--AS ONLY THE X-MEN CAN!
YOU DUMB BROAD--COME BACK HERE! YOU GO CHARSIN' UP THERE ALONE, YOU'LL JUST GET YOURSELF KILLED!
F'R CRYIN' OUT LOUD, LADY! HOW'RE WE SUPPOSED TA FOLLOW YA, HUH?!
WOLVERINE...
HEEYYYY!
...I TOLD YOU NEVER TO CALL STORM A "BROAD" AGAIN. AND I MEANT IT.
HAPPY LANDINGS, TOVARISCH.
KRAKT!
IT'S A PITY, THOUGH, THAT THERE'S NO ONE LEFT TO THROW ME.
I'M AFRAID I'LL HAVE TO CLIMB THIS WALL...
...THE HARD WAY.
"HARD WAY" IS RIGHT, YOU STEEL-SKINNED CHUMP--
--'CAUSE CLIMBIN' THE WALL LIKE THAT MAKES YOU A SITTIN' DUCK A BLIND MAN COULDN'T MISS!

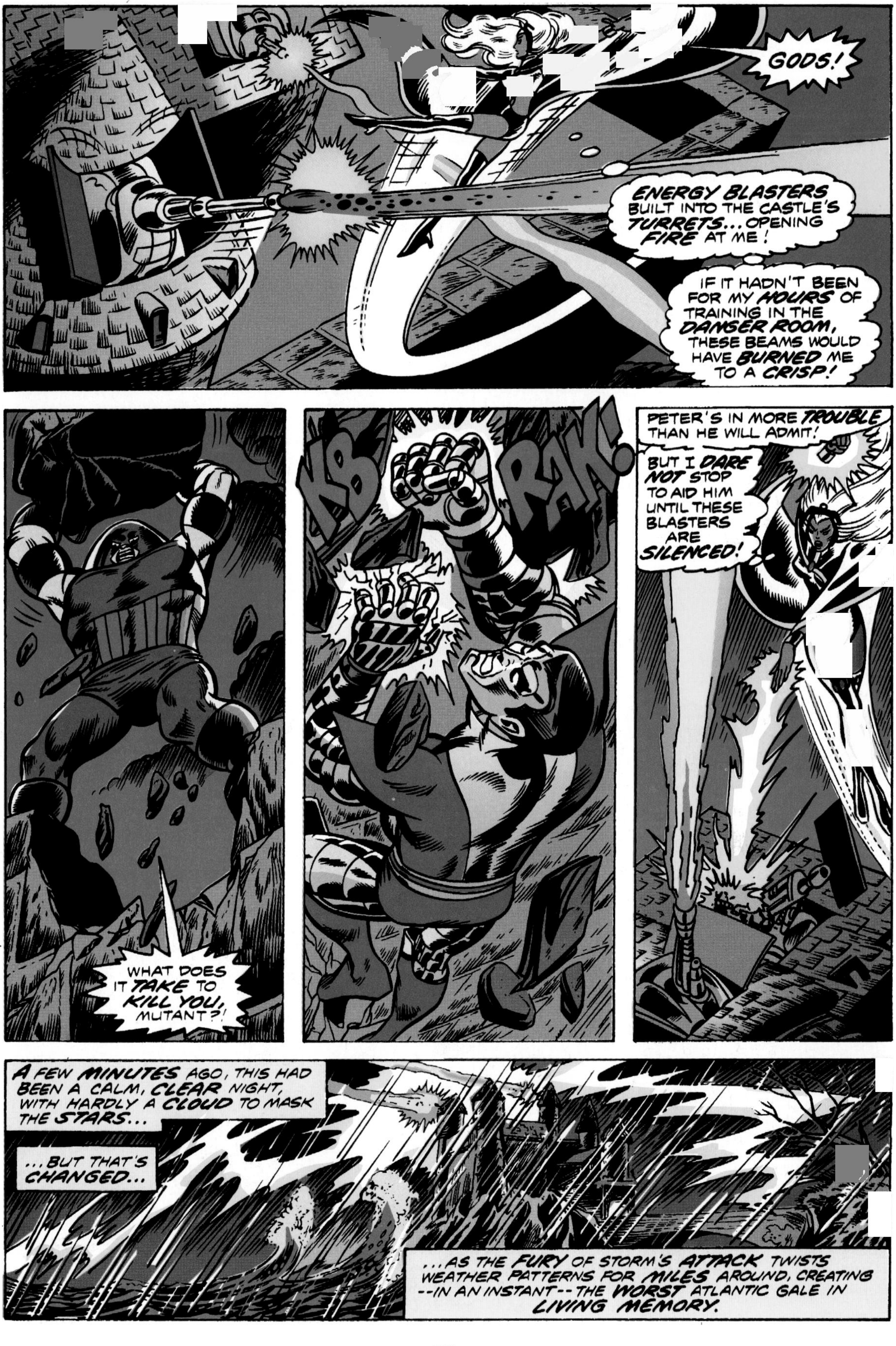
GODS!
ENERGY BLASTERS BUILT INTO THE CASTLE'S TURRETS... OPENING FIRE AT ME!
IF IT HADN'T BEEN FOR MY HOURS OF TRAINING IN THE DANGER ROOM, THESE BEAMS WOULD HAVE BURNED ME TO A CRISP!
WHAT DOES IT TAKE TO KILL YOU, MUTANT?!
KA-BRAK!
PETER'S IN MORE TROUBLE THAN HE WILL ADMIT!
BUT I DARE NOT STOP TO AID HIM UNTIL THESE BLASTERS ARE SILENCED!
A FEW MINUTES AGO, THIS HAD BEEN A CALM, CLEAR NIGHT, WITH HARDLY A CLOUD TO MASK THE STARS...
...BUT THAT'S CHANGED...
...AS THE FURY OF STORM'S ATTACK TWISTS WEATHER PATTERNS FOR MILES AROUND, CREATING --IN AN INSTANT-- THE WORST ATLANTIC GALE IN LIVING MEMORY.

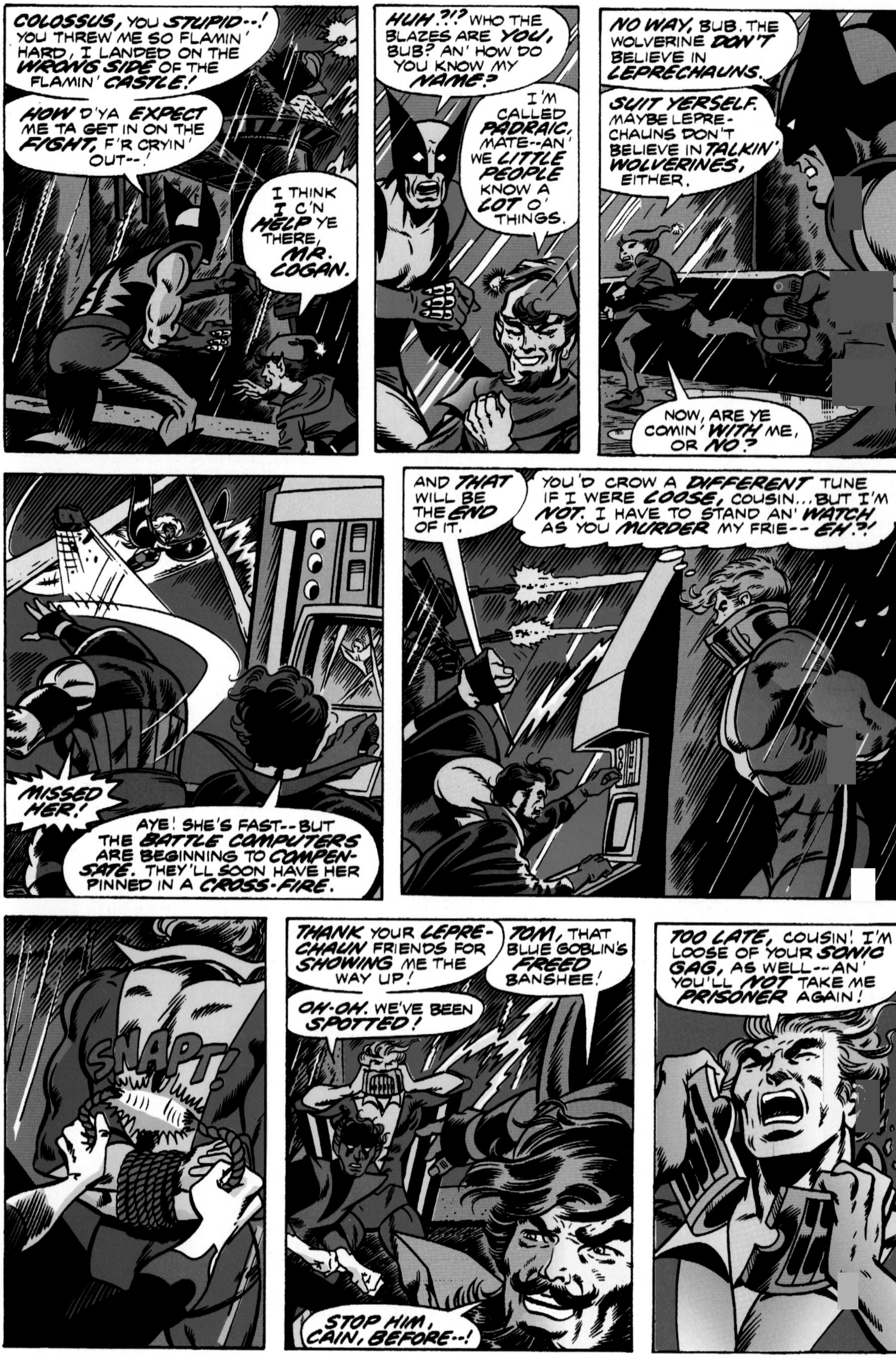
COLOSSUS, YOU STUPID--! YOU THREW ME SO FLAMIN' HARD, I LANDED ON THE WRONG SIDE OF THE FLAMIN' CASTLE!
HOW D'YA EXPECT ME TA GET IN ON THE FIGHT, F'R CRYIN' OUT--!
I THINK I C'N HELP YE THERE, MR. COGAN.
HUH?!? WHO THE BLAZES ARE YOU, BUB? AN' HOW DO YOU KNOW MY NAME?
I'M CALLED PADRAIC, MATE--AN' WE LITTLE PEOPLE KNOW A LOT O' THINGS.
NO WAY, BUB. THE WOLVERINE DON'T BELIEVE IN LEPRECHAUNS.
SUIT YERSELF. MAYBE LEPRECHAUNS DON'T BELIEVE IN TALKIN' WOLVERINES, EITHER.
NOW, ARE YE COMIN' WITH ME, OR NO?
MISSED HER!
AYE! SHE'S FAST--BUT THE BATTLE COMPUTERS ARE BEGINNING TO COMPENSATE. THEY'LL SOON HAVE HER PINNED IN A CROSS-FIRE.
AND THAT WILL BE THE END OF IT.
YOU'D CROW A DIFFERENT TUNE IF I WERE LOOSE, COUSIN... BUT I'M NOT. I HAVE TO STAND AN' WATCH AS YOU MURDER MY FRIE-- EH?!
SNAPT!
THANK YOUR LEPRECHAUN FRIENDS FOR SHOWING ME THE WAY UP!
OH-OH. WE'VE BEEN SPOTTED!
TOM, THAT BLUE GOBLIN'S FREED BANSHEE!
STOP HIM, CAIN, BEFORE--!
TOO LATE, COUSIN! I'M LOOSE OF YOUR SONIC GAG, AS WELL--AN' YOU'LL NOT TAKE ME PRISONER AGAIN!

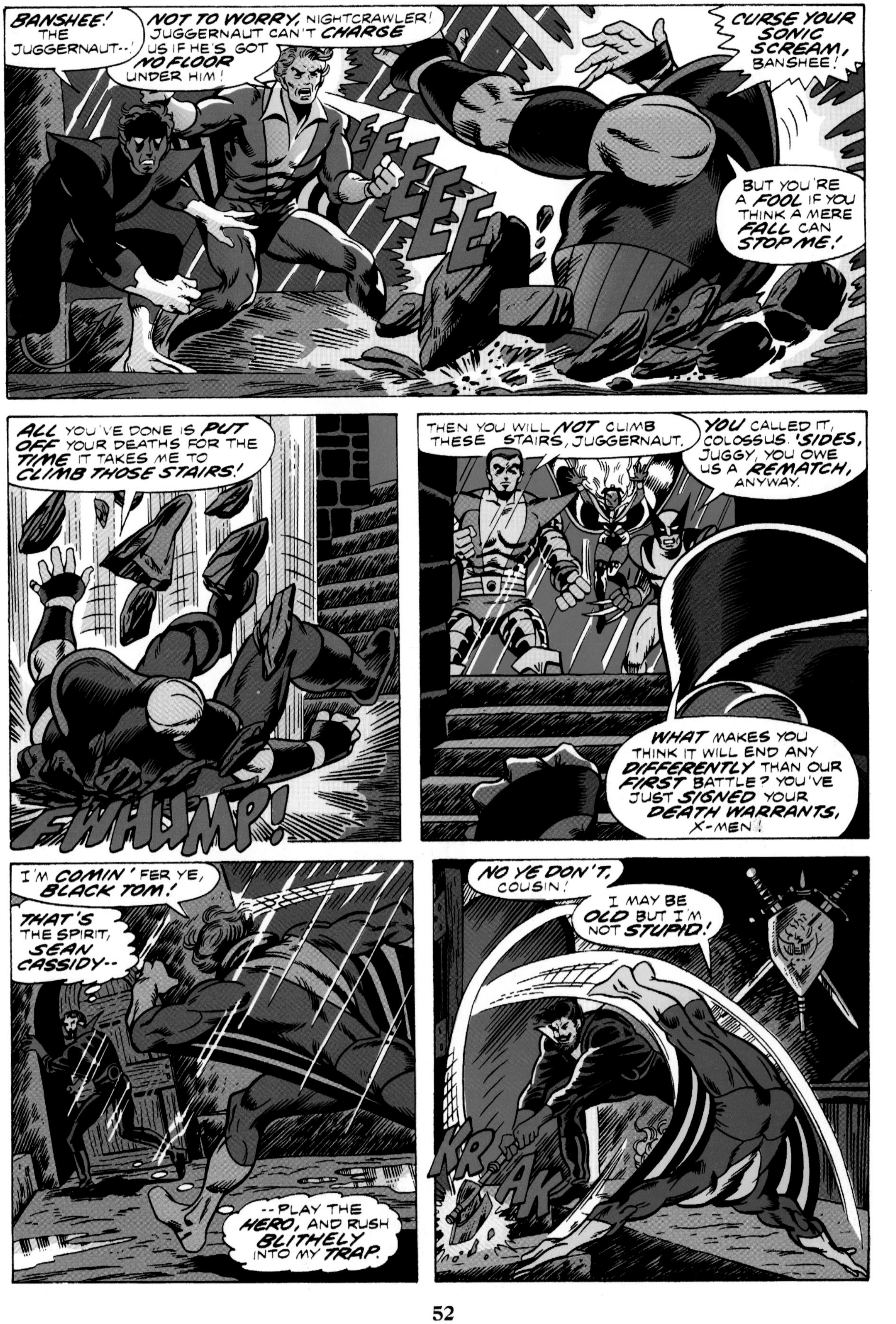
BANSHEE! THE JUGGERNAUT--!
NOT TO WORRY, NIGHTCRAWLER! JUGGERNAUT CAN'T CHARGE US IF HE'S GOT NO FLOOR UNDER HIM!
CURSE YOUR SONIC SCREAM, BANSHEE!
BUT YOU'RE A FOOL IF YOU THINK A MERE FALL CAN STOP ME!
ALL YOU'VE DONE IS PUT OFF YOUR DEATHS FOR THE TIME IT TAKES ME TO CLIMB THOSE STAIRS!
FWHUMP!
THEN YOU WILL NOT CLIMB THESE STAIRS, JUGGERNAUT.
YOU CALLED IT, COLOSSUS. 'SIDES, JUGGY, YOU OWE US A REMATCH, ANYWAY.
WHAT MAKES YOU THINK IT WILL END ANY DIFFERENTLY THAN OUR FIRST BATTLE? YOU'VE JUST SIGNED YOUR DEATH WARRANTS, X-MEN!
I'M COMIN' FER YE, BLACK TOM!
THAT'S THE SPIRIT, SEAN CASSIDY--
--PLAY THE HERO, AND RUSH BLITHELY INTO MY TRAP.
NO YE DON'T, COUSIN!
I MAY BE OLD BUT I'M NOT STUPID!
KRAK

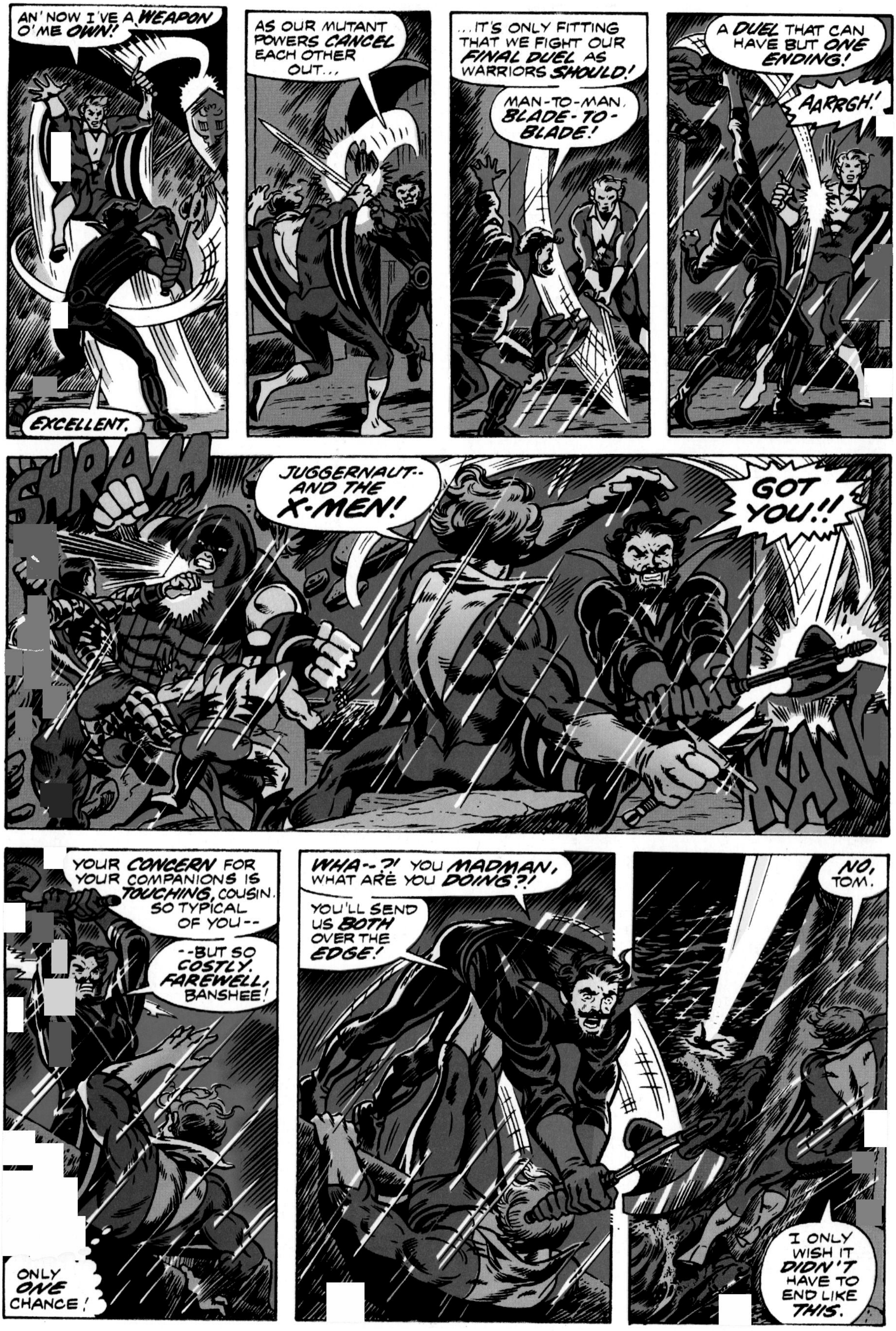
AN' NOW I'VE A WEAPON O' ME OWN!
EXCELLENT.
AS OUR MUTANT POWERS CANCEL EACH OTHER OUT...
...IT'S ONLY FITTING THAT WE FIGHT OUR FINAL DUEL AS WARRIORS SHOULD!
MAN-TO-MAN. BLADE-TO-BLADE!
A DUEL THAT CAN HAVE BUT ONE ENDING!
AARRGH!
SHRAM
JUGGERNAUT-- AND THE X-MEN!
GOT YOU!!
KANG
YOUR CONCERN FOR YOUR COMPANIONS IS TOUCHING, COUSIN. SO TYPICAL OF YOU--
--BUT SO COSTLY. FAREWELL, BANSHEE!
ONLY ONE CHANCE!
WHA--?! YOU MADMAN, WHAT ARE YOU DOING?!
YOU'LL SEND US BOTH OVER THE EDGE!
NO, TOM.
I ONLY WISH IT DIDN'T HAVE TO END LIKE THIS.

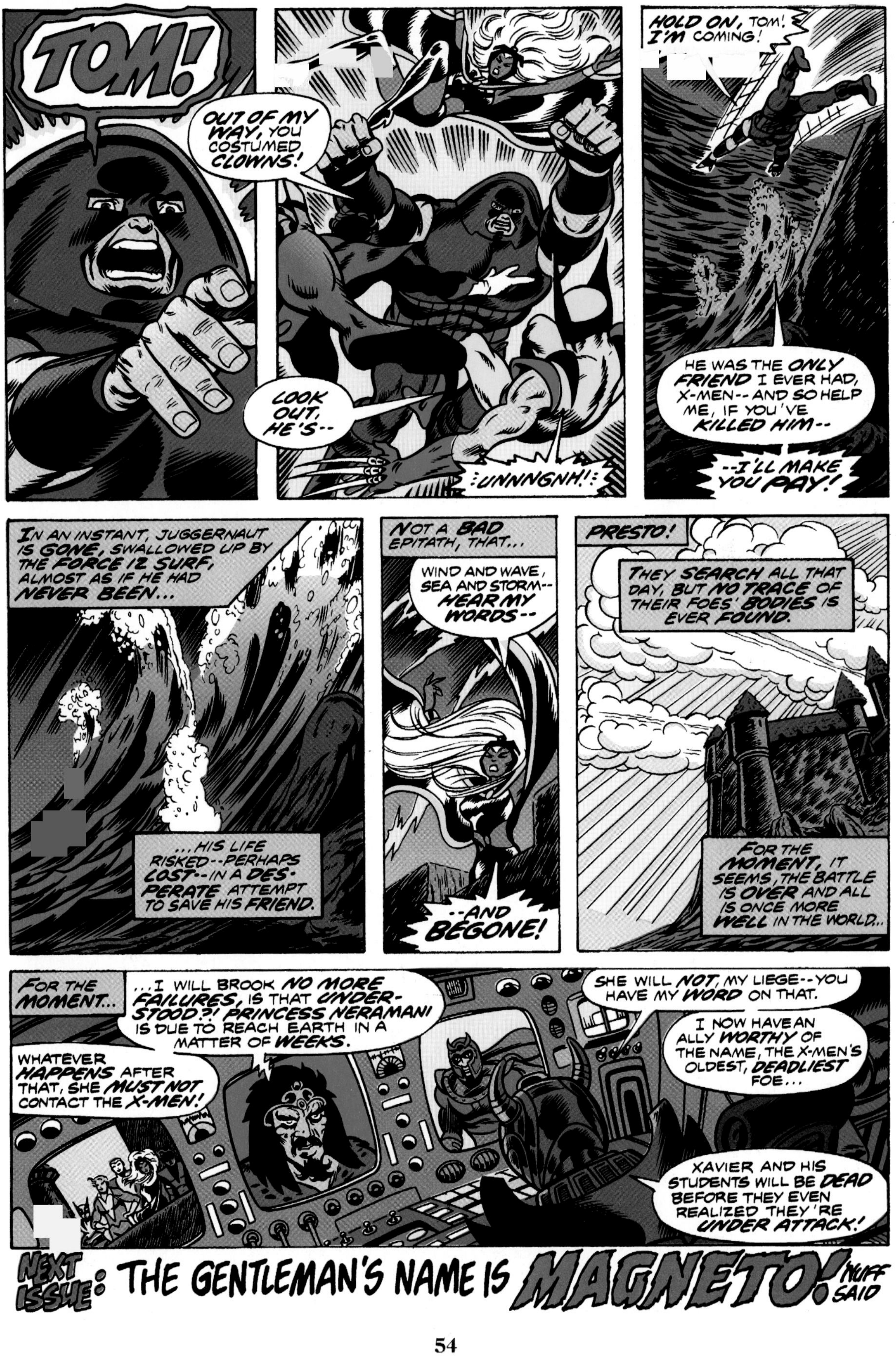
TOM!
OUT OF MY WAY, YOU COSTUMED CLOWNS!
LOOK OUT. HE'S--
UNNNGNH!
HOLD ON, TOM! I'M COMING!
HE WAS THE ONLY FRIEND I EVER HAD, X-MEN--AND SO HELP ME, IF YOU'VE KILLED HIM--
--I'LL MAKE YOU PAY!
IN AN INSTANT, JUGGERNAUT IS GONE, SWALLOWED UP BY THE FORCE 12 SURF, ALMOST AS IF HE HAD NEVER BEEN...
...HIS LIFE RISKED--PERHAPS LOST--IN A DESPERATE ATTEMPT TO SAVE HIS FRIEND.
NOT A BAD EPITATH, THAT...
WIND AND WAVE, SEA AND STORM--HEAR MY WORDS--
--AND BEGONE!
PRESTO!
THEY SEARCH ALL THAT DAY, BUT NO TRACE OF THEIR FOES' BODIES IS EVER FOUND.
FOR THE MOMENT, IT SEEMS, THE BATTLE IS OVER AND ALL IS ONCE MORE WELL IN THE WORLD...
FOR THE MOMENT...
...I WILL BROOK NO MORE FAILURES, IS THAT UNDERSTOOD?! PRINCESS NERAMANI IS DUE TO REACH EARTH IN A MATTER OF WEEKS.
WHATEVER HAPPENS AFTER THAT, SHE MUST NOT CONTACT THE X-MEN!
SHE WILL NOT, MY LIEGE--YOU HAVE MY WORD ON THAT.
I NOW HAVE AN ALLY WORTHY OF THE NAME, THE X-MEN'S OLDEST, DEADLIEST FOE...
XAVIER AND HIS STUDENTS WILL BE DEAD BEFORE THEY EVEN REALIZED THEY'RE UNDER ATTACK!
NEXT ISSUE: THE GENTLEMAN'S NAME IS MAGNETO! 'NUFF SAID

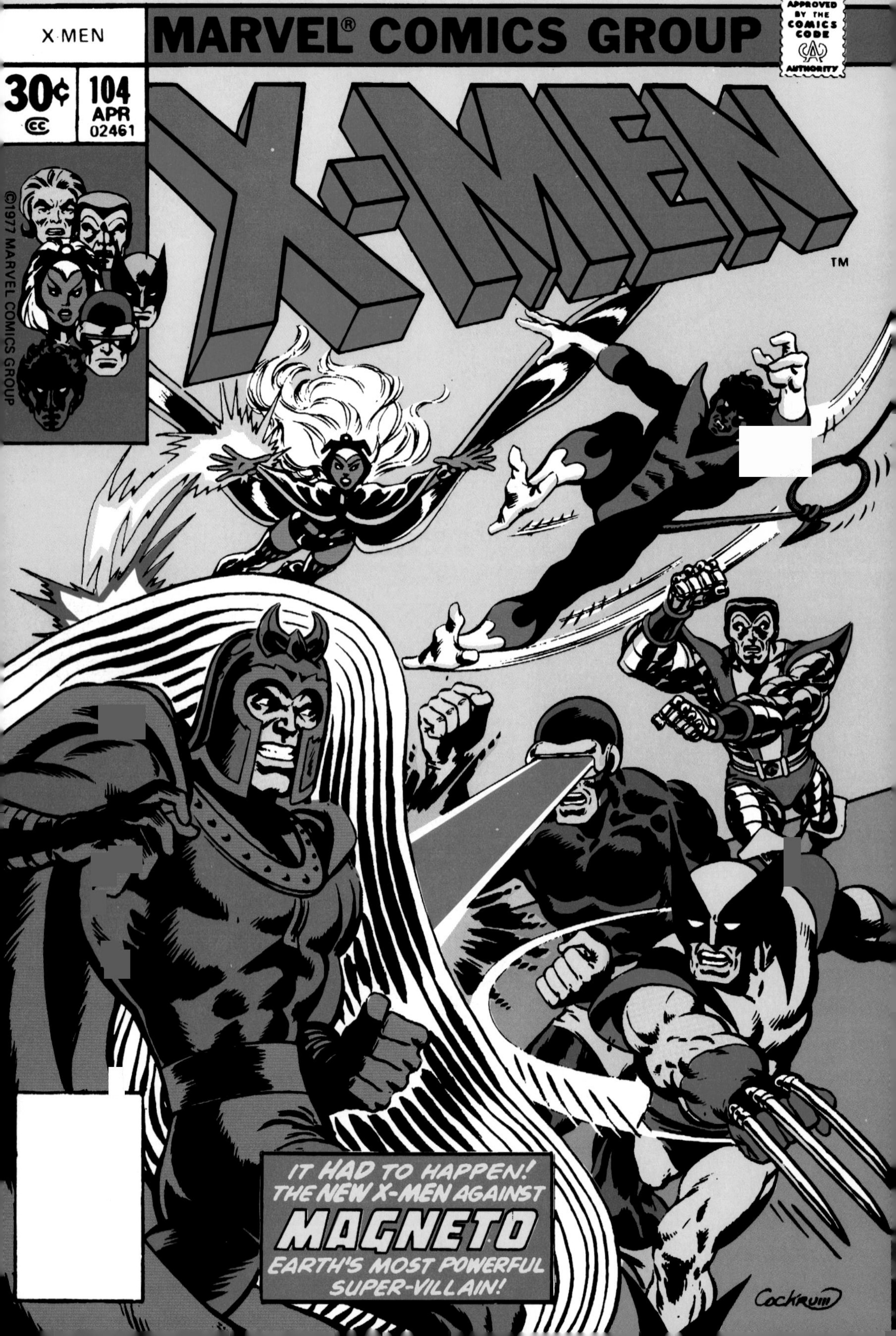
X-MEN
MARVEL® COMICS GROUP
APPROVED BY THE COMICS CODE AUTHORITY
30¢
104
APR
02461
©1977 MARVEL COMICS GROUP
X-MEN
TM
IT HAD TO HAPPEN!
THE NEW X-MEN AGAINST
MAGNETO
EARTH'S MOST POWERFUL
SUPER-VILLAIN!
Cockrum

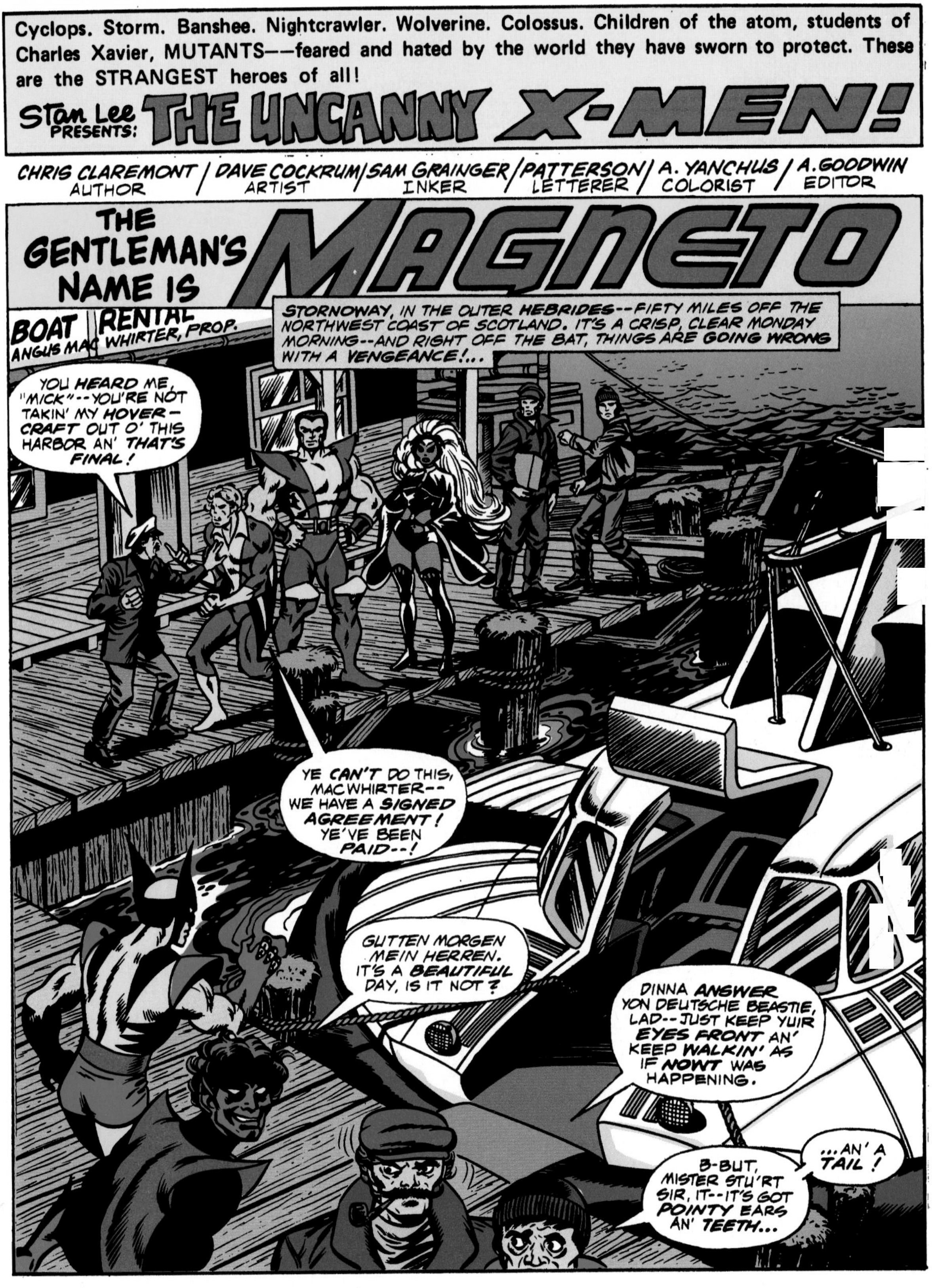
Cyclops. Storm. Banshee. Nightcrawler. Wolverine. Colossus. Children of the atom, students of Charles Xavier, MUTANTS––feared and hated by the world they have sworn to protect. These are the STRANGEST heroes of all!
Stan Lee PRESENTS: THE UNCANNY X-MEN!
CHRIS CLAREMONT AUTHOR / DAVE COCKRUM ARTIST / SAM GRAINGER INKER / PATTERSON LETTERER / A. YANCHUS COLORIST / A. GOODWIN EDITOR
THE GENTLEMAN'S NAME IS MAGNETO
BOAT RENTAL ANGUS MAC WHIRTER, PROP.
STORNOWAY, IN THE OUTER HEBRIDES--FIFTY MILES OFF THE NORTHWEST COAST OF SCOTLAND. IT'S A CRISP, CLEAR MONDAY MORNING--AND RIGHT OFF THE BAT, THINGS ARE GOING WRONG WITH A VENGEANCE!...
YOU HEARD ME, "MICK"--YOU'RE NOT TAKIN' MY HOVER-CRAFT OUT O' THIS HARBOR AN' THAT'S FINAL!
YE CAN'T DO THIS, MACWHIRTER--WE HAVE A SIGNED AGREEMENT! YE'VE BEEN PAID--!
GUTTEN MORGEN MEIN HERREN. IT'S A BEAUTIFUL DAY, IS IT NOT?
DINNA ANSWER YON DEUTSCHE BEASTIE, LAD--JUST KEEP YUIR EYES FRONT AN' KEEP WALKIN' AS IF NOWT WAS HAPPENING.
B-BUT, MISTER STU'RT SIR, IT--IT'S GOT POINTY EARS AN' TEETH...
...AN' A TAIL!

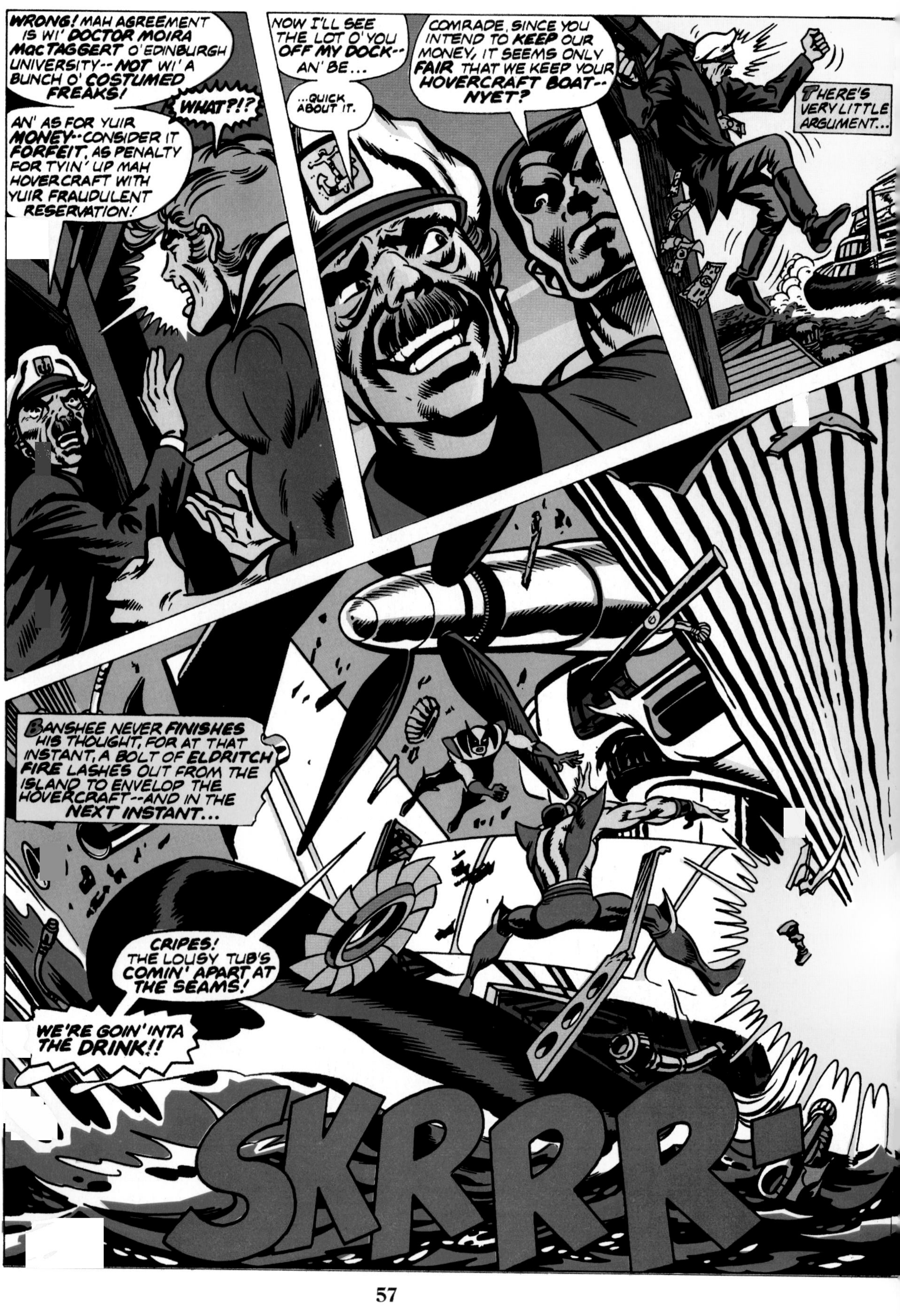
WRONG! MAH AGREEMENT IS WI' DOCTOR MOIRA MacTAGGERT O'EDINBURGH UNIVERSITY-- NOT WI' A BUNCH O' COSTUMED FREAKS!
WHAT?!?
AN' AS FOR YUIR MONEY--CONSIDER IT FORFEIT, AS PENALTY FOR TYIN' UP MAH HOVERCRAFT WITH YUIR FRAUDULENT RESERVATION!
NOW I'LL SEE THE LOT O'YOU OFF MY DOCK-- AN' BE...
...QUICK ABOUT IT.
COMRADE, SINCE YOU INTEND TO KEEP OUR MONEY, IT SEEMS ONLY FAIR THAT WE KEEP YOUR HOVERCRAFT BOAT-- NYET?
THERE'S VERY LITTLE ARGUMENT...
BANSHEE NEVER FINISHES HIS THOUGHT, FOR AT THAT INSTANT, A BOLT OF ELDRITCH FIRE LASHES OUT FROM THE ISLAND TO ENVELOP THE HOVERCRAFT--AND IN THE NEXT INSTANT...
CRIPES! THE LOUSY TUB'S COMIN' APART AT THE SEAMS!
WE'RE GOIN' INTA THE DRINK!!
SKRRR-

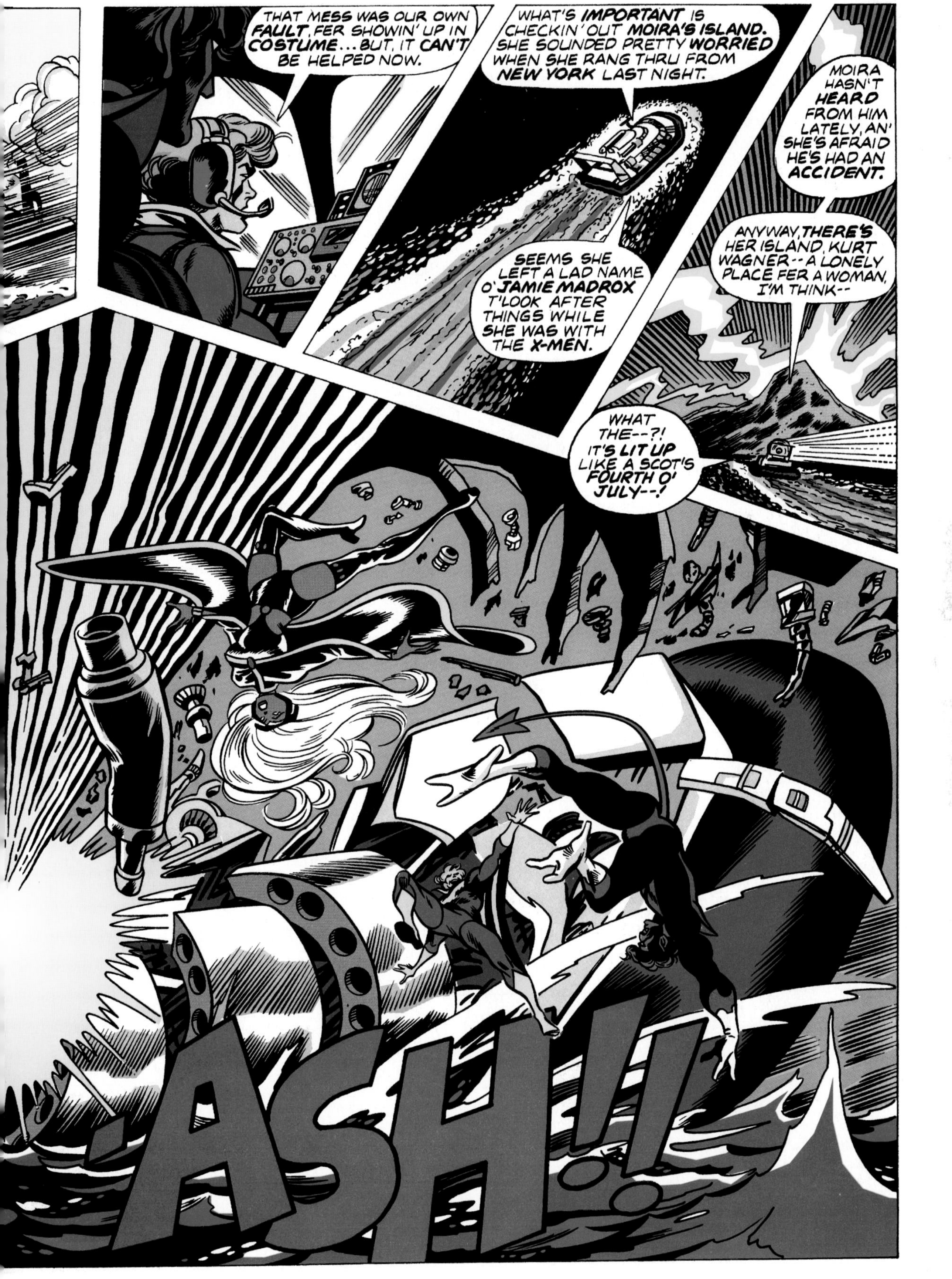
THAT MESS WAS OUR OWN FAULT, FER SHOWIN' UP IN COSTUME... BUT, IT CAN'T BE HELPED NOW.
WHAT'S IMPORTANT IS CHECKIN' OUT MOIRA'S ISLAND. SHE SOUNDED PRETTY WORRIED WHEN SHE RANG THRU FROM NEW YORK LAST NIGHT.
SEEMS SHE LEFT A LAD NAME O' JAMIE MADROX T'LOOK AFTER THINGS WHILE SHE WAS WITH THE X-MEN.
MOIRA HASN'T HEARD FROM HIM LATELY, AN' SHE'S AFRAID HE'S HAD AN ACCIDENT.
ANYWAY, THERE'S HER ISLAND, KURT WAGNER -- A LONELY PLACE FER A WOMAN, I'M THINK--
WHAT THE--?! IT'S LIT UP LIKE A SCOT'S FOURTH O' JULY--!
'ASH!!

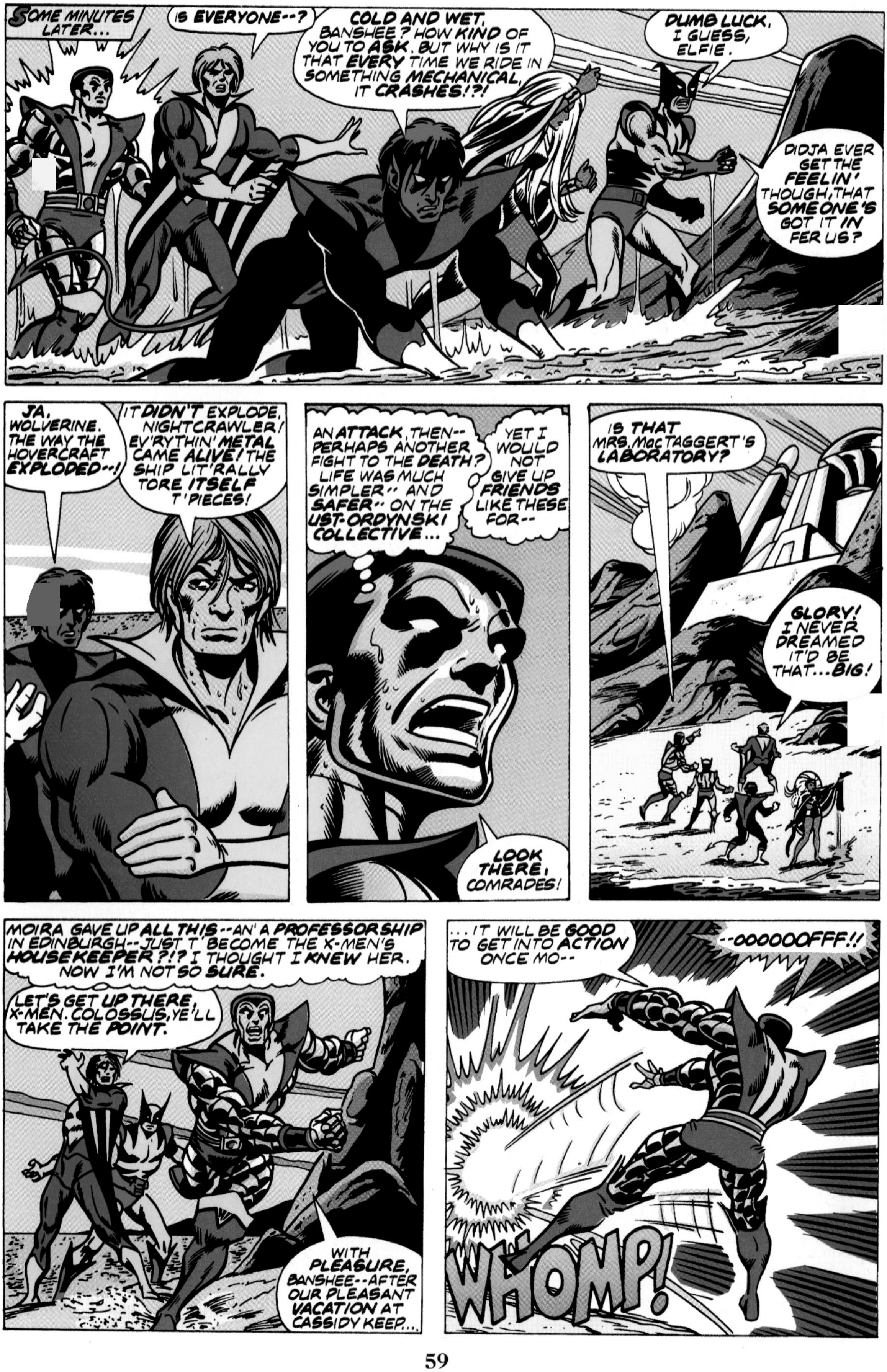
SOME MINUTES LATER...
IS EVERYONE--?
COLD AND WET, BANSHEE? HOW KIND OF YOU TO ASK. BUT WHY IS IT THAT EVERY TIME WE RIDE IN SOMETHING MECHANICAL, IT CRASHES!?!
DUMB LUCK, I GUESS, ELFIE.
DIDJA EVER GET THE FEELIN' THOUGH, THAT SOMEONE'S GOT IT IN FER US?
JA, WOLVERINE. THE WAY THE HOVERCRAFT EXPLODED--!
IT DIDN'T EXPLODE, NIGHTCRAWLER! EV'RYTHIN' METAL CAME ALIVE! THE SHIP LIT'RALLY TORE ITSELF T'PIECES!
AN ATTACK, THEN-- PERHAPS ANOTHER FIGHT TO THE DEATH? LIFE WAS MUCH SIMPLER-- AND SAFER-- ON THE UST-ORDYNSKI COLLECTIVE...
YET I WOULD NOT GIVE UP FRIENDS LIKE THESE FOR--
LOOK THERE, COMRADES!
IS THAT MRS. MacTAGGERT'S LABORATORY?
GLORY! I NEVER DREAMED IT'D BE THAT...BIG!
MOIRA GAVE UP ALL THIS--AN' A PROFESSORSHIP IN EDINBURGH--JUST T' BECOME THE X-MEN'S HOUSEKEEPER?!? I THOUGHT I KNEW HER. NOW I'M NOT SO SURE.
LET'S GET UP THERE, X-MEN. COLOSSUS, YE'LL TAKE THE POINT.
WITH PLEASURE, BANSHEE--AFTER OUR PLEASANT VACATION AT CASSIDY KEEP...
...IT WILL BE GOOD TO GET INTO ACTION ONCE MO--
--OOOOOOFFF!!
WHOMP!

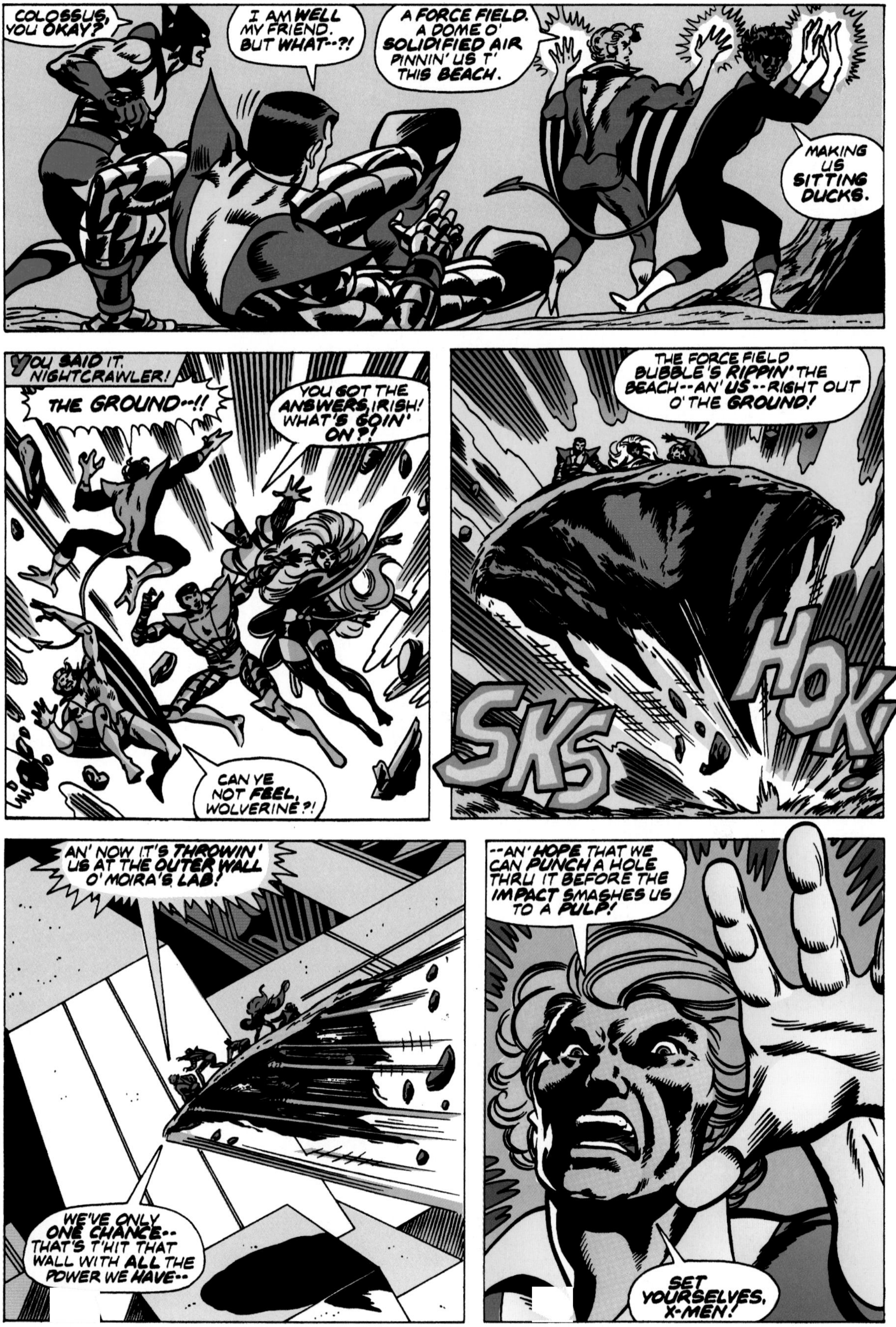
COLOSSUS, YOU OKAY?
I AM WELL MY FRIEND. BUT WHAT--?!
A FORCE FIELD. A DOME O' SOLIDIFIED AIR PINNIN' US T' THIS BEACH.
MAKING US SITTING DUCKS.
YOU SAID IT, NIGHTCRAWLER!
THE GROUND--!!
YOU GOT THE ANSWERS, IRISH! WHAT'S GOIN' ON?!
CAN YE NOT FEEL, WOLVERINE?!
THE FORCE FIELD BUBBLE'S RIPPIN' THE BEACH--AN' US--RIGHT OUT O' THE GROUND!
SKS
HOK!
AN' NOW IT'S THROWIN' US AT THE OUTER WALL O' MOIRA'S LAB!
WE'VE ONLY ONE CHANCE-- THAT'S T'HIT THAT WALL WITH ALL THE POWER WE HAVE--
--AN' HOPE THAT WE CAN PUNCH A HOLE THRU IT BEFORE THE IMPACT SMASHES US TO A PULP!
SET YOURSELVES, X-MEN!

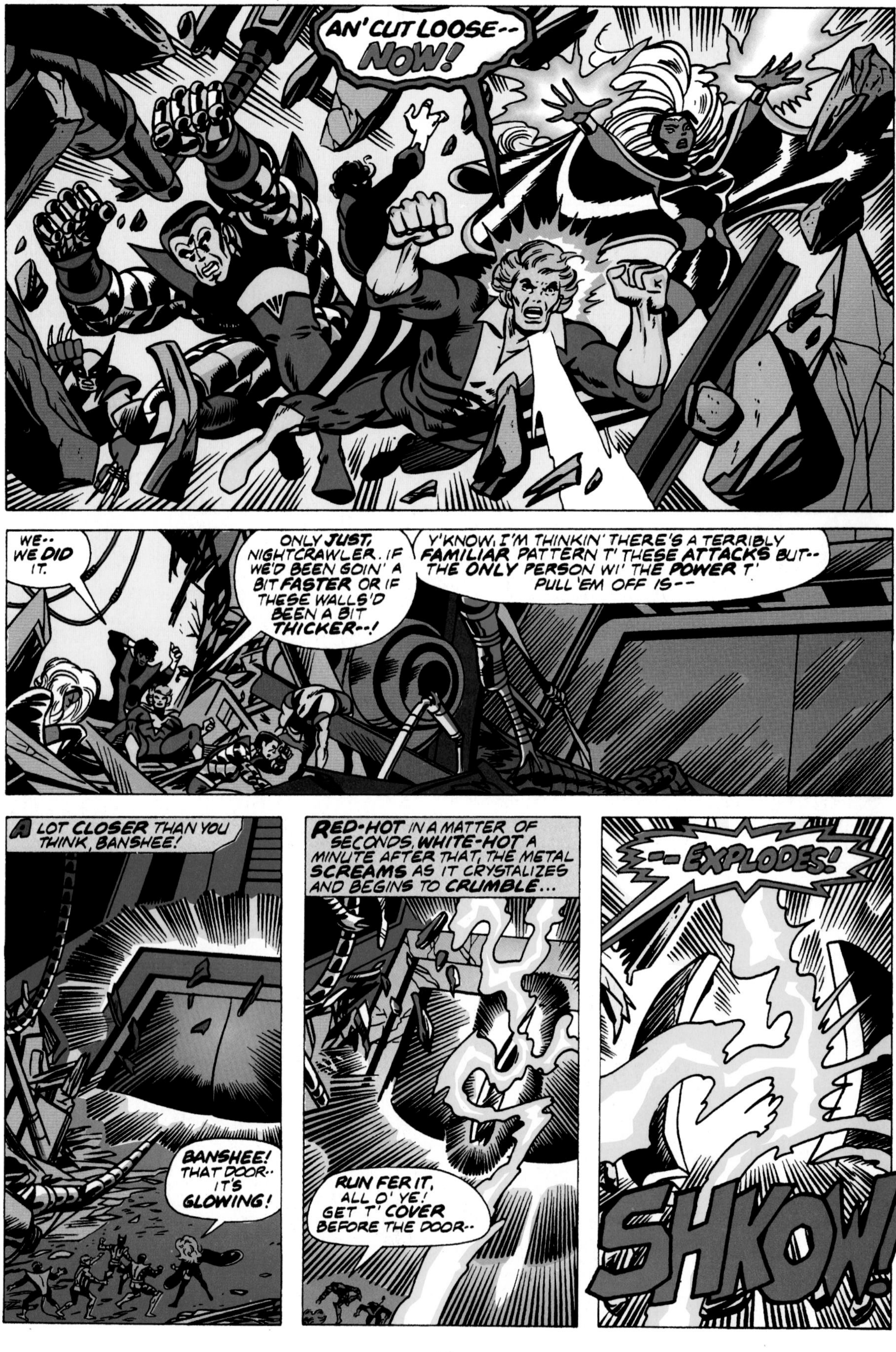
AN' CUT LOOSE-- NOW!
WE-- WE DID IT.
ONLY JUST, NIGHTCRAWLER. IF WE'D BEEN GOIN' A BIT FASTER OR IF THESE WALLS'D BEEN A BIT THICKER--!
Y'KNOW, I'M THINKIN' THERE'S A TERRIBLY FAMILIAR PATTERN T' THESE ATTACKS BUT-- THE ONLY PERSON WI' THE POWER T' PULL 'EM OFF IS--
A LOT CLOSER THAN YOU THINK, BANSHEE!
BANSHEE! THAT DOOR-- IT'S GLOWING!
RED-HOT IN A MATTER OF SECONDS, WHITE-HOT A MINUTE AFTER THAT, THE METAL SCREAMS AS IT CRYSTALIZES AND BEGINS TO CRUMBLE...
RUN FER IT, ALL O' YE! GET T' COVER BEFORE THE DOOR--
--EXPLODES!
SHKOW!

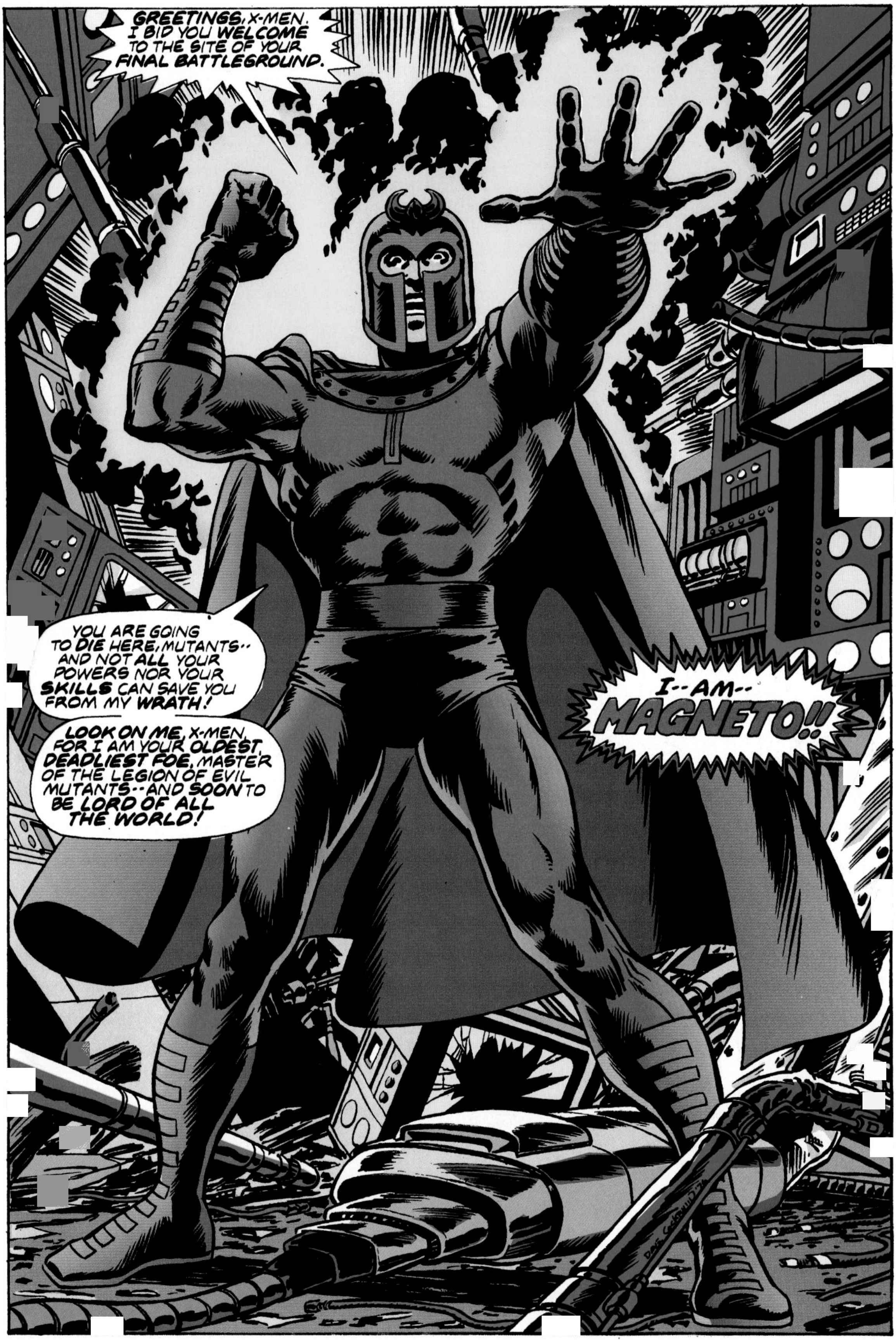
GREETINGS, X-MEN. I BID YOU WELCOME TO THE SITE OF YOUR FINAL BATTLEGROUND.
YOU ARE GOING TO DIE HERE, MUTANTS-- AND NOT ALL YOUR POWERS NOR YOUR SKILLS CAN SAVE YOU FROM MY WRATH!
LOOK ON ME, X-MEN, FOR I AM YOUR OLDEST, DEADLIEST FOE, MASTER OF THE LEGION OF EVIL MUTANTS--AND SOON TO BE LORD OF ALL THE WORLD!
I--AM-- MAGNETO!!

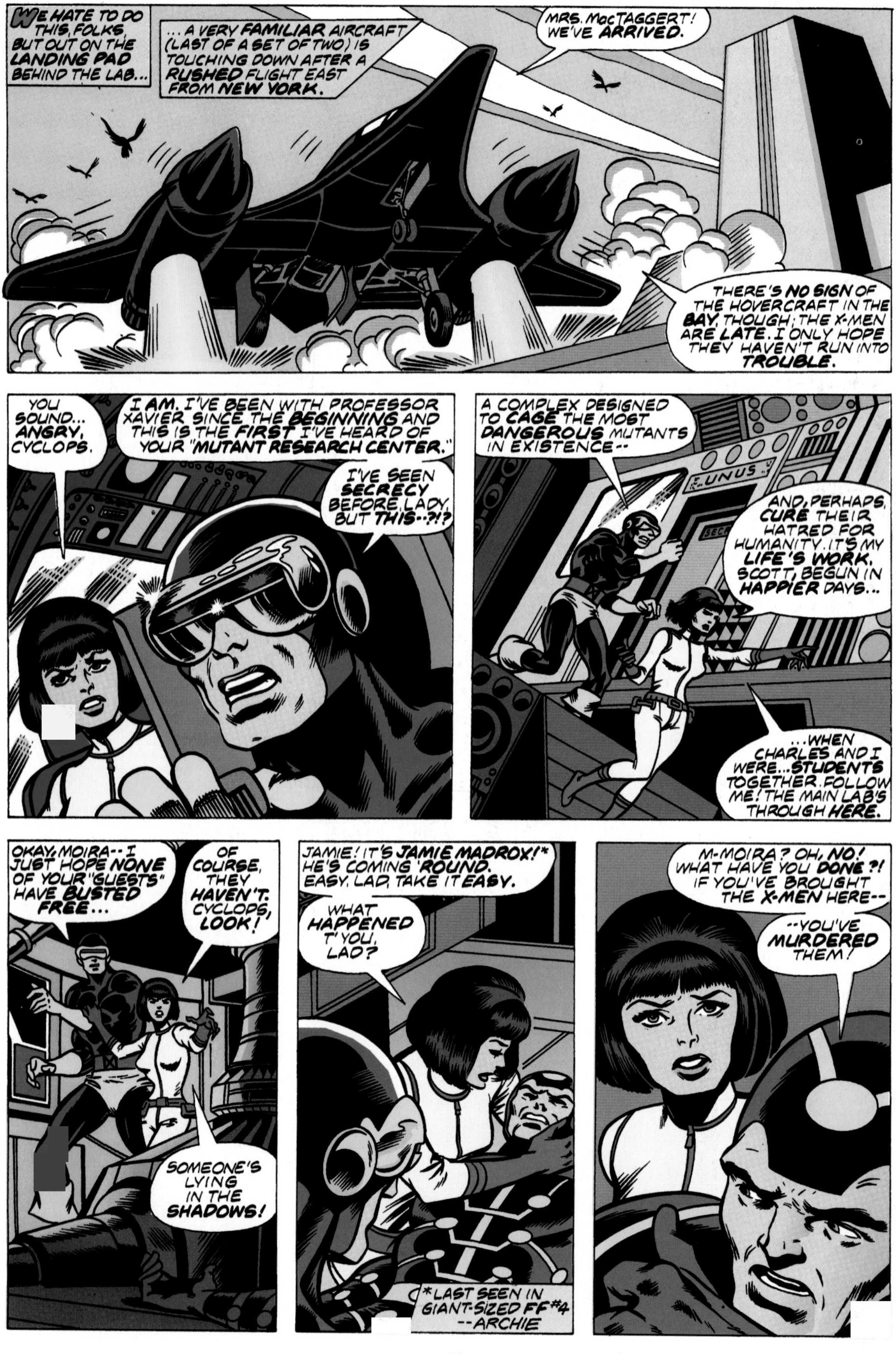
WE HATE TO DO THIS, FOLKS, BUT OUT ON THE LANDING PAD BEHIND THE LAB...
...A VERY FAMILIAR AIRCRAFT (LAST OF A SET OF TWO) IS TOUCHING DOWN AFTER A RUSHED FLIGHT EAST FROM NEW YORK.
MRS. MacTAGGERT! WE'VE ARRIVED.
THERE'S NO SIGN OF THE HOVERCRAFT IN THE BAY, THOUGH; THE X-MEN ARE LATE. I ONLY HOPE THEY HAVEN'T RUN INTO TROUBLE.
YOU SOUND... ANGRY, CYCLOPS.
I AM. I'VE BEEN WITH PROFESSOR XAVIER SINCE THE BEGINNING AND THIS IS THE FIRST I'VE HEARD OF YOUR "MUTANT RESEARCH CENTER."
I'VE SEEN SECRECY BEFORE, LADY, BUT THIS--?!?
A COMPLEX DESIGNED TO CAGE THE MOST DANGEROUS MUTANTS IN EXISTENCE--
UNUS
AND, PERHAPS, CURE THEIR HATRED FOR HUMANITY. IT'S MY LIFE'S WORK, SCOTT, BEGUN IN HAPPIER DAYS...
...WHEN CHARLES AND I WERE...STUDENTS TOGETHER. FOLLOW ME! THE MAIN LAB'S THROUGH HERE.
OKAY, MOIRA-- I JUST HOPE NONE OF YOUR "GUESTS" HAVE BUSTED FREE...
OF COURSE, THEY HAVEN'T. CYCLOPS, LOOK!
SOMEONE'S LYING IN THE SHADOWS!
JAMIE! IT'S JAMIE MADROX!* HE'S COMING 'ROUND. EASY, LAD, TAKE IT EASY.
WHAT HAPPENED T'YOU, LAD?
*LAST SEEN IN GIANT-SIZED FF #4 --ARCHIE
M-MOIRA? OH, NO! WHAT HAVE YOU DONE?! IF YOU'VE BROUGHT THE X-MEN HERE--
--YOU'VE MURDERED THEM!

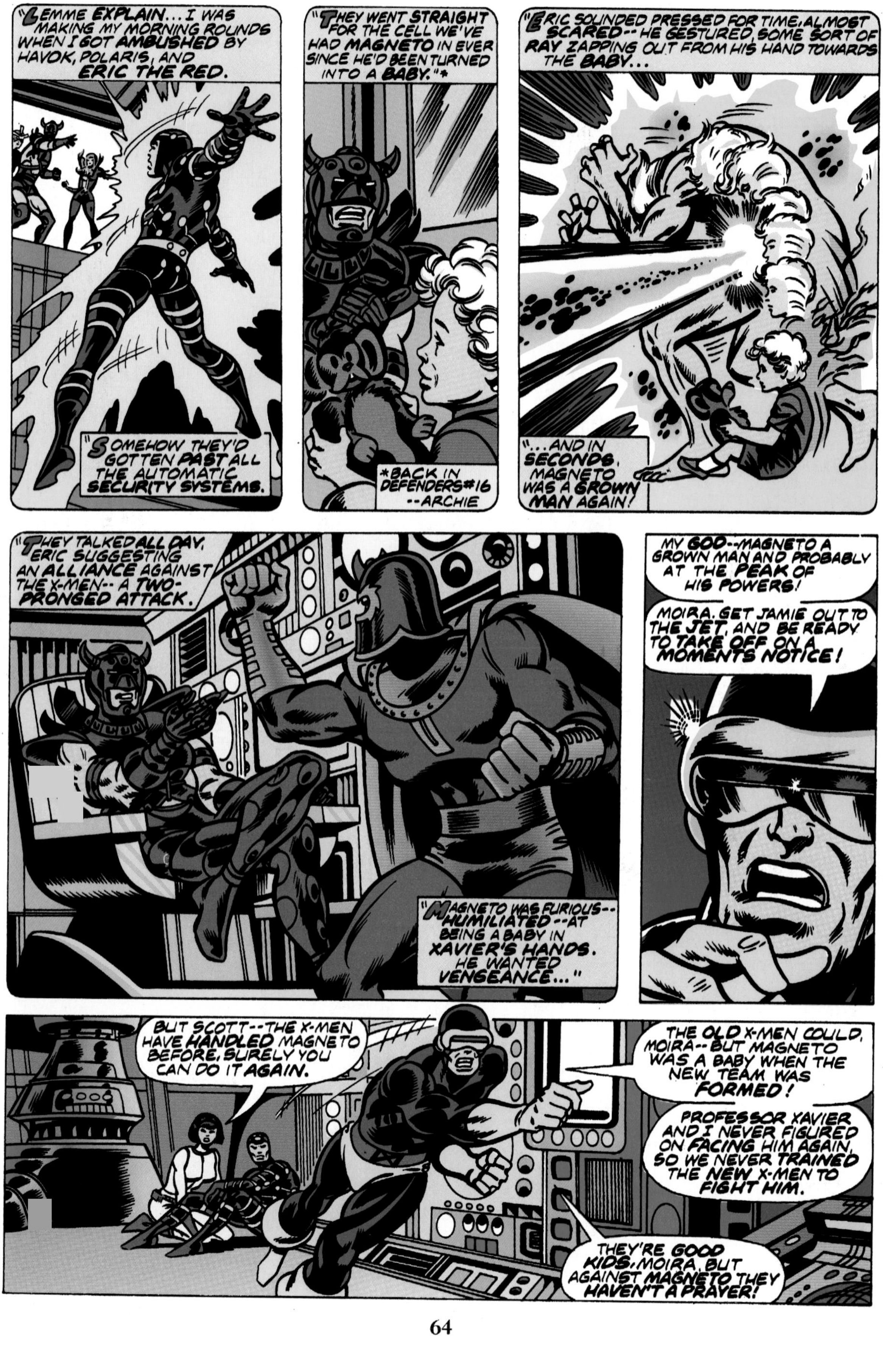
"LEMME EXPLAIN... I WAS MAKING MY MORNING ROUNDS WHEN I GOT AMBUSHED BY HAVOK, POLARIS, AND ERIC THE RED.
"SOMEHOW THEY'D GOTTEN PAST ALL THE AUTOMATIC SECURITY SYSTEMS.
"THEY WENT STRAIGHT FOR THE CELL WE'VE HAD MAGNETO IN EVER SINCE HE'D BEEN TURNED INTO A BABY."*
*BACK IN DEFENDERS #16 --ARCHIE
"ERIC SOUNDED PRESSED FOR TIME, ALMOST SCARED-- HE GESTURED, SOME SORT OF RAY ZAPPING OUT FROM HIS HAND TOWARDS THE BABY...
"...AND IN SECONDS, MAGNETO WAS A GROWN MAN AGAIN!
"THEY TALKED ALL DAY, ERIC SUGGESTING AN ALLIANCE AGAINST THE X-MEN-- A TWO-PRONGED ATTACK.
"MAGNETO WAS FURIOUS-- HUMILIATED --AT BEING A BABY IN XAVIER'S HANDS. HE WANTED VENGEANCE..."
MY GOD--MAGNETO A GROWN MAN AND PROBABLY AT THE PEAK OF HIS POWERS!
MOIRA, GET JAMIE OUT TO THE JET, AND BE READY TO TAKE OFF ON A MOMENTS NOTICE!
BUT SCOTT--THE X-MEN HAVE HANDLED MAGNETO BEFORE, SURELY YOU CAN DO IT AGAIN.
THE OLD X-MEN COULD, MOIRA-- BUT MAGNETO WAS A BABY WHEN THE NEW TEAM WAS FORMED!
PROFESSOR XAVIER AND I NEVER FIGURED ON FACING HIM AGAIN, SO WE NEVER TRAINED THE NEW X-MEN TO FIGHT HIM.
THEY'RE GOOD KIDS, MOIRA, BUT AGAINST MAGNETO THEY HAVEN'T A PRAYER!

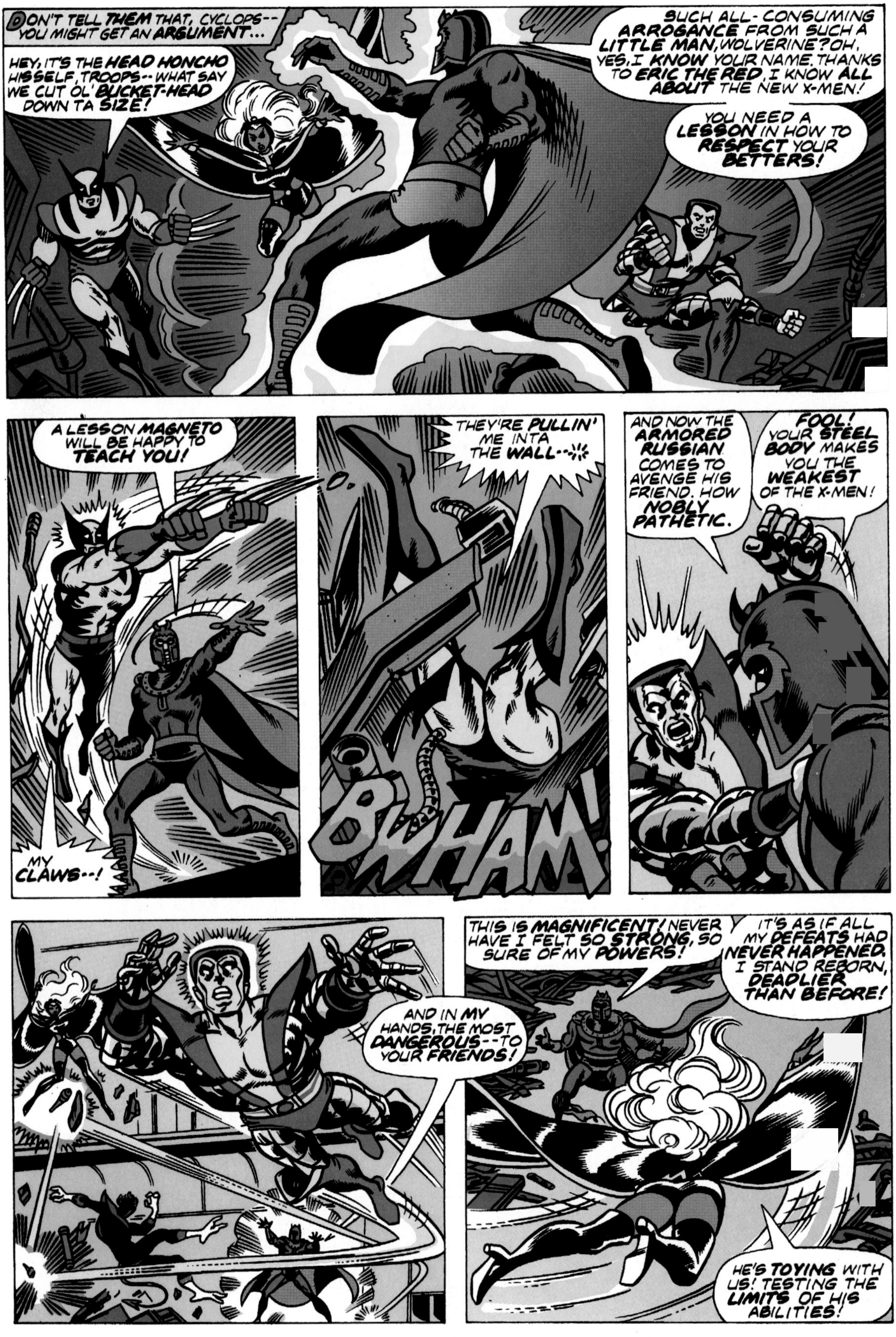
DON'T TELL THEM THAT, CYCLOPS-- YOU MIGHT GET AN ARGUMENT...
HEY, IT'S THE HEAD HONCHO HISSELF, TROOPS-- WHAT SAY WE CUT OL' BUCKET-HEAD DOWN TA SIZE!
SUCH ALL-CONSUMING ARROGANCE FROM SUCH A LITTLE MAN, WOLVERINE? OH, YES, I KNOW YOUR NAME. THANKS TO ERIC THE RED, I KNOW ALL ABOUT THE NEW X-MEN!
YOU NEED A LESSON IN HOW TO RESPECT YOUR BETTERS!
A LESSON MAGNETO WILL BE HAPPY TO TEACH YOU!
MY CLAWS--!
THEY'RE PULLIN' ME INTA THE WALL--!
BWHAM!
AND NOW THE ARMORED RUSSIAN COMES TO AVENGE HIS FRIEND. HOW NOBLY PATHETIC.
FOOL! YOUR STEEL BODY MAKES YOU THE WEAKEST OF THE X-MEN!
AND IN MY HANDS, THE MOST DANGEROUS--TO YOUR FRIENDS!
THIS IS MAGNIFICENT! NEVER HAVE I FELT SO STRONG, SO SURE OF MY POWERS!
IT'S AS IF ALL MY DEFEATS HAD NEVER HAPPENED. I STAND REBORN, DEADLIER THAN BEFORE!
HE'S TOYING WITH US! TESTING THE LIMITS OF HIS ABILITIES!

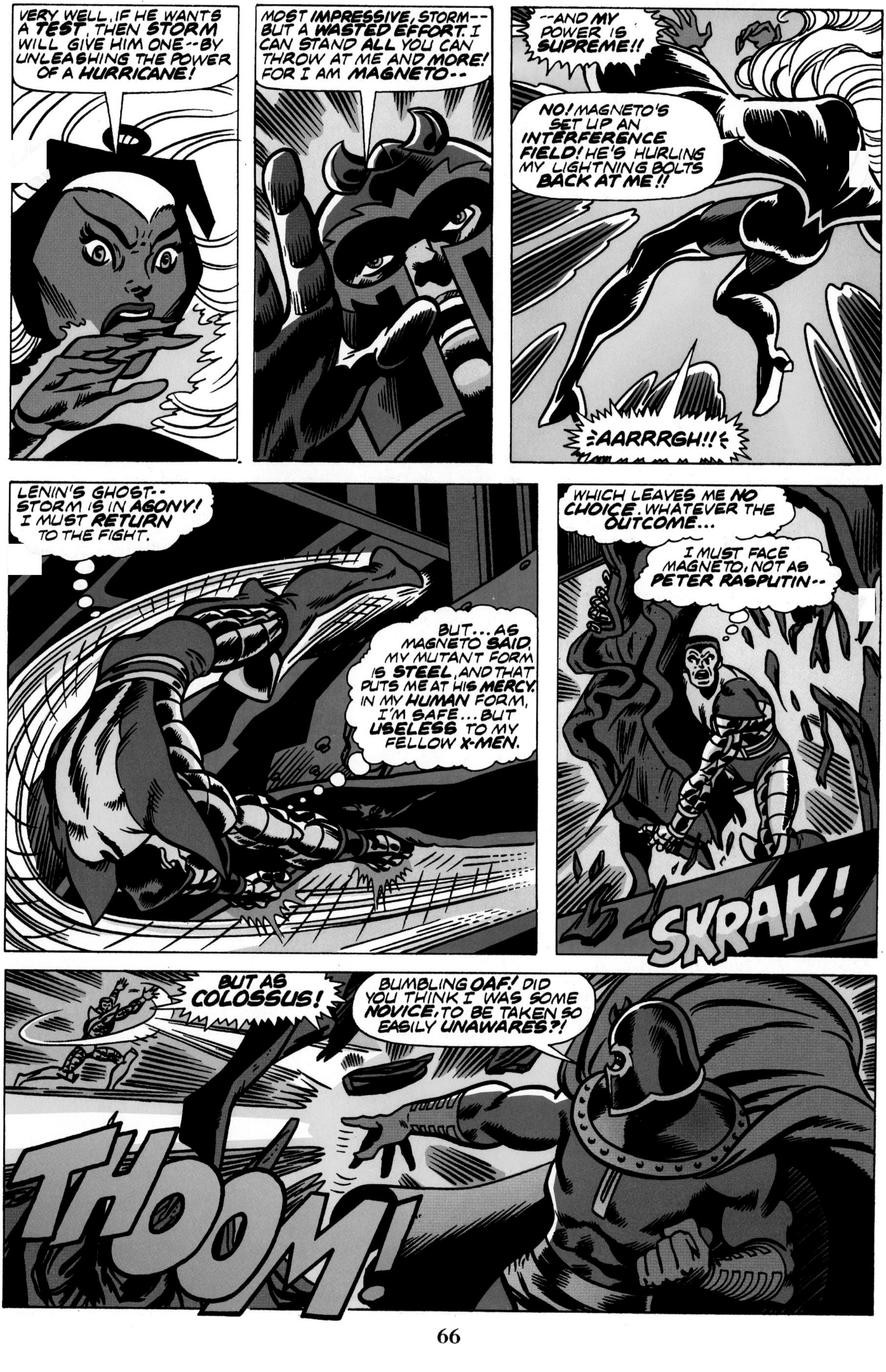

VERY WELL, IF HE WANTS A TEST, THEN STORM WILL GIVE HIM ONE--BY UNLEASHING THE POWER OF A HURRICANE!
MOST IMPRESSIVE, STORM--BUT A WASTED EFFORT. I CAN STAND ALL YOU CAN THROW AT ME AND MORE! FOR I AM MAGNETO--
--AND MY POWER IS SUPREME!!
NO! MAGNETO'S SET UP AN INTERFERENCE FIELD! HE'S HURLING MY LIGHTNING BOLTS BACK AT ME!!
AARRRGH!!
LENIN'S GHOST--STORM IS IN AGONY! I MUST RETURN TO THE FIGHT.
BUT... AS MAGNETO SAID, MY MUTANT FORM IS STEEL, AND THAT PUTS ME AT HIS MERCY. IN MY HUMAN FORM, I'M SAFE... BUT USELESS TO MY FELLOW X-MEN.
WHICH LEAVES ME NO CHOICE. WHATEVER THE OUTCOME...
I MUST FACE MAGNETO, NOT AS PETER RASPUTIN--
SKRAK!
BUT AS COLOSSUS!
BUMBLING OAF! DID YOU THINK I WAS SOME NOVICE, TO BE TAKEN SO EASILY UNAWARES?!
THOOM!

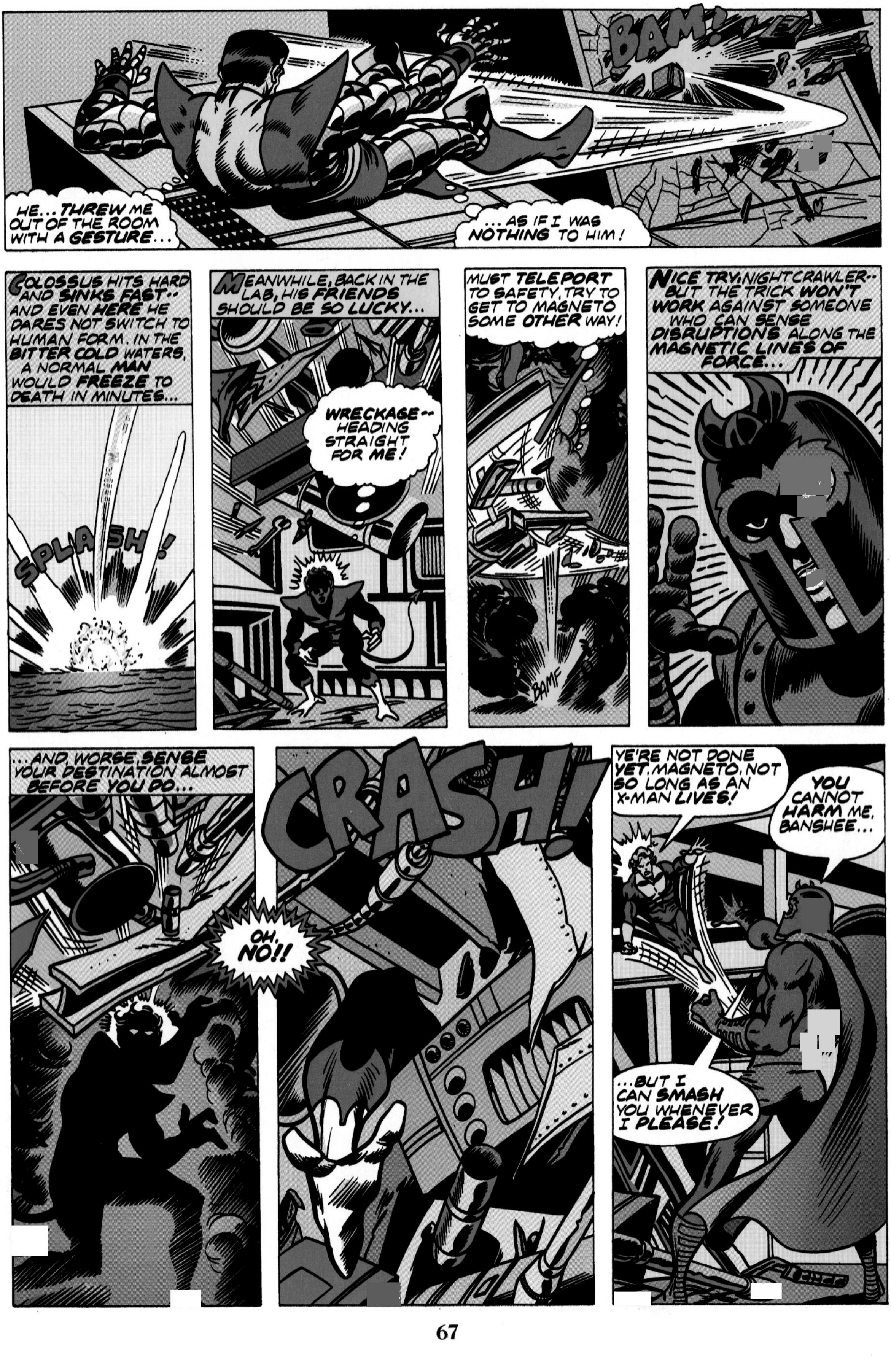
HE... THREW ME OUT OF THE ROOM WITH A GESTURE...
BAM!
...AS IF I WAS NOTHING TO HIM!
COLOSSUS HITS HARD AND SINKS FAST-- AND EVEN HERE HE DARES NOT SWITCH TO HUMAN FORM. IN THE BITTER COLD WATERS, A NORMAL MAN WOULD FREEZE TO DEATH IN MINUTES...
SPLASH!
MEANWHILE, BACK IN THE LAB, HIS FRIENDS SHOULD BE SO LUCKY...
WRECKAGE-- HEADING STRAIGHT FOR ME!
MUST TELEPORT TO SAFETY, TRY TO GET TO MAGNETO SOME OTHER WAY!
BAMF
NICE TRY, NIGHTCRAWLER-- BUT THE TRICK WON'T WORK AGAINST SOMEONE WHO CAN SENSE DISRUPTIONS ALONG THE MAGNETIC LINES OF FORCE...
...AND, WORSE, SENSE YOUR DESTINATION ALMOST BEFORE YOU DO...
OH, NO!!
CRASH!
YE'RE NOT DONE YET, MAGNETO, NOT SO LONG AS AN X-MAN LIVES!
YOU CANNOT HARM ME, BANSHEE...
...BUT I CAN SMASH YOU WHENEVER I PLEASE!

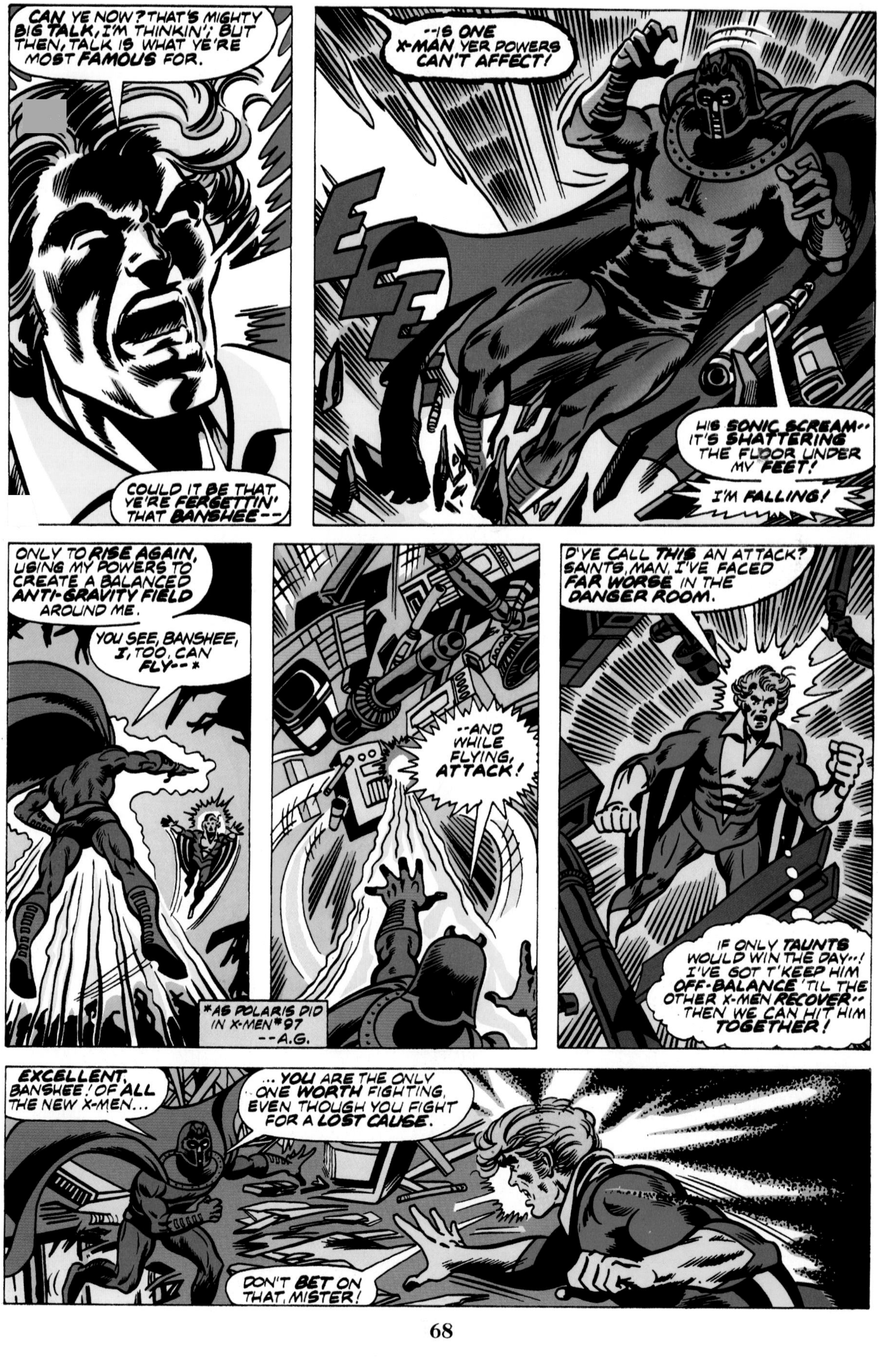

CAN YE NOW? THAT'S MIGHTY BIG TALK, I'M THINKIN'; BUT THEN, TALK IS WHAT YE'RE MOST FAMOUS FOR.
COULD IT BE THAT YE'RE FERGETTIN' THAT BANSHEE--
--IS ONE X-MAN YER POWERS CAN'T AFFECT!
EEE
HIS SONIC SCREAM-- IT'S SHATTERING THE FLOOR UNDER MY FEET!
I'M FALLING!
ONLY TO RISE AGAIN, USING MY POWERS TO CREATE A BALANCED ANTI-GRAVITY FIELD AROUND ME.
YOU SEE, BANSHEE, I, TOO, CAN FLY--*
*AS POLARIS DID IN X-MEN #97 --A.G.
--AND WHILE FLYING, ATTACK!
D'YE CALL THIS AN ATTACK? SAINTS, MAN, I'VE FACED FAR WORSE IN THE DANGER ROOM.
IF ONLY TAUNTS WOULD WIN THE DAY--! I'VE GOT T'KEEP HIM OFF-BALANCE 'TIL THE OTHER X-MEN RECOVER-- THEN WE CAN HIT HIM TOGETHER!
EXCELLENT, BANSHEE! OF ALL THE NEW X-MEN...
...YOU ARE THE ONLY ONE WORTH FIGHTING, EVEN THOUGH YOU FIGHT FOR A LOST CAUSE.
DON'T BET ON THAT, MISTER!

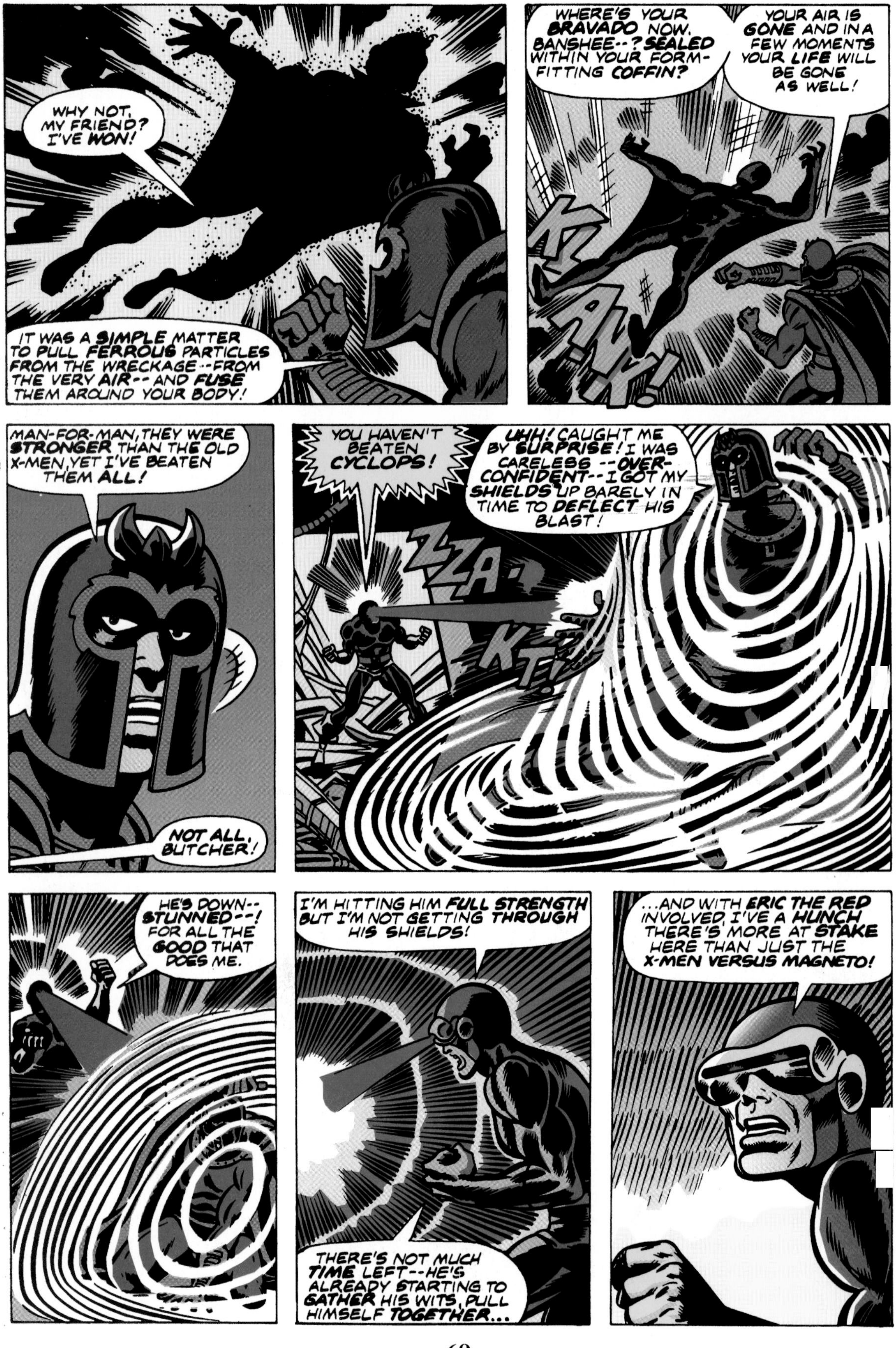
WHY NOT, MY FRIEND? I'VE WON!
IT WAS A SIMPLE MATTER TO PULL FERROUS PARTICLES FROM THE WRECKAGE--FROM THE VERY AIR--AND FUSE THEM AROUND YOUR BODY!
WHERE'S YOUR BRAVADO NOW, BANSHEE--? SEALED WITHIN YOUR FORM-FITTING COFFIN?
YOUR AIR IS GONE AND IN A FEW MOMENTS YOUR LIFE WILL BE GONE AS WELL!
KLANK!
MAN-FOR-MAN, THEY WERE STRONGER THAN THE OLD X-MEN, YET I'VE BEATEN THEM ALL!
NOT ALL, BUTCHER!
YOU HAVEN'T BEATEN CYCLOPS!
UHH! CAUGHT ME BY SURPRISE! I WAS CARELESS --OVER-CONFIDENT--I GOT MY SHIELDS UP BARELY IN TIME TO DEFLECT HIS BLAST!
ZZA-KT!
HE'S DOWN--STUNNED--! FOR ALL THE GOOD THAT DOES ME.
I'M HITTING HIM FULL STRENGTH BUT I'M NOT GETTING THROUGH HIS SHIELDS!
THERE'S NOT MUCH TIME LEFT--HE'S ALREADY STARTING TO GATHER HIS WITS, PULL HIMSELF TOGETHER...
...AND WITH ERIC THE RED INVOLVED, I'VE A HUNCH THERE'S MORE AT STAKE HERE THAN JUST THE X-MEN VERSUS MAGNETO!

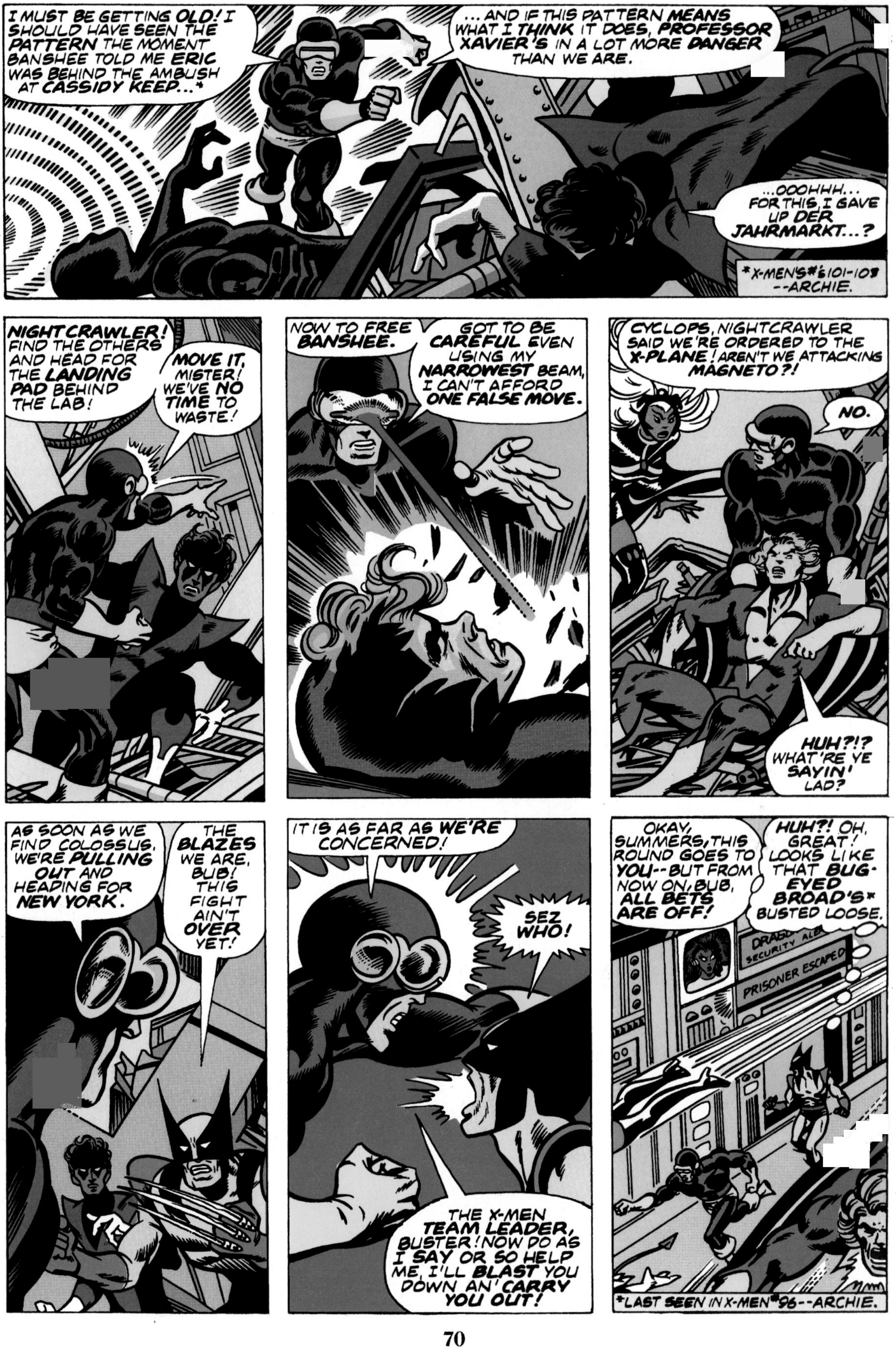

I MUST BE GETTING OLD! I SHOULD HAVE SEEN THE PATTERN THE MOMENT BANSHEE TOLD ME ERIC WAS BEHIND THE AMBUSH AT CASSIDY KEEP...*
... AND IF THIS PATTERN MEANS WHAT I THINK IT DOES, PROFESSOR XAVIER'S IN A LOT MORE DANGER THAN WE ARE.
...OOOHHH... FOR THIS, I GAVE UP DER JAHRMARKT...?
*X-MEN'S #'S 101-103 --ARCHIE.
NIGHTCRAWLER! FIND THE OTHERS AND HEAD FOR THE LANDING PAD BEHIND THE LAB!
MOVE IT, MISTER! WE'VE NO TIME TO WASTE!
NOW TO FREE BANSHEE.
GOT TO BE CAREFUL EVEN USING MY NARROWEST BEAM, I CAN'T AFFORD ONE FALSE MOVE.
CYCLOPS, NIGHTCRAWLER SAID WE'RE ORDERED TO THE X-PLANE! AREN'T WE ATTACKING MAGNETO?!
NO.
HUH?!? WHAT'RE YE SAYIN' LAD?
AS SOON AS WE FIND COLOSSUS, WE'RE PULLING OUT AND HEADING FOR NEW YORK.
THE BLAZES WE ARE, BUB! THIS FIGHT AIN'T OVER YET!
IT IS AS FAR AS WE'RE CONCERNED!
SEZ WHO!
THE X-MEN TEAM LEADER, BUSTER! NOW DO AS I SAY OR SO HELP ME, I'LL BLAST YOU DOWN AN' CARRY YOU OUT!
OKAY, SUMMERS, THIS ROUND GOES TO YOU--BUT FROM NOW ON, BUB, ALL BETS ARE OFF!
HUH?! OH, GREAT! LOOKS LIKE THAT BUG-EYED BROAD'S* BUSTED LOOSE.
SECURITY ALERT
PRISONER ESCAPED
*LAST SEEN IN X-MEN #96--ARCHIE.

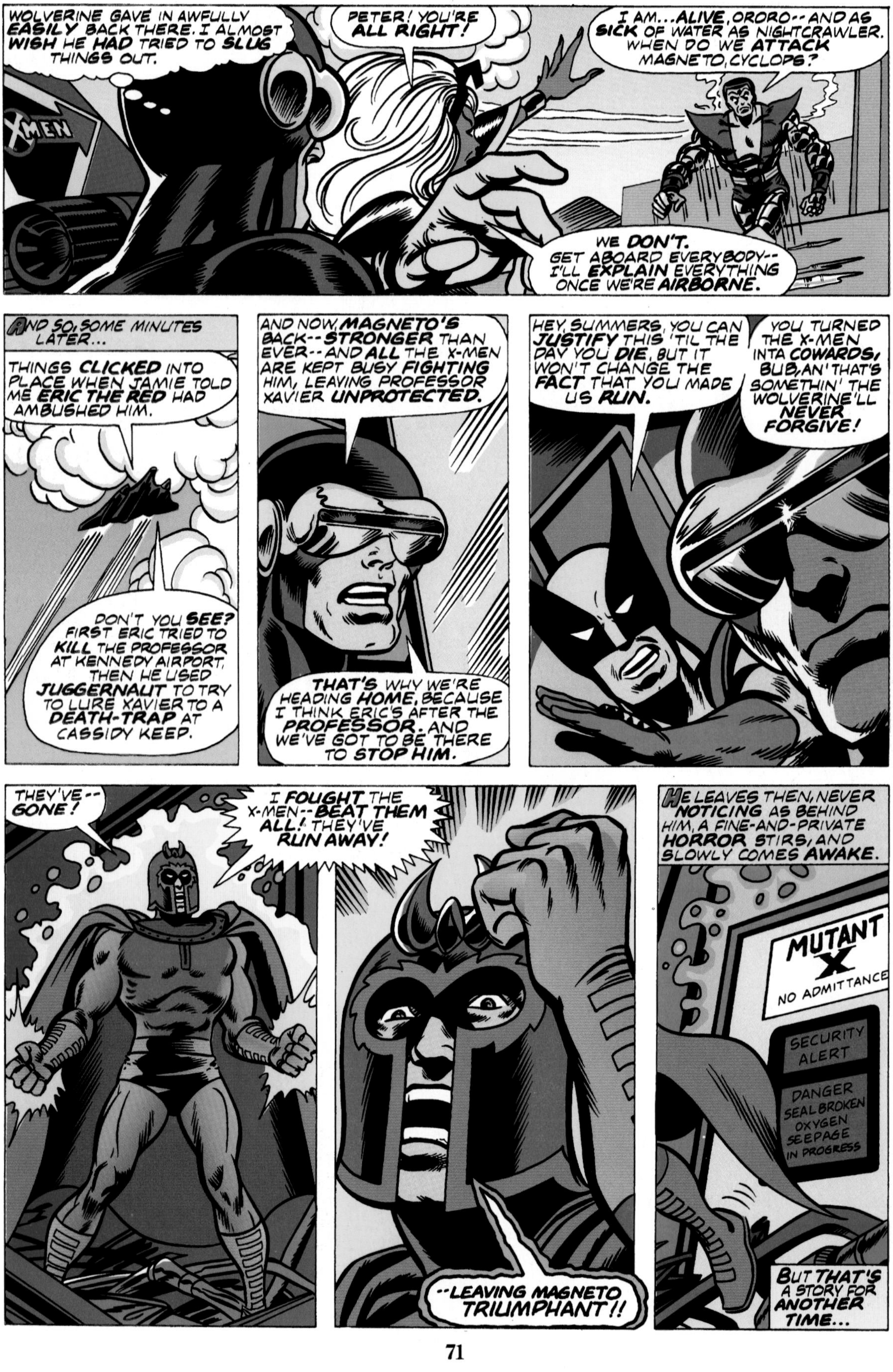
WOLVERINE GAVE IN AWFULLY EASILY BACK THERE. I ALMOST WISH HE HAD TRIED TO SLUG THINGS OUT.
PETER! YOU'RE ALL RIGHT!
I AM...ALIVE, ORORO--AND AS SICK OF WATER AS NIGHTCRAWLER. WHEN DO WE ATTACK MAGNETO, CYCLOPS?
X-MEN
WE DON'T. GET ABOARD EVERYBODY--I'LL EXPLAIN EVERYTHING ONCE WE'RE AIRBORNE.
AND SO, SOME MINUTES LATER...
THINGS CLICKED INTO PLACE WHEN JAMIE TOLD ME ERIC THE RED HAD AMBUSHED HIM.
DON'T YOU SEE? FIRST ERIC TRIED TO KILL THE PROFESSOR AT KENNEDY AIRPORT, THEN HE USED JUGGERNAUT TO TRY TO LURE XAVIER TO A DEATH-TRAP AT CASSIDY KEEP.
AND NOW, MAGNETO'S BACK--STRONGER THAN EVER--AND ALL THE X-MEN ARE KEPT BUSY FIGHTING HIM, LEAVING PROFESSOR XAVIER UNPROTECTED.
THAT'S WHY WE'RE HEADING HOME, BECAUSE I THINK ERIC'S AFTER THE PROFESSOR. AND WE'VE GOT TO BE THERE TO STOP HIM.
HEY, SUMMERS, YOU CAN JUSTIFY THIS 'TIL THE DAY YOU DIE, BUT IT WON'T CHANGE THE FACT THAT YOU MADE US RUN.
YOU TURNED THE X-MEN INTA COWARDS, BUB, AN' THAT'S SOMETHIN' THE WOLVERINE'LL NEVER FORGIVE!
THEY'VE--GONE!
I FOUGHT THE X-MEN--BEAT THEM ALL! THEY'VE RUN AWAY!
--LEAVING MAGNETO TRIUMPHANT!!
HE LEAVES THEN, NEVER NOTICING AS BEHIND HIM, A FINE-AND-PRIVATE HORROR STIRS, AND SLOWLY COMES AWAKE.
MUTANT X
NO ADMITTANCE
SECURITY ALERT
DANGER SEAL BROKEN OXYGEN SEEPAGE IN PROGRESS
BUT THAT'S A STORY FOR ANOTHER TIME...

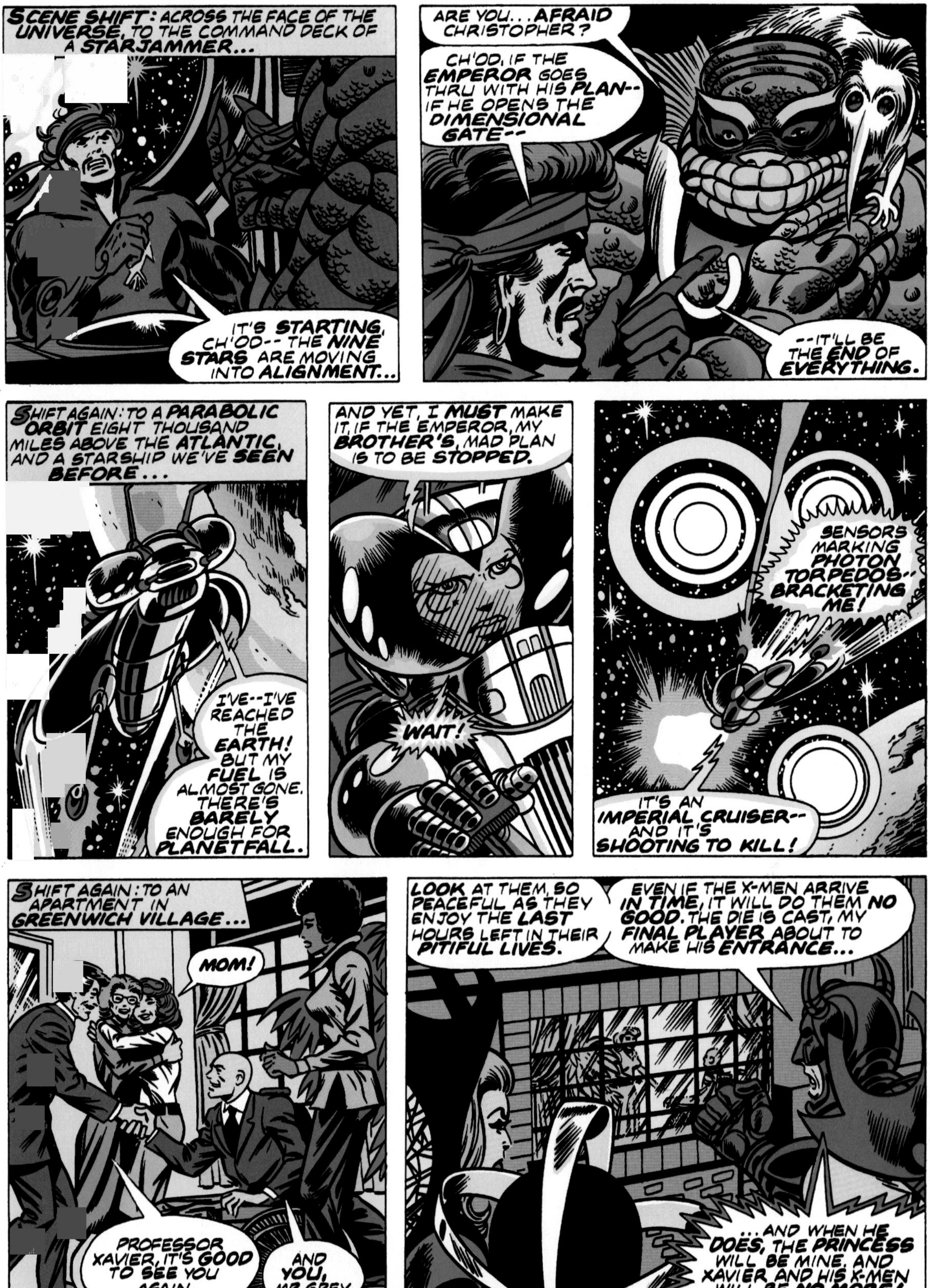
SCENE SHIFT: ACROSS THE FACE OF THE UNIVERSE, TO THE COMMAND DECK OF A STARJAMMER...
IT'S STARTING, CH'OD-- THE NINE STARS ARE MOVING INTO ALIGNMENT...
ARE YOU... AFRAID CHRISTOPHER?
CH'OD, IF THE EMPEROR GOES THRU WITH HIS PLAN-- IF HE OPENS THE DIMENSIONAL GATE--
--IT'LL BE THE END OF EVERYTHING.
SHIFT AGAIN: TO A PARABOLIC ORBIT EIGHT THOUSAND MILES ABOVE THE ATLANTIC, AND A STARSHIP WE'VE SEEN BEFORE...
I'VE--I'VE REACHED THE EARTH! BUT MY FUEL IS ALMOST GONE. THERE'S BARELY ENOUGH FOR PLANETFALL.
AND YET, I MUST MAKE IT, IF THE EMPEROR, MY BROTHER'S, MAD PLAN IS TO BE STOPPED.
WAIT!
SENSORS MARKING PHOTON TORPEDOS-- BRACKETING ME!
IT'S AN IMPERIAL CRUISER-- AND IT'S SHOOTING TO KILL!
SHIFT AGAIN: TO AN APARTMENT IN GREENWICH VILLAGE...
MOM!
PROFESSOR XAVIER, IT'S GOOD TO SEE YOU AGAIN.
AND YOU, MR. GREY.
LOOK AT THEM, SO PEACEFUL AS THEY ENJOY THE LAST HOURS LEFT IN THEIR PITIFUL LIVES.
EVEN IF THE X-MEN ARRIVE IN TIME, IT WILL DO THEM NO GOOD. THE DIE IS CAST, MY FINAL PLAYER ABOUT TO MAKE HIS ENTRANCE...
...AND WHEN HE DOES, THE PRINCESS WILL BE MINE. AND XAVIER AND HIS X-MEN WILL BE NO MORE!
EXT ISSUE: PHOENIX UNLEASHED!

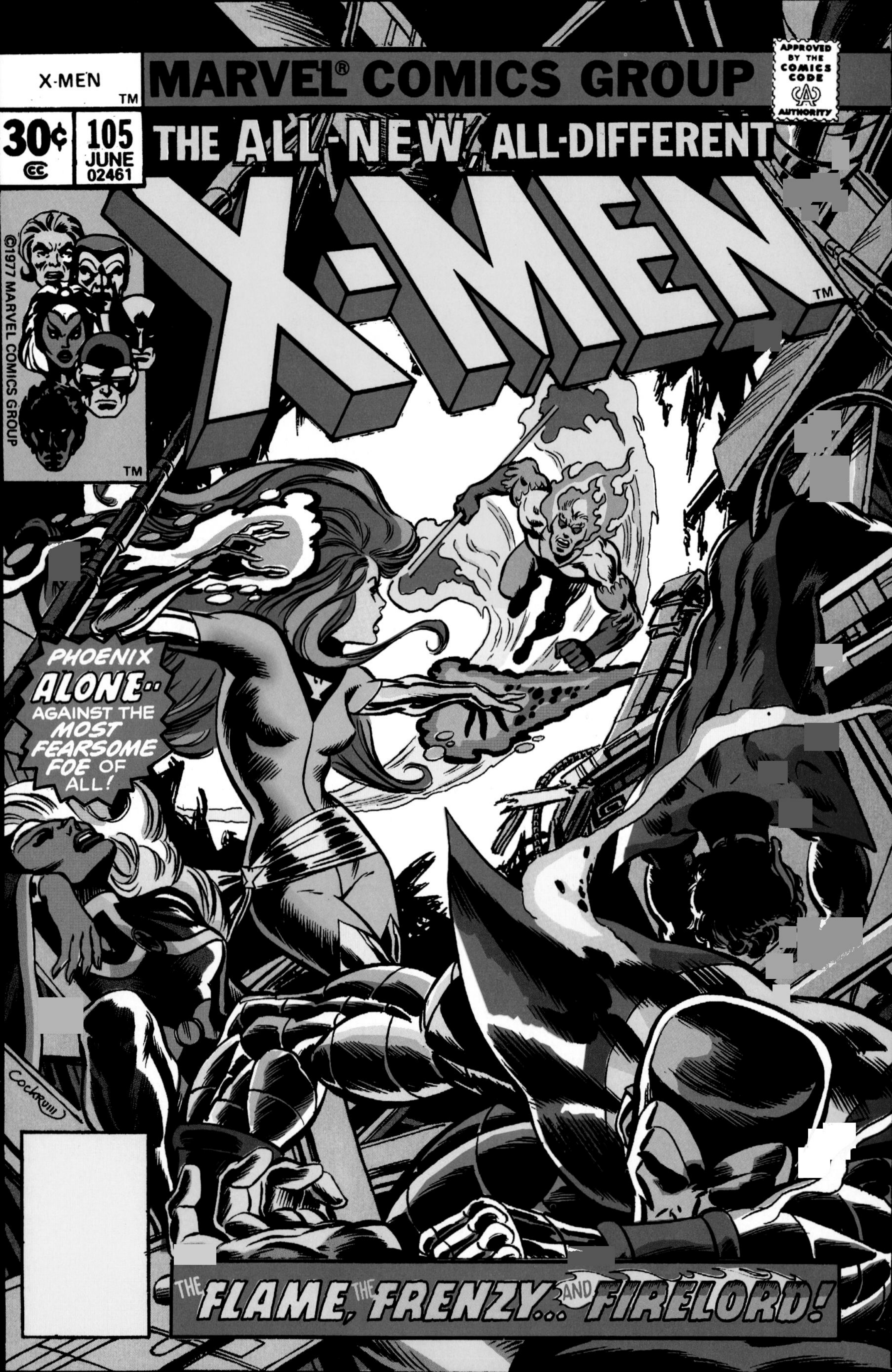
X-MEN
MARVEL® COMICS GROUP
APPROVED BY THE COMICS CODE AUTHORITY
30¢
105
JUNE
02461
THE ALL-NEW, ALL-DIFFERENT
X-MEN
©1977 MARVEL COMICS GROUP
PHOENIX ALONE.. AGAINST THE MOST FEARSOME FOE OF ALL!
COCKRUM
THE FLAME, THE FRENZY... AND FIRELORD!

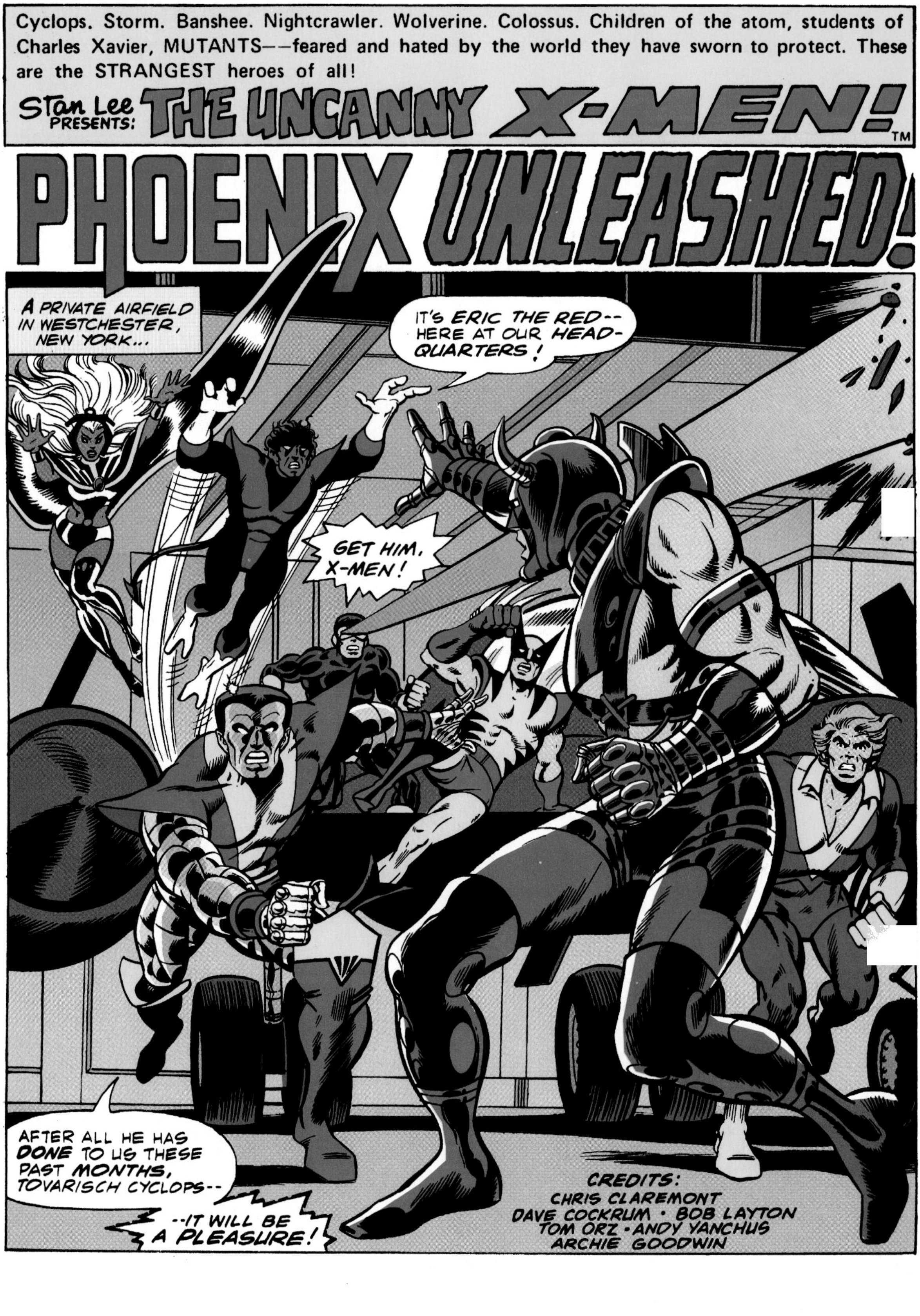
Cyclops. Storm. Banshee. Nightcrawler. Wolverine. Colossus. Children of the atom, students of Charles Xavier, MUTANTS——feared and hated by the world they have sworn to protect. These are the STRANGEST heroes of all!
Stan Lee PRESENTS: THE UNCANNY X-MEN! TM
PHOENIX UNLEASHED!
A PRIVATE AIRFIELD IN WESTCHESTER, NEW YORK...
IT'S ERIC THE RED-- HERE AT OUR HEAD-QUARTERS!
GET HIM, X-MEN!
AFTER ALL HE HAS DONE TO US THESE PAST MONTHS, TOVARISCH CYCLOPS--
--IT WILL BE A PLEASURE!
CREDITS: CHRIS CLAREMONT
DAVE COCKRUM • BOB LAYTON
TOM ORZ • ANDY YANCHUS
ARCHIE GOODWIN

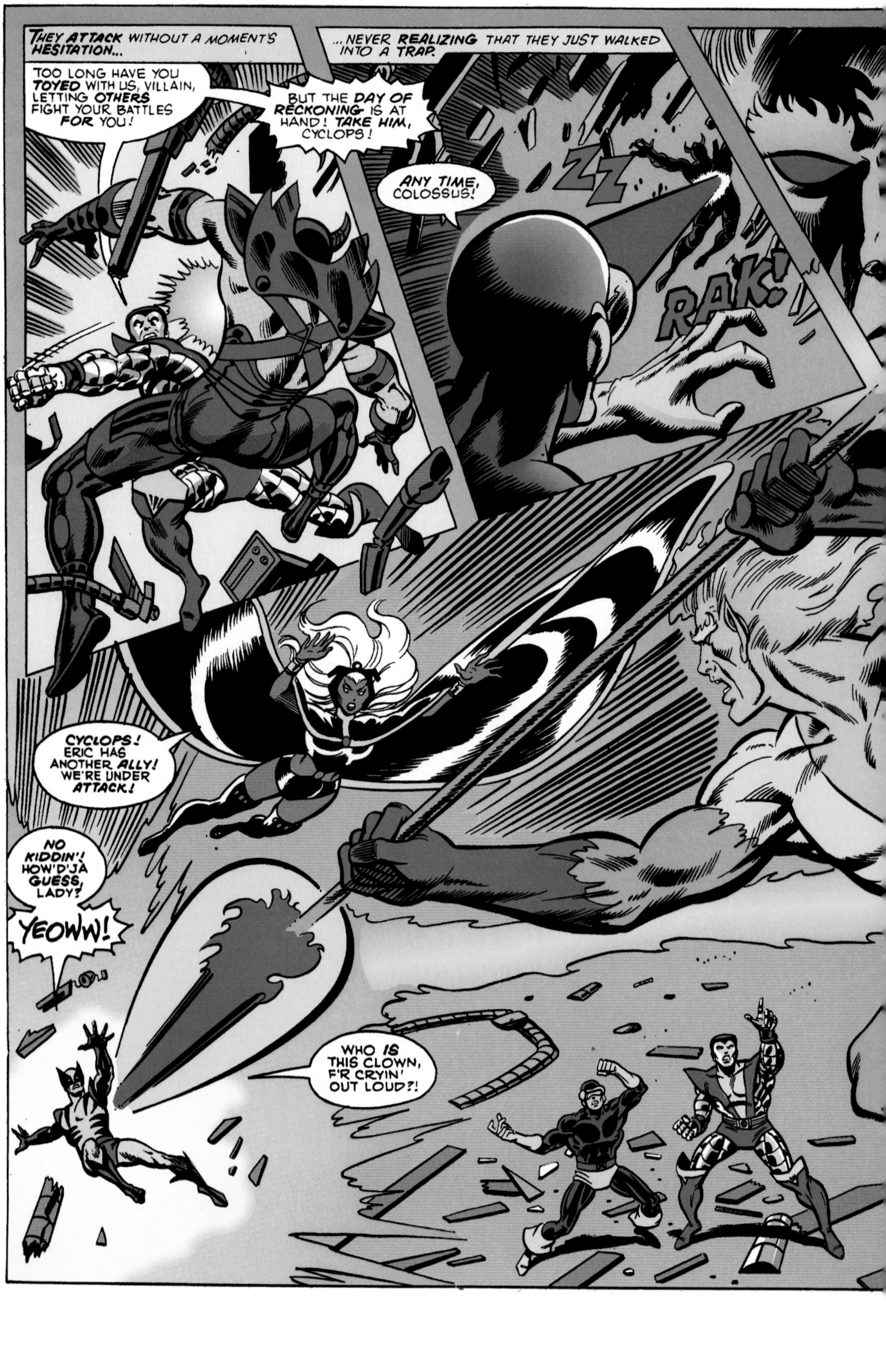
THEY ATTACK WITHOUT A MOMENT'S HESITATION...
...NEVER REALIZING THAT THEY JUST WALKED INTO A TRAP.
TOO LONG HAVE YOU TOYED WITH US, VILLAIN, LETTING OTHERS FIGHT YOUR BATTLES FOR YOU!
BUT THE DAY OF RECKONING IS AT HAND! TAKE HIM, CYCLOPS!
ANY TIME, COLOSSUS!
ZZ
RAK!
CYCLOPS! ERIC HAS ANOTHER ALLY! WE'RE UNDER ATTACK!
NO KIDDIN'! HOW'D'JA GUESS, LADY?
YEOWW!
WHO IS THIS CLOWN, F'R CRYIN' OUT LOUD?!

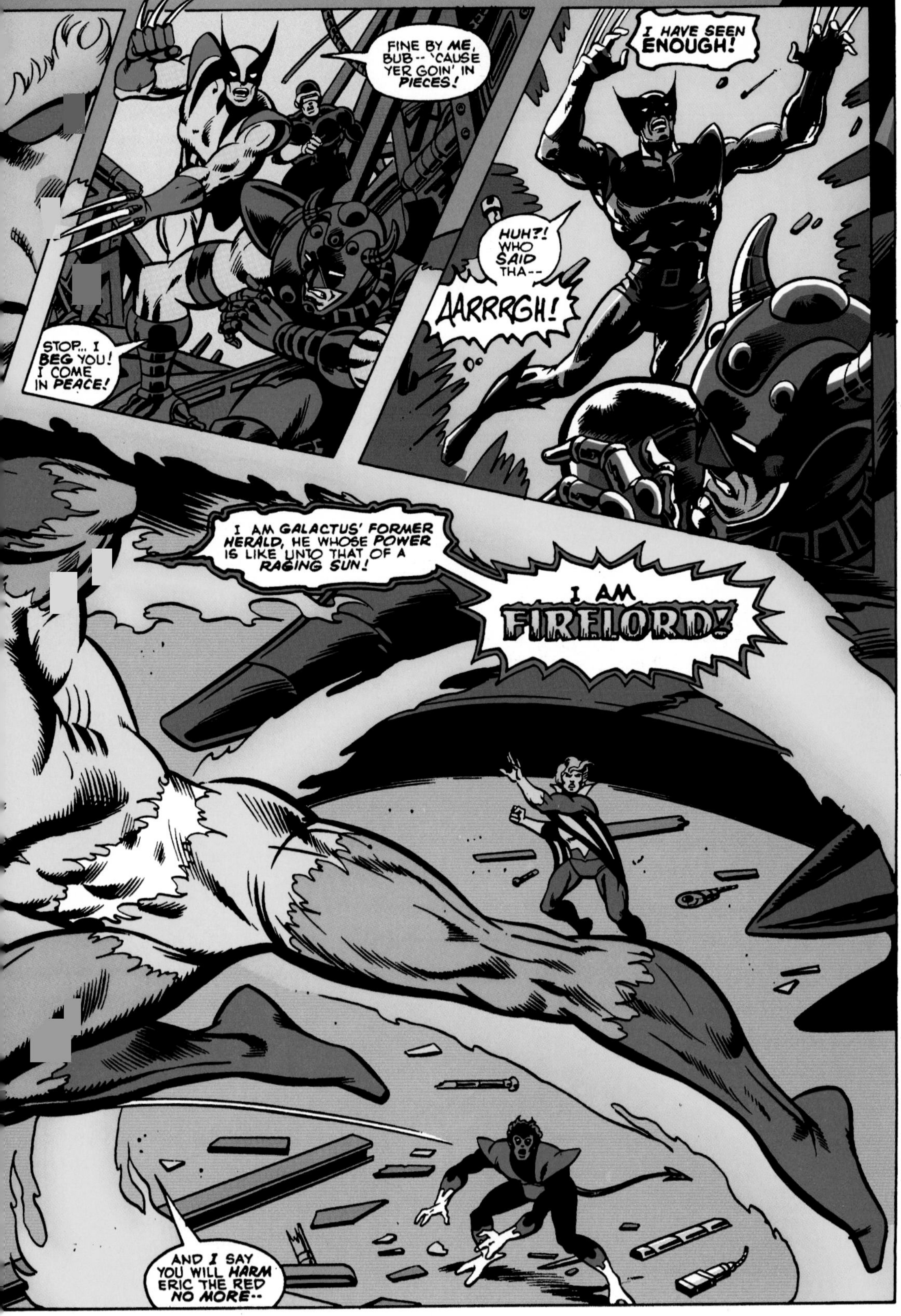

FINE BY ME, BUB -- 'CAUSE YER GOIN' IN PIECES!
STOP... I BEG YOU! I COME IN PEACE!
I HAVE SEEN ENOUGH!
HUH?! WHO SAID THA--
AARRRGH!
I AM GALACTUS' FORMER HERALD, HE WHOSE POWER IS LIKE UNTO THAT OF A RAGING SUN!
I AM FIRELORD!
AND I SAY YOU WILL HARM ERIC THE RED NO MORE--

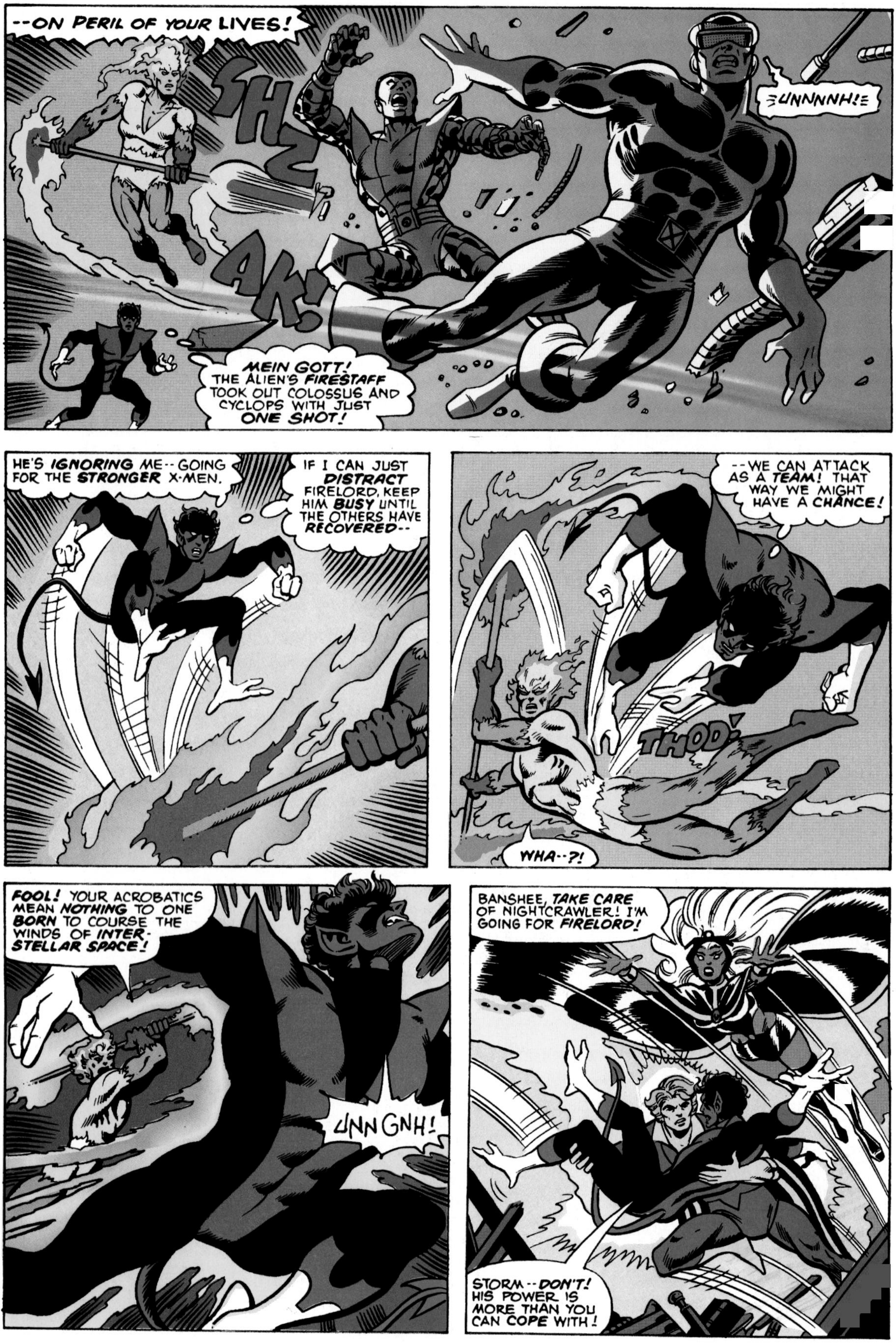
--ON PERIL OF YOUR LIVES!
SHZZAK!
UNNNNH!
MEIN GOTT! THE ALIEN'S FIRESTAFF TOOK OUT COLOSSUS AND CYCLOPS WITH JUST ONE SHOT!
HE'S IGNORING ME--GOING FOR THE STRONGER X-MEN.
IF I CAN JUST DISTRACT FIRELORD, KEEP HIM BUSY UNTIL THE OTHERS HAVE RECOVERED--
--WE CAN ATTACK AS A TEAM! THAT WAY WE MIGHT HAVE A CHANCE!
THOD!
WHA--?!
FOOL! YOUR ACROBATICS MEAN NOTHING TO ONE BORN TO COURSE THE WINDS OF INTER-STELLAR SPACE!
UNNGNH!
BANSHEE, TAKE CARE OF NIGHTCRAWLER! I'M GOING FOR FIRELORD!
STORM--DON'T! HIS POWER IS MORE THAN YOU CAN COPE WITH!

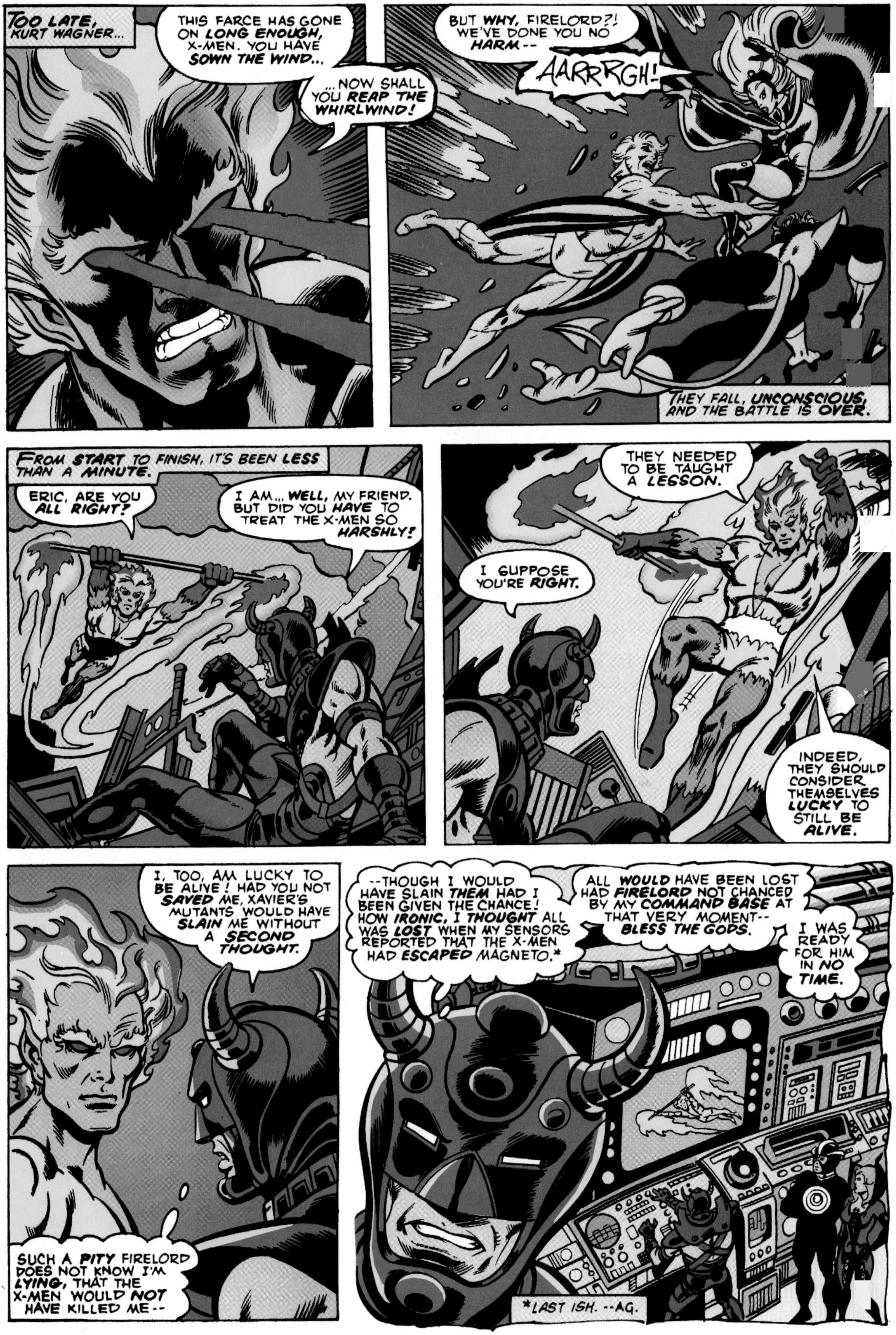

TOO LATE, KURT WAGNER...
THIS FARCE HAS GONE ON LONG ENOUGH, X-MEN. YOU HAVE SOWN THE WIND...
...NOW SHALL YOU REAP THE WHIRLWIND!
BUT WHY, FIRELORD?! WE'VE DONE YOU NO HARM--
AARRRGH!
THEY FALL, UNCONSCIOUS, AND THE BATTLE IS OVER.
FROM START TO FINISH, IT'S BEEN LESS THAN A MINUTE.
ERIC, ARE YOU ALL RIGHT?
I AM... WELL, MY FRIEND. BUT DID YOU HAVE TO TREAT THE X-MEN SO HARSHLY!
THEY NEEDED TO BE TAUGHT A LESSON.
I SUPPOSE YOU'RE RIGHT.
INDEED, THEY SHOULD CONSIDER THEMSELVES LUCKY TO STILL BE ALIVE.
I, TOO, AM LUCKY TO BE ALIVE! HAD YOU NOT SAVED ME, XAVIER'S MUTANTS WOULD HAVE SLAIN ME WITHOUT A SECOND THOUGHT.
SUCH A PITY FIRELORD DOES NOT KNOW I'M LYING, THAT THE X-MEN WOULD NOT HAVE KILLED ME--
--THOUGH I WOULD HAVE SLAIN THEM HAD I BEEN GIVEN THE CHANCE! HOW IRONIC, I THOUGHT ALL WAS LOST WHEN MY SENSORS REPORTED THAT THE X-MEN HAD ESCAPED MAGNETO.*
ALL WOULD HAVE BEEN LOST HAD FIRELORD NOT CHANCED BY MY COMMAND BASE AT THAT VERY MOMENT-- BLESS THE GODS.
I WAS READY FOR HIM IN NO TIME.
*LAST ISH. --AG.

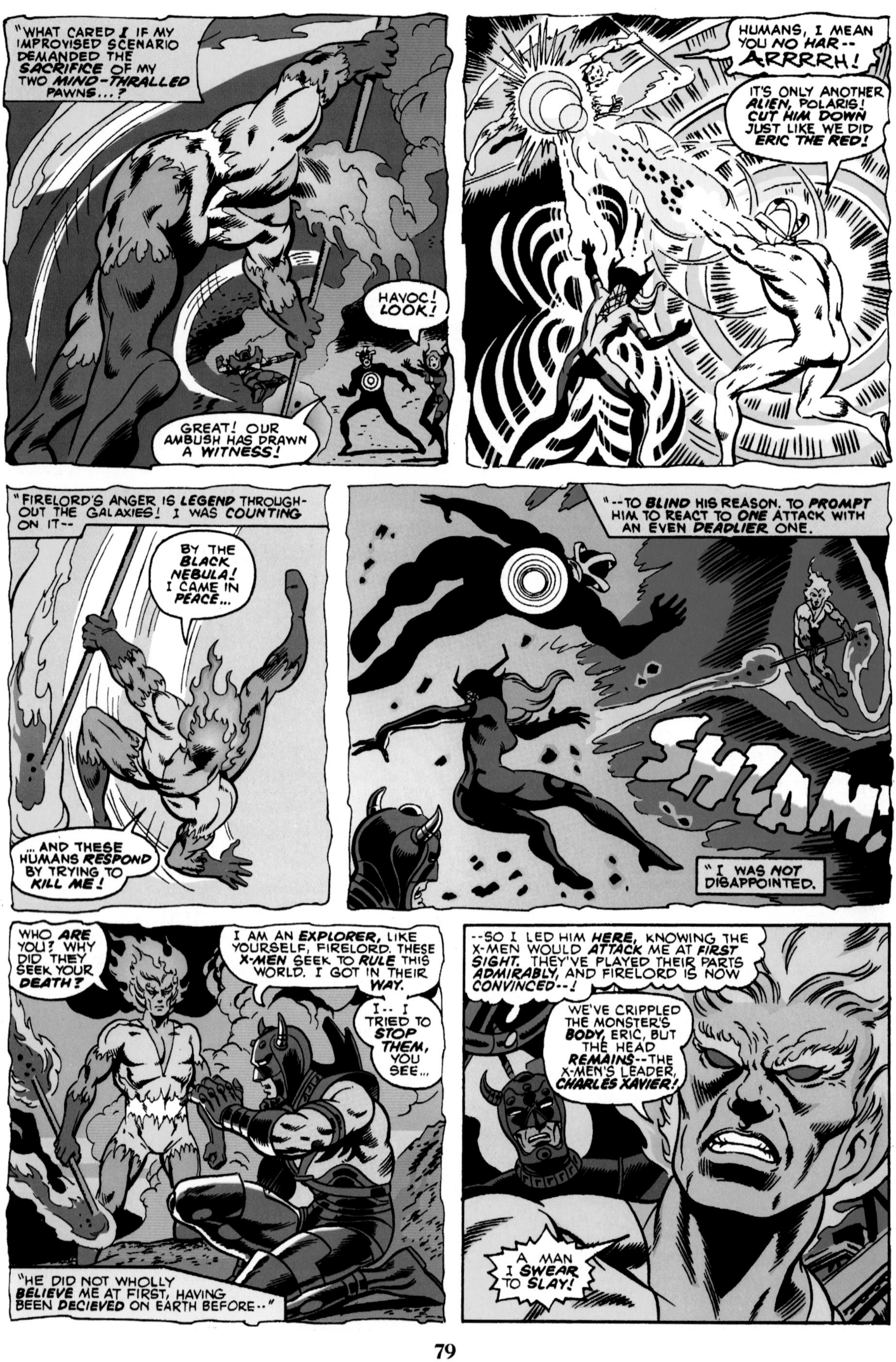
"WHAT CARED I IF MY IMPROVISED SCENARIO DEMANDED THE SACRIFICE OF MY TWO MIND-THRALLED PAWNS...?
HAVOC! LOOK!
GREAT! OUR AMBUSH HAS DRAWN A WITNESS!
HUMANS, I MEAN YOU NO HAR-- ARRRRH!
IT'S ONLY ANOTHER ALIEN, POLARIS! CUT HIM DOWN JUST LIKE WE DID ERIC THE RED!
"FIRELORD'S ANGER IS LEGEND THROUGHOUT THE GALAXIES! I WAS COUNTING ON IT--
BY THE BLACK NEBULA! I CAME IN PEACE...
...AND THESE HUMANS RESPOND BY TRYING TO KILL ME!
"--TO BLIND HIS REASON. TO PROMPT HIM TO REACT TO ONE ATTACK WITH AN EVEN DEADLIER ONE.
SHLAM!
"I WAS NOT DISAPPOINTED.
WHO ARE YOU? WHY DID THEY SEEK YOUR DEATH?
I AM AN EXPLORER, LIKE YOURSELF, FIRELORD. THESE X-MEN SEEK TO RULE THIS WORLD. I GOT IN THEIR WAY.
I-- I TRIED TO STOP THEM, YOU SEE...
"HE DID NOT WHOLLY BELIEVE ME AT FIRST, HAVING BEEN DECIEVED ON EARTH BEFORE--"
--SO I LED HIM HERE, KNOWING THE X-MEN WOULD ATTACK ME AT FIRST SIGHT. THEY'VE PLAYED THEIR PARTS ADMIRABLY, AND FIRELORD IS NOW CONVINCED--!
WE'VE CRIPPLED THE MONSTER'S BODY, ERIC, BUT THE HEAD REMAINS--THE X-MEN'S LEADER, CHARLES XAVIER!
A MAN I SWEAR TO SLAY!

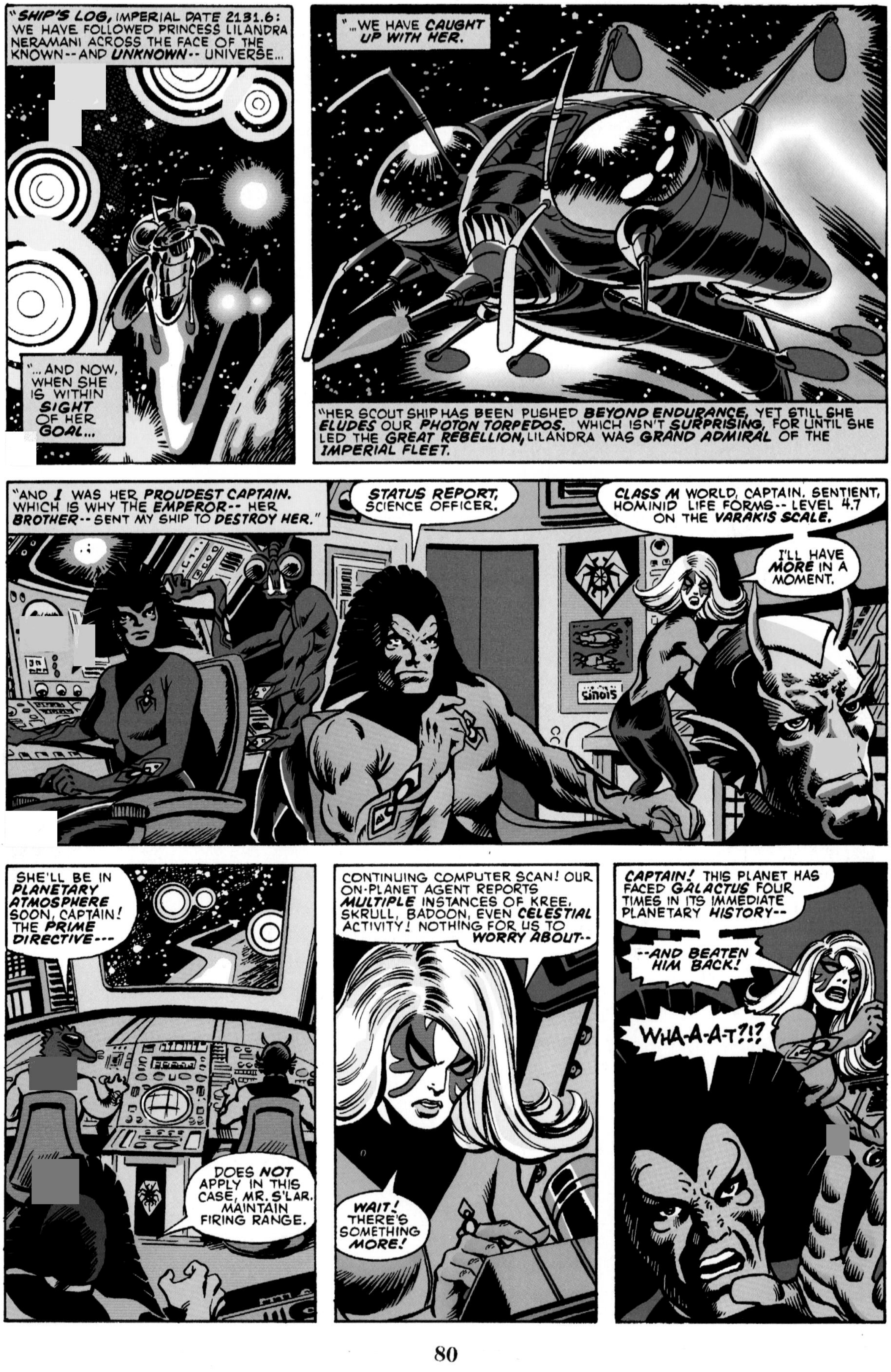
"SHIP'S LOG, IMPERIAL DATE 2131.6: WE HAVE FOLLOWED PRINCESS LILANDRA NERAMANI ACROSS THE FACE OF THE KNOWN--AND UNKNOWN--UNIVERSE...
"...AND NOW, WHEN SHE IS WITHIN SIGHT OF HER GOAL...
"...WE HAVE CAUGHT UP WITH HER.
"HER SCOUT SHIP HAS BEEN PUSHED BEYOND ENDURANCE, YET STILL SHE ELUDES OUR PHOTON TORPEDOS. WHICH ISN'T SURPRISING, FOR UNTIL SHE LED THE GREAT REBELLION, LILANDRA WAS GRAND ADMIRAL OF THE IMPERIAL FLEET.
"AND I WAS HER PROUDEST CAPTAIN. WHICH IS WHY THE EMPEROR--HER BROTHER--SENT MY SHIP TO DESTROY HER."
STATUS REPORT, SCIENCE OFFICER.
CLASS M WORLD, CAPTAIN. SENTIENT, HOMINID LIFE FORMS--LEVEL 4.7 ON THE VARAKIS SCALE.
I'LL HAVE MORE IN A MOMENT.
SHE'LL BE IN PLANETARY ATMOSPHERE SOON, CAPTAIN! THE PRIME DIRECTIVE---
DOES NOT APPLY IN THIS CASE, MR. S'LAR. MAINTAIN FIRING RANGE.
CONTINUING COMPUTER SCAN! OUR ON-PLANET AGENT REPORTS MULTIPLE INSTANCES OF KREE, SKRULL, BADOON, EVEN CELESTIAL ACTIVITY! NOTHING FOR US TO WORRY ABOUT--
WAIT! THERE'S SOMETHING MORE!
CAPTAIN! THIS PLANET HAS FACED GALACTUS FOUR TIMES IN ITS IMMEDIATE PLANETARY HISTORY--
--AND BEATEN HIM BACK!
WHA-A-A-T?!?

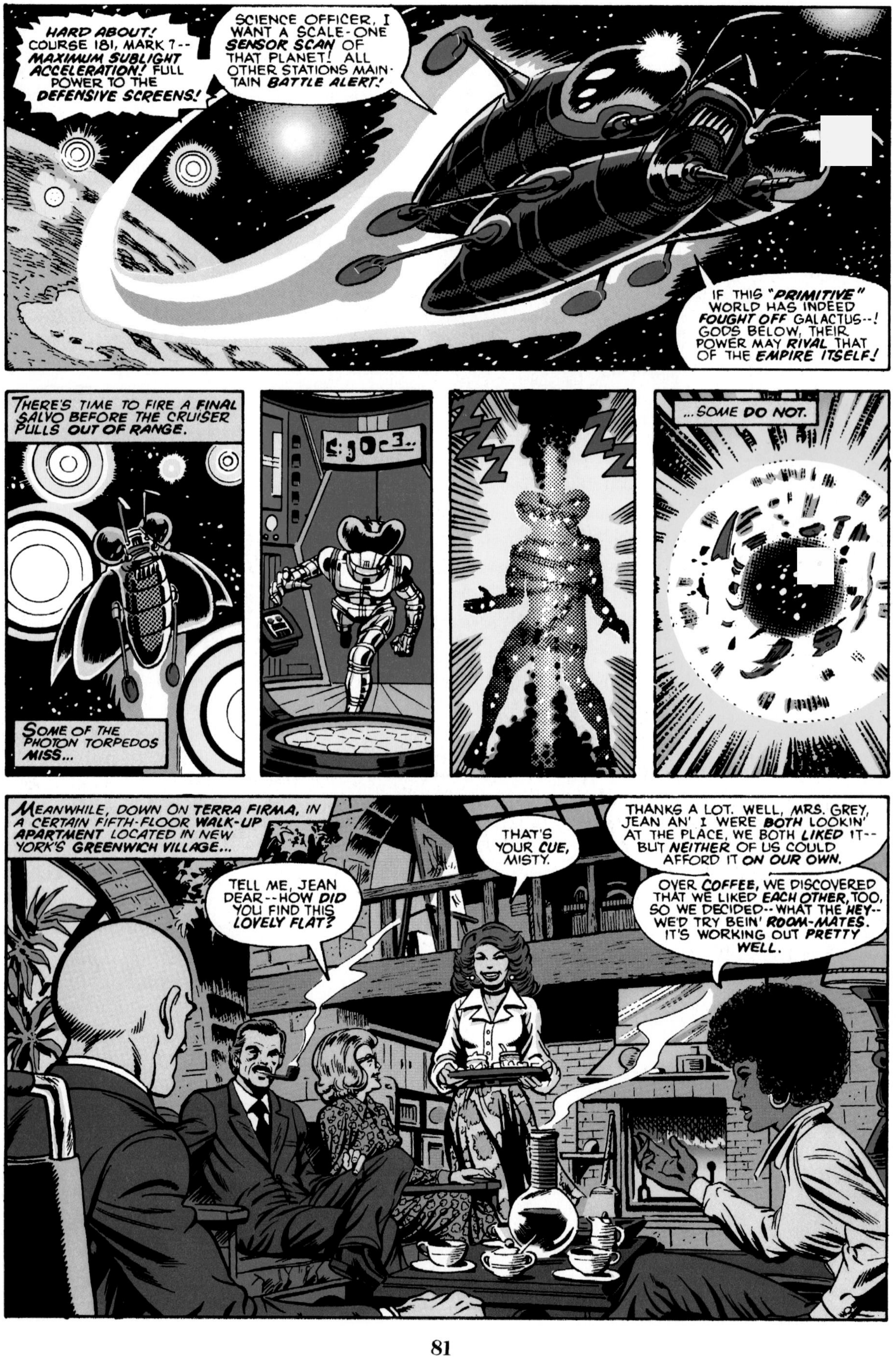
HARD ABOUT! COURSE 181, MARK 7-- MAXIMUM SUBLIGHT ACCELERATION! FULL POWER TO THE DEFENSIVE SCREENS!
SCIENCE OFFICER, I WANT A SCALE-ONE SENSOR SCAN OF THAT PLANET! ALL OTHER STATIONS MAINTAIN BATTLE ALERT!
IF THIS "PRIMITIVE" WORLD HAS INDEED FOUGHT OFF GALACTUS--! GODS BELOW, THEIR POWER MAY RIVAL THAT OF THE EMPIRE ITSELF!
THERE'S TIME TO FIRE A FINAL SALVO BEFORE THE CRUISER PULLS OUT OF RANGE.
SOME OF THE PHOTON TORPEDOS MISS...
...SOME DO NOT.
MEANWHILE, DOWN ON TERRA FIRMA, IN A CERTAIN FIFTH-FLOOR WALK-UP APARTMENT LOCATED IN NEW YORK'S GREENWICH VILLAGE...
TELL ME, JEAN DEAR--HOW DID YOU FIND THIS LOVELY FLAT?
THAT'S YOUR CUE, MISTY.
THANKS A LOT. WELL, MRS. GREY, JEAN AN' I WERE BOTH LOOKIN' AT THE PLACE, WE BOTH LIKED IT-- BUT NEITHER OF US COULD AFFORD IT ON OUR OWN.
OVER COFFEE, WE DISCOVERED THAT WE LIKED EACH OTHER, TOO, SO WE DECIDED--WHAT THE HEY-- WE'D TRY BEIN' ROOM-MATES. IT'S WORKING OUT PRETTY WELL.

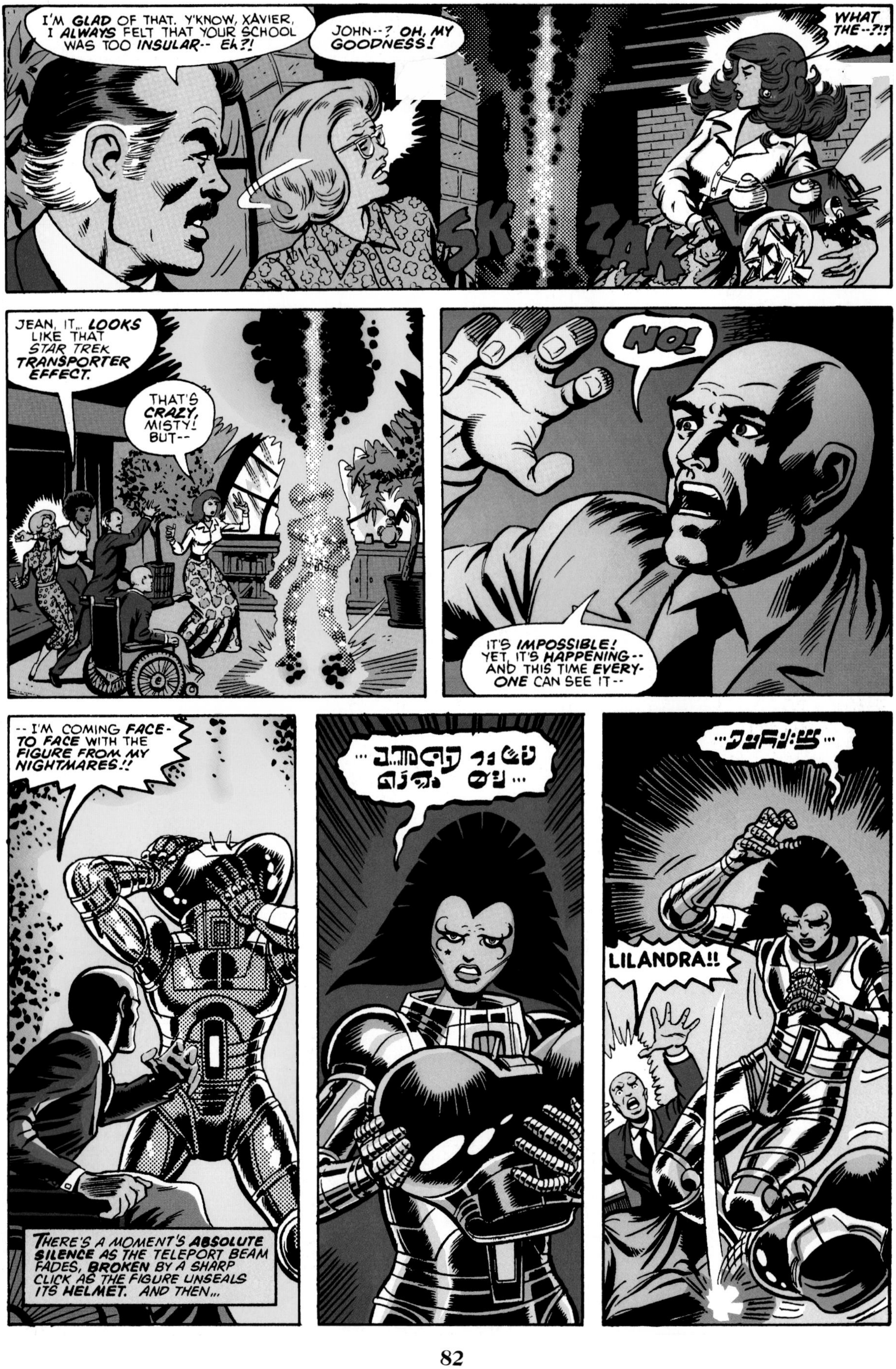
I'M GLAD OF THAT. Y'KNOW, XAVIER, I ALWAYS FELT THAT YOUR SCHOOL WAS TOO INSULAR-- Eh?!
JOHN--? OH, MY GOODNESS!
WHAT THE--?!?
SK ZAK
JEAN, IT... LOOKS LIKE THAT STAR TREK TRANSPORTER EFFECT.
THAT'S CRAZY, MISTY! BUT--
NO!
IT'S IMPOSSIBLE! YET, IT'S HAPPENING-- AND THIS TIME EVERY-ONE CAN SEE IT--
--I'M COMING FACE-TO FACE WITH THE FIGURE FROM MY NIGHTMARES!!
THERE'S A MOMENT'S ABSOLUTE SILENCE AS THE TELEPORT BEAM FADES, BROKEN BY A SHARP CLICK AS THE FIGURE UNSEALS ITS HELMET. AND THEN...
LILANDRA!!

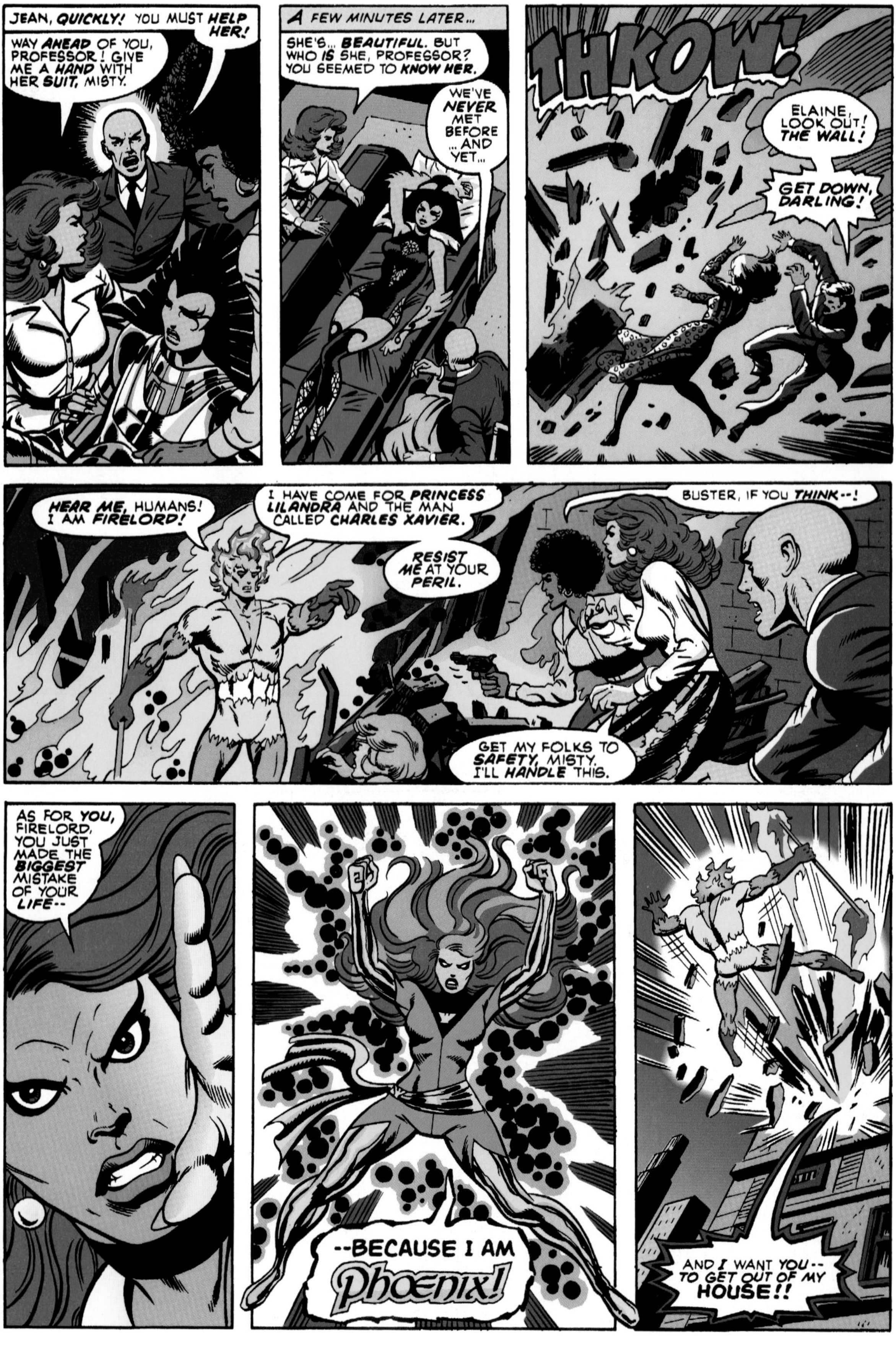
JEAN, QUICKLY! YOU MUST HELP HER!
WAY AHEAD OF YOU, PROFESSOR! GIVE ME A HAND WITH HER SUIT, MISTY.
A FEW MINUTES LATER...
SHE'S... BEAUTIFUL. BUT WHO IS SHE, PROFESSOR? YOU SEEMED TO KNOW HER.
WE'VE NEVER MET BEFORE ...AND YET...
THKOW!
ELAINE, LOOK OUT! THE WALL!
GET DOWN, DARLING!
HEAR ME, HUMANS! I AM FIRELORD!
I HAVE COME FOR PRINCESS LILANDRA AND THE MAN CALLED CHARLES XAVIER.
RESIST ME AT YOUR PERIL.
BUSTER, IF YOU THINK--!
GET MY FOLKS TO SAFETY, MISTY. I'LL HANDLE THIS.
AS FOR YOU, FIRELORD, YOU JUST MADE THE BIGGEST MISTAKE OF YOUR LIFE--
--BECAUSE I AM Phoenix!
AND I WANT YOU-- TO GET OUT OF MY HOUSE!!

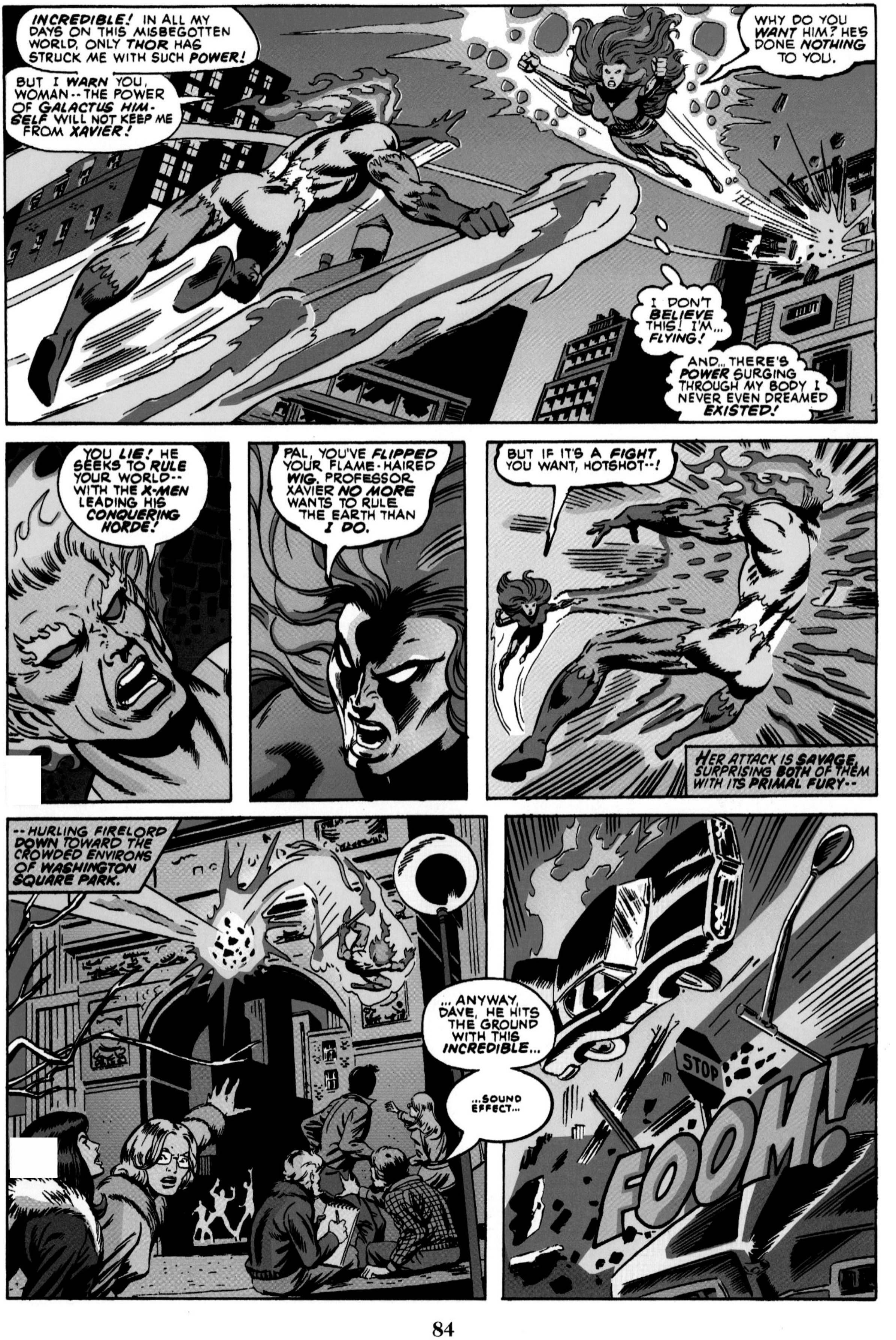
INCREDIBLE! IN ALL MY DAYS ON THIS MISBEGOTTEN WORLD, ONLY THOR HAS STRUCK ME WITH SUCH POWER!
BUT I WARN YOU, WOMAN -- THE POWER OF GALACTUS HIMSELF WILL NOT KEEP ME FROM XAVIER!
WHY DO YOU WANT HIM? HE'S DONE NOTHING TO YOU.
I DON'T BELIEVE THIS! I'M... FLYING!
AND... THERE'S POWER SURGING THROUGH MY BODY I NEVER EVEN DREAMED EXISTED!
YOU LIE! HE SEEKS TO RULE YOUR WORLD -- WITH THE X-MEN LEADING HIS CONQUERING HORDE!
PAL, YOU'VE FLIPPED YOUR FLAME-HAIRED WIG. PROFESSOR XAVIER NO MORE WANTS TO RULE THE EARTH THAN I DO.
BUT IF IT'S A FIGHT YOU WANT, HOTSHOT --!
HER ATTACK IS SAVAGE, SURPRISING BOTH OF THEM WITH ITS PRIMAL FURY --
-- HURLING FIRELORD DOWN TOWARD THE CROWDED ENVIRONS OF WASHINGTON SQUARE PARK.
... ANYWAY, DAVE, HE HITS THE GROUND WITH THIS INCREDIBLE...
...SOUND EFFECT...
STOP
FOOM!

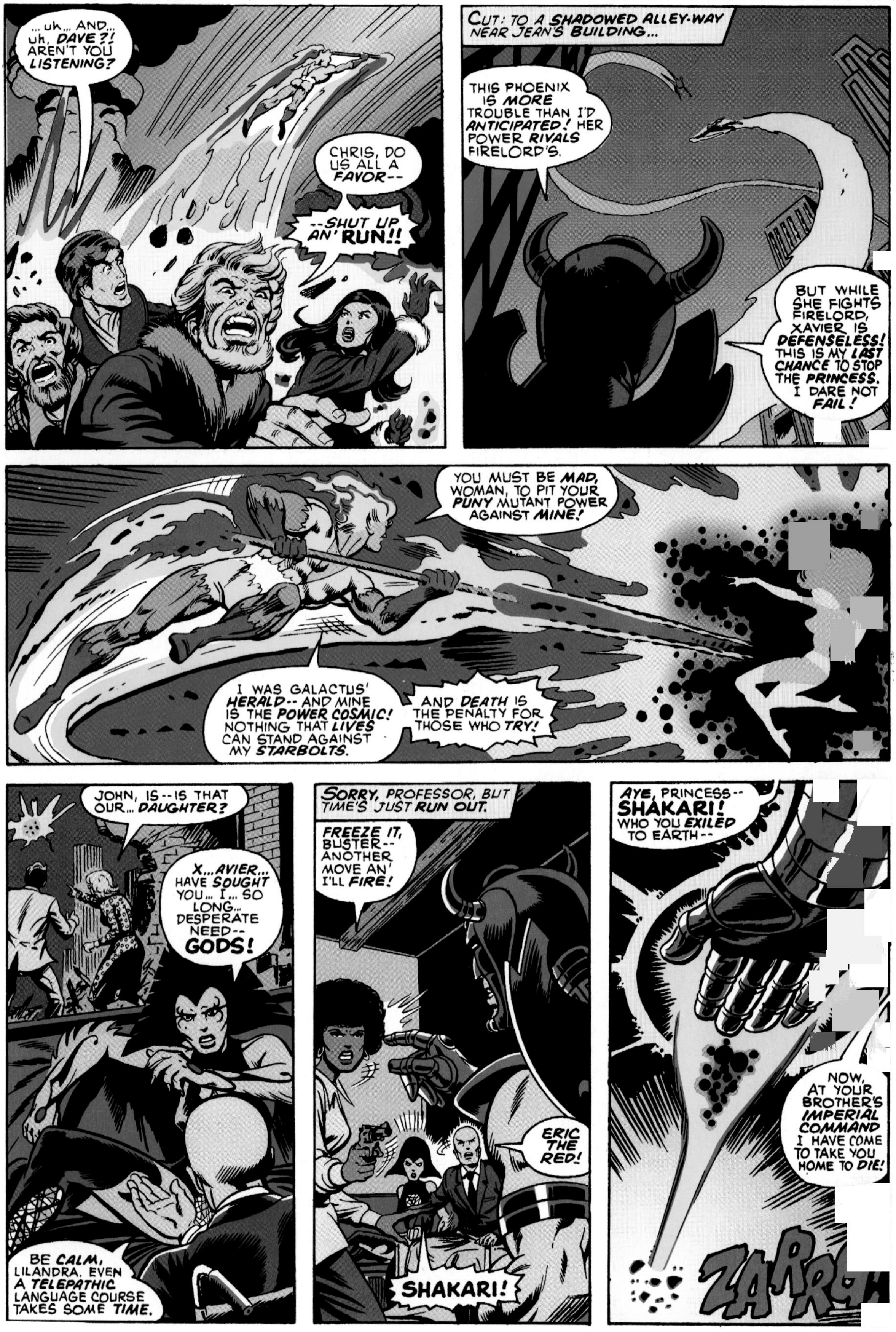
... uh... AND... uh, DAVE?! AREN'T YOU LISTENING?
CHRIS, DO US ALL A FAVOR--
--SHUT UP AN' RUN!!
CUT: TO A SHADOWED ALLEY-WAY NEAR JEAN'S BUILDING...
THIS PHOENIX IS MORE TROUBLE THAN I'D ANTICIPATED! HER POWER RIVALS FIRELORD'S.
BUT WHILE SHE FIGHTS FIRELORD, XAVIER IS DEFENSELESS! THIS IS MY LAST CHANCE TO STOP THE PRINCESS. I DARE NOT FAIL!
YOU MUST BE MAD, WOMAN, TO PIT YOUR PUNY MUTANT POWER AGAINST MINE!
I WAS GALACTUS' HERALD-- AND MINE IS THE POWER COSMIC! NOTHING THAT LIVES CAN STAND AGAINST MY STARBOLTS.
AND DEATH IS THE PENALTY FOR THOSE WHO TRY!
JOHN, IS--IS THAT OUR... DAUGHTER?
X... AVIER... HAVE SOUGHT YOU... I... SO LONG... DESPERATE NEED-- GODS!
BE CALM, LILANDRA. EVEN A TELEPATHIC LANGUAGE COURSE TAKES SOME TIME.
SORRY, PROFESSOR, BUT TIME'S JUST RUN OUT.
FREEZE IT, BUSTER-- ANOTHER MOVE AN' I'LL FIRE!
ERIC THE RED!
SHAKARI!
AYE, PRINCESS-- SHAKARI! WHO YOU EXILED TO EARTH--
NOW, AT YOUR BROTHER'S IMPERIAL COMMAND I HAVE COME TO TAKE YOU HOME TO DIE!
ZARRGH

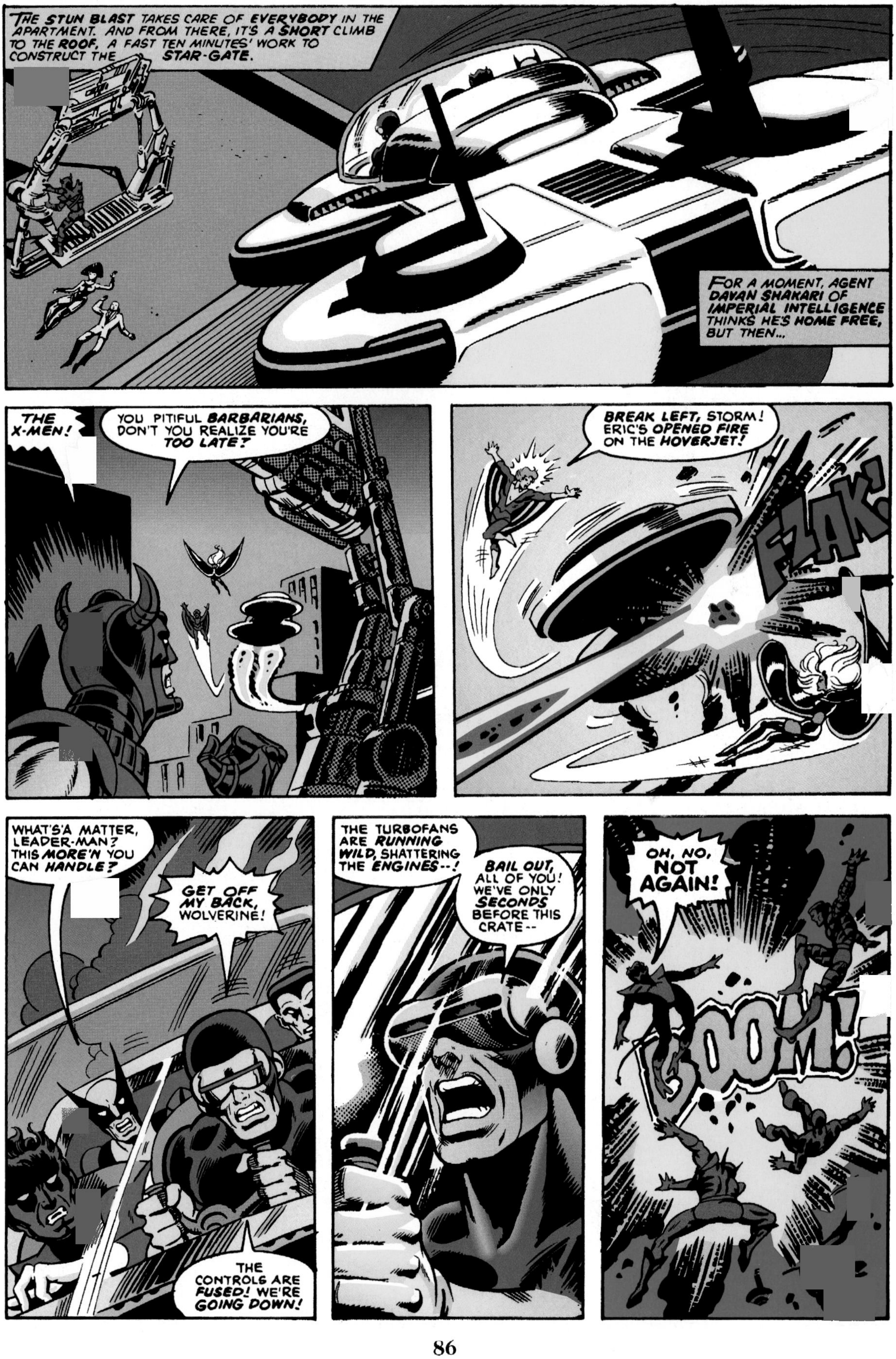
THE STUN BLAST TAKES CARE OF EVERYBODY IN THE APARTMENT. AND FROM THERE, IT'S A SHORT CLIMB TO THE ROOF, A FAST TEN MINUTES' WORK TO CONSTRUCT THE STAR-GATE.
FOR A MOMENT, AGENT DAVAN SHAKARI OF IMPERIAL INTELLIGENCE THINKS HE'S HOME FREE, BUT THEN...
THE X-MEN!
YOU PITIFUL BARBARIANS, DON'T YOU REALIZE YOU'RE TOO LATE?
BREAK LEFT, STORM! ERIC'S OPENED FIRE ON THE HOVERJET!
FZAK!
WHAT'S'A MATTER, LEADER-MAN? THIS MORE'N YOU CAN HANDLE?
GET OFF MY BACK, WOLVERINE!
THE CONTROLS ARE FUSED! WE'RE GOING DOWN!
THE TURBOFANS ARE RUNNING WILD, SHATTERING THE ENGINES--!
BAIL OUT, ALL OF YOU! WE'VE ONLY SECONDS BEFORE THIS CRATE--
OH, NO, NOT AGAIN!
BOOM!

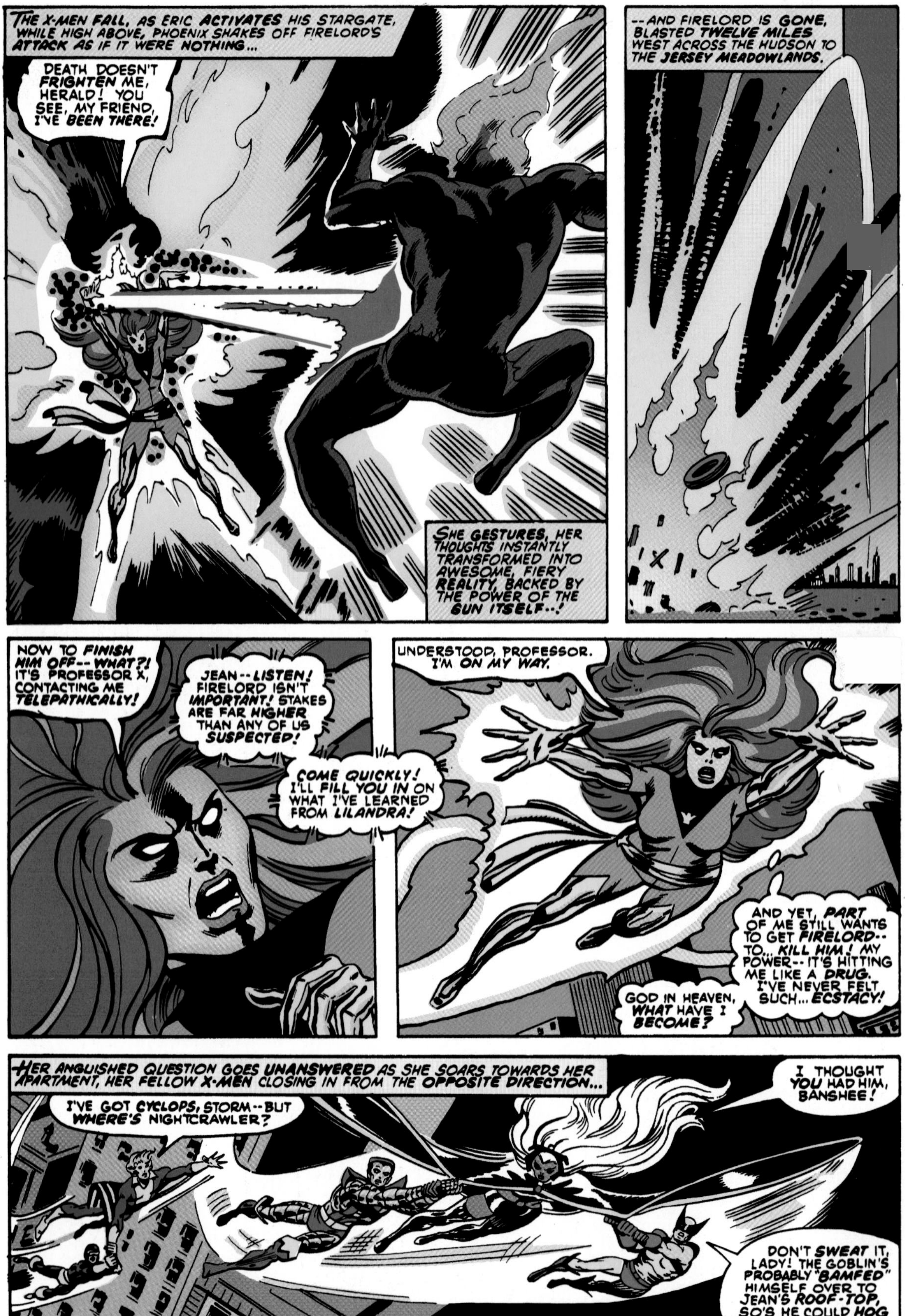

THE X-MEN FALL, AS ERIC ACTIVATES HIS STARGATE, WHILE HIGH ABOVE, PHOENIX SHAKES OFF FIRELORD'S ATTACK AS IF IT WERE NOTHING...
DEATH DOESN'T FRIGHTEN ME, HERALD! YOU SEE, MY FRIEND, I'VE BEEN THERE!
SHE GESTURES, HER THOUGHTS INSTANTLY TRANSFORMED INTO AWESOME, FIERY REALITY, BACKED BY THE POWER OF THE SUN ITSELF..!
--AND FIRELORD IS GONE, BLASTED TWELVE MILES WEST ACROSS THE HUDSON TO THE JERSEY MEADOWLANDS.
NOW TO FINISH HIM OFF-- WHAT?! IT'S PROFESSOR X, CONTACTING ME TELEPATHICALLY!
JEAN--LISTEN! FIRELORD ISN'T IMPORTANT! STAKES ARE FAR HIGHER THAN ANY OF US SUSPECTED!
COME QUICKLY! I'LL FILL YOU IN ON WHAT I'VE LEARNED FROM LILANDRA!
UNDERSTOOD, PROFESSOR. I'M ON MY WAY.
AND YET, PART OF ME STILL WANTS TO GET FIRELORD-- TO... KILL HIM! MY POWER--IT'S HITTING ME LIKE A DRUG. I'VE NEVER FELT SUCH... ECSTACY!
GOD IN HEAVEN, WHAT HAVE I BECOME?
HER ANGUISHED QUESTION GOES UNANSWERED AS SHE SOARS TOWARDS HER APARTMENT, HER FELLOW X-MEN CLOSING IN FROM THE OPPOSITE DIRECTION...
I'VE GOT CYCLOPS, STORM--BUT WHERE'S NIGHTCRAWLER?
I THOUGHT YOU HAD HIM, BANSHEE!
DON'T SWEAT IT, LADY! THE GOBLIN'S PROBABLY "BAMFED" HIMSELF OVER TO JEAN'S ROOF-TOP, SO'S HE COULD HOG ALL THE ACTION!

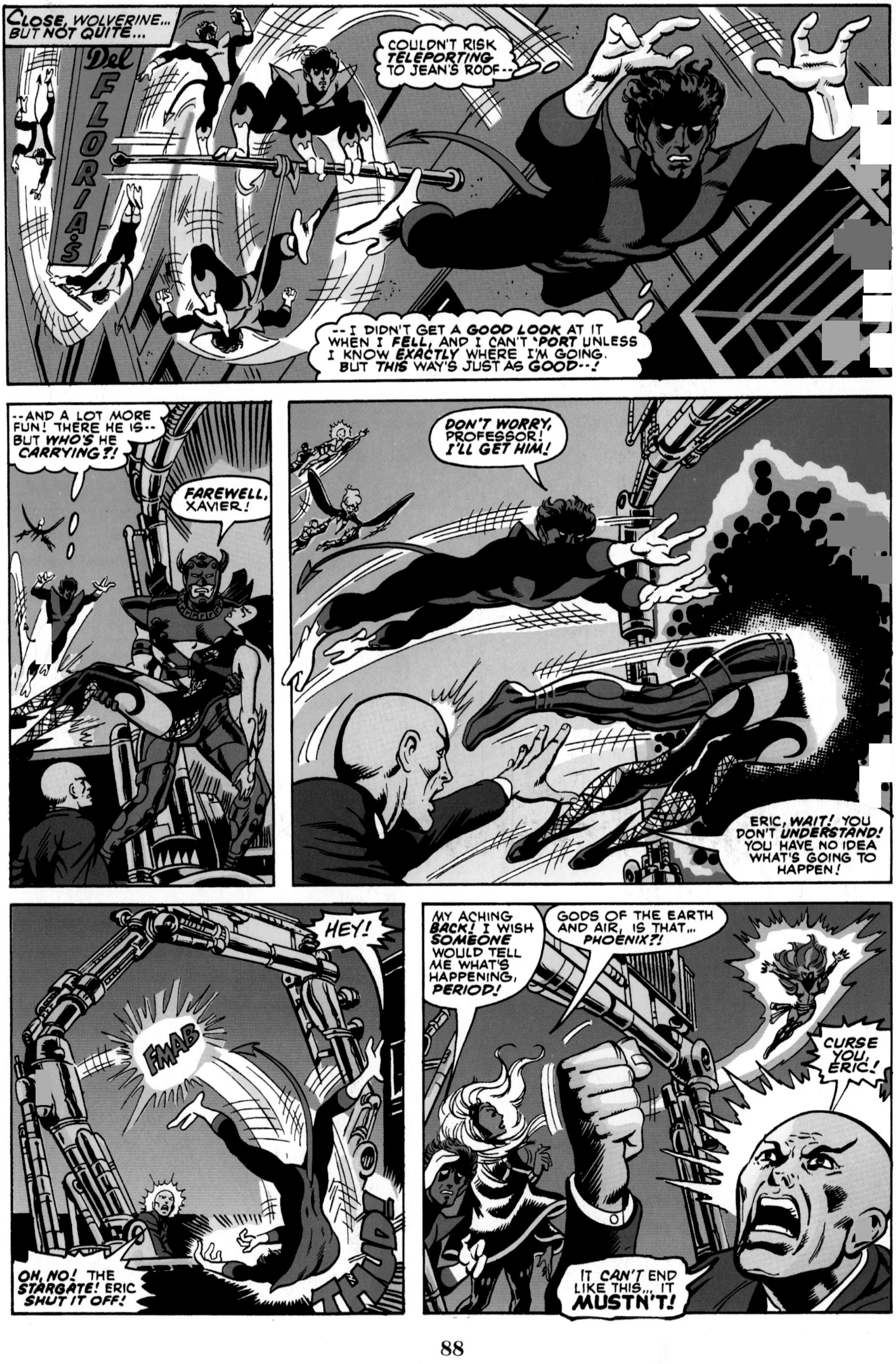
CLOSE, WOLVERINE... BUT NOT QUITE...
Del FLORIA'S
COULDN'T RISK TELEPORTING TO JEAN'S ROOF--
--I DIDN'T GET A GOOD LOOK AT IT WHEN I FELL, AND I CAN'T 'PORT UNLESS I KNOW EXACTLY WHERE I'M GOING. BUT THIS WAY'S JUST AS GOOD--!
--AND A LOT MORE FUN! THERE HE IS-- BUT WHO'S HE CARRYING?!
FAREWELL, XAVIER!
DON'T WORRY, PROFESSOR! I'LL GET HIM!
ERIC, WAIT! YOU DON'T UNDERSTAND! YOU HAVE NO IDEA WHAT'S GOING TO HAPPEN!
HEY!
FMAB
OH, NO! THE STARGATE! ERIC SHUT IT OFF!
THUD
MY ACHING BACK! I WISH SOMEONE WOULD TELL ME WHAT'S HAPPENING, PERIOD!
GODS OF THE EARTH AND AIR, IS THAT... PHOENIX?!
CURSE YOU, ERIC!
IT CAN'T END LIKE THIS... IT MUSTN'T!

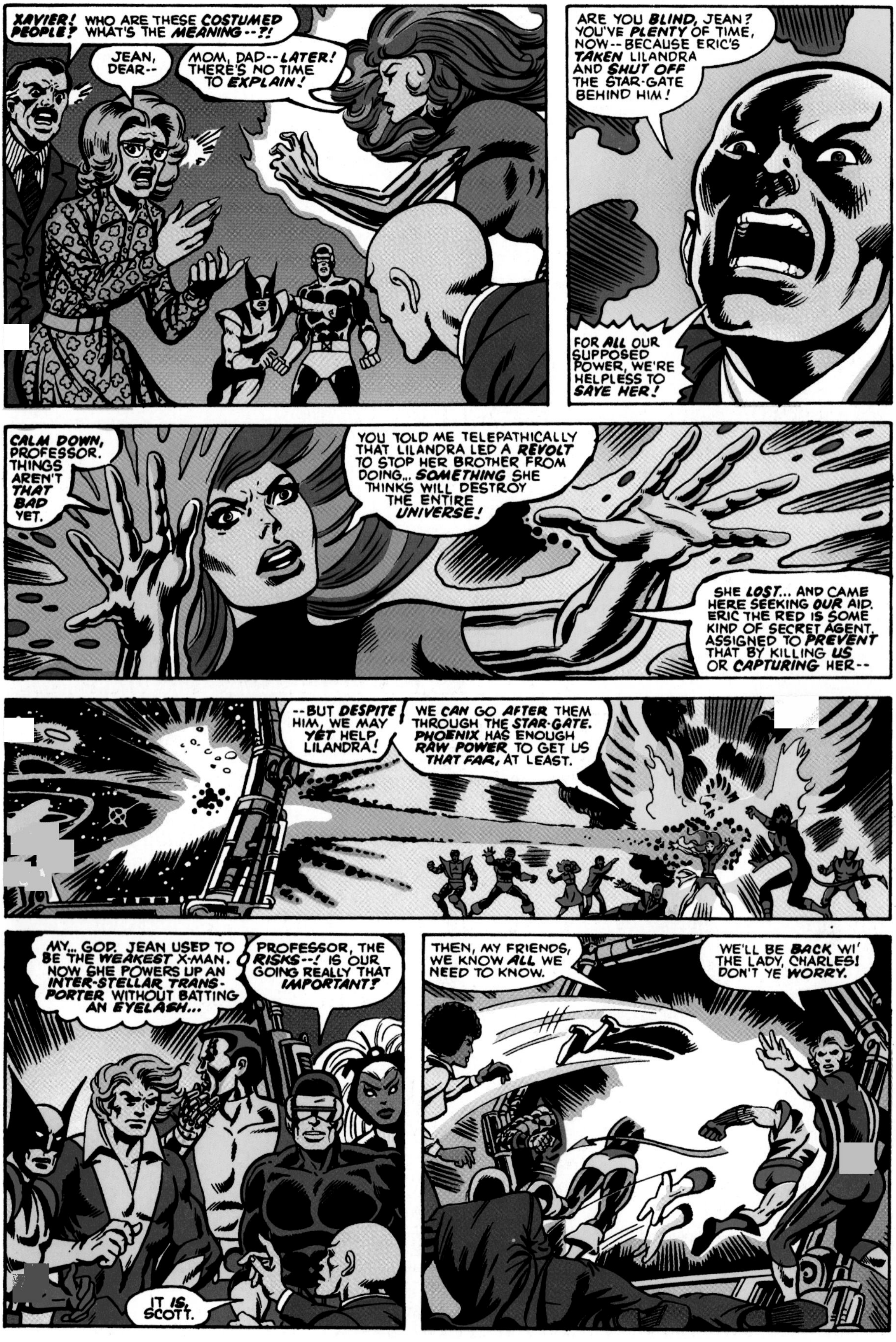
XAVIER! WHO ARE THESE COSTUMED PEOPLE? WHAT'S THE MEANING--?!
JEAN, DEAR--
MOM, DAD--LATER! THERE'S NO TIME TO EXPLAIN!
ARE YOU BLIND, JEAN? YOU'VE PLENTY OF TIME, NOW--BECAUSE ERIC'S TAKEN LILANDRA AND SHUT OFF THE STAR-GATE BEHIND HIM!
FOR ALL OUR SUPPOSED POWER, WE'RE HELPLESS TO SAVE HER!
CALM DOWN, PROFESSOR. THINGS AREN'T THAT BAD YET.
YOU TOLD ME TELEPATHICALLY THAT LILANDRA LED A REVOLT TO STOP HER BROTHER FROM DOING... SOMETHING SHE THINKS WILL DESTROY THE ENTIRE UNIVERSE!
SHE LOST... AND CAME HERE SEEKING OUR AID. ERIC THE RED IS SOME KIND OF SECRET AGENT. ASSIGNED TO PREVENT THAT BY KILLING US OR CAPTURING HER--
--BUT DESPITE HIM, WE MAY YET HELP LILANDRA!
WE CAN GO AFTER THEM THROUGH THE STAR-GATE. PHOENIX HAS ENOUGH RAW POWER TO GET US THAT FAR, AT LEAST.
MY... GOD. JEAN USED TO BE THE WEAKEST X-MAN. NOW SHE POWERS UP AN INTER-STELLAR TRANS-PORTER WITHOUT BATTING AN EYELASH...
PROFESSOR, THE RISKS--! IS OUR GOING REALLY THAT IMPORTANT?
IT IS, SCOTT.
THEN, MY FRIENDS, WE KNOW ALL WE NEED TO KNOW.
WE'LL BE BACK WI' THE LADY, CHARLES! DON'T YE WORRY.

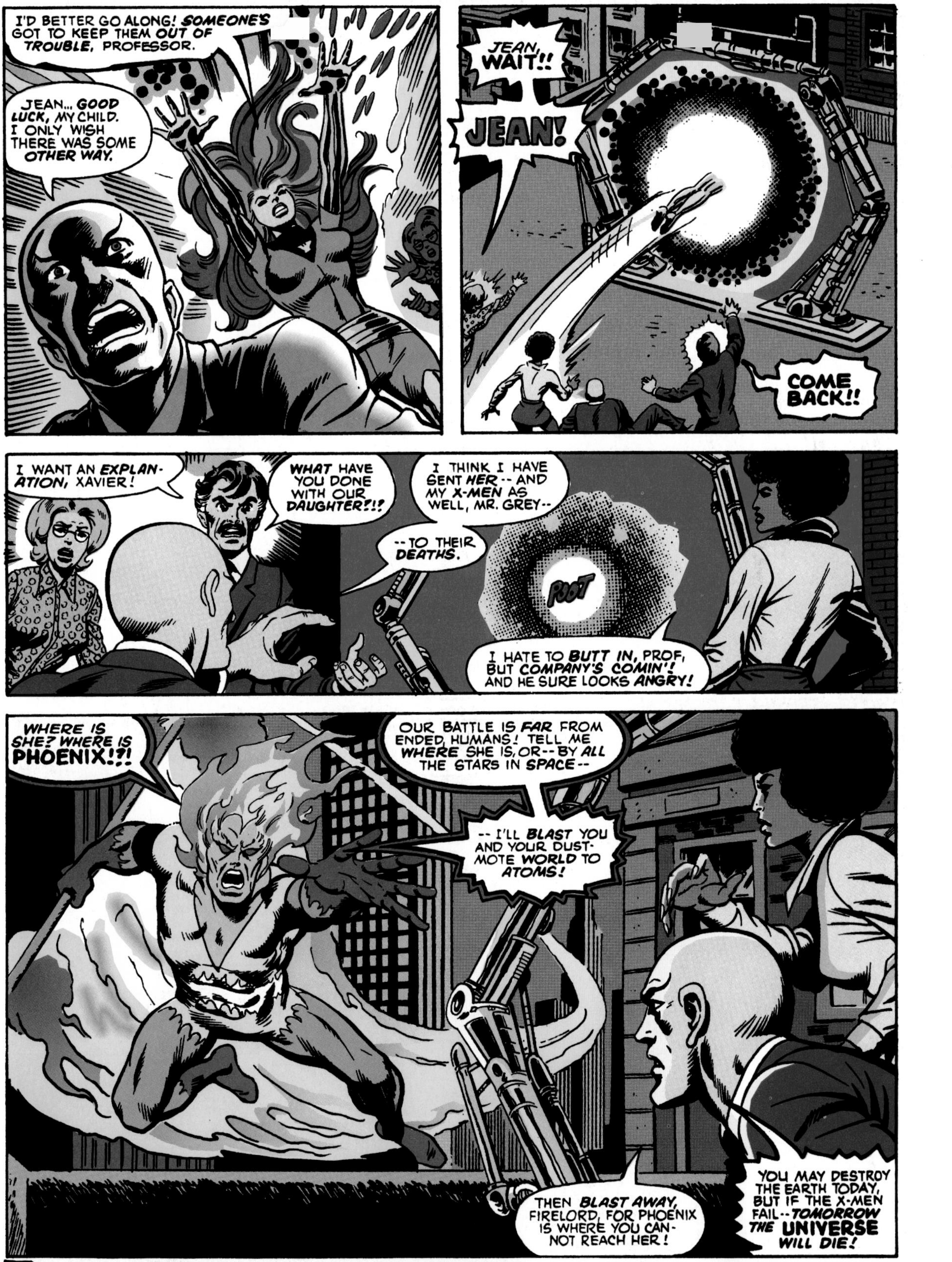
I'D BETTER GO ALONG! SOMEONE'S GOT TO KEEP THEM OUT OF TROUBLE, PROFESSOR.
JEAN... GOOD LUCK, MY CHILD. I ONLY WISH THERE WAS SOME OTHER WAY.
JEAN, WAIT!!
JEAN!
COME BACK!!
I WANT AN EXPLANATION, XAVIER!
WHAT HAVE YOU DONE WITH OUR DAUGHTER?!?
I THINK I HAVE SENT HER -- AND MY X-MEN AS WELL, MR. GREY--
--TO THEIR DEATHS.
POOT
I HATE TO BUTT IN, PROF, BUT COMPANY'S COMIN'! AND HE SURE LOOKS ANGRY!
WHERE IS SHE? WHERE IS PHOENIX!?!
OUR BATTLE IS FAR FROM ENDED, HUMANS! TELL ME WHERE SHE IS, OR-- BY ALL THE STARS IN SPACE--
--I'LL BLAST YOU AND YOUR DUST-MOTE WORLD TO ATOMS!
THEN BLAST AWAY, FIRELORD, FOR PHOENIX IS WHERE YOU CANNOT REACH HER!
YOU MAY DESTROY THE EARTH TODAY, BUT IF THE X-MEN FAIL--TOMORROW THE UNIVERSE WILL DIE!
NEXT
THE BEGINNING OF THE END!

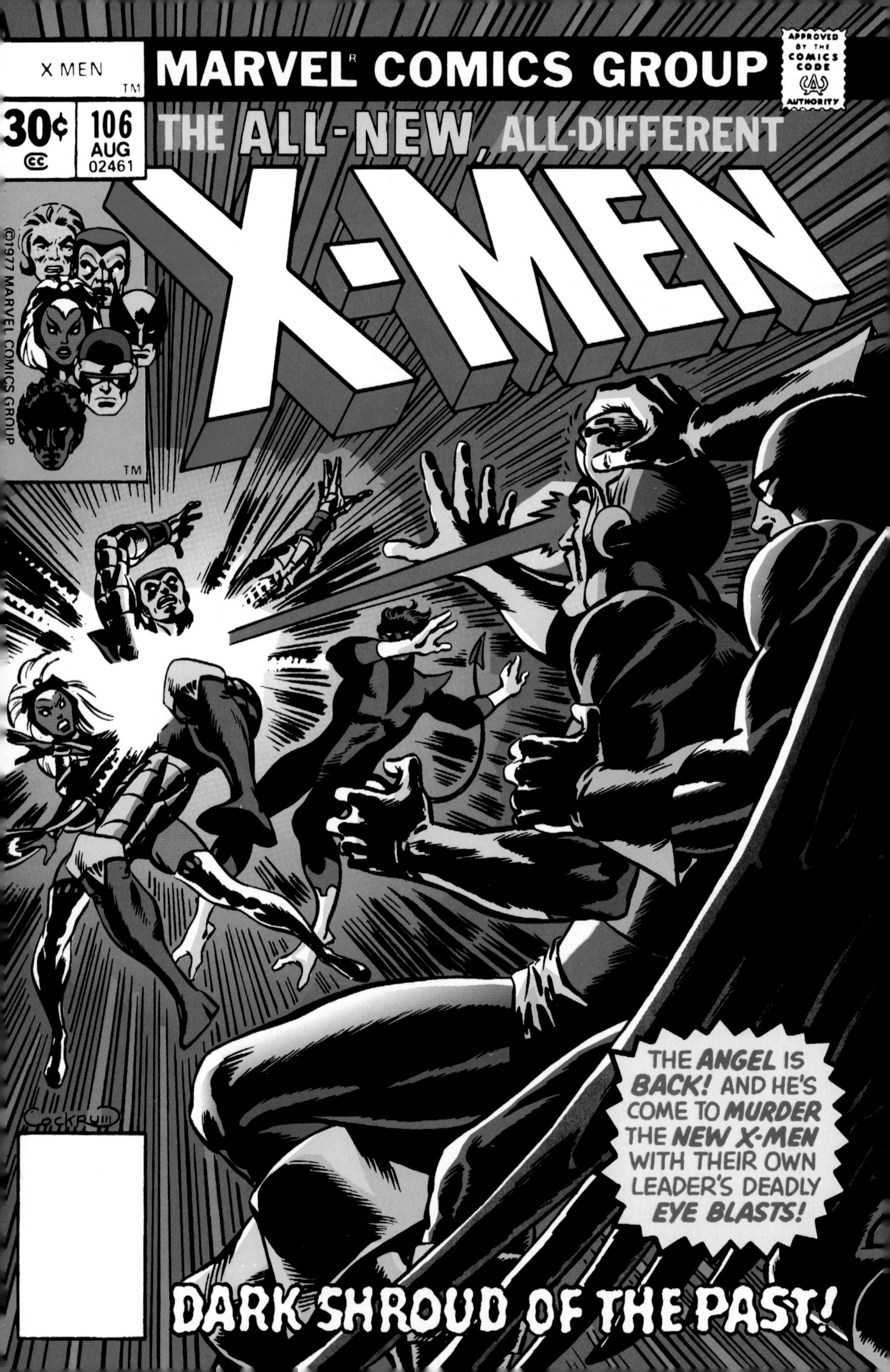
X MEN TM
MARVEL® COMICS GROUP
APPROVED BY THE COMICS CODE AUTHORITY
30¢
106 AUG 02461
THE ALL-NEW, ALL-DIFFERENT
X-MEN
©1977 MARVEL COMICS GROUP
TM
THE ANGEL IS BACK! AND HE'S COME TO MURDER THE NEW X-MEN WITH THEIR OWN LEADER'S DEADLY EYE BLASTS!
DARK SHROUD OF THE PAST!

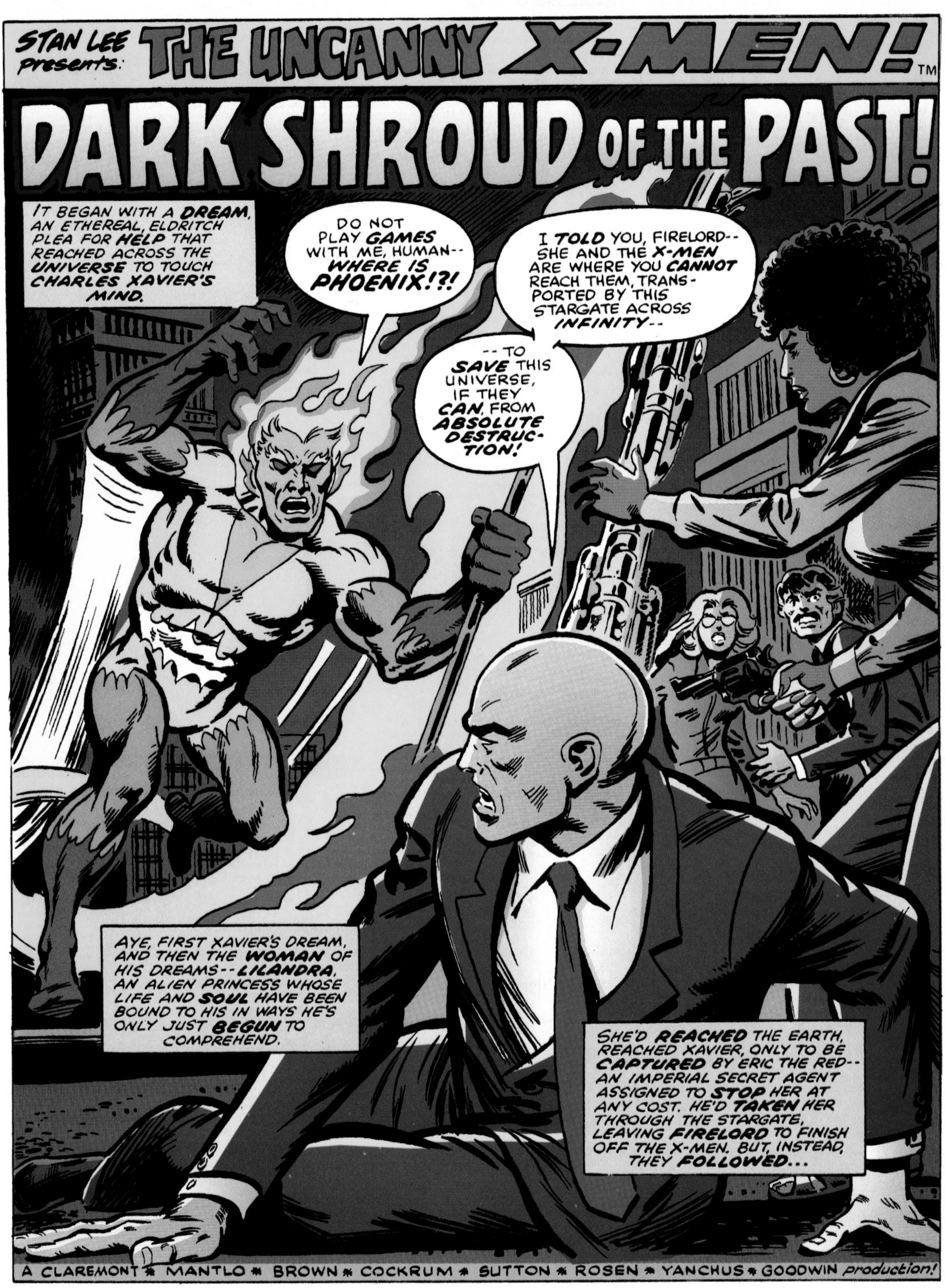
STAN LEE presents: THE UNCANNY X-MEN! TM
DARK SHROUD OF THE PAST!
IT BEGAN WITH A DREAM, AN ETHEREAL, ELDRITCH PLEA FOR HELP THAT REACHED ACROSS THE UNIVERSE TO TOUCH CHARLES XAVIER'S MIND.
DO NOT PLAY GAMES WITH ME, HUMAN-- WHERE IS PHOENIX!?!
I TOLD YOU, FIRELORD-- SHE AND THE X-MEN ARE WHERE YOU CANNOT REACH THEM, TRANS-PORTED BY THIS STARGATE ACROSS INFINITY--
-- TO SAVE THIS UNIVERSE, IF THEY CAN, FROM ABSOLUTE DESTRUC-TION!
AYE, FIRST XAVIER'S DREAM, AND THEN THE WOMAN OF HIS DREAMS--LILANDRA, AN ALIEN PRINCESS WHOSE LIFE AND SOUL HAVE BEEN BOUND TO HIS IN WAYS HE'S ONLY JUST BEGUN TO COMPREHEND.
SHE'D REACHED THE EARTH, REACHED XAVIER, ONLY TO BE CAPTURED BY ERIC THE RED-- AN IMPERIAL SECRET AGENT ASSIGNED TO STOP HER AT ANY COST. HE'D TAKEN HER THROUGH THE STARGATE, LEAVING FIRELORD TO FINISH OFF THE X-MEN. BUT, INSTEAD, THEY FOLLOWED...
A CLAREMONT * MANTLO * BROWN * COCKRUM * SUTTON * ROSEN * YANCHUS * GOODWIN production!

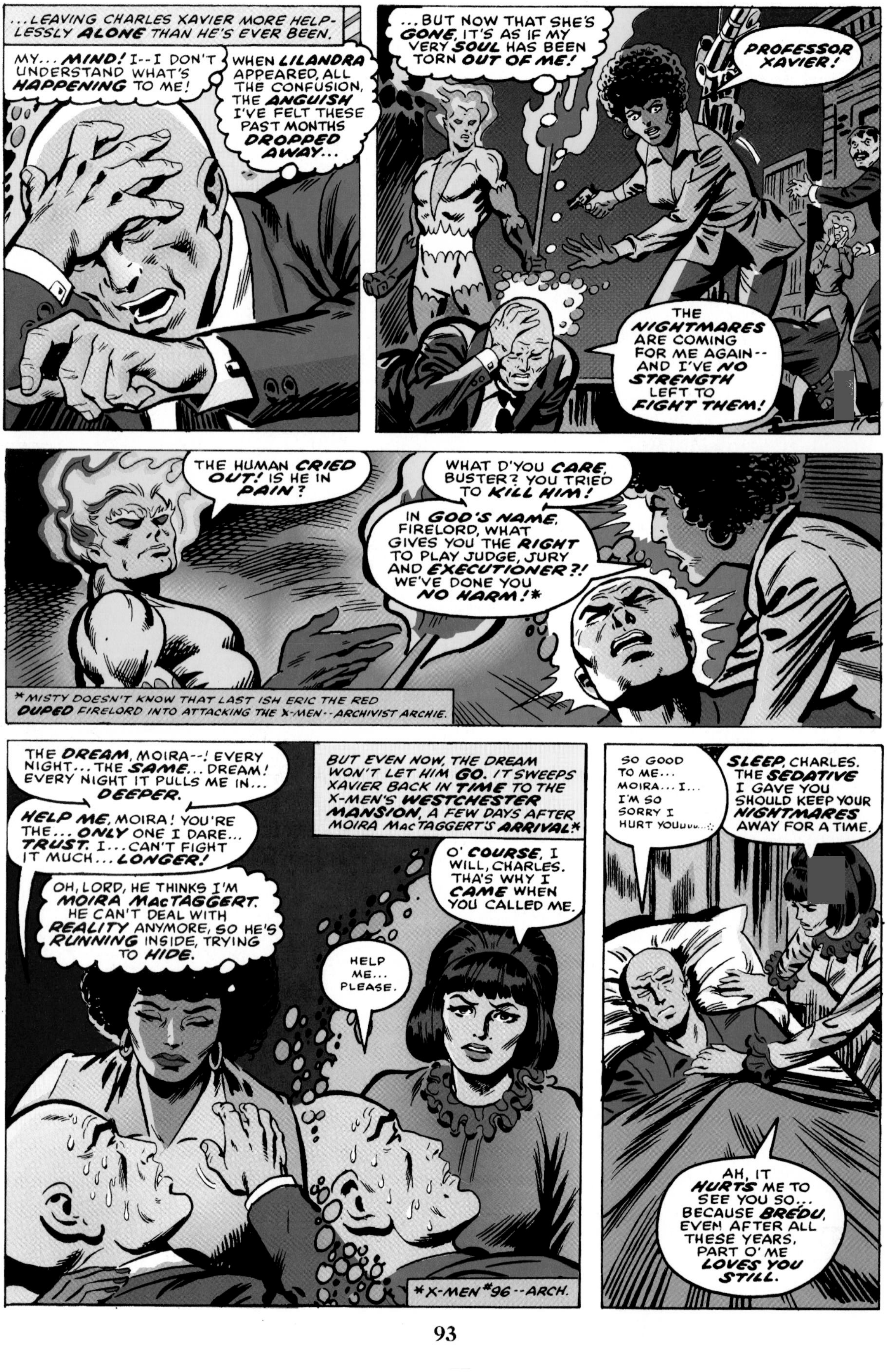
...LEAVING CHARLES XAVIER MORE HELPLESSLY ALONE THAN HE'S EVER BEEN.
MY... MIND! I--I DON'T UNDERSTAND WHAT'S HAPPENING TO ME!
WHEN LILANDRA APPEARED, ALL THE CONFUSION, THE ANGUISH I'VE FELT THESE PAST MONTHS DROPPED AWAY...
...BUT NOW THAT SHE'S GONE, IT'S AS IF MY VERY SOUL HAS BEEN TORN OUT OF ME!
PROFESSOR XAVIER!
THE NIGHTMARES ARE COMING FOR ME AGAIN-- AND I'VE NO STRENGTH LEFT TO FIGHT THEM!
THE HUMAN CRIED OUT! IS HE IN PAIN?
WHAT D'YOU CARE, BUSTER? YOU TRIED TO KILL HIM!
IN GOD'S NAME, FIRELORD, WHAT GIVES YOU THE RIGHT TO PLAY JUDGE, JURY AND EXECUTIONER?! WE'VE DONE YOU NO HARM!*
*MISTY DOESN'T KNOW THAT LAST ISH ERIC THE RED DUPED FIRELORD INTO ATTACKING THE X-MEN--ARCHIVIST ARCHIE.
THE DREAM, MOIRA--! EVERY NIGHT... THE SAME... DREAM! EVERY NIGHT IT PULLS ME IN... DEEPER.
HELP ME, MOIRA! YOU'RE THE... ONLY ONE I DARE... TRUST. I... CAN'T FIGHT IT MUCH... LONGER!
OH, LORD, HE THINKS I'M MOIRA MacTAGGERT. HE CAN'T DEAL WITH REALITY ANYMORE, SO HE'S RUNNING INSIDE, TRYING TO HIDE.
BUT EVEN NOW, THE DREAM WON'T LET HIM GO. IT SWEEPS XAVIER BACK IN TIME TO THE X-MEN'S WESTCHESTER MANSION, A FEW DAYS AFTER MOIRA MacTAGGERT'S ARRIVAL*
O' COURSE, I WILL, CHARLES. THA'S WHY I CAME WHEN YOU CALLED ME.
HELP ME... PLEASE.
*X-MEN #96--ARCH.
SO GOOD TO ME... MOIRA... I... I'M SO SORRY I HURT YOUuuu...
SLEEP, CHARLES. THE SEDATIVE I GAVE YOU SHOULD KEEP YOUR NIGHTMARES AWAY FOR A TIME.
AH, IT HURTS ME TO SEE YOU SO... BECAUSE BREDU, EVEN AFTER ALL THESE YEARS, PART O' ME LOVES YOU STILL.

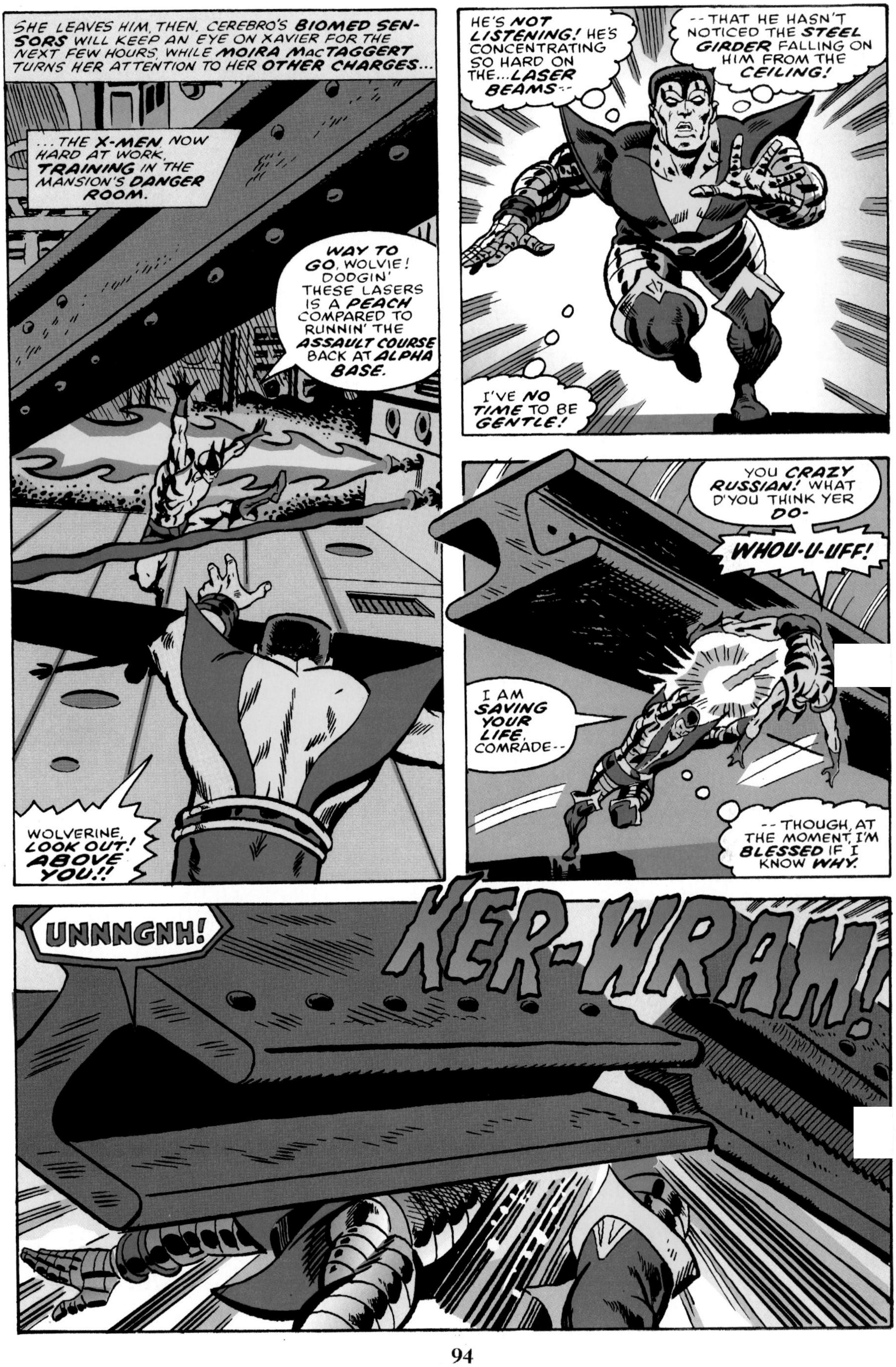
SHE LEAVES HIM, THEN. CEREBRO'S BIOMED SENSORS WILL KEEP AN EYE ON XAVIER FOR THE NEXT FEW HOURS, WHILE MOIRA MacTAGGERT TURNS HER ATTENTION TO HER OTHER CHARGES...
...THE X-MEN, NOW HARD AT WORK, TRAINING IN THE MANSION'S DANGER ROOM.
WAY TO GO, WOLVIE! DODGIN' THESE LASERS IS A PEACH COMPARED TO RUNNIN' THE ASSAULT COURSE BACK AT ALPHA BASE.
WOLVERINE, LOOK OUT! ABOVE YOU!!
HE'S NOT LISTENING! HE'S CONCENTRATING SO HARD ON THE...LASER BEAMS--
--THAT HE HASN'T NOTICED THE STEEL GIRDER FALLING ON HIM FROM THE CEILING!
I'VE NO TIME TO BE GENTLE!
YOU CRAZY RUSSIAN! WHAT D'YOU THINK YER DO-
WHOU-U-UFF!
I AM SAVING YOUR LIFE, COMRADE--
--THOUGH, AT THE MOMENT, I'M BLESSED IF I KNOW WHY.
UNNNGNH!
KER-WRAM!

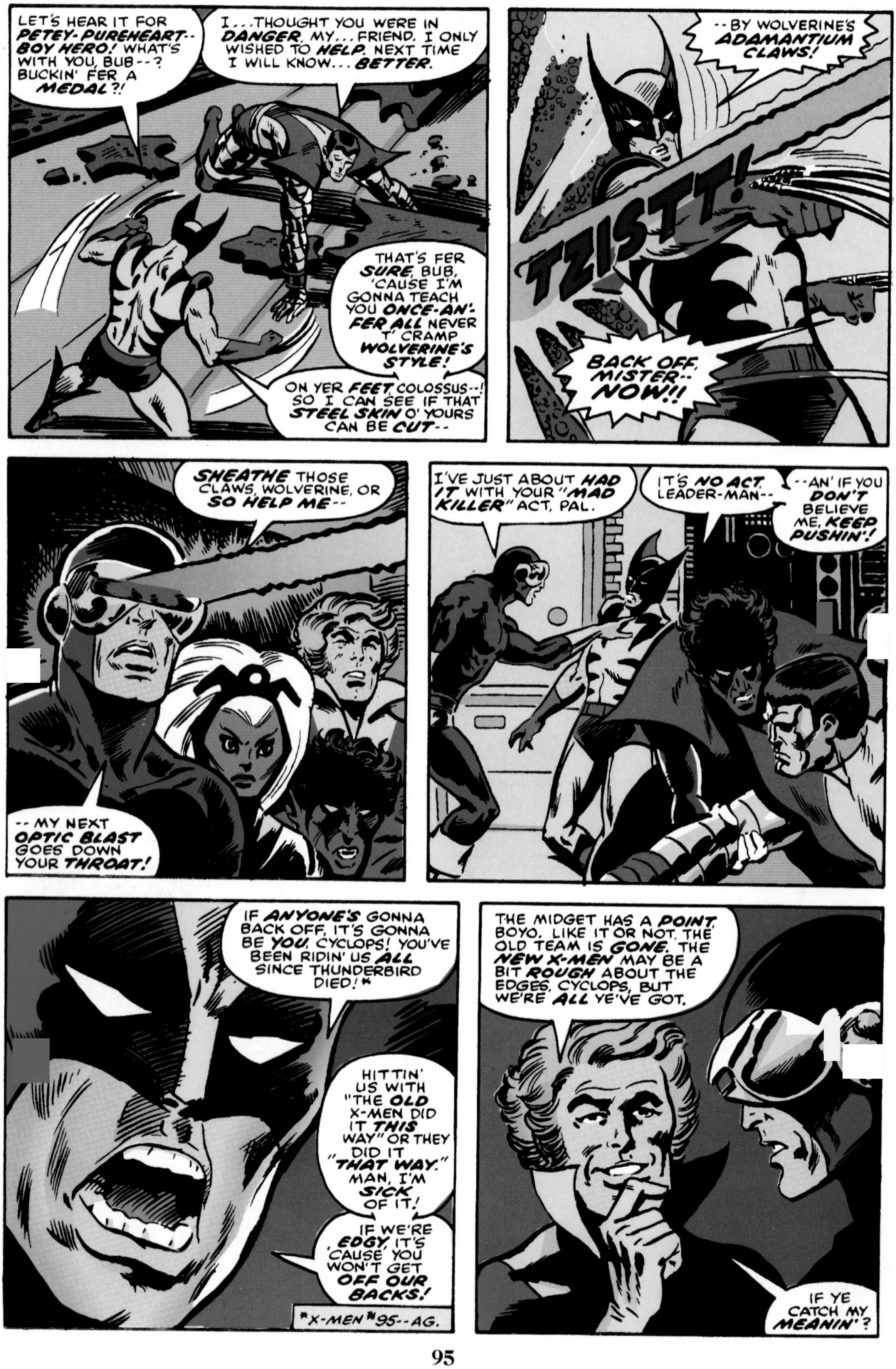
LET'S HEAR IT FOR PETEY-PUREHEART-BOY HERO! WHAT'S WITH YOU, BUB--? BUCKIN' FER A MEDAL?!
I...THOUGHT YOU WERE IN DANGER, MY...FRIEND. I ONLY WISHED TO HELP. NEXT TIME I WILL KNOW...BETTER.
THAT'S FER SURE, BUB, 'CAUSE I'M GONNA TEACH YOU ONCE-AN'-FER ALL NEVER T' CRAMP WOLVERINE'S STYLE!
ON YER FEET, COLOSSUS--! SO I CAN SEE IF THAT STEEL SKIN O' YOURS CAN BE CUT--
--BY WOLVERINE'S ADAMANTIUM CLAWS!
TZISTT!
BACK OFF, MISTER--NOW!!
SHEATHE THOSE CLAWS, WOLVERINE, OR SO HELP ME--
--MY NEXT OPTIC BLAST GOES DOWN YOUR THROAT!
I'VE JUST ABOUT HAD IT WITH YOUR "MAD KILLER" ACT, PAL.
IT'S NO ACT, LEADER-MAN--
--AN' IF YOU DON'T BELIEVE ME, KEEP PUSHIN'!
IF ANYONE'S GONNA BACK OFF, IT'S GONNA BE YOU, CYCLOPS! YOU'VE BEEN RIDIN' US ALL SINCE THUNDERBIRD DIED!*
HITTIN' US WITH "THE OLD X-MEN DID IT THIS WAY" OR THEY DID IT "THAT WAY." MAN, I'M SICK OF IT!
IF WE'RE EDGY, IT'S 'CAUSE YOU WON'T GET OFF OUR BACKS!
*X-MEN #95--AG.
THE MIDGET HAS A POINT, BOYO. LIKE IT OR NOT, THE OLD TEAM IS GONE. THE NEW X-MEN MAY BE A BIT ROUGH ABOUT THE EDGES, CYCLOPS, BUT WE'RE ALL YE'VE GOT.
IF YE CATCH MY MEANIN'?

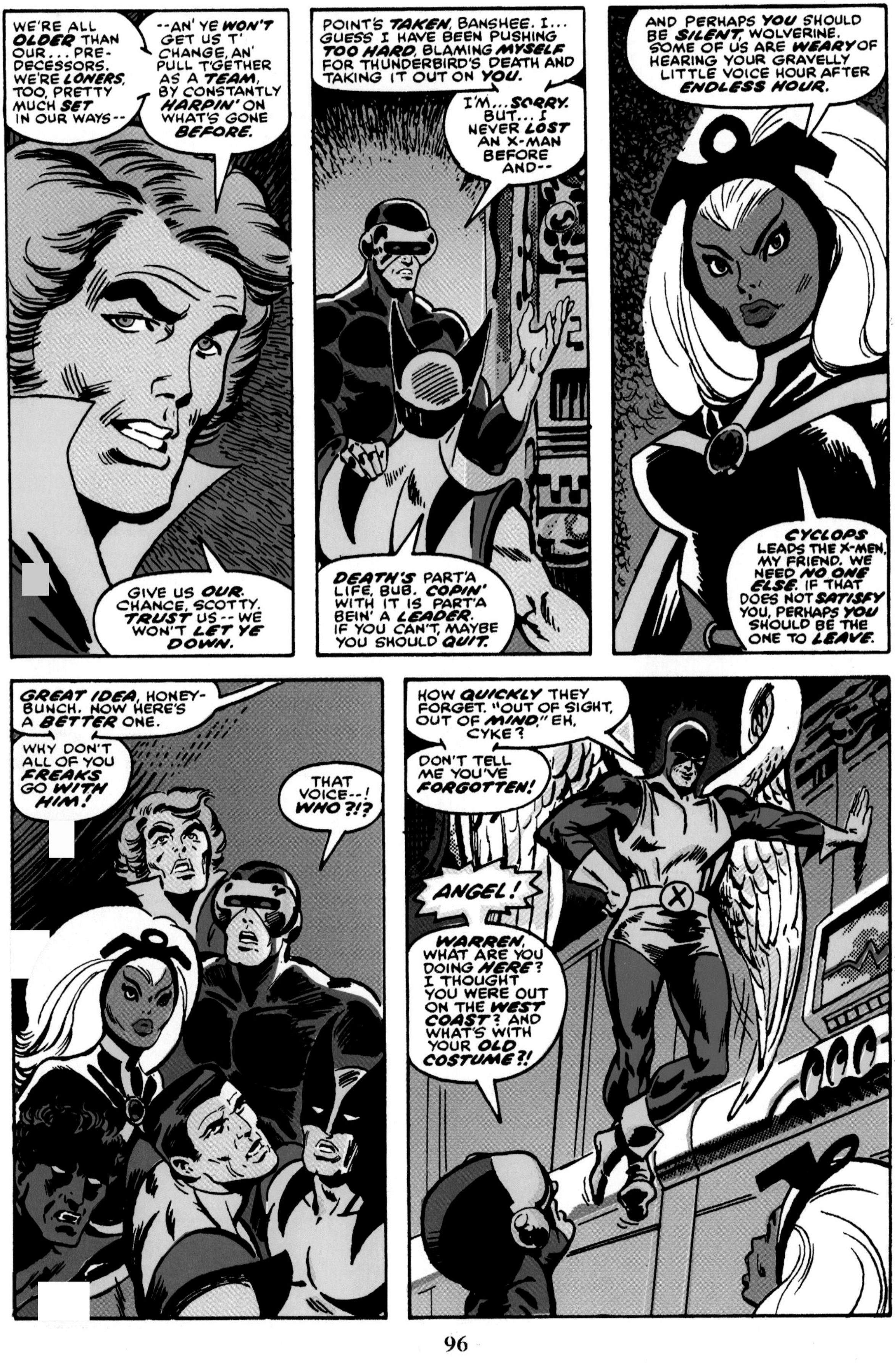

WE'RE ALL OLDER THAN OUR... PRE-DECESSORS. WE'RE LONERS, TOO, PRETTY MUCH SET IN OUR WAYS--
--AN' YE WON'T GET US T' CHANGE, AN' PULL T'GETHER AS A TEAM, BY CONSTANTLY HARPIN' ON WHAT'S GONE BEFORE.
GIVE US OUR CHANCE, SCOTTY. TRUST US -- WE WON'T LET YE DOWN.
POINT'S TAKEN, BANSHEE. I... GUESS I HAVE BEEN PUSHING TOO HARD, BLAMING MYSELF FOR THUNDERBIRD'S DEATH AND TAKING IT OUT ON YOU.
I'M... SORRY. BUT... I NEVER LOST AN X-MAN BEFORE AND--
DEATH'S PART'A LIFE, BUB. COPIN' WITH IT IS PART'A BEIN' A LEADER. IF YOU CAN'T, MAYBE YOU SHOULD QUIT.
AND PERHAPS YOU SHOULD BE SILENT, WOLVERINE. SOME OF US ARE WEARY OF HEARING YOUR GRAVELLY LITTLE VOICE HOUR AFTER ENDLESS HOUR.
CYCLOPS LEADS THE X-MEN, MY FRIEND. WE NEED NO ONE ELSE. IF THAT DOES NOT SATISFY YOU, PERHAPS YOU SHOULD BE THE ONE TO LEAVE.
GREAT IDEA, HONEY-BUNCH. NOW HERE'S A BETTER ONE.
WHY DON'T ALL OF YOU FREAKS GO WITH HIM!
THAT VOICE--! WHO?!?
HOW QUICKLY THEY FORGET. "OUT OF SIGHT, OUT OF MIND," EH, CYKE?
DON'T TELL ME YOU'VE FORGOTTEN!
ANGEL!
WARREN, WHAT ARE YOU DOING HERE? I THOUGHT YOU WERE OUT ON THE WEST COAST? AND WHAT'S WITH YOUR OLD COSTUME?!

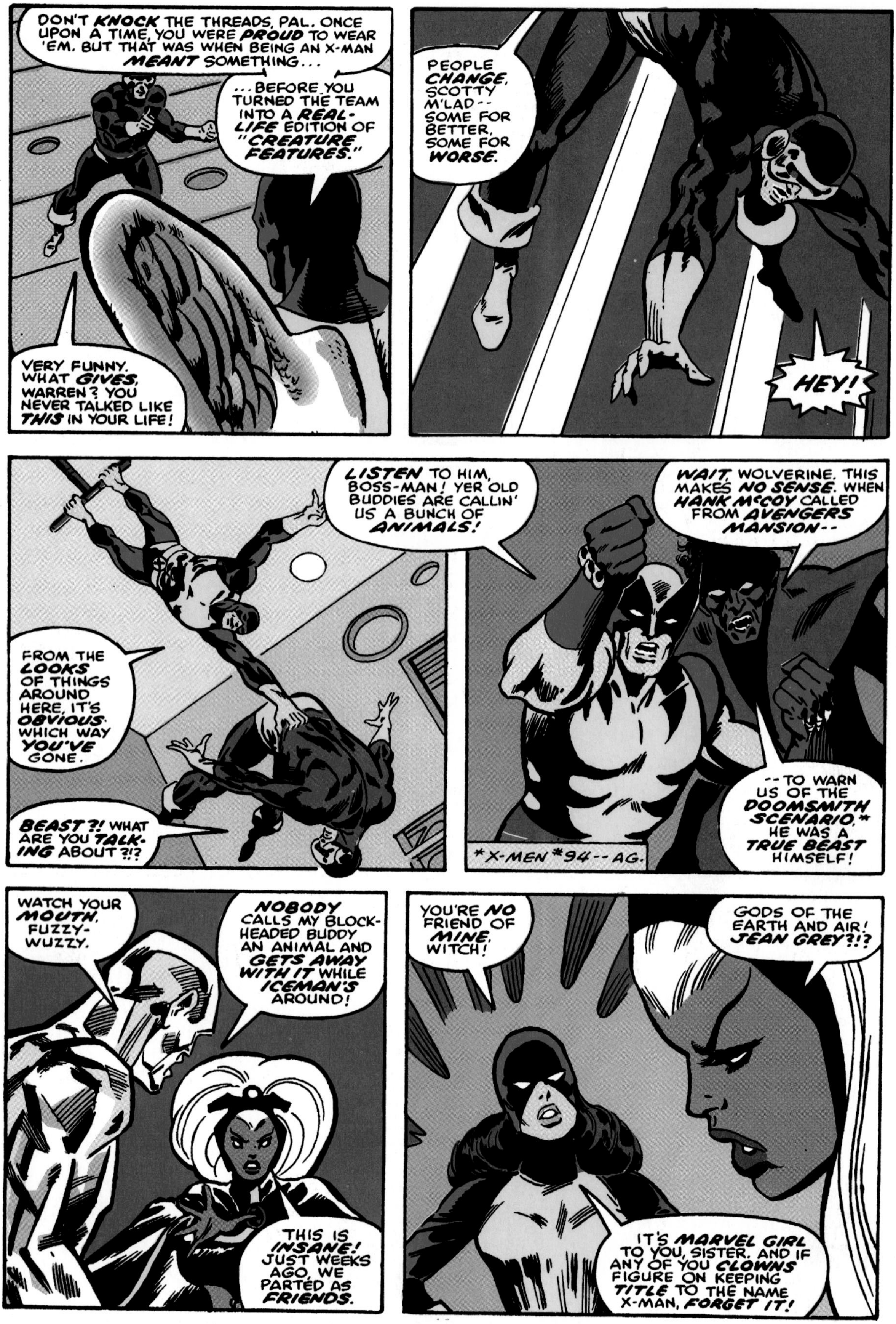

DON'T KNOCK THE THREADS, PAL. ONCE UPON A TIME, YOU WERE PROUD TO WEAR 'EM. BUT THAT WAS WHEN BEING AN X-MAN MEANT SOMETHING...
...BEFORE YOU TURNED THE TEAM INTO A REAL-LIFE EDITION OF "CREATURE FEATURES."
VERY FUNNY. WHAT GIVES, WARREN? YOU NEVER TALKED LIKE THIS IN YOUR LIFE!
PEOPLE CHANGE, SCOTTY M'LAD-- SOME FOR BETTER, SOME FOR WORSE.
HEY!
LISTEN TO HIM, BOSS-MAN! YER OLD BUDDIES ARE CALLIN' US A BUNCH OF ANIMALS!
FROM THE LOOKS OF THINGS AROUND HERE, IT'S OBVIOUS WHICH WAY YOU'VE GONE.
BEAST?! WHAT ARE YOU TALKING ABOUT?!?
WAIT, WOLVERINE. THIS MAKES NO SENSE. WHEN HANK McCOY CALLED FROM AVENGERS MANSION--
--TO WARN US OF THE DOOMSMITH SCENARIO,* HE WAS A TRUE BEAST HIMSELF!
*X-MEN #94--AG.
WATCH YOUR MOUTH, FUZZY-WUZZY.
NOBODY CALLS MY BLOCK-HEADED BUDDY AN ANIMAL AND GETS AWAY WITH IT WHILE ICEMAN'S AROUND!
THIS IS INSANE! JUST WEEKS AGO, WE PARTED AS FRIENDS.
YOU'RE NO FRIEND OF MINE, WITCH!
GODS OF THE EARTH AND AIR! JEAN GREY?!?
IT'S MARVEL GIRL TO YOU, SISTER. AND IF ANY OF YOU CLOWNS FIGURE ON KEEPING TITLE TO THE NAME X-MAN, FORGET IT!

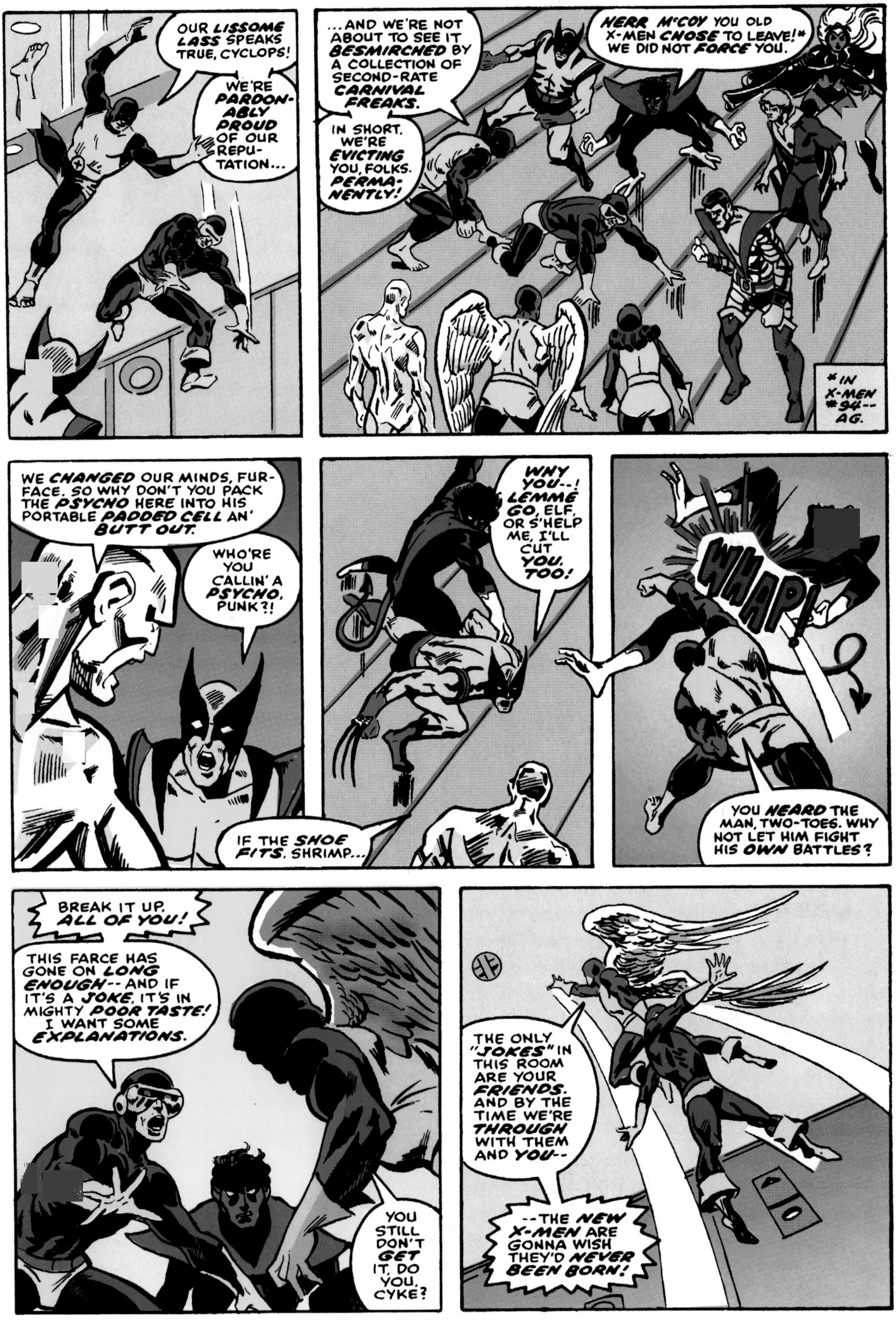

OUR LISSOME LASS SPEAKS TRUE, CYCLOPS!
WE'RE PARDON-ABLY PROUD OF OUR REPU-TATION...
...AND WE'RE NOT ABOUT TO SEE IT BESMIRCHED BY A COLLECTION OF SECOND-RATE CARNIVAL FREAKS.
IN SHORT, WE'RE EVICTING YOU, FOLKS. PERMA-NENTLY!
HERR M'COY YOU OLD X-MEN CHOSE TO LEAVE!* WE DID NOT FORCE YOU.
*IN X-MEN #94--AG.
WE CHANGED OUR MINDS, FUR-FACE. SO WHY DON'T YOU PACK THE PSYCHO HERE INTO HIS PORTABLE PADDED CELL AN' BUTT OUT.
WHO'RE YOU CALLIN' A PSYCHO, PUNK?!
IF THE SHOE FITS, SHRIMP...
WHY YOU--! LEMME GO, ELF, OR S'HELP ME, I'LL CUT YOU, TOO!
WHAP!
YOU HEARD THE MAN, TWO-TOES. WHY NOT LET HIM FIGHT HIS OWN BATTLES?
BREAK IT UP, ALL OF YOU!
THIS FARCE HAS GONE ON LONG ENOUGH-- AND IF IT'S A JOKE, IT'S IN MIGHTY POOR TASTE! I WANT SOME EXPLANATIONS.
YOU STILL DON'T GET IT, DO YOU, CYKE?
THE ONLY "JOKES" IN THIS ROOM ARE YOUR FRIENDS. AND BY THE TIME WE'RE THROUGH WITH THEM AND YOU--
--THE NEW X-MEN ARE GONNA WISH THEY'D NEVER BEEN BORN!

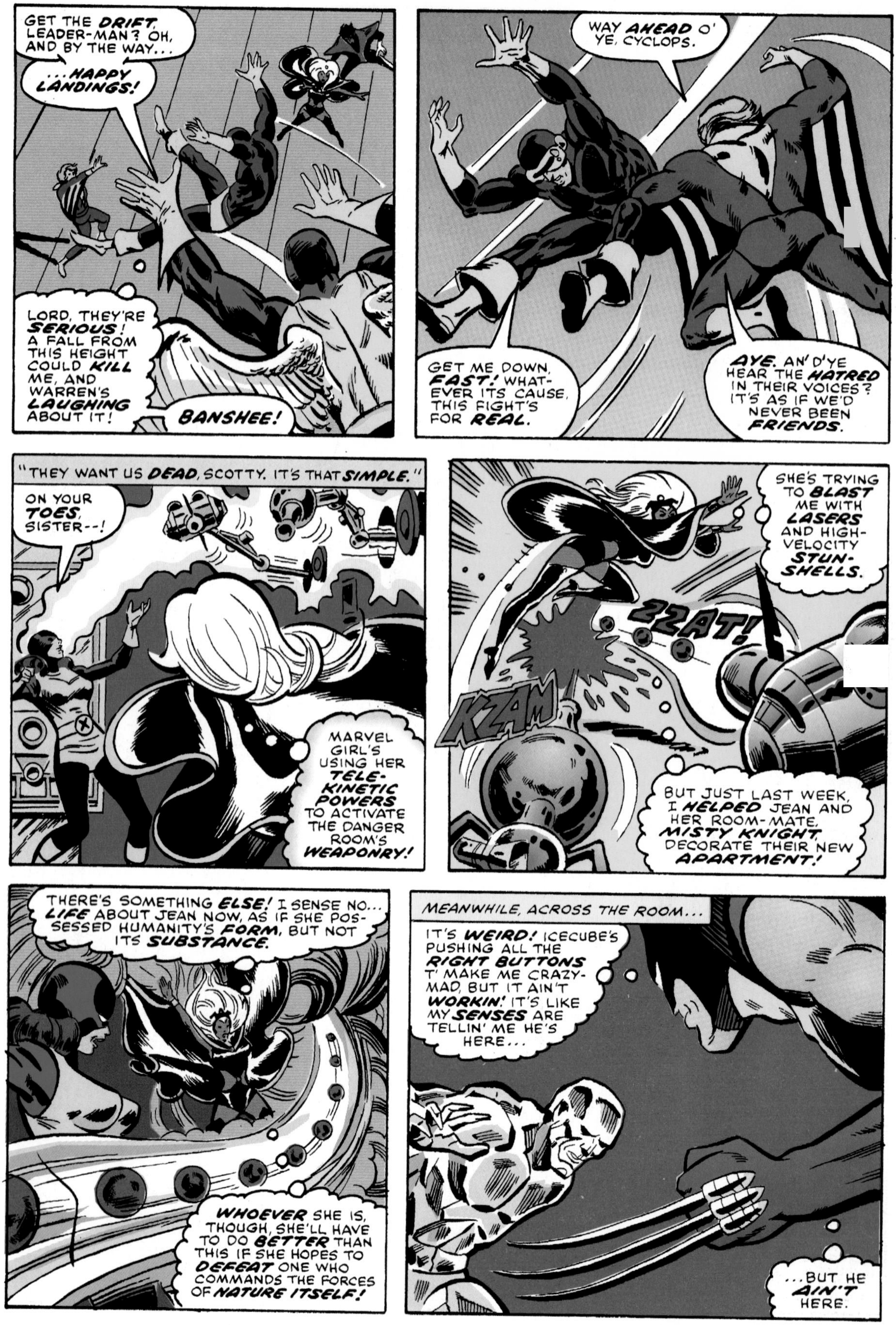
GET THE DRIFT, LEADER-MAN? OH, AND BY THE WAY...
...HAPPY LANDINGS!
LORD, THEY'RE SERIOUS! A FALL FROM THIS HEIGHT COULD KILL ME, AND WARREN'S LAUGHING ABOUT IT!
BANSHEE!
WAY AHEAD O' YE, CYCLOPS.
GET ME DOWN, FAST! WHAT-EVER ITS CAUSE, THIS FIGHT'S FOR REAL.
AYE. AN' D'YE HEAR THE HATRED IN THEIR VOICES? IT'S AS IF WE'D NEVER BEEN FRIENDS.
"THEY WANT US DEAD, SCOTTY. IT'S THAT SIMPLE."
ON YOUR TOES, SISTER--!
MARVEL GIRL'S USING HER TELE-KINETIC POWERS TO ACTIVATE THE DANGER ROOM'S WEAPONRY!
SHE'S TRYING TO BLAST ME WITH LASERS AND HIGH-VELOCITY STUN-SHELLS.
ZZAT!
KZAM
BUT JUST LAST WEEK, I HELPED JEAN AND HER ROOM-MATE, MISTY KNIGHT, DECORATE THEIR NEW APARTMENT!
THERE'S SOMETHING ELSE! I SENSE NO... LIFE ABOUT JEAN NOW, AS IF SHE POS-SESSED HUMANITY'S FORM, BUT NOT ITS SUBSTANCE.
WHOEVER SHE IS, THOUGH, SHE'LL HAVE TO DO BETTER THAN THIS IF SHE HOPES TO DEFEAT ONE WHO COMMANDS THE FORCES OF NATURE ITSELF!
MEANWHILE, ACROSS THE ROOM...
IT'S WEIRD! ICECUBE'S PUSHING ALL THE RIGHT BUTTONS T' MAKE ME CRAZY-MAD, BUT IT AIN'T WORKIN'! IT'S LIKE MY SENSES ARE TELLIN' ME HE'S HERE...
...BUT HE AIN'T HERE.

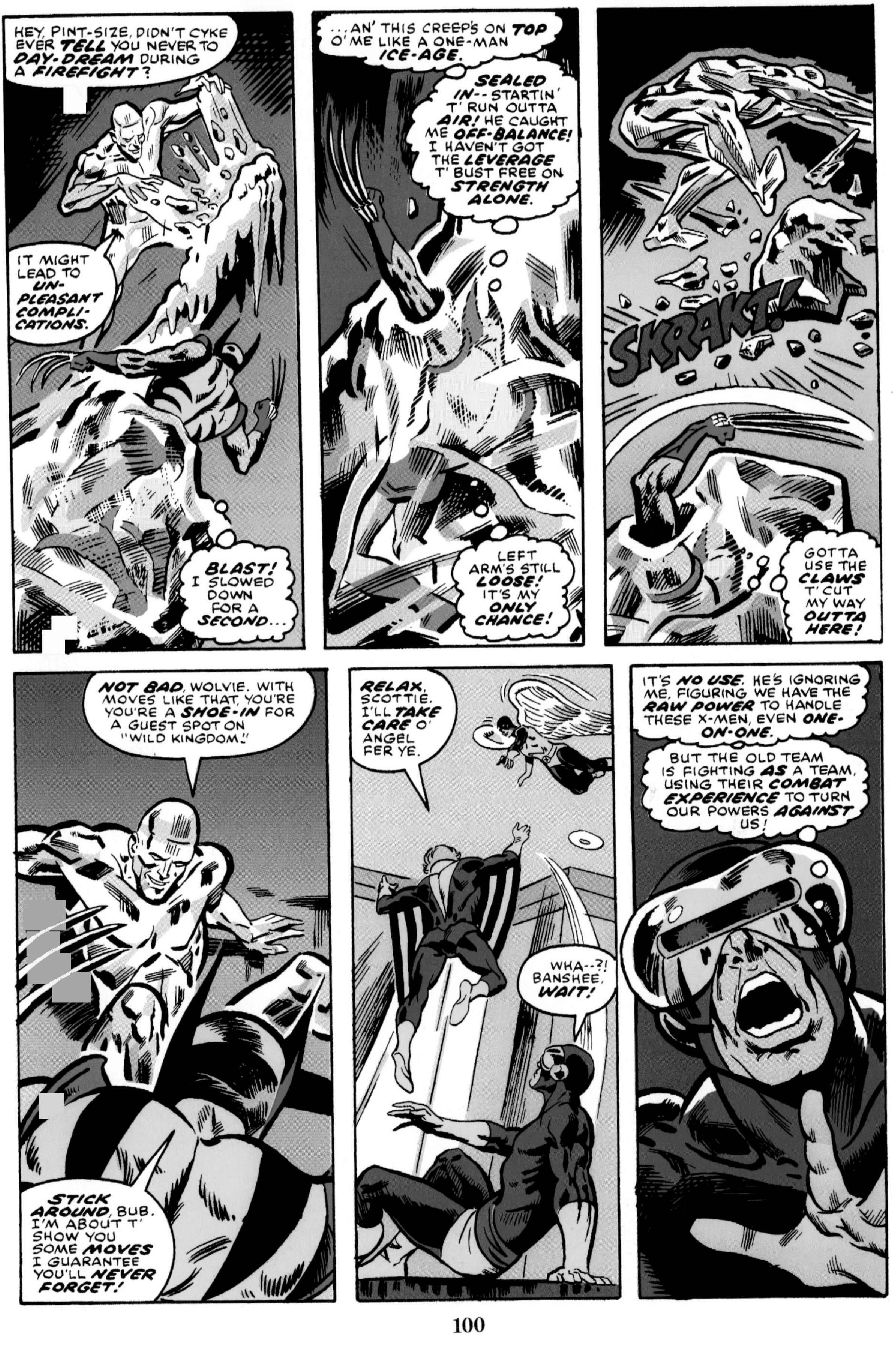
HEY, PINT-SIZE, DIDN'T CYKE EVER TELL YOU NEVER TO DAY-DREAM DURING A FIREFIGHT?
IT MIGHT LEAD TO UN-PLEASANT COMPLI-CATIONS.
BLAST! I SLOWED DOWN FOR A SECOND...
...AN' THIS CREEP'S ON TOP O' ME LIKE A ONE-MAN ICE-AGE.
SEALED IN-- STARTIN' T' RUN OUTTA AIR! HE CAUGHT ME OFF-BALANCE! I HAVEN'T GOT THE LEVERAGE T' BUST FREE ON STRENGTH ALONE.
LEFT ARM'S STILL LOOSE! IT'S MY ONLY CHANCE!
SKRAKT!
GOTTA USE THE CLAWS T' CUT MY WAY OUTTA HERE!
NOT BAD, WOLVIE. WITH MOVES LIKE THAT, YOU'RE YOU'RE A SHOE-IN FOR A GUEST SPOT ON "WILD KINGDOM."
STICK AROUND, BUB. I'M ABOUT T' SHOW YOU SOME MOVES I GUARANTEE YOU'LL NEVER FORGET!
RELAX, SCOTTIE. I'LL TAKE CARE O' ANGEL FER YE.
WHA--?! BANSHEE, WAIT!
IT'S NO USE. HE'S IGNORING ME, FIGURING WE HAVE THE RAW POWER TO HANDLE THESE X-MEN, EVEN ONE-ON-ONE.
BUT THE OLD TEAM IS FIGHTING AS A TEAM, USING THEIR COMBAT EXPERIENCE TO TURN OUR POWERS AGAINST US!

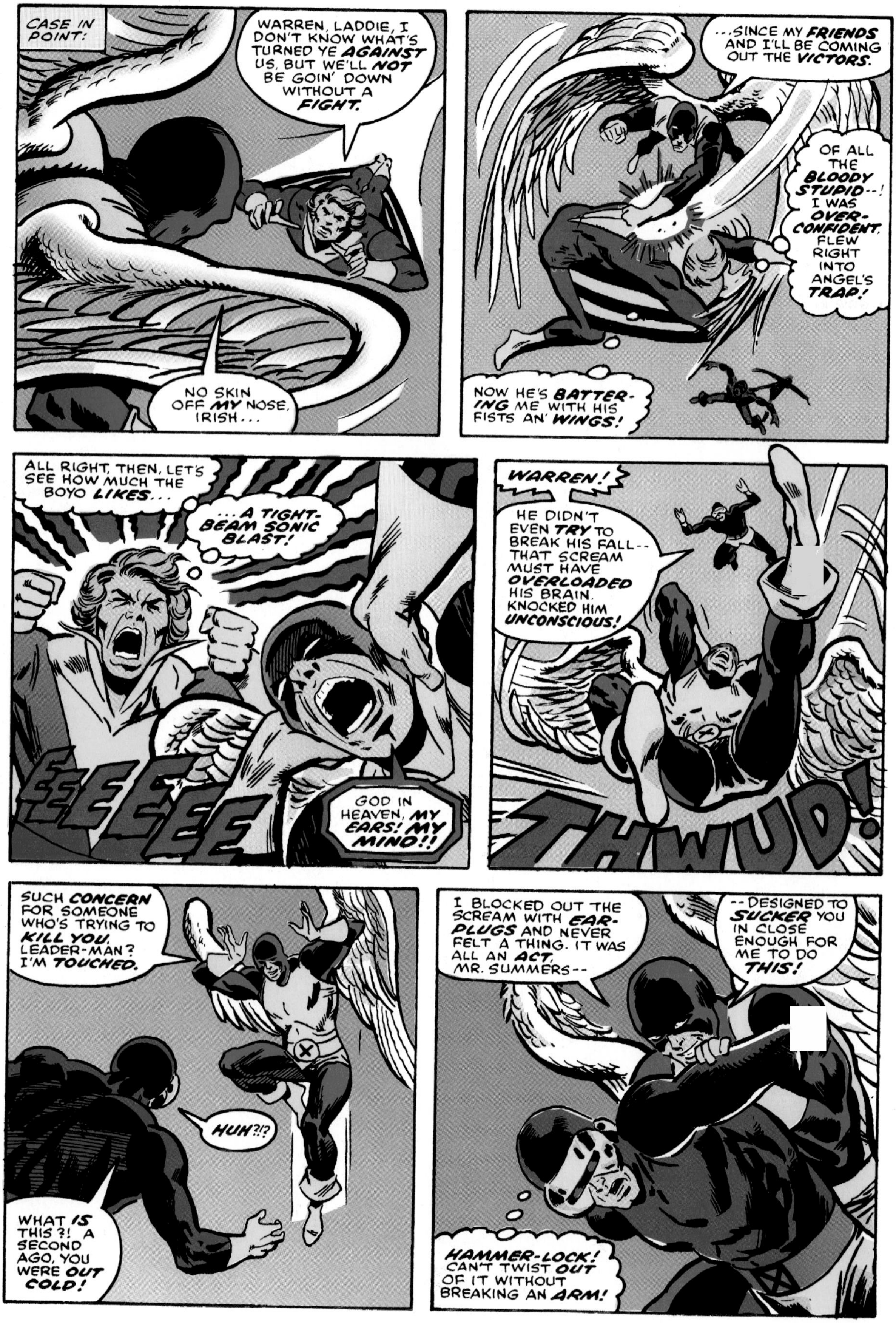

CASE IN POINT:
WARREN, LADDIE, I DON'T KNOW WHAT'S TURNED YE AGAINST US, BUT WE'LL NOT BE GOIN' DOWN WITHOUT A FIGHT.
NO SKIN OFF MY NOSE, IRISH...
...SINCE MY FRIENDS AND I'LL BE COMING OUT THE VICTORS.
OF ALL THE BLOODY STUPID--! I WAS OVER-CONFIDENT. FLEW RIGHT INTO ANGEL'S TRAP!
NOW HE'S BATTER-ING ME WITH HIS FISTS AN' WINGS!
ALL RIGHT, THEN, LET'S SEE HOW MUCH THE BOYO LIKES...
...A TIGHT-BEAM SONIC BLAST!
EEEEEEE
GOD IN HEAVEN, MY EARS! MY MIND!!
WARREN!
HE DIDN'T EVEN TRY TO BREAK HIS FALL-- THAT SCREAM MUST HAVE OVERLOADED HIS BRAIN. KNOCKED HIM UNCONSCIOUS!
THWUD!
SUCH CONCERN FOR SOMEONE WHO'S TRYING TO KILL YOU, LEADER-MAN? I'M TOUCHED.
HUH?!?
WHAT IS THIS?! A SECOND AGO, YOU WERE OUT COLD!
I BLOCKED OUT THE SCREAM WITH EAR-PLUGS AND NEVER FELT A THING. IT WAS ALL AN ACT, MR. SUMMERS--
--DESIGNED TO SUCKER YOU IN CLOSE ENOUGH FOR ME TO DO THIS!
HAMMER-LOCK! CAN'T TWIST OUT OF IT WITHOUT BREAKING AN ARM!

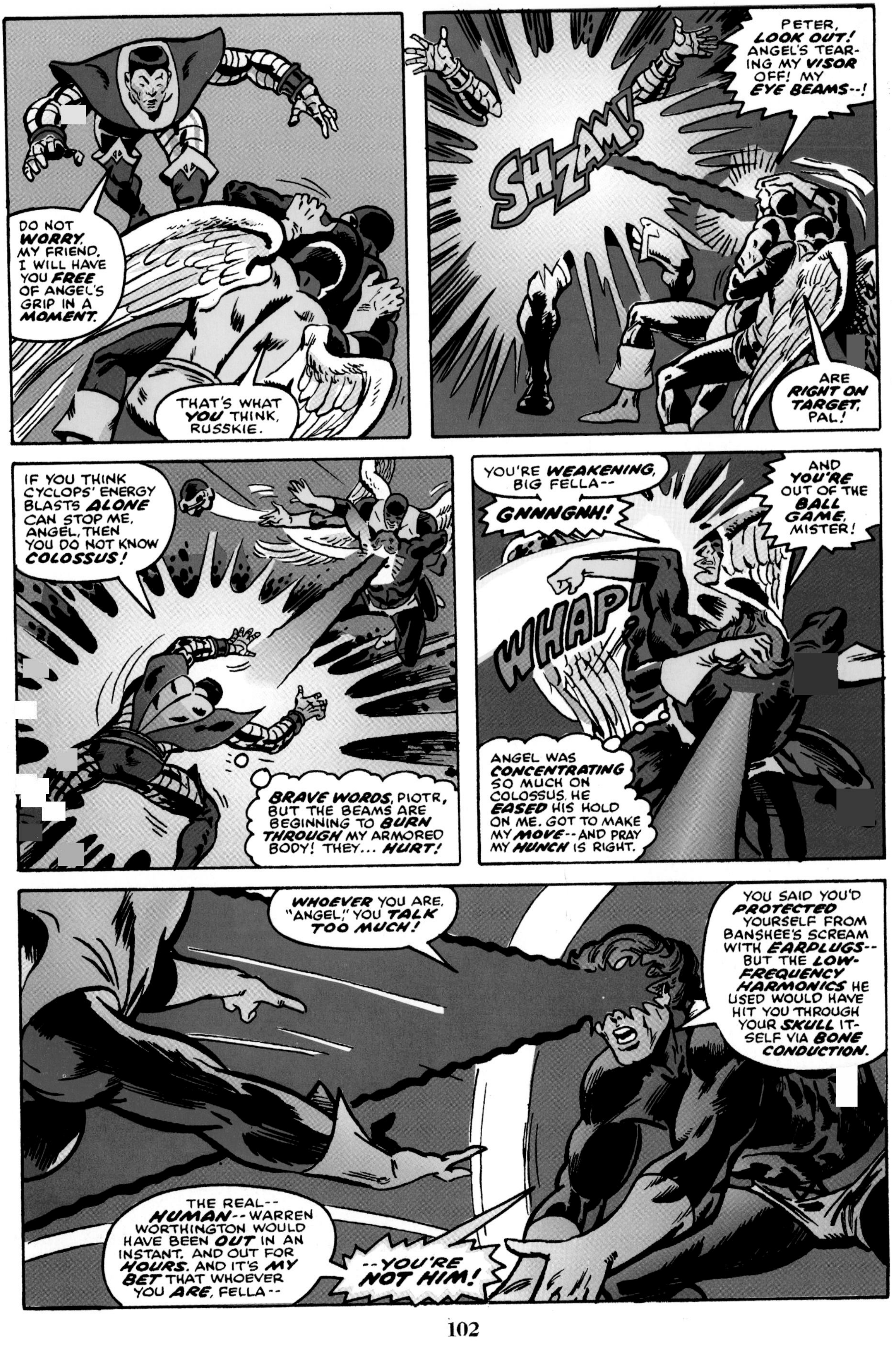

DO NOT WORRY, MY FRIEND, I WILL HAVE YOU FREE OF ANGEL'S GRIP IN A MOMENT.
THAT'S WHAT YOU THINK, RUSSKIE.
PETER, LOOK OUT! ANGEL'S TEARING MY VISOR OFF! MY EYE BEAMS--!
SHZAM!
ARE RIGHT ON TARGET, PAL!
IF YOU THINK CYCLOPS' ENERGY BLASTS ALONE CAN STOP ME, ANGEL, THEN YOU DO NOT KNOW COLOSSUS!
BRAVE WORDS, PIOTR, BUT THE BEAMS ARE BEGINNING TO BURN THROUGH MY ARMORED BODY! THEY... HURT!
YOU'RE WEAKENING, BIG FELLA--
GNNNGNH!
AND YOU'RE OUT OF THE BALL GAME, MISTER!
WHAP!
ANGEL WAS CONCENTRATING SO MUCH ON COLOSSUS, HE EASED HIS HOLD ON ME. GOT TO MAKE MY MOVE--AND PRAY MY HUNCH IS RIGHT.
WHOEVER YOU ARE, "ANGEL," YOU TALK TOO MUCH!
YOU SAID YOU'D PROTECTED YOURSELF FROM BANSHEE'S SCREAM WITH EARPLUGS--BUT THE LOW-FREQUENCY HARMONICS HE USED WOULD HAVE HIT YOU THROUGH YOUR SKULL ITSELF VIA BONE CONDUCTION.
THE REAL--HUMAN--WARREN WORTHINGTON WOULD HAVE BEEN OUT IN AN INSTANT, AND OUT FOR HOURS. AND IT'S MY BET THAT WHOEVER YOU ARE, FELLA--
--YOU'RE NOT HIM!

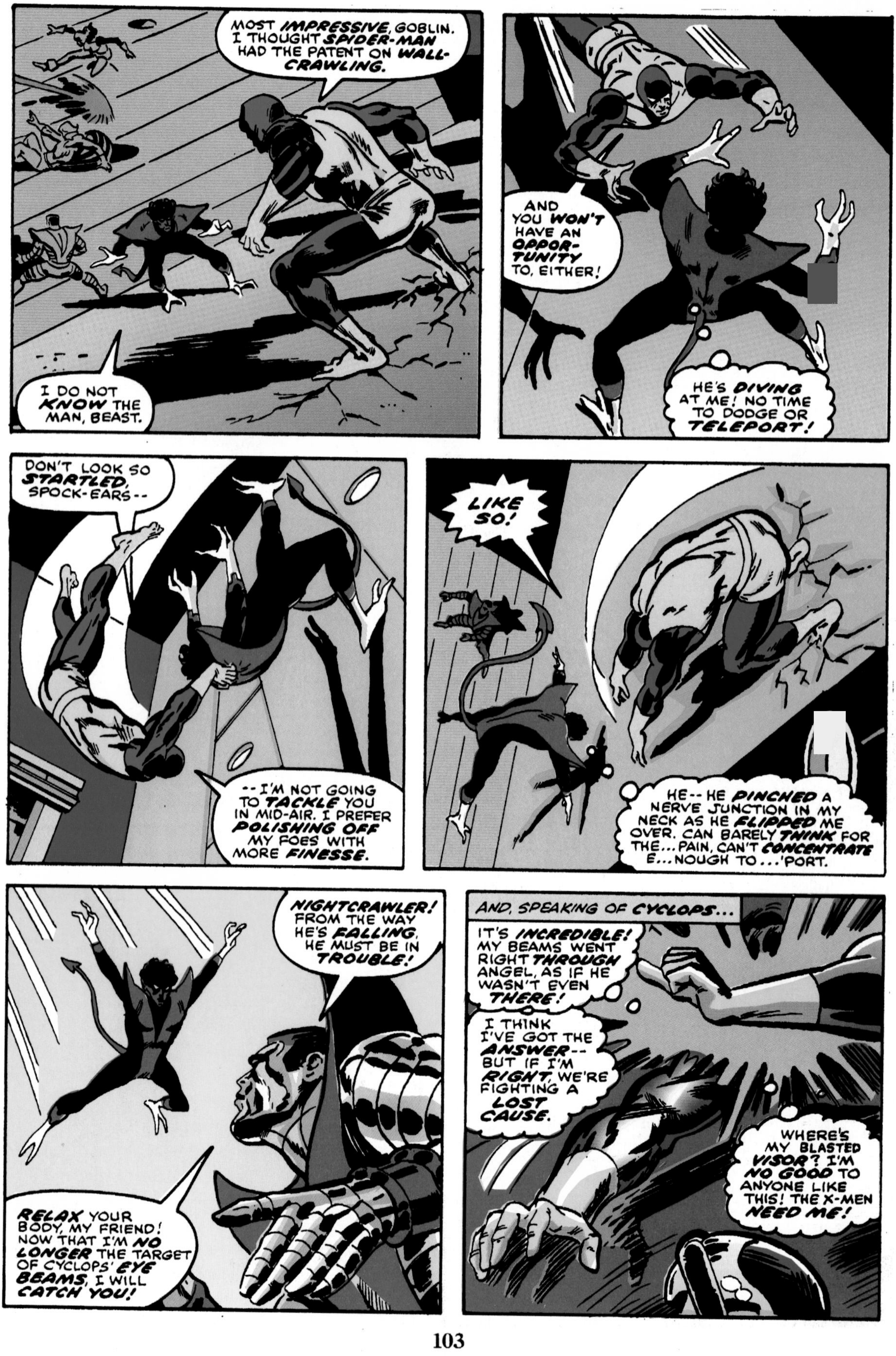
MOST IMPRESSIVE, GOBLIN. I THOUGHT SPIDER-MAN HAD THE PATENT ON WALL-CRAWLING.
I DO NOT KNOW THE MAN, BEAST.
AND YOU WON'T HAVE AN OPPORTUNITY TO, EITHER!
HE'S DIVING AT ME! NO TIME TO DODGE OR TELEPORT!
DON'T LOOK SO STARTLED, SPOCK-EARS--
--I'M NOT GOING TO TACKLE YOU IN MID-AIR. I PREFER POLISHING OFF MY FOES WITH MORE FINESSE.
LIKE SO!
HE--HE PINCHED A NERVE JUNCTION IN MY NECK AS HE FLIPPED ME OVER. CAN BARELY THINK FOR THE... PAIN, CAN'T CONCENTRATE E...NOUGH TO...'PORT.
NIGHTCRAWLER! FROM THE WAY HE'S FALLING, HE MUST BE IN TROUBLE!
RELAX YOUR BODY, MY FRIEND! NOW THAT I'M NO LONGER THE TARGET OF CYCLOPS' EYE BEAMS, I WILL CATCH YOU!
AND, SPEAKING OF CYCLOPS...
IT'S INCREDIBLE! MY BEAMS WENT RIGHT THROUGH ANGEL, AS IF HE WASN'T EVEN THERE!
I THINK I'VE GOT THE ANSWER--BUT IF I'M RIGHT, WE'RE FIGHTING A LOST CAUSE.
WHERE'S MY BLASTED VISOR? I'M NO GOOD TO ANYONE LIKE THIS! THE X-MEN NEED ME!

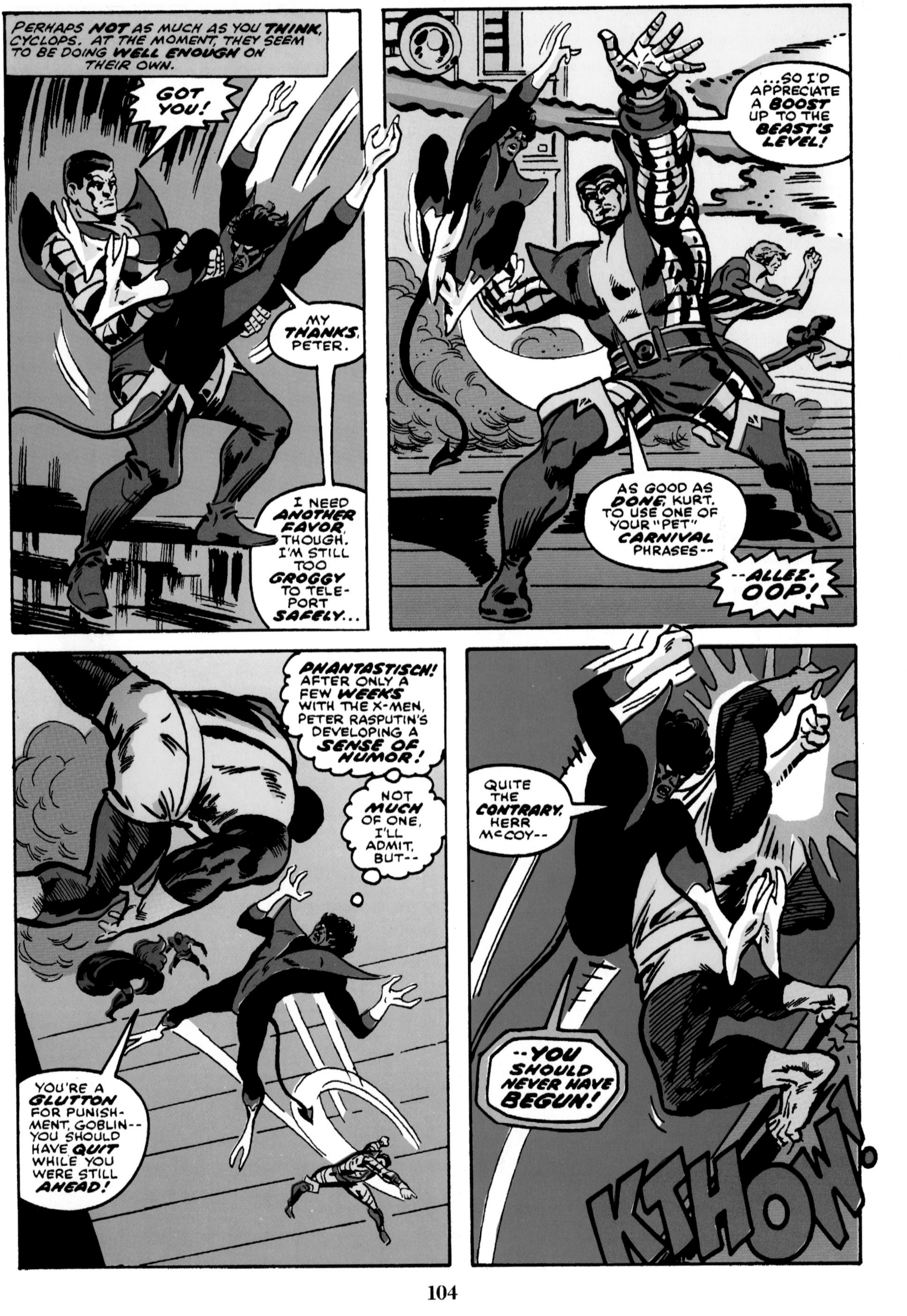
PERHAPS NOT AS MUCH AS YOU THINK, CYCLOPS. AT THE MOMENT, THEY SEEM TO BE DOING WELL ENOUGH ON THEIR OWN.
GOT YOU!
MY THANKS, PETER.
I NEED ANOTHER FAVOR, THOUGH. I'M STILL TOO GROGGY TO TELE-PORT SAFELY...
...SO I'D APPRECIATE A BOOST UP TO THE BEAST'S LEVEL!
AS GOOD AS DONE, KURT. TO USE ONE OF YOUR "PET" CARNIVAL PHRASES--
--ALLEZ-OOP!
PHANTASTISCH! AFTER ONLY A FEW WEEKS WITH THE X-MEN, PETER RASPUTIN'S DEVELOPING A SENSE OF HUMOR!
NOT MUCH OF ONE, I'LL ADMIT, BUT--
YOU'RE A GLUTTON FOR PUNISH-MENT, GOBLIN-- YOU SHOULD HAVE QUIT WHILE YOU WERE STILL AHEAD!
QUITE THE CONTRARY, HERR McCOY--
--YOU SHOULD NEVER HAVE BEGUN!
KTHOW!

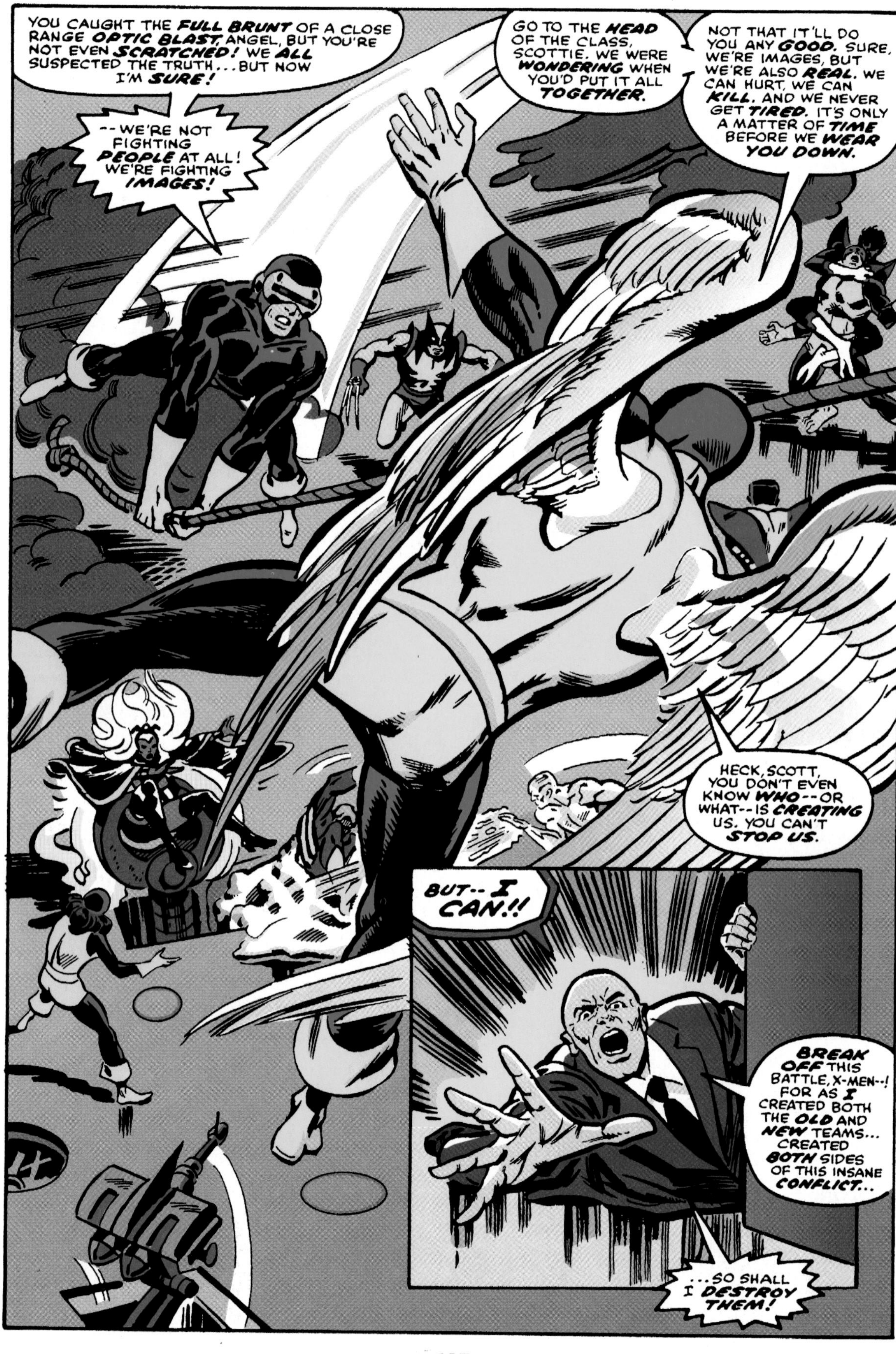

YOU CAUGHT THE FULL BRUNT OF A CLOSE RANGE OPTIC BLAST, ANGEL, BUT YOU'RE NOT EVEN SCRATCHED! WE ALL SUSPECTED THE TRUTH... BUT NOW I'M SURE!
--WE'RE NOT FIGHTING PEOPLE AT ALL! WE'RE FIGHTING IMAGES!
GO TO THE HEAD OF THE CLASS, SCOTTIE. WE WERE WONDERING WHEN YOU'D PUT IT ALL TOGETHER.
NOT THAT IT'LL DO YOU ANY GOOD. SURE, WE'RE IMAGES, BUT WE'RE ALSO REAL. WE CAN HURT, WE CAN KILL. AND WE NEVER GET TIRED. IT'S ONLY A MATTER OF TIME BEFORE WE WEAR YOU DOWN.
HECK, SCOTT, YOU DON'T EVEN KNOW WHO--OR WHAT--IS CREATING US. YOU CAN'T STOP US.
BUT--I CAN!!
BREAK OFF THIS BATTLE, X-MEN--! FOR AS I CREATED BOTH THE OLD AND NEW TEAMS... CREATED BOTH SIDES OF THIS INSANE CONFLICT...
...SO SHALL I DESTROY THEM!

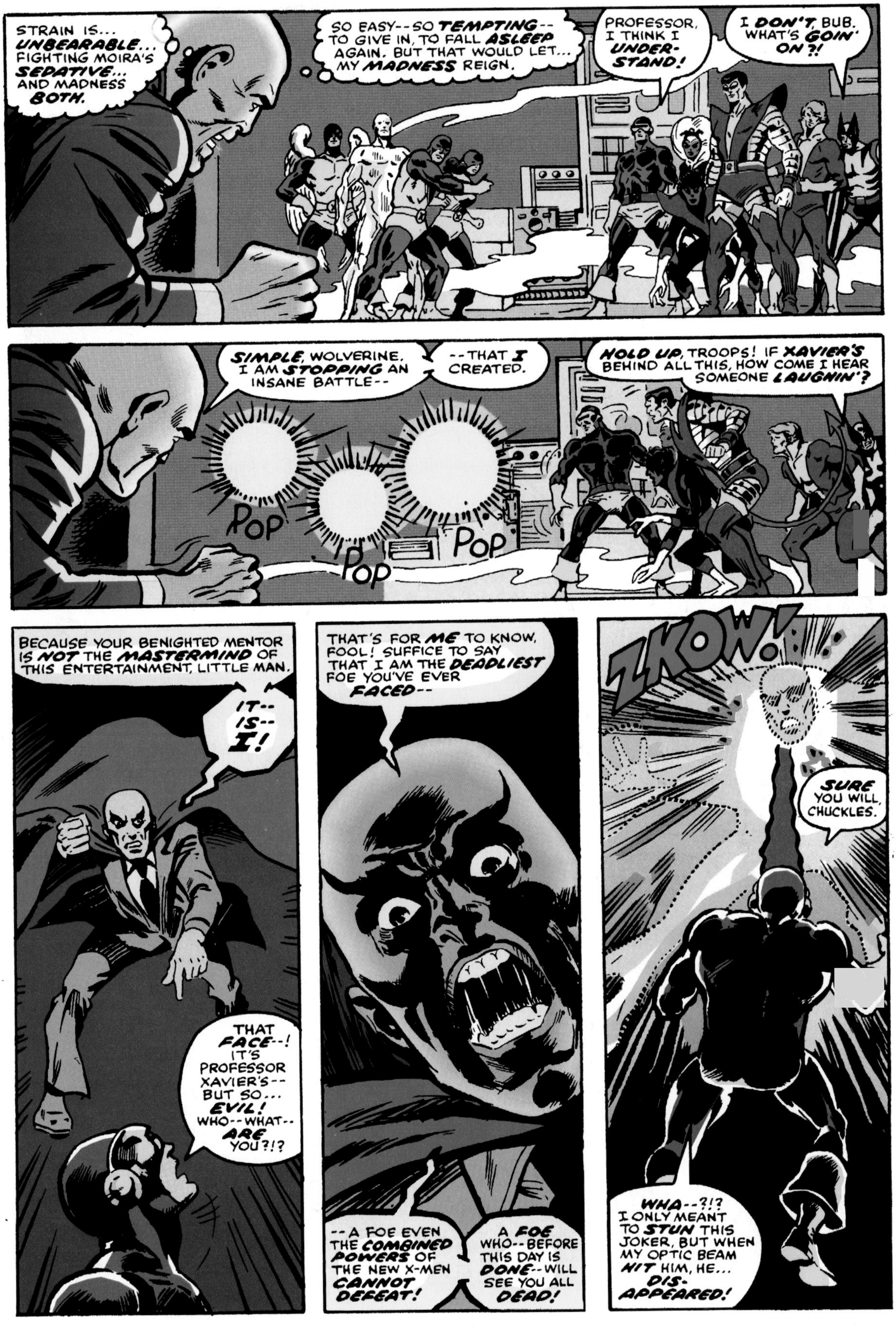

STRAIN IS... UNBEARABLE... FIGHTING MOIRA'S SEDATIVE... AND MADNESS BOTH.
SO EASY--SO TEMPTING--TO GIVE IN, TO FALL ASLEEP AGAIN. BUT THAT WOULD LET... MY MADNESS REIGN.
PROFESSOR, I THINK I UNDER-STAND!
I DON'T, BUB. WHAT'S GOIN' ON?!
SIMPLE, WOLVERINE. I AM STOPPING AN INSANE BATTLE--
--THAT I CREATED.
HOLD UP, TROOPS! IF XAVIER'S BEHIND ALL THIS, HOW COME I HEAR SOMEONE LAUGHIN'?
POP
POP
POP
BECAUSE YOUR BENIGHTED MENTOR IS NOT THE MASTERMIND OF THIS ENTERTAINMENT, LITTLE MAN.
IT--IS--I!
THAT FACE--! IT'S PROFESSOR XAVIER'S--BUT SO... EVIL! WHO--WHAT--ARE YOU?!?
THAT'S FOR ME TO KNOW, FOOL! SUFFICE TO SAY THAT I AM THE DEADLIEST FOE YOU'VE EVER FACED--
--A FOE EVEN THE COMBINED POWERS OF THE NEW X-MEN CANNOT DEFEAT!
A FOE WHO--BEFORE THIS DAY IS DONE--WILL SEE YOU ALL DEAD!
ZKOW!
SURE YOU WILL, CHUCKLES.
WHA--?!? I ONLY MEANT TO STUN THIS JOKER, BUT WHEN MY OPTIC BEAM HIT HIM, HE... DIS-APPEARED!

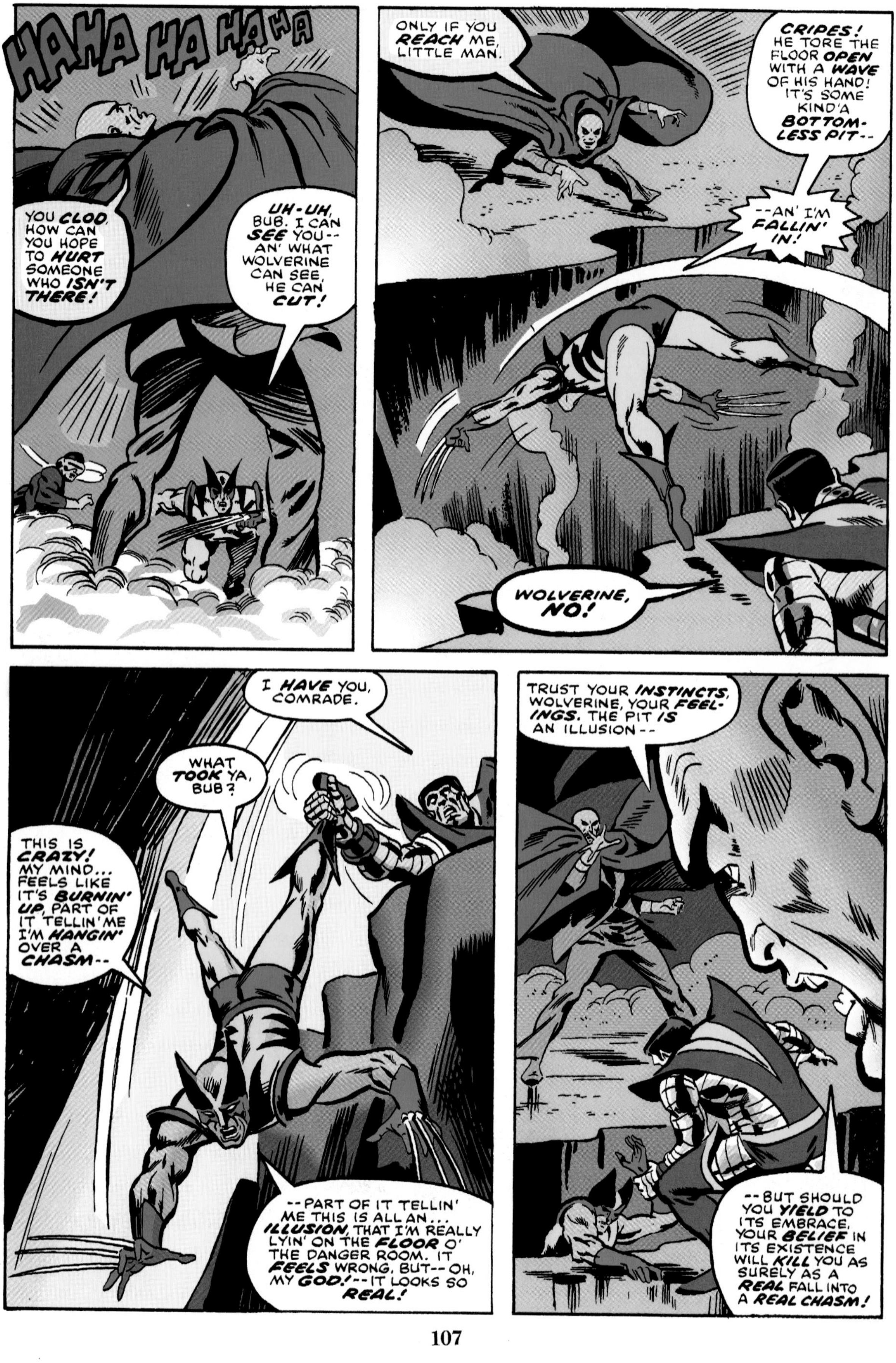
HAHA HA HAHA
YOU CLOD, HOW CAN YOU HOPE TO HURT SOMEONE WHO ISN'T THERE!
UH-UH, BUB. I CAN SEE YOU-- AN' WHAT WOLVERINE CAN SEE, HE CAN CUT!
ONLY IF YOU REACH ME, LITTLE MAN.
CRIPES! HE TORE THE FLOOR OPEN WITH A WAVE OF HIS HAND! IT'S SOME KIND'A BOTTOM-LESS PIT--
--AN' I'M FALLIN' IN!
WOLVERINE, NO!
I HAVE YOU, COMRADE.
WHAT TOOK YA, BUB?
THIS IS CRAZY! MY MIND... FEELS LIKE IT'S BURNIN' UP, PART OF IT TELLIN' ME I'M HANGIN' OVER A CHASM--
--PART OF IT TELLIN' ME THIS IS ALL AN... ILLUSION, THAT I'M REALLY LYIN' ON THE FLOOR O' THE DANGER ROOM. IT FEELS WRONG, BUT--OH, MY GOD!--IT LOOKS SO REAL!
TRUST YOUR INSTINCTS, WOLVERINE, YOUR FEEL-INGS. THE PIT IS AN ILLUSION--
--BUT SHOULD YOU YIELD TO ITS EMBRACE, YOUR BELIEF IN ITS EXISTENCE WILL KILL YOU AS SURELY AS A REAL FALL INTO A REAL CHASM!

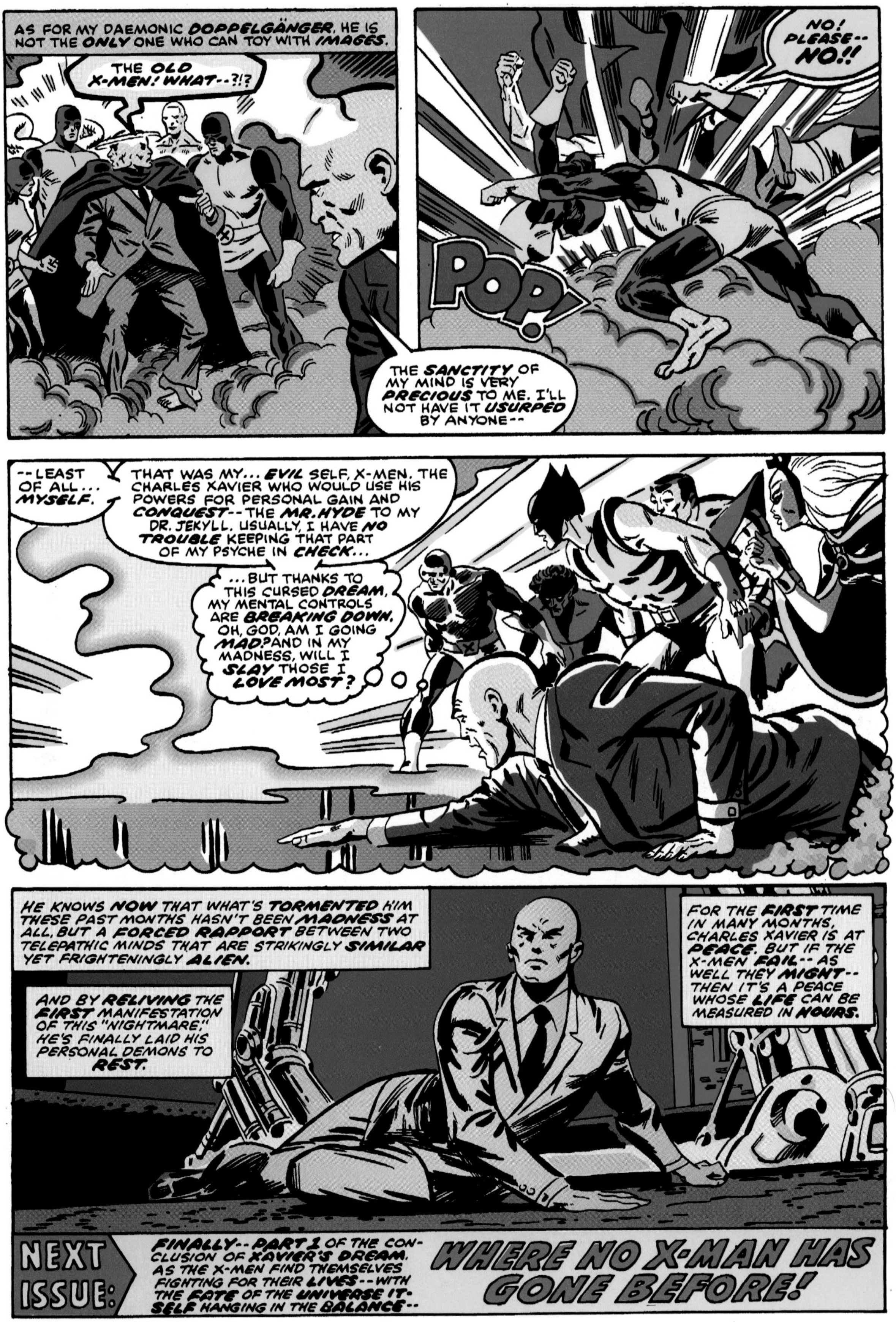

AS FOR MY DAEMONIC DOPPELGÄNGER, HE IS NOT THE ONLY ONE WHO CAN TOY WITH IMAGES.
THE OLD X-MEN! WHAT--?!?
NO! PLEASE-- NO!!
POP!
THE SANCTITY OF MY MIND IS VERY PRECIOUS TO ME. I'LL NOT HAVE IT USURPED BY ANYONE--
--LEAST OF ALL... MYSELF.
THAT WAS MY... EVIL SELF, X-MEN. THE CHARLES XAVIER WHO WOULD USE HIS POWERS FOR PERSONAL GAIN AND CONQUEST--THE MR. HYDE TO MY DR. JEKYLL. USUALLY, I HAVE NO TROUBLE KEEPING THAT PART OF MY PSYCHE IN CHECK...
...BUT THANKS TO THIS CURSED DREAM, MY MENTAL CONTROLS ARE BREAKING DOWN. OH, GOD, AM I GOING MAD? AND IN MY MADNESS, WILL I SLAY THOSE I LOVE MOST?
HE KNOWS NOW THAT WHAT'S TORMENTED HIM THESE PAST MONTHS HASN'T BEEN MADNESS AT ALL, BUT A FORCED RAPPORT BETWEEN TWO TELEPATHIC MINDS THAT ARE STRIKINGLY SIMILAR YET FRIGHTENINGLY ALIEN.
AND BY RELIVING THE FIRST MANIFESTATION OF THIS "NIGHTMARE," HE'S FINALLY LAID HIS PERSONAL DEMONS TO REST.
FOR THE FIRST TIME IN MANY MONTHS, CHARLES XAVIER IS AT PEACE. BUT IF THE X-MEN FAIL-- AS WELL THEY MIGHT-- THEN IT'S A PEACE WHOSE LIFE CAN BE MEASURED IN HOURS.
NEXT ISSUE:
FINALLY-- PART 1 OF THE CONCLUSION OF XAVIER'S DREAM, AS THE X-MEN FIND THEMSELVES FIGHTING FOR THEIR LIVES--WITH THE FATE OF THE UNIVERSE IT-SELF HANGING IN THE BALANCE--
WHERE NO X-MAN HAS GONE BEFORE!

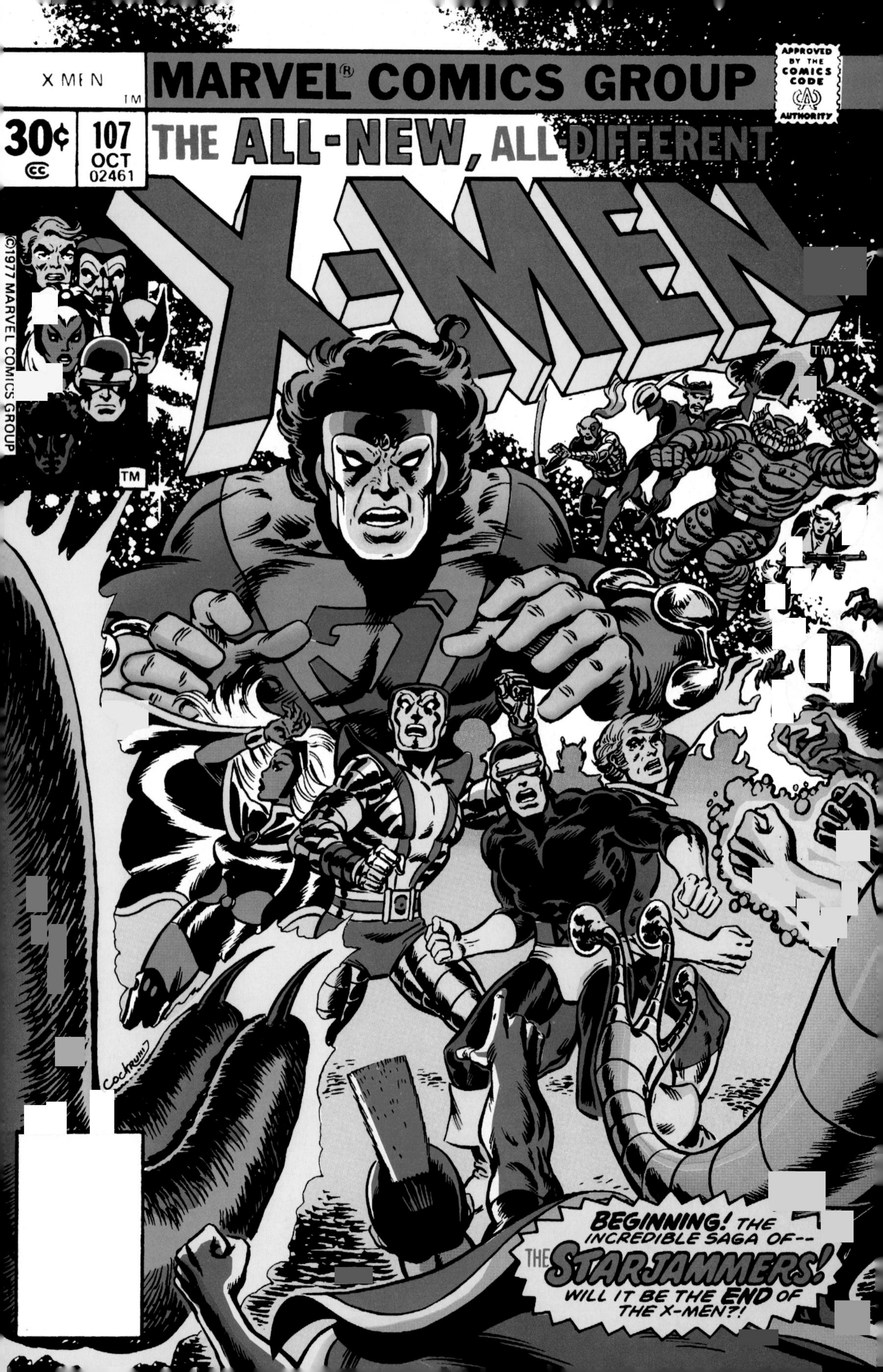
X-MEN TM
MARVEL® COMICS GROUP
APPROVED BY THE COMICS CODE AUTHORITY
30¢
107
OCT
02461
THE ALL-NEW, ALL-DIFFERENT
X-MEN TM
©1977 MARVEL COMICS GROUP
COCKRUM
BEGINNING! THE INCREDIBLE SAGA OF--
THE STARJAMMERS!
WILL IT BE THE END OF THE X-MEN?!

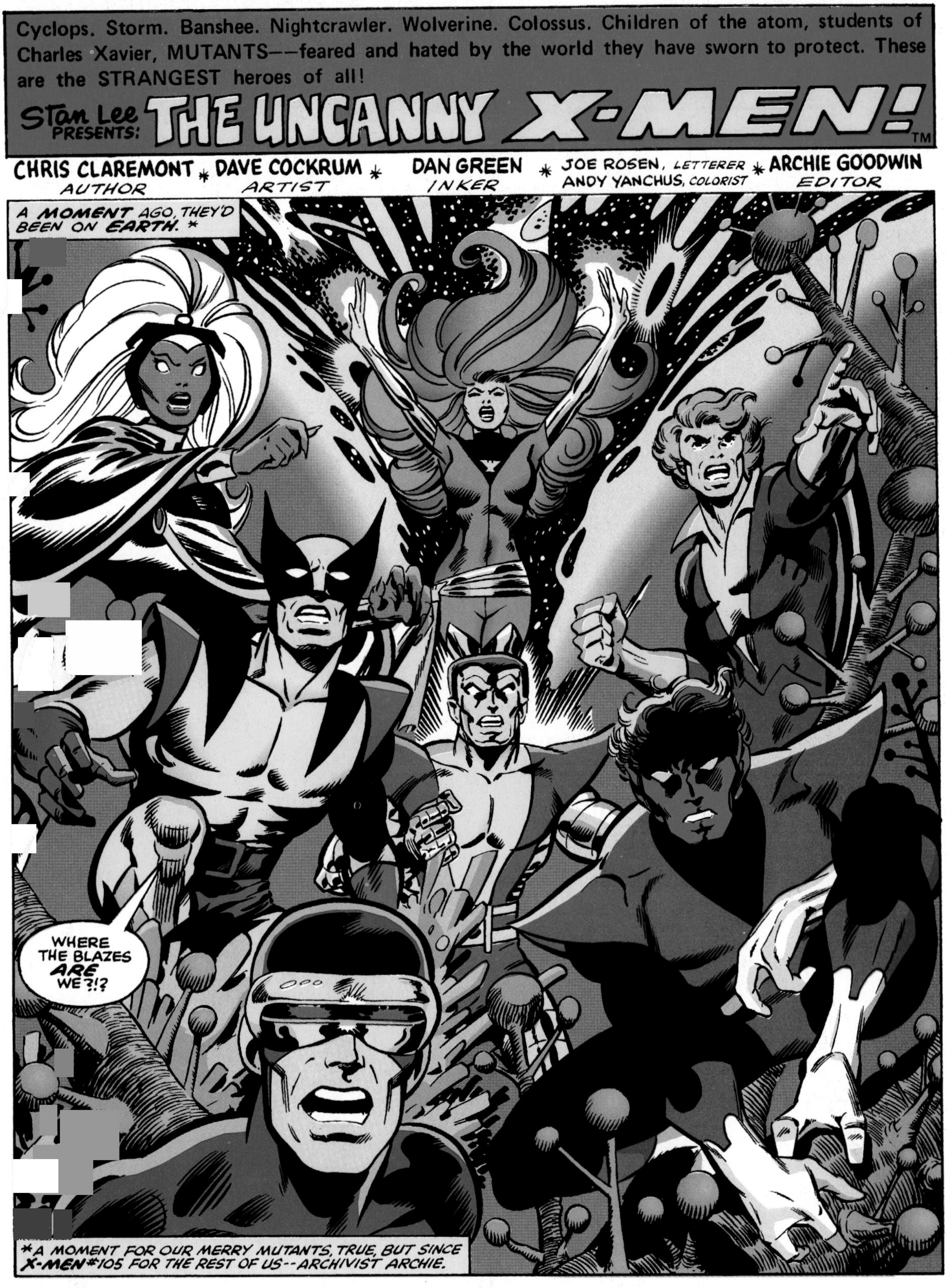

Cyclops. Storm. Banshee. Nightcrawler. Wolverine. Colossus. Children of the atom, students of Charles Xavier, MUTANTS—feared and hated by the world they have sworn to protect. These are the STRANGEST heroes of all!
Stan Lee PRESENTS: THE UNCANNY X-MEN!
TM
CHRIS CLAREMONT AUTHOR
DAVE COCKRUM ARTIST
DAN GREEN INKER
JOE ROSEN, LETTERER
ANDY YANCHUS, COLORIST
ARCHIE GOODWIN EDITOR
A MOMENT AGO, THEY'D BEEN ON EARTH.*
WHERE THE BLAZES ARE WE?!?
*A MOMENT FOR OUR MERRY MUTANTS, TRUE, BUT SINCE X-MEN #105 FOR THE REST OF US--ARCHIVIST ARCHIE.

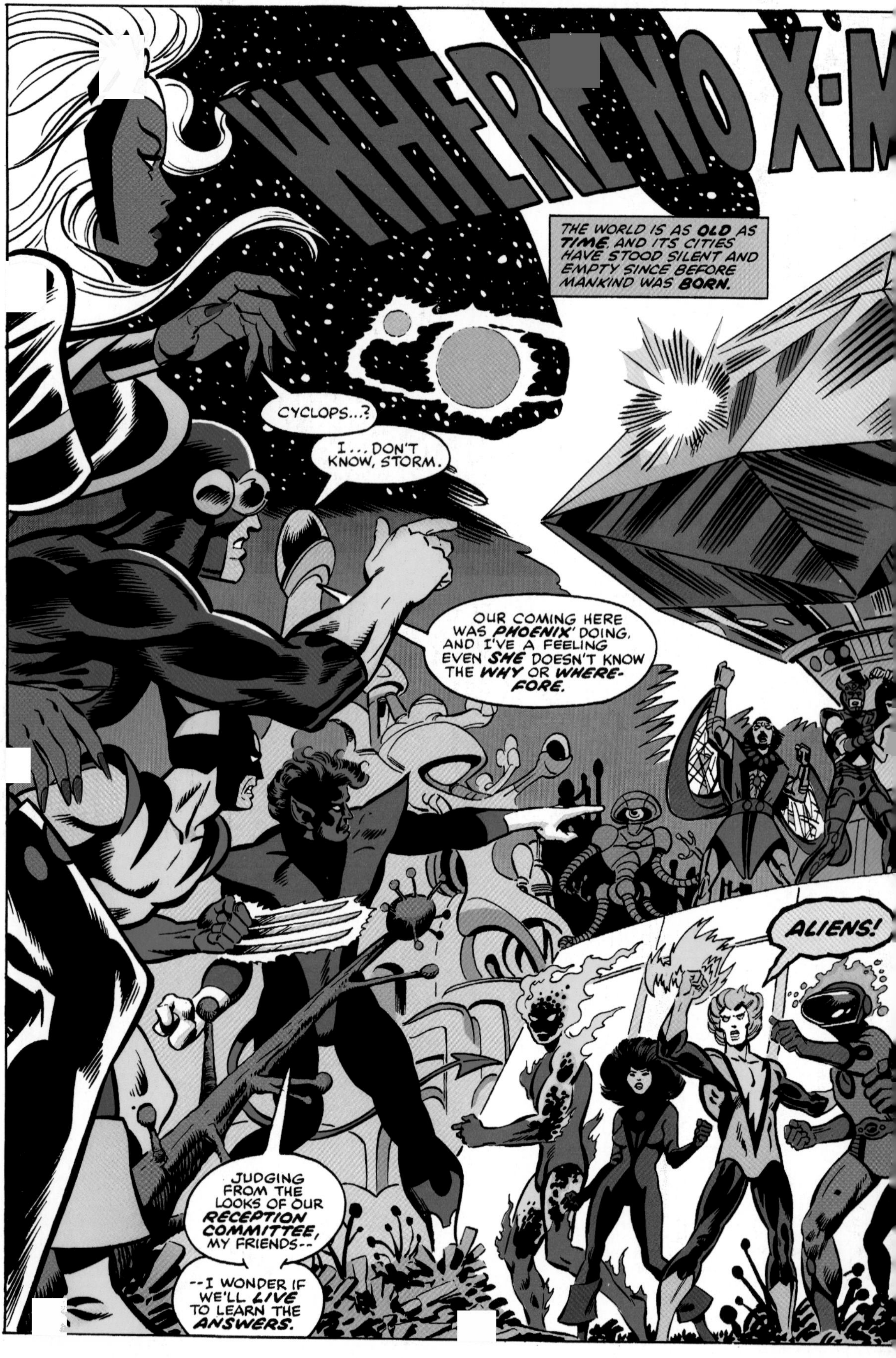
WHERE NO X-M
THE WORLD IS AS OLD AS TIME, AND ITS CITIES HAVE STOOD SILENT AND EMPTY SINCE BEFORE MANKIND WAS BORN.
CYCLOPS...?
I... DON'T KNOW, STORM.
OUR COMING HERE WAS PHOENIX' DOING, AND I'VE A FEELING EVEN SHE DOESN'T KNOW THE WHY OR WHERE-FORE.
ALIENS!
JUDGING FROM THE LOOKS OF OUR RECEPTION COMMITTEE, MY FRIENDS--
--I WONDER IF WE'LL LIVE TO LEARN THE ANSWERS.

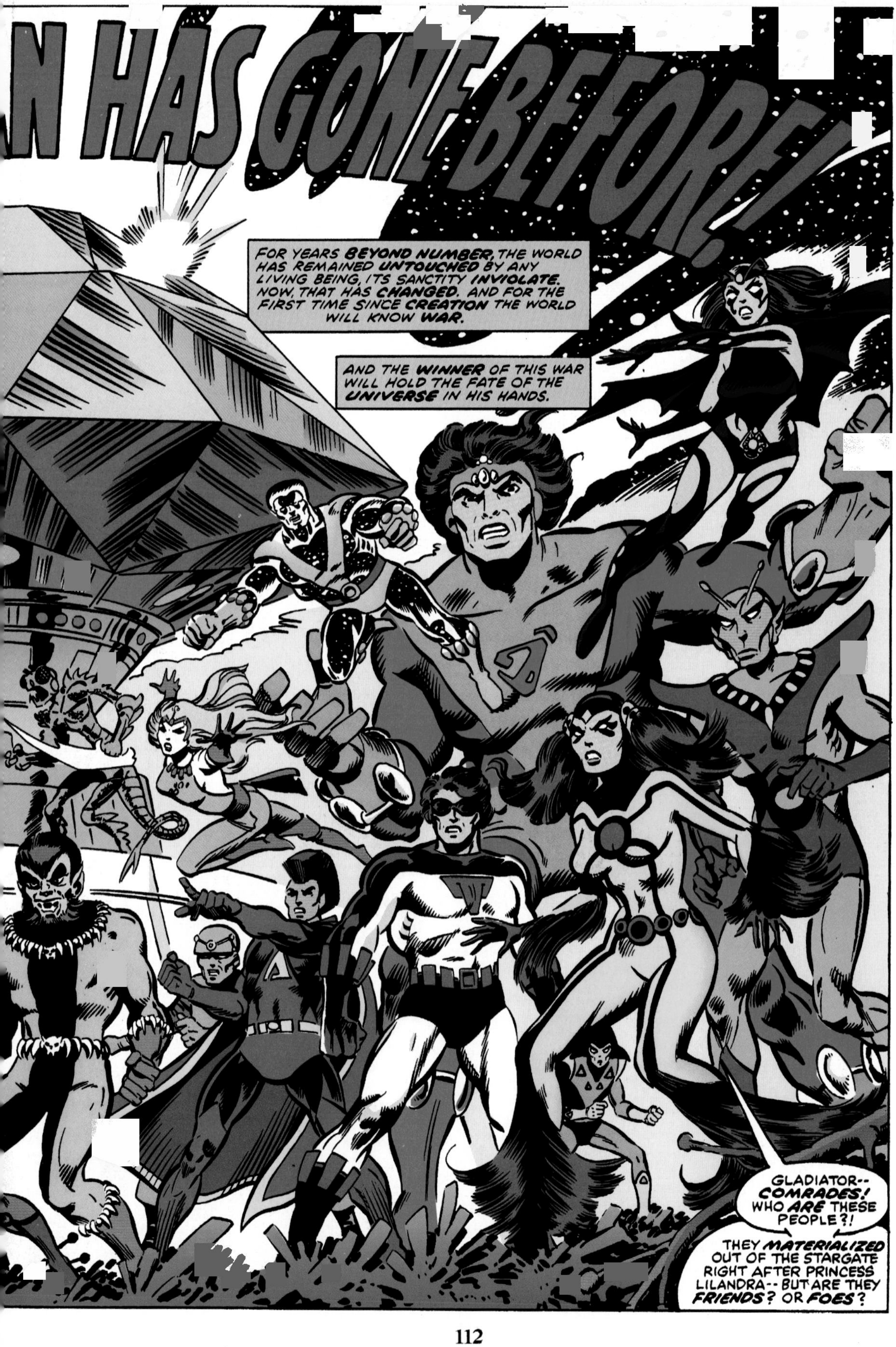

...N HAS GONE BEFORE!
FOR YEARS BEYOND NUMBER, THE WORLD HAS REMAINED UNTOUCHED BY ANY LIVING BEING, ITS SANCTITY INVIOLATE. NOW, THAT HAS CHANGED. AND FOR THE FIRST TIME SINCE CREATION THE WORLD WILL KNOW WAR.
AND THE WINNER OF THIS WAR WILL HOLD THE FATE OF THE UNIVERSE IN HIS HANDS.
GLADIATOR-- COMRADES! WHO ARE THESE PEOPLE?!
THEY MATERIALIZED OUT OF THE STARGATE RIGHT AFTER PRINCESS LILANDRA-- BUT ARE THEY FRIENDS? OR FOES?

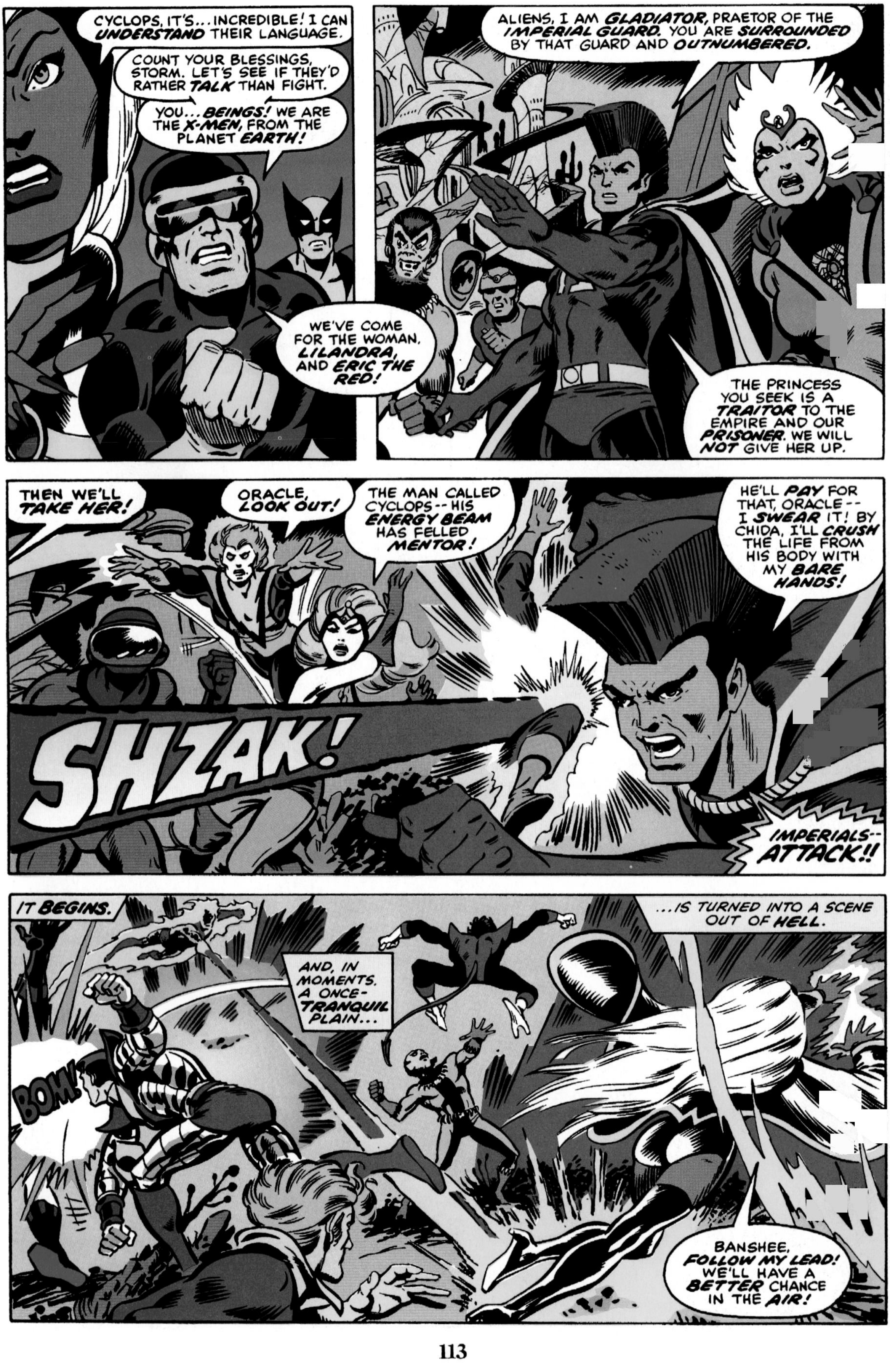
CYCLOPS, IT'S... INCREDIBLE! I CAN UNDERSTAND THEIR LANGUAGE.
COUNT YOUR BLESSINGS, STORM. LET'S SEE IF THEY'D RATHER TALK THAN FIGHT.
YOU... BEINGS! WE ARE THE X-MEN, FROM THE PLANET EARTH!
WE'VE COME FOR THE WOMAN, LILANDRA, AND ERIC THE RED!
ALIENS, I AM GLADIATOR, PRAETOR OF THE IMPERIAL GUARD. YOU ARE SURROUNDED BY THAT GUARD AND OUTNUMBERED.
THE PRINCESS YOU SEEK IS A TRAITOR TO THE EMPIRE AND OUR PRISONER. WE WILL NOT GIVE HER UP.
THEN WE'LL TAKE HER!
ORACLE, LOOK OUT!
THE MAN CALLED CYCLOPS -- HIS ENERGY BEAM HAS FELLED MENTOR!
HE'LL PAY FOR THAT, ORACLE -- I SWEAR IT! BY CHIDA, I'LL CRUSH THE LIFE FROM HIS BODY WITH MY BARE HANDS!
SHZAK!
IMPERIALS -- ATTACK!!
IT BEGINS.
AND, IN MOMENTS, A ONCE-TRANQUIL PLAIN...
...IS TURNED INTO A SCENE OUT OF HELL.
BOM!
BANSHEE, FOLLOW MY LEAD! WE'LL HAVE A BETTER CHANCE IN THE AIR!

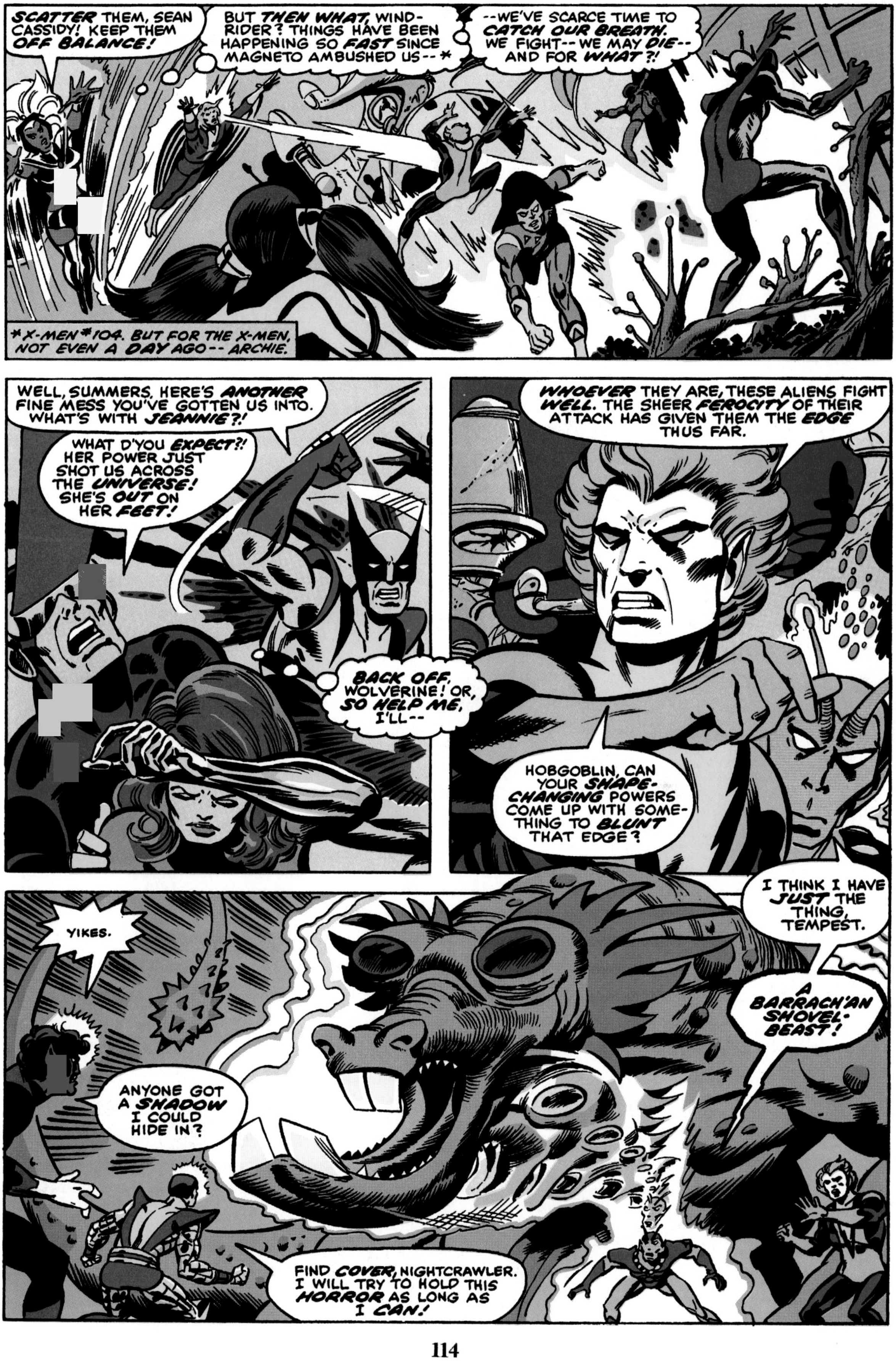
SCATTER THEM, SEAN CASSIDY! KEEP THEM OFF BALANCE!
BUT THEN WHAT, WIND-RIDER? THINGS HAVE BEEN HAPPENING SO FAST SINCE MAGNETO AMBUSHED US-- *
--WE'VE SCARCE TIME TO CATCH OUR BREATH. WE FIGHT-- WE MAY DIE-- AND FOR WHAT?!
* X-MEN # 104. BUT FOR THE X-MEN, NOT EVEN A DAY AGO-- ARCHIE.
WELL, SUMMERS, HERE'S ANOTHER FINE MESS YOU'VE GOTTEN US INTO. WHAT'S WITH JEANNIE?!
WHAT D'YOU EXPECT?! HER POWER JUST SHOT US ACROSS THE UNIVERSE! SHE'S OUT ON HER FEET!
BACK OFF, WOLVERINE! OR, SO HELP ME, I'LL--
WHOEVER THEY ARE, THESE ALIENS FIGHT WELL. THE SHEER FEROCITY OF THEIR ATTACK HAS GIVEN THEM THE EDGE THUS FAR.
HOBGOBLIN, CAN YOUR SHAPE-CHANGING POWERS COME UP WITH SOME-THING TO BLUNT THAT EDGE?
YIKES.
I THINK I HAVE JUST THE THING, TEMPEST.
A BARRACH'AN SHOVEL-BEAST!
ANYONE GOT A SHADOW I COULD HIDE IN?
FIND COVER, NIGHTCRAWLER. I WILL TRY TO HOLD THIS HORROR AS LONG AS I CAN!

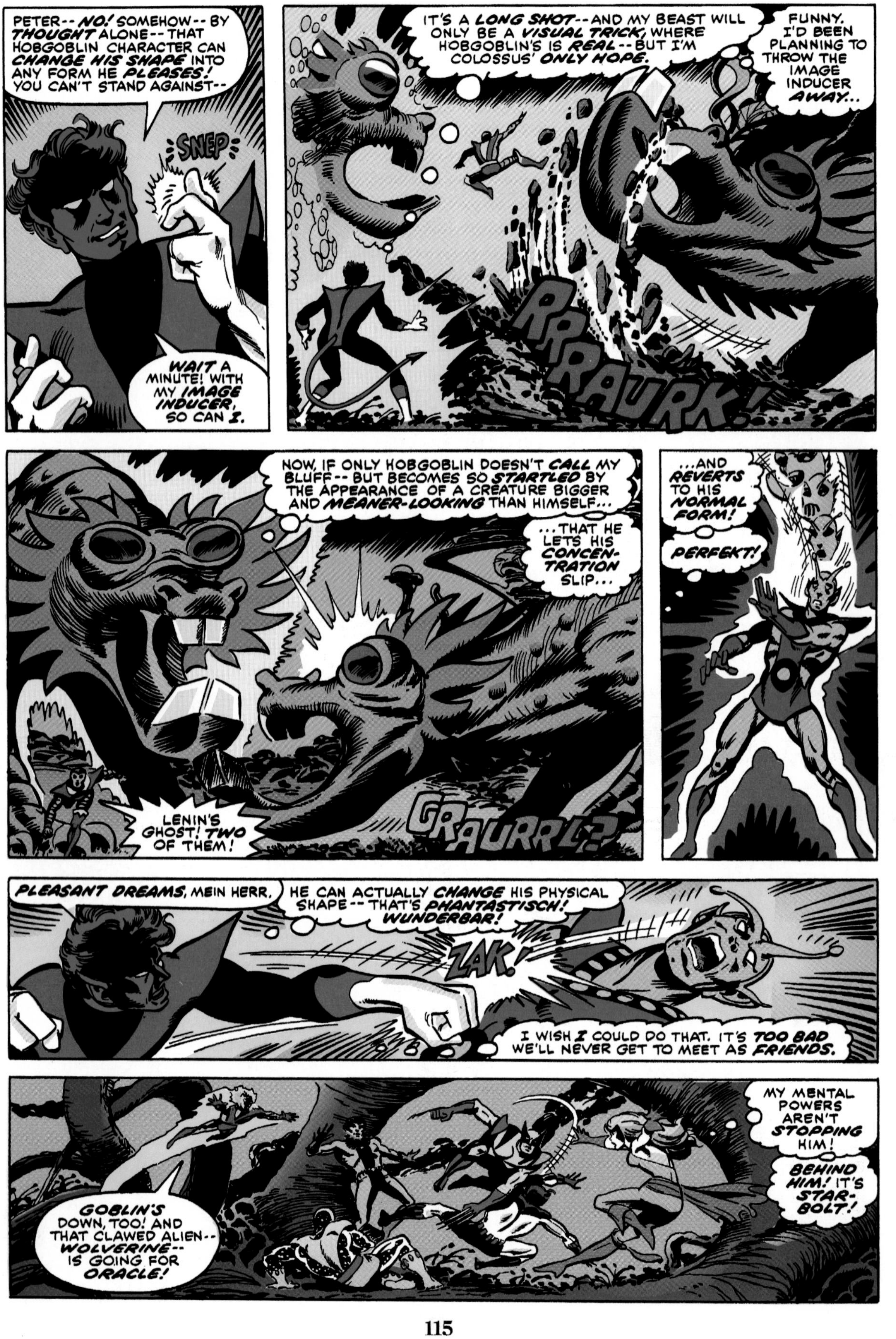

PETER-- NO! SOMEHOW-- BY THOUGHT ALONE-- THAT HOBGOBLIN CHARACTER CAN CHANGE HIS SHAPE INTO ANY FORM HE PLEASES! YOU CAN'T STAND AGAINST--
SNEP
WAIT A MINUTE! WITH MY IMAGE INDUCER, SO CAN I.
IT'S A LONG SHOT-- AND MY BEAST WILL ONLY BE A VISUAL TRICK, WHERE HOBGOBLIN'S IS REAL-- BUT I'M COLOSSUS' ONLY HOPE.
FUNNY. I'D BEEN PLANNING TO THROW THE IMAGE INDUCER AWAY...
RRRAURK!
NOW, IF ONLY HOBGOBLIN DOESN'T CALL MY BLUFF-- BUT BECOMES SO STARTLED BY THE APPEARANCE OF A CREATURE BIGGER AND MEANER-LOOKING THAN HIMSELF...
...THAT HE LETS HIS CONCEN-TRATION SLIP...
LENIN'S GHOST! TWO OF THEM!
GRAURRL?
...AND REVERTS TO HIS NORMAL FORM!
PERFEKT!
PLEASANT DREAMS, MEIN HERR.
HE CAN ACTUALLY CHANGE HIS PHYSICAL SHAPE-- THAT'S PHANTASTISCH! WUNDERBAR!
ZAK!
I WISH I COULD DO THAT. IT'S TOO BAD WE'LL NEVER GET TO MEET AS FRIENDS.
GOBLIN'S DOWN, TOO! AND THAT CLAWED ALIEN-- WOLVERINE-- IS GOING FOR ORACLE!
MY MENTAL POWERS AREN'T STOPPING HIM!
BEHIND HIM! IT'S STAR-BOLT!

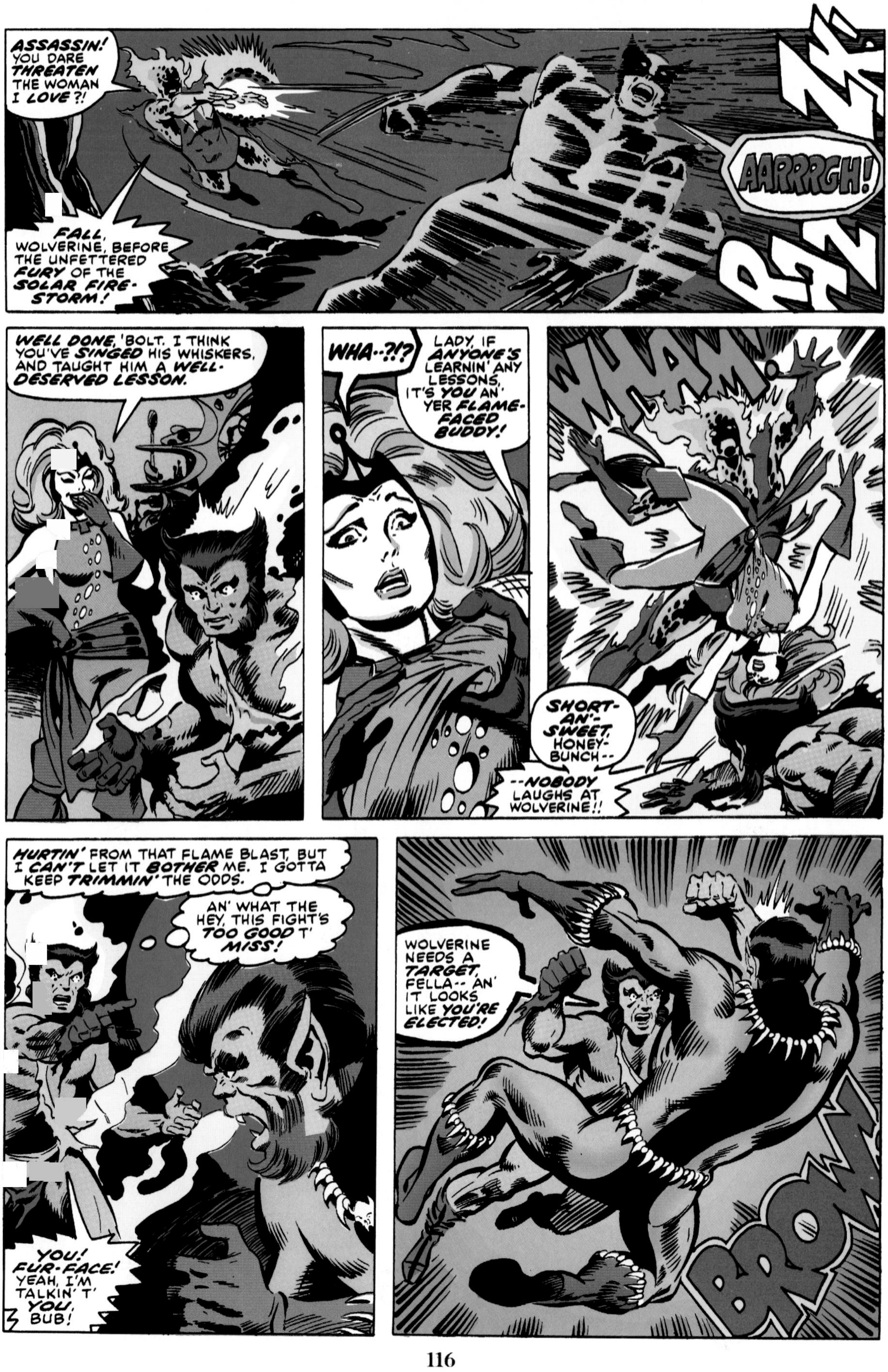
ASSASSIN! YOU DARE THREATEN THE WOMAN I LOVE?!
RZZZK!
AARRRGH!
FALL, WOLVERINE, BEFORE THE UNFETTERED FURY OF THE SOLAR FIRE-STORM!
WELL DONE, 'BOLT. I THINK YOU'VE SINGED HIS WHISKERS, AND TAUGHT HIM A WELL-DESERVED LESSON.
WHA--?!?
LADY, IF ANYONE'S LEARNIN' ANY LESSONS, IT'S YOU AN' YER FLAME-FACED BUDDY!
WHAM!
SHORT-AN'-SWEET, HONEY-BUNCH--
--NOBODY LAUGHS AT WOLVERINE!!
HURTIN' FROM THAT FLAME BLAST, BUT I CAN'T LET IT BOTHER ME. I GOTTA KEEP TRIMMIN' THE ODDS.
AN' WHAT THE HEY, THIS FIGHT'S TOO GOOD T' MISS!
YOU! FUR-FACE! YEAH, I'M TALKIN' T' YOU, BUB!
WOLVERINE NEEDS A TARGET, FELLA-- AN' IT LOOKS LIKE YOU'RE ELECTED!
BROOM!

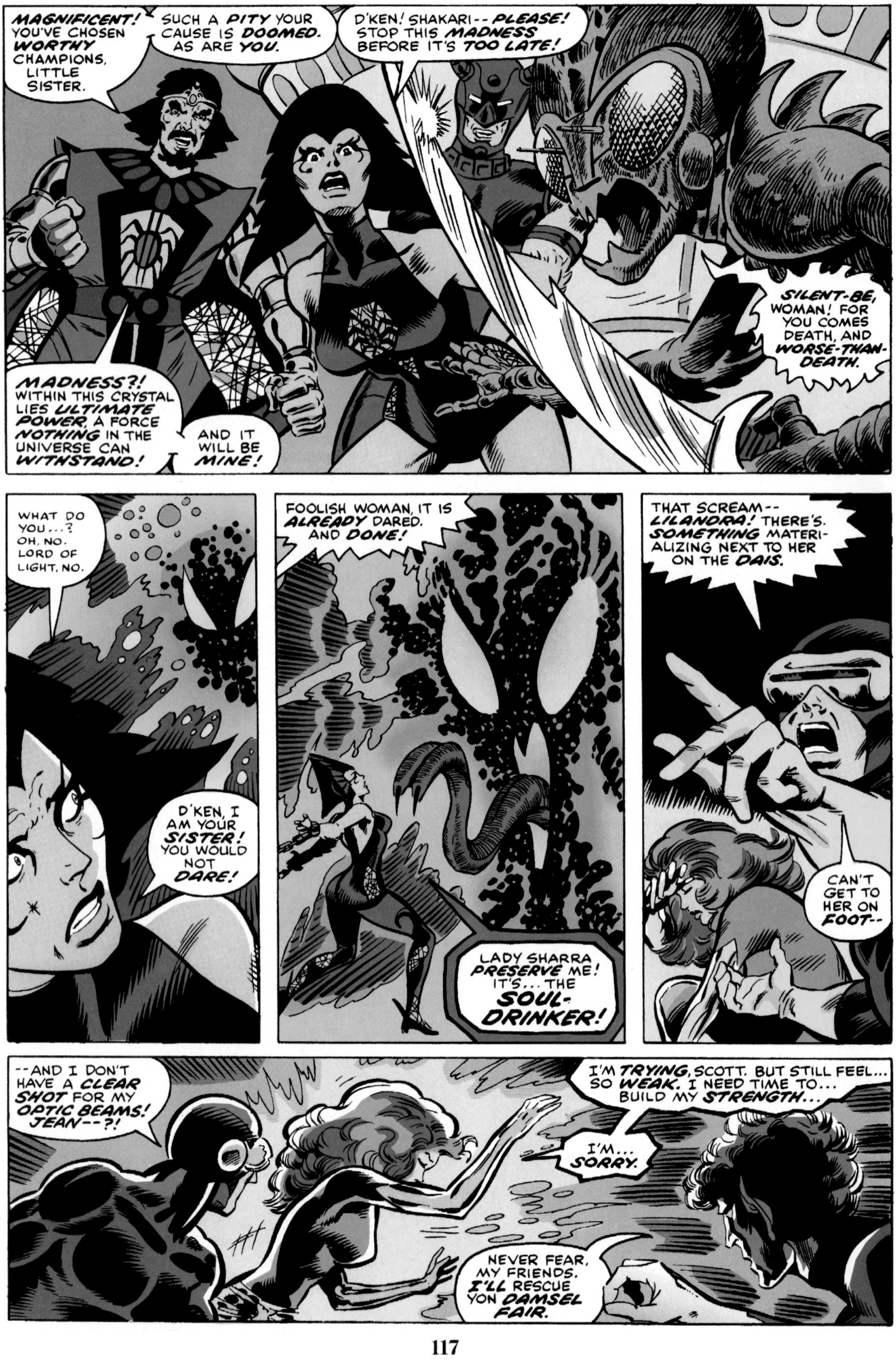
MAGNIFICENT! YOU'VE CHOSEN WORTHY CHAMPIONS, LITTLE SISTER.
SUCH A PITY YOUR CAUSE IS DOOMED. AS ARE YOU.
D'KEN! SHAKARI-- PLEASE! STOP THIS MADNESS BEFORE IT'S TOO LATE!
SILENT-BE, WOMAN! FOR YOU COMES DEATH, AND WORSE-THAN-DEATH.
MADNESS?! WITHIN THIS CRYSTAL LIES ULTIMATE POWER, A FORCE NOTHING IN THE UNIVERSE CAN WITHSTAND!
AND IT WILL BE MINE!
WHAT DO YOU...? OH, NO. LORD OF LIGHT, NO.
D'KEN, I AM YOUR SISTER! YOU WOULD NOT DARE!
FOOLISH WOMAN, IT IS ALREADY DARED. AND DONE!
LADY SHARRA PRESERVE ME! IT'S... THE SOUL-DRINKER!
THAT SCREAM-- LILANDRA! THERE'S. SOMETHING MATERIALIZING NEXT TO HER ON THE DAIS.
CAN'T GET TO HER ON FOOT--
--AND I DON'T HAVE A CLEAR SHOT FOR MY OPTIC BEAMS! JEAN--?!
I'M TRYING, SCOTT. BUT STILL FEEL... SO WEAK. I NEED TIME TO... BUILD MY STRENGTH...
I'M... SORRY.
NEVER FEAR, MY FRIENDS. I'LL RESCUE YON DAMSEL FAIR.

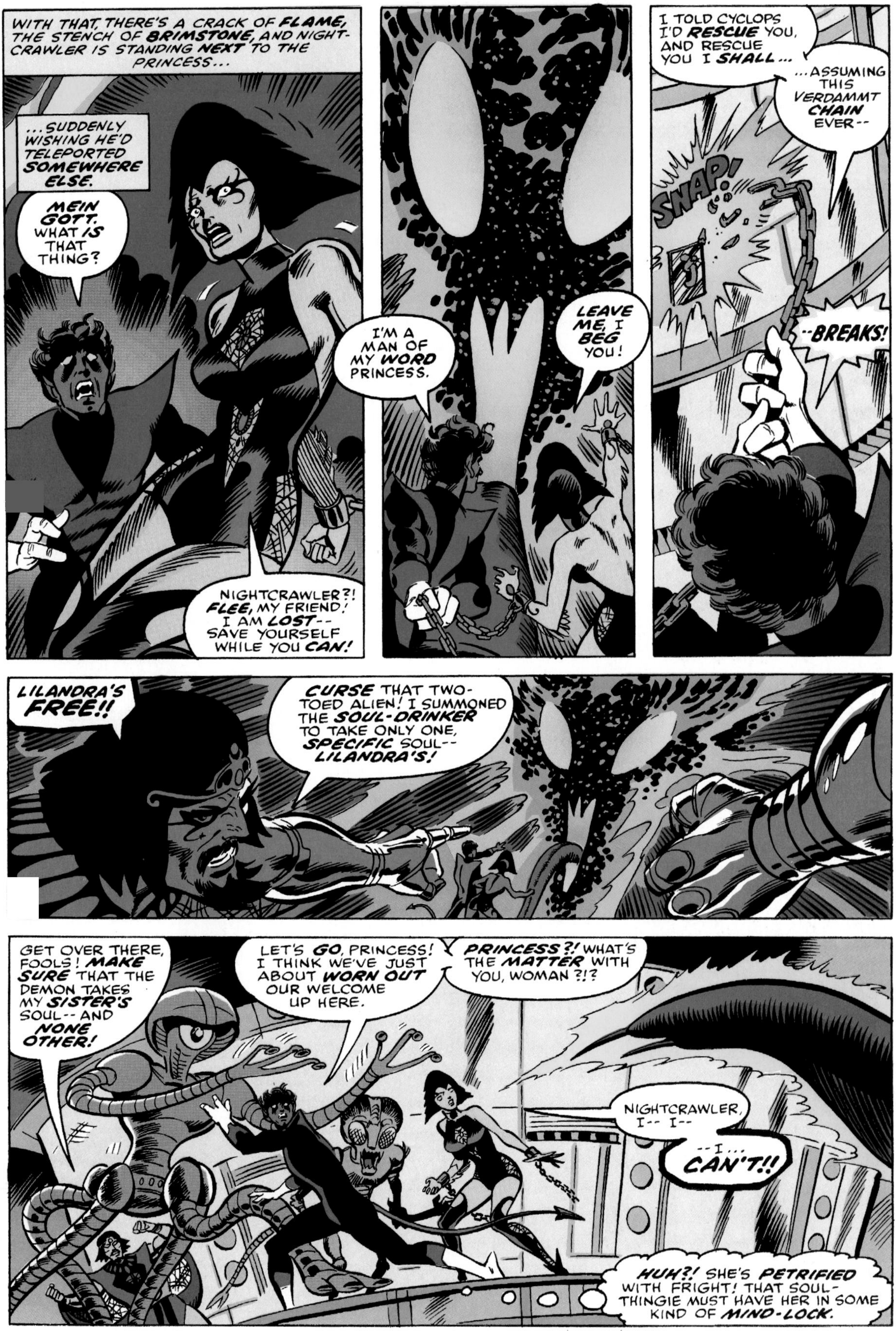
WITH THAT, THERE'S A CRACK OF FLAME, THE STENCH OF BRIMSTONE, AND NIGHTCRAWLER IS STANDING NEXT TO THE PRINCESS...
...SUDDENLY WISHING HE'D TELEPORTED SOMEWHERE ELSE.
MEIN GOTT. WHAT IS THAT THING?
NIGHTCRAWLER?! FLEE, MY FRIEND! I AM LOST-- SAVE YOURSELF WHILE YOU CAN!
I'M A MAN OF MY WORD PRINCESS.
LEAVE ME, I BEG YOU!
I TOLD CYCLOPS I'D RESCUE YOU, AND RESCUE YOU I SHALL...
...ASSUMING THIS VERDAMMT CHAIN EVER--
SNAP!
--BREAKS!
LILANDRA'S FREE!!
CURSE THAT TWO-TOED ALIEN! I SUMMONED THE SOUL-DRINKER TO TAKE ONLY ONE, SPECIFIC SOUL-- LILANDRA'S!
GET OVER THERE, FOOLS! MAKE SURE THAT THE DEMON TAKES MY SISTER'S SOUL-- AND NONE OTHER!
LET'S GO, PRINCESS! I THINK WE'VE JUST ABOUT WORN OUT OUR WELCOME UP HERE.
PRINCESS?! WHAT'S THE MATTER WITH YOU, WOMAN?!?
NIGHTCRAWLER, I-- I--
--I... CAN'T!!
HUH?! SHE'S PETRIFIED WITH FRIGHT! THAT SOUL-THINGIE MUST HAVE HER IN SOME KIND OF MIND-LOCK.

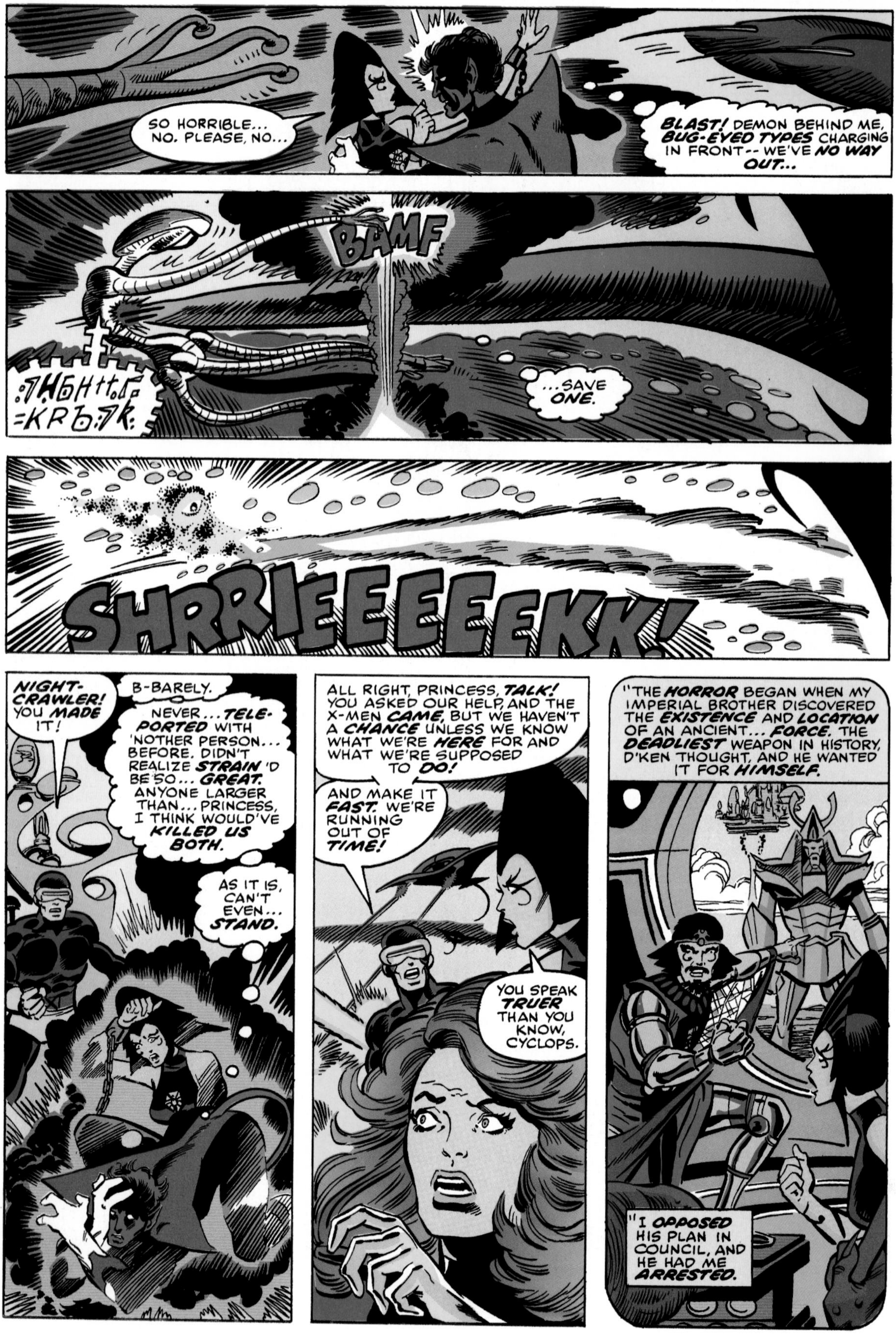
SO HORRIBLE... NO. PLEASE, NO...
BLAST! DEMON BEHIND ME, BUG-EYED TYPES CHARGING IN FRONT-- WE'VE NO WAY OUT...
BAMF
...SAVE ONE.
SHRRIEEEEEKK!
NIGHT-CRAWLER! YOU MADE IT!
B-BARELY.
NEVER... TELE-PORTED WITH 'NOTHER PERSON... BEFORE. DIDN'T REALIZE STRAIN 'D BE SO... GREAT. ANYONE LARGER THAN... PRINCESS, I THINK WOULD'VE KILLED US BOTH.
AS IT IS, CAN'T EVEN... STAND.
ALL RIGHT, PRINCESS, TALK! YOU ASKED OUR HELP, AND THE X-MEN CAME, BUT WE HAVEN'T A CHANCE UNLESS WE KNOW WHAT WE'RE HERE FOR AND WHAT WE'RE SUPPOSED TO DO!
AND MAKE IT FAST. WE'RE RUNNING OUT OF TIME!
YOU SPEAK TRUER THAN YOU KNOW, CYCLOPS.
"THE HORROR BEGAN WHEN MY IMPERIAL BROTHER DISCOVERED THE EXISTENCE AND LOCATION OF AN ANCIENT... FORCE. THE DEADLIEST WEAPON IN HISTORY, D'KEN THOUGHT, AND HE WANTED IT FOR HIMSELF.
"I OPPOSED HIS PLAN IN COUNCIL, AND HE HAD ME ARRESTED.

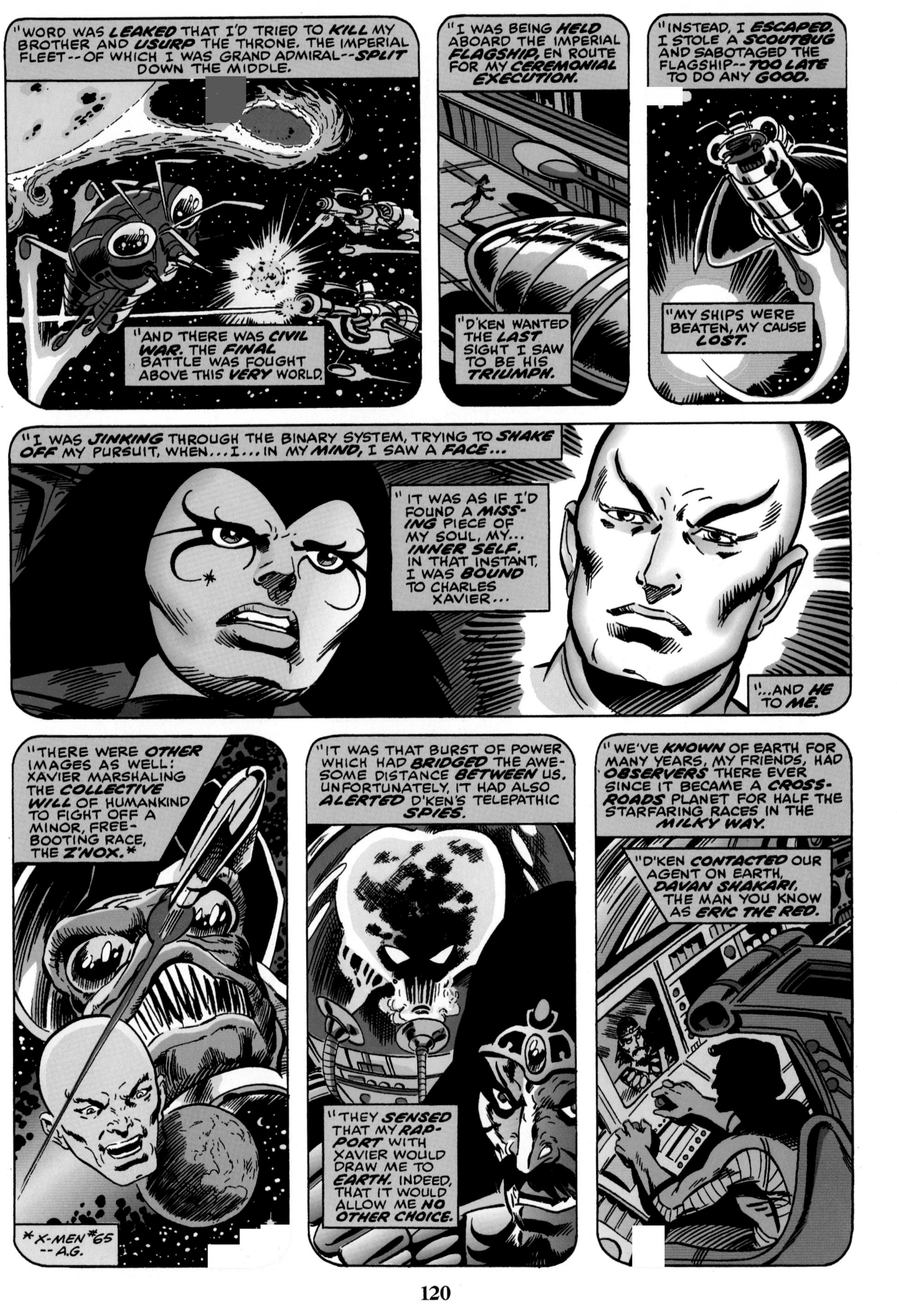
"WORD WAS LEAKED THAT I'D TRIED TO KILL MY BROTHER AND USURP THE THRONE. THE IMPERIAL FLEET--OF WHICH I WAS GRAND ADMIRAL--SPLIT DOWN THE MIDDLE.
"AND THERE WAS CIVIL WAR. THE FINAL BATTLE WAS FOUGHT ABOVE THIS VERY WORLD.
"I WAS BEING HELD ABOARD THE IMPERIAL FLAGSHIP, EN ROUTE FOR MY CEREMONIAL EXECUTION.
"D'KEN WANTED THE LAST SIGHT I SAW TO BE HIS TRIUMPH.
"INSTEAD, I ESCAPED. I STOLE A SCOUTBUG AND SABOTAGED THE FLAGSHIP--TOO LATE TO DO ANY GOOD.
"MY SHIPS WERE BEATEN, MY CAUSE LOST.
"I WAS JINKING THROUGH THE BINARY SYSTEM, TRYING TO SHAKE OFF MY PURSUIT, WHEN...I...IN MY MIND, I SAW A FACE...
"IT WAS AS IF I'D FOUND A MISSING PIECE OF MY SOUL, MY... INNER SELF. IN THAT INSTANT, I WAS BOUND TO CHARLES XAVIER...
"...AND HE TO ME.
"THERE WERE OTHER IMAGES AS WELL: XAVIER MARSHALING THE COLLECTIVE WILL OF HUMANKIND TO FIGHT OFF A MINOR, FREE-BOOTING RACE, THE Z'NOX.*
*X-MEN #65 --A.G.
"IT WAS THAT BURST OF POWER WHICH HAD BRIDGED THE AWESOME DISTANCE BETWEEN US. UNFORTUNATELY, IT HAD ALSO ALERTED D'KEN'S TELEPATHIC SPIES.
"THEY SENSED THAT MY RAPPORT WITH XAVIER WOULD DRAW ME TO EARTH. INDEED, THAT IT WOULD ALLOW ME NO OTHER CHOICE.
"WE'VE KNOWN OF EARTH FOR MANY YEARS, MY FRIENDS, HAD OBSERVERS THERE EVER SINCE IT BECAME A CROSSROADS PLANET FOR HALF THE STARFARING RACES IN THE MILKY WAY.
"D'KEN CONTACTED OUR AGENT ON EARTH, DAVAN SHAKARI, THE MAN YOU KNOW AS ERIC THE RED.

"HIS ORDERS WERE SIMPLE: *KILL* XAVIER OR, FAILING THAT, *PREVENT* ME FROM CONTACTING HIM-- WHAT-EVER THE *COST.* WHICH MEANT, FIRST OF ALL, THE *X-MEN* HAD TO BE *ELIMINATED.*

"SHAKARI TOLD ME HE *LEARNED* OF YOU FROM LORNA DANE-- *POLARIS*-- THOUGH HE REFUSED TO SAY HOW HE LEARNED OF *HER.*

"HE TRIED TIME AND AGAIN TO *DESTROY* YOU -- USING POLARIS AND *HAVOK,* AND THEN YOUR OLDEST, *DEADLI-EST* FOES -- YET EACH TIME HE *FAILED.* *

* X-MEN'S #'S 97,101-105--AG.

"WITH *FIRELORD'S* UNWITTING AID, HE FINALLY SUC-CEEDED IN *CAPTURING* ME. HE THOUGHT HE'D *WON*-- UNTIL *PHOENIX'* POWER SENT YOU THROUGH THE STARGATE *AFTER ME.*

FINE, LILANDRA, BUT WHAT'S THIS ALL BEEN *FOR*?!?

THE *OLDEST* OF ALL REASONS, CYCLOPS.

POWER. THIS GREAT *M'KRAAN CRYSTAL* IS A ...*GATEWAY* TO THE POWER MY BROTHER SEEKS, A GATE THAT OPENS *ONCE* EVERY *MILLION YEARS...*

...WHEN THOSE NINE *DEATH-STARS* ENTER A CERTAIN *ALIGN-MENT.*

AND *WITHIN* THE CRYSTAL, SO THE LEGEND SAYS, CAN BE FOUND *POWER ABSOLUTE.*

AYE, PRINCESS! AND WHAT RIGHT HAVE *YOU* TO DENY IT TO YOUR *EMPEROR* ?! YOU SWORE AN OATH TO *SERVE* D'KEN!

THIS *TRANSCENDS* AN OATH SWORN TO A *MADMAN!*

OPEN YOUR EYES, GLADIATOR, BEFORE MY BROTHER'S DREAMS OF IMPERIAL *GLORY* CLOSE THEM *FOREVER!*

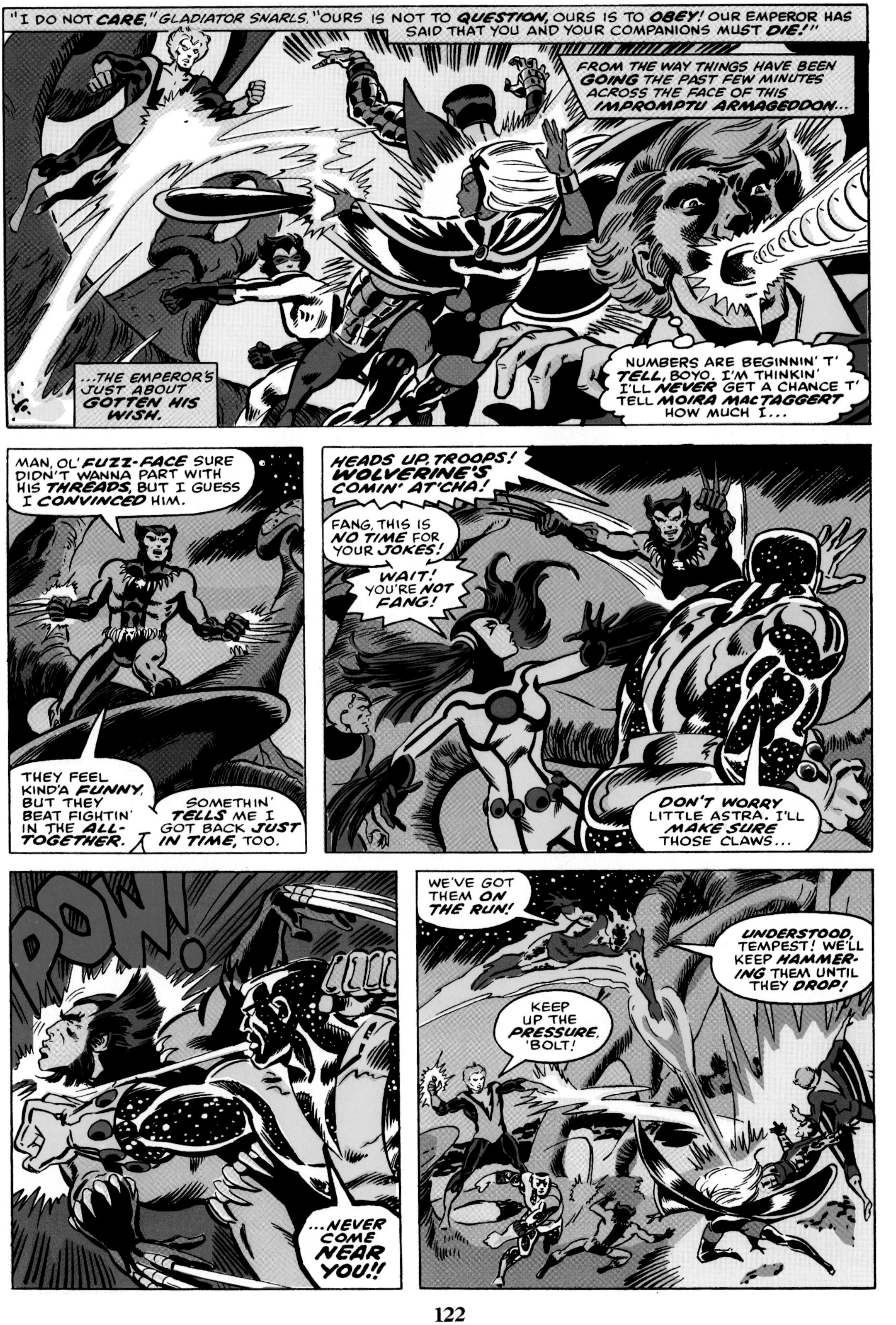
"I DO NOT CARE," GLADIATOR SNARLS, "OURS IS NOT TO QUESTION, OURS IS TO OBEY! OUR EMPEROR HAS SAID THAT YOU AND YOUR COMPANIONS MUST DIE!"
FROM THE WAY THINGS HAVE BEEN GOING THE PAST FEW MINUTES ACROSS THE FACE OF THIS IMPROMPTU ARMAGEDDON...
...THE EMPEROR'S JUST ABOUT GOTTEN HIS WISH.
NUMBERS ARE BEGINNIN' T' TELL, BOYO. I'M THINKIN' I'LL NEVER GET A CHANCE T' TELL MOIRA MACTAGGERT HOW MUCH I...
MAN, OL' FUZZ-FACE SURE DIDN'T WANNA PART WITH HIS THREADS, BUT I GUESS I CONVINCED HIM.
THEY FEEL KIND'A FUNNY, BUT THEY BEAT FIGHTIN' IN THE ALL-TOGETHER.
SOMETHIN' TELLS ME I GOT BACK JUST IN TIME, TOO.
HEADS UP, TROOPS! WOLVERINE'S COMIN' AT'CHA!
FANG, THIS IS NO TIME FOR YOUR JOKES!
WAIT! YOU'RE NOT FANG!
DON'T WORRY LITTLE ASTRA. I'LL MAKE SURE THOSE CLAWS...
POW!
...NEVER COME NEAR YOU!!
WE'VE GOT THEM ON THE RUN!
UNDERSTOOD, TEMPEST! WE'LL KEEP HAMMER-ING THEM UNTIL THEY DROP!
KEEP UP THE PRESSURE, 'BOLT!

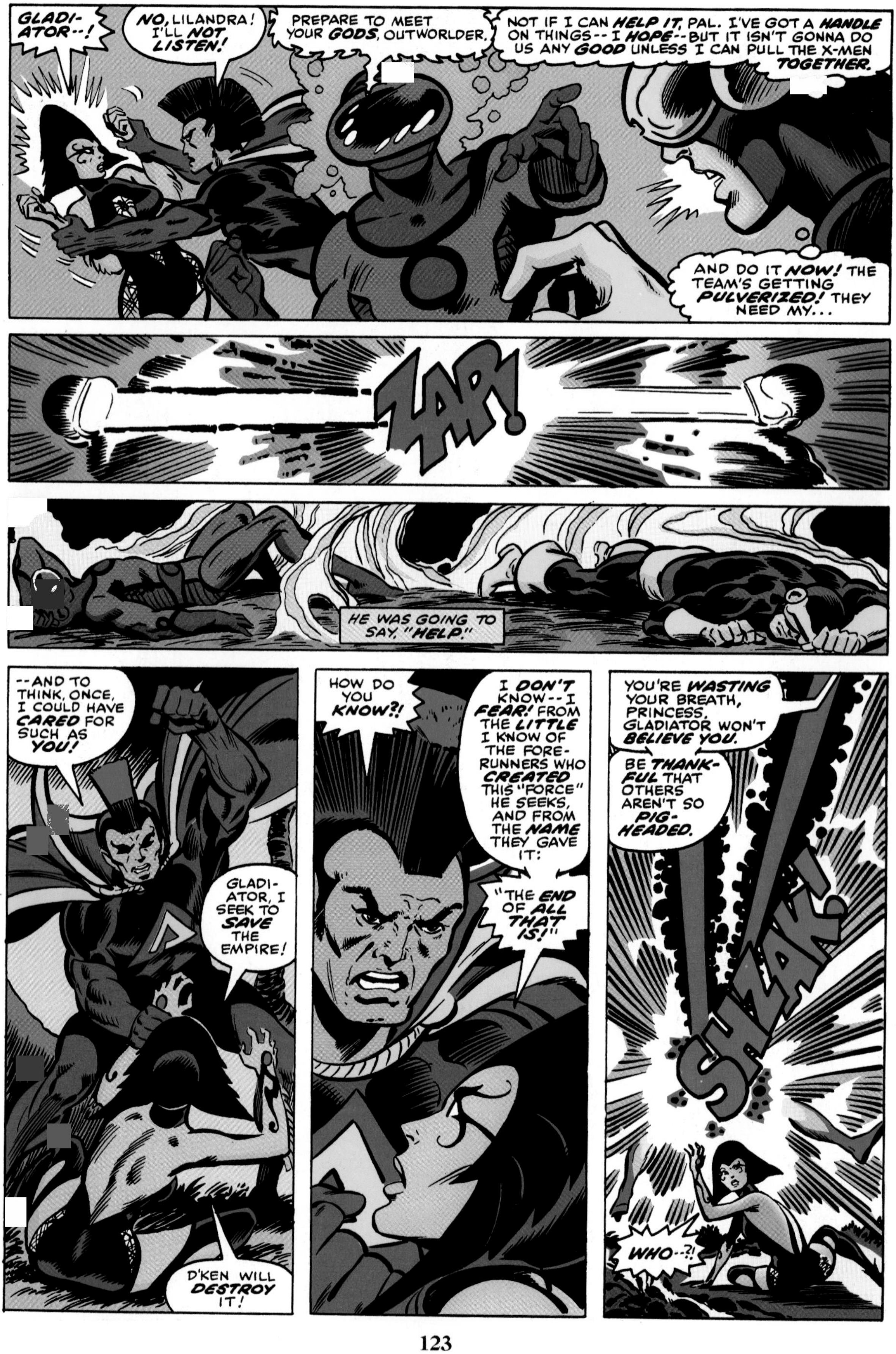
GLADI-ATOR--!
NO, LILANDRA! I'LL NOT LISTEN!
PREPARE TO MEET YOUR GODS, OUTWORLDER.
NOT IF I CAN HELP IT, PAL. I'VE GOT A HANDLE ON THINGS-- I HOPE--BUT IT ISN'T GONNA DO US ANY GOOD UNLESS I CAN PULL THE X-MEN TOGETHER.
AND DO IT NOW! THE TEAM'S GETTING PULVERIZED! THEY NEED MY...
ZAP!
HE WAS GOING TO SAY, "HELP."
--AND TO THINK, ONCE, I COULD HAVE CARED FOR SUCH AS YOU!
GLADI-ATOR, I SEEK TO SAVE THE EMPIRE!
D'KEN WILL DESTROY IT!
HOW DO YOU KNOW?!
I DON'T KNOW--I FEAR! FROM THE LITTLE I KNOW OF THE FORE-RUNNERS WHO CREATED THIS "FORCE" HE SEEKS, AND FROM THE NAME THEY GAVE IT:
"THE END OF ALL THAT IS!"
YOU'RE WASTING YOUR BREATH, PRINCESS. GLADIATOR WON'T BELIEVE YOU.
BE THANK-FUL THAT OTHERS AREN'T SO PIG-HEADED.
SHZAK!
WHO--?!

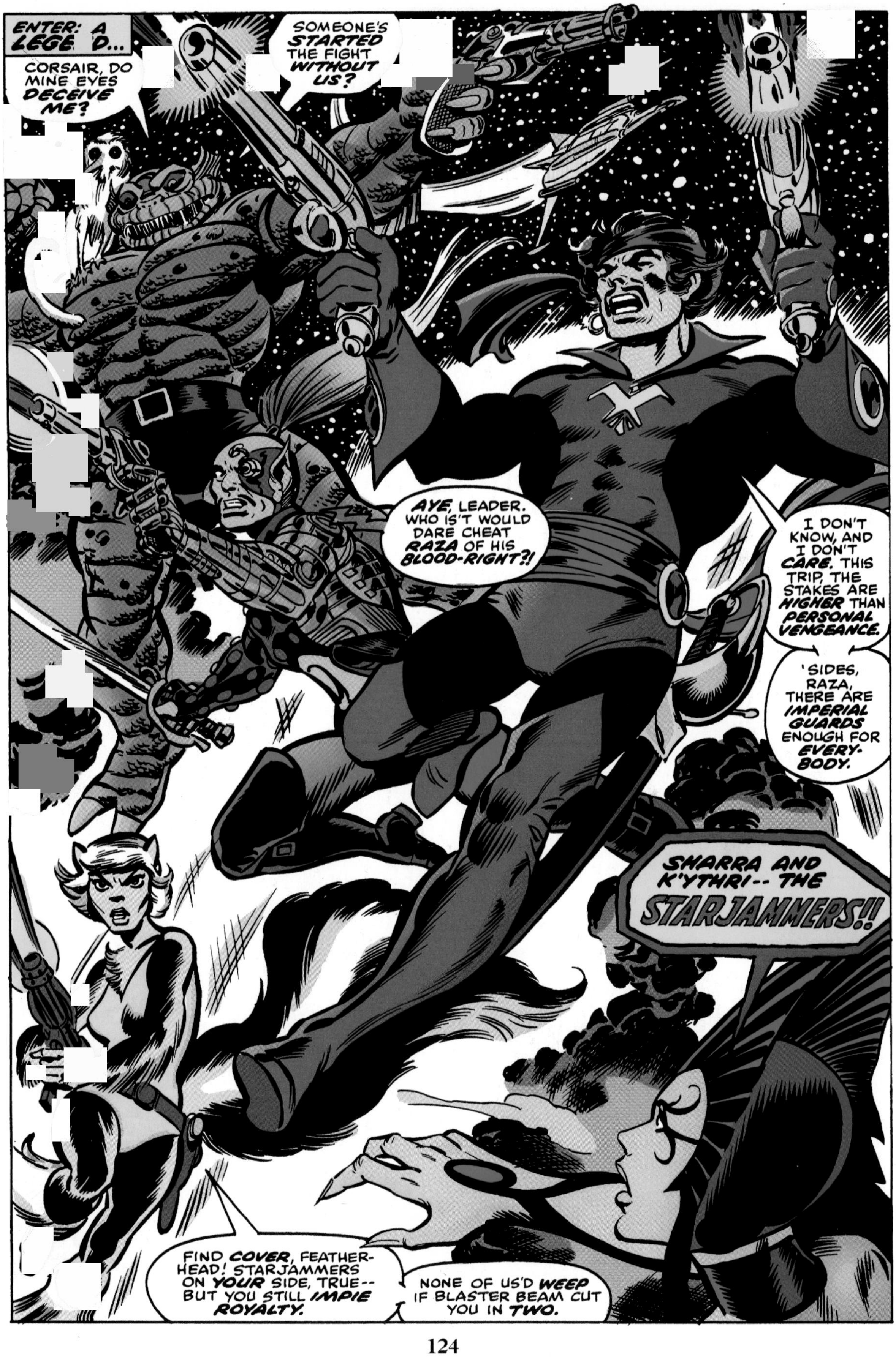

ENTER: A LEGE D...
CORSAIR, DO MINE EYES DECEIVE ME?
SOMEONE'S STARTED THE FIGHT WITHOUT US?
AYE, LEADER. WHO IS'T WOULD DARE CHEAT RAZA OF HIS BLOOD-RIGHT?!
I DON'T KNOW, AND I DON'T CARE. THIS TRIP, THE STAKES ARE HIGHER THAN PERSONAL VENGEANCE.
'SIDES, RAZA, THERE ARE IMPERIAL GUARDS ENOUGH FOR EVERY-BODY.
SHARRA AND K'YTHRI-- THE STARJAMMERS!!
FIND COVER, FEATHER-HEAD! STARJAMMERS ON YOUR SIDE, TRUE-- BUT YOU STILL IMPIE ROYALTY.
NONE OF US'D WEEP IF BLASTER BEAM CUT YOU IN TWO.

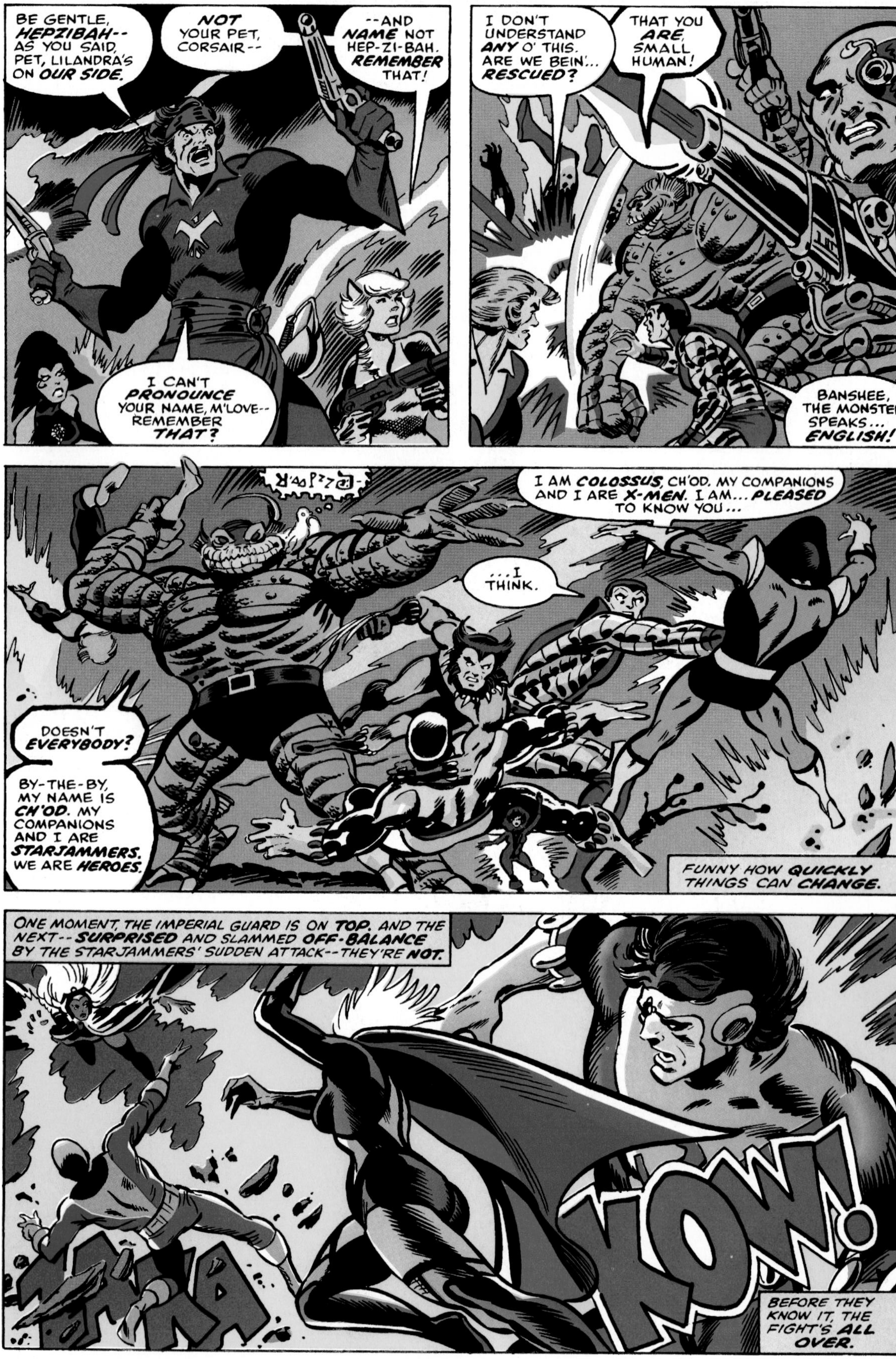
BE GENTLE, HEPZIBAH-- AS YOU SAID, PET, LILANDRA'S ON OUR SIDE.
NOT YOUR PET, CORSAIR--
--AND NAME NOT HEP-ZI-BAH. REMEMBER THAT!
I CAN'T PRONOUNCE YOUR NAME, M'LOVE-- REMEMBER THAT?
I DON'T UNDERSTAND ANY O' THIS. ARE WE BEIN'... RESCUED?
THAT YOU ARE, SMALL HUMAN!
BANSHEE, THE MONSTER SPEAKS... ENGLISH!
I AM COLOSSUS, CH'OD. MY COMPANIONS AND I ARE X-MEN. I AM... PLEASED TO KNOW YOU...
...I THINK.
DOESN'T EVERYBODY?
BY-THE-BY, MY NAME IS CH'OD. MY COMPANIONS AND I ARE STARJAMMERS. WE ARE HEROES.
FUNNY HOW QUICKLY THINGS CAN CHANGE.
ONE MOMENT, THE IMPERIAL GUARD IS ON TOP, AND THE NEXT-- SURPRISED AND SLAMMED OFF-BALANCE BY THE STARJAMMERS' SUDDEN ATTACK--THEY'RE NOT.
KOW!
BEFORE THEY KNOW IT, THE FIGHT'S ALL OVER.

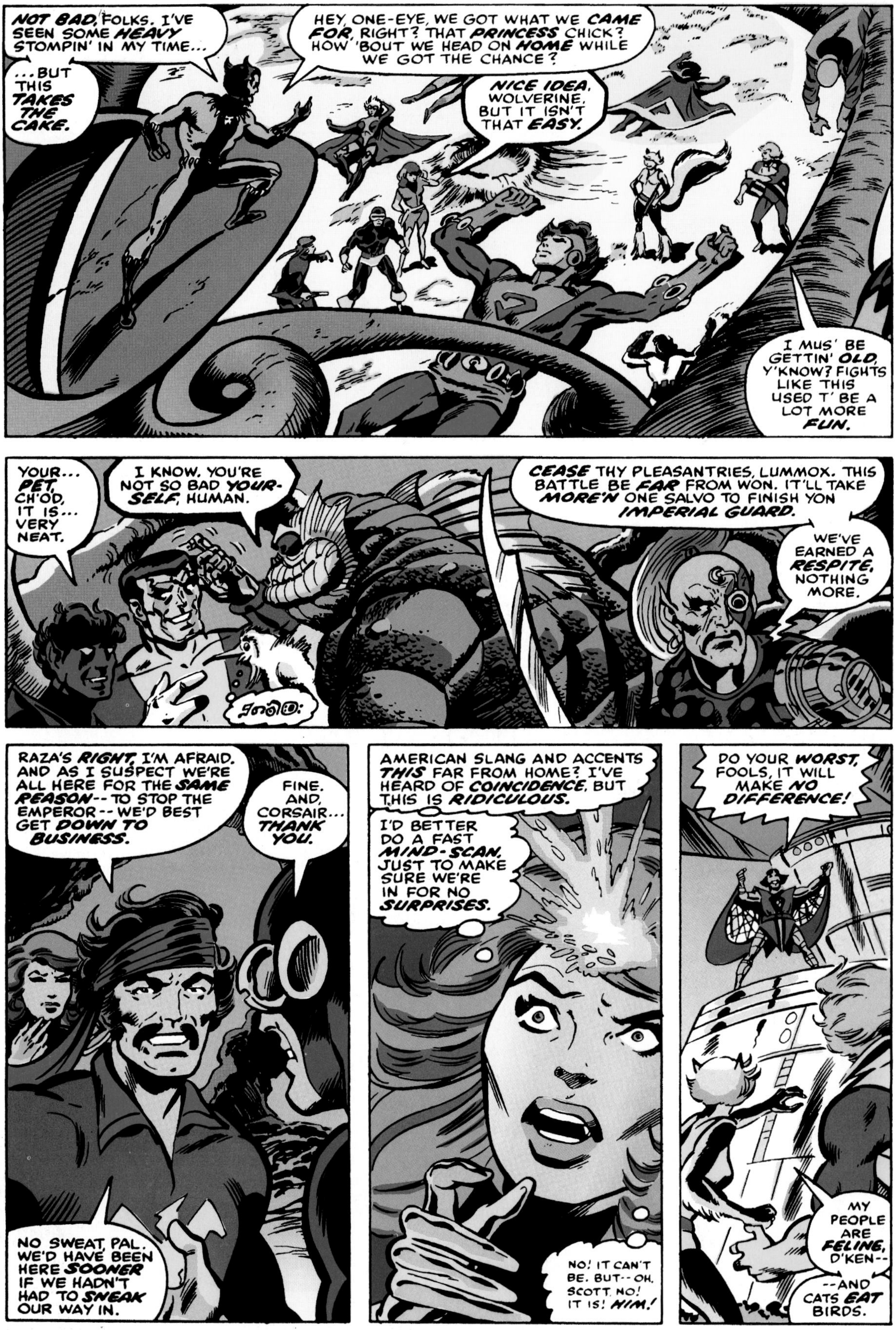
NOT BAD, FOLKS. I'VE SEEN SOME HEAVY STOMPIN' IN MY TIME...
...BUT THIS TAKES THE CAKE.
HEY, ONE-EYE, WE GOT WHAT WE CAME FOR, RIGHT? THAT PRINCESS CHICK? HOW 'BOUT WE HEAD ON HOME WHILE WE GOT THE CHANCE?
NICE IDEA, WOLVERINE, BUT IT ISN'T THAT EASY.
I MUS' BE GETTIN' OLD, Y'KNOW? FIGHTS LIKE THIS USED T' BE A LOT MORE FUN.
YOUR... PET, CH'OD, IT IS... VERY NEAT.
I KNOW. YOU'RE NOT SO BAD YOURSELF, HUMAN.
CEASE THY PLEASANTRIES, LUMMOX. THIS BATTLE BE FAR FROM WON. IT'LL TAKE MORE'N ONE SALVO TO FINISH YON IMPERIAL GUARD.
WE'VE EARNED A RESPITE, NOTHING MORE.
RAZA'S RIGHT, I'M AFRAID. AND AS I SUSPECT WE'RE ALL HERE FOR THE SAME REASON -- TO STOP THE EMPEROR -- WE'D BEST GET DOWN TO BUSINESS.
FINE. AND, CORSAIR... THANK YOU.
NO SWEAT, PAL. WE'D HAVE BEEN HERE SOONER IF WE HADN'T HAD TO SNEAK OUR WAY IN.
AMERICAN SLANG AND ACCENTS THIS FAR FROM HOME? I'VE HEARD OF COINCIDENCE, BUT THIS IS RIDICULOUS.
I'D BETTER DO A FAST MIND-SCAN, JUST TO MAKE SURE WE'RE IN FOR NO SURPRISES.
NO! IT CAN'T BE. BUT -- OH, SCOTT, NO! IT IS! HIM!
DO YOUR WORST, FOOLS, IT WILL MAKE NO DIFFERENCE!
MY PEOPLE ARE FELINE, D'KEN --
-- AND CATS EAT BIRDS.

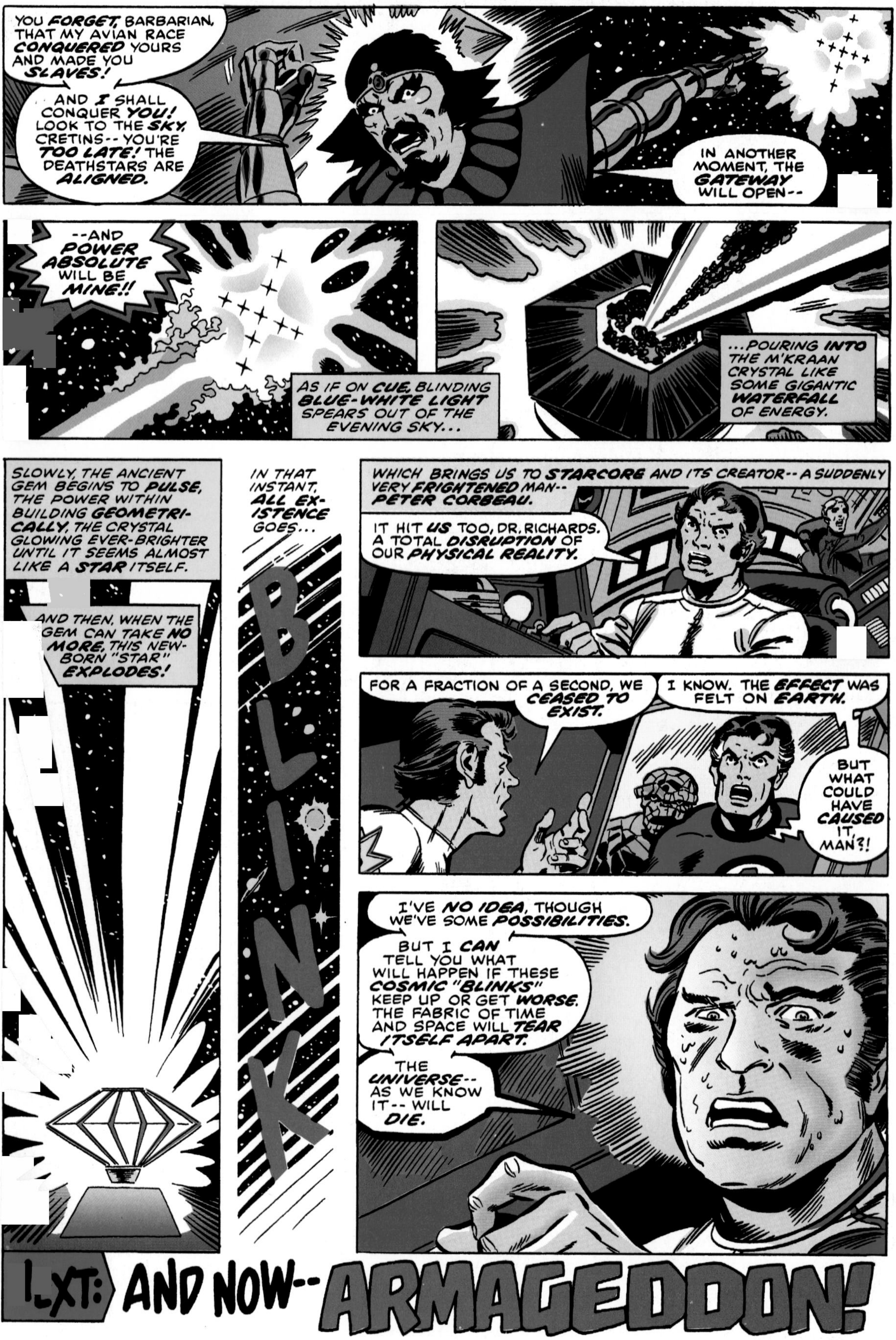

YOU FORGET, BARBARIAN, THAT MY AVIAN RACE CONQUERED YOURS AND MADE YOU SLAVES!
AND I SHALL CONQUER YOU! LOOK TO THE SKY, CRETINS-- YOU'RE TOO LATE! THE DEATHSTARS ARE ALIGNED.
IN ANOTHER MOMENT, THE GATEWAY WILL OPEN--
--AND POWER ABSOLUTE WILL BE MINE!!
AS IF ON CUE, BLINDING BLUE-WHITE LIGHT SPEARS OUT OF THE EVENING SKY...
...POURING INTO THE M'KRAAN CRYSTAL LIKE SOME GIGANTIC WATERFALL OF ENERGY.
SLOWLY, THE ANCIENT GEM BEGINS TO PULSE, THE POWER WITHIN BUILDING GEOMETRICALLY, THE CRYSTAL GLOWING EVER-BRIGHTER UNTIL IT SEEMS ALMOST LIKE A STAR ITSELF.
AND THEN, WHEN THE GEM CAN TAKE NO MORE, THIS NEW-BORN "STAR" EXPLODES!
IN THAT INSTANT, ALL EXISTENCE GOES...
BLINK
WHICH BRINGS US TO STARCORE AND ITS CREATOR-- A SUDDENLY VERY FRIGHTENED MAN-- PETER CORBEAU.
IT HIT US TOO, DR. RICHARDS. A TOTAL DISRUPTION OF OUR PHYSICAL REALITY.
FOR A FRACTION OF A SECOND, WE CEASED TO EXIST.
I KNOW. THE EFFECT WAS FELT ON EARTH.
BUT WHAT COULD HAVE CAUSED IT, MAN?!
I'VE NO IDEA, THOUGH WE'VE SOME POSSIBILITIES.
BUT I CAN TELL YOU WHAT WILL HAPPEN IF THESE COSMIC "BLINKS" KEEP UP OR GET WORSE. THE FABRIC OF TIME AND SPACE WILL TEAR ITSELF APART.
THE UNIVERSE-- AS WE KNOW IT-- WILL DIE.
NEXT: AND NOW-- ARMAGEDDON!

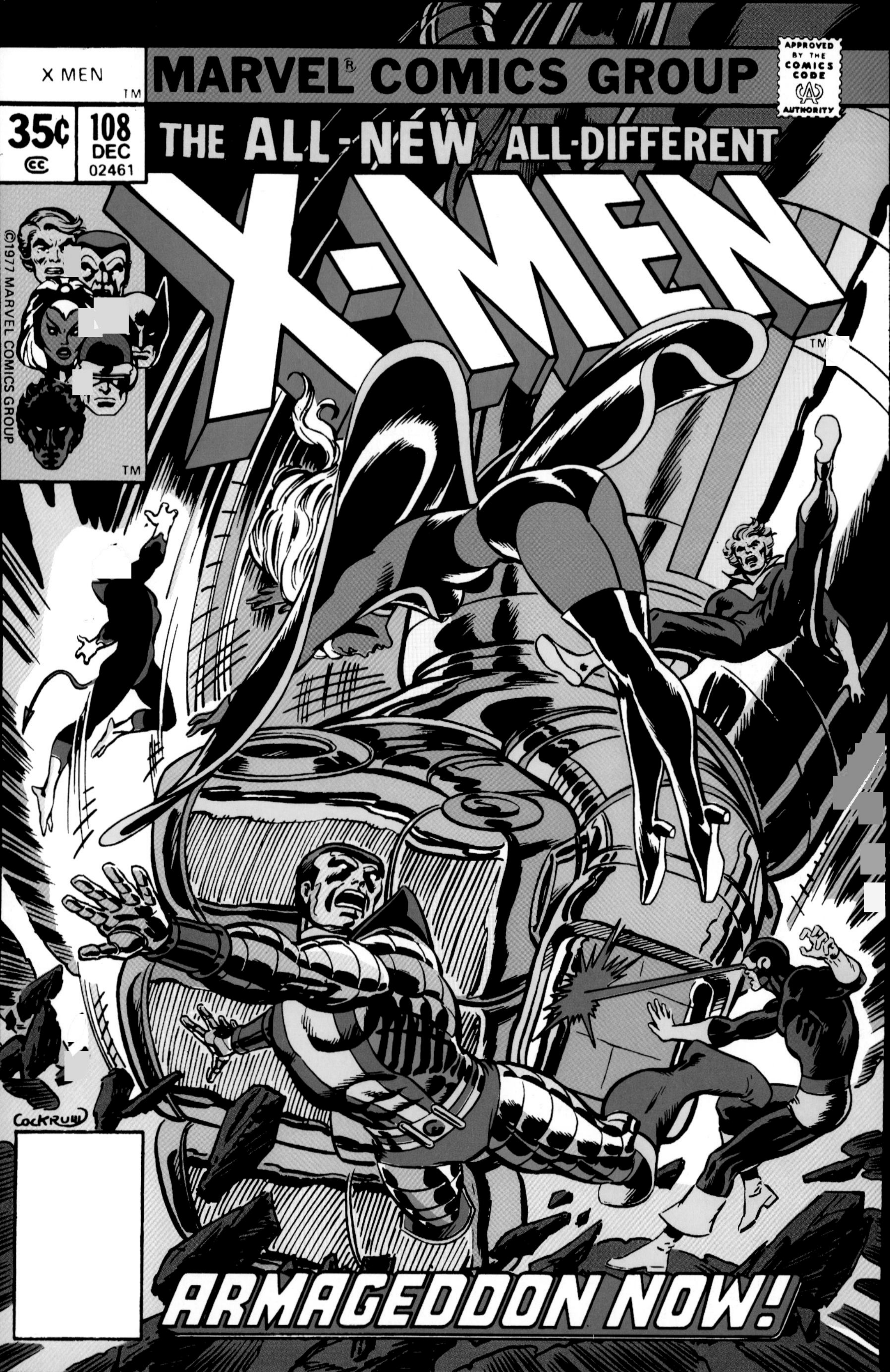
X MEN
MARVEL® COMICS GROUP
APPROVED BY THE COMICS CODE AUTHORITY
35¢
108
DEC
02461
THE ALL-NEW ALL-DIFFERENT
X-MEN
©1977 MARVEL COMICS GROUP
COCKRUM
ARMAGEDDON NOW!

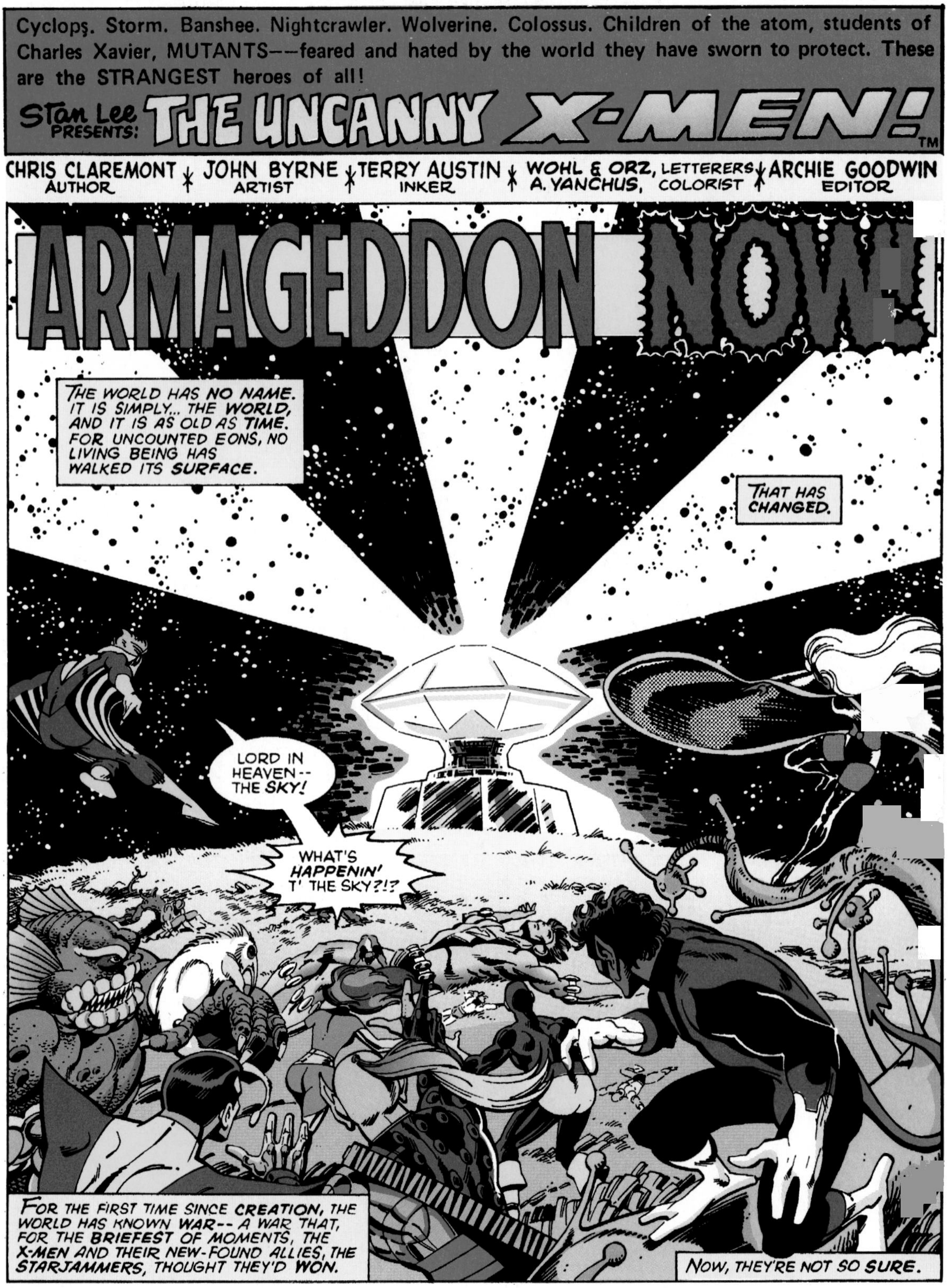
Cyclops. Storm. Banshee. Nightcrawler. Wolverine. Colossus. Children of the atom, students of Charles Xavier, MUTANTS---feared and hated by the world they have sworn to protect. These are the STRANGEST heroes of all!
Stan Lee PRESENTS: THE UNCANNY X-MEN! TM
CHRIS CLAREMONT AUTHOR * JOHN BYRNE ARTIST * TERRY AUSTIN INKER * WOHL & ORZ, LETTERERS A. YANCHUS, COLORIST * ARCHIE GOODWIN EDITOR
ARMAGEDDON NOW!
THE WORLD HAS NO NAME. IT IS SIMPLY... THE WORLD, AND IT IS AS OLD AS TIME. FOR UNCOUNTED EONS, NO LIVING BEING HAS WALKED ITS SURFACE.
THAT HAS CHANGED.
LORD IN HEAVEN-- THE SKY!
WHAT'S HAPPENIN' T' THE SKY?!?
FOR THE FIRST TIME SINCE CREATION, THE WORLD HAS KNOWN WAR-- A WAR THAT, FOR THE BRIEFEST OF MOMENTS, THE X-MEN AND THEIR NEW-FOUND ALLIES, THE STARJAMMERS, THOUGHT THEY'D WON.
NOW, THEY'RE NOT SO SURE.

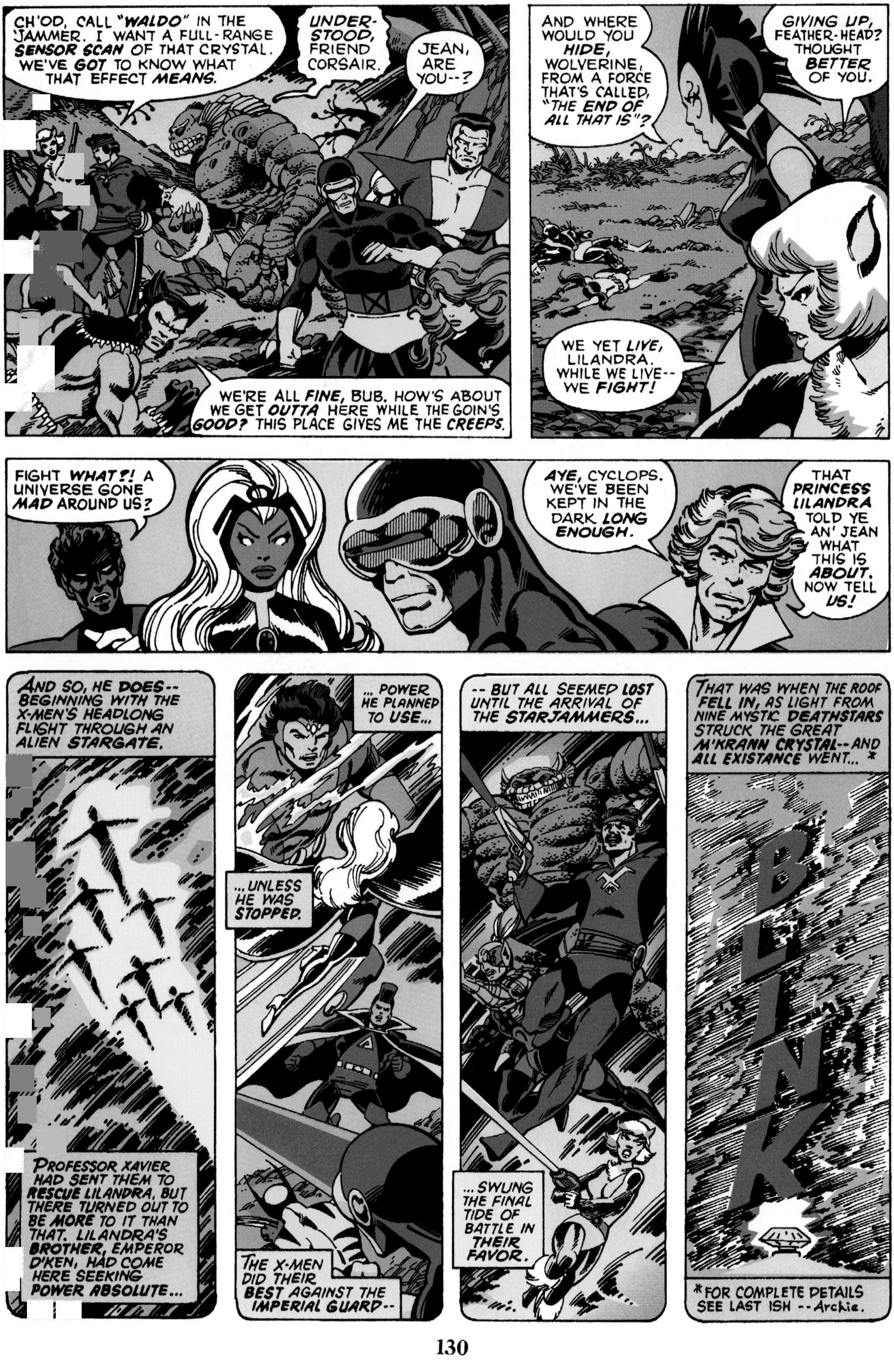

CH'OD, CALL "WALDO" IN THE 'JAMMER. I WANT A FULL-RANGE SENSOR SCAN OF THAT CRYSTAL. WE'VE GOT TO KNOW WHAT THAT EFFECT MEANS.
UNDER-STOOD, FRIEND CORSAIR.
JEAN, ARE YOU--?
WE'RE ALL FINE, BUB. HOW'S ABOUT WE GET OUTTA HERE WHILE THE GOIN'S GOOD? THIS PLACE GIVES ME THE CREEPS.
AND WHERE WOULD YOU HIDE, WOLVERINE, FROM A FORCE THAT'S CALLED, "THE END OF ALL THAT IS"?
GIVING UP, FEATHER-HEAD? THOUGHT BETTER OF YOU.
WE YET LIVE, LILANDRA. WHILE WE LIVE-- WE FIGHT!
FIGHT WHAT?! A UNIVERSE GONE MAD AROUND US?
AYE, CYCLOPS. WE'VE BEEN KEPT IN THE DARK LONG ENOUGH.
THAT PRINCESS LILANDRA TOLD YE AN' JEAN WHAT THIS IS ABOUT. NOW TELL US!
AND SO, HE DOES-- BEGINNING WITH THE X-MEN'S HEADLONG FLIGHT THROUGH AN ALIEN STARGATE.
PROFESSOR XAVIER HAD SENT THEM TO RESCUE LILANDRA, BUT THERE TURNED OUT TO BE MORE TO IT THAN THAT. LILANDRA'S BROTHER, EMPEROR D'KEN, HAD COME HERE SEEKING POWER ABSOLUTE...
... POWER HE PLANNED TO USE...
...UNLESS HE WAS STOPPED.
THE X-MEN DID THEIR BEST AGAINST THE IMPERIAL GUARD--
-- BUT ALL SEEMED LOST UNTIL THE ARRIVAL OF THE STARJAMMERS...
...SWUNG THE FINAL TIDE OF BATTLE IN THEIR FAVOR.
THAT WAS WHEN THE ROOF FELL IN, AS LIGHT FROM NINE MYSTIC DEATHSTARS STRUCK THE GREAT M'KRANN CRYSTAL-- AND ALL EXISTANCE WENT... *
BLINK
*FOR COMPLETE DETAILS SEE LAST ISH --Archie.

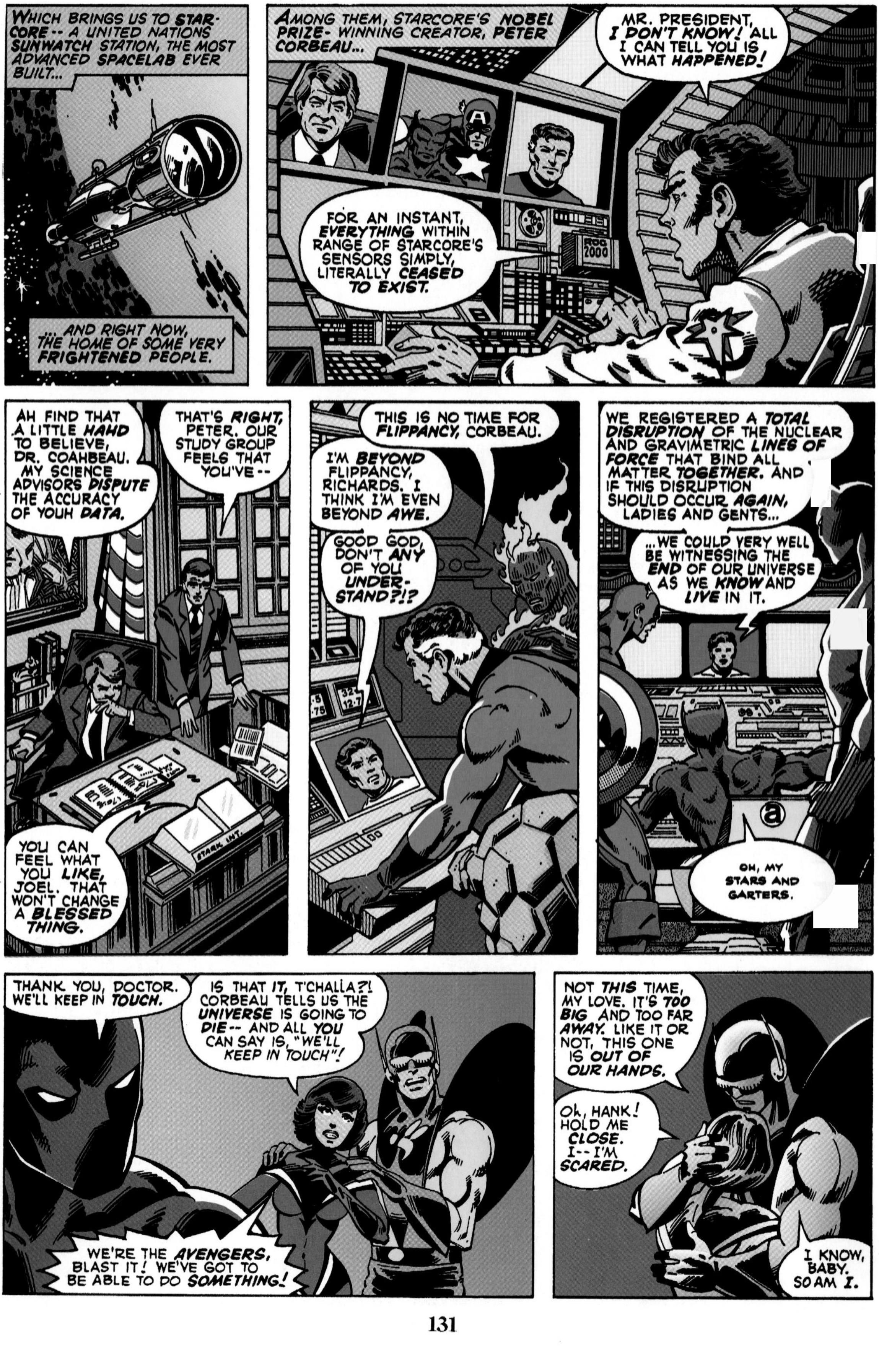
WHICH BRINGS US TO STARCORE -- A UNITED NATIONS SUNWATCH STATION, THE MOST ADVANCED SPACELAB EVER BUILT...
...AND RIGHT NOW, THE HOME OF SOME VERY FRIGHTENED PEOPLE.
AMONG THEM, STARCORE'S NOBEL PRIZE- WINNING CREATOR, PETER CORBEAU...
MR. PRESIDENT, I DON'T KNOW! ALL I CAN TELL YOU IS WHAT HAPPENED!
FOR AN INSTANT, EVERYTHING WITHIN RANGE OF STARCORE'S SENSORS SIMPLY, LITERALLY CEASED TO EXIST.
ROG 2000
AH FIND THAT A LITTLE HAHD TO BELIEVE, DR. COAHBEAU. MY SCIENCE ADVISORS DISPUTE THE ACCURACY OF YOUH DATA.
THAT'S RIGHT, PETER. OUR STUDY GROUP FEELS THAT YOU'VE --
YOU CAN FEEL WHAT YOU LIKE, JOEL. THAT WON'T CHANGE A BLESSED THING.
STARK INT.
THIS IS NO TIME FOR FLIPPANCY, CORBEAU.
I'M BEYOND FLIPPANCY, RICHARDS. I THINK I'M EVEN BEYOND AWE.
GOOD GOD, DON'T ANY OF YOU UNDERSTAND?!?
WE REGISTERED A TOTAL DISRUPTION OF THE NUCLEAR AND GRAVIMETRIC LINES OF FORCE THAT BIND ALL MATTER TOGETHER. AND IF THIS DISRUPTION SHOULD OCCUR AGAIN, LADIES AND GENTS...
...WE COULD VERY WELL BE WITNESSING THE END OF OUR UNIVERSE AS WE KNOW AND LIVE IN IT.
OH, MY STARS AND GARTERS.
THANK YOU, DOCTOR. WE'LL KEEP IN TOUCH.
IS THAT IT, T'CHALLA?! CORBEAU TELLS US THE UNIVERSE IS GOING TO DIE -- AND ALL YOU CAN SAY IS, "WE'LL KEEP IN TOUCH"!
WE'RE THE AVENGERS, BLAST IT! WE'VE GOT TO BE ABLE TO DO SOMETHING!
NOT THIS TIME, MY LOVE. IT'S TOO BIG AND TOO FAR AWAY. LIKE IT OR NOT, THIS ONE IS OUT OF OUR HANDS.
OH, HANK! HOLD ME CLOSE. I -- I'M SCARED.
I KNOW, BABY. SO AM I.

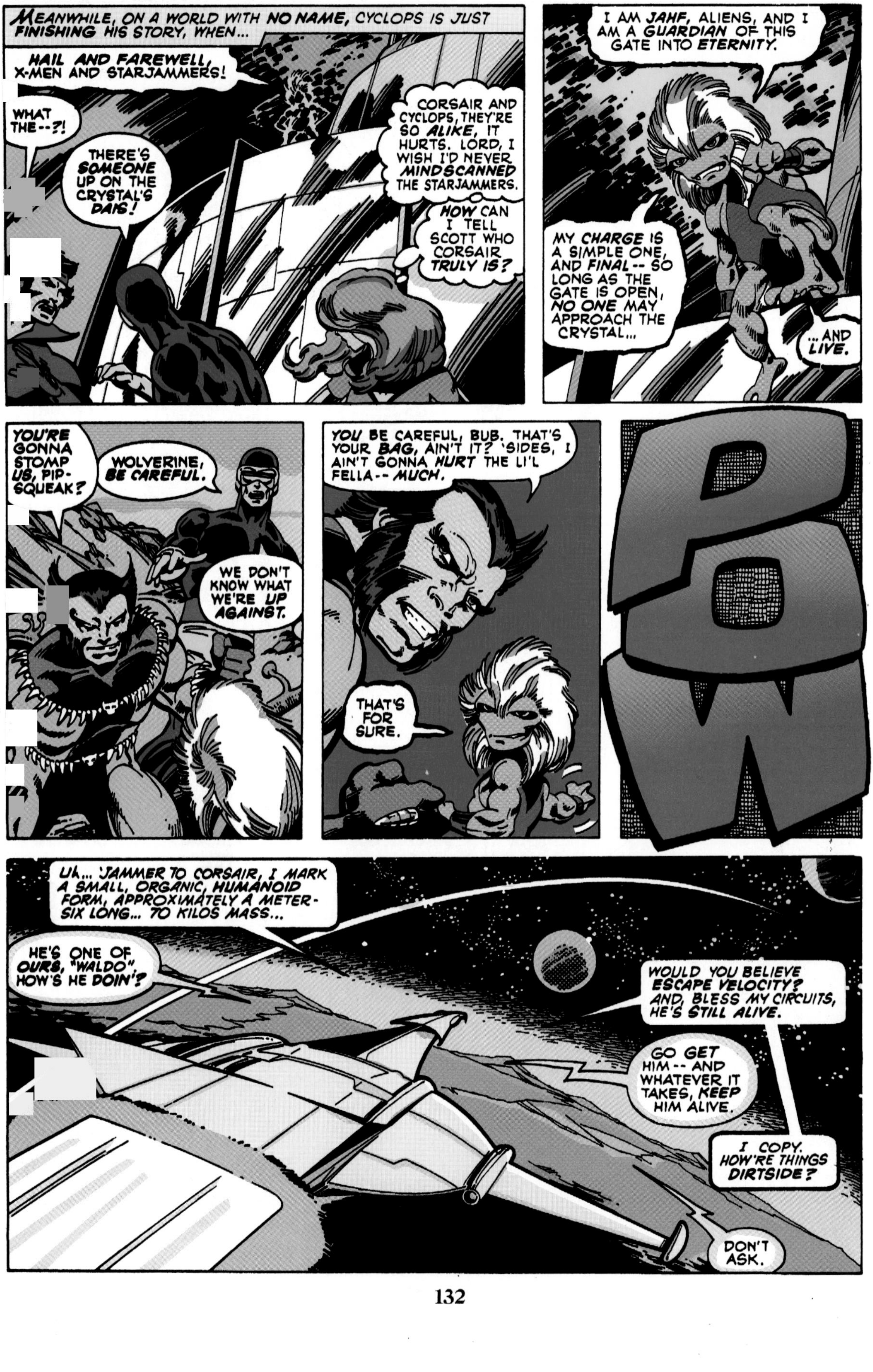

MEANWHILE, ON A WORLD WITH NO NAME, CYCLOPS IS JUST FINISHING HIS STORY, WHEN...
HAIL AND FAREWELL, X-MEN AND STARJAMMERS!
WHAT THE--?!
THERE'S SOMEONE UP ON THE CRYSTAL'S DAIS!
CORSAIR AND CYCLOPS, THEY'RE SO ALIKE, IT HURTS. LORD, I WISH I'D NEVER MINDSCANNED THE STARJAMMERS.
HOW CAN I TELL SCOTT WHO CORSAIR TRULY IS?
I AM JAHF, ALIENS, AND I AM A GUARDIAN OF THIS GATE INTO ETERNITY.
MY CHARGE IS A SIMPLE ONE, AND FINAL -- SO LONG AS THE GATE IS OPEN, NO ONE MAY APPROACH THE CRYSTAL...
...AND LIVE.
YOU'RE GONNA STOMP US, PIP-SQUEAK?
WOLVERINE, BE CAREFUL.
WE DON'T KNOW WHAT WE'RE UP AGAINST.
YOU BE CAREFUL, BUB. THAT'S YOUR BAG, AIN'T IT? 'SIDES, I AIN'T GONNA HURT THE LI'L FELLA-- MUCH.
THAT'S FOR SURE.
BOW
UH... 'JAMMER TO CORSAIR, I MARK A SMALL, ORGANIC, HUMANOID FORM, APPROXIMATELY A METER-SIX LONG... 70 KILOS MASS...
HE'S ONE OF OURS, "WALDO". HOW'S HE DOIN'?
WOULD YOU BELIEVE ESCAPE VELOCITY? AND, BLESS MY CIRCUITS, HE'S STILL ALIVE.
GO GET HIM -- AND WHATEVER IT TAKES, KEEP HIM ALIVE.
I COPY. HOW'RE THINGS DIRTSIDE?
DON'T ASK.

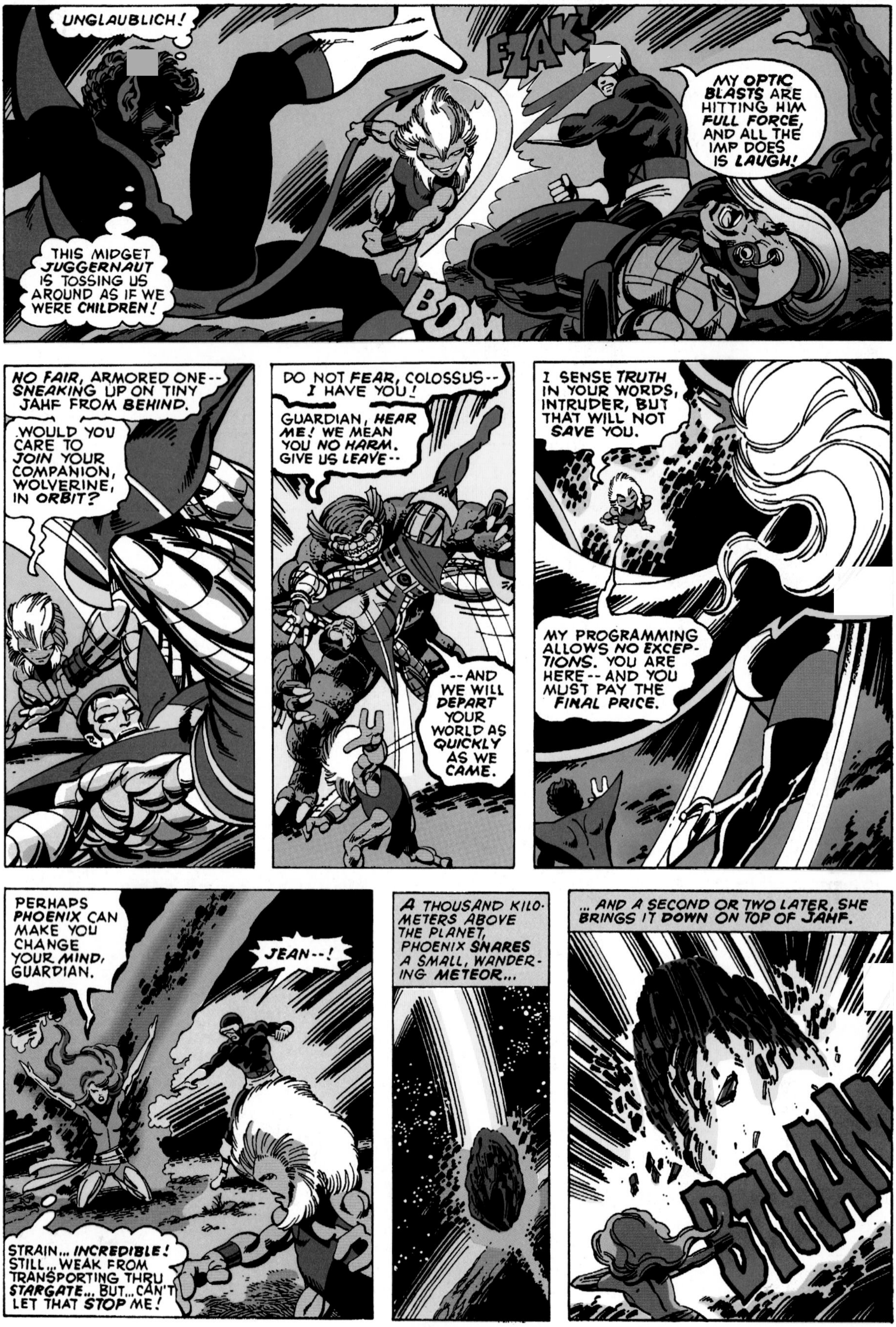
UNGLAUBLICH!
FZAK!
MY OPTIC BLASTS ARE HITTING HIM FULL FORCE, AND ALL THE IMP DOES IS LAUGH!
THIS MIDGET JUGGERNAUT IS TOSSING US AROUND AS IF WE WERE CHILDREN!
BOM
NO FAIR, ARMORED ONE-- SNEAKING UP ON TINY JAHF FROM BEHIND.
WOULD YOU CARE TO JOIN YOUR COMPANION, WOLVERINE, IN ORBIT?
DO NOT FEAR, COLOSSUS-- I HAVE YOU!
GUARDIAN, HEAR ME! WE MEAN YOU NO HARM. GIVE US LEAVE--
--AND WE WILL DEPART YOUR WORLD AS QUICKLY AS WE CAME.
I SENSE TRUTH IN YOUR WORDS, INTRUDER, BUT THAT WILL NOT SAVE YOU.
MY PROGRAMMING ALLOWS NO EXCEPTIONS. YOU ARE HERE-- AND YOU MUST PAY THE FINAL PRICE.
PERHAPS PHOENIX CAN MAKE YOU CHANGE YOUR MIND, GUARDIAN.
JEAN--!
STRAIN... INCREDIBLE! STILL... WEAK FROM TRANSPORTING THRU STARGATE... BUT... CAN'T LET THAT STOP ME!
A THOUSAND KILOMETERS ABOVE THE PLANET, PHOENIX SNARES A SMALL, WANDERING METEOR...
... AND A SECOND OR TWO LATER, SHE BRINGS IT DOWN ON TOP OF JAHF.
BTHAM

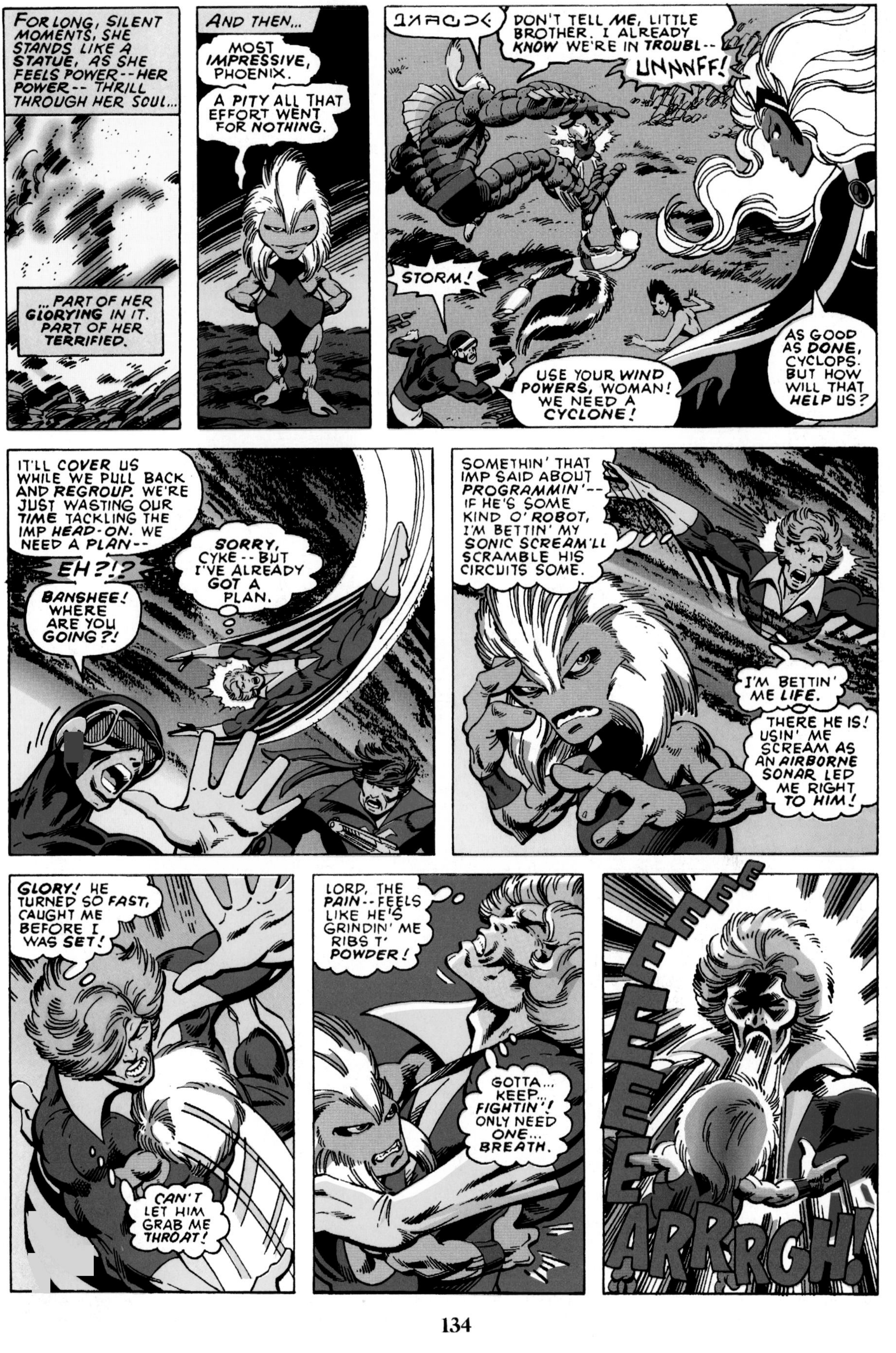

FOR LONG, SILENT MOMENTS, SHE STANDS LIKE A STATUE, AS SHE FEELS POWER--HER POWER-- THRILL THROUGH HER SOUL...
...PART OF HER GLORYING IN IT. PART OF HER TERRIFIED.
AND THEN...
MOST IMPRESSIVE, PHOENIX.
A PITY ALL THAT EFFORT WENT FOR NOTHING.
DON'T TELL ME, LITTLE BROTHER. I ALREADY KNOW WE'RE IN TROUBL--
UNNNFF!
STORM!
USE YOUR WIND POWERS, WOMAN! WE NEED A CYCLONE!
AS GOOD AS DONE, CYCLOPS. BUT HOW WILL THAT HELP US?
IT'LL COVER US WHILE WE PULL BACK AND REGROUP. WE'RE JUST WASTING OUR TIME TACKLING THE IMP HEAD-ON. WE NEED A PLAN--
EH?!?
BANSHEE! WHERE ARE YOU GOING?!
SORRY, CYKE--BUT I'VE ALREADY GOT A PLAN.
SOMETHIN' THAT IMP SAID ABOUT PROGRAMMIN'-- IF HE'S SOME KIND O' ROBOT, I'M BETTIN' MY SONIC SCREAM'LL SCRAMBLE HIS CIRCUITS SOME.
I'M BETTIN' ME LIFE.
THERE HE IS! USIN' ME SCREAM AS AN AIRBORNE SONAR LED ME RIGHT TO HIM!
GLORY! HE TURNED SO FAST, CAUGHT ME BEFORE I WAS SET!
CAN'T LET HIM GRAB ME THROAT!
LORD, THE PAIN--FEELS LIKE HE'S GRINDIN' ME RIBS T' POWDER!
GOTTA... KEEP... FIGHTIN'! ONLY NEED ONE... BREATH.
EEEEEEEEEE
ARRRGH!

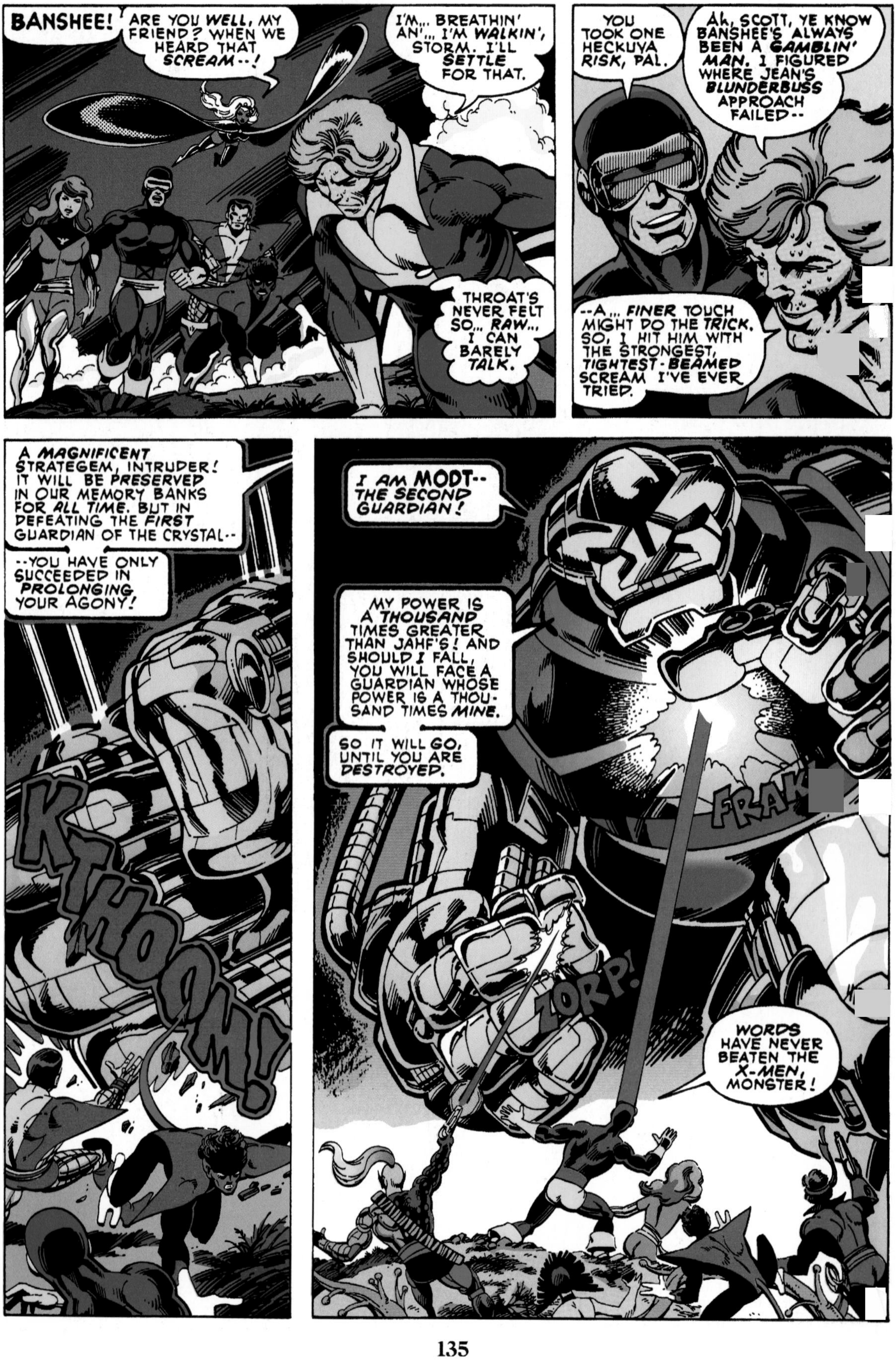
BANSHEE!
ARE YOU WELL, MY FRIEND? WHEN WE HEARD THAT SCREAM--!
I'M... BREATHIN' AN'... I'M WALKIN', STORM. I'LL SETTLE FOR THAT.
THROAT'S NEVER FELT SO... RAW... I CAN BARELY TALK.
YOU TOOK ONE HECKUVA RISK, PAL.
Ah, SCOTT, YE KNOW BANSHEE'S ALWAYS BEEN A GAMBLIN' MAN. I FIGURED WHERE JEAN'S BLUNDERBUSS APPROACH FAILED--
--A... FINER TOUCH MIGHT DO THE TRICK. SO, I HIT HIM WITH THE STRONGEST, TIGHTEST-BEAMED SCREAM I'VE EVER TRIED.
A MAGNIFICENT STRATEGEM, INTRUDER! IT WILL BE PRESERVED IN OUR MEMORY BANKS FOR ALL TIME. BUT IN DEFEATING THE FIRST GUARDIAN OF THE CRYSTAL--
--YOU HAVE ONLY SUCCEEDED IN PROLONGING YOUR AGONY!
KTHOOOM!
I AM MODT-- THE SECOND GUARDIAN!
MY POWER IS A THOUSAND TIMES GREATER THAN JAHF'S! AND SHOULD I FALL, YOU WILL FACE A GUARDIAN WHOSE POWER IS A THOUSAND TIMES MINE.
SO IT WILL GO, UNTIL YOU ARE DESTROYED.
FRAK
ZORP!
WORDS HAVE NEVER BEATEN THE X-MEN, MONSTER!

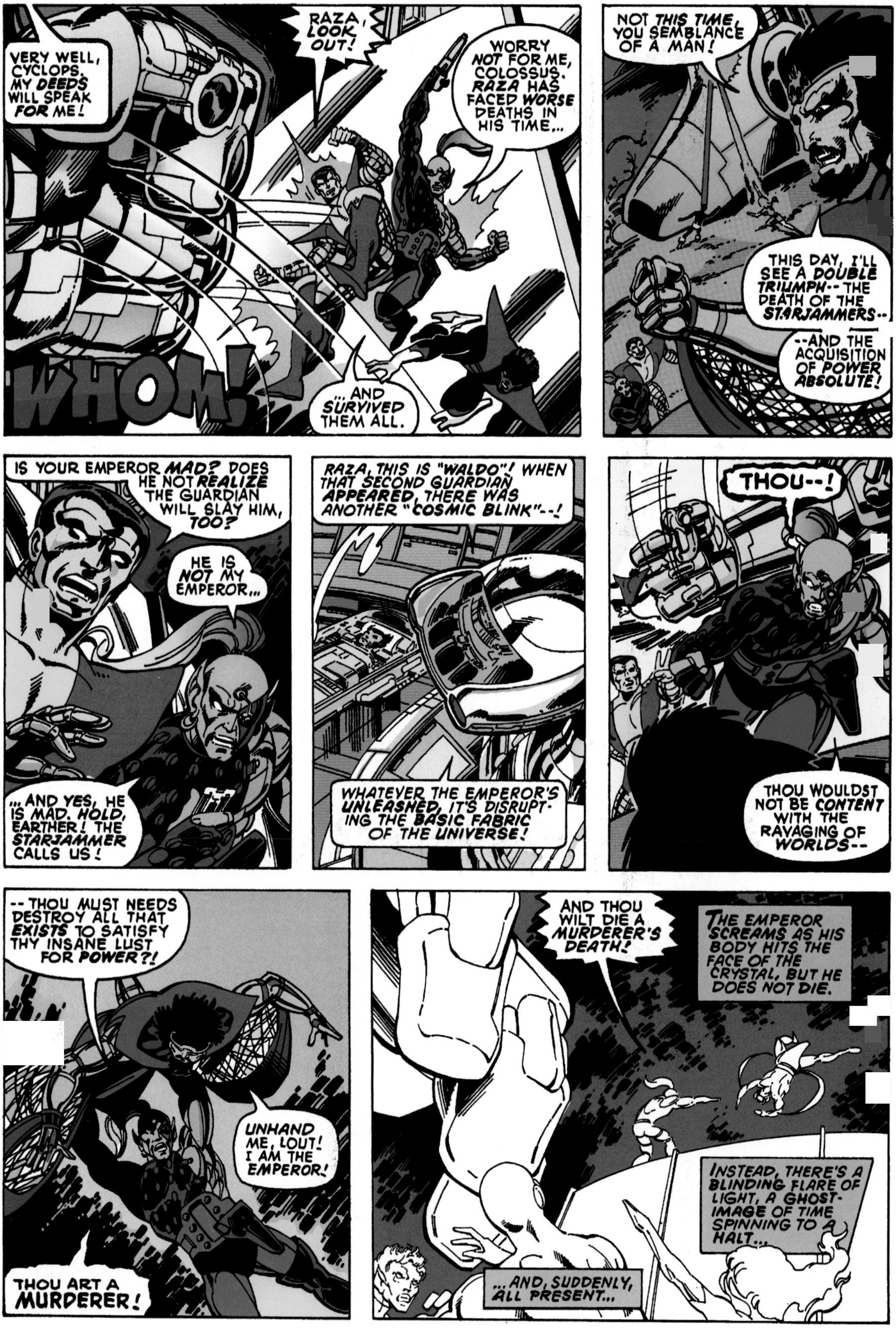
VERY WELL, CYCLOPS. MY DEEDS WILL SPEAK FOR ME!
RAZA, LOOK OUT!
WORRY NOT FOR ME, COLOSSUS. RAZA HAS FACED WORSE DEATHS IN HIS TIME...
WHOM!
...AND SURVIVED THEM ALL.
NOT THIS TIME, YOU SEMBLANCE OF A MAN!
THIS DAY, I'LL SEE A DOUBLE TRIUMPH--THE DEATH OF THE STARJAMMERS--
--AND THE ACQUISITION OF POWER ABSOLUTE!
IS YOUR EMPEROR MAD? DOES HE NOT REALIZE THE GUARDIAN WILL SLAY HIM, TOO?
HE IS NOT MY EMPEROR...
...AND YES, HE IS MAD. HOLD, EARTHER! THE STARJAMMER CALLS US!
RAZA, THIS IS "WALDO"! WHEN THAT SECOND GUARDIAN APPEARED, THERE WAS ANOTHER "COSMIC BLINK"--!
WHATEVER THE EMPEROR'S UNLEASHED, IT'S DISRUPTING THE BASIC FABRIC OF THE UNIVERSE!
THOU--!
THOU WOULDST NOT BE CONTENT WITH THE RAVAGING OF WORLDS--
--THOU MUST NEEDS DESTROY ALL THAT EXISTS TO SATISFY THY INSANE LUST FOR POWER?!
UNHAND ME, LOUT! I AM THE EMPEROR!
THOU ART A MURDERER!
AND THOU WILT DIE A MURDERER'S DEATH!
THE EMPEROR SCREAMS AS HIS BODY HITS THE FACE OF THE CRYSTAL, BUT HE DOES NOT DIE.
INSTEAD, THERE'S A BLINDING FLARE OF LIGHT, A GHOST-IMAGE OF TIME SPINNING TO A HALT...
...AND, SUDDENLY, ALL PRESENT...

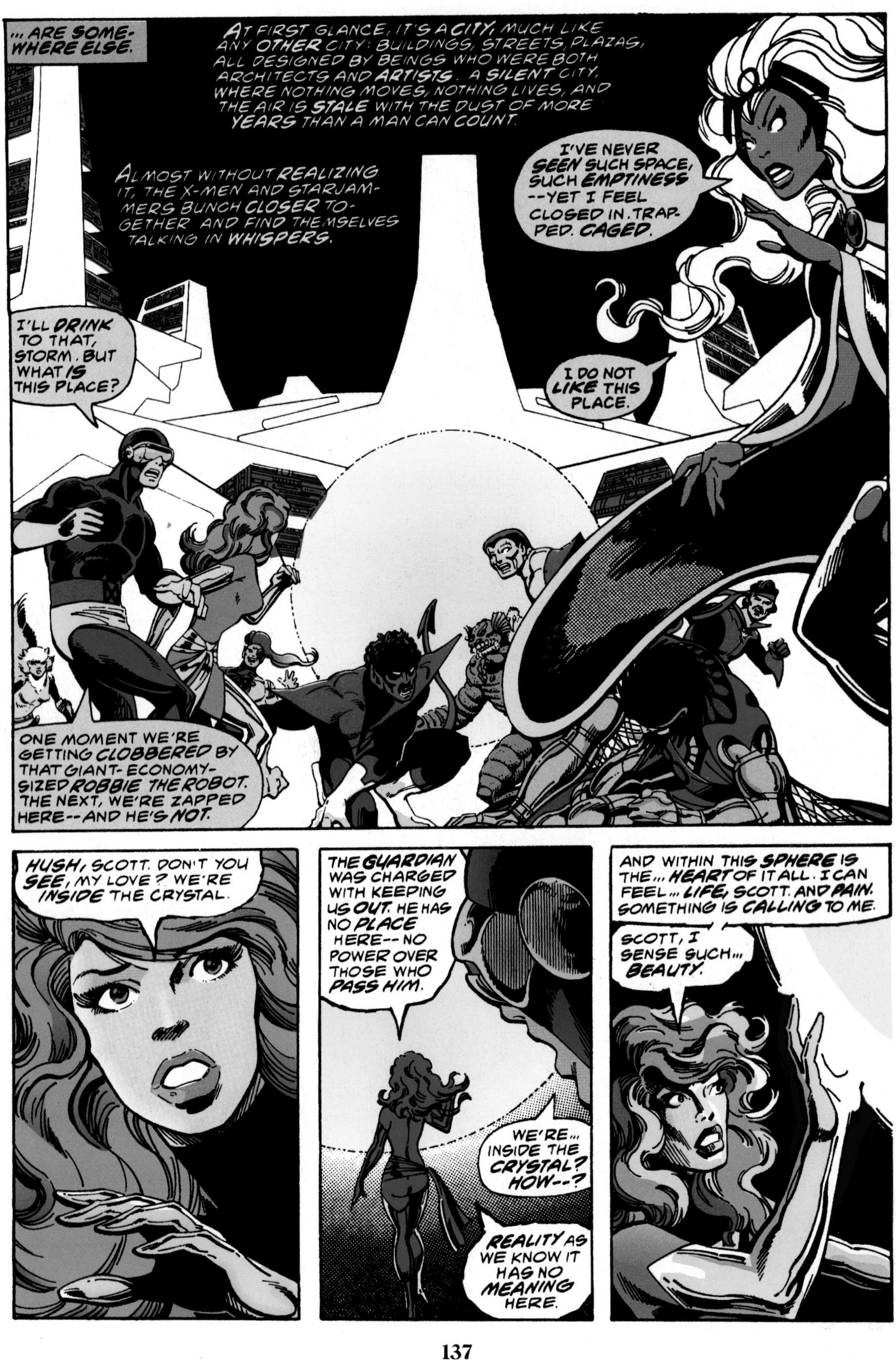
...ARE SOME-WHERE ELSE.
AT FIRST GLANCE, IT'S A CITY, MUCH LIKE ANY OTHER CITY: BUILDINGS, STREETS, PLAZAS, ALL DESIGNED BY BEINGS WHO WERE BOTH ARCHITECTS AND ARTISTS. A SILENT CITY, WHERE NOTHING MOVES, NOTHING LIVES, AND THE AIR IS STALE WITH THE DUST OF MORE YEARS THAN A MAN CAN COUNT.
ALMOST WITHOUT REALIZING IT, THE X-MEN AND STARJAMMERS BUNCH CLOSER TOGETHER AND FIND THEMSELVES TALKING IN WHISPERS.
I'VE NEVER SEEN SUCH SPACE, SUCH EMPTINESS --YET I FEEL CLOSED IN. TRAPPED. CAGED.
I'LL DRINK TO THAT, STORM. BUT WHAT IS THIS PLACE?
I DO NOT LIKE THIS PLACE.
ONE MOMENT WE'RE GETTING CLOBBERED BY THAT GIANT-ECONOMY-SIZED ROBBIE THE ROBOT. THE NEXT, WE'RE ZAPPED HERE--AND HE'S NOT.
HUSH, SCOTT. DON'T YOU SEE, MY LOVE? WE'RE INSIDE THE CRYSTAL.
THE GUARDIAN WAS CHARGED WITH KEEPING US OUT. HE HAS NO PLACE HERE--NO POWER OVER THOSE WHO PASS HIM.
WE'RE... INSIDE THE CRYSTAL? HOW--?
REALITY AS WE KNOW IT HAS NO MEANING HERE.
AND WITHIN THIS SPHERE IS THE... HEART OF IT ALL. I CAN FEEL... LIFE, SCOTT. AND PAIN. SOMETHING IS CALLING TO ME.
SCOTT, I SENSE SUCH... BEAUTY.

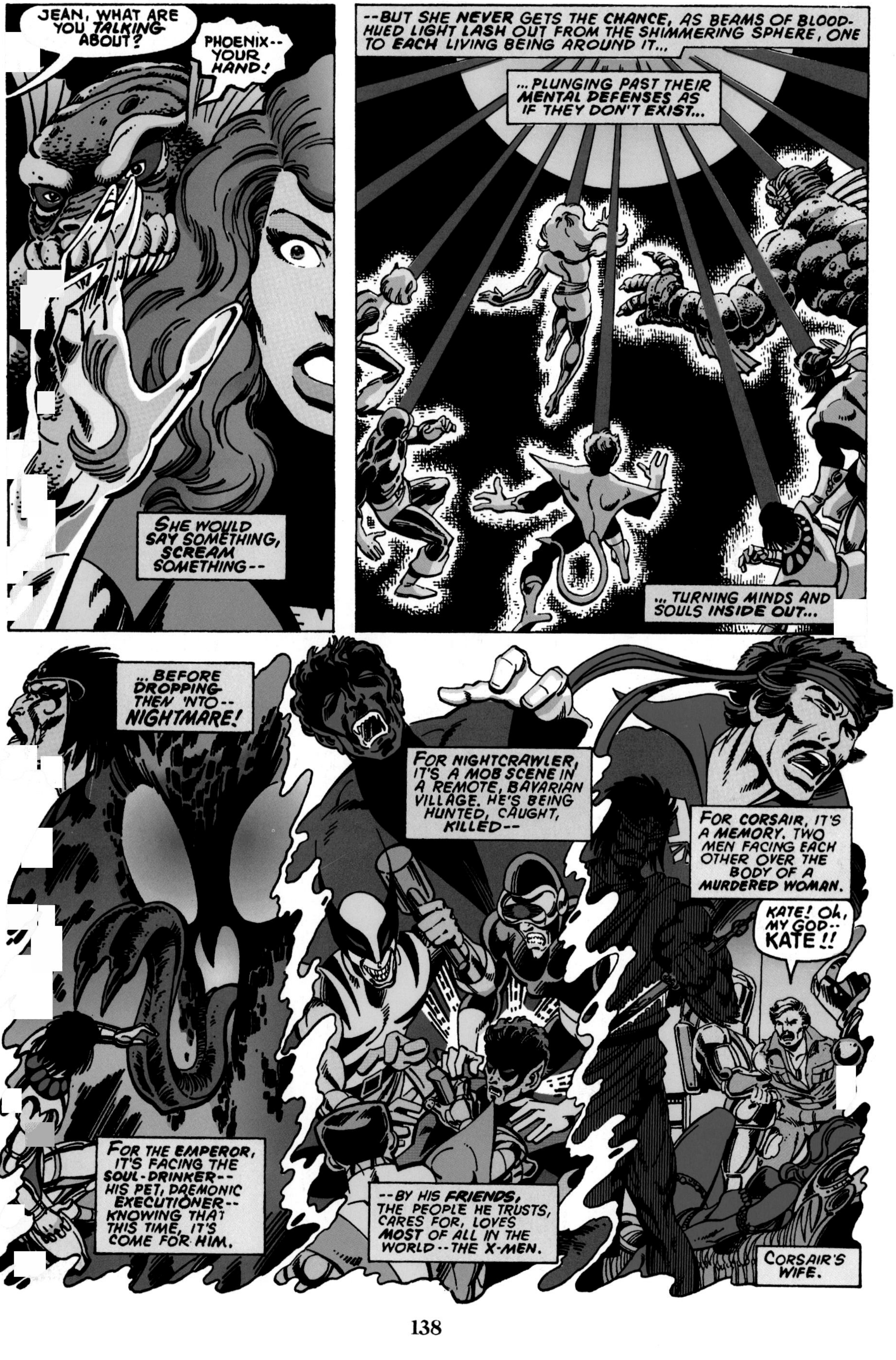
JEAN, WHAT ARE YOU TALKING ABOUT?
PHOENIX-- YOUR HAND!
SHE WOULD SAY SOMETHING, SCREAM SOMETHING--
--BUT SHE NEVER GETS THE CHANCE, AS BEAMS OF BLOOD-HUED LIGHT LASH OUT FROM THE SHIMMERING SPHERE, ONE TO EACH LIVING BEING AROUND IT...
...PLUNGING PAST THEIR MENTAL DEFENSES AS IF THEY DON'T EXIST...
...TURNING MINDS AND SOULS INSIDE OUT...
...BEFORE DROPPING THEN 'NTO-- NIGHTMARE!
FOR NIGHTCRAWLER, IT'S A MOB SCENE IN A REMOTE, BAVARIAN VILLAGE. HE'S BEING HUNTED, CAUGHT, KILLED--
--BY HIS FRIENDS, THE PEOPLE HE TRUSTS, CARES FOR, LOVES MOST OF ALL IN THE WORLD--THE X-MEN.
FOR CORSAIR, IT'S A MEMORY. TWO MEN FACING EACH OTHER OVER THE BODY OF A MURDERED WOMAN.
KATE! Oh, MY GOD-- KATE!!
CORSAIR'S WIFE.
FOR THE EMPEROR, IT'S FACING THE SOUL-DRINKER-- HIS PET, DAEMONIC EXECUTIONER-- KNOWING THAT THIS TIME, IT'S COME FOR HIM.

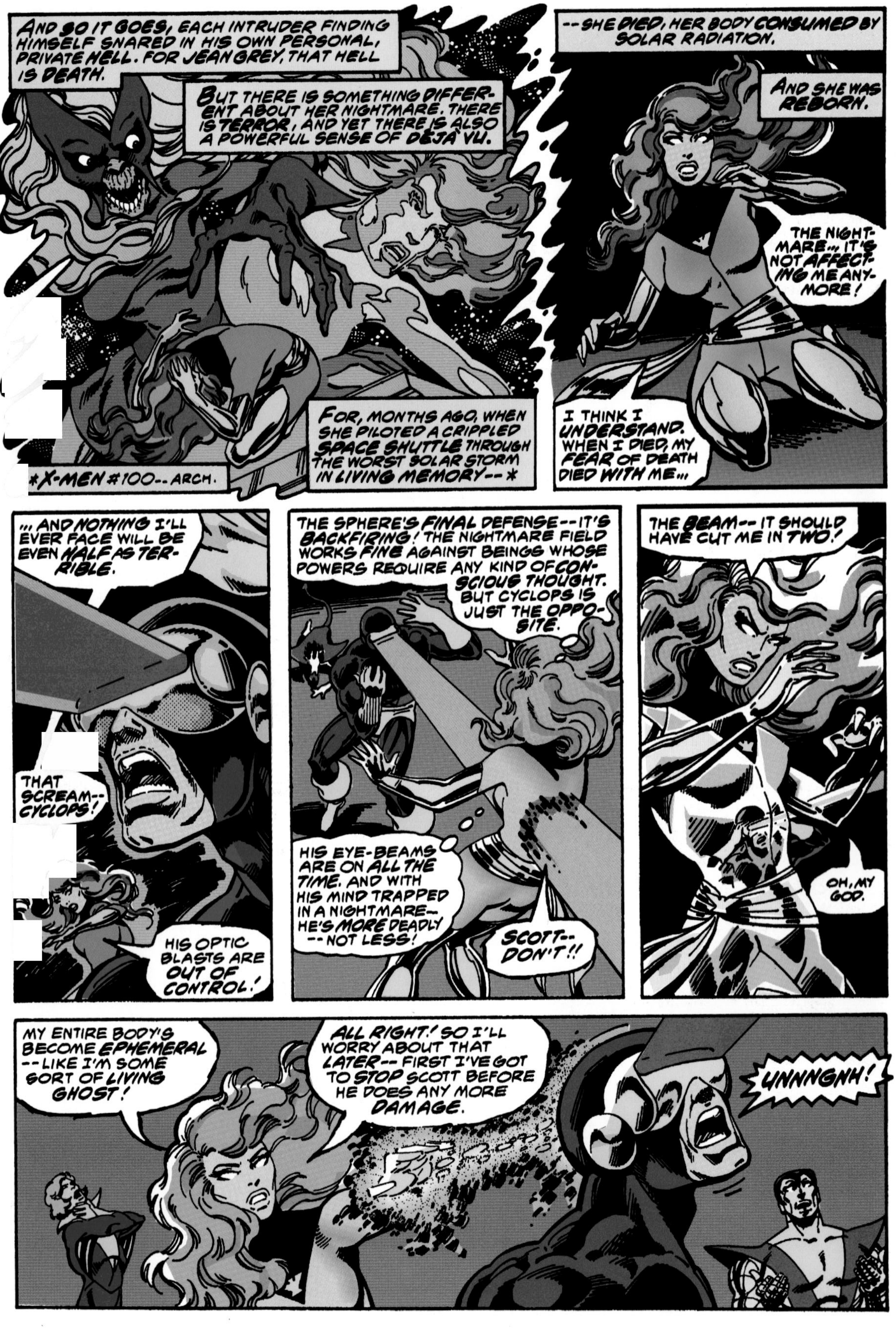
AND SO IT GOES, EACH INTRUDER FINDING HIMSELF SNARED IN HIS OWN PERSONAL, PRIVATE HELL. FOR JEAN GREY, THAT HELL IS DEATH.
BUT THERE IS SOMETHING DIFFERENT ABOUT HER NIGHTMARE. THERE IS TERROR, AND YET THERE IS ALSO A POWERFUL SENSE OF DÉJÀ VU.
FOR, MONTHS AGO, WHEN SHE PILOTED A CRIPPLED SPACE SHUTTLE THROUGH THE WORST SOLAR STORM IN LIVING MEMORY-- *
*X-MEN #100-- ARCH.
--SHE DIED, HER BODY CONSUMED BY SOLAR RADIATION.
AND SHE WAS REBORN.
THE NIGHTMARE... IT'S NOT AFFECTING ME ANYMORE!
I THINK I UNDERSTAND. WHEN I DIED, MY FEAR OF DEATH DIED WITH ME...
...AND NOTHING I'LL EVER FACE WILL BE EVEN HALF AS TERRIBLE.
THAT SCREAM-- CYCLOPS!
HIS OPTIC BLASTS ARE OUT OF CONTROL!
THE SPHERE'S FINAL DEFENSE--IT'S BACKFIRING! THE NIGHTMARE FIELD WORKS FINE AGAINST BEINGS WHOSE POWERS REQUIRE ANY KIND OF CONSCIOUS THOUGHT. BUT CYCLOPS IS JUST THE OPPOSITE.
HIS EYE-BEAMS ARE ON ALL THE TIME. AND WITH HIS MIND TRAPPED IN A NIGHTMARE-- HE'S MORE DEADLY --NOT LESS!
SCOTT-- DON'T!!
THE BEAM-- IT SHOULD HAVE CUT ME IN TWO!
OH, MY GOD.
MY ENTIRE BODY'S BECOME EPHEMERAL --LIKE I'M SOME SORT OF LIVING GHOST!
ALL RIGHT! SO I'LL WORRY ABOUT THAT LATER-- FIRST I'VE GOT TO STOP SCOTT BEFORE HE DOES ANY MORE DAMAGE.
UNNNGNH!

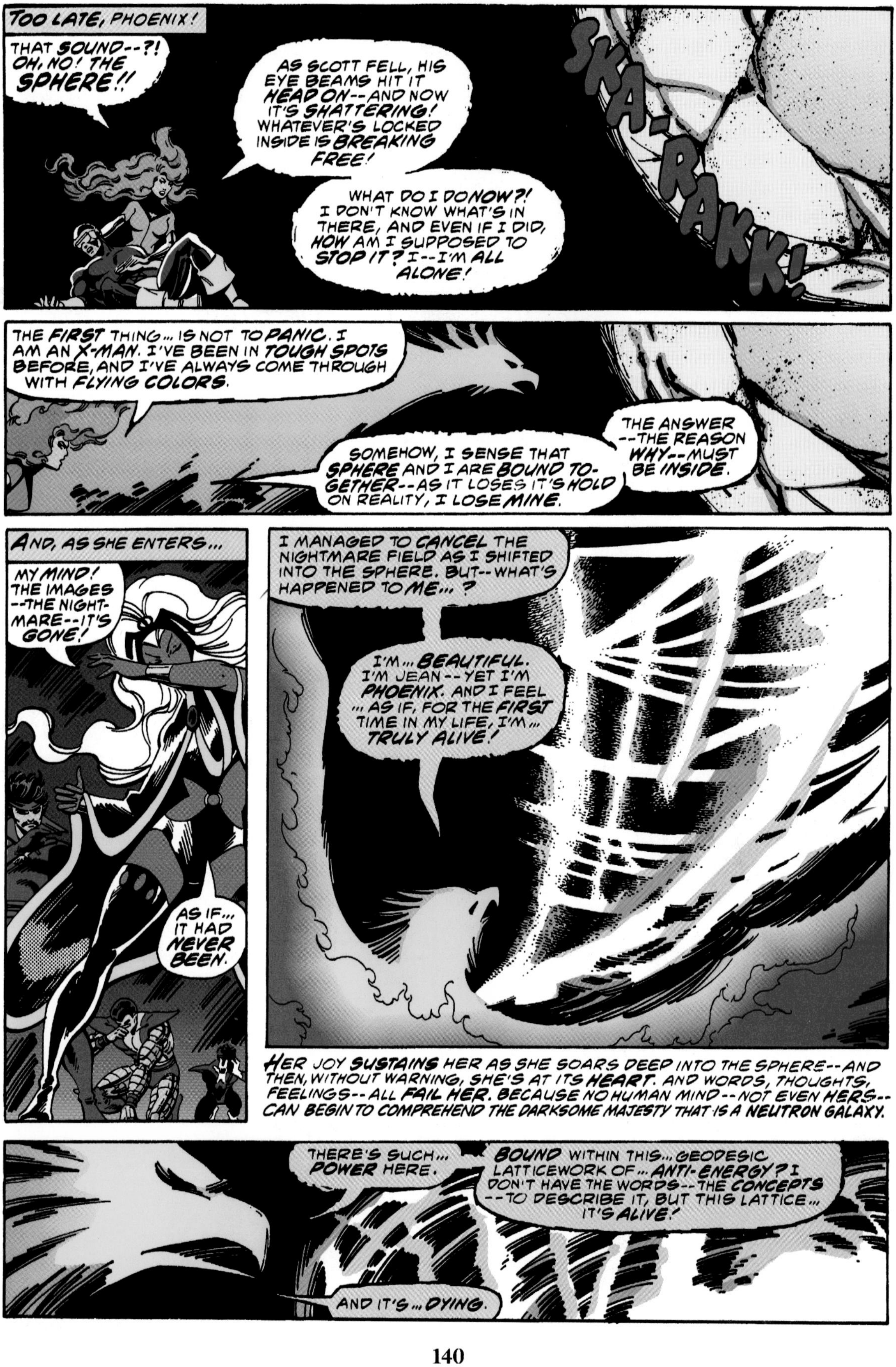
TOO LATE, PHOENIX!
THAT SOUND--?! OH, NO! THE SPHERE!!
AS SCOTT FELL, HIS EYE BEAMS HIT IT HEAD ON--AND NOW IT'S SHATTERING! WHATEVER'S LOCKED INSIDE IS BREAKING FREE!
WHAT DO I DO NOW?! I DON'T KNOW WHAT'S IN THERE, AND EVEN IF I DID, HOW AM I SUPPOSED TO STOP IT? I--I'M ALL ALONE!
SKA-RAKK!
THE FIRST THING... IS NOT TO PANIC. I AM AN X-MAN. I'VE BEEN IN TOUGH SPOTS BEFORE, AND I'VE ALWAYS COME THROUGH WITH FLYING COLORS.
SOMEHOW, I SENSE THAT SPHERE AND I ARE BOUND TOGETHER--AS IT LOSES IT'S HOLD ON REALITY, I LOSE MINE.
THE ANSWER--THE REASON WHY--MUST BE INSIDE.
AND, AS SHE ENTERS...
MY MIND! THE IMAGES--THE NIGHTMARE--IT'S GONE!
AS IF... IT HAD NEVER BEEN.
I MANAGED TO CANCEL THE NIGHTMARE FIELD AS I SHIFTED INTO THE SPHERE. BUT--WHAT'S HAPPENED TO ME...?
I'M... BEAUTIFUL. I'M JEAN--YET I'M PHOENIX. AND I FEEL... AS IF, FOR THE FIRST TIME IN MY LIFE, I'M... TRULY ALIVE!
HER JOY SUSTAINS HER AS SHE SOARS DEEP INTO THE SPHERE--AND THEN, WITHOUT WARNING, SHE'S AT ITS HEART. AND WORDS, THOUGHTS, FEELINGS--ALL FAIL HER. BECAUSE NO HUMAN MIND--NOT EVEN HERS--CAN BEGIN TO COMPREHEND THE DARKSOME MAJESTY THAT IS A NEUTRON GALAXY.
THERE'S SUCH... POWER HERE.
BOUND WITHIN THIS... GEODESIC LATTICEWORK OF... ANTI-ENERGY? I DON'T HAVE THE WORDS--THE CONCEPTS--TO DESCRIBE IT, BUT THIS LATTICE... IT'S ALIVE!
AND IT'S... DYING.

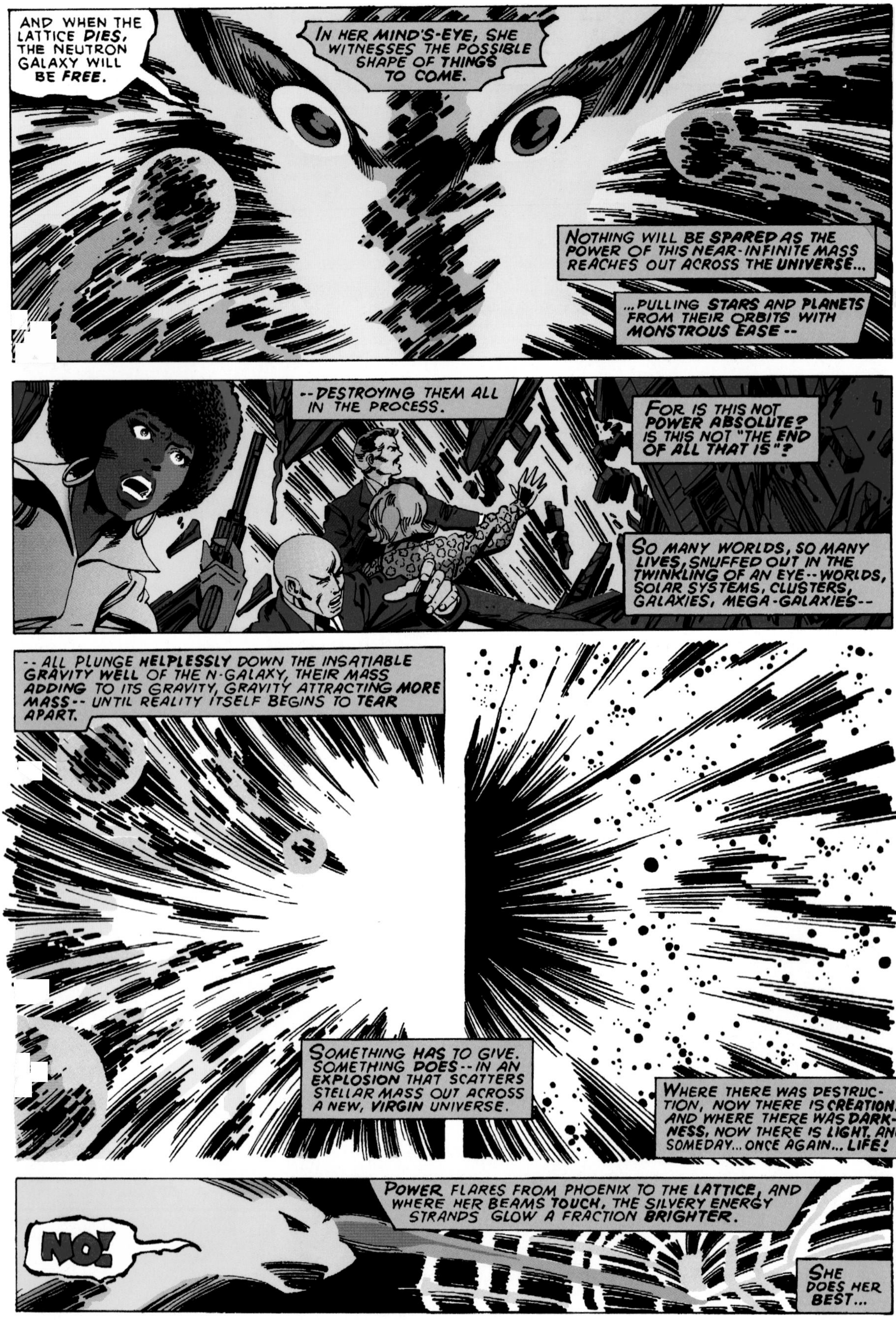

AND WHEN THE LATTICE DIES, THE NEUTRON GALAXY WILL BE FREE.
IN HER MIND'S-EYE, SHE WITNESSES THE POSSIBLE SHAPE OF THINGS TO COME.
NOTHING WILL BE SPARED AS THE POWER OF THIS NEAR-INFINITE MASS REACHES OUT ACROSS THE UNIVERSE...
...PULLING STARS AND PLANETS FROM THEIR ORBITS WITH MONSTROUS EASE --
--DESTROYING THEM ALL IN THE PROCESS.
FOR IS THIS NOT POWER ABSOLUTE? IS THIS NOT "THE END OF ALL THAT IS"?
SO MANY WORLDS, SO MANY LIVES, SNUFFED OUT IN THE TWINKLING OF AN EYE--WORLDS, SOLAR SYSTEMS, CLUSTERS, GALAXIES, MEGA-GALAXIES--
--ALL PLUNGE HELPLESSLY DOWN THE INSATIABLE GRAVITY WELL OF THE N-GALAXY, THEIR MASS ADDING TO ITS GRAVITY, GRAVITY ATTRACTING MORE MASS-- UNTIL REALITY ITSELF BEGINS TO TEAR APART.
SOMETHING HAS TO GIVE. SOMETHING DOES--IN AN EXPLOSION THAT SCATTERS STELLAR MASS OUT ACROSS A NEW, VIRGIN UNIVERSE.
WHERE THERE WAS DESTRUCTION, NOW THERE IS CREATION. AND WHERE THERE WAS DARKNESS, NOW THERE IS LIGHT. AND SOMEDAY...ONCE AGAIN...LIFE!
POWER FLARES FROM PHOENIX TO THE LATTICE, AND WHERE HER BEAMS TOUCH, THE SILVERY ENERGY STRANDS GLOW A FRACTION BRIGHTER.
NO!
SHE DOES HER BEST...

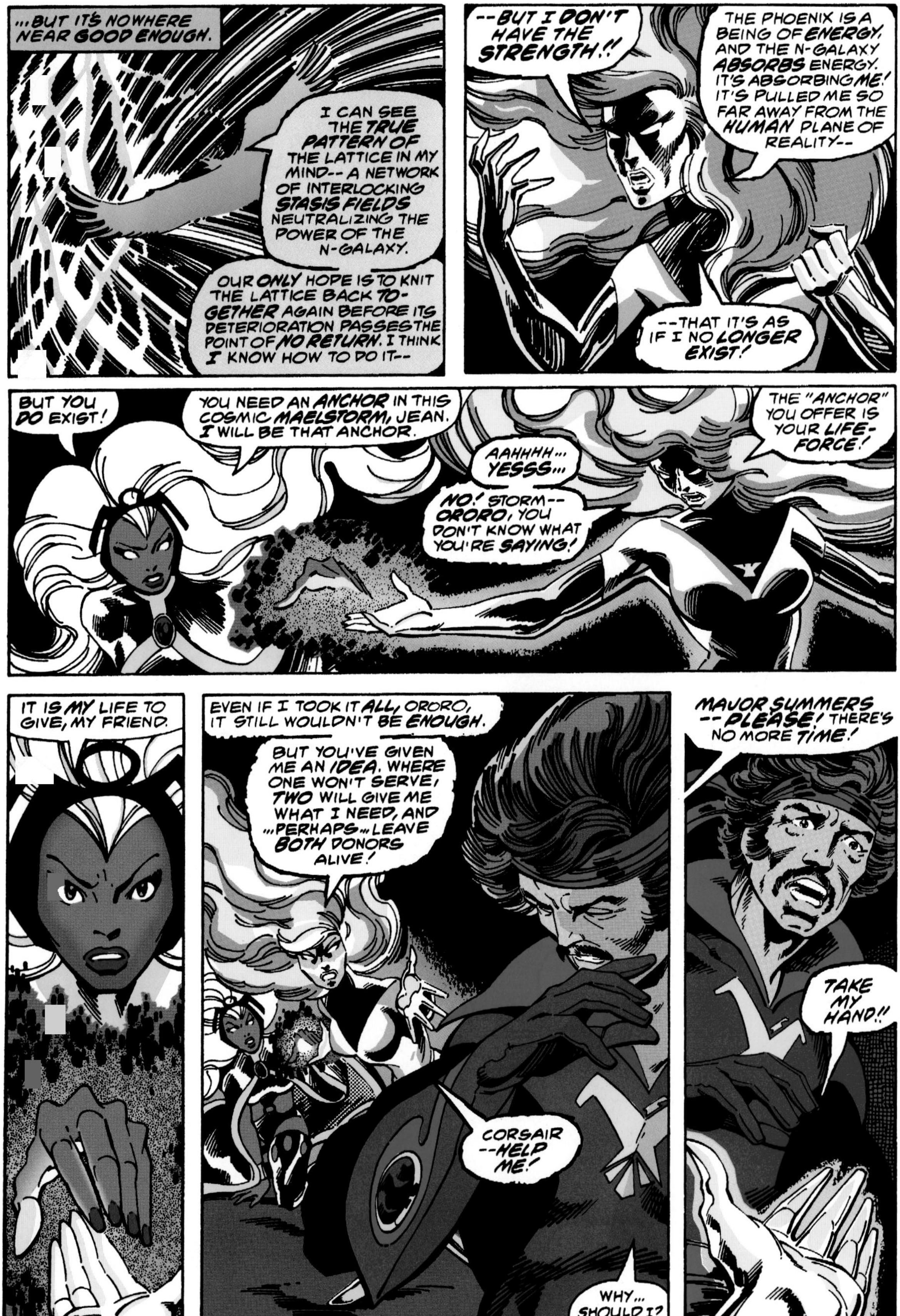

...BUT IT'S NOWHERE NEAR GOOD ENOUGH.
I CAN SEE THE TRUE PATTERN OF THE LATTICE IN MY MIND-- A NETWORK OF INTERLOCKING STASIS FIELDS NEUTRALIZING THE POWER OF THE N-GALAXY.
OUR ONLY HOPE IS TO KNIT THE LATTICE BACK TO-GETHER AGAIN BEFORE ITS DETERIORATION PASSES THE POINT OF NO RETURN. I THINK I KNOW HOW TO DO IT--
--BUT I DON'T HAVE THE STRENGTH!!
THE PHOENIX IS A BEING OF ENERGY, AND THE N-GALAXY ABSORBS ENERGY. IT'S ABSORBING ME! IT'S PULLED ME SO FAR AWAY FROM THE HUMAN PLANE OF REALITY--
--THAT IT'S AS IF I NO LONGER EXIST!
BUT YOU DO EXIST!
YOU NEED AN ANCHOR IN THIS COSMIC MAELSTORM, JEAN. I WILL BE THAT ANCHOR.
AAHHHH... YESSS...
NO! STORM-- ORORO, YOU DON'T KNOW WHAT YOU'RE SAYING!
THE "ANCHOR" YOU OFFER IS YOUR LIFE-FORCE!
IT IS MY LIFE TO GIVE, MY FRIEND.
EVEN IF I TOOK IT ALL, ORORO, IT STILL WOULDN'T BE ENOUGH.
BUT YOU'VE GIVEN ME AN IDEA. WHERE ONE WON'T SERVE, TWO WILL GIVE ME WHAT I NEED, AND ...PERHAPS... LEAVE BOTH DONORS ALIVE!
CORSAIR --HELP ME!
WHY... SHOULD I?
MAJOR SUMMERS --PLEASE! THERE'S NO MORE TIME!
TAKE MY HAND!!

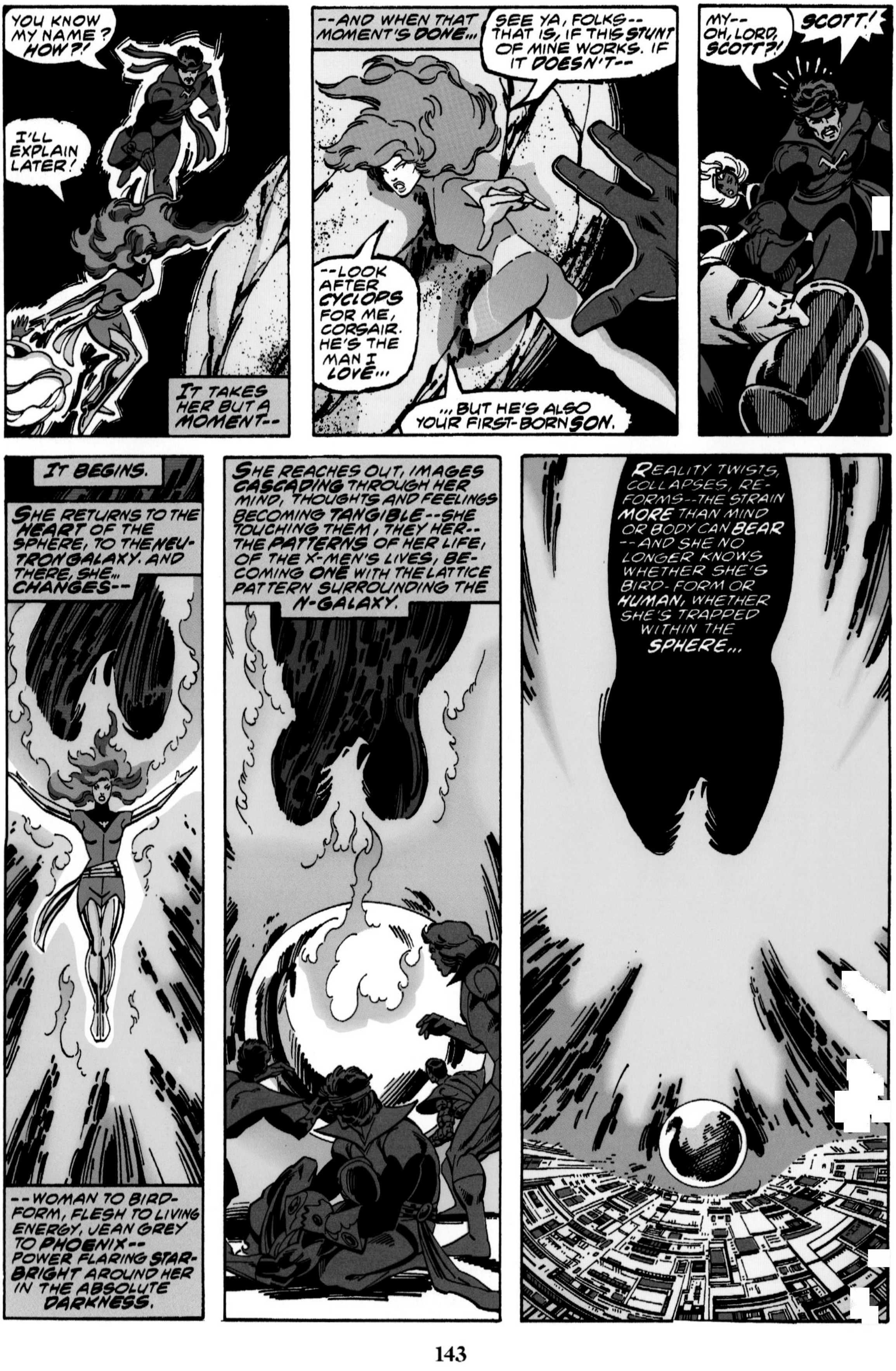
YOU KNOW MY NAME? HOW?!
I'LL EXPLAIN LATER!
IT TAKES HER BUT A MOMENT--
--AND WHEN THAT MOMENT'S DONE...
SEE YA, FOLKS-- THAT IS, IF THIS STUNT OF MINE WORKS. IF IT DOESN'T--
--LOOK AFTER CYCLOPS FOR ME, CORSAIR. HE'S THE MAN I LOVE...
...BUT HE'S ALSO YOUR FIRST-BORN SON.
MY-- OH, LORD, SCOTT?!
SCOTT!
IT BEGINS.
SHE RETURNS TO THE HEART OF THE SPHERE, TO THE NEUTRON GALAXY. AND THERE, SHE... CHANGES--
--WOMAN TO BIRD-FORM, FLESH TO LIVING ENERGY, JEAN GREY TO PHOENIX-- POWER FLARING STAR-BRIGHT AROUND HER IN THE ABSOLUTE DARKNESS.
SHE REACHES OUT, IMAGES CASCADING THROUGH HER MIND, THOUGHTS AND FEELINGS BECOMING TANGIBLE--SHE TOUCHING THEM, THEY HER-- THE PATTERNS OF HER LIFE, OF THE X-MEN'S LIVES, BECOMING ONE WITH THE LATTICE PATTERN SURROUNDING THE N-GALAXY.
REALITY TWISTS, COLLAPSES, REFORMS--THE STRAIN MORE THAN MIND OR BODY CAN BEAR --AND SHE NO LONGER KNOWS WHETHER SHE'S BIRD-FORM OR HUMAN, WHETHER SHE'S TRAPPED WITHIN THE SPHERE...

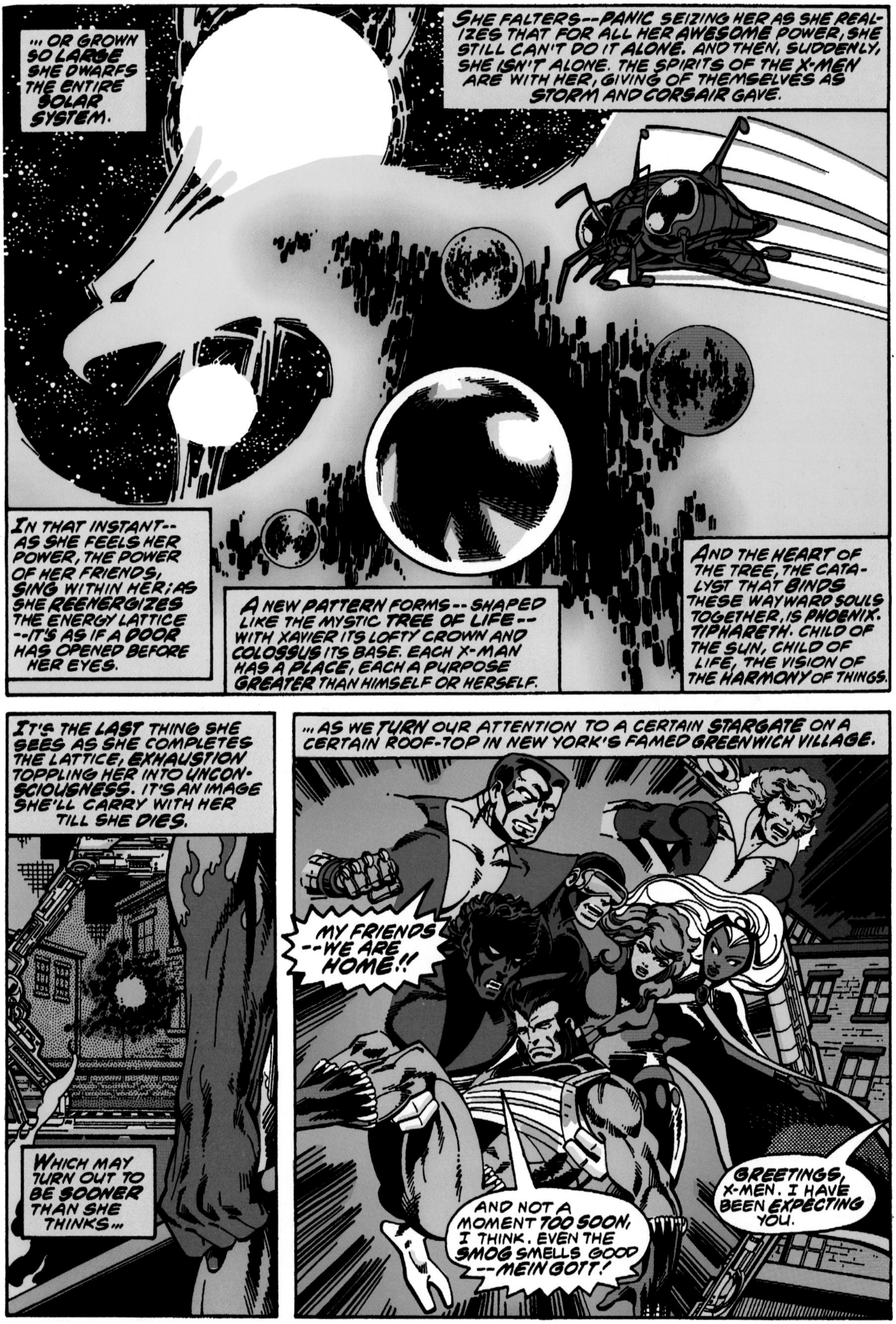
...OR GROWN SO LARGE SHE DWARFS THE ENTIRE SOLAR SYSTEM.
SHE FALTERS--PANIC SEIZING HER AS SHE REALIZES THAT FOR ALL HER AWESOME POWER, SHE STILL CAN'T DO IT ALONE. AND THEN, SUDDENLY, SHE ISN'T ALONE. THE SPIRITS OF THE X-MEN ARE WITH HER, GIVING OF THEMSELVES AS STORM AND CORSAIR GAVE.
IN THAT INSTANT--AS SHE FEELS HER POWER, THE POWER OF HER FRIENDS, SING WITHIN HER; AS SHE REENERGIZES THE ENERGY LATTICE--IT'S AS IF A DOOR HAS OPENED BEFORE HER EYES.
A NEW PATTERN FORMS--SHAPED LIKE THE MYSTIC TREE OF LIFE--WITH XAVIER ITS LOFTY CROWN AND COLOSSUS ITS BASE. EACH X-MAN HAS A PLACE, EACH A PURPOSE GREATER THAN HIMSELF OR HERSELF.
AND THE HEART OF THE TREE, THE CATALYST THAT BINDS THESE WAYWARD SOULS TOGETHER, IS PHOENIX. TIPHARETH. CHILD OF THE SUN, CHILD OF LIFE, THE VISION OF THE HARMONY OF THINGS.
IT'S THE LAST THING SHE SEES AS SHE COMPLETES THE LATTICE, EXHAUSTION TOPPLING HER INTO UNCONSCIOUSNESS. IT'S AN IMAGE SHE'LL CARRY WITH HER TILL SHE DIES.
WHICH MAY TURN OUT TO BE SOONER THAN SHE THINKS...
...AS WE TURN OUR ATTENTION TO A CERTAIN STARGATE ON A CERTAIN ROOF-TOP IN NEW YORK'S FAMED GREENWICH VILLAGE.
MY FRIENDS--WE ARE HOME!!
AND NOT A MOMENT TOO SOON, I THINK. EVEN THE SMOG SMELLS GOOD--MEIN GOTT!
GREETINGS, X-MEN. I HAVE BEEN EXPECTING YOU.

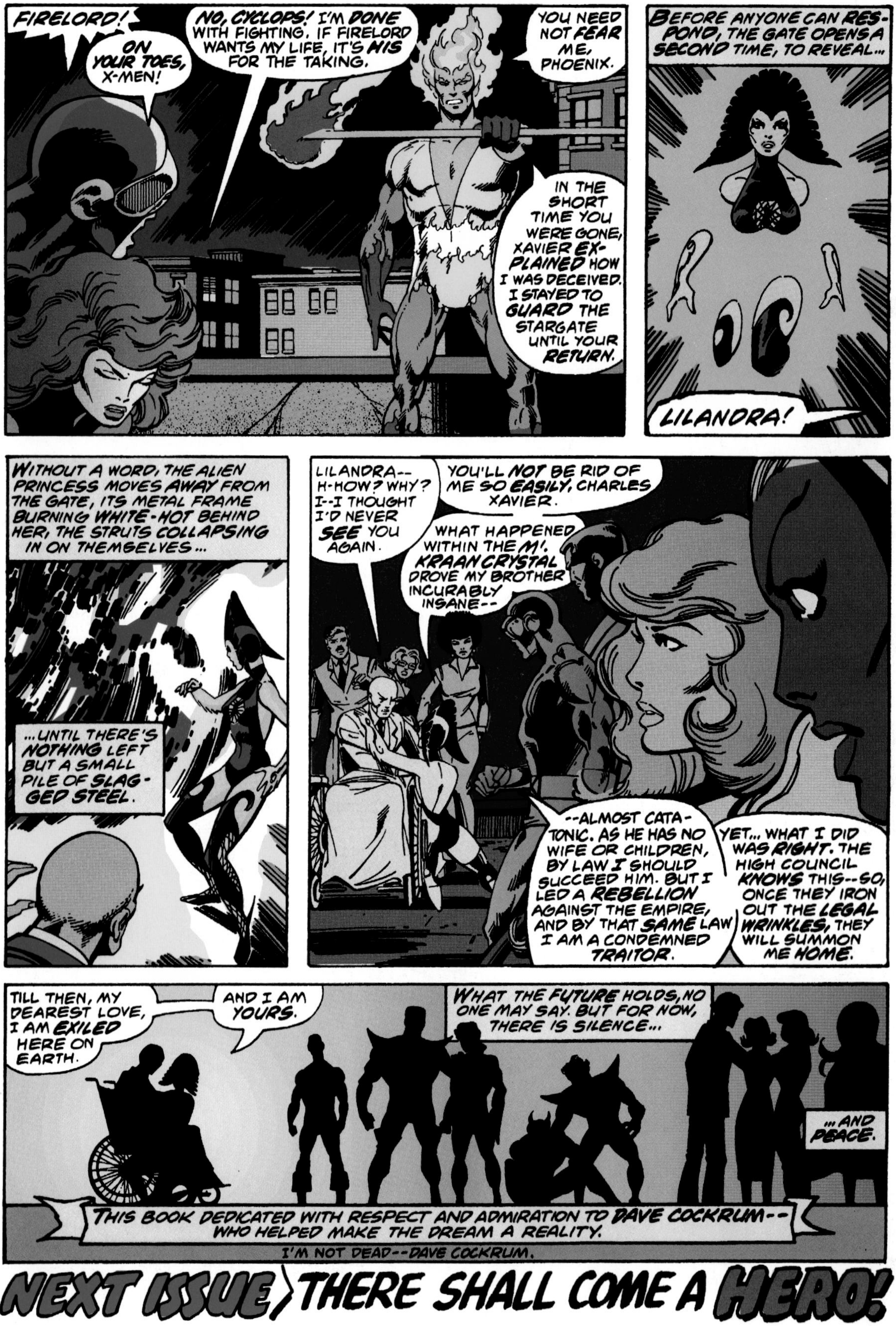
FIRELORD!
ON YOUR TOES, X-MEN!
NO, CYCLOPS! I'M DONE WITH FIGHTING. IF FIRELORD WANTS MY LIFE, IT'S HIS FOR THE TAKING.
YOU NEED NOT FEAR ME, PHOENIX.
IN THE SHORT TIME YOU WERE GONE, XAVIER EXPLAINED HOW I WAS DECEIVED. I STAYED TO GUARD THE STARGATE UNTIL YOUR RETURN.
BEFORE ANYONE CAN RESPOND, THE GATE OPENS A SECOND TIME, TO REVEAL...
LILANDRA!
WITHOUT A WORD, THE ALIEN PRINCESS MOVES AWAY FROM THE GATE, ITS METAL FRAME BURNING WHITE-HOT BEHIND HER, THE STRUTS COLLAPSING IN ON THEMSELVES...
...UNTIL THERE'S NOTHING LEFT BUT A SMALL PILE OF SLAGGED STEEL.
LILANDRA-- H-HOW? WHY? I--I THOUGHT I'D NEVER SEE YOU AGAIN.
YOU'LL NOT BE RID OF ME SO EASILY, CHARLES XAVIER.
WHAT HAPPENED WITHIN THE M'KRAAN CRYSTAL DROVE MY BROTHER INCURABLY INSANE--
--ALMOST CATATONIC. AS HE HAS NO WIFE OR CHILDREN, BY LAW I SHOULD SUCCEED HIM. BUT I LED A REBELLION AGAINST THE EMPIRE, AND BY THAT SAME LAW I AM A CONDEMNED TRAITOR.
YET... WHAT I DID WAS RIGHT. THE HIGH COUNCIL KNOWS THIS--SO, ONCE THEY IRON OUT THE LEGAL WRINKLES, THEY WILL SUMMON ME HOME.
TILL THEN, MY DEAREST LOVE, I AM EXILED HERE ON EARTH.
AND I AM YOURS.
WHAT THE FUTURE HOLDS, NO ONE MAY SAY. BUT FOR NOW, THERE IS SILENCE...
...AND PEACE.
THIS BOOK DEDICATED WITH RESPECT AND ADMIRATION TO DAVE COCKRUM-- WHO HELPED MAKE THE DREAM A REALITY.
I'M NOT DEAD--DAVE COCKRUM.

NEXT ISSUE › THERE SHALL COME A HERO!

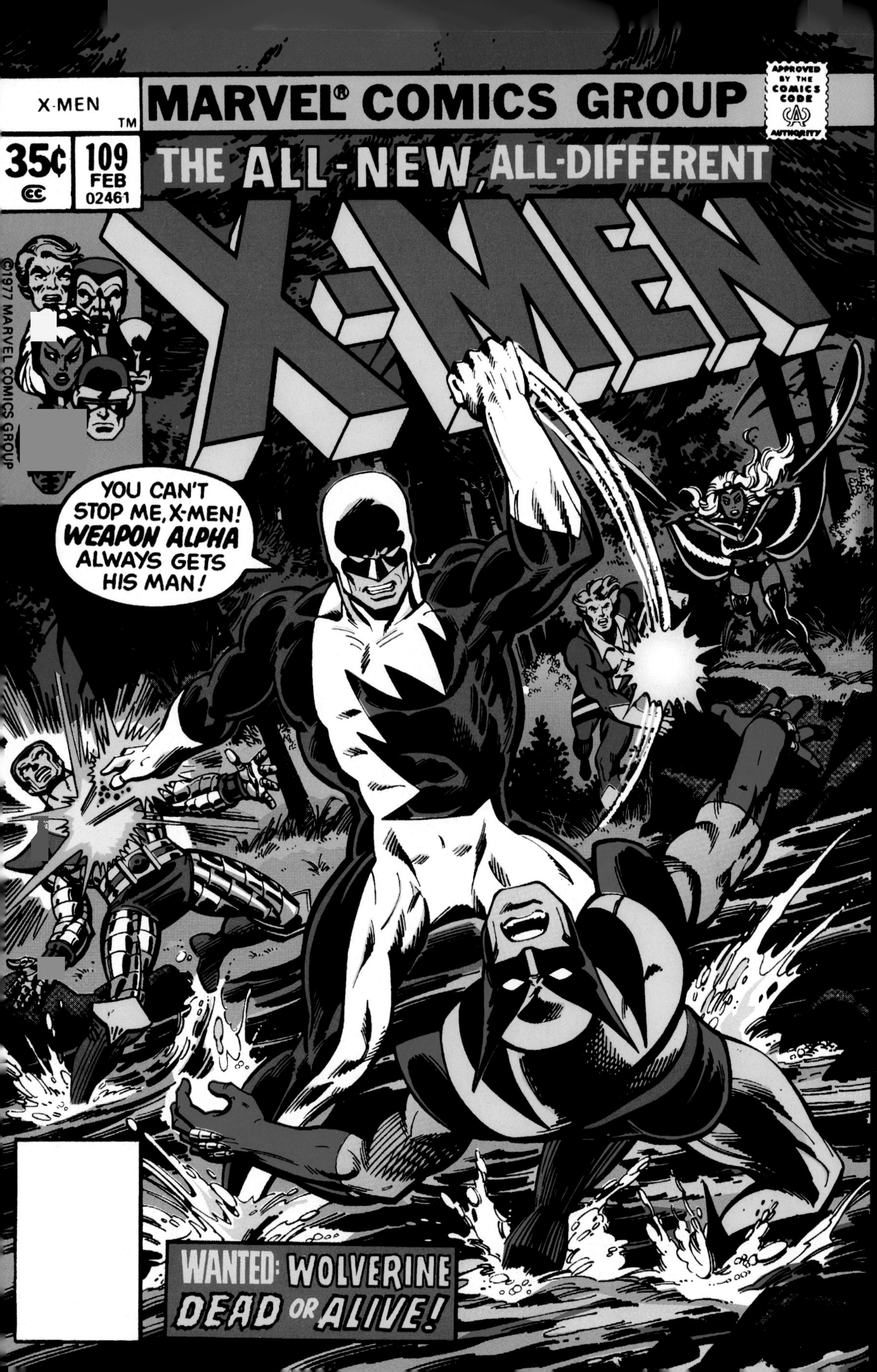
X-MEN ™
MARVEL® COMICS GROUP
APPROVED BY THE COMICS CODE AUTHORITY
35¢
109 FEB 02461
THE ALL-NEW, ALL-DIFFERENT
X-MEN ™
©1977 MARVEL COMICS GROUP
YOU CAN'T STOP ME, X-MEN! WEAPON ALPHA ALWAYS GETS HIS MAN!
WANTED: WOLVERINE DEAD OR ALIVE!

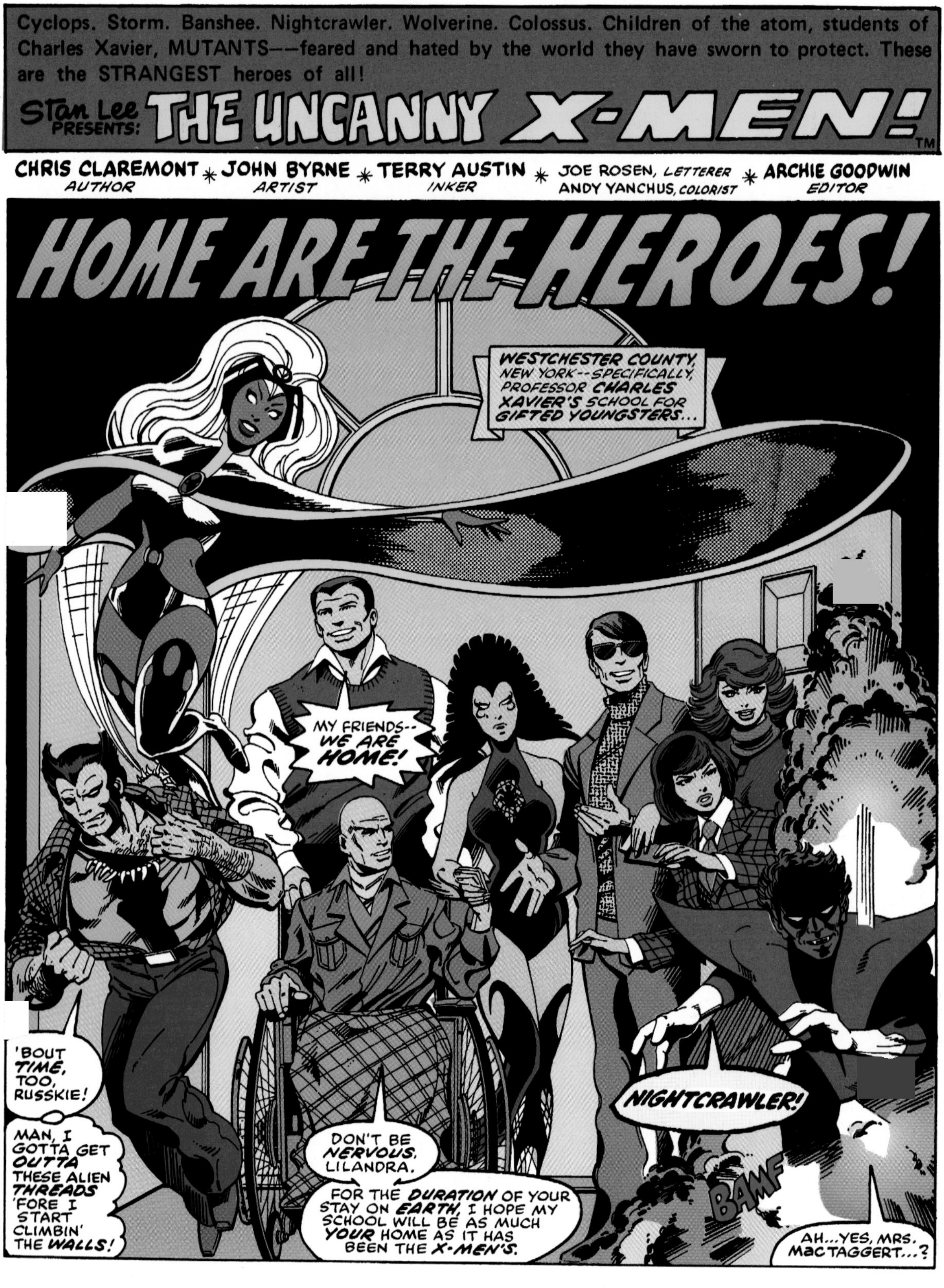

Cyclops. Storm. Banshee. Nightcrawler. Wolverine. Colossus. Children of the atom, students of Charles Xavier, MUTANTS––feared and hated by the world they have sworn to protect. These are the STRANGEST heroes of all!
Stan Lee PRESENTS: THE UNCANNY X-MEN!
CHRIS CLAREMONT AUTHOR * JOHN BYRNE ARTIST * TERRY AUSTIN INKER * JOE ROSEN, LETTERER ANDY YANCHUS, COLORIST * ARCHIE GOODWIN EDITOR
HOME ARE THE HEROES!
WESTCHESTER COUNTY, NEW YORK--SPECIFICALLY, PROFESSOR CHARLES XAVIER'S SCHOOL FOR GIFTED YOUNGSTERS...
MY FRIENDS-- WE ARE HOME!
'BOUT TIME, TOO, RUSSKIE!
MAN, I GOTTA GET OUTTA THESE ALIEN THREADS 'FORE I START CLIMBIN' THE WALLS!
DON'T BE NERVOUS, LILANDRA.
FOR THE DURATION OF YOUR STAY ON EARTH, I HOPE MY SCHOOL WILL BE AS MUCH YOUR HOME AS IT HAS BEEN THE X-MEN'S.
NIGHTCRAWLER!
BAMF
AH...YES, MRS. MacTAGGERT...?

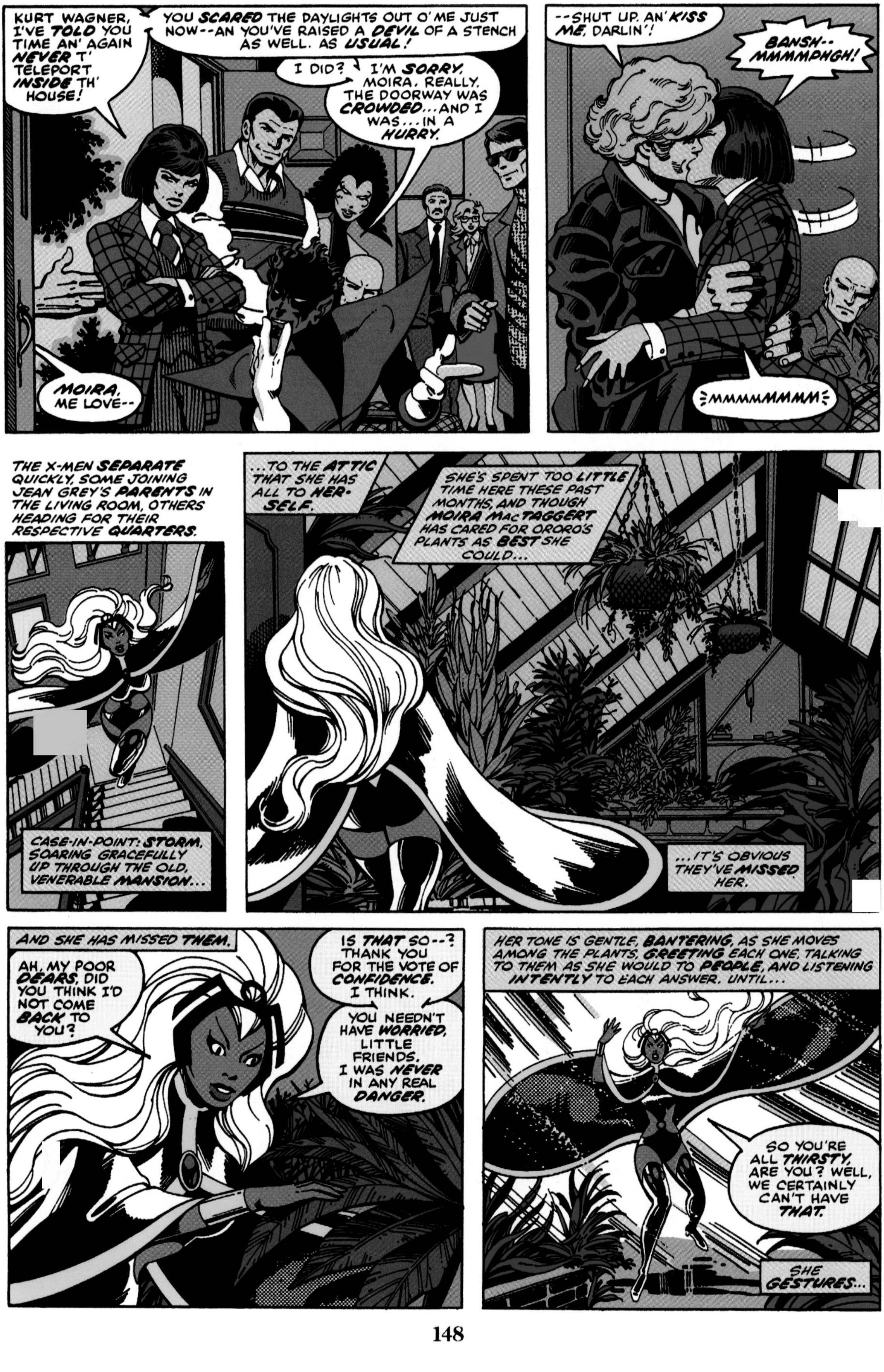
KURT WAGNER, I'VE TOLD YOU TIME AN' AGAIN NEVER T' TELEPORT INSIDE TH' HOUSE!
YOU SCARED THE DAYLIGHTS OUT O' ME JUST NOW--AN YOU'VE RAISED A DEVIL OF A STENCH AS WELL. AS USUAL!
I DID?
I'M SORRY, MOIRA. REALLY. THE DOORWAY WAS CROWDED...AND I WAS...IN A HURRY.
MOIRA, ME LOVE--
--SHUT UP. AN' KISS ME, DARLIN'!
BANSH--MMMMPHGH!
MMMMMMMM
THE X-MEN SEPARATE QUICKLY, SOME JOINING JEAN GREY'S PARENTS IN THE LIVING ROOM, OTHERS HEADING FOR THEIR RESPECTIVE QUARTERS.
CASE-IN-POINT: STORM, SOARING GRACEFULLY UP THROUGH THE OLD, VENERABLE MANSION...
...TO THE ATTIC THAT SHE HAS ALL TO HER-SELF.
SHE'S SPENT TOO LITTLE TIME HERE THESE PAST MONTHS, AND THOUGH MOIRA MacTAGGERT HAS CARED FOR ORORO'S PLANTS AS BEST SHE COULD...
...IT'S OBVIOUS THEY'VE MISSED HER.
AND SHE HAS MISSED THEM.
AH, MY POOR DEARS, DID YOU THINK I'D NOT COME BACK TO YOU?
IS THAT SO--? THANK YOU FOR THE VOTE OF CONFIDENCE. I THINK.
YOU NEEDN'T HAVE WORRIED, LITTLE FRIENDS. I WAS NEVER IN ANY REAL DANGER.
HER TONE IS GENTLE, BANTERING, AS SHE MOVES AMONG THE PLANTS, GREETING EACH ONE, TALKING TO THEM AS SHE WOULD TO PEOPLE, AND LISTENING INTENTLY TO EACH ANSWER. UNTIL...
SO YOU'RE ALL THIRSTY, ARE YOU? WELL, WE CERTAINLY CAN'T HAVE THAT.
SHE GESTURES...

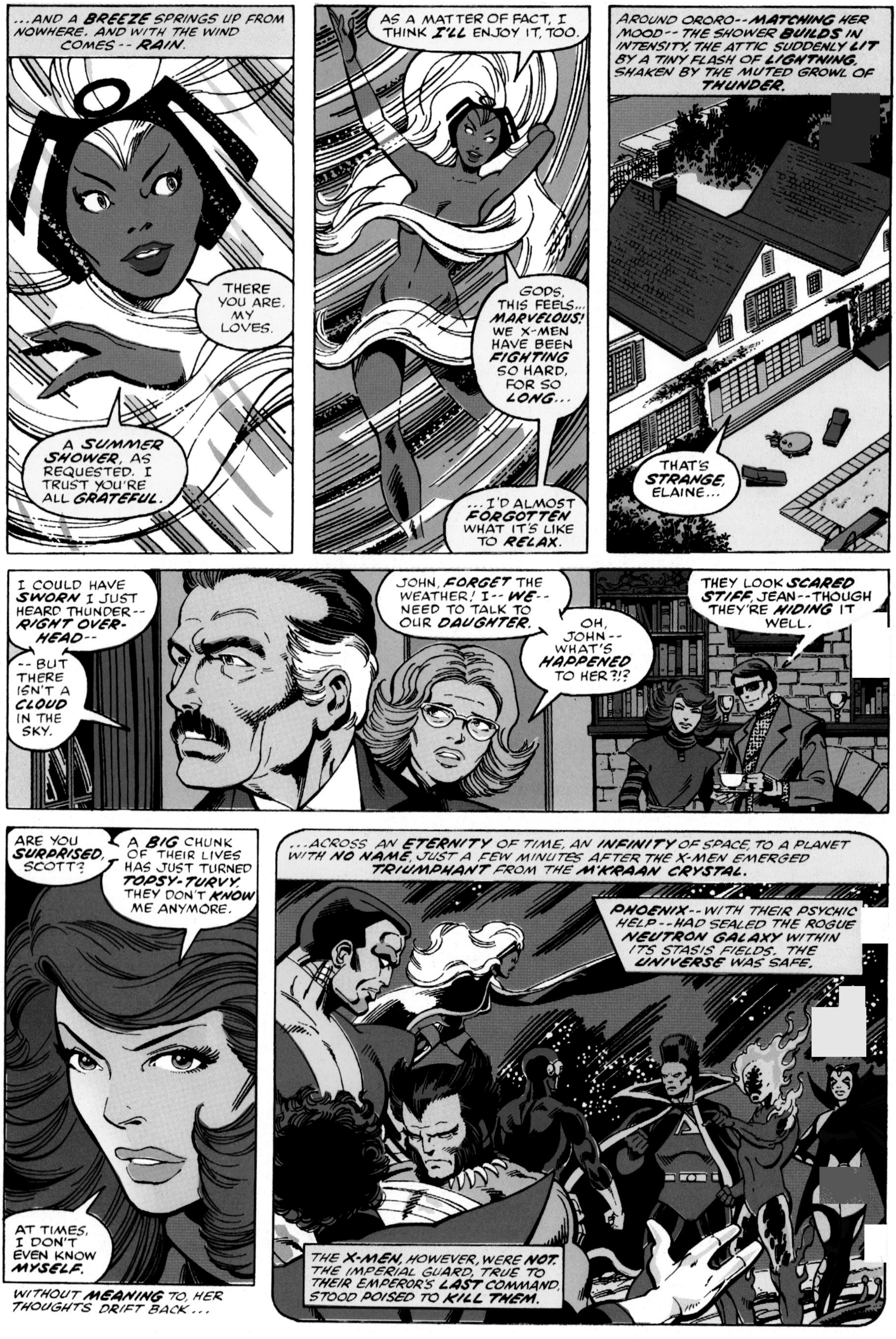
...AND A BREEZE SPRINGS UP FROM NOWHERE. AND WITH THE WIND COMES-- RAIN.
THERE YOU ARE, MY LOVES.
A SUMMER SHOWER, AS REQUESTED. I TRUST YOU'RE ALL GRATEFUL.
AS A MATTER OF FACT, I THINK I'LL ENJOY IT, TOO.
GODS, THIS FEELS... MARVELOUS! WE X-MEN HAVE BEEN FIGHTING SO HARD, FOR SO LONG...
...I'D ALMOST FORGOTTEN WHAT IT'S LIKE TO RELAX.
AROUND ORORO--MATCHING HER MOOD--THE SHOWER BUILDS IN INTENSITY, THE ATTIC SUDDENLY LIT BY A TINY FLASH OF LIGHTNING, SHAKEN BY THE MUTED GROWL OF THUNDER.
THAT'S STRANGE, ELAINE...
I COULD HAVE SWORN I JUST HEARD THUNDER--RIGHT OVER-HEAD--
--BUT THERE ISN'T A CLOUD IN THE SKY.
JOHN, FORGET THE WEATHER! I--WE--NEED TO TALK TO OUR DAUGHTER.
OH, JOHN--WHAT'S HAPPENED TO HER?!?
THEY LOOK SCARED STIFF, JEAN--THOUGH THEY'RE HIDING IT WELL.
ARE YOU SURPRISED, SCOTT?
A BIG CHUNK OF THEIR LIVES HAS JUST TURNED TOPSY-TURVY. THEY DON'T KNOW ME ANYMORE.
AT TIMES, I DON'T EVEN KNOW MYSELF.
WITHOUT MEANING TO, HER THOUGHTS DRIFT BACK...
...ACROSS AN ETERNITY OF TIME, AN INFINITY OF SPACE, TO A PLANET WITH NO NAME, JUST A FEW MINUTES AFTER THE X-MEN EMERGED TRIUMPHANT FROM THE M'KRAAN CRYSTAL.
PHOENIX--WITH THEIR PSYCHIC HELP--HAD SEALED THE ROGUE NEUTRON GALAXY WITHIN ITS STASIS FIELDS. THE UNIVERSE WAS SAFE.
THE X-MEN, HOWEVER, WERE NOT. THE IMPERIAL GUARD, TRUE TO THEIR EMPEROR'S LAST COMMAND, STOOD POISED TO KILL THEM.

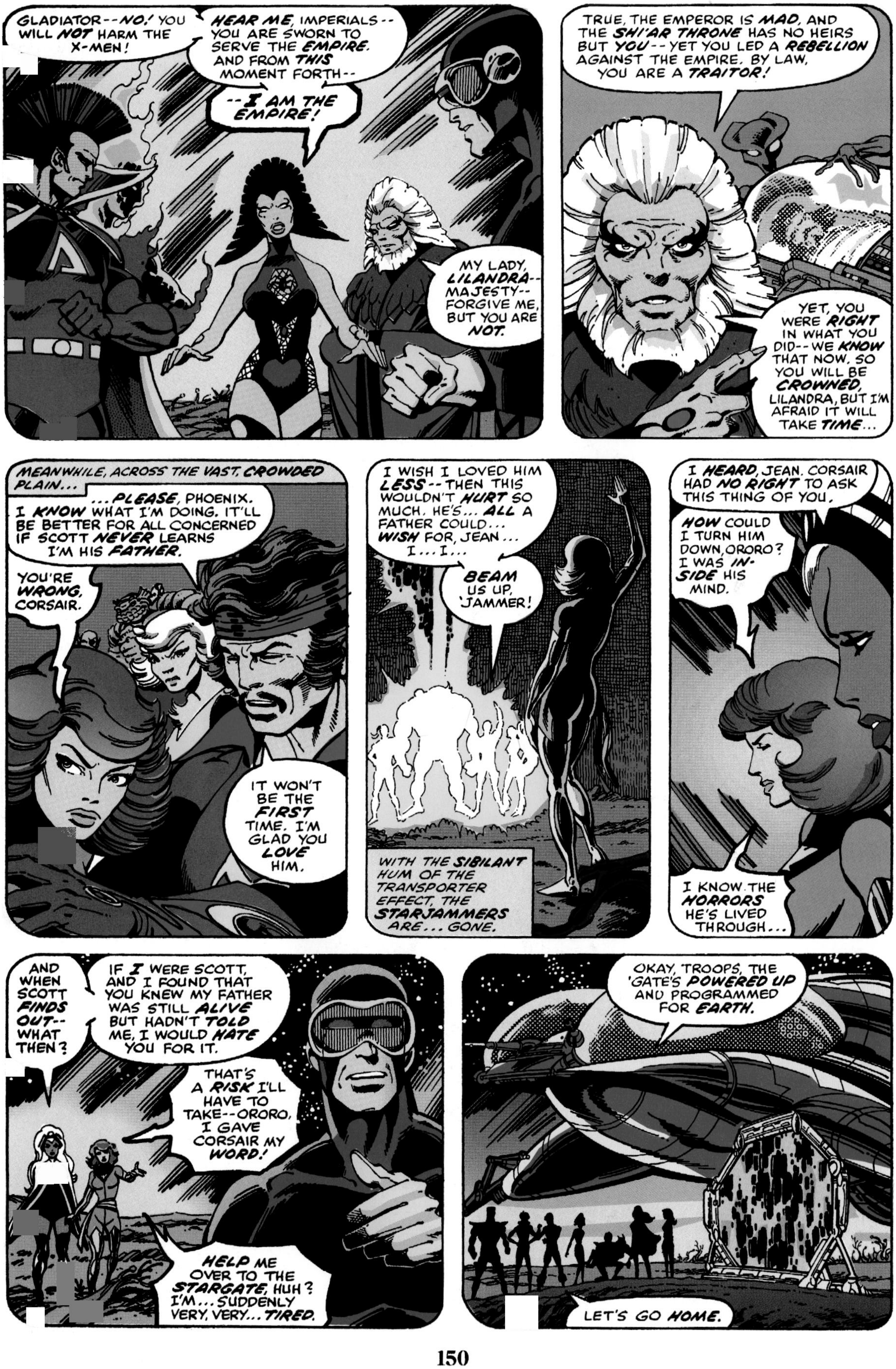
GLADIATOR--NO! YOU WILL NOT HARM THE X-MEN!
HEAR ME, IMPERIALS--YOU ARE SWORN TO SERVE THE EMPIRE. AND FROM THIS MOMENT FORTH--
--I AM THE EMPIRE!
MY LADY, LILANDRA--MAJESTY--FORGIVE ME, BUT YOU ARE NOT.
TRUE, THE EMPEROR IS MAD, AND THE SHI'AR THRONE HAS NO HEIRS BUT YOU--YET YOU LED A REBELLION AGAINST THE EMPIRE. BY LAW, YOU ARE A TRAITOR!
YET, YOU WERE RIGHT IN WHAT YOU DID--WE KNOW THAT NOW. SO YOU WILL BE CROWNED, LILANDRA, BUT I'M AFRAID IT WILL TAKE TIME...
MEANWHILE, ACROSS THE VAST, CROWDED PLAIN...
...PLEASE, PHOENIX. I KNOW WHAT I'M DOING. IT'LL BE BETTER FOR ALL CONCERNED IF SCOTT NEVER LEARNS I'M HIS FATHER.
YOU'RE WRONG, CORSAIR.
IT WON'T BE THE FIRST TIME. I'M GLAD YOU LOVE HIM.
I WISH I LOVED HIM LESS--THEN THIS WOULDN'T HURT SO MUCH. HE'S... ALL A FATHER COULD... WISH FOR, JEAN... I... I...
BEAM US UP, 'JAMMER!
WITH THE SIBILANT HUM OF THE TRANSPORTER EFFECT, THE STARJAMMERS ARE... GONE.
I HEARD, JEAN. CORSAIR HAD NO RIGHT TO ASK THIS THING OF YOU.
HOW COULD I TURN HIM DOWN, ORORO? I WAS IN-SIDE HIS MIND.
I KNOW THE HORRORS HE'S LIVED THROUGH...
AND WHEN SCOTT FINDS OUT--WHAT THEN?
IF I WERE SCOTT, AND I FOUND THAT YOU KNEW MY FATHER WAS STILL ALIVE BUT HADN'T TOLD ME, I WOULD HATE YOU FOR IT.
THAT'S A RISK I'LL HAVE TO TAKE--ORORO, I GAVE CORSAIR MY WORD!
HELP ME OVER TO THE STARGATE, HUH? I'M... SUDDENLY VERY, VERY... TIRED.
OKAY, TROOPS, THE 'GATE'S POWERED UP AND PROGRAMMED FOR EARTH.
LET'S GO HOME.

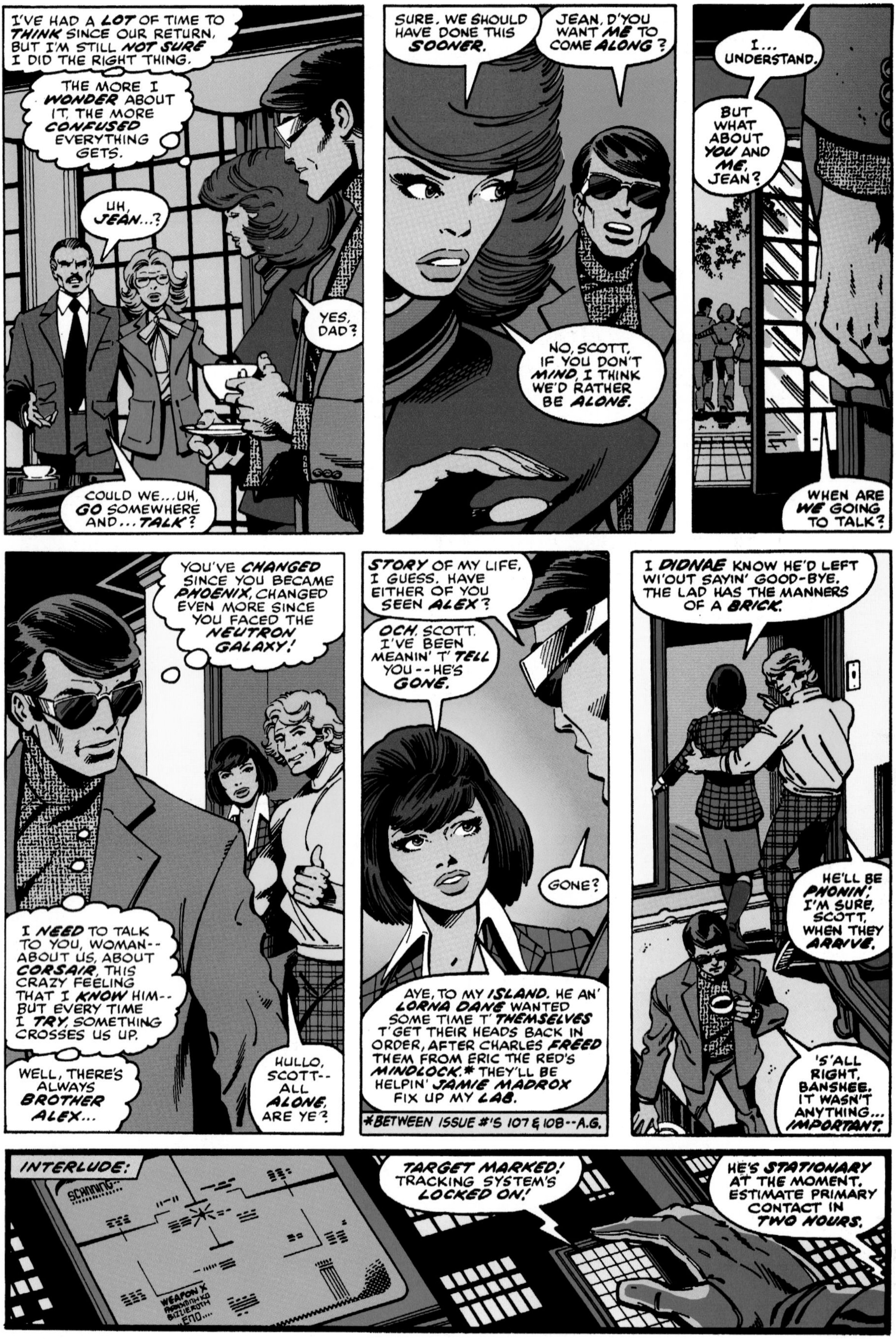
I'VE HAD A LOT OF TIME TO THINK SINCE OUR RETURN, BUT I'M STILL NOT SURE I DID THE RIGHT THING.
THE MORE I WONDER ABOUT IT, THE MORE CONFUSED EVERYTHING GETS.
UH, JEAN...?
YES, DAD?
COULD WE...UH, GO SOMEWHERE AND...TALK?
SURE. WE SHOULD HAVE DONE THIS SOONER.
JEAN, D'YOU WANT ME TO COME ALONG?
NO, SCOTT, IF YOU DON'T MIND, I THINK WE'D RATHER BE ALONE.
I... UNDERSTAND.
BUT WHAT ABOUT YOU AND ME, JEAN?
WHEN ARE WE GOING TO TALK?
YOU'VE CHANGED SINCE YOU BECAME PHOENIX, CHANGED EVEN MORE SINCE YOU FACED THE NEUTRON GALAXY!
I NEED TO TALK TO YOU, WOMAN-- ABOUT US, ABOUT CORSAIR, THIS CRAZY FEELING THAT I KNOW HIM-- BUT EVERY TIME I TRY, SOMETHING CROSSES US UP.
WELL, THERE'S ALWAYS BROTHER ALEX...
HULLO, SCOTT-- ALL ALONE, ARE YE?
STORY OF MY LIFE, I GUESS. HAVE EITHER OF YOU SEEN ALEX?
OCH, SCOTT, I'VE BEEN MEANIN' T' TELL YOU--HE'S GONE.
GONE?
AYE, TO MY ISLAND. HE AN' LORNA DANE WANTED SOME TIME T' THEMSELVES T'GET THEIR HEADS BACK IN ORDER, AFTER CHARLES FREED THEM FROM ERIC THE RED'S MINDLOCK.* THEY'LL BE HELPIN' JAMIE MADROX FIX UP MY LAB.
*BETWEEN ISSUE #'S 107 & 108--A.G.
I DIDNAE KNOW HE'D LEFT WI'OUT SAYIN' GOOD-BYE. THE LAD HAS THE MANNERS OF A BRICK.
HE'LL BE PHONIN', I'M SURE, SCOTT, WHEN THEY ARRIVE.
'S'ALL RIGHT, BANSHEE. IT WASN'T ANYTHING... IMPORTANT.
INTERLUDE:
SCANNING...
TARGET MARKED! TRACKING SYSTEM'S LOCKED ON!
HE'S STATIONARY AT THE MOMENT. ESTIMATE PRIMARY CONTACT IN TWO HOURS.

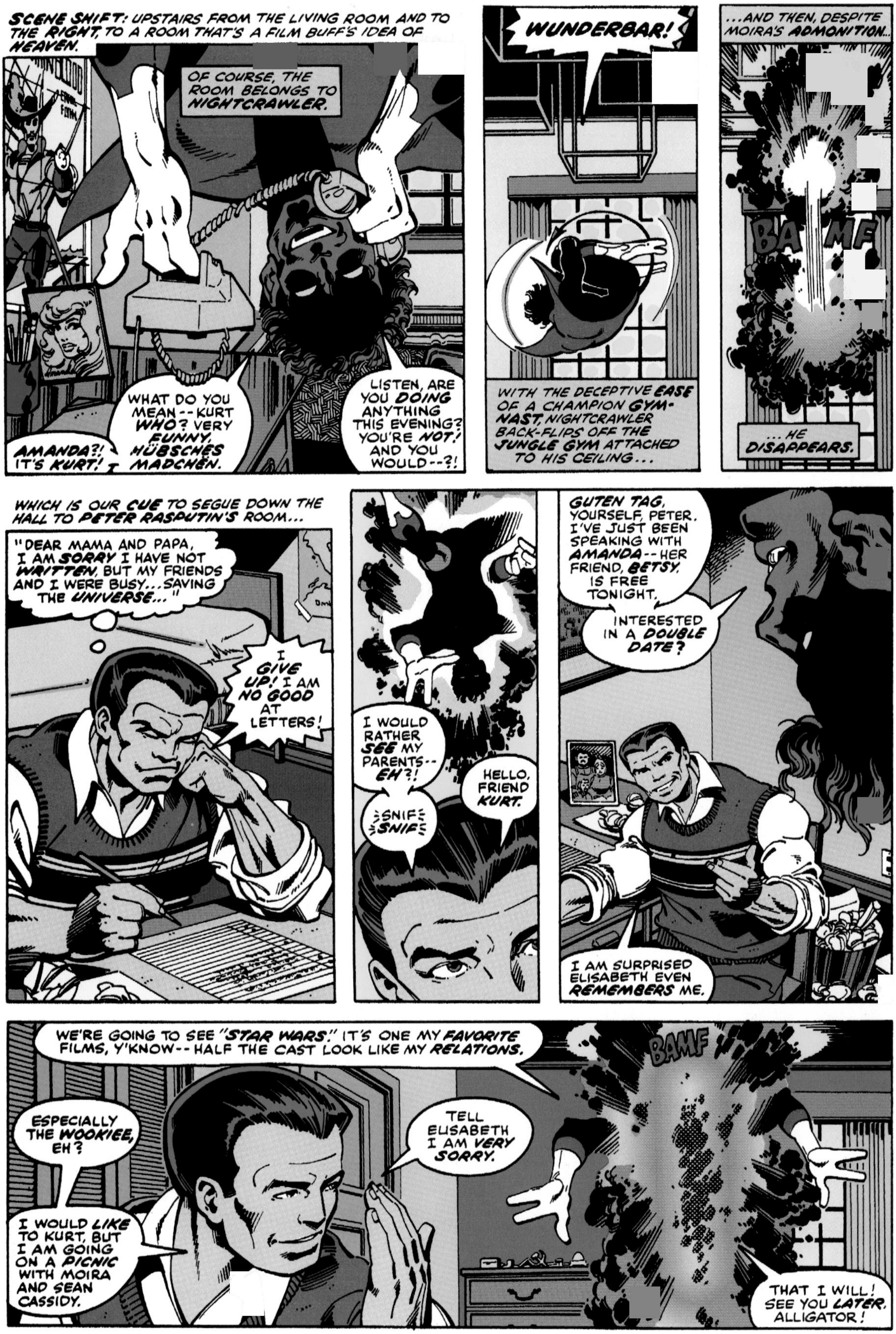

SCENE SHIFT: UPSTAIRS FROM THE LIVING ROOM AND TO THE RIGHT, TO A ROOM THAT'S A FILM BUFF'S IDEA OF HEAVEN.
OF COURSE, THE ROOM BELONGS TO NIGHTCRAWLER.
AMANDA?! IT'S KURT!
WHAT DO YOU MEAN--KURT WHO? VERY FUNNY, HÜBSCHES MADCHEN.
LISTEN, ARE YOU DOING ANYTHING THIS EVENING? YOU'RE NOT! AND YOU WOULD--?!
WUNDERBAR!
WITH THE DECEPTIVE EASE OF A CHAMPION GYMNAST, NIGHTCRAWLER BACK-FLIPS OFF THE JUNGLE GYM ATTACHED TO HIS CEILING...
...AND THEN, DESPITE MOIRA'S ADMONITION...
BAMF
...HE DISAPPEARS.
WHICH IS OUR CUE TO SEGUE DOWN THE HALL TO PETER RASPUTIN'S ROOM...
"DEAR MAMA AND PAPA, I AM SORRY I HAVE NOT WRITTEN, BUT MY FRIENDS AND I WERE BUSY...SAVING THE UNIVERSE..."
I GIVE UP! I AM NO GOOD AT LETTERS!
I WOULD RATHER SEE MY PARENTS--EH?!
SNIF SNIF
HELLO, FRIEND KURT.
GUTEN TAG, YOURSELF, PETER. I'VE JUST BEEN SPEAKING WITH AMANDA--HER FRIEND, BETSY, IS FREE TONIGHT.
INTERESTED IN A DOUBLE DATE?
I AM SURPRISED ELISABETH EVEN REMEMBERS ME.
WE'RE GOING TO SEE "STAR WARS." IT'S ONE MY FAVORITE FILMS, Y'KNOW--HALF THE CAST LOOK LIKE MY RELATIONS.
BAMF
ESPECIALLY THE WOOKIEE, EH?
TELL ELISABETH I AM VERY SORRY.
I WOULD LIKE TO KURT, BUT I AM GOING ON A PICNIC WITH MOIRA AND SEAN CASSIDY.
THAT I WILL! SEE YOU LATER, ALLIGATOR!

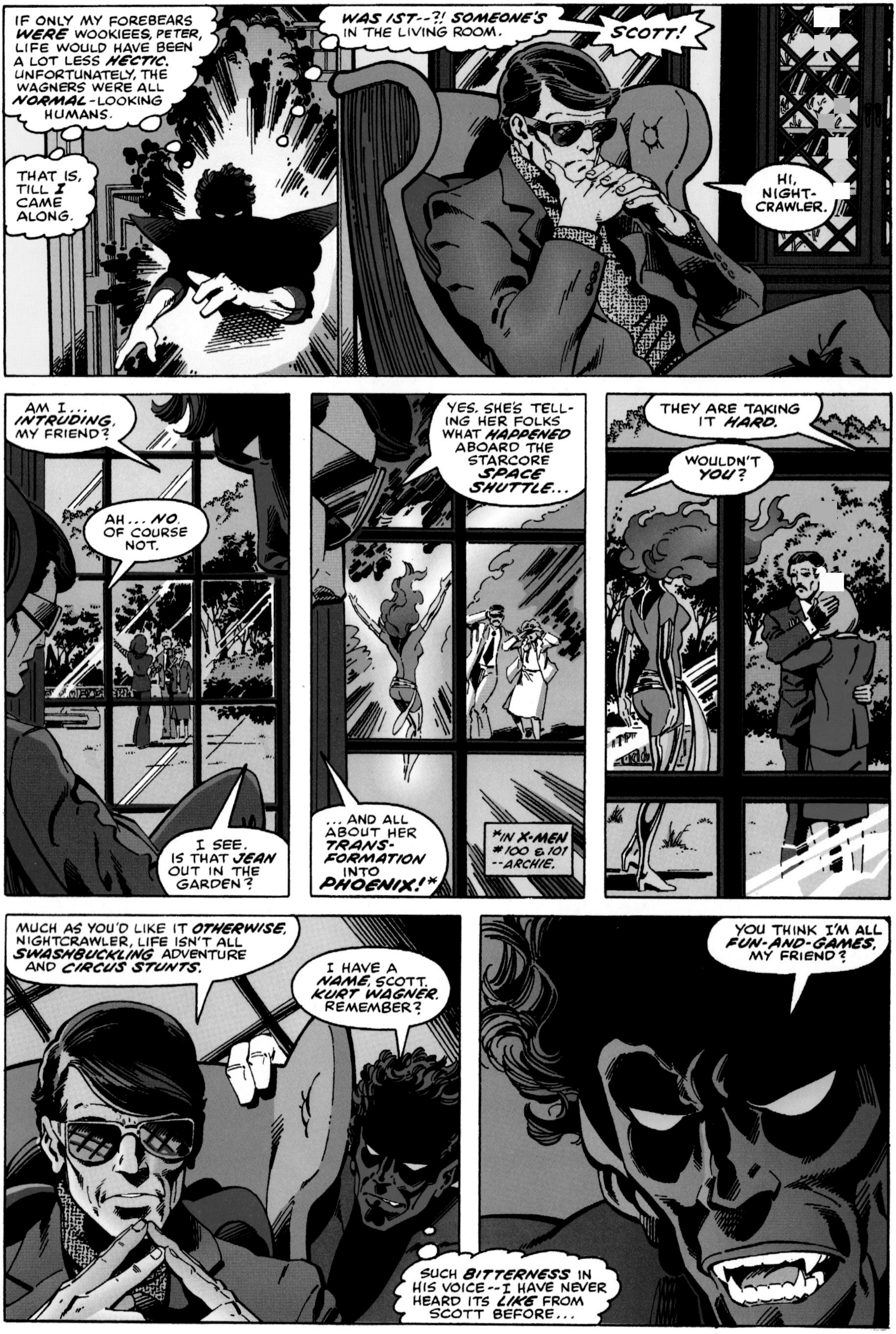
IF ONLY MY FOREBEARS WERE WOOKIEES, PETER, LIFE WOULD HAVE BEEN A LOT LESS HECTIC. UNFORTUNATELY, THE WAGNERS WERE ALL NORMAL-LOOKING HUMANS.
THAT IS, TILL I CAME ALONG.
WAS IST--?! SOMEONE'S IN THE LIVING ROOM.
SCOTT!
HI, NIGHT-CRAWLER.
AM I... INTRUDING, MY FRIEND?
AH... NO. OF COURSE NOT.
I SEE. IS THAT JEAN OUT IN THE GARDEN?
YES. SHE'S TELLING HER FOLKS WHAT HAPPENED ABOARD THE STARCORE SPACE SHUTTLE...
... AND ALL ABOUT HER TRANSFORMATION INTO PHOENIX!*
*IN X-MEN #100 & 101 --ARCHIE.
THEY ARE TAKING IT HARD.
WOULDN'T YOU?
MUCH AS YOU'D LIKE IT OTHERWISE, NIGHTCRAWLER, LIFE ISN'T ALL SWASHBUCKLING ADVENTURE AND CIRCUS STUNTS.
I HAVE A NAME, SCOTT. KURT WAGNER. REMEMBER?
SUCH BITTERNESS IN HIS VOICE--I HAVE NEVER HEARD ITS LIKE FROM SCOTT BEFORE...
YOU THINK I'M ALL FUN-AND-GAMES, MY FRIEND?

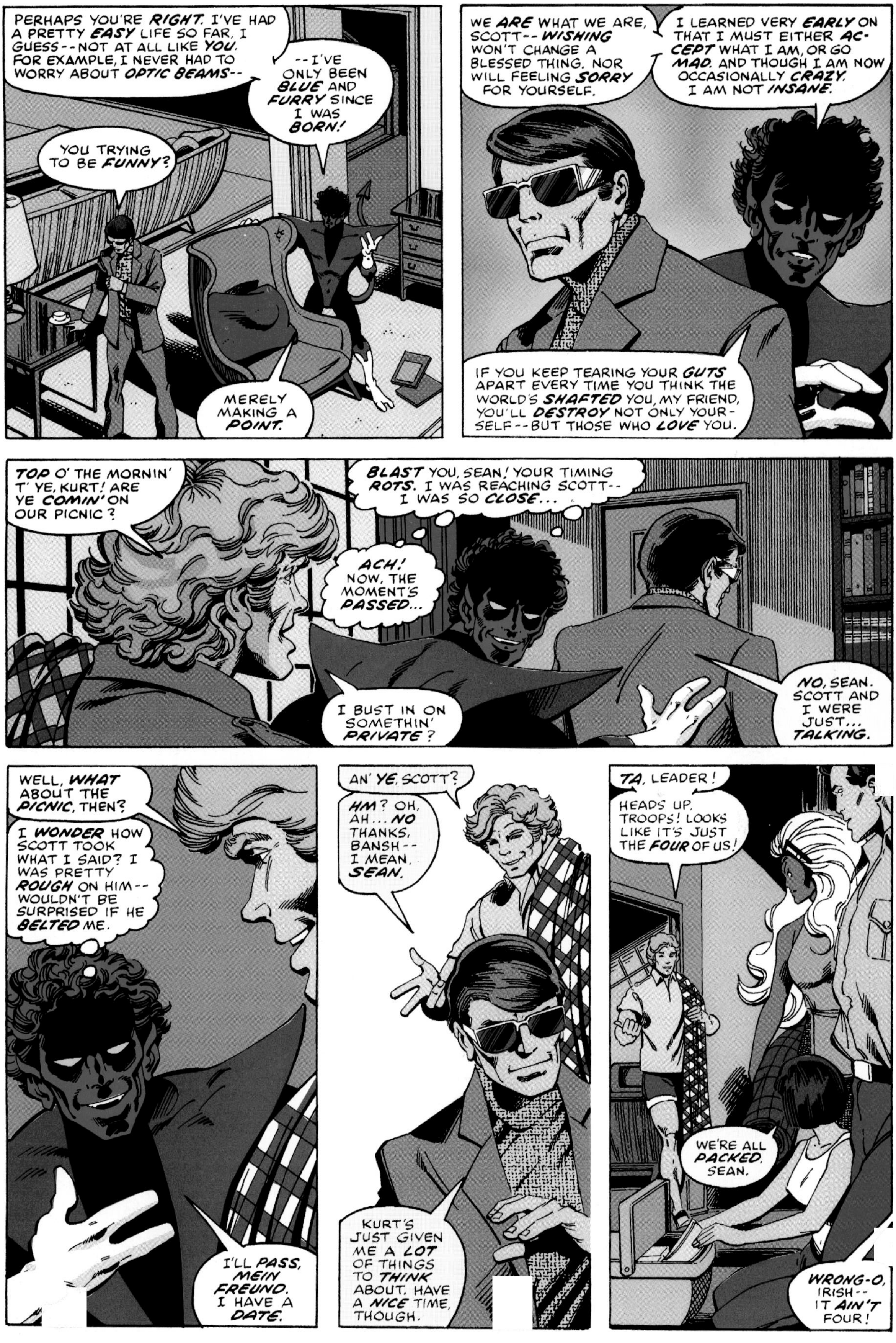

PERHAPS YOU'RE RIGHT. I'VE HAD A PRETTY EASY LIFE SO FAR, I GUESS--NOT AT ALL LIKE YOU. FOR EXAMPLE, I NEVER HAD TO WORRY ABOUT OPTIC BEAMS--
--I'VE ONLY BEEN BLUE AND FURRY SINCE I WAS BORN!
YOU TRYING TO BE FUNNY?
MERELY MAKING A POINT.
WE ARE WHAT WE ARE, SCOTT--WISHING WON'T CHANGE A BLESSED THING. NOR WILL FEELING SORRY FOR YOURSELF.
I LEARNED VERY EARLY ON THAT I MUST EITHER ACCEPT WHAT I AM, OR GO MAD. AND THOUGH I AM NOW OCCASIONALLY CRAZY, I AM NOT INSANE.
IF YOU KEEP TEARING YOUR GUTS APART EVERY TIME YOU THINK THE WORLD'S SHAFTED YOU, MY FRIEND, YOU'LL DESTROY NOT ONLY YOURSELF--BUT THOSE WHO LOVE YOU.
TOP O' THE MORNIN' T' YE, KURT! ARE YE COMIN' ON OUR PICNIC?
BLAST YOU, SEAN! YOUR TIMING ROTS. I WAS REACHING SCOTT-- I WAS SO CLOSE...
ACH! NOW, THE MOMENT'S PASSED...
I BUST IN ON SOMETHIN' PRIVATE?
NO, SEAN. SCOTT AND I WERE JUST... TALKING.
WELL, WHAT ABOUT THE PICNIC, THEN?
I WONDER HOW SCOTT TOOK WHAT I SAID? I WAS PRETTY ROUGH ON HIM--WOULDN'T BE SURPRISED IF HE BELTED ME.
I'LL PASS, MEIN FREUND. I HAVE A DATE.
AN' YE, SCOTT?
HM? OH, AH... NO THANKS, BANSH-- I MEAN, SEAN.
KURT'S JUST GIVEN ME A LOT OF THINGS TO THINK ABOUT. HAVE A NICE TIME, THOUGH.
TA, LEADER!
HEADS UP, TROOPS! LOOKS LIKE IT'S JUST THE FOUR OF US!
WE'RE ALL PACKED, SEAN.
WRONG-O, IRISH-- IT AIN'T FOUR!

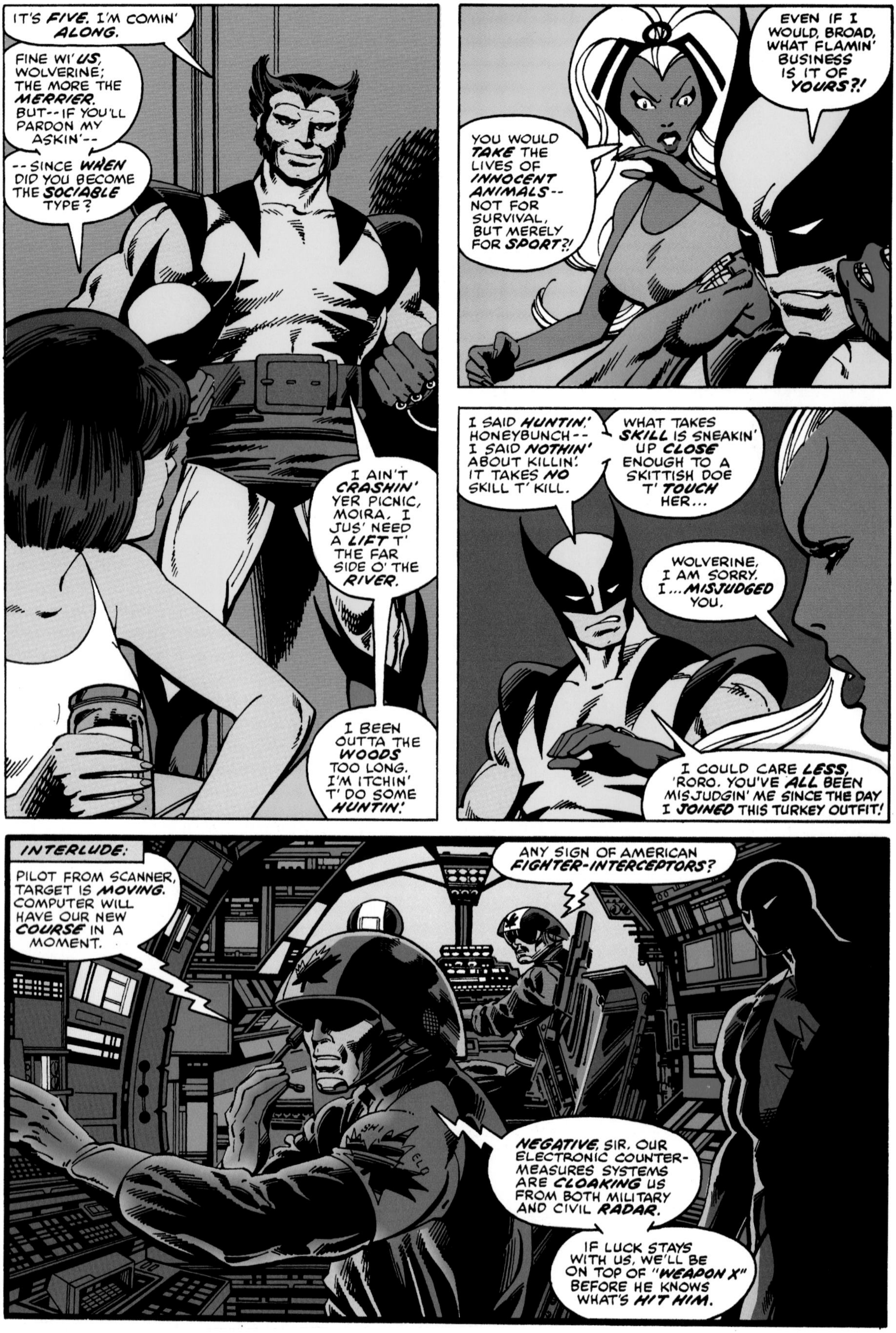
IT'S FIVE. I'M COMIN' ALONG.
FINE WI' US, WOLVERINE; THE MORE THE MERRIER. BUT--IF YOU'LL PARDON MY ASKIN'--
--SINCE WHEN DID YOU BECOME THE SOCIABLE TYPE?
I AIN'T CRASHIN' YER PICNIC, MOIRA. I JUS' NEED A LIFT T' THE FAR SIDE O' THE RIVER.
I BEEN OUTTA THE WOODS TOO LONG. I'M ITCHIN' T' DO SOME HUNTIN'.
YOU WOULD TAKE THE LIVES OF INNOCENT ANIMALS--NOT FOR SURVIVAL, BUT MERELY FOR SPORT?!
EVEN IF I WOULD, BROAD, WHAT FLAMIN' BUSINESS IS IT OF YOURS?!
I SAID HUNTIN.' HONEYBUNCH--I SAID NOTHIN' ABOUT KILLIN'. IT TAKES NO SKILL T' KILL.
WHAT TAKES SKILL IS SNEAKIN' UP CLOSE ENOUGH TO A SKITTISH DOE T' TOUCH HER...
WOLVERINE, I AM SORRY. I...MISJUDGED YOU.
I COULD CARE LESS, 'RORO. YOU'VE ALL BEEN MISJUDGIN' ME SINCE THE DAY I JOINED THIS TURKEY OUTFIT!
INTERLUDE:
PILOT FROM SCANNER, TARGET IS MOVING. COMPUTER WILL HAVE OUR NEW COURSE IN A MOMENT.
ANY SIGN OF AMERICAN FIGHTER-INTERCEPTORS?
NEGATIVE, SIR. OUR ELECTRONIC COUNTER-MEASURES SYSTEMS ARE CLOAKING US FROM BOTH MILITARY AND CIVIL RADAR.
IF LUCK STAYS WITH US, WE'LL BE ON TOP OF "WEAPON X" BEFORE HE KNOWS WHAT'S HIT HIM.

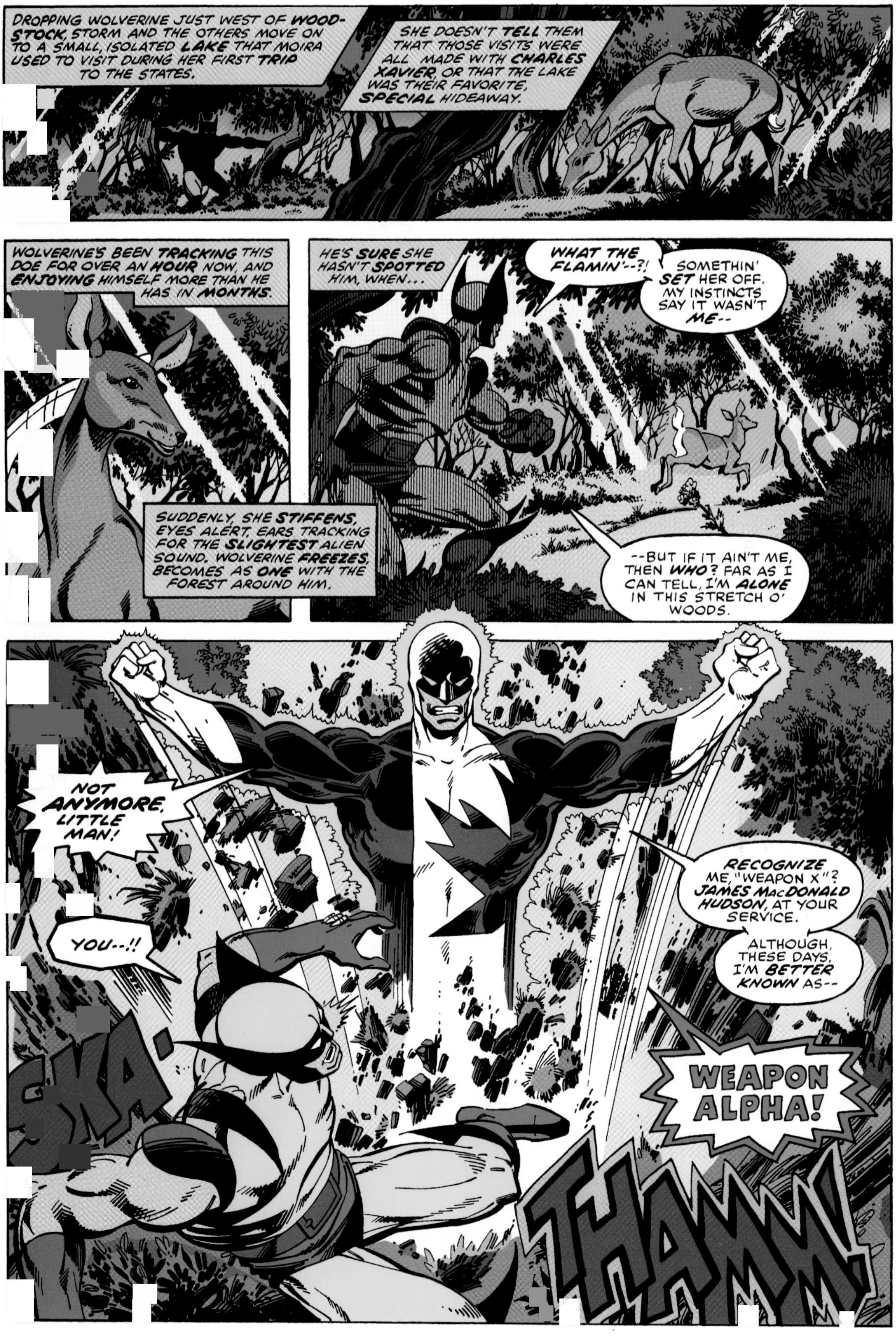
DROPPING WOLVERINE JUST WEST OF WOODSTOCK, STORM AND THE OTHERS MOVE ON TO A SMALL, ISOLATED LAKE THAT MOIRA USED TO VISIT DURING HER FIRST TRIP TO THE STATES.
SHE DOESN'T TELL THEM THAT THOSE VISITS WERE ALL MADE WITH CHARLES XAVIER, OR THAT THE LAKE WAS THEIR FAVORITE, SPECIAL HIDEAWAY.
WOLVERINE'S BEEN TRACKING THIS DOE FOR OVER AN HOUR NOW, AND ENJOYING HIMSELF MORE THAN HE HAS IN MONTHS.
SUDDENLY, SHE STIFFENS, EYES ALERT, EARS TRACKING FOR THE SLIGHTEST ALIEN SOUND. WOLVERINE FREEZES, BECOMES AS ONE WITH THE FOREST AROUND HIM.
HE'S SURE SHE HASN'T SPOTTED HIM, WHEN...
WHAT THE FLAMIN'--?!
SOMETHIN' SET HER OFF. MY INSTINCTS SAY IT WASN'T ME--
--BUT IF IT AIN'T ME, THEN WHO? FAR AS I CAN TELL, I'M ALONE IN THIS STRETCH O' WOODS.
NOT ANYMORE, LITTLE MAN!
YOU--!!
RECOGNIZE ME, "WEAPON X"? JAMES MacDONALD HUDSON, AT YOUR SERVICE.
ALTHOUGH, THESE DAYS, I'M BETTER KNOWN AS--
WEAPON ALPHA!
SKA-
THAMM!

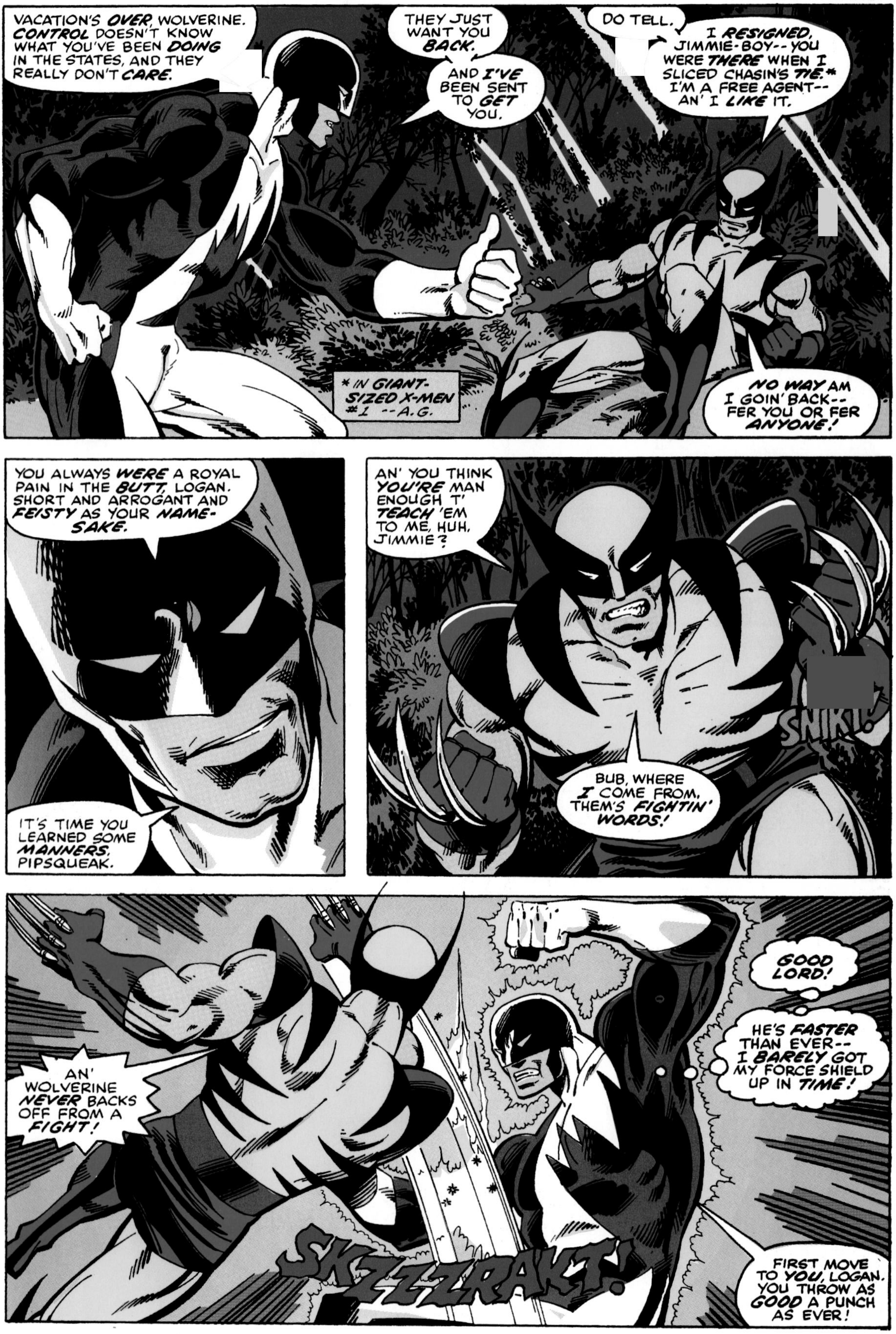

VACATION'S OVER, WOLVERINE. CONTROL DOESN'T KNOW WHAT YOU'VE BEEN DOING IN THE STATES, AND THEY REALLY DON'T CARE.
THEY JUST WANT YOU BACK.
AND I'VE BEEN SENT TO GET YOU.
DO TELL.
I RESIGNED, JIMMIE-BOY-- YOU WERE THERE WHEN I SLICED CHASIN'S TIE.* I'M A FREE AGENT-- AN' I LIKE IT.
NO WAY AM I GOIN' BACK-- FER YOU OR FER ANYONE!
* IN GIANT-SIZED X-MEN #1 --A.G.
YOU ALWAYS WERE A ROYAL PAIN IN THE BUTT, LOGAN. SHORT AND ARROGANT AND FEISTY AS YOUR NAME-SAKE.
IT'S TIME YOU LEARNED SOME MANNERS, PIPSQUEAK.
AN' YOU THINK YOU'RE MAN ENOUGH T' TEACH 'EM TO ME, HUH, JIMMIE?
BUB, WHERE I COME FROM, THEM'S FIGHTIN' WORDS!
AN' WOLVERINE NEVER BACKS OFF FROM A FIGHT!
GOOD LORD!
HE'S FASTER THAN EVER-- I BARELY GOT MY FORCE SHIELD UP IN TIME!
SKZZZRAKT!
FIRST MOVE TO YOU, LOGAN. YOU THROW AS GOOD A PUNCH AS EVER!

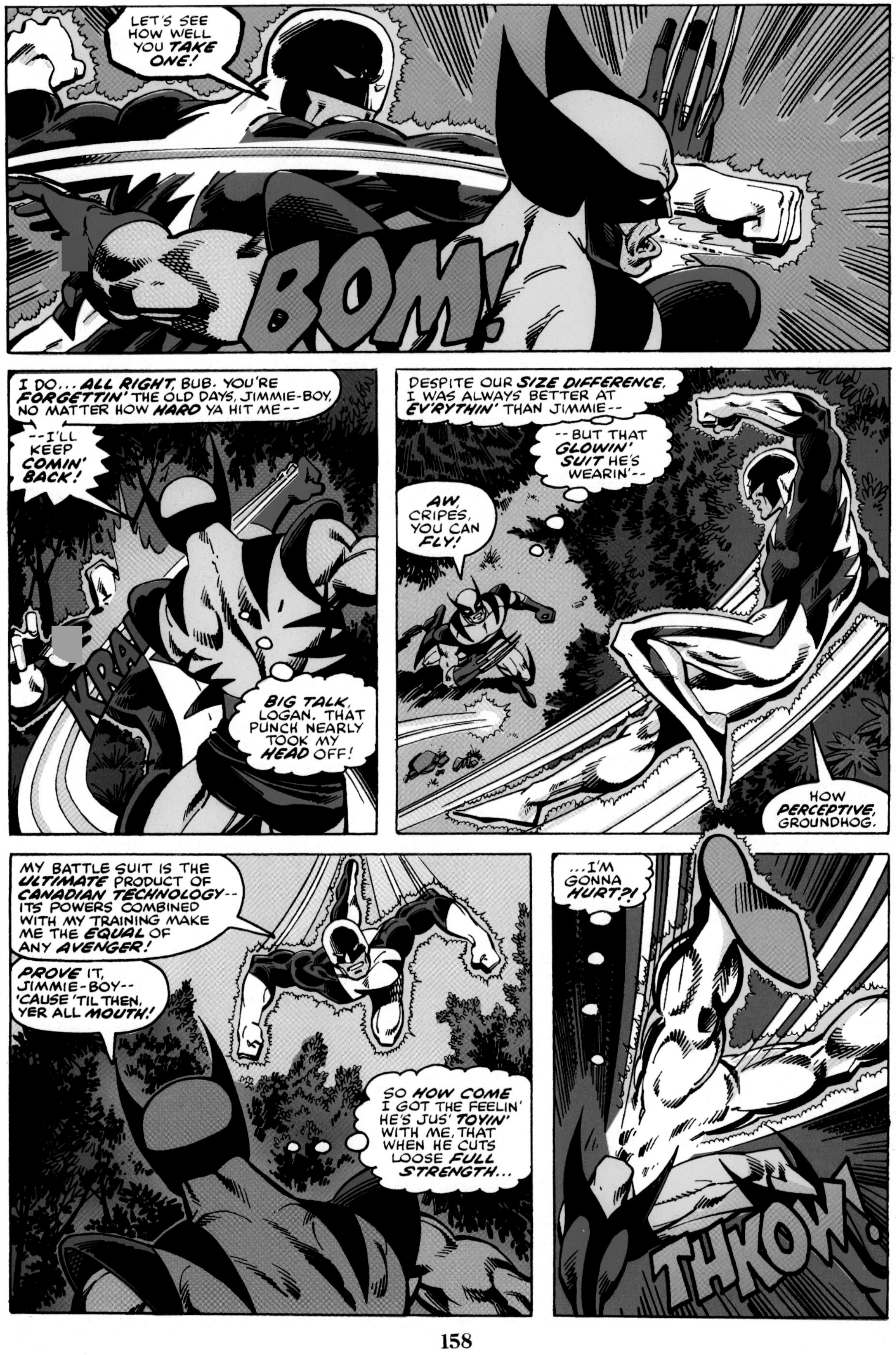

LET'S SEE HOW WELL YOU TAKE ONE!
BOM!
I DO... ALL RIGHT, BUB. YOU'RE FORGETTIN' THE OLD DAYS, JIMMIE-BOY, NO MATTER HOW HARD YA HIT ME--
--I'LL KEEP COMIN' BACK!
BIG TALK, LOGAN. THAT PUNCH NEARLY TOOK MY HEAD OFF!
DESPITE OUR SIZE DIFFERENCE, I WAS ALWAYS BETTER AT EV'RYTHIN' THAN JIMMIE--
--BUT THAT GLOWIN' SUIT HE'S WEARIN'--
AW, CRIPES, YOU CAN FLY!
HOW PERCEPTIVE, GROUNDHOG.
MY BATTLE SUIT IS THE ULTIMATE PRODUCT OF CANADIAN TECHNOLOGY-- ITS POWERS COMBINED WITH MY TRAINING MAKE ME THE EQUAL OF ANY AVENGER!
PROVE IT, JIMMIE-BOY-- 'CAUSE 'TIL THEN, YER ALL MOUTH!
SO HOW COME I GOT THE FEELIN' HE'S JUS' TOYIN' WITH ME, THAT WHEN HE CUTS LOOSE FULL STRENGTH...
...I'M GONNA HURT?!
THKOW!

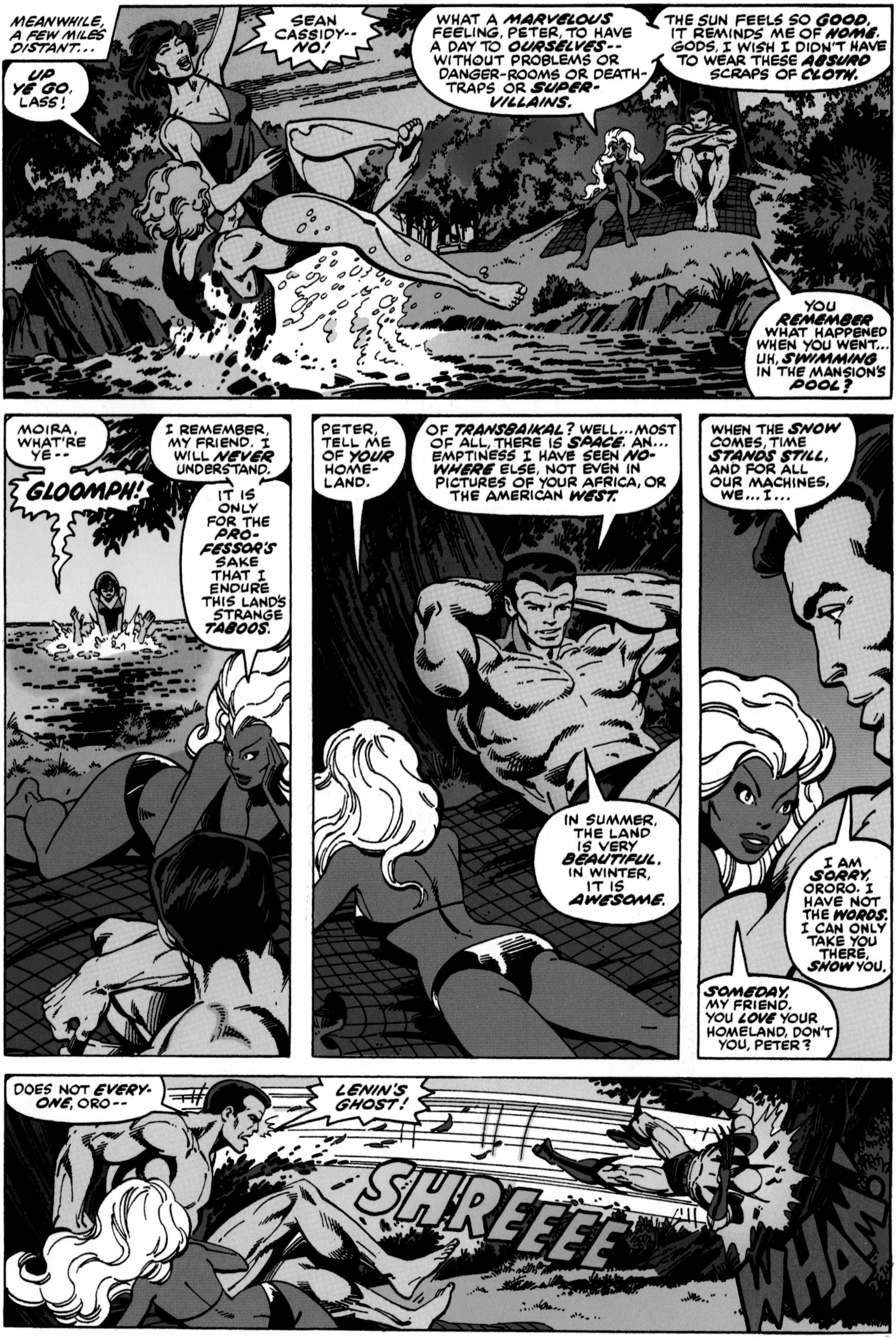

MEANWHILE, A FEW MILES DISTANT...
UP YE GO, LASS!
SEAN CASSIDY-- NO!
WHAT A MARVELOUS FEELING, PETER, TO HAVE A DAY TO OURSELVES-- WITHOUT PROBLEMS OR DANGER-ROOMS OR DEATH-TRAPS OR SUPER-VILLAINS.
THE SUN FEELS SO GOOD. IT REMINDS ME OF HOME. GODS, I WISH I DIDN'T HAVE TO WEAR THESE ABSURD SCRAPS OF CLOTH.
YOU REMEMBER WHAT HAPPENED WHEN YOU WENT... UH, SWIMMING IN THE MANSION'S POOL?
MOIRA, WHAT'RE YE--
GLOOMPH!
I REMEMBER, MY FRIEND. I WILL NEVER UNDERSTAND.
IT IS ONLY FOR THE PROFESSOR'S SAKE THAT I ENDURE THIS LAND'S STRANGE TABOOS.
PETER, TELL ME OF YOUR HOMELAND.
OF TRANSBAIKAL? WELL... MOST OF ALL, THERE IS SPACE. AN... EMPTINESS I HAVE SEEN NOWHERE ELSE, NOT EVEN IN PICTURES OF YOUR AFRICA, OR THE AMERICAN WEST.
IN SUMMER, THE LAND IS VERY BEAUTIFUL. IN WINTER, IT IS AWESOME.
WHEN THE SNOW COMES, TIME STANDS STILL, AND FOR ALL OUR MACHINES, WE... I...
I AM SORRY, ORORO. I HAVE NOT THE WORDS. I CAN ONLY TAKE YOU THERE, SHOW YOU.
SOMEDAY, MY FRIEND. YOU LOVE YOUR HOMELAND, DON'T YOU, PETER?
DOES NOT EVERYONE, ORO--
LENIN'S GHOST!
SHREEEEE
WHAM!

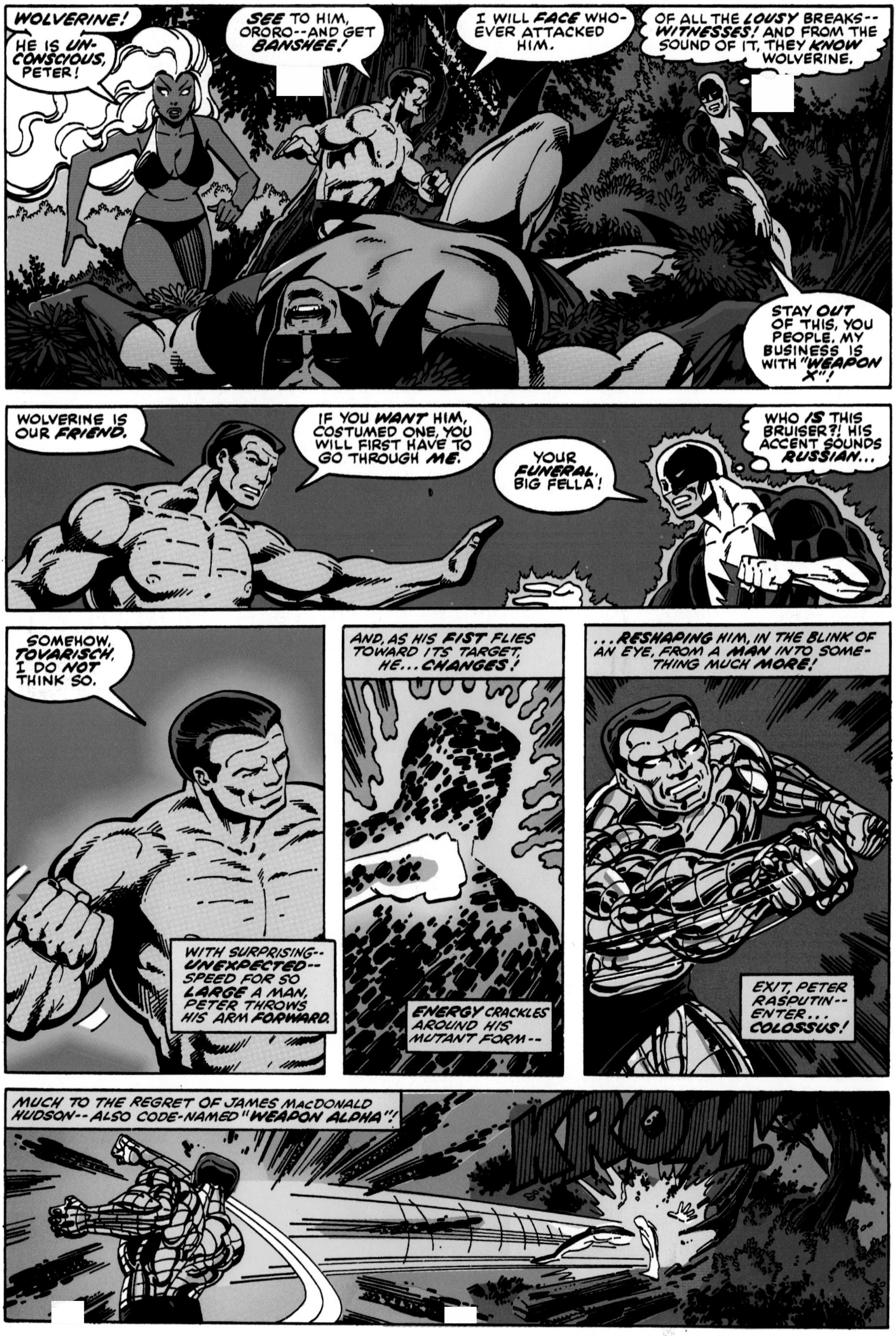
WOLVERINE! HE IS UN-CONSCIOUS, PETER!
SEE TO HIM, ORORO--AND GET BANSHEE!
I WILL FACE WHO-EVER ATTACKED HIM.
OF ALL THE LOUSY BREAKS-- WITNESSES! AND FROM THE SOUND OF IT, THEY KNOW WOLVERINE.
STAY OUT OF THIS, YOU PEOPLE. MY BUSINESS IS WITH "WEAPON X"!
WOLVERINE IS OUR FRIEND.
IF YOU WANT HIM, COSTUMED ONE, YOU WILL FIRST HAVE TO GO THROUGH ME.
YOUR FUNERAL, BIG FELLA!
WHO IS THIS BRUISER?! HIS ACCENT SOUNDS RUSSIAN...
SOMEHOW, TOVARISCH, I DO NOT THINK SO.
WITH SURPRISING-- UNEXPECTED-- SPEED FOR SO LARGE A MAN, PETER THROWS HIS ARM FORWARD.
AND, AS HIS FIST FLIES TOWARD ITS TARGET, HE... CHANGES!
ENERGY CRACKLES AROUND HIS MUTANT FORM--
...RESHAPING HIM, IN THE BLINK OF AN EYE, FROM A MAN INTO SOME-THING MUCH MORE!
EXIT, PETER RASPUTIN-- ENTER... COLOSSUS!
MUCH TO THE REGRET OF JAMES MACDONALD HUDSON-- ALSO CODE-NAMED "WEAPON ALPHA"!

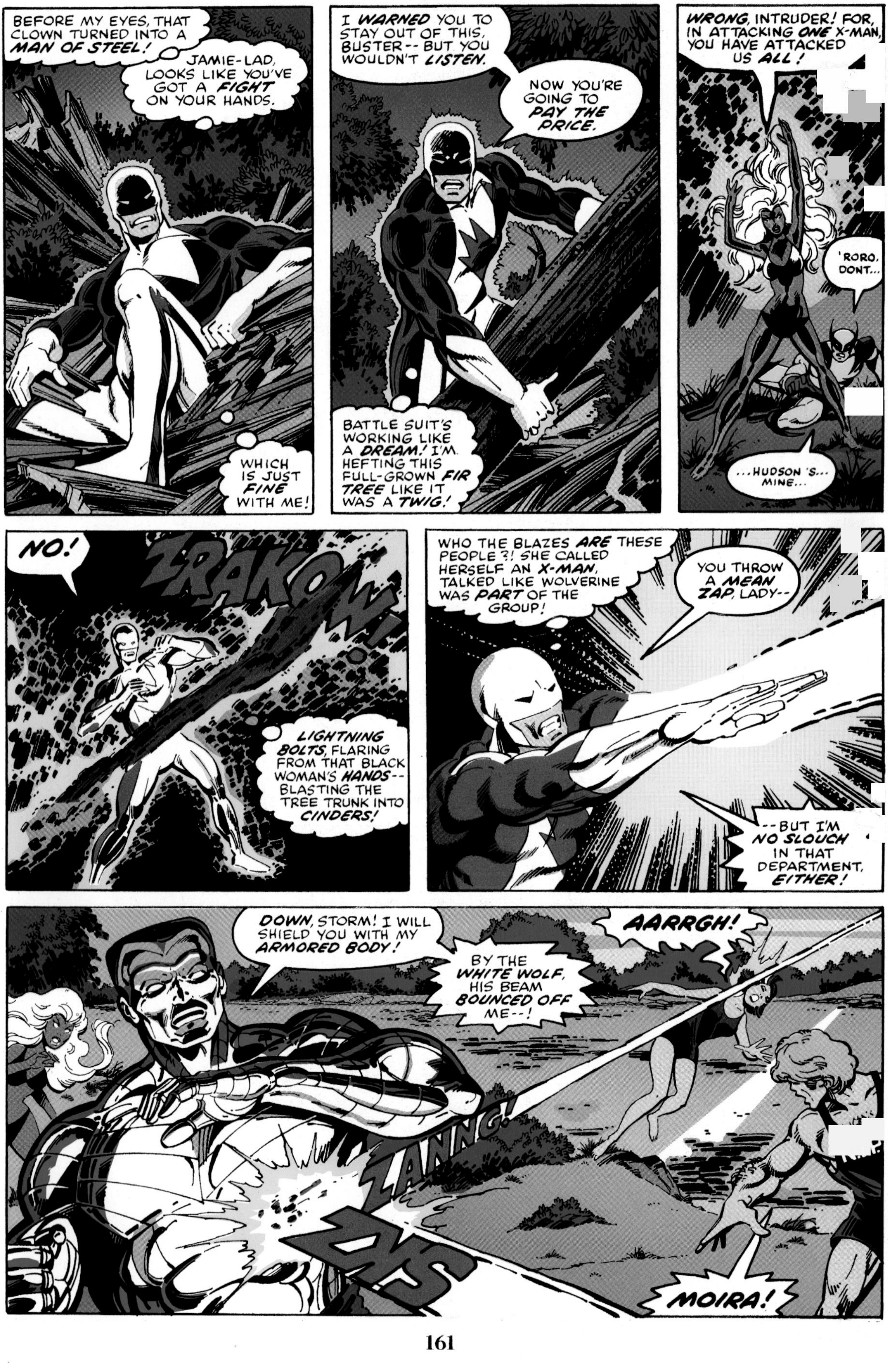

BEFORE MY EYES, THAT CLOWN TURNED INTO A MAN OF STEEL!
JAMIE-LAD, LOOKS LIKE YOU'VE GOT A FIGHT ON YOUR HANDS.
WHICH IS JUST FINE WITH ME!
I WARNED YOU TO STAY OUT OF THIS, BUSTER -- BUT YOU WOULDN'T LISTEN.
NOW YOU'RE GOING TO PAY THE PRICE.
BATTLE SUIT'S WORKING LIKE A DREAM! I'M HEFTING THIS FULL-GROWN FIR TREE LIKE IT WAS A TWIG!
WRONG, INTRUDER! FOR, IN ATTACKING ONE X-MAN, YOU HAVE ATTACKED US ALL!
'RORO, DONT...
...HUDSON 'S... MINE...
NO!
ZRAKOW!
LIGHTNING BOLTS, FLARING FROM THAT BLACK WOMAN'S HANDS-- BLASTING THE TREE TRUNK INTO CINDERS!
WHO THE BLAZES ARE THESE PEOPLE ?! SHE CALLED HERSELF AN X-MAN, TALKED LIKE WOLVERINE WAS PART OF THE GROUP!
YOU THROW A MEAN ZAP, LADY--
--BUT I'M NO SLOUCH IN THAT DEPARTMENT, EITHER!
DOWN, STORM! I WILL SHIELD YOU WITH MY ARMORED BODY!
BY THE WHITE WOLF, HIS BEAM BOUNCED OFF ME--!
AARRGH!
ZANNG!
ZAS
MOIRA!

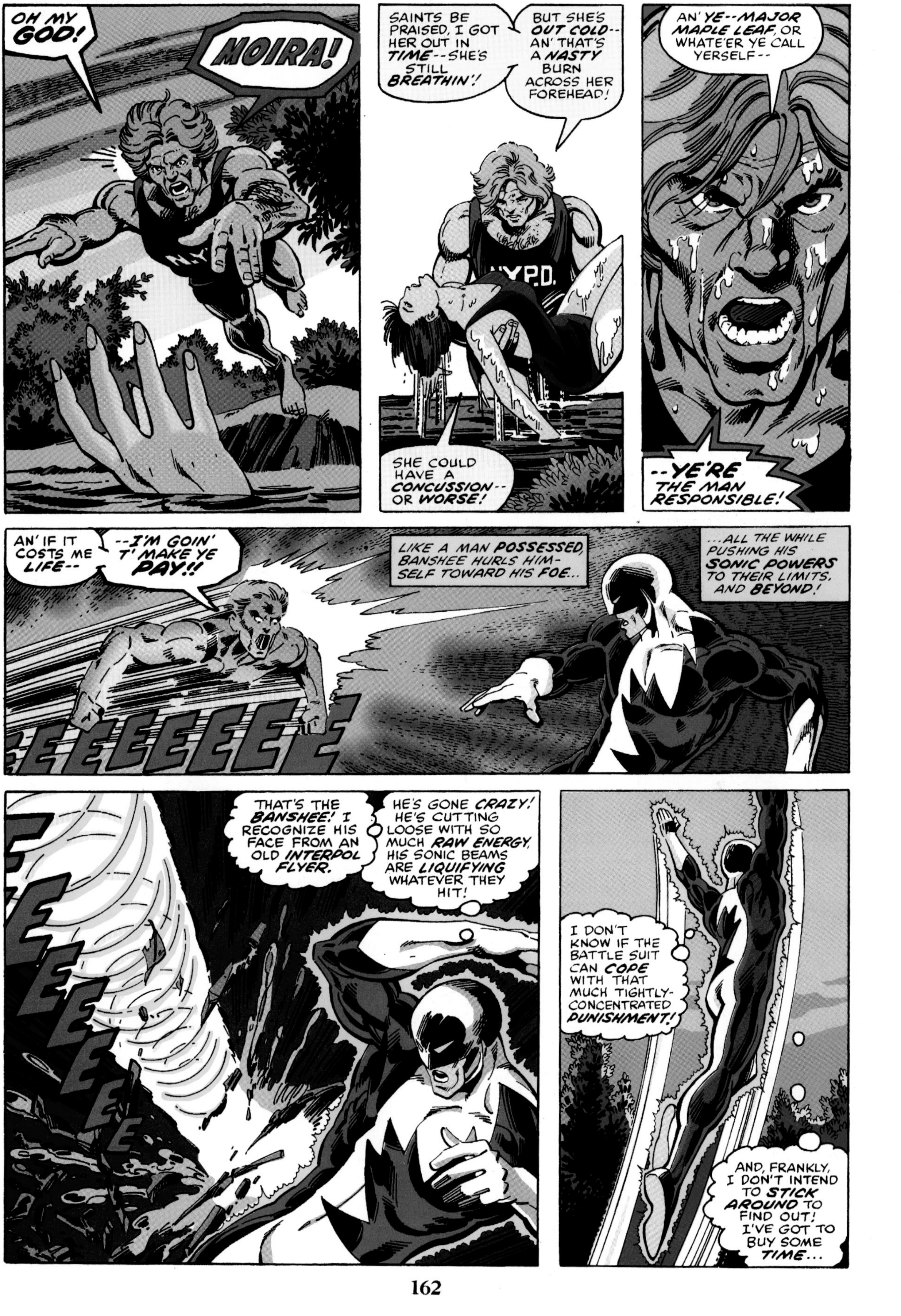

OH MY GOD!
MOIRA!
SAINTS BE PRAISED, I GOT HER OUT IN TIME--SHE'S STILL BREATHIN'!
BUT SHE'S OUT COLD--AN' THAT'S A NASTY BURN ACROSS HER FOREHEAD!
SHE COULD HAVE A CONCUSSION--OR WORSE!
AN' YE--MAJOR MAPLE LEAF, OR WHATE'ER YE CALL YERSELF--
--YE'RE THE MAN RESPONSIBLE!
AN' IF IT COSTS ME LIFE--
--I'M GOIN' T' MAKE YE PAY!!
LIKE A MAN POSSESSED, BANSHEE HURLS HIMSELF TOWARD HIS FOE...
...ALL THE WHILE PUSHING HIS SONIC POWERS TO THEIR LIMITS, AND BEYOND!
EEEEEEEE
THAT'S THE BANSHEE! I RECOGNIZE HIS FACE FROM AN OLD INTERPOL FLYER.
HE'S GONE CRAZY! HE'S CUTTING LOOSE WITH SO MUCH RAW ENERGY, HIS SONIC BEAMS ARE LIQUIFYING WHATEVER THEY HIT!
EEEEEEE
I DON'T KNOW IF THE BATTLE SUIT CAN COPE WITH THAT MUCH TIGHTLY-CONCENTRATED PUNISHMENT!
AND, FRANKLY, I DON'T INTEND TO STICK AROUND TO FIND OUT! I'VE GOT TO BUY SOME TIME...

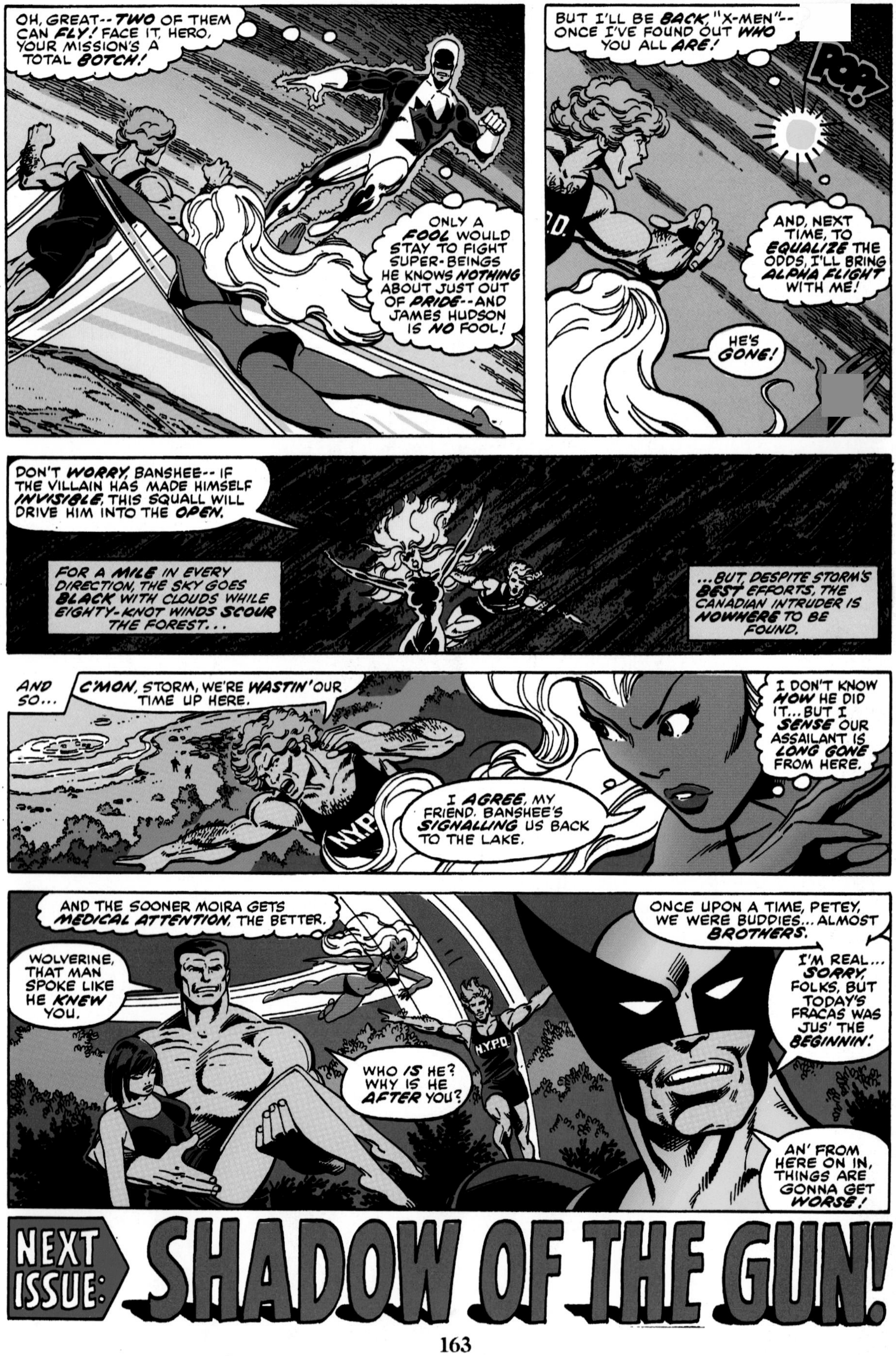

OH, GREAT--TWO OF THEM CAN FLY! FACE IT, HERO, YOUR MISSION'S A TOTAL BOTCH!
ONLY A FOOL WOULD STAY TO FIGHT SUPER-BEINGS HE KNOWS NOTHING ABOUT JUST OUT OF PRIDE--AND JAMES HUDSON IS NO FOOL!
BUT I'LL BE BACK, "X-MEN"-- ONCE I'VE FOUND OUT WHO YOU ALL ARE!
POP!
AND, NEXT TIME, TO EQUALIZE THE ODDS, I'LL BRING ALPHA FLIGHT WITH ME!
HE'S GONE!
DON'T WORRY, BANSHEE-- IF THE VILLAIN HAS MADE HIMSELF INVISIBLE, THIS SQUALL WILL DRIVE HIM INTO THE OPEN.
FOR A MILE IN EVERY DIRECTION, THE SKY GOES BLACK WITH CLOUDS WHILE EIGHTY-KNOT WINDS SCOUR THE FOREST...
...BUT, DESPITE STORM'S BEST EFFORTS, THE CANADIAN INTRUDER IS NOWHERE TO BE FOUND.
AND SO...
C'MON, STORM, WE'RE WASTIN' OUR TIME UP HERE.
I DON'T KNOW HOW HE DID IT... BUT I SENSE OUR ASSAILANT IS LONG GONE FROM HERE.
I AGREE, MY FRIEND. BANSHEE'S SIGNALLING US BACK TO THE LAKE.
AND THE SOONER MOIRA GETS MEDICAL ATTENTION, THE BETTER.
WOLVERINE, THAT MAN SPOKE LIKE HE KNEW YOU.
WHO IS HE? WHY IS HE AFTER YOU?
ONCE UPON A TIME, PETEY, WE WERE BUDDIES... ALMOST BROTHERS.
I'M REAL... SORRY, FOLKS, BUT TODAY'S FRACAS WAS JUS' THE BEGINNIN'.
AN' FROM HERE ON IN, THINGS ARE GONNA GET WORSE!
NEXT ISSUE: SHADOW OF THE GUN!

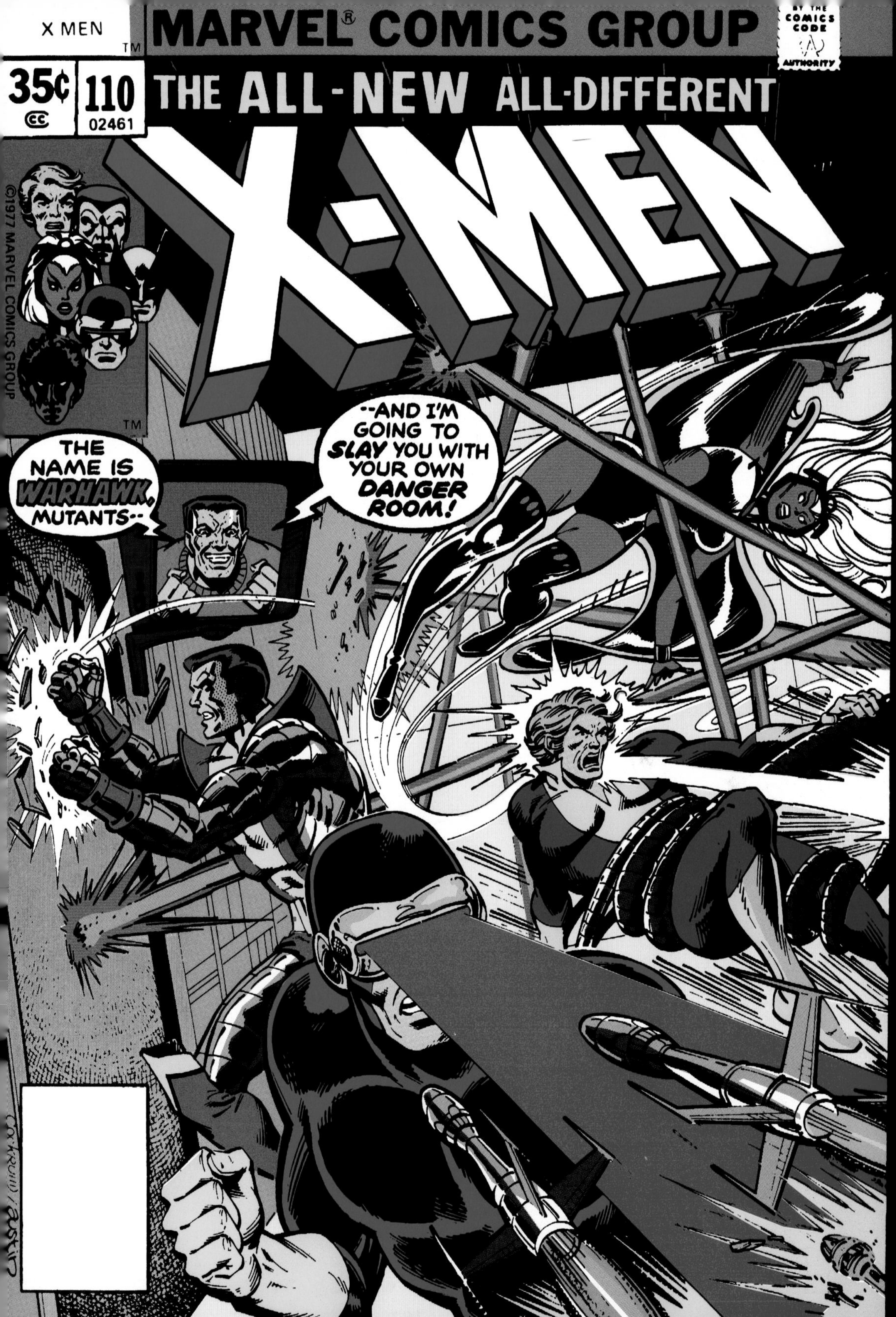
X MEN
MARVEL® COMICS GROUP
BY THE COMICS CODE AUTHORITY
35¢ 110
02461
THE ALL-NEW ALL-DIFFERENT
X-MEN
©1977 MARVEL COMICS GROUP
THE NAME IS WARHAWK, MUTANTS--
--AND I'M GOING TO SLAY YOU WITH YOUR OWN DANGER ROOM!
EXIT

Cyclops. Storm. Banshee. Nightcrawler. Wolverine. Colossus. Children of the atom, students of Charles Xavier, MUTANTS––feared and hated by the world they have sworn to protect. These are the STRANGEST heroes of all!

STAN LEE PRESENTS: THE UNCANNY X-MEN!™

CHRIS CLAREMONT AUTHOR * TONY DeZUNIGA GUEST ARTIST * ANNETTE KAWECKI, LETTERER * ANDY YANCHUS, COLORIST * ARCHIE GOODWIN EDITOR
—AND THANKS TO DAVE COCKRUM FOR A WELCOME ART ASSIST.

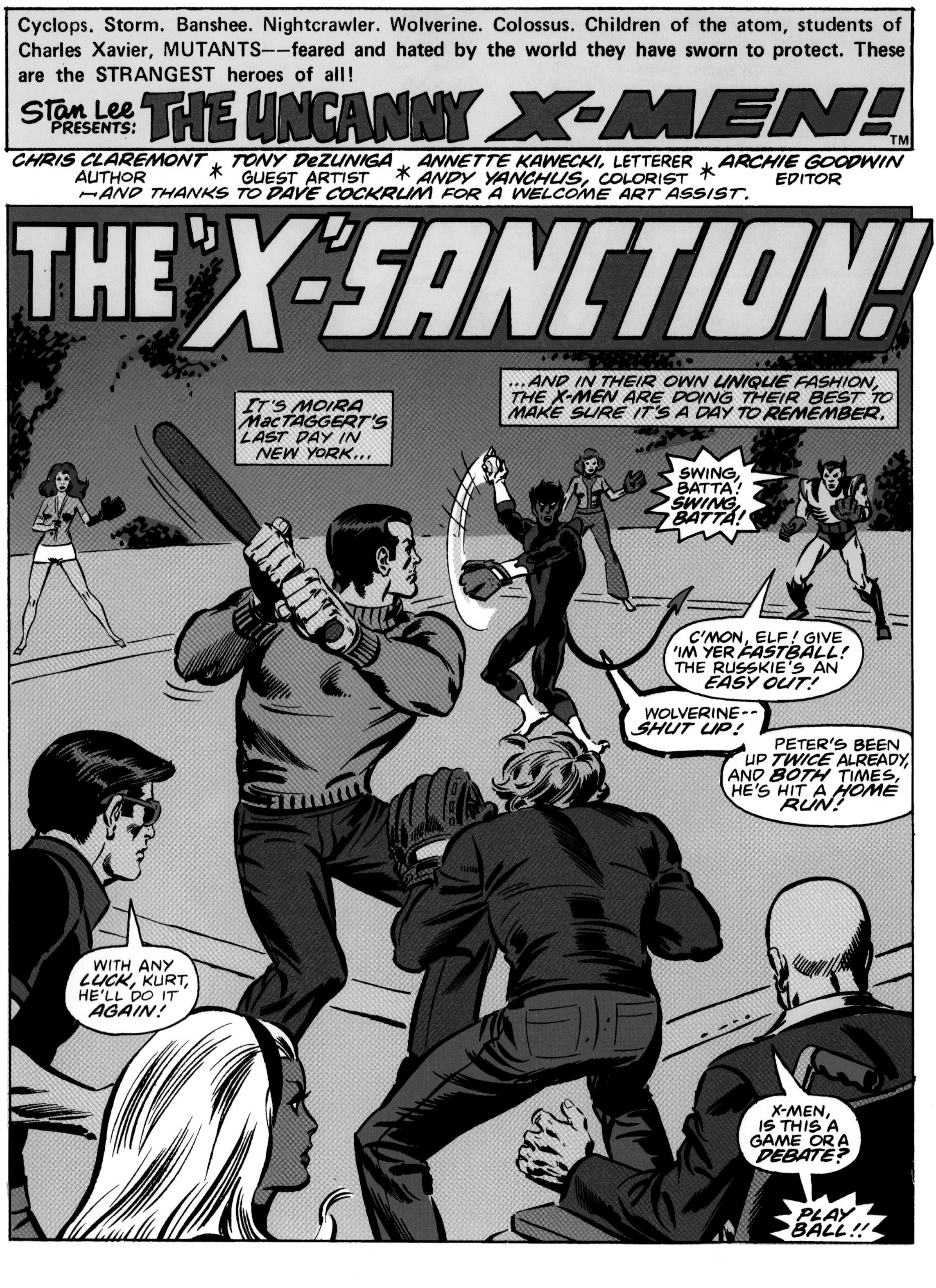
THE "X"-SANCTION!
IT'S MOIRA MacTAGGERT'S LAST DAY IN NEW YORK...
...AND IN THEIR OWN UNIQUE FASHION, THE X-MEN ARE DOING THEIR BEST TO MAKE SURE IT'S A DAY TO REMEMBER.
SWING, BATTA! SWING, BATTA!
C'MON, ELF! GIVE 'IM YER FASTBALL! THE RUSSKIE'S AN EASY OUT!
WOLVERINE-- SHUT UP!
PETER'S BEEN UP TWICE ALREADY, AND BOTH TIMES, HE'S HIT A HOME RUN!
WITH ANY LUCK, KURT, HE'LL DO IT AGAIN!
X-MEN, IS THIS A GAME OR A DEBATE?
PLAY BALL!!

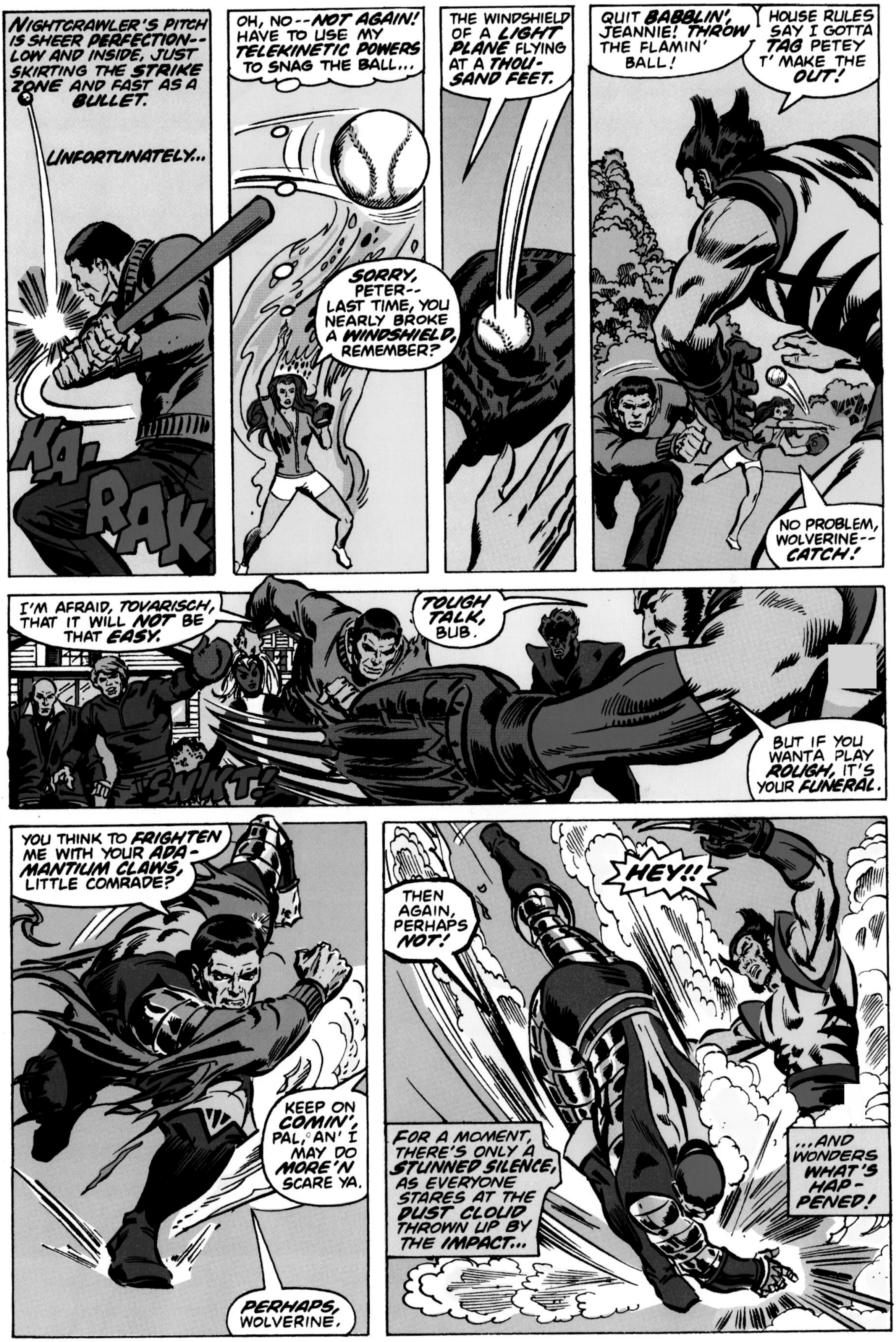

NIGHTCRAWLER'S PITCH IS SHEER PERFECTION-- LOW AND INSIDE, JUST SKIRTING THE STRIKE ZONE AND FAST AS A BULLET.
UNFORTUNATELY...
KA-RAK!
OH, NO--NOT AGAIN! HAVE TO USE MY TELEKINETIC POWERS TO SNAG THE BALL...
SORRY, PETER-- LAST TIME, YOU NEARLY BROKE A WINDSHIELD, REMEMBER?
THE WINDSHIELD OF A LIGHT PLANE FLYING AT A THOUSAND FEET.
QUIT BABBLIN', JEANNIE! THROW THE FLAMIN' BALL!
HOUSE RULES SAY I GOTTA TAG PETEY T' MAKE THE OUT!
NO PROBLEM, WOLVERINE-- CATCH!
I'M AFRAID, TOVARISCH, THAT IT WILL NOT BE THAT EASY.
TOUGH TALK, BUB.
SNIKT!
BUT IF YOU WANTA PLAY ROUGH, IT'S YOUR FUNERAL.
YOU THINK TO FRIGHTEN ME WITH YOUR ADAMANTIUM CLAWS, LITTLE COMRADE?
KEEP ON COMIN', PAL, AN' I MAY DO MORE'N SCARE YA.
PERHAPS, WOLVERINE.
HEY!!
THEN AGAIN, PERHAPS NOT!
FOR A MOMENT, THERE'S ONLY A STUNNED SILENCE, AS EVERYONE STARES AT THE DUST CLOUD THROWN UP BY THE IMPACT...
...AND WONDERS WHAT'S HAPPENED!

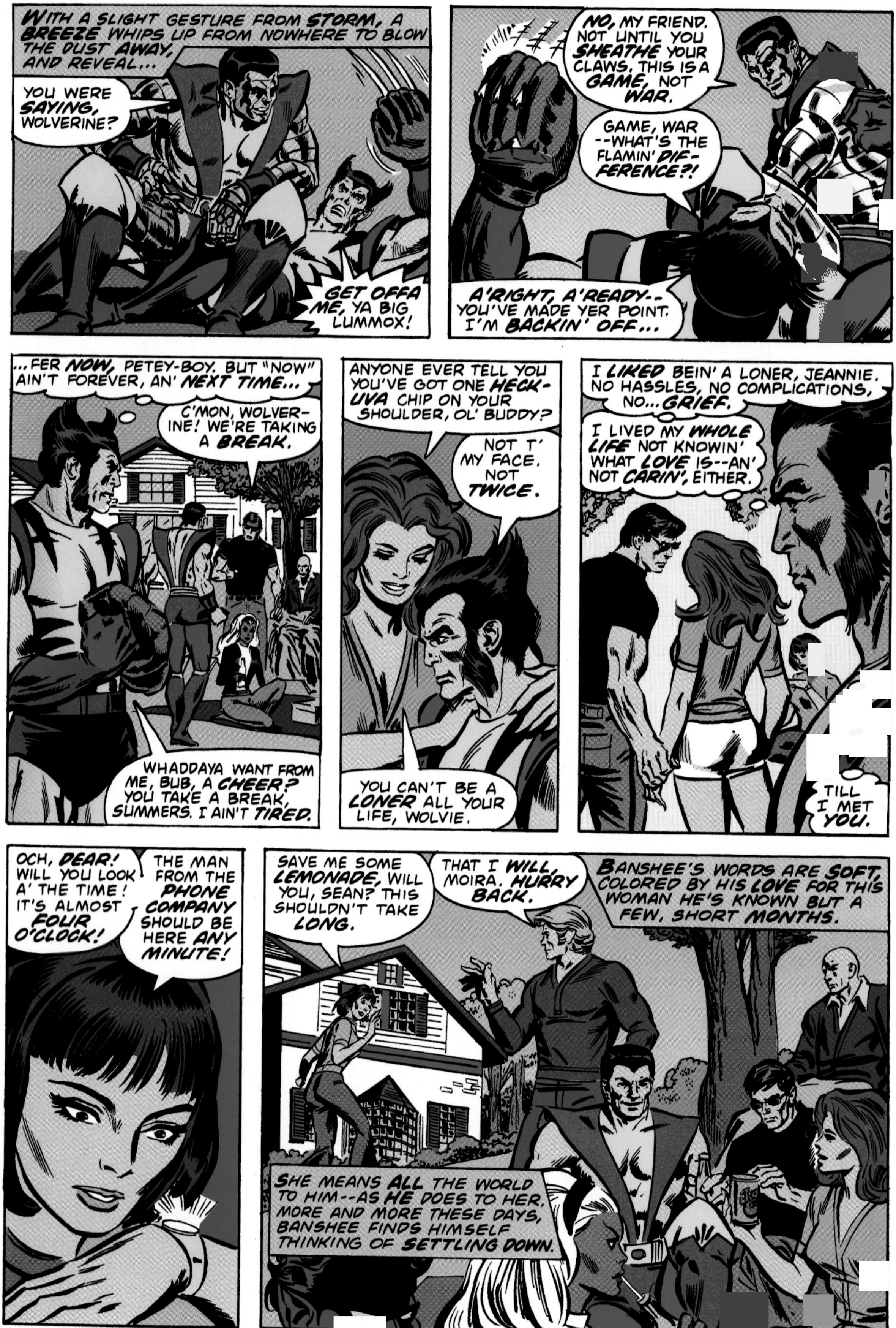
WITH A SLIGHT GESTURE FROM STORM, A BREEZE WHIPS UP FROM NOWHERE TO BLOW THE DUST AWAY, AND REVEAL...
YOU WERE SAYING, WOLVERINE?
GET OFFA ME, YA BIG LUMMOX!
NO, MY FRIEND. NOT UNTIL YOU SHEATHE YOUR CLAWS. THIS IS A GAME, NOT WAR.
GAME, WAR --WHAT'S THE FLAMIN' DIF-FERENCE?!
A'RIGHT, A'READY-- YOU'VE MADE YER POINT. I'M BACKIN' OFF...
...FER NOW, PETEY-BOY. BUT "NOW" AIN'T FOREVER, AN' NEXT TIME...
C'MON, WOLVERINE! WE'RE TAKING A BREAK.
WHADDAYA WANT FROM ME, BUB, A CHEER? YOU TAKE A BREAK, SUMMERS. I AIN'T TIRED.
ANYONE EVER TELL YOU YOU'VE GOT ONE HECK-UVA CHIP ON YOUR SHOULDER, OL' BUDDY?
NOT T' MY FACE. NOT TWICE.
YOU CAN'T BE A LONER ALL YOUR LIFE, WOLVIE.
I LIKED BEIN' A LONER, JEANNIE. NO HASSLES, NO COMPLICATIONS, NO... GRIEF.
I LIVED MY WHOLE LIFE NOT KNOWIN' WHAT LOVE IS--AN' NOT CARIN', EITHER.
TILL I MET YOU.
OCH, DEAR! WILL YOU LOOK A' THE TIME! IT'S ALMOST FOUR O'CLOCK!
THE MAN FROM THE PHONE COMPANY SHOULD BE HERE ANY MINUTE!
SAVE ME SOME LEMONADE, WILL YOU, SEAN? THIS SHOULDN'T TAKE LONG.
THAT I WILL, MOIRA. HURRY BACK.
BANSHEE'S WORDS ARE SOFT, COLORED BY HIS LOVE FOR THIS WOMAN HE'S KNOWN BUT A FEW, SHORT MONTHS.
SHE MEANS ALL THE WORLD TO HIM--AS HE DOES TO HER. MORE AND MORE THESE DAYS, BANSHEE FINDS HIMSELF THINKING OF SETTLING DOWN.

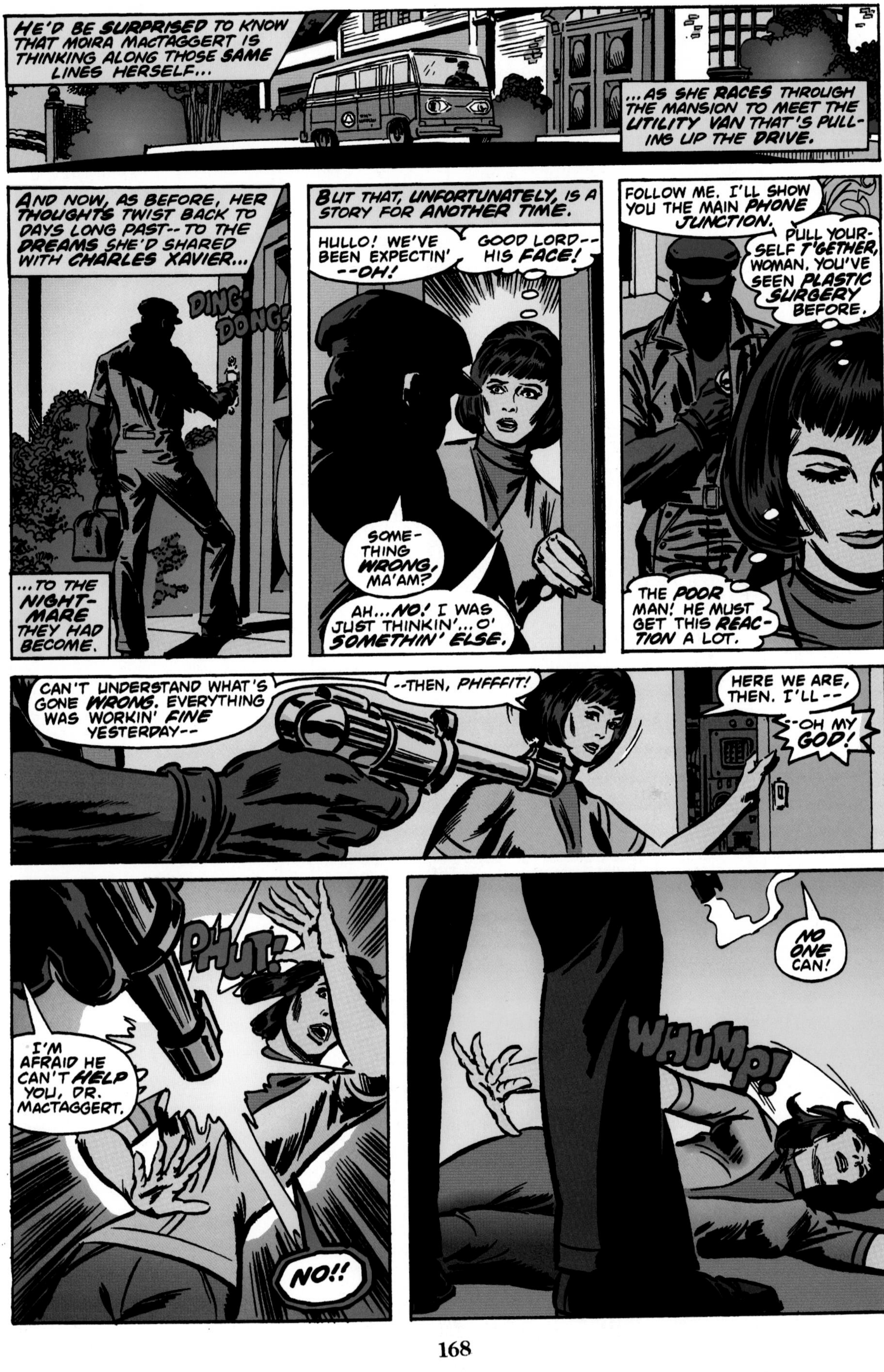
HE'D BE SURPRISED TO KNOW THAT MOIRA MACTAGGERT IS THINKING ALONG THOSE SAME LINES HERSELF...
...AS SHE RACES THROUGH THE MANSION TO MEET THE UTILITY VAN THAT'S PULLING UP THE DRIVE.
AND NOW, AS BEFORE, HER THOUGHTS TWIST BACK TO DAYS LONG PAST--TO THE DREAMS SHE'D SHARED WITH CHARLES XAVIER...
DING-DONG!
...TO THE NIGHTMARE THEY HAD BECOME.
BUT THAT, UNFORTUNATELY, IS A STORY FOR ANOTHER TIME.
HULLO! WE'VE BEEN EXPECTIN' --OH!
GOOD LORD-- HIS FACE!
SOMETHING WRONG, MA'AM?
AH...NO! I WAS JUST THINKIN'...O' SOMETHIN' ELSE.
FOLLOW ME. I'LL SHOW YOU THE MAIN PHONE JUNCTION.
PULL YOURSELF T'GETHER, WOMAN. YOU'VE SEEN PLASTIC SURGERY BEFORE.
THE POOR MAN! HE MUST GET THIS REACTION A LOT.
CAN'T UNDERSTAND WHAT'S GONE WRONG. EVERYTHING WAS WORKIN' FINE YESTERDAY--
--THEN, PHFFFIT!
HERE WE ARE, THEN. I'LL--
--OH MY GOD!
PHUT!
I'M AFRAID HE CAN'T HELP YOU, DR. MACTAGGERT.
NO!!
NO ONE CAN!
WHUMP!

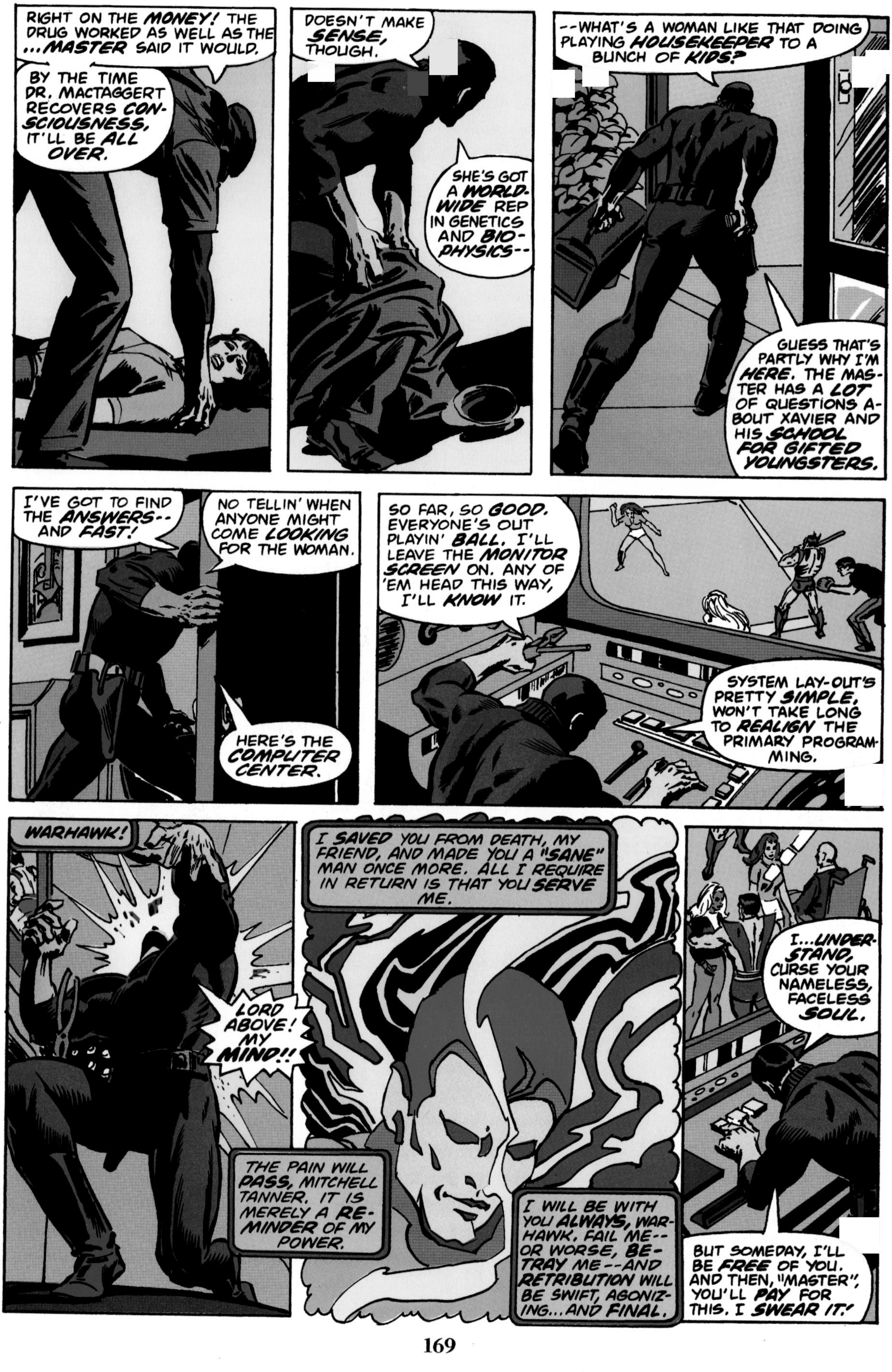
RIGHT ON THE MONEY! THE DRUG WORKED AS WELL AS THE ...MASTER SAID IT WOULD.
BY THE TIME DR. MACTAGGERT RECOVERS CONSCIOUSNESS, IT'LL BE ALL OVER.
DOESN'T MAKE SENSE, THOUGH.
SHE'S GOT A WORLD-WIDE REP IN GENETICS AND BIO-PHYSICS--
--WHAT'S A WOMAN LIKE THAT DOING PLAYING HOUSEKEEPER TO A BUNCH OF KIDS?
GUESS THAT'S PARTLY WHY I'M HERE. THE MASTER HAS A LOT OF QUESTIONS ABOUT XAVIER AND HIS SCHOOL FOR GIFTED YOUNGSTERS.
I'VE GOT TO FIND THE ANSWERS-- AND FAST!
NO TELLIN' WHEN ANYONE MIGHT COME LOOKING FOR THE WOMAN.
HERE'S THE COMPUTER CENTER.
SO FAR, SO GOOD. EVERYONE'S OUT PLAYIN' BALL. I'LL LEAVE THE MONITOR SCREEN ON. ANY OF 'EM HEAD THIS WAY, I'LL KNOW IT.
SYSTEM LAY-OUT'S PRETTY SIMPLE, WON'T TAKE LONG TO REALIGN THE PRIMARY PROGRAMMING.
WARHAWK!
LORD ABOVE! MY MIND!!
I SAVED YOU FROM DEATH, MY FRIEND, AND MADE YOU A "SANE" MAN ONCE MORE. ALL I REQUIRE IN RETURN IS THAT YOU SERVE ME.
THE PAIN WILL PASS, MITCHELL TANNER. IT IS MERELY A REMINDER OF MY POWER.
I WILL BE WITH YOU ALWAYS, WARHAWK. FAIL ME-- OR WORSE, BETRAY ME--AND RETRIBUTION WILL BE SWIFT, AGONIZING...AND FINAL.
I...UNDERSTAND, CURSE YOUR NAMELESS, FACELESS SOUL.
BUT SOMEDAY, I'LL BE FREE OF YOU. AND THEN, "MASTER", YOU'LL PAY FOR THIS. I SWEAR IT!

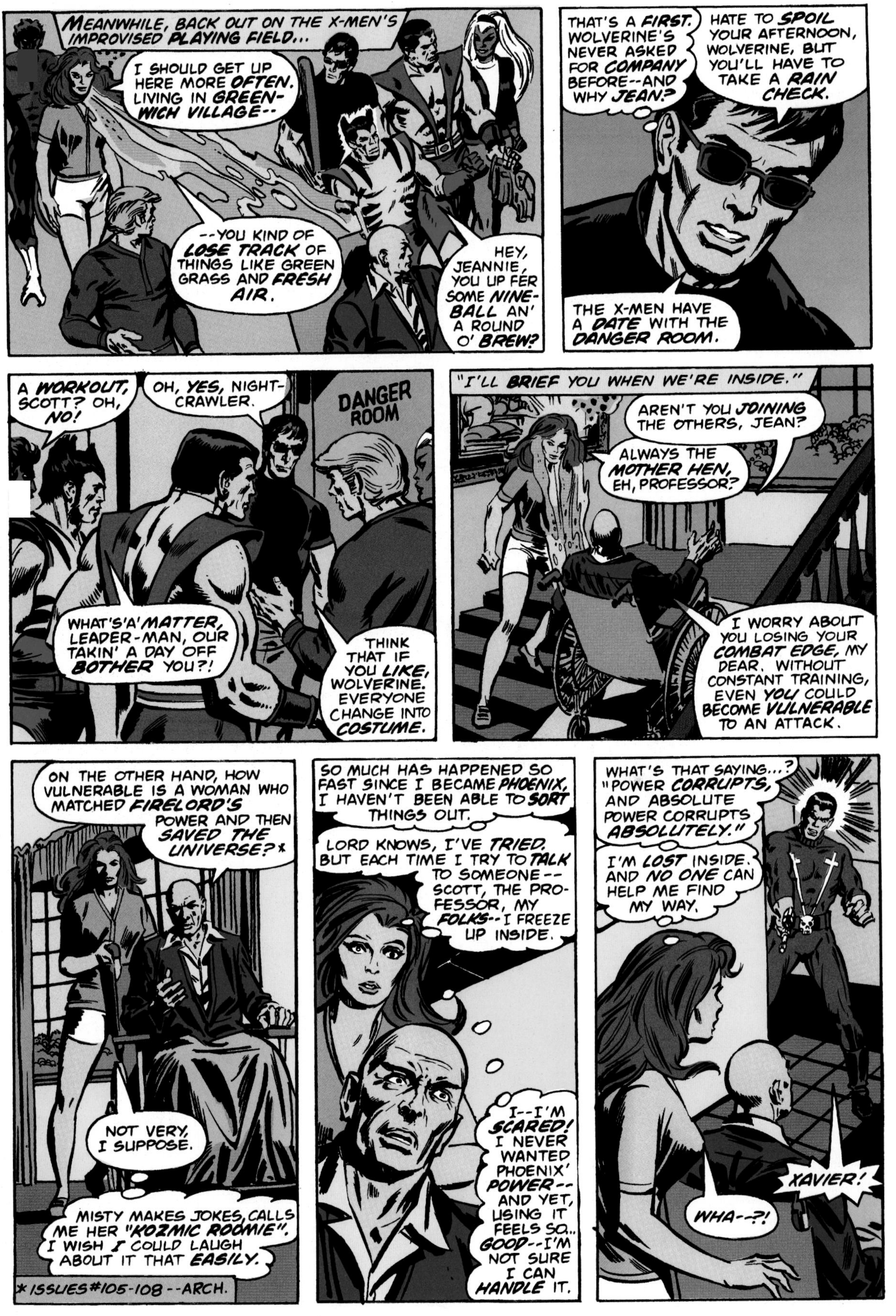
MEANWHILE, BACK OUT ON THE X-MEN'S IMPROVISED PLAYING FIELD...
I SHOULD GET UP HERE MORE OFTEN. LIVING IN GREENWICH VILLAGE--
--YOU KIND OF LOSE TRACK OF THINGS LIKE GREEN GRASS AND FRESH AIR.
HEY, JEANNIE, YOU UP FER SOME NINE-BALL AN' A ROUND O' BREW?
THAT'S A FIRST. WOLVERINE'S NEVER ASKED FOR COMPANY BEFORE--AND WHY JEAN?
HATE TO SPOIL YOUR AFTERNOON, WOLVERINE, BUT YOU'LL HAVE TO TAKE A RAIN CHECK.
THE X-MEN HAVE A DATE WITH THE DANGER ROOM.
A WORKOUT, SCOTT? OH, NO!
OH, YES, NIGHTCRAWLER.
DANGER ROOM
WHAT'S'A'MATTER, LEADER-MAN, OUR TAKIN' A DAY OFF BOTHER YOU?!
THINK THAT IF YOU LIKE, WOLVERINE. EVERYONE CHANGE INTO COSTUME.
"I'LL BRIEF YOU WHEN WE'RE INSIDE."
AREN'T YOU JOINING THE OTHERS, JEAN?
ALWAYS THE MOTHER HEN, EH, PROFESSOR?
I WORRY ABOUT YOU LOSING YOUR COMBAT EDGE, MY DEAR. WITHOUT CONSTANT TRAINING, EVEN YOU COULD BECOME VULNERABLE TO AN ATTACK.
ON THE OTHER HAND, HOW VULNERABLE IS A WOMAN WHO MATCHED FIRELORD'S POWER AND THEN SAVED THE UNIVERSE?*
NOT VERY, I SUPPOSE.
MISTY MAKES JOKES, CALLS ME HER "KOZMIC ROOMIE". I WISH I COULD LAUGH ABOUT IT THAT EASILY.
*ISSUES #105-108 --ARCH.
SO MUCH HAS HAPPENED SO FAST SINCE I BECAME PHOENIX, I HAVEN'T BEEN ABLE TO SORT THINGS OUT.
LORD KNOWS, I'VE TRIED. BUT EACH TIME I TRY TO TALK TO SOMEONE -- SCOTT, THE PROFESSOR, MY FOLKS-- I FREEZE UP INSIDE.
I--I'M SCARED! I NEVER WANTED PHOENIX' POWER-- AND YET, USING IT FEELS SO... GOOD--I'M NOT SURE I CAN HANDLE IT.
WHAT'S THAT SAYING...? "POWER CORRUPTS, AND ABSOLUTE POWER CORRUPTS ABSOLUTELY."
I'M LOST INSIDE. AND NO ONE CAN HELP ME FIND MY WAY.
XAVIER!
WHA--?!

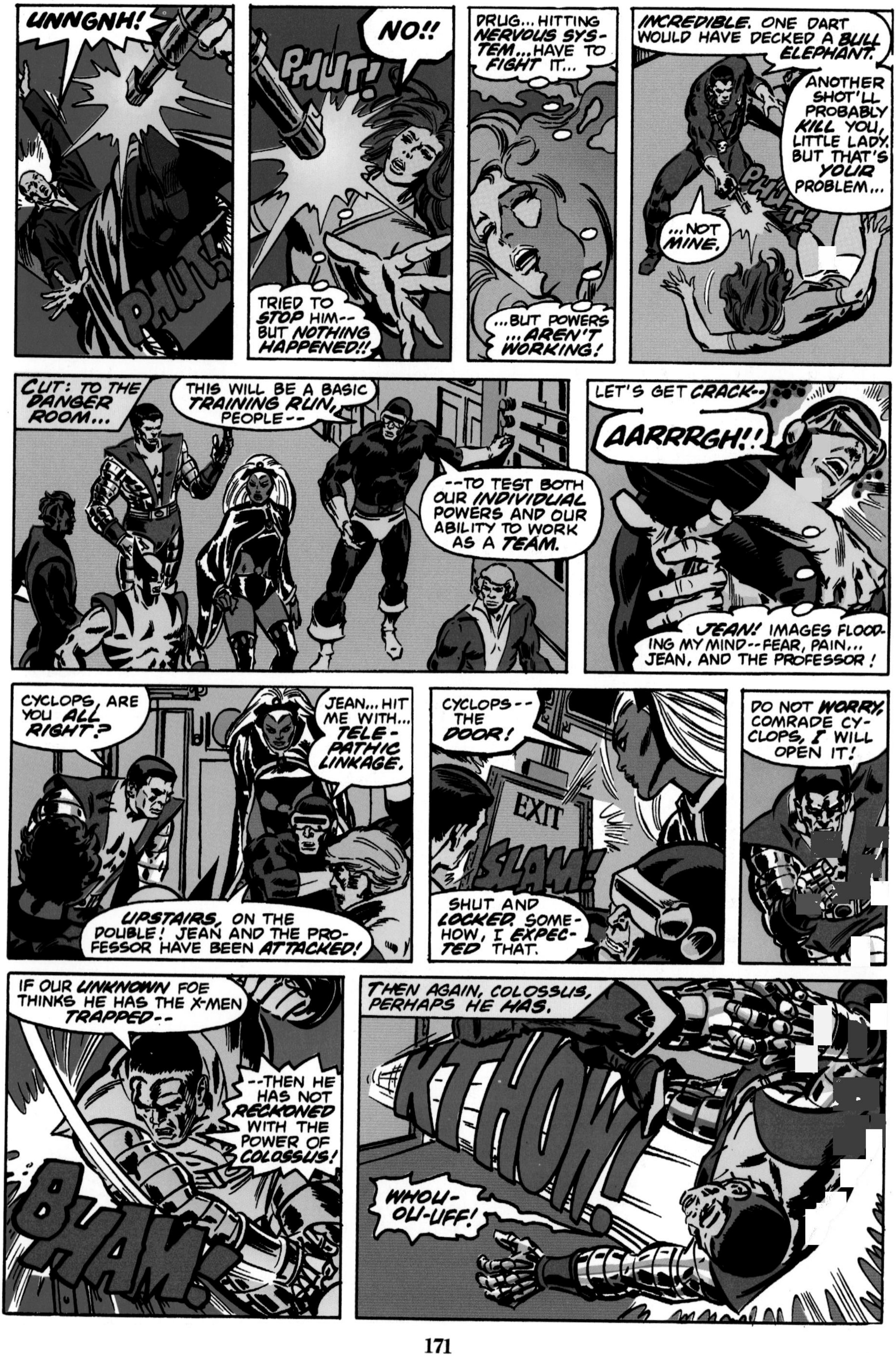

UNNGNH!
PHUT!
NO!!
PHUT!
TRIED TO STOP HIM--BUT NOTHING HAPPENED!!
DRUG... HITTING NERVOUS SYSTEM... HAVE TO FIGHT IT...
...BUT POWERS ...AREN'T WORKING!
INCREDIBLE. ONE DART WOULD HAVE DECKED A BULL ELEPHANT.
ANOTHER SHOT'LL PROBABLY KILL YOU, LITTLE LADY. BUT THAT'S YOUR PROBLEM...
...NOT MINE.
CUT: TO THE DANGER ROOM...
THIS WILL BE A BASIC TRAINING RUN, PEOPLE--
--TO TEST BOTH OUR INDIVIDUAL POWERS AND OUR ABILITY TO WORK AS A TEAM.
LET'S GET CRACK--
AARRRGH!!
JEAN! IMAGES FLOODING MY MIND--FEAR, PAIN... JEAN, AND THE PROFESSOR!
CYCLOPS, ARE YOU ALL RIGHT?
JEAN... HIT ME WITH... TELEPATHIC LINKAGE.
UPSTAIRS, ON THE DOUBLE! JEAN AND THE PROFESSOR HAVE BEEN ATTACKED!
CYCLOPS--THE DOOR!
EXIT
SLAM!
SHUT AND LOCKED. SOMEHOW, I EXPECTED THAT.
DO NOT WORRY, COMRADE CYCLOPS, I WILL OPEN IT!
IF OUR UNKNOWN FOE THINKS HE HAS THE X-MEN TRAPPED--
--THEN HE HAS NOT RECKONED WITH THE POWER OF COLOSSUS!
BLAM!
THEN AGAIN, COLOSSUS, PERHAPS HE HAS.
KTHOW
WHOUOU-UFF!

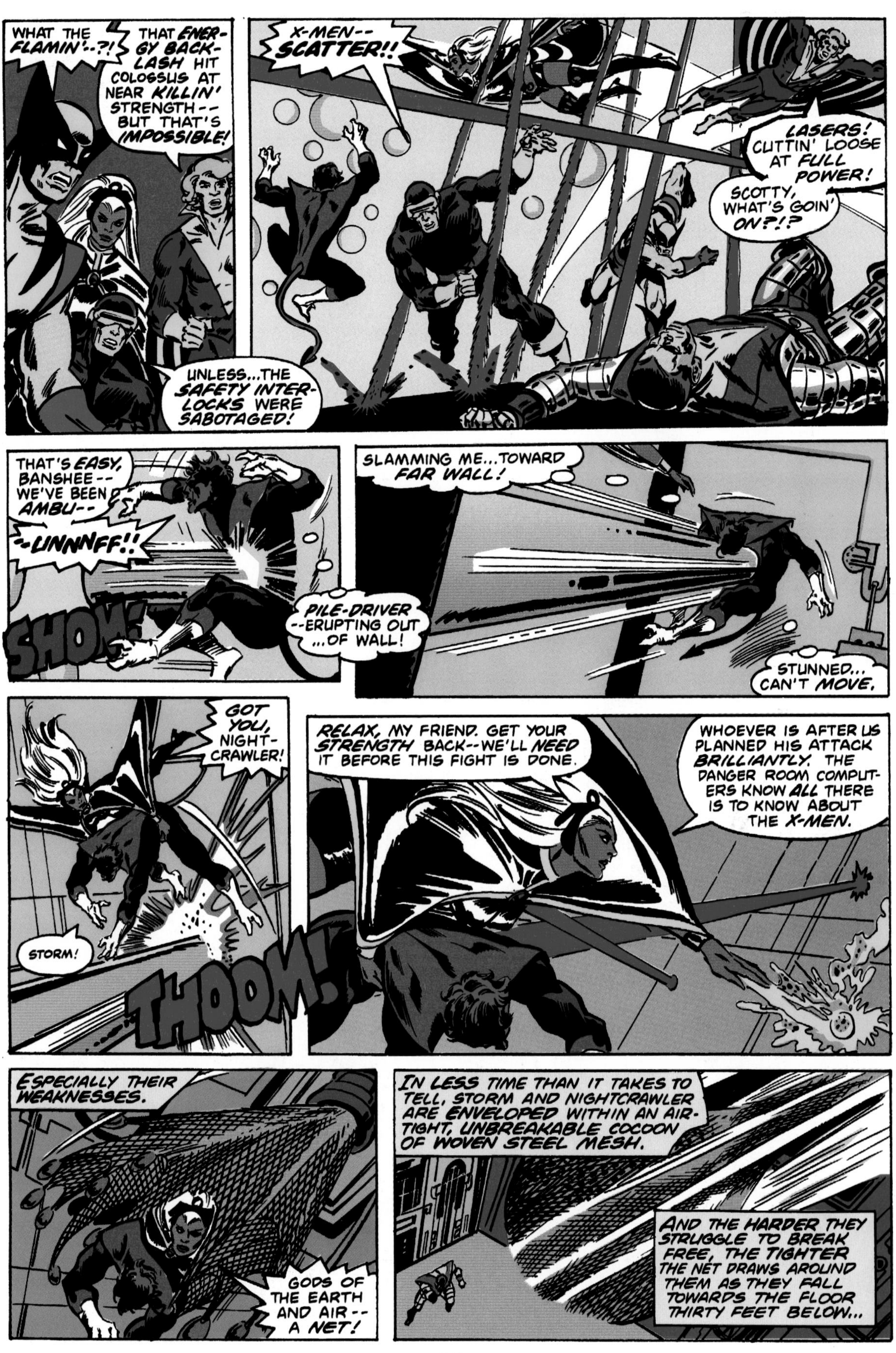
WHAT THE FLAMIN'..?!
THAT ENERGY BACKLASH HIT COLOSSUS AT NEAR KILLIN' STRENGTH--BUT THAT'S IMPOSSIBLE!
UNLESS... THE SAFETY INTERLOCKS WERE SABOTAGED!
X-MEN--SCATTER!!
LASERS! CUTTIN' LOOSE AT FULL POWER!
SCOTTY, WHAT'S GOIN' ON?!?
THAT'S EASY, BANSHEE--WE'VE BEEN AMBU--
--UNNNFF!!
SHOM!
PILE-DRIVER--ERUPTING OUT ...OF WALL!
SLAMMING ME... TOWARD FAR WALL!
STUNNED... CAN'T MOVE.
GOT YOU, NIGHTCRAWLER!
STORM!
THOOM!
RELAX, MY FRIEND. GET YOUR STRENGTH BACK--WE'LL NEED IT BEFORE THIS FIGHT IS DONE.
WHOEVER IS AFTER US PLANNED HIS ATTACK BRILLIANTLY. THE DANGER ROOM COMPUTERS KNOW ALL THERE IS TO KNOW ABOUT THE X-MEN.
ESPECIALLY THEIR WEAKNESSES.
GODS OF THE EARTH AND AIR--A NET!
IN LESS TIME THAN IT TAKES TO TELL, STORM AND NIGHTCRAWLER ARE ENVELOPED WITHIN AN AIR-TIGHT, UNBREAKABLE COCOON OF WOVEN STEEL MESH.
AND THE HARDER THEY STRUGGLE TO BREAK FREE, THE TIGHTER THE NET DRAWS AROUND THEM AS THEY FALL TOWARDS THE FLOOR THIRTY FEET BELOW...

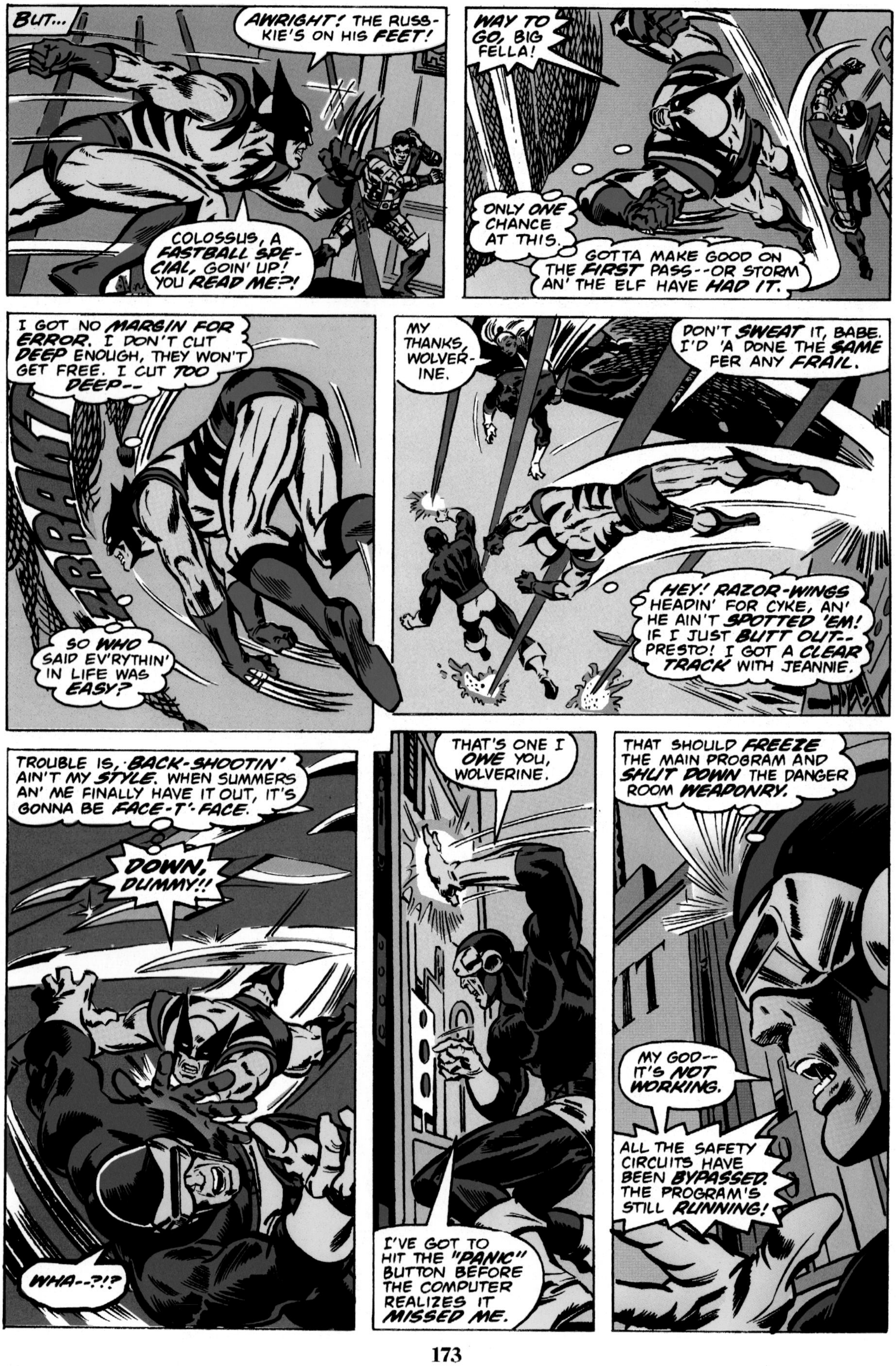

BUT...
AWRIGHT! THE RUSS-KIE'S ON HIS FEET!
COLOSSUS, A FASTBALL SPE-CIAL, GOIN' UP! YOU READ ME?!
WAY TO GO, BIG FELLA!
ONLY ONE CHANCE AT THIS.
GOTTA MAKE GOOD ON THE FIRST PASS--OR STORM AN' THE ELF HAVE HAD IT.
I GOT NO MARGIN FOR ERROR. I DON'T CUT DEEP ENOUGH, THEY WON'T GET FREE. I CUT TOO DEEP--
SO WHO SAID EV'RYTHIN' IN LIFE WAS EASY?
MY THANKS, WOLVER-INE.
DON'T SWEAT IT, BABE. I'D 'A DONE THE SAME FER ANY FRAIL.
HEY! RAZOR-WINGS HEADIN' FOR CYKE, AN' HE AIN'T SPOTTED 'EM! IF I JUST BUTT OUT--PRESTO! I GOT A CLEAR TRACK WITH JEANNIE.
TROUBLE IS, BACK-SHOOTIN' AIN'T MY STYLE. WHEN SUMMERS AN' ME FINALLY HAVE IT OUT, IT'S GONNA BE FACE-T'-FACE.
DOWN, DUMMY!!
WHA--?!?
THAT'S ONE I OWE YOU, WOLVERINE.
I'VE GOT TO HIT THE "PANIC" BUTTON BEFORE THE COMPUTER REALIZES IT MISSED ME.
THAT SHOULD FREEZE THE MAIN PROGRAM AND SHUT DOWN THE DANGER ROOM WEAPONRY.
MY GOD--IT'S NOT WORKING.
ALL THE SAFETY CIRCUITS HAVE BEEN BYPASSED. THE PROGRAM'S STILL RUNNING!

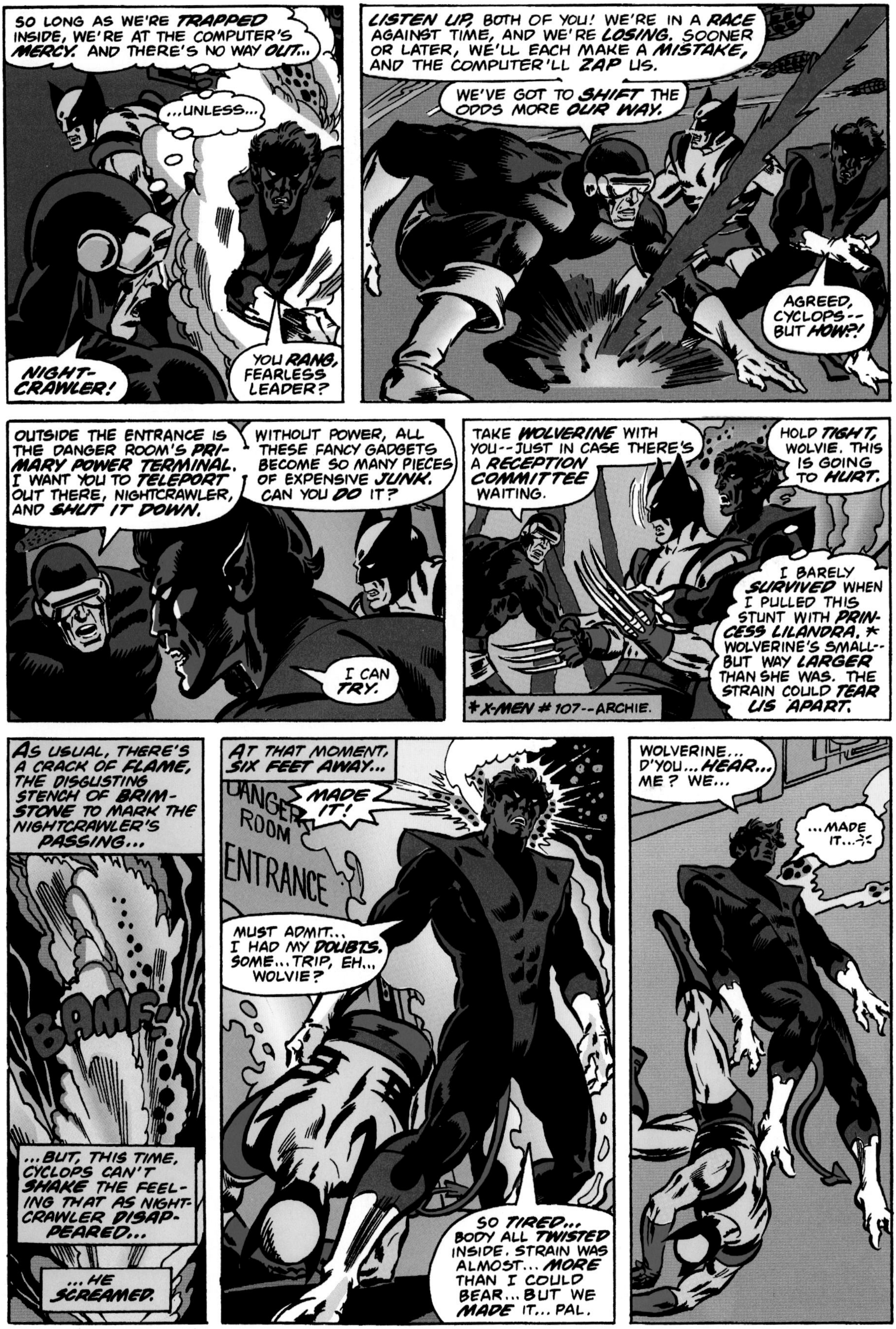
SO LONG AS WE'RE TRAPPED INSIDE, WE'RE AT THE COMPUTER'S MERCY. AND THERE'S NO WAY OUT...
...UNLESS...
NIGHT-CRAWLER!
YOU RANG, FEARLESS LEADER?
LISTEN UP, BOTH OF YOU! WE'RE IN A RACE AGAINST TIME, AND WE'RE LOSING. SOONER OR LATER, WE'LL EACH MAKE A MISTAKE, AND THE COMPUTER'LL ZAP US.
WE'VE GOT TO SHIFT THE ODDS MORE OUR WAY.
AGREED, CYCLOPS--BUT HOW?!
OUTSIDE THE ENTRANCE IS THE DANGER ROOM'S PRIMARY POWER TERMINAL. I WANT YOU TO TELEPORT OUT THERE, NIGHTCRAWLER, AND SHUT IT DOWN.
WITHOUT POWER, ALL THESE FANCY GADGETS BECOME SO MANY PIECES OF EXPENSIVE JUNK. CAN YOU DO IT?
I CAN TRY.
TAKE WOLVERINE WITH YOU--JUST IN CASE THERE'S A RECEPTION COMMITTEE WAITING.
HOLD TIGHT, WOLVIE. THIS IS GOING TO HURT.
I BARELY SURVIVED WHEN I PULLED THIS STUNT WITH PRINCESS LILANDRA.* WOLVERINE'S SMALL--BUT WAY LARGER THAN SHE WAS. THE STRAIN COULD TEAR US APART.
*X-MEN #107--ARCHIE.
AS USUAL, THERE'S A CRACK OF FLAME, THE DISGUSTING STENCH OF BRIMSTONE TO MARK THE NIGHTCRAWLER'S PASSING...
BAMF!
...BUT, THIS TIME, CYCLOPS CAN'T SHAKE THE FEELING THAT AS NIGHTCRAWLER DISAPPEARED...
...HE SCREAMED.
AT THAT MOMENT, SIX FEET AWAY...
DANGER ROOM ENTRANCE
MADE IT!
MUST ADMIT... I HAD MY DOUBTS. SOME... TRIP, EH... WOLVIE?
SO TIRED... BODY ALL TWISTED INSIDE. STRAIN WAS ALMOST... MORE THAN I COULD BEAR... BUT WE MADE IT... PAL.
WOLVERINE... D'YOU... HEAR... ME? WE...
...MADE IT...

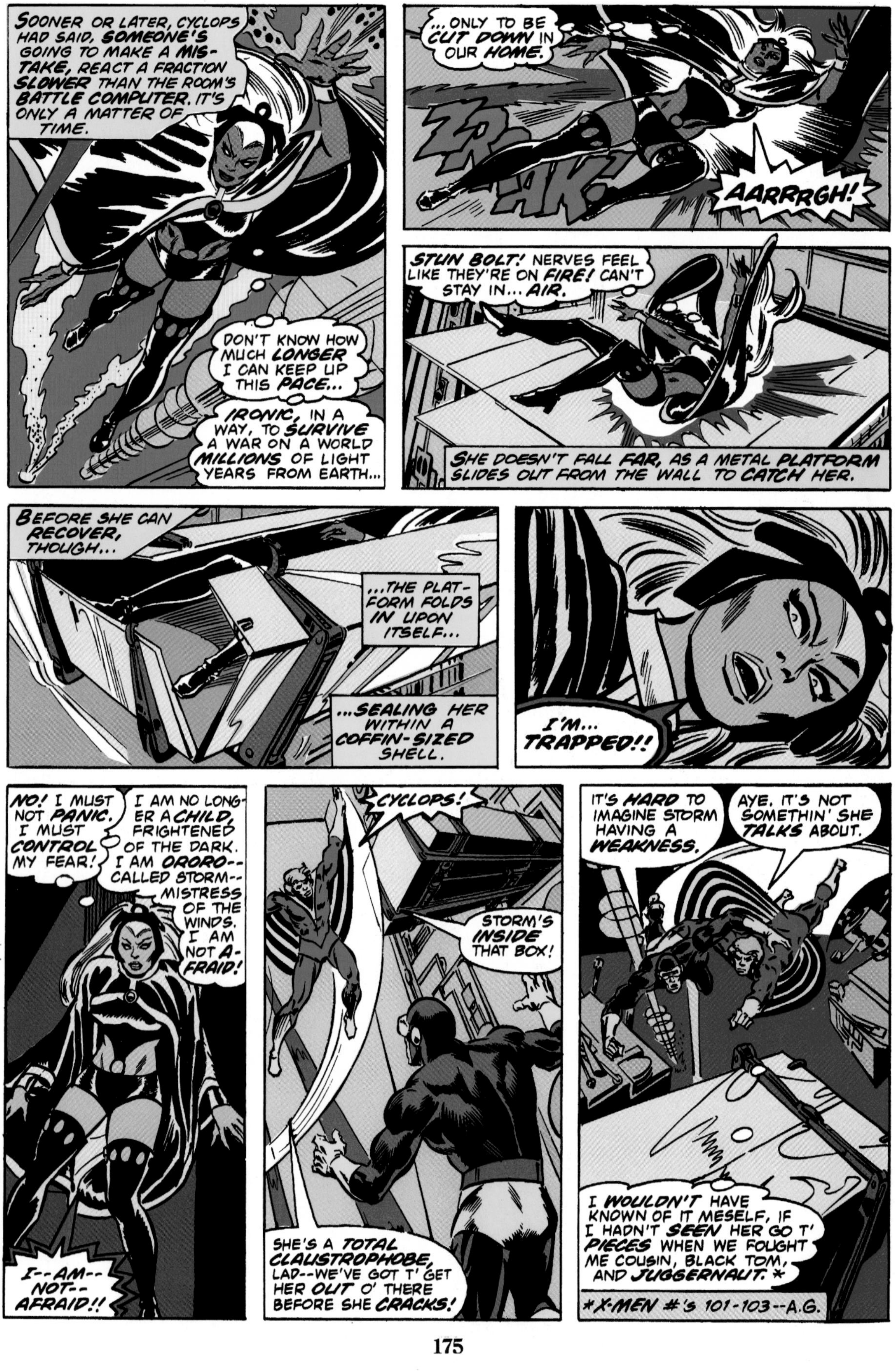
SOONER OR LATER, CYCLOPS HAD SAID, SOMEONE'S GOING TO MAKE A MISTAKE, REACT A FRACTION SLOWER THAN THE ROOM'S BATTLE COMPUTER. IT'S ONLY A MATTER OF TIME.
DON'T KNOW HOW MUCH LONGER I CAN KEEP UP THIS PACE...
IRONIC, IN A WAY, TO SURVIVE A WAR ON A WORLD MILLIONS OF LIGHT YEARS FROM EARTH...
...ONLY TO BE CUT DOWN IN OUR HOME.
ZRAAK!
AARRRGH!
STUN BOLT! NERVES FEEL LIKE THEY'RE ON FIRE! CAN'T STAY IN... AIR.
SHE DOESN'T FALL FAR, AS A METAL PLATFORM SLIDES OUT FROM THE WALL TO CATCH HER.
BEFORE SHE CAN RECOVER, THOUGH...
...THE PLATFORM FOLDS IN UPON ITSELF...
...SEALING HER WITHIN A COFFIN-SIZED SHELL.
I'M... TRAPPED!!
NO! I MUST NOT PANIC. I MUST CONTROL MY FEAR!
I AM NO LONGER A CHILD, FRIGHTENED OF THE DARK. I AM ORORO--CALLED STORM--MISTRESS OF THE WINDS. I AM NOT AFRAID!
I--AM--NOT--AFRAID!!
CYCLOPS!
STORM'S INSIDE THAT BOX!
SHE'S A TOTAL CLAUSTROPHOBE, LAD--WE'VE GOT T' GET HER OUT O' THERE BEFORE SHE CRACKS!
IT'S HARD TO IMAGINE STORM HAVING A WEAKNESS.
AYE. IT'S NOT SOMETHIN' SHE TALKS ABOUT.
I WOULDN'T HAVE KNOWN OF IT MESELF, IF I HADN'T SEEN HER GO T' PIECES WHEN WE FOUGHT ME COUSIN, BLACK TOM, AND JUGGERNAUT. *
*X-MEN #'s 101-103--A.G.

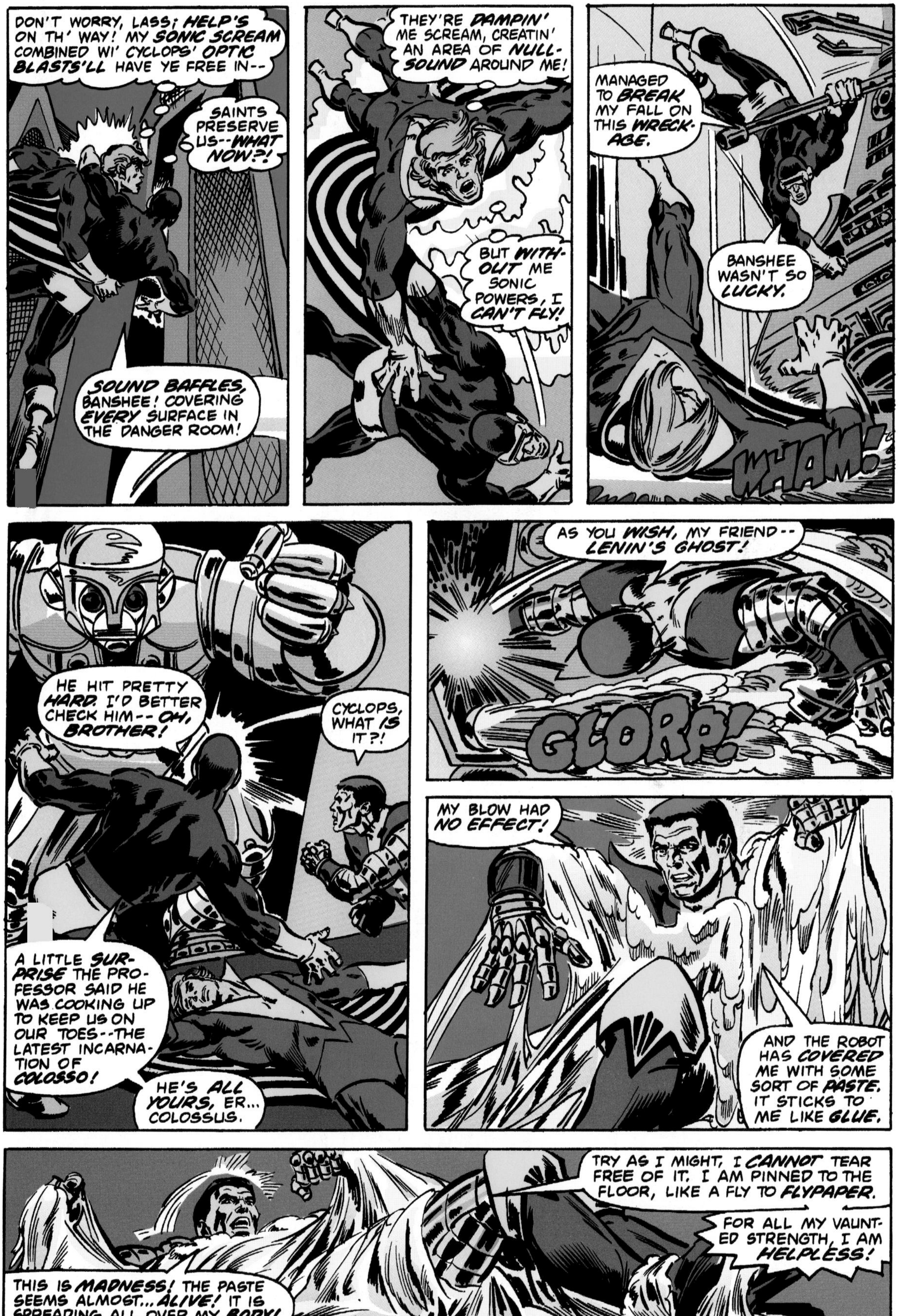
DON'T WORRY, LASS; HELP'S ON TH' WAY! MY SONIC SCREAM COMBINED WI' CYCLOPS' OPTIC BLASTS'LL HAVE YE FREE IN--
SAINTS PRESERVE US--WHAT NOW?!
SOUND BAFFLES, BANSHEE! COVERING EVERY SURFACE IN THE DANGER ROOM!
THEY'RE DAMPIN' ME SCREAM, CREATIN' AN AREA OF NULL-SOUND AROUND ME!
BUT WITH-OUT ME SONIC POWERS, I CAN'T FLY!
MANAGED TO BREAK MY FALL ON THIS WRECK-AGE.
BANSHEE WASN'T SO LUCKY.
WHAM!
HE HIT PRETTY HARD. I'D BETTER CHECK HIM-- OH, BROTHER!
CYCLOPS, WHAT IS IT?!
A LITTLE SUR-PRISE THE PRO-FESSOR SAID HE WAS COOKING UP TO KEEP US ON OUR TOES--THE LATEST INCARNA-TION OF COLOSSO!
HE'S ALL YOURS, ER... COLOSSUS.
AS YOU WISH, MY FRIEND-- LENIN'S GHOST!
GLORP!
MY BLOW HAD NO EFFECT!
AND THE ROBOT HAS COVERED ME WITH SOME SORT OF PASTE. IT STICKS TO ME LIKE GLUE.
TRY AS I MIGHT, I CANNOT TEAR FREE OF IT. I AM PINNED TO THE FLOOR, LIKE A FLY TO FLYPAPER.
FOR ALL MY VAUNT-ED STRENGTH, I AM HELPLESS!
THIS IS MADNESS! THE PASTE SEEMS ALMOST... ALIVE! IT IS SPREADING ALL OVER MY BODY!

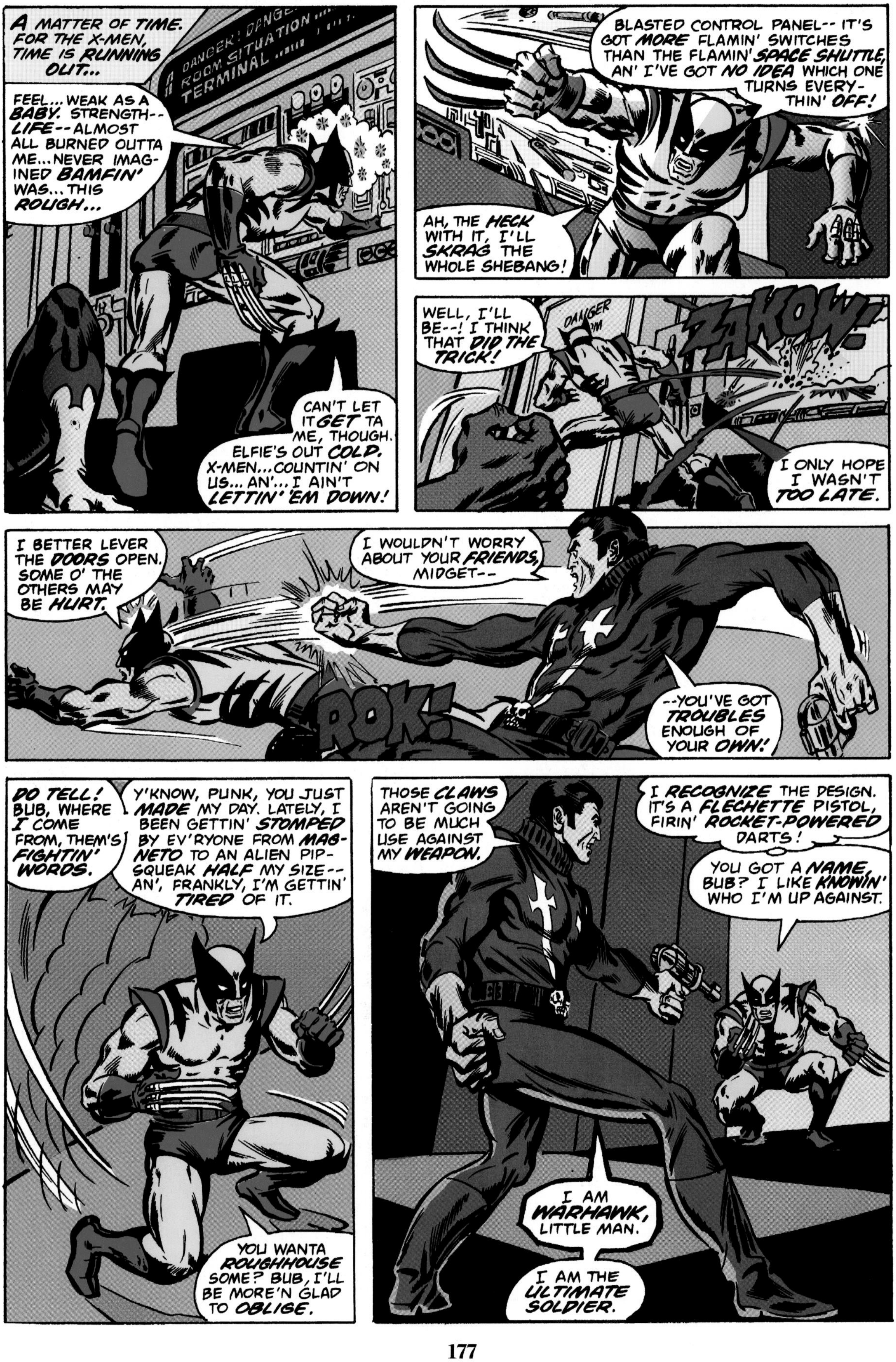
A MATTER OF TIME. FOR THE X-MEN, TIME IS RUNNING OUT...
DANGER! DANGE... ROOM SITUATION ... TERMINAL ...
FEEL... WEAK AS A BABY. STRENGTH-- LIFE--ALMOST ALL BURNED OUTTA ME...NEVER IMAGINED BAMFIN' WAS... THIS ROUGH...
CAN'T LET IT GET TA ME, THOUGH. ELFIE'S OUT COLD. X-MEN...COUNTIN' ON US... AN'... I AIN'T LETTIN' 'EM DOWN!
BLASTED CONTROL PANEL-- IT'S GOT MORE FLAMIN' SWITCHES THAN THE FLAMIN' SPACE SHUTTLE, AN' I'VE GOT NO IDEA WHICH ONE TURNS EVERY-THIN' OFF!
AH, THE HECK WITH IT, I'LL SKRAG THE WHOLE SHEBANG!
WELL, I'LL BE--! I THINK THAT DID THE TRICK!
ZAKOW!
I ONLY HOPE I WASN'T TOO LATE.
I BETTER LEVER THE DOORS OPEN. SOME O' THE OTHERS MAY BE HURT.
I WOULDN'T WORRY ABOUT YOUR FRIENDS, MIDGET--
ROK!
--YOU'VE GOT TROUBLES ENOUGH OF YOUR OWN!
DO TELL! BUB, WHERE I COME FROM, THEM'S FIGHTIN' WORDS.
Y'KNOW, PUNK, YOU JUST MADE MY DAY. LATELY, I BEEN GETTIN' STOMPED BY EV'RYONE FROM MAGNETO TO AN ALIEN PIPSQUEAK HALF MY SIZE--AN', FRANKLY, I'M GETTIN' TIRED OF IT.
YOU WANTA ROUGHHOUSE SOME? BUB, I'LL BE MORE'N GLAD TO OBLIGE.
THOSE CLAWS AREN'T GOING TO BE MUCH USE AGAINST MY WEAPON.
I RECOGNIZE THE DESIGN. IT'S A FLECHETTE PISTOL, FIRIN' ROCKET-POWERED DARTS!
YOU GOT A NAME, BUB? I LIKE KNOWIN' WHO I'M UP AGAINST.
I AM WARHAWK, LITTLE MAN.
I AM THE ULTIMATE SOLDIER.

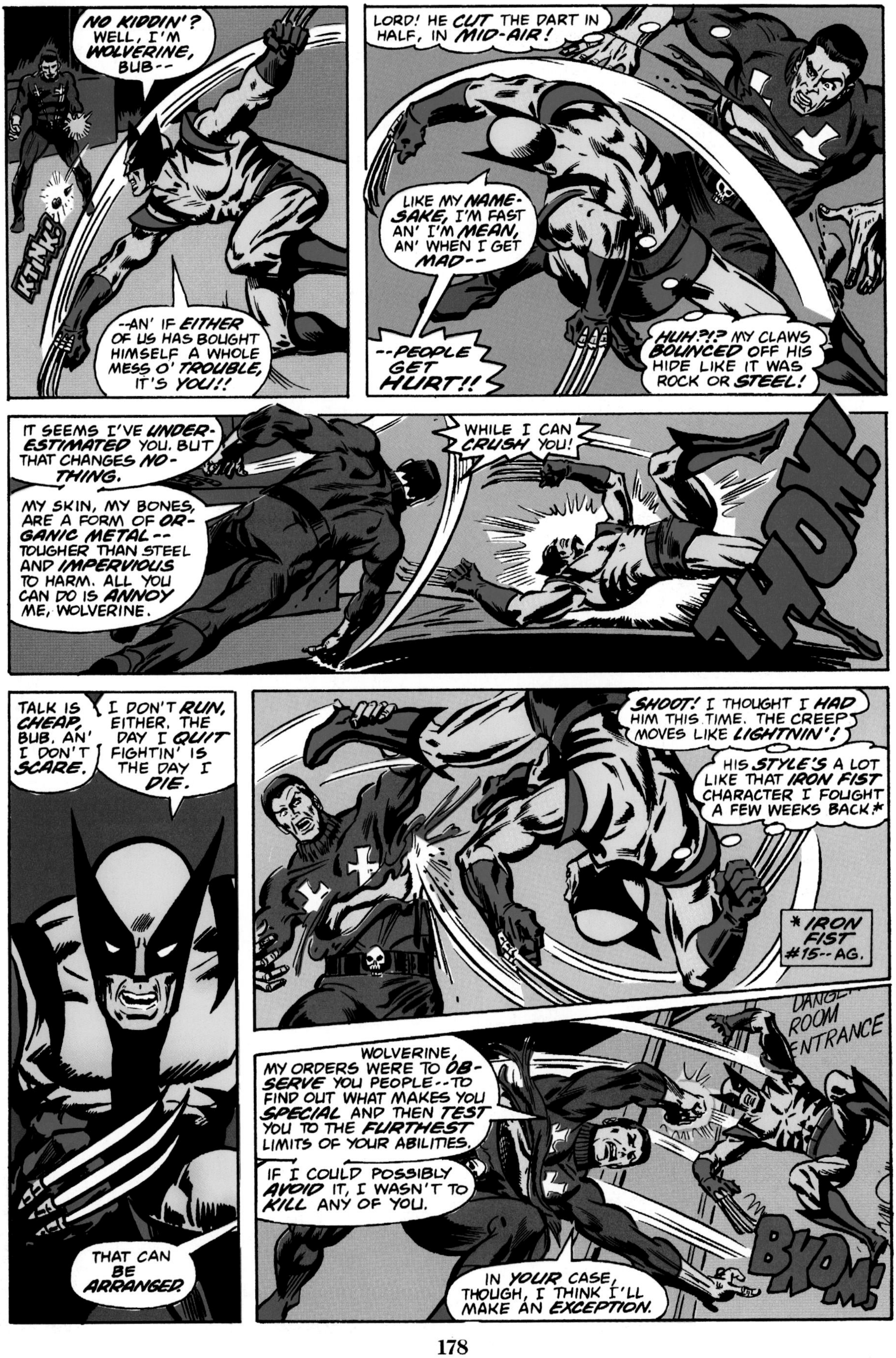
NO KIDDIN'? WELL, I'M WOLVERINE, BUB--
KTINK!
--AN' IF EITHER OF US HAS BOUGHT HIMSELF A WHOLE MESS O' TROUBLE, IT'S YOU!!
LORD! HE CUT THE DART IN HALF, IN MID-AIR!
LIKE MY NAME-SAKE, I'M FAST AN' I'M MEAN, AN' WHEN I GET MAD--
--PEOPLE GET HURT!!
HUH?!? MY CLAWS BOUNCED OFF HIS HIDE LIKE IT WAS ROCK OR STEEL!
IT SEEMS I'VE UNDER-ESTIMATED YOU. BUT THAT CHANGES NO-THING.
MY SKIN, MY BONES, ARE A FORM OF OR-GANIC METAL-- TOUGHER THAN STEEL AND IMPERVIOUS TO HARM. ALL YOU CAN DO IS ANNOY ME, WOLVERINE.
WHILE I CAN CRUSH YOU!
THOK!
TALK IS CHEAP, BUB. AN' I DON'T SCARE.
I DON'T RUN, EITHER. THE DAY I QUIT FIGHTIN' IS THE DAY I DIE.
THAT CAN BE ARRANGED.
SHOOT! I THOUGHT I HAD HIM THIS TIME. THE CREEP MOVES LIKE LIGHTNIN'!
HIS STYLE'S A LOT LIKE THAT IRON FIST CHARACTER I FOUGHT A FEW WEEKS BACK.*
*IRON FIST #15--AG.
ROOM ENTRANCE
WOLVERINE, MY ORDERS WERE TO OB-SERVE YOU PEOPLE--TO FIND OUT WHAT MAKES YOU SPECIAL AND THEN TEST YOU TO THE FURTHEST LIMITS OF YOUR ABILITIES.
IF I COULD POSSIBLY AVOID IT, I WASN'T TO KILL ANY OF YOU.
IN YOUR CASE, THOUGH, I THINK I'LL MAKE AN EXCEPTION.
BKOM!

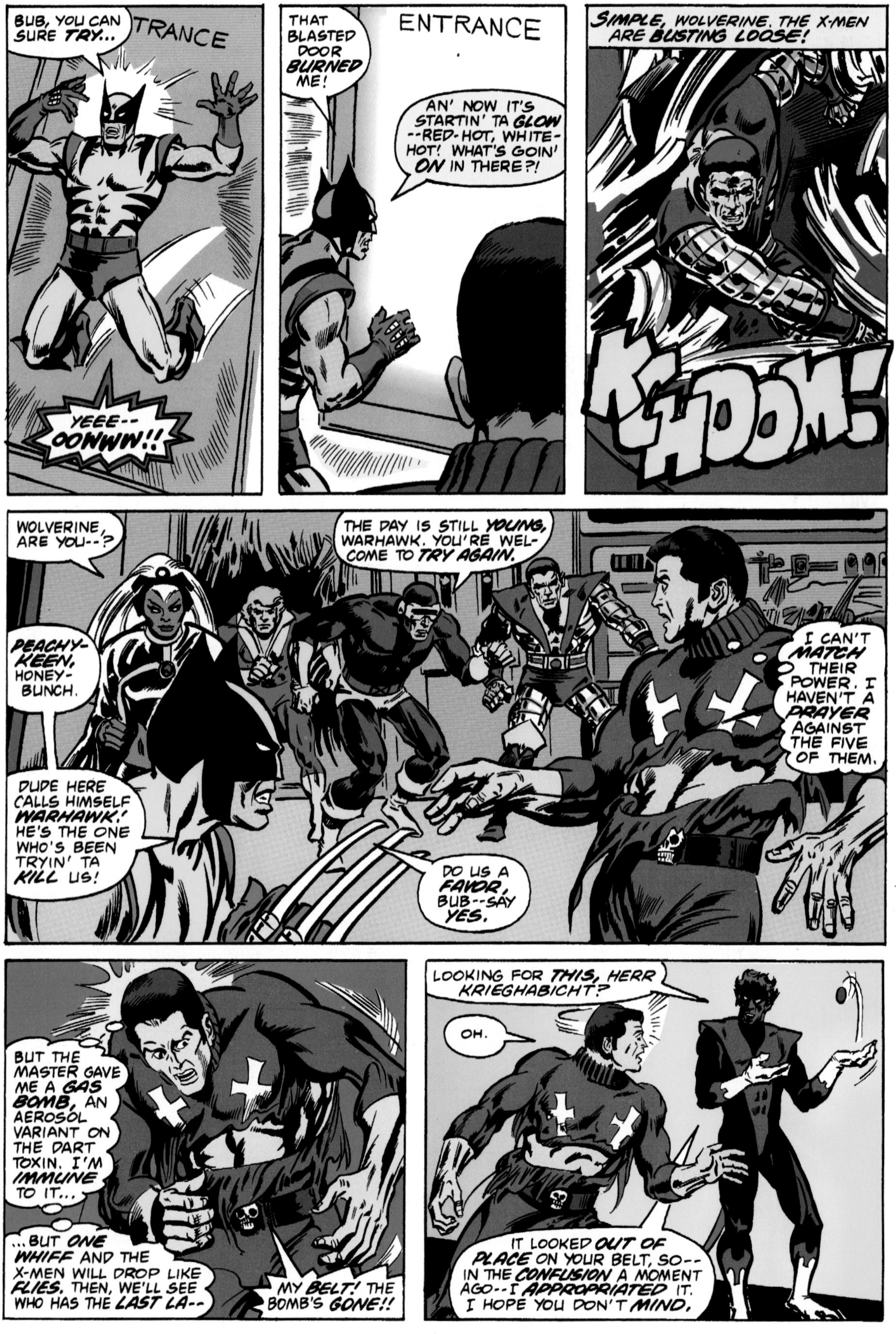
BUB, YOU CAN SURE TRY...
TRANCE
YEEE-- OONWW!!
THAT BLASTED DOOR BURNED ME!
ENTRANCE
AN' NOW IT'S STARTIN' TA GLOW --RED-HOT, WHITE-HOT! WHAT'S GOIN' ON IN THERE?!
SIMPLE, WOLVERINE. THE X-MEN ARE BUSTING LOOSE!
K-THOOM!
WOLVERINE, ARE YOU--?
THE DAY IS STILL YOUNG, WARHAWK. YOU'RE WEL-COME TO TRY AGAIN.
PEACHY-KEEN, HONEY-BUNCH.
DUDE HERE CALLS HIMSELF WARHAWK! HE'S THE ONE WHO'S BEEN TRYIN' TA KILL US!
DO US A FAVOR, BUB--SAY YES.
I CAN'T MATCH THEIR POWER. I HAVEN'T A PRAYER AGAINST THE FIVE OF THEM.
BUT THE MASTER GAVE ME A GAS BOMB, AN AEROSOL VARIANT ON THE DART TOXIN. I'M IMMUNE TO IT...
...BUT ONE WHIFF AND THE X-MEN WILL DROP LIKE FLIES. THEN, WE'LL SEE WHO HAS THE LAST LA--
MY BELT! THE BOMB'S GONE!!
LOOKING FOR THIS, HERR KRIEGHABICHT?
OH.
IT LOOKED OUT OF PLACE ON YOUR BELT, SO--IN THE CONFUSION A MOMENT AGO--I APPROPRIATED IT. I HOPE YOU DON'T MIND.

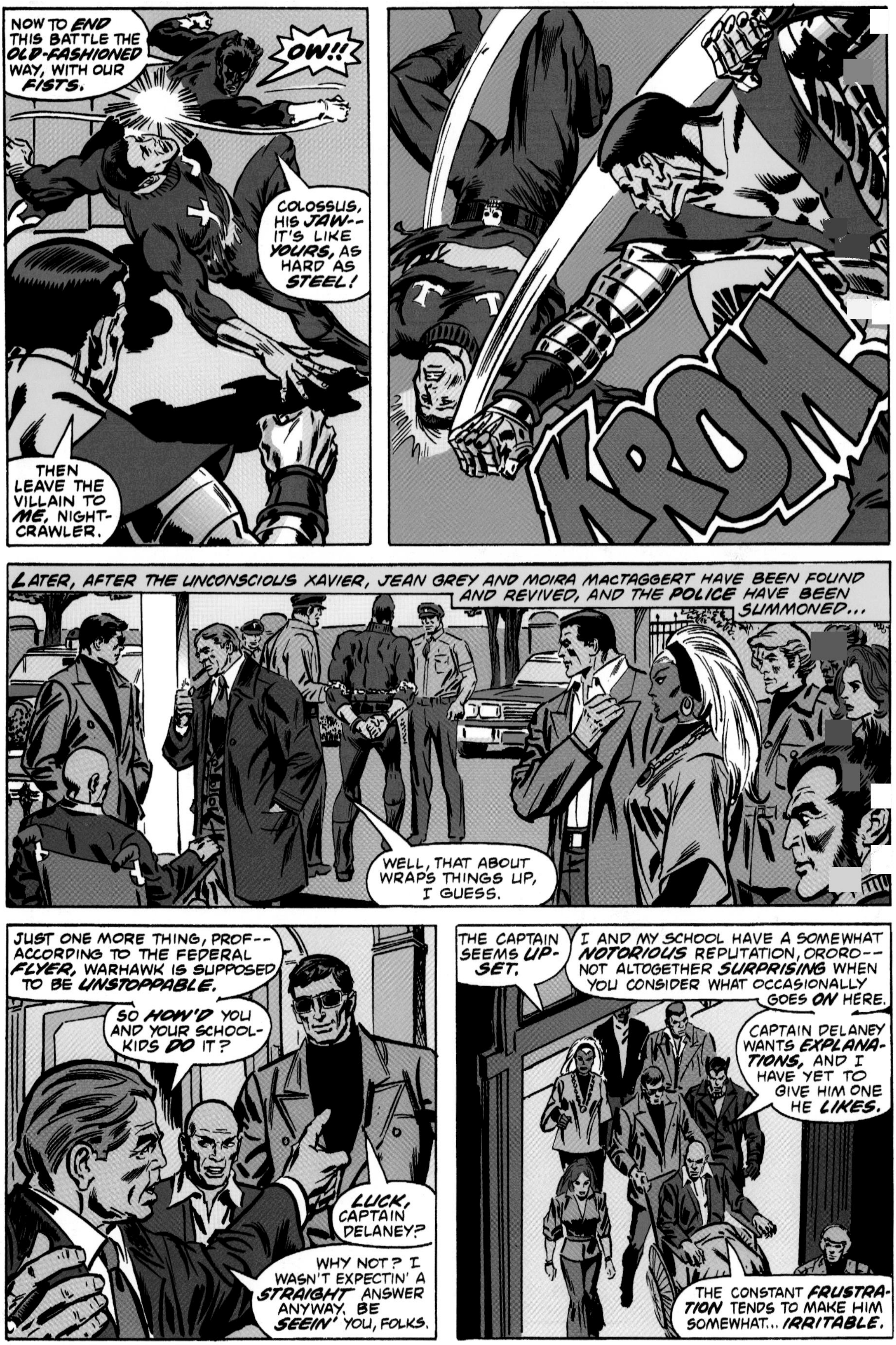
NOW TO END THIS BATTLE THE OLD-FASHIONED WAY, WITH OUR FISTS.
OW!!
COLOSSUS, HIS JAW-- IT'S LIKE YOURS, AS HARD AS STEEL!
THEN LEAVE THE VILLAIN TO ME, NIGHT-CRAWLER.
KROM!
LATER, AFTER THE UNCONSCIOUS XAVIER, JEAN GREY AND MOIRA MACTAGGERT HAVE BEEN FOUND AND REVIVED, AND THE POLICE HAVE BEEN SUMMONED...
WELL, THAT ABOUT WRAPS THINGS UP, I GUESS.
JUST ONE MORE THING, PROF-- ACCORDING TO THE FEDERAL FLYER, WARHAWK IS SUPPOSED TO BE UNSTOPPABLE.
SO HOW'D YOU AND YOUR SCHOOL-KIDS DO IT?
LUCK, CAPTAIN DELANEY?
WHY NOT? I WASN'T EXPECTIN' A STRAIGHT ANSWER ANYWAY. BE SEEIN' YOU, FOLKS.
THE CAPTAIN SEEMS UP-SET.
I AND MY SCHOOL HAVE A SOMEWHAT NOTORIOUS REPUTATION, ORORO-- NOT ALTOGETHER SURPRISING WHEN YOU CONSIDER WHAT OCCASIONALLY GOES ON HERE.
CAPTAIN DELANEY WANTS EXPLANA-TIONS, AND I HAVE YET TO GIVE HIM ONE HE LIKES.
THE CONSTANT FRUSTRA-TION TENDS TO MAKE HIM SOMEWHAT... IRRITABLE.

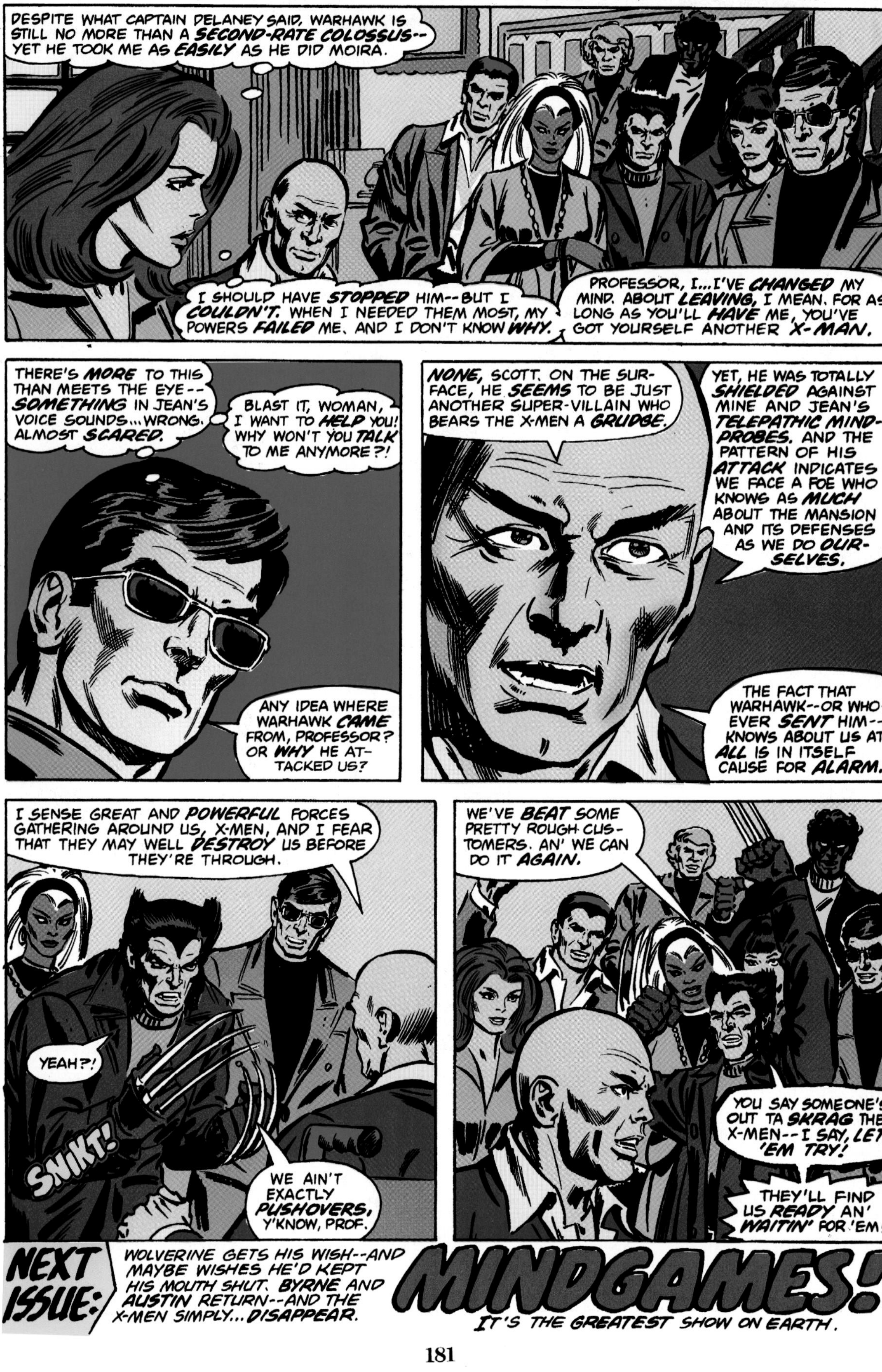
DESPITE WHAT CAPTAIN DELANEY SAID, WARHAWK IS STILL NO MORE THAN A SECOND-RATE COLOSSUS--YET HE TOOK ME AS EASILY AS HE DID MOIRA.
I SHOULD HAVE STOPPED HIM--BUT I COULDN'T. WHEN I NEEDED THEM MOST, MY POWERS FAILED ME. AND I DON'T KNOW WHY.
PROFESSOR, I...I'VE CHANGED MY MIND. ABOUT LEAVING, I MEAN. FOR AS LONG AS YOU'LL HAVE ME, YOU'VE GOT YOURSELF ANOTHER X-MAN.
THERE'S MORE TO THIS THAN MEETS THE EYE--SOMETHING IN JEAN'S VOICE SOUNDS... WRONG. ALMOST SCARED.
BLAST IT, WOMAN, I WANT TO HELP YOU! WHY WON'T YOU TALK TO ME ANYMORE?!
ANY IDEA WHERE WARHAWK CAME FROM, PROFESSOR? OR WHY HE ATTACKED US?
NONE, SCOTT. ON THE SURFACE, HE SEEMS TO BE JUST ANOTHER SUPER-VILLAIN WHO BEARS THE X-MEN A GRUDGE.
YET, HE WAS TOTALLY SHIELDED AGAINST MINE AND JEAN'S TELEPATHIC MIND-PROBES. AND THE PATTERN OF HIS ATTACK INDICATES WE FACE A FOE WHO KNOWS AS MUCH ABOUT THE MANSION AND ITS DEFENSES AS WE DO OURSELVES.
THE FACT THAT WARHAWK--OR WHOEVER SENT HIM--KNOWS ABOUT US AT ALL IS IN ITSELF CAUSE FOR ALARM.
I SENSE GREAT AND POWERFUL FORCES GATHERING AROUND US, X-MEN, AND I FEAR THAT THEY MAY WELL DESTROY US BEFORE THEY'RE THROUGH.
YEAH?!
SNIKT!
WE AIN'T EXACTLY PUSHOVERS, Y'KNOW, PROF.
WE'VE BEAT SOME PRETTY ROUGH CUSTOMERS. AN' WE CAN DO IT AGAIN.
YOU SAY SOMEONE'S OUT TA SKRAG THE X-MEN--I SAY, LET 'EM TRY!
THEY'LL FIND US READY AN' WAITIN' FOR 'EM!
NEXT ISSUE:
WOLVERINE GETS HIS WISH--AND MAYBE WISHES HE'D KEPT HIS MOUTH SHUT. BYRNE AND AUSTIN RETURN--AND THE X-MEN SIMPLY... DISAPPEAR.
MINDGAMES!
IT'S THE GREATEST SHOW ON EARTH.

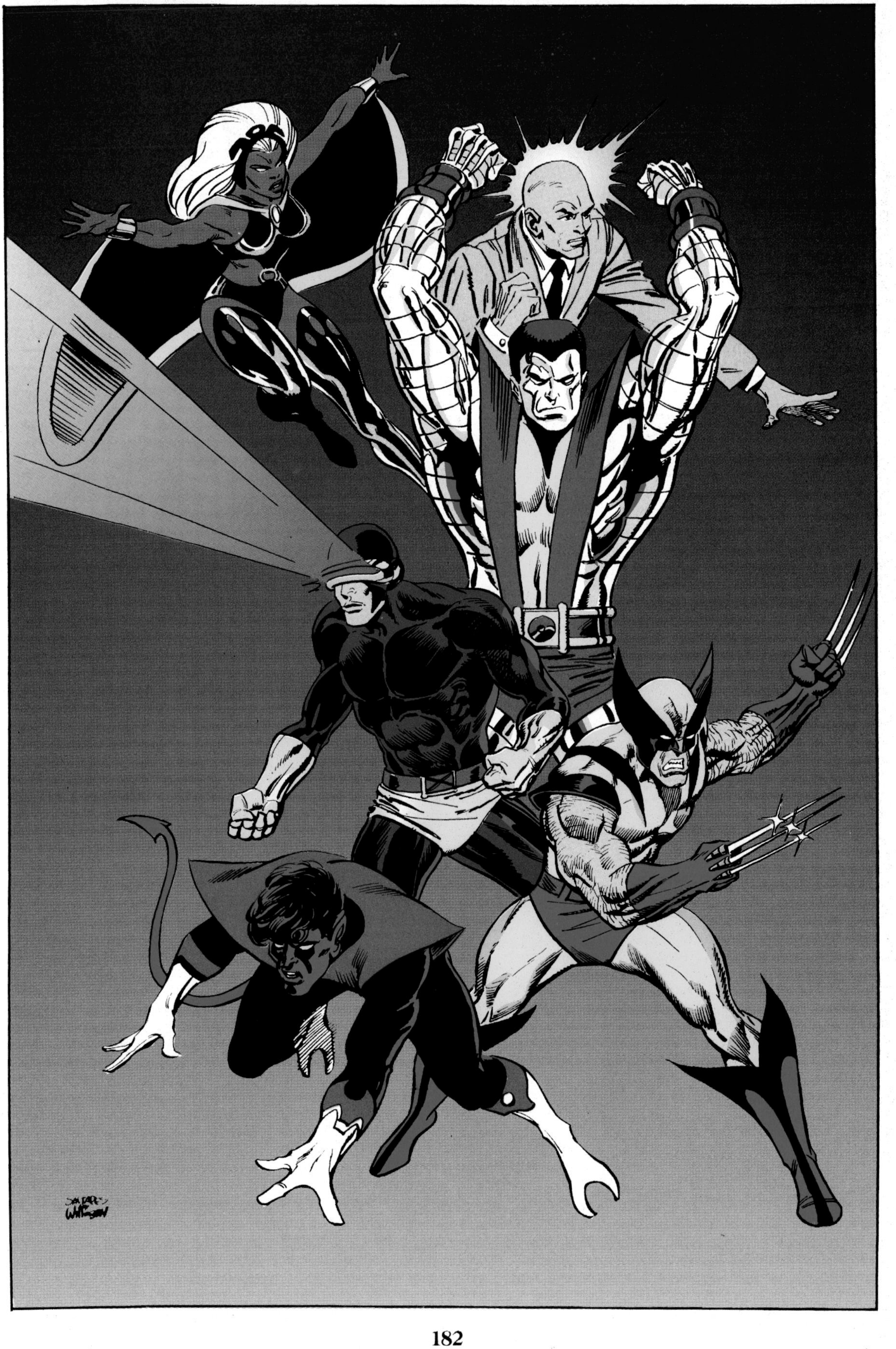

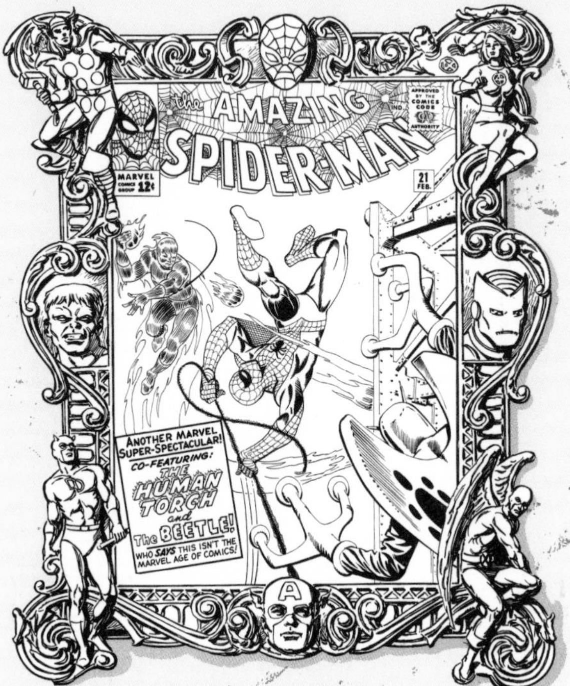

the AMAZING SPIDER-MAN
MARVEL COMICS GROUP 12¢
21 FEB.
ANOTHER MARVEL SUPER-SPECTACULAR!
CO-FEATURING:
THE HUMAN TORCH and The BEETLE!
WHO SAYS THIS ISN'T THE MARVEL AGE OF COMICS!

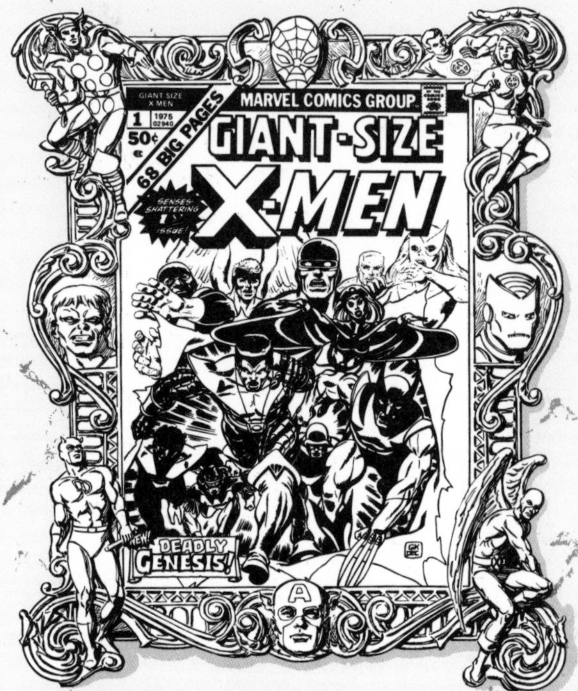

GIANT SIZE X MEN
MARVEL COMICS GROUP
1
50¢
68 BIG PAGES
GIANT-SIZE X-MEN
SENSES-SHATTERING 1st ISSUE!
NEW!
DEADLY GENESIS!

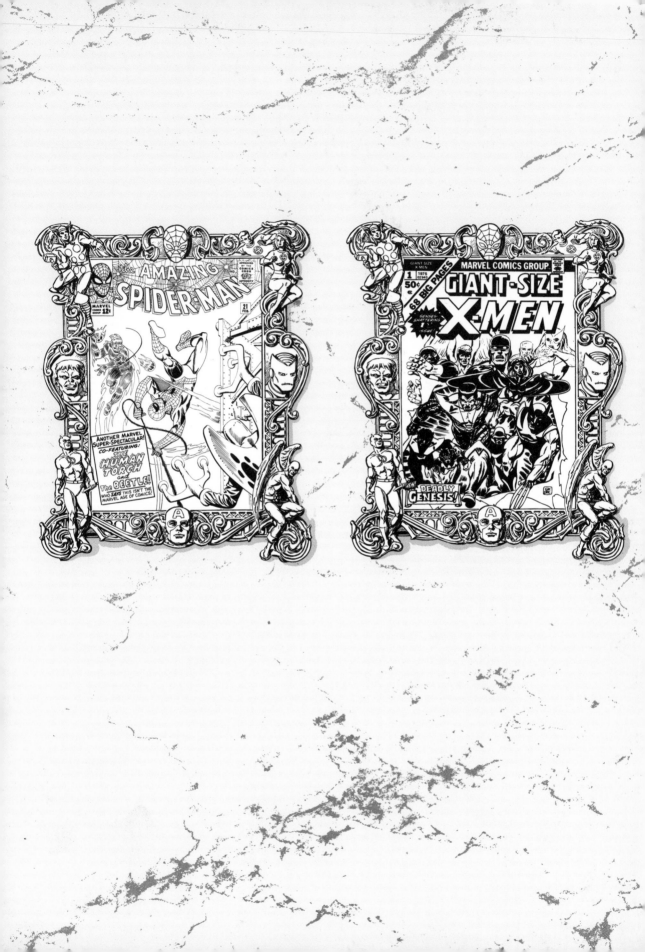